FUNDAMENTALS
of Game Design

THIRD EDITION

Ernest Adams

FUNDAMENTALS OF GAME DESIGN, THIRD EDITION
Ernest Adams

New Riders
www.newriders.com

To report errors, please send a note to errata@peachpit.com
New Riders is an imprint of Peachpit, a division of Pearson Education
Copyright © 2014 by Pearson Education, Inc.

Senior Editor: Karyn Johnson
Development Editor: Robyn G. Thomas
Production Editor: Maureen Forys, Happenstance Type-O-Rama
Copy Editor: Rebecca Rider
Technical Editor: Tobi Saulnier
Compositor: WolfsonDesign
Proofreader: Emily K. Wolman
Indexer: Jack Lewis
Interior Design: WolfsonDesign
Cover Design: Peachpit Press/Aren Howell

ISBN-13: 978-0-321-92967-9
ISBN-10:   0-321-92967-5

20 2024

Printed and bound in the United States of America

To Mary Ellen Foley, for love and wisdom.

Omnia vincit amor.

Acknowledgments

It would be a rare developer indeed who had worked on all the kinds of games addressed in this book, and certainly I cannot make that claim. When it came time to speak about subjects of which I had little direct experience, I relied heavily on the advice and wisdom of my professional colleagues. I owe particular gratitude to

Monty Clark	Mike Lopez	Michelle Hinn and the IGDA Accessibility Special Interest Group
Jesyca Durchin	Steve Meretzky	
Joseph Ganetakos	Carolyn Handler Miller	
Scott Kim	Brian Moriarty	
Rick Knowles	Tess Snider	
Raph Koster	Chris Taylor	

I owe special thanks to Jason VandenBerghe, Creative Director at UbiSoft, whose research on player motivation has been enormously valuable, and I'm grateful for his and UbiSoft's willingness to share it with the world. I hasten to add that any errors in the book are mine and not theirs.

I am also indebted to MobyGames (www.mobygames.com) and Giant Bomb (www.giantbomb.com), whose vast databases of games I consulted daily, and sometimes hourly, in my research.

My technical editor, Tobi Saulnier, gave me advice and feedback about every aspect of the book. This is the second time Tobi has worked with me in this capacity, and her experience, especially with casual games and games for children, has been invaluable. A number of other colleagues offered useful suggestions about different parts of the manuscript; I am particularly grateful to Chris Bateman, Ben Cousins, Melissa Federoff, Ola Holmdahl, and Lucy Joyner for their advice.

Several people and institutions generously gave me permission to reproduce images:

MobyGames (www.mobygames.com)

Giant Bomb (www.giantbomb.com)

Björn Hurri (www.bjornhurri.com)

Cecropia, Inc.

Pseudo Interactive (www.pseudointeractive.com)

Martin Stever

Finally, no list of acknowledgments would be complete without recognizing the help of my editor. Robyn Thomas worked hard with me to get the book done under severe deadline pressure (as always). Mary Ellen Foley, The Word Boffin (www.wordboffin.com), also provided occasional advice and staunch support. I'm grateful for the assistance of Margot Hutchison, my agent at Waterside Productions, in helping to finalize the contract.

Suggestions, corrections, and even complaints are always welcome; please send them to ewadams@designersnotebook.com.

About the Author

Ernest Adams is a game design consultant and part-time professor at University of Uppsala Campus Gotland in Sweden. He lives in England and holds a Ph.D. in Computer Science from Teesside University for his contributions to the field of interactive storytelling. In addition to his consulting and teaching, he gives game design workshops and is a popular speaker at conferences and on college campuses. Dr. Adams has worked in the interactive entertainment industry since 1989, and he founded the International Game Developers' Association in 1994. He was most recently employed as a lead designer at Bullfrog Productions, and for several years before that he was the audio/video producer on the *Madden NFL* line of football games at Electronic Arts. In his early career, Dr. Adams was a software engineer, and he has developed games for machines from the IBM 360 mainframe to the present day. He is the author of five other books and the "Designer's Notebook" series of columns on the *Gamasutra* developers' webzine. His professional website is at www.designersnotebook.com.

About the Technical Editor

Tobi Saulnier is founder and CEO of 1st Playable Productions, a game development studio that specializes in design and development of games tailored to specific audiences. Games developed by 1st Playable span numerous genres to appeal to play styles and preferences of each group and include games for young children, girls, middle schoolers, and young adults, and some that appeal to broad audiences. The studio also creates games for education. Before joining the game industry in 2000, Tobi managed R&D in embedded and distributed systems at General Electric Research and Development, where she also led initiatives in new product development, software quality, business strategy, and outsourcing. She earned her BS, MS, and Ph.D. in Electrical Engineering from Rensselaer Polytechnic Institute.

CONTENTS

INTRODUCTION

This is the third edition of *Fundamentals of Game Design,* a series of books that began ten years ago with *Andrew Rollings and Ernest Adams on Game Design.* This version has been updated and reorganized to reflect the latest changes to games, game technology, and even the gamers themselves.

Since the previous edition of *Fundamentals of Game Design,* the game industry has undergone a transformation more profound than any other in its history. The explosive growth of casual games, free-to-play games, and mobile gaming has challenged the traditional console and PC game publishing models. It is now easier than ever to build a video game thanks to middleware such as Unity and the many free tools for making art, animation, and audio. How we play has changed too. Most input devices have three-axis accelerometers to detect player movements, and the Kinect camera-based motion-capture device from Microsoft is just about to enter its second generation. (It was still called "Project Natal" in the previous edition of this book!)

In order to reflect all these changes, I have added four new chapters: Chapter 3, "The Major Genres," a brief overview of game genres; Chapter 4, "Understanding Your Player," which is about different kinds of players and their motivations and preferred play styles; Chapter 5, "Understanding Your Machine," a general overview of the different game platforms and how players use them; and Chapter 6, "Making Money from Your Game," which is about the various business models you can use to earn money as a game developer.

In order to make room for all this new material, the old Part Two from the second edition, which contained chapters about the individual game genres, has become a series of inexpensive e-books. The e-books are named *Fundamentals of <genre name> Design,* so the second edition's Chapter 16, "Sports Games," has been updated and now is an e-book called *Fundamentals of Sports Game Design.* I have also broken out shooter games and music games from action games as separate genres. All of these e-books are available from the Peachpit website at www.peachpit.com/ernestadams.

Two things set this book apart from its competitors: First, *Fundamentals of Game Design, Third Edition* is aimed squarely at designing complete, commercial video games. It's not an esoteric book of theory, and it tries to cover the whole of the player's experience, not just the gameplay or the mechanics. Second, it doesn't contain a lot of interviews with famous designers. Interviews can spice up a book with entertaining anecdotes, but I prefer to use that space for practical advice to the working designer or design student.

Fundamentals of Game Design is entirely about game design. It does not cover programming, art, animation, music, audio engineering, or writing. Nor is it about project management, budgeting, scheduling, or producing. However, it does refer to all these things, because your design decisions will affect them all significantly. A budding game designer should learn something about all these subjects, and I encourage you to consult other books to broaden your education as much as you can. All the greatest game designers are Renaissance men and women, interested in everything.

Most chapters end with two sections called "Design Practice Exercises" and "Design Practice Questions." The exercises are intended for your instructor to assign to you (or for you to do on your own, if you're not a student). The questions are ones that you should ask yourself about the game that you're designing. Deciding on the answers to these questions is the essence of game design.

Whom Is This Book For?

This book is aimed at anyone who is interested in designing video games but doesn't know how to begin. More specifically, it is intended for university students and junior professionals in the game industry. Although it is a general, introductory text, more experienced professionals may find it a useful reference as well.

TIP To get the most out of the book while you're actually working on a game design, be sure to ask yourself the questions at the end of most chapters.

My only explicit prerequisite for reading the book is some knowledge of video games, especially the more famous ones. It would be impossible to write a book on game design for someone who has never played a game; I have to assume basic familiarity with video games and game hardware. For a thorough and deeply insightful history of video games, read Steven Poole's *Trigger Happy: Videogames and the Entertainment Revolution* (Poole, 2004).

I do expect that you are able to write succinctly and unambiguously; this skill is an absolute requirement for a game designer, and many of the exercises are writing assignments. I also expect you to be familiar with basic high school algebra and probability; you'll find this especially important when you study the chapters on core mechanics and game balancing.

The book assumes that you are designing an entire game by yourself. I have two reasons for taking this approach. First, to become a skilled game designer, you should be familiar with all aspects of design, so I cover the subject as if you will do it all. Second, even if you do have a team of designers, I cannot tell you how to structure or manage your team beyond a few generalities. The way you divide up their responsibilities will depend a great deal on the kind of game you are designing and the skills of the individuals on the team. From the standpoint of teaching the material, it is simplest to write it as if one person will do all the work.

How Is This Book Organized?

Fundamentals of Game Design, Third Edition consists of 17 chapters, plus the companion e-books devoted to the individual genres (see www.peachpit.com/ernestadams for more details). The first six chapters introduce games, game design, genres, players, machines, and business models for making money from games. The next ten chapters delve deeply into the different aspects of a game and how to design them:

worlds, characters, mechanics, stories, the user experience, and many other issues. The final chapter addresses some of the special design considerations of online gaming.

Chapter Overviews

Chapter 1 introduces games in general and video games in particular, including formal definitions of the terms *game* and *gameplay*. It also discusses what computers bring to games and lists the important ways that video games entertain.

Chapter 2 introduces the key components of a video game: the core mechanics, user interface, and storytelling engine. It also presents the concept of a gameplay mode and the structure of a video game. The last half of the chapter is devoted to the practice of game design, including my recommended approach, player-centric design.

Chapter 3 explains what game genres are and gives a brief introduction to the major genres of games.

Chapter 4 discusses players. It addresses the psychological traits that cause players to prefer different kinds of games. It also reviews key demographic categories—men and women, boys and girls—and looks at the phenomenon of gamer dedication.

Chapter 5 is about the different types of machines people play games on: home consoles, personal computers, and portable devices, and how designing and developing for these devices varies.

Chapter 6 examines the various business models by which you can make money from your game. These include traditional direct payment models such as retail sales and subscription-based games, and new indirect payment models such as freemium and advertising-supported games.

Chapter 7 is about game concepts: where the idea for a game comes from and how to refine the idea. The audience and the target hardware (the machine the game will run on) both have a strong influence on the direction the game will take.

Chapter 8 speaks to the game's setting and world: the place where the gameplay happens and the way things work there. As the designer, you're the god of your world, and it's up to you to define its concepts of time and space, mechanics, and natural laws, as well as many other things: its logic, emotions, culture, and values.

Chapter 9 addresses creative and expressive play, listing different ways your game can support the players' creativity and self-expression.

Chapter 10 addresses character design, inventing the people or beings who populate your game world—especially the character who will represent the player there (his avatar), if there is one. Every successful entertainer from Homer onward has understood the importance of having an appealing protagonist.

Chapter 11 delves into the problems of storytelling and narrative, introducing the issues of linear, branching, and foldback story structures. It also discusses a number of related issues such as scripted conversations and episodic story structures.

Chapter 12 is about user experience design: the way the player experiences and interacts with the game world. A bad user interface can kill an otherwise brilliant game, so you must get this right.

Chapter 13 discusses gameplay, the heart of the player's mental experience of a game. The gameplay consists of the challenges the player faces and the actions he takes to overcome them. It also analyzes the nature of difficulty in gameplay.

Chapter 14 introduces the five types of core mechanics: physics, economics, tactical maneuvering, progression, and social interactions. It examines each of these (except physics) and looks in depth as internal economies. These govern the flow of resources (money, points, ammunition, or whatever) throughout the game.

Chapter 15 considers the issue of game balancing, the process of making multiplayer games fair to all players, and controlling the difficulty of single-player games.

Chapter 16 introduces the general principles of level design, both universal principles and genre-specific ones. It also considers a variety of level layouts and proposes a process for level design.

Chapter 17 looks at online gaming, which is not a genre but a technology. Online games enable people to play with, or against, each other in numbers from two up to hundreds of thousands. Playing against real people that you cannot see has enormous consequences for the game's design. The second half of the chapter addresses the particular problems of persistent worlds like *World of Warcraft,* and some of the social problems that can occur in online games that you will have to prepare for.

The Glossary defines many of the game design terms that appear in italics throughout the book.

The Companion E-Books

As mentioned earlier in the introduction, the old Part Two from the second edition, which contained chapters about the individual game genres, has become a series of inexpensive e-books. All of these e-books are available from the Peachpit website at www.peachpit.com/ernestadams.

Two of these e-books are available for free with this book; the details of that are in the next section, "A Note on the Downloadable Files."

Fundamentals of Shooter Game Design discusses designing for this huge and specialized market. It examines both the frenetic deathmatch style of play and the stealthier, more tactical approach.

Fundamentals of Action and Arcade Game Design is about the earliest, and still most popular, genre of interactive entertainment: action games. This genre may be divided into numerous subgenres such as fighting games, platformers, and others, which the chapter addresses in as much detail as there is room for. It also looks at the most popular hybrid genre, the action-adventure.

Fundamentals of Music, Dance, and Exercise Game Design addresses a popular new genre that has made gaming more accessible to new players than conventional action games are.

Fundamentals of Strategy Game Design discusses another genre that has been part of gaming since the beginning: strategy games, both real-time and turn-based.

Fundamentals of Role-Playing Game Design is about role-playing games, a natural outgrowth of pencil and paper games such as *Dungeons & Dragons*.

Fundamentals of Sports Game Design looks at sports games, which have a number of peculiar design challenges. The actual contest itself is designed by others; the trick is to map human athletic activities onto a screen and control devices.

Fundamentals of Vehicle Simulation Design addresses vehicle simulations: cars, planes, boats, and other, more exotic modes of transportation such as tanks.

Fundamentals of Construction and Simulation Game Design is about construction and management simulations in which the player tries to build and maintain something—a city, a theme park, a planet—within the limitations of an economic system.

Fundamentals of Adventure Game Design explores adventure games, an old and unique genre of gaming that continues to earn a great deal of critical attention by its strong storytelling and its visual aesthetics.

Fundamentals of Puzzle and Casual Game Design examines puzzle games and casual games in general.

A Note on the Downloadable Files

NOTE If updates to this book are posted, those updates will also appear in your Account page at www.peachpit.com.

At the publisher's website you'll find design document templates, a list of suggestions for further reading, and two free e-books (*Fundamentals of Strategy Game Design* and *Fundamentals of Construction and Simulation Game Design*).

At the back of this book is a card with an access code. To access the files, please do the following:

1. On a Mac or Windows computer, go to www.peachpit.com/redeem and enter the code at the back of your book.

2. If you do not have a Peachpit.com account, you will be prompted to create one.

The downloadable files will be listed in the Lesson & Update Files tab on your Account page.

3. Click the file links to download them to your computer.

This process may take some time to complete, depending on the speed of your computer and Internet connection.

Games and Video Games

Before we talk about game design, we have to talk about games themselves. We'll start by identifying the essential elements that a game must have and then define what a game is based on those elements. Then we'll go on to discuss what computers bring to gaming and how video games are different from conventional games. Finally, we'll look at the specific ways in which video games entertain people and note some other enjoyable features of video games that this book will teach you how to design.

What Is a Game?

Work consists of whatever a body is obliged to do, and… Play consists of whatever a body is not obliged to do.

—MARK TWAIN, *THE ADVENTURES OF TOM SAWYER*

Games arise from the human desire for play and from our capacity to pretend. *Play* is a wide category of nonessential, and usually recreational, human activities that are often socially significant as well. *Pretending* is the mental ability to establish an imaginary reality that the pretender knows is different from the real world and that the pretender can create, abandon, or change at will. Playing and pretending are essential elements of playing games. Both have been studied extensively as cultural and psychological phenomena.

Toys, Puzzles, and Games

In English, we use the word *play* to describe how we entertain ourselves with toys, puzzles, and games—although with puzzles, we more frequently say that we *solve* them. However, even though we use the same word, we do not play with all types of entertainment in the same way. What differentiates these types of play is the presence, or absence, of rules and goals.

Rules are instructions that dictate how to play. A toy does not come with any rules about the right way to play with it, nor does it come with a particular goal that the player should try to achieve. You may play with a ball or a stick any way you like. In fact, you can pretend that either one is something else entirely. Toys that model other objects (such as a doll that resembles a real baby) might *suggest* an appropriate way to play, but the suggestion is not a rule. In fact, young children get special enjoyment by playing with toys in a way that subverts their intended purpose, such as treating a doll as a car.

If you add a distinct *goal* to playing—a particular objective that you are trying to achieve—then the article you're playing with is not a toy but a *puzzle*. Puzzles have one rule that defines the goal, but they seldom have rules that dictate how you must get to the goal. Some approaches might be fruitless, but none are actually prohibited.

A *game* includes both rules and a goal. Playing a game is a more structured activity than playing with toys or puzzles, and it requires more maturity. As children develop longer attention spans, they start to play with puzzles and then to play games. Multiplayer games also require social cooperation, another thing that children learn as they mature.

The Definition of a Game

Games are so diverse that it's difficult to create a satisfactory definition of the word. Instead, we'll use a convenient description to cover the majority of cases, without trying to be rigorous.

> **GAMES** *are a type of play activity, conducted in the context of a pretended reality, in which the participant(s) try to achieve at least one arbitrary, nontrivial goal by acting in accordance with rules.*

There may be exceptions—activities that someone would instantly recognize as a game but that don't conform to this definition. So be it. The definition is intended to be practical rather than complete.

OTHER VIEWS

Many people in fields as diverse as anthropology, philosophy, history, and, of course, game design have attempted to define the word *game* over the years. In *Rules of Play*, Salen and Zimmerman examine several of these definitions (Salen and Zimmerman, 2003, pp. 73–80). Most, but not all, make some reference to rules, goals, play, and pretending. Some include other elements such as decision-making or the quality of being a system. This book doesn't try to replace any of these; it just presents a new definition to stand beside the others. Note that some commentators, such as Raph Koster in *A Theory of Fun for Game Design*, disparage the distinctions between toys, puzzles, and games as irrelevant (Koster, 2004, p. 36). However, it is important to address them in an introductory text.

The Essential Elements of a Game

The essential elements of a game are play, pretending, a goal, and rules. Our definition of games refers to each of these elements and includes some additional conditions as well. In the next few sections, we'll look at each of these elements and their significance in the definition more closely.

PLAY

Play is a participatory form of entertainment, whereas books, films, and theater are presentational forms. When you read a book, the author entertains you; when you play, you entertain yourself. A book doesn't change, no matter how often you read it, but when you play, you make choices that affect the course of events.

Theoreticians of drama often argue that watching a play or film is a conscious, active process and that the audience *is* an active participant in those forms of entertainment. The theoreticians have a point, but the issue here is with the actual content and not the audience's interpretation of it. With the rare exception of some experimental works, the audience does not actually create or change the content of a play, even if their comprehension or interpretation does change over time. Reading a book or watching a play is not *passive*, but it is not *interactive* in the sense of modifying the text.

NOTE Games are interactive. They require active players whose participation changes the course of events.

In contrast, each time you play a game, you can make different choices and have a different experience. Play ultimately includes the freedom to act and the freedom to choose *how* you act. This freedom is not unlimited, however. Your choices are constrained by the rules, and this requires you to be clever, imaginative, or skillful in your play.

This book will continue to use the term *play* despite the fact that you can play games for a serious purpose such as learning or exercise.

PRETENDING

David: Is this a game, or is it real?

Joshua: What's the difference?

—Exchange between a boy (David) and a computer in the movie *WarGames*

Pretending is the act of creating a notional reality in the mind, which is one element of our definition of a game. Another name for the reality created by pretending is the *magic circle*. This is an idea that Dutch historian Johan Huizinga originally identified in his book *Homo Ludens* (Huizinga, 1971), and others expanded upon in later theories of play. The magic circle is related to the concept of imaginary worlds in fiction and drama, and Huizinga also felt that it was connected to ceremonial, spiritual, legal, and other activities. For our purposes, however, the magic circle simply refers to the boundary between reality and make-believe.

THE MAGIC CIRCLE

Huizinga did not use the term *magic circle* as a generic name for the concept. His text actually refers to the *play-ground*, a physical space for play, of which he considers the tennis court, the court of law, the stage, the magic circle (a sacred outdoor space for worship in "primitive" religions), the temple, and many others to be examples. However, theoreticians of play have since adopted the term *magic circle* to refer to the *mental* universe established when a player pretends. That is the sense that this book uses.

In recent years a few scholars have begun to argue that the magic circle is so fluid and permeable that the concept isn't really of much value (Consalvo, 2009). However, we still need a way to discuss the mental state of pretending that an artificial and arbitrary world is meaningful. People become emotionally invested in purely imaginary things. The term *magic circle* is as good as any to describe this phenomenon.

Players can even pretend things in the magic circle that are impossible in the real world, for example, "Let's pretend that I'm moving at the speed of light." **Figure 1.1** illustrates the magic circle.

FIGURE 1.1
The magic circle, separating the real world from the pretended reality

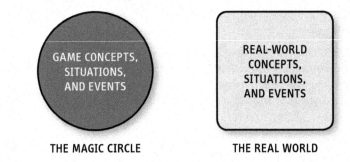

THE MAGIC CIRCLE   THE REAL WORLD

NOTE Within the magic circle, the players agree to attach a temporary, artificial significance to situations and events in the game. The magic circle comes into existence when the players join the game—in effect, when they agree to abide by the rules. It disappears again when they abandon the game or the game ends.

The definition of a game used the term *pretended reality* rather than *magic circle* because the former is self-explanatory and the latter is not. However, from now on, we'll refer to the magic circle because it is the more widely accepted term.

In single-player games, the player establishes the magic circle simply by choosing to play. In multiplayer games, players agree upon a convention, which in turn establishes the magic circle. In other words, they all pretend together, and more important, they all agree to pretend the same things—that is, to accept the same rules (see **Figure 1.2**). Although the pretended reality can seem very real to a deeply immersed player, it is still only a convention and can be renounced by the player refusing to play.

The boundary between make-believe and reality is not always well-defined. If the events in the game are also meaningful in the real world, the magic circle becomes blurred. For example, gambling crosses the line between the real world and the magic circle because when you gamble, you bet real money on the outcome of a game. So do games, such as *EVE Online,* in which you can pay real money for better in-game equipment that improves your chances of winning battles.

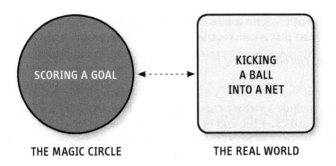

THE MAGIC CIRCLE   THE REAL WORLD

FIGURE 1.2
We pretend that real-world events have special meanings inside the magic circle.

A GOAL

A game must have a goal (or *object;* these terms are used interchangeably throughout the book), and it can have more than one. As observed previously, goalless play is not the same as game play. Even creative, noncompetitive play still has a goal: creation. The object of *SimCity* is to build and manage a city without going bankrupt; as long as the player does not go bankrupt, the game continues indefinitely without any outcome. In fact, the object of a game need not even be achievable, as long as the players *try* to achieve it. Most early arcade games, such as *Space Invaders* and *Missile Command*, gave the players an unachievable goal. In the case of *Missile Command*, this resonated emotionally with Cold War fears: Sooner or later, nuclear war spelled inevitable doom. The player can never win; the only thing he can actually achieve is to play longer or earn a higher score than he (or other players) have done before.

NOTE There must be some challenge (non-trivial effort) involved in trying to achieve a game's goal. The difficulty of a challenge is perceived differently by different players, however.

The goal of the game is defined by the rules and is arbitrary because the game designers can define it any way they like. The goal of the children's card game Go Fish is to obtain *books*—collections of four cards of the same suit—but this can change if the rules change. The goal must be nontrivial because a game must include some element of challenge. In a creative game, creation itself challenges the players. To do well requires skill. If the object can be achieved in a single moment, without either physical or mental effort, then the activity is not really a game. Betting on a coin flip, for example, is not a game because it does not include a challenge.

The rules of a game frequently characterize the game's ultimate goal as a *victory condition*—an unambiguous situation in the game at which point one or more of the players are declared the winners. For example, the victory condition for chess states that the first player to checkmate her opponent's king (an unambiguous situation) is the winner. In timed sports such as basketball, the victory condition states that when time runs out (the unambiguous situation), whichever team has the most points wins the game and the other team loses. Game designers can also establish additional rules about ties and tie-breaking mechanisms if they think it is important to have a clear winner.

NOTE The concepts of winning and losing are not essential to games, but they make a game more exciting. A game must have a goal, but the goal need not be characterized as victory or defeat.

The rule that determines when the game is over is called the *termination condition.* In two-player competitive games, the termination condition is usually taken for granted: The game ends when one player achieves victory. Note that victory does not necessarily end the game, however. In a game with more than two players, play can

as "interaction that entertains" (Dini, 2004, p. 31). Although neither of these is obviously wrong, these definitions are too general for practical use and not much help as you learn how to design a game. Again, this book uses a nonrigorous definition that might not cover all possible cases but that provides a basis for thinking about game design. The definition hinges on challenges and actions, so we look at them first.

CHALLENGES

A *challenge* is any task set for the player that is nontrivial to accomplish. Overcoming a challenge must require either mental or physical effort. Challenges can be as simple as getting a ball through a hoop or as complex as making a business profitable. Challenges can be unique, recurring, or continuing. In action video games, players frequently face a recurring challenge to defeat a number of identical enemies, and then having done so, they must overcome a unique challenge to defeat a particular *boss* enemy. In a combat flight simulator, shooting down enemy planes is a recurring challenge, whereas avoiding being hit by them is a continuing challenge. The players must do both at once to be successful.

You can also define a challenge in terms of other, smaller challenges. For example, you can give your player an overall challenge of completing an obstacle course, and you can set up the obstacle course in terms of smaller challenges such as climbing over a fence, crawling under a barrier, jumping across a gap, and so on. The largest challenge of all in a game is to achieve its goal, but unless the game is extremely simple (such as tic-tac-toe), the players always have to surmount other challenges along the way.

Most challenges in a game are direct obstacles to achieving the goal, although games might include optional challenges as well. You can include optional challenges to help the player practice or simply to provide more things for the player to do. In sports games, a team needs only to score more goals than its opponent(s) to win the game, but the team may consider an optional challenge to prevent the opposing team from ever scoring at all.

The challenges in a game are established by the rules, although the rules don't always specify them precisely. In some cases, the players must figure out what the challenges are by thinking logically about the rules or by playing the game a few times. For example, the rules of *Othello* (Reversi) state only how pieces are converted from one color to another and that the object of the game is to have the most pieces of your own color when the board is filled. As you play the game, however, you discover that the corner spaces on the board are extremely valuable because they can never be converted to your opponent's color. Gaining control of a corner space is one of the major challenges of the game, but it's not spelled out explicitly in the rules.

A challenge must be nontrivial, but that doesn't mean that it must be difficult. Young children and inexperienced players often prefer to play games with easy challenges.

ACTIONS

The rules specify what *actions* the players may take to overcome the challenges and achieve the goal of the game. The rules define not only what actions are allowed but also which ones are prohibited and which ones are required, and under what circumstances. Games also permit optional actions that are not required to surmount a challenge but add to the player's enjoyment in other ways. For example, in the *Grand Theft Auto* games, you can listen to the radio in the car.

Many conventional games allow any action that is not prohibited by the rules. For example, in paintball, you may run, jump, crouch, crawl, climb, or make any other movement that you can think of to take enemy ground. Because video games are implemented by computer software, however, they can allow only actions that are built into the game. A video game offers a player a fixed suite of actions to choose from, which limits the number of ways in which a player can attack a challenge.

THE DEFINITION OF GAMEPLAY

Combining the concepts of challenges and actions produces the following definition:

GAMEPLAY *consists of*

- ▦ *The challenges that a player must face to arrive at the object of the game.*
- ▦ *The actions that the player is permitted to take to address those challenges.*

This definition lies at the heart of game design. Gameplay consists of challenges and actions, and you will see this idea throughout the rest of the book. As a designer, you must create them both together. It's not enough to invent interesting challenges without the actions that will surmount them, nor is it enough to think of exciting actions without the challenges that they are intended to address. Games often permit additional actions that are not intended to solve a challenge, but the *essence* of gameplay is the challenge/action relationship.

Fantasy and imagination play an important role in entertaining the player, and some designers consider them to be elements of gameplay; in other words, the act of pretending that you are a pilot or a princess is an explicit part of the gameplay. However, these elements unnecessarily complicate the definition of gameplay. The player's imaginary role is not the gameplay; the gameplay *arises from* the role, as we will see in the next chapter.

Fairness

Generally speaking, players expect that the rules will guarantee that the game is *fair*. Different societies, and indeed individual players, have varying notions of what is and is not fair. Fairness is not an essential element of a game but a culturally constructed notion that lies outside the magic circle. It is, in fact, a social metarule that the players can use to pass judgment on the rules themselves. Players sometimes decide spontaneously to change the rules of a game during play if they perceive that the rules are unfair or that the rules are permitting unfair behavior. For all the players to enjoy a game, they must all be in general agreement about what constitutes fair play.

CHANGING THE RULES

Whether the rules can be changed during play is usually determined by an unwritten social convention, but in some cases, the rules themselves describe the procedure for changing the rules. Games in which rules can be changed usually define two types of rules: the *mutable* (changeable) and the *immutable*. The immutable rules include instructions about when and how the mutable rules may be changed. *Nomic*, created by philosopher Peter Suber, is such a game.

It is particularly important that the players perceive a video game to be fair because, unlike conventional games, video games seldom give the players any way to change the rules if the players don't like them. One widely accepted definition of fairness is that all the players in a multiplayer game must have an equal chance of winning at the beginning of the game. The simplest way to achieve this is to make the game symmetric, as you'll see in the next section. In single-player video games, fairness is a complex issue that has to do with balance and with meeting players' expectations. Chapter 15, "Game Balancing," discusses this at much greater length.

Symmetry and Asymmetry

In a *symmetric* game, all the players play by the same rules and try to achieve the same victory condition. Basketball is a symmetric game. The initial conditions, the actions allowed, and the victory condition are identical for both teams. Many traditional games such as chess and backgammon are symmetric in every respect except that one player must move first.

WHO GOES FIRST?

In turn-based games, the fact that one player moves first can confer an advantage to one side or the other. For example, in tic-tac-toe among experienced players, *only* the person who goes first can win. However, if a game is designed in such a way that the advantage of going first is slight or nonexistent, this asymmetry can be ignored. In chess, only the weakest pieces on the board, pawns or knights, can move on the first turn, and they cannot move very far or establish a dominant position. The asymmetry of going first is considered irrelevant, so for practical purposes chess is a symmetric game.

People usually feel that if all players start in the same state, they all have an equal chance of winning. This assumes that the definition of fairness ignores the differences in the players' skill levels. Occasionally, people agree that a highly skilled player must take a *handicap*—that is, they impose a disadvantage on a skilled player to give the less-skilled players a better chance of winning. Amateur golf is the best-known example: Poor players are allotted a certain number of strokes per match that do not count against their score. On the other hand, professional golf, in which prize money is at stake, does not use this system and is purely symmetric. Parents playing against their own children often handicap themselves, too.

In an *asymmetric* game, different players may play by different rules and try to achieve different victory conditions. Many games that represent real-world situations (for example, war games based on historical events) are asymmetric. If you play a war game about World War II, one side is the Axis and one is the Allied powers. The two sides necessarily begin at different locations on the map, with different numbers of troops and different kinds of weapons. As a result, it is often necessary for the two sides to have different objectives to make the game fair.

In asymmetric games, it is much more difficult to determine in advance whether players of equal skill have an equal chance of winning. As a result, people often adjust the rules of asymmetric games to suit their own notions of fairness. **Figure 1.3** shows an asymmetric medieval board game called Fox and Geese. One player moves the fox (F) and the other moves the geese (G).

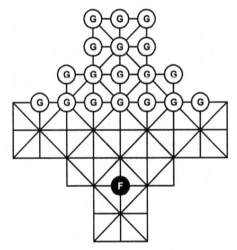

The players take turns each moving one piece. The objective for the fox is to jump over the geese and remove them from the board, while the objective for the geese is to push the fox into a corner so that it cannot move. The geese cannot jump over the fox. Several variants of this game exist because people

FIGURE 1.3 Fox and Geese, an asymmetric medieval board game

have adjusted the rules to align it closer to their sense of fairness. Some versions have two foxes; other versions have smaller numbers of geese; in some, the geese may not move on the diagonal lines, and so on.

Competition and Cooperation

Competition occurs when players have conflicting interests; that is, when the players try to accomplish mutually exclusive goals. *Cooperation* occurs when the players try to achieve the same or related goals by working together. Players who are trying to achieve different, unrelated goals that are not mutually exclusive are neither competing nor cooperating—they are not really playing the same game. *Competition modes* are ways to build cooperation and competition into games:

▪ **Two-player competitive ("you versus me")** is the best-known mode; this is found in the most ancient games such as chess and backgammon.

▪ **Multiplayer competitive ("everyone for himself")** is familiar from games such as *Monopoly*, poker, and of course, many individual sports such as track and field athletics. This is also known as *deathmatch*, although the term is usually used only in shooter games.

▪ **Multiplayer cooperative ("all of us together")** occurs when all the players cooperate to accomplish the same goal. Conventional cooperative games are somewhat rare, but they are more common in video games. Many games, such as *LEGO Star Wars* and *LittleBigPlanet*, offer a cooperative mode as a variant of their normal single-player mode.

▪ **Team-based ("us versus them")** mode occurs when the members of a team cooperate, and the team collectively competes against one or more other teams. This mode is familiar to fans of soccer and many other team sports as well as partner games such as bridge.

▪ **Single-player ("me versus the situation")** is familiar to those who play solitaire card games as well as the vast majority of arcade and other video games such as the *Mario* series from Nintendo.

▪ **Hybrid competition modes** occur in a few games such as *Diplomacy*. Such games specifically permit cooperation at times, even if the overall context of the game is competitive. In *Diplomacy*, players may coordinate their strategies, but they also may renege on their agreements to their own advantage if they wish. The standard rules for *Monopoly*, by contrast, does not permit cooperation because it gives the cooperating players too much of an advantage against the others.

Many video games let the players choose a competition mode at the beginning of the game: single-player, team-based, or multiplayer competitive. A choice of competition modes broadens the market for these games but adds considerably to the work of designing them. Chapter 4, "Understanding Your Player," discusses how players feel about different cooperation modes.

Conventional Games Versus Video Games

A game designer should be able to design all kinds of games, not just video games. She must have a thorough understanding of the essential elements—play, rules, goals, and so on—and should be able to design an enjoyable game with nothing but paper and pencil. That's part of the reason the beginning of this chapter included so much material on games in general. However, the purpose of this book is to teach you to design video games, and from now on it concentrates on that (although it will still sometimes refer to conventional games such as *Monopoly* when they illustrate a point particularly well). If you'd like to learn more about general game design, read *Rules of Play* by Salen and Zimmerman (Salen and Zimmerman, 2003).

You now know the formal definition of a game, but from this point on, we'll use the word *game* in an informal sense to refer to the game software. Phrases like "the game is smart" or "the game offers the player certain options" mean the software, not the play activity itself.

Video games are a subset of the universe of all games. A *video game* is a game mediated by a computer, whether the computer is installed in a tiny keychain device such as a Tamagotchi or in a huge electronic play environment at a theme park. The computer enables video games to borrow entertainment techniques from other media such as books, film, karaoke, and so on. This section looks at what the computer brings to gaming.

Hiding the Rules

Unlike conventional games, video games ordinarily do not require written rules. The game still *has* rules, but the machine implements and enforces them for the players. The players do not need to even know exactly what the rules are, although they do need to be told how to play. The computer also determines when the player reaches the goal. It adjudicates victory and defeat if those concepts are programmed into the game.

This means players no longer have to think about the game as a system of rules. A player contemplating an action can simply try it, without having to read the rules to see whether the game permits it. This lets players become much more deeply immersed in the experience, to see it not as a temporary artificial environment with arbitrary rules, but as an alternate universe of which the player is a part.

Hiding the rules has one big disadvantage. If the players don't know the rules, they don't know how to optimize their choices. They can learn the rules only by playing the game. This is a reasonable design technique provided that the game includes hints about how to play it and what to expect. However, some video games force the player to learn by trial and error, which can make the game extremely frustrating.

NOTE Multiplayer video games, especially online games, often do have explicit written rules to prohibit cheating and abusive behavior. These games are usually less immersive than single-player games.

DESIGN RULE Avoid Trial and Error

Provide adequate clues that enable players to deduce the correct resolution to a problem. Avoid creating challenges that they can surmount only by trial and error. (Challenges that require physical skill and that may be overcome with practice are an exception.)

Setting the Pace

In conventional games that don't use a timer, either the players or an independent referee sets the *pace* of the game—the rate at which the events required by the rules take place. In effect, it is up to the players to make the game go. In video games, the computer sets the pace and makes the game go. Unless specifically waiting for the player's input, the computer keeps the game moving forward at whatever pace the designer has set. This allows us to design fast and furious games that constantly throw enemies or other challenges at the players, or to design slow and deliberative games in which the players can stop to think for as long as they want. Games can also modulate the pace, giving players a rest between periods of intense activity.

Presenting a Game World

Because a game world is fictional—a fantasy world—the game designer can include imaginary people, places, and situations. The players can think of themselves as make-believe characters in a make-believe place. With conventional games, this takes place primarily in the player's imagination, although printed boards, cards, and so on can help.

Video games can go much further. By using a screen and speakers, video games present a fictional world the players can sense directly. Modern video games are full of pictures, animation, movies, music, dialog, sound effects, and so on that conventional games cannot possibly provide. In fact, video games have become so photorealistic in recent years that some designers now experiment with a wider range of visual styles such as Impressionism, traditional Japanese brush painting, and so on. *Minecraft,* with its retro pixelated look, is a perfect example.

Some people are also making games of *augmented reality*, or *mixed reality*, in which computers are used in conjunction with real-world activities to play a game. Such games often use mobile phones, video cameras, or global positioning systems as well as web servers and a browser-based interface for some of the players. This book doesn't discuss how to design such games, but use the resources in the references if you're interested in learning more.

Creating Artificial Intelligence

In 1959, IBM scientist Arthur Samuels devised a program that played checkers (Samuels, 1959). The program could also learn from its mistakes, and eventually it became good enough to beat expert human players. Much of the earliest research on artificial intelligence (AI) and games was of this sort, as computer scientists tried to create artificial opponents that could play traditional games as competently as humans could. AI lets us play multiplayer games even when we don't have other people to play with.

However, AI brings considerably more to video gaming than artificial opponents for traditional games. Game developers use AI techniques for the following:

■ **Strategy.** This means determining the optimal action to take by considering the possible consequences of a variety of available actions. Samuels's checker-playing program did this, but checkers is a game of *perfect information,* which means it does not have any hidden information or element of chance. Modern video games usually have both hidden information and a large element of chance, so a strategy is more difficult to compute.

■ **Pathfinding.** This means finding the most advantageous routes through a simulated landscape filled with obstacles.

■ **Natural language parsing.** Despite decades of research, computers still cannot understand ordinary written or spoken language well, but researchers are still very interested in using it for games. When this problem is solved, players will be able to give commands using natural sentences.

■ **Natural language generation.** Video games currently produce language by playing combinations of previously recorded phrases or sentences. At the moment, they cannot generate language on their own. In time perhaps they will, which will make simulated people seem far more realistic. In the meantime, games use AI to select a sentence from their library of prerecorded material that is most appropriate for the current game situation.

■ **Pattern recognition.** This valuable technique has numerous applications including voice recognition, face recognition, pattern detection in ongoing processes, and pattern detection in player behavior. Human poker players use pattern recognition to establish a correlation between their opponent's behavior and their opponent's cards, which players can use to their advantage later. Eventually, a computer might be programmed to do the same thing.

■ **Simulated people and creatures.** Many games use simple AI techniques to create a behavioral model for simulated people or creatures. The simulated character seems to respond intelligently to the human player's actions, at least within certain limits. The models are seldom complex, and a player can usually tell the difference between a simulated person and a real one within a few minutes. Simulating human beings is the most difficult and also the most important problem in game AI research.

Many games do not need sophisticated AI. The point of video games is to entertain, not to simulate intelligence in depth, so as designers, we need to match the AI to our goals for the experience. We still have a lot of room for improvement, however. Artificial intelligence is one of the most important areas of research in game development.

Games for Entertainment

The vast majority of video games in the world are designed to entertain people, either for profit or for free. To make games for entertainment, you must learn to be an entertainer. This section looks at how games entertain people.

Different people enjoy different things, so we have both grand opera and motorcycle races, as well as long, slow adventure games and short, frenetic arcade games. As a well-rounded game designer, you should be able to create games that entertain in a variety of ways.

DESIGN RULE You Can't Please Everyone

It is not possible to design an ideal game that pleases everyone, because everyone does not enjoy the same thing. Do not try.

Gameplay

Games provide *gameplay,* that is, challenges and actions that entertain. People enjoy a challenge, as long as they can reasonably expect to accomplish it. People also try a challenge they do not expect to meet if the risk is low and the reward is high. Challenges create tension and drama. At the simplest level, presenting players with a challenge amounts to asking the question, "Can you do it?" They'll enjoy trying to prove that they can.

People also enjoy executing the actions that the game offers. It's fun to fly a plane, shoot a rifle, design clothing, build a castle, or sing and dance. Video games let us do many things that are impossible or too expensive for us to do in real life, which is an important part of their appeal. The actions don't all have to be tied to a specific challenge; some things are fun to do even if they don't affect the outcome of the game. Many children's video games include toy-like elements to play with that light up, ring, change color, and so on.

DESIGN RULE Gameplay Comes First

Gameplay is the primary source of entertainment in all video games. When designing a game, it is the *first* thing to consider.

Table 1.1 lists several types of challenges that video games offer, along with well-known examples from individual games or game series.

TABLE 1.1 Video Game Challenges

CHALLENGE TYPE	FAMILIAR EXAMPLE
Physical Coordination Challenges	
Speed and reaction time	*Tetris*
Accuracy or precision (steering, shooting)	*OutRun, Rainbow Six*
Timing and rhythm	*Just Dance*
Learning combination moves	*Street Fighter II*
Formal Logic Challenges	
Deduction and decoding	*Minesweeper, Mastermind*
Pattern Recognition Challenges	
Static patterns	*Brain Age, Bejeweled*
Patterns of movement and change	*Sonic the Hedgehog*, behavior patterns of enemies
Time Pressure	
Beating the clock	*Frogger, Diner Dash*
Achieving something before someone else	*Need for Speed*
Memory and Knowledge Challenges	
Trivia	*You Don't Know Jack*
Recollection of objects or patterns	*Brain Age*
Exploration Challenges	
Identifying spatial relationships	*Descent*, navigating in three dimensions
Finding keys (unlocking any space)	*Ultima*
Finding hidden passages	*Doom*
Mazes and illogical spaces	*Zork*
Conflict	
Strategy, tactics, and logistics	*Warcraft*, commanding armies
Survival	*Pac-Man*, avoiding being caught
Reduction of enemy forces	*Space Invaders*, killing aliens
Defending vulnerable items or units	*Ico*, looking after a little girl who can't fight
Stealth	*Assassin's Creed*, avoiding being seen
Economic Challenges	
Accumulating resources or points (growth)	*Civilization*
Establishing efficient production systems	*The Settlers*
Achieving balance or stability in a system	*SimEarth*
Caring for living things	*The Sims*

continues on next page

IMMERSION

In 1817, the English poet Samuel Taylor Coleridge coined an important term, *the willing suspension of disbelief:*

…it was agreed, that my endeavours should be directed to persons and characters supernatural, or at least romantic, yet so as to transfer from our inward nature a human interest and a semblance of truth sufficient to procure for these shadows of imagination that willing suspension of disbelief for the moment, which constitutes poetic faith.

—Samuel Taylor Coleridge, *Biographia Litteraria*, Chapter XIV

Coleridge was originally referring not to immersion but to an absence of skepticism. He wanted people who read his poems to accept the poems' romantic, imaginary people ("shadows of imagination") on "poetic faith," without asking questions. However, the term *suspension of disbelief,* as used by the game industry, has come to mean *immersion:* losing track of the outside world. Immersion is the feeling of being submerged in a form of entertainment, or rather, being unaware that you are experiencing an artificial world. When you are immersed in a book, movie, or game, you devote all your attention to it and it seems real. You have lost track of the boundaries of the magic circle. The pretended reality in which you are immersed seems as real as, or at least as meaningful as, the real world.

This feeling of immersion is deeply and satisfyingly entertaining to some players; others prefer not to become immersed and to remember that it's only a game while they play. People who take the game seriously find interruptions that break their sense of immersion jarring and disappointing. This is part of the reason that harmony is so important.

Players become immersed in games in several ways:

■ **Tactical immersion** is the sense of being "in the groove" in high-speed action games. It's sometimes called the *Tetris trance.* When playing such a game, the action is so fast that your brain has no time for anything else. You don't have time to think about strategy or a story line; the game is mostly about survival. To encourage tactical immersion, you must offer the player dozens of small challenges that can each be met in a fraction of a second. These small challenges must be fairly similar to one another—such as in an arcade shooter. Abrupt changes in the gameplay destroy tactical immersion.

■ **Strategic immersion** occurs when you are deeply involved in trying to win a game, like the immersion of the chess master: observing, calculating, and planning. You don't think about a story, characters, or the game world but focus strictly on optimizing your choices. To experience strategic immersion, the players must understand the rules of the game clearly so that they can plan actions to their maximum advantage. Strategic immersion breaks down if a game confronts players with a situation they have never seen before or if the game contains too many unpredictable elements. Unexpected or erratic behavior makes it impossible to plan.

▪ **Spatial immersion** is the sense of being in a place other than the one you're actually in. This is what virtual reality equipment is designed to achieve, although it's not necessary; with a good 3D engine, people can feel spatially immersed in an environment even without stereo vision or 360-degree sound. Some players set up multiple monitors so even their peripheral vision is seeing the game world, which heightens their sense of spatial immersion.

▪ **Narrative immersion** is the feeling of being inside a story; the player is completely involved and accepts the world and events of the story as real. It is the same immersion as that produced by a good book or movie, but in video games, the player is also an actor within the story. Good storytelling—interesting characters, exciting plots, dramatic situations—produces narrative immersion. Bad storytelling—two-dimensional characters, implausible plots, or trite situations—destroys narrative immersion, and so does gameplay that is inappropriate in the context of the story. If a player is immersed in a story about being a dancer, the gameplay should be about dancing, not about flying a plane or commanding an army.

You cannot create immersion purely by design. The game must also be attractive and well constructed, or its flaws break the player's sense of immersion. Also, you cannot design a game that pleases everyone, and players do not become immersed in a game they don't like. If you want to create an immersive game, you first must have a clear understanding of how your player likes to be entertained; then deliver the best entertainment experience that you can. Chapter 7, "Game Concepts," discusses the question of understanding your hypothetical player in more detail.

EMOTIONAL RESONANCE

Every game designer must ask herself what she wants her player to feel. As explained earlier, the term *fun* is too broad, and not all players feel that the same things are fun. Rather, we can try to evoke specific emotions in a player. If we do so successfully, the game possesses *emotional resonance.*

The game designer Chris Bateman conducted a survey of over 1000 players to identify the emotions that players most frequently feel and enjoy while playing games (Bateman, 2008). After analyzing the results, these were his top 10 emotions that people both experience and enjoy:

1. Amusement. Surprisingly, this was by far the most prevalent emotional experience in games and the second most desired one after wonderment (number 3, below). Bateman suggested that perhaps this indicates that we should be working harder to make games funny.

2. Contentment. Another surprise, when the stereotype of gamers is that they seek out adrenaline rushes. Contentment is that sense of satisfaction you get when you solve a puzzle, collect a full set of something, or complete a series of tasks.

3. Wonderment. This was the most desired (though not the most commonly felt) emotion. Players love to be amazed.

4. **Excitement.** This needs no introduction. Almost all players sometimes feel excitement when playing, although not all of them make active efforts to find it.

5. **Curiosity.** Players want to know what's around the corner, behind the mountain, or in the locked chest. They also want to know what's going to happen next. Engaging players' curiosity is an important skill in level design.

6. **Triumph,** which Bateman calls *fiero*. This is the feeling of elation at having overcome adversity.

7. **Surprise.** Surprises can be pleasurable or they can be startling or even frightening, but however they appear, players like them.

8. **Naches.** This is a Yiddish word that refers to the pleasure of seeing one's students or children do well. People feel this when they help a friend or a child learn a game. The players who hang around the entrance portals of massively multiplayer online games (MMOGs) giving advice to newcomers are seeking *naches*.

9. **Relief.** We all know this one. Barely surviving a particularly tough challenge sometimes creates a sense of relief more than a sense of triumph.

10. **Bliss.** Utter joyfulness without stress. This is not that common in games but may become more so in the future. New kinds of games might emphasize relaxed gameplay rather than the more demanding forms that dominate commercial games at the moment.

To achieve emotional resonance in your game, you will have to think about what causes players to feel the emotions you seek to evoke: personal conflict, physical or logical challenges, caring for an endangered character, mysterious circumstances, and so on. The mood of the game is also part of its emotional resonance, and it can be affected by your choices of lighting and ambient audio. We'll discuss these issues more in Chapter 12, "Creating the User Experience."

Storytelling

Many games incorporate some kind of story as part of the entertainment. In conventional games, players can find it difficult to become immersed in a story because the players must also implement the rules. Stopping to implement the rules interrupts the players' sense of being in another place or being actors in a plot. Video games can mix storylike entertainment and gamelike entertainment almost seamlessly. To some extent, they can make players feel as if they are *inside* a story, affecting its flow of events. This has enormous implications for game design and is one of the reasons that video games are more than simply a new kind of game; they are a completely new medium. Many video games—even those that involve the most frenetic action—now include elements of storytelling. Chapter 11, "Storytelling," will discuss this concept in detail.

In fact, storytelling is *so* powerful as an entertainment device that one genre of video game—the adventure game—is starting to move away from the formal concept of a game entirely. Although we still call them games, adventure games are in fact a new hybrid form of interactive entertainment—the *interactive story*. As time goes on, we can expect to see more new kinds of game/story/play experiences emerge that defy conventional descriptions. Video games aren't just games any more.

Risks and Rewards

Risks and rewards as sources of entertainment are most familiar to us from gambling. You risk money by placing a bet, and you are rewarded with more money if you win the bet. However, risk and reward are key parts of *any* kind of competitive gameplay, even if no money is at stake. Whenever you play a competitive game, you risk losing in the hope that you will get the reward of winning. Risk and reward also occur on a smaller scale within the game. In a war game, when you choose a place to begin an attack, you risk the attack being detected and repulsed, but if you are successful, you are rewarded by controlling new territory or depleting the enemy's resources. In *Monopoly,* you risk money by purchasing a property in the hope that you will be rewarded with income from rents later on.

Risk is produced by uncertainty. If a player knows exactly what the consequences of an action will be, then there is no risk. In gambling, uncertainty is often produced by chance (which way will the dice fall?), but other features produce uncertainty as well. A game might have hidden information (where are the enemy's troops hiding?) that is revealed only after you take the risk. Even in a game such as chess, which has no hidden information and no element of chance, not knowing what your opponent will do produces uncertainty.

The risk/reward mechanism makes gameplay more exciting. Gameplay is entertaining all by itself because it lets the player attempt the challenges and perform the actions, but adding risks and rewards raises the level of tension and makes success or failure more meaningful.

A game should always reward achievement, whether it is risky or not. The more difficult the achievement, the bigger the reward should be. Rewards can take various forms. Usually they advance the player's interests somehow, either by giving him something tangible that helps him play (such as money or a key to a locked area) or something intangible but still valuable, such as a strategic advantage. However, rewards don't have to affect the gameplay. Games that include a story reward the player's achievements by advancing the plot of the story by presenting a little more of it, often in a noninteractive video sequence. Games for children often reward achievements with flashing lights and ringing sounds.

Players' attitudes toward risk-taking vary. Some take an aggressive, inherently risky approach, whereas others prefer a defensive approach in which they try to minimize risk. You can design your game to suit one style or the other, or try to balance the game so that neither really has an advantage. For example, *Cooking Mama* was designed specifically to accommodate players who prefer less risk and want to be successful most of the time that they're playing.

> ### DESIGN RULE Risks Need Rewards
>
> A risk must *always* be accompanied by a reward. Otherwise the player has no incentive to take the risk.

Novelty

People enjoy novelty: new things to see, to hear, and to do. Early video games were extremely repetitive and developed an unfortunate reputation for being monotonous. Nowadays, however, video games can offer more variety and content than any traditional game, no matter how complex. Not only can video games give the player new worlds to play in, but they can easily change the gameplay as the game progresses. So, for example, the *Battlefield* series not only lets the player play as a foot soldier (one of several types, in fact), but also allows her to hop in a tank, an airplane, or a ship and play from those perspectives.

Novelty can even be an end in itself. In the *WarioWare* series from Nintendo, the player must play dozens of strange *microgames,* each of which lasts only a few seconds. Their constantly changing goals and graphical styles make *WarioWare* quite challenging, if rather disorienting. There aren't many games like this on the market, however. Novelty alone is not enough to sustain player interest. Most games rely more on theme-and-variations approaches—introducing a new element and giving the player the chance to explore it for a while before introducing the next one.

Progression

Progression refers to a sequence of challenges planned explicitly by the game designer, as opposed to arising naturally from the operation of the mechanics. Players enjoy the sense that they are advancing toward a goal along a well-designed path, particularly if it includes a feeling of growing power. *Bejeweled* offers the player an experience that is different each time she plays, but it contains no progression because each game is unrelated to the last game. *Candy Crush Saga* improves on this idea by providing the player with a sequence of different kinds of playfields, with different victory conditions for each one. In order to move to the next playfield, the player must complete the current one, and this is called *progression.*

People often think of progression in terms of the game's sequence of levels (or missions, scenarios, or athletic matches). Progression does not only refer to moving from level to level, however; progression can exist within a level, too. The game scholar Jesper Juul has argued that any game with a walkthrough is a game of progression (Juul, 2002).

Exploration

If the player moves through an unfamiliar space, and especially a nonlinear space, he is said to be exploring a major feature of adventure and action-adventure games. We can make exploration more difficult and exciting by including locked doors, traps, and dangerous or confusing spaces. *Portal* is a brilliant game of exploration in which the players must navigate their way through a complicated space by creating portals that teleport them from one place to another instantly. Most games are not this complex, however, and simply require the player to navigate around in a conventional space. This space can be three-dimensional, as in the *Assassin's Creed* series, but sometimes it is two-dimensional, as in side-scrolling games. Point-and-click adventures provide individual scenes that the player moves among by clicking certain locations on the screen.

Learning

In this context, *learning* doesn't refer to educational software. Learning is an aspect of playing a game, even just for entertainment, and people enjoy the learning process. This is the central thesis of Raph Koster's book, *A Theory of Fun for Game Design* (Koster, 2004). Although some of the things Koster says conflict with ideas in this book, *A Theory of Fun for Game Design* is well worth reading. Players have to learn the rules of a game and then learn how to optimize their chances of winning. As long as a game keeps offering you new things to learn, it remains enjoyable—assuming it was enjoyable to begin with! After you have learned everything about a game and have complete mastery over it, you might start to think that the game is boring. Koster asserts that this is inevitable, which is why people eventually abandon a game and pick up a new one. (This is more true of single-player games than it is of multiplayer games, because in multiplayer games the unpredictability of human opponents keeps them fresh.)

Learning isn't always easy, and it isn't guaranteed to be fun, as we all remember from our days in school. People enjoy learning when at least one of two conditions is met: It takes place in an enjoyable context; it provides useful mastery. A game should *always* provide an enjoyable context for learning; if it doesn't, there's something wrong with the game. A game should also offer useful mastery; the things that players learn should help them play the game more successfully. For further discussion of this issue, consider reading James Paul Gee's books *What Video Games Have to Teach Us About Learning and Literacy* (Gee, 2004) and *Why Video Games Are Good for Your Soul* (Gee, 2005).

Simulation and Study

Many games (such as flight and driving simulators) reproduce a real process of some kind, so the boundary between games and simulations is indistinct. Generally speaking, a pure simulation makes no concessions to entertainment at all and tries to be as accurate as possible within the limitations of its hardware. Serious games for the purpose of simulation try to retain the accuracy but to incorporate more game-like qualities to provide player feedback and engagement. For example, the online puzzle game *Foldit* lets players search for proteins with shapes that can be useful in chemistry and medicine.

Persuasive Games

Some people use games to convey a particular message or point of view, either to advertise a product or to promote a political or charitable cause. The web-based *Virtual Pilot* game by Lufthansa airline tests the players' knowledge of the names and locations of European cities…but it includes only the cities that Lufthansa flies to, so it subtly promotes awareness of their route map. If a game conveys its message primarily through its mechanics rather than through explicit narration, we say that is uses *procedural rhetoric*. The game *PeaceMaker*'s explicit goal is to establish peace between Israel and Palestine. The player has many choices of how to achieve this, but it is impossible to win the game if he takes a hard-line attitude. The game seeks to persuade players that reconciliation is the best way.

Games for Health and Growth

It's now well known that mental exercise helps to prevent loss of brain function as humans age, and this accounts for the popularity of brain-training games. But games can be used in many other aspects of health care and personal growth as well. *Wii Fit* has become popular in care homes for the elderly and as a way of making physical therapy less boring. Games can also reduce the need for morphine during painful procedures by distracting the patient. The University of Washington's Medical Center created a game called *Snow World*, which—with the addition of virtual reality gear—helps people undergoing burn treatment. The same institution also created a game called *Spider World* to assist people in overcoming a fear of spiders. In addition, games have been used to teach people to manage their diseases and to learn to control stress. We have really only begun to scratch the surface of what can be done with games for health.

Summary

In this chapter, you have learned that play, pretending, a goal, and rules are the essential elements of a game, and you've learned how they work together to create the experience of playing one. You have been taught to think of gameplay in terms of challenges and actions, and you have looked at such important issues as winning and losing, fairness, competition, and cooperation. You should now be aware of some of the special benefits that computers bring to playing games and the manifold ways that video games entertain people. We also looked at ways we can use games to solve real-world problems. With this as a foundation, you're ready to proceed to the next chapter. There, you'll learn how games are structured, an approach to designing them, and what it takes to be a game designer.

Design Practice EXERCISES

1. Create a competitive game for two players and a ball that does *not* involve throwing it or kicking it. Prove that it is a game by showing how it contains all the essential elements.

2. Using a chessboard and the types of pieces and moves available in chess, devise a cooperative game of some kind for two people, in which they must work together to achieve a victory condition. (You do not need to use the starting conditions of chess, nor all the pieces.) Document the rules and the victory condition.

3. Define a competitive game with a single winner, for an unlimited number of players, in which only creative actions are available. Be sure to document the termination and victory conditions.

4. Describe the elements of the gameplay in each of the following games: backgammon, poker, bowling, and Botticelli. (Use the Internet to look up the rules if you do not know them.)

5. List examples not already mentioned in this book of video games designed for single-player, multiplayer local, and multiplayer distributed play. Explain how the games' design supports these different modes.

Design Practice QUESTIONS

1. As a potential designer, do you see yourself as an artist, an engineer, a craftsman, or something else? Why do you see yourself that way?

2. Do you agree or disagree with the definition of a game? If you disagree, what would you add, remove, or change?

3. We have defined gameplay strictly in terms of challenges and actions, leaving out the game world or the story. Do you feel that this is appropriate? Why or why not?

4. Why is it considered to be fair if one athlete trains to become better but it is not fair if he takes drugs to become better? What does this say about our notions of fairness?

5. We've listed only the most important things that computers bring to gaming. What other things can you think of?

6. The list of ways that video games entertain people is only a beginning. What else would you add?

CHAPTER 2

Designing and Developing Games

Game design is the process of

- Imagining a game

- Defining the way it works

- Describing the elements that make up the game (conceptual, functional, artistic, and others)

- Transmitting information about the game to the team who will build it

- Refining and tuning the game during development and testing

A game designer's job includes all these tasks. This chapter begins by discussing an approach called player-centric game design. Then you learn about the central components of any video game—the core mechanics and the user interface (UI)—and you see how these components are defined in the design process. Finally, we explore the various job roles on a design team and some of the qualities that it takes to be a game designer.

In the video game industry, all but the smallest games are designed by teams of anywhere from 3 to 20 people. (The entire development team is often much larger, but we're concerned only with the design team.) This book is written as if you are the lead designer, responsible for overseeing everything. If your team is small, or if you are designing alone, you may perform many of the different design roles yourself.

An Approach to the Task

Over the years, people have tried many approaches to game design, and some of them are better than others. A few tend to result in catastrophic failures. This book teaches you a way to think about what you are actually trying to accomplish so that you'll be more likely to succeed than fail.

Art, Engineering, or Craft?

Some people like to think of game design as an art, a process of imagination that draws on a mysterious wellspring of creativity. They think of game designers as

NOTE Game design is a craft, combining both aesthetic and functional elements. Craftsmanship of a high quality produces elegance.

artists, and they suppose that game designers spend their time indulging in flights of imagination. Other people, often more mathematically or technologically oriented, see game design as a type of engineering. They concentrate on the methodology for determining and balancing the rules of play. Game design to these people is a set of techniques. Aesthetics are a minor consideration.

Each of these views is incomplete. Game design is not purely an art because it is not primarily a means of aesthetic expression. Nor is game design an act of pure engineering. It's not bound by rigorous standards or formal methods. The goal of a game is to entertain through play, and designing a game requires both creativity and careful planning.

Interactive entertainment is an art form, but like film and television, it is a collaborative art form. In fact, it is far more collaborative than either of those media, and development companies seldom grant the game designer the level of creative control that a film director enjoys. Designing games is a *craft*, like cinematography or costume design. A game includes both artistic and functional elements: It must be aesthetically pleasing, but it also must work well and be enjoyable to play. The greatest games combine their artistic and functional elements brilliantly, achieving a quality for which the best word is *elegance*. Elegance is the sign of craftsmanship of the highest order.

The Player-Centric Approach

This book teaches you an approach called *player-centric game design*. This approach helps you produce an enjoyable game, which, in turn, helps it be a commercially successful one. Many other factors affect the commercial success of a game as well: marketing, distribution, and the experience of the development team. These are beyond the control of the game designer, so no design or development methodology can guarantee a hit. However, a well-designed game undoubtedly has a better chance of being a hit than a poorly designed one.

> **PLAYER-CENTRIC GAME DESIGN** *is a philosophy of design in which the designer envisions a representative player of a game the designer wants to create. The designer then undertakes two key obligations to that player:*
>
> ▪ *The duty to entertain: A game's primary function is to entertain the player, and it is the designer's obligation to create a game that does so. Other motivations are secondary.*
>
> ▪ *The duty to empathize: To design a game that entertains the player, the designer must imagine that he is the player and must build the game to meet the player's desires and preferences for entertainment.*

You can adapt the designer's first obligation, the duty to entertain, in a player-centric game design somewhat if you're designing the game for education, research, advertising, political, or other purposes, but for recreational video games it is imperative. If a player is going to spend time and money on your game, your first concern *must* be to see that he enjoys himself. You must have a creative vision for your game, but if some aspect of your vision is incompatible with entertaining the player, you should modify or eliminate it.

The second obligation, the duty to empathize, requires you to place yourself in the position of a representative player and imagine what it is like to play your game. You must mentally become the player and stand in his shoes. For every design decision that you make—and there will be thousands—you must ask yourself how it affects the player's experience. Note the mention of a *representative player.* It is up to you to decide what that means, but this hypothetical being must bear some resemblance to the customers whom you want to actually buy the game. Smart game designers conduct audience research if they're planning to make a game for an audience that they don't know enough about to understand their preferences.

When you employ player-centric game design, you need to think about how the player will react to everything in your game: its artwork, its user interface, its gameplay, and so on. But that is only the surface. At a deeper level, you must understand what the player wants from the entire experience you are offering—what motivates her to play your game at all? To design a game around the player, you must have a clear answer to the following questions: Who *is* your intended player, anyway? What does she like and dislike? What games is she playing now? Why would she want to play your game? The answer is also influenced by the game concept that you choose for your game. Chapter 4, "Understanding Your Player," discusses player-centric design in more detail.

This act of empathizing with your player is one of the aspects that differentiate games from presentational forms of entertainment. With books, paintings, and music, it is considered artistically virtuous to create your work without worrying about how it is received, and it's thought to be rather mercenary to modify the content based on sales considerations. But with a video game—whether you are concerned about sales or not—you *must* think about the player's feelings about the game, because the player participates in the game with both thought and action.

There are two common misconceptions about player-centric design that you must avoid.

MISCONCEPTION 1: I AM MY OWN TYPICAL PLAYER

For years, designers built video games, in effect, for themselves. They assumed that whatever they liked, their customers would like. Because most designers were young men, they took it for granted that their customer base was also made up of young men. This is a dangerous fallacy. Today the game industry serves all kinds of people. In the player-centric approach, this means learning to think like your intended players, whoever they may be: little girls, old men, busy mothers, disabled people, and so on. You cannot assume that players like what you like. Rather, you must learn to design for what *they* like. (You may also find that you grow to like a game that you didn't think you would as you work to design it!)

3D graphics engine and encourage other developers to use it. Console manufacturers often write technology-driven games when they release a new platform to show everyone the features of their machine. The main risk in designing a technology-driven game is that you'll spend too much time concentrating on the technology and not enough on making sure your game is really enjoyable. As with a hot license, a hot technology alone is not enough to guarantee success.

Art-driven games are comparatively rare. An art-driven game exists to show off someone's artwork and aesthetic sensibilities. Although such games are visually innovative, they're seldom very good because the designer has spent more time thinking about ways to present his material than about the player's experience of the game. A game must have enjoyable gameplay as well as great visuals. *Myst* is a game that got this right; it is an art-driven game with strong gameplay.

Integrating for Entertainment

When one particular motivation drives the development of a game, the result is often a substandard product. A good designer seeks not to maximize one characteristic at the expense of others but to integrate them all in support of a higher goal: entertaining the player. You should keep the following points in mind as you integrate all the design motivations:

▦ A game must present an imaginative, coherent experience, so the designer must have a vision.

▦ A game must sell well, so the designer must consider the audience's preferences (without becoming a slave to them).

▦ A game with a license must pay back the license's cost, so the designer must understand what the fans love about the brand and create a game that resonates with them and meets their expectations.

▦ A game must offer an intelligent challenge and a smooth, seamless experience, so the designer must understand the technology.

▦ A game must be attractive, so the designer must think about its aesthetic style.

Player-centric game design means testing every element and every feature against the standard: Does this contribute to the player's enjoyment? Does it entertain her? If so, it stays; if not, you should consider eliminating it. There's no easy formula for deciding this; the main thing is to make the effort. As Brian Moriarty said in the section quoted in Chapter 1, "Games and Video Games," too many designers "pile on gratuitous features just so that they can boast about them," which means they're not designing player-centrically.

Sometimes there are reasons for including features that don't directly entertain: They might be necessary to make other parts of the game work, or they might be required by the licensor. But you should regard them with great suspicion and do your best to minimize their impact on the player.

Key Components of Video Games

Chapter 1 looked at what a game is and what gameplay is. But where does gameplay come from, and how does the player interact with it? To create gameplay and offer it to the player, you need to make sure your video game is composed of two key components. These are not technical components but conceptual ones. They are the *core mechanics* and the *user interface*. Some games also use a third important component called the *storytelling engine*, but we will deal with it in Chapter 11, "Storytelling." This section introduces the core mechanics and the user interface and shows how they work together to produce entertainment. Each of these components has a complete chapter devoted to it later in the book, so the discussion here is limited to defining their functions, not explaining how to design them.

Core Mechanics

One of a game designer's tasks is to turn the general rules of the game into a symbolic and mathematical model that can be implemented algorithmically. This model is called the *core mechanics* of the game. The model is more specific than the rules. For example, the general rules might say, "Caterpillars move faster than snails," but the core mechanics state exactly how fast each moves in centimeters per minute. The programmers then turn the core mechanics into algorithms and write the software that implements the algorithms. This book doesn't address technical design or programming but concentrates on the first part of the process, creating the core mechanics. Chapter 14, "Core Mechanics," addresses this process at length.

The core mechanics are at the heart of any game because they generate the gameplay. They define the challenges that the game can offer and the actions that the player can take to meet those challenges. The core mechanics also determine the effect of the player's actions upon the game world. The mechanics state the conditions for achieving the goals of the game and what consequences follow from succeeding or failing to achieve them.

One quality of the core mechanics is their degree of *realism*. An ordinary game is created for the purpose of entertainment. Even if it represents the real world to some degree, it always includes compromises to make it more playable and more fun. For example, a real army requires a large general staff to make sure the army has all the ammunition and supplies it needs. In a game, a single player has to manage everything, so to avoid overwhelming him, the designer abstracts these logistical considerations out of the model—that is to say, out of the core mechanics. The game simply pretends that soldiers never need food or sleep, and they never run out of ammunition. All games fall along a continuum between the *abstract* and the *representational*. *Pac-Man* is a purely abstract game; it's not a simulation of anything real. Its location is imaginary, and its rules are arbitrary. *Grand Prix Legends* is a highly representational game: It accurately simulates the extraordinary danger of driving racing cars before the spoiler was invented. Although no game is completely realistic, gamers (and game developers) often refer to this variable quality of games as their degree of realism. For the most part, however, this book uses the terms *abstract* and *representational* to characterize games at opposite ends of the realism scale.

You will decide what degree of realism your game will have when you decide upon its concept. The decision you make determines how complex the core mechanics are.

User Interface

The concept of a *user interface* should be familiar to you from computer software, but in a game the user interface has a more complex role. Most computer programs are tools of some kind: word-processing tools, web-browsing tools, painting tools, and so on. They are designed to be as efficient as possible and to present the user's work clearly. Games are different because the player's actions are *not* supposed to be as efficient as possible; they are obstructed by the challenges of the game. Most games also hide information from the player, revealing it only as the player advances. A game's user interface is supposed to entertain as well as to facilitate. Chapter 12, "Creating the User Experience," discusses this in detail.

The user interface mediates between the core mechanics of the game and the player (**Figure 2.1**). It takes the challenges that are generated by the core mechanics (driving a racing car, for example) and turns them into graphics on the screen and sound from the speakers. It also turns the player's button presses and movements on the keyboard or controller into actions within the context of the game.

FIGURE 2.1
The relationships among the core mechanics, the user interface, and the player

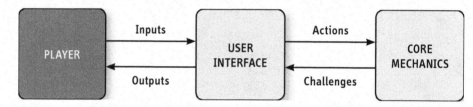

Because the user interface lies between the player and the core mechanics, it is sometimes referred to as the *presentation layer*.

The user interface does more than display the outputs and receive the inputs. It also presents the story of the game, if there is any, and creates the sensory embodiment of the game world—all the images and sounds of the world and, if the game machine has other output devices (such as a vibration feature, as mobile phones usually do), those sensations as well. All the artwork and all the audio of the game are part of its user interface, also known as its presentation layer. Two essential features of the user interface of a game are its *camera model* and its *interaction model*, as shown in **Figure 2.2**.

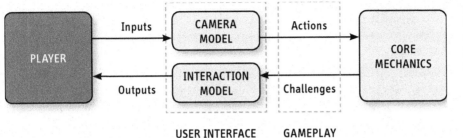

FIGURE 2.2
The camera model
and interaction model
are features of the
user interface.

CHAPTER 2

INTERACTION MODELS

The user interface turns the player's inputs on the hardware into actions within the game world. The relationship between the player's inputs and the resulting actions is dictated by the game's *interaction model*. The model determines how the player projects her will, her choices, and her commands, into the game. In particular, it defines what she may and may not act upon at any given moment. Video games use a number of standard interaction models, including multipresence, avatar-based models, contestant models, and so on. In a multipresent model, for example, the player can act on different parts of the game world whenever she wants to, reaching "into" it from the "outside." In an avatar-based model, the player is represented by a character who already *is* inside the game world, and the player acts on the world through that character. Just as the visible parts of a game's user interface change during play, a game can have more than one interaction model depending on what is happening at the time. Chapter 12 discusses interaction models at greater length.

CAMERA MODELS

If a game includes a simulated physical space, or *game world,* then it almost certainly uses graphics to display that space to the player. The user interface displays the space from a particular angle or point of view (which may move around). Designers imagine this as a hypothetical camera, creating the image that the player sees. The system that controls the behavior of this imaginary camera is called the *camera model.* To define the camera model, think about how you want the player to view the game world and specify a system in your design documents that the programmers can implement.

Camera models may be static or dynamic. Early arcade games, and many small games today, use a static camera model in which the camera always shows the virtual space from a fixed perspective. In a dynamic model, the camera moves in response to player actions or events in the game world. Dynamic camera models require more effort to design and implement, but they make the player's experience livelier and more cinematic.

If a game doesn't have a virtual space (for example, if it's a business simulation and its graphics are mostly numbers and charts), the term *camera model* doesn't apply, and you have to explain the layout of your screen in your design documents in more detail.

The most commonly used camera models are first person and third person for presenting 3D game worlds and top-down, side-scrolling, and isometric for presenting 2D worlds. Chapter 8, "Game Worlds," discusses the question of game-world dimensionality. Chapter 12 addresses the merits of the different camera models.

GAMES WITHOUT GRAPHICS

Many of the early computer games were text-based, designed to be played on a printing terminal attached to a mainframe computer. Text-only games still exist in the form of quizzes or trivia games, especially for small devices such as cell phones. *Interactive fiction*—text-only adventure games—has long since ceased to be a commercial genre, but it is still popular with a small group of hobbyists. Blind players can play text-only games using text-to-speech synthesizers. Also, a small number of experimental audio-only games are intended for the blind.

The Structure of a Video Game

You now know how the core mechanics of a game work with the user interface to create gameplay for the player. A game seldom presents all its challenges at one time, however, nor does it permit the player to take any actions at any time. Instead, most video games present a subset of their complete gameplay, often with a particular user interface to support it. Both the gameplay available and the user interface change from time to time as the player meets new challenges or views the game world from a different point of view. These changes sometimes occur in response to something the player has done, and at other times they occur automatically when the core mechanics have determined that they should. How and why the changes occur are determined by the game's *structure*. The structure is made up of *gameplay modes*, a vitally important concept in game design, and *shell menus*. This section explores gameplay modes and shell menus and discusses how they interact to form the structure.

Gameplay Modes

If a game is to be coherent, the challenges and actions available to the player at any given time should be conceptually related to one another. In hand-to-hand combat, for example, the player should be able to move around, wield his weapons, quaff a healing potion, and perhaps run away or surrender. He should not be able to pull out a map or sit down to inventory his assets, even if those are actions he may take at other times in the game.

In short, unless a game is very simple, not all the challenges and actions that it offers make sense at all times. The user interface, too, must be designed to facilitate whatever activity is taking place. The camera and interaction models may vary. When driving a race car, the vehicle is the player's avatar on the racetrack, and the player usually sees the world from the cockpit; when tuning up the car, the player has omnipresent control over all of its parts, but the rest of the game world (the racetrack) is not accessible.

This combination of related items—the available gameplay and its supporting user interface at a given point in the game—collectively describe something called a *gameplay mode* (**Figure 2.3**) for an illustration. In a given gameplay mode, the features of the game combine to give the player a certain experience that feels different from other parts of the game—that is, other gameplay modes. Because the game offers only a subset of all its challenges and actions in a given gameplay mode, the player is focused on a limited number of goals.

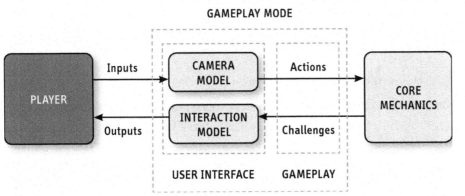

GAMEPLAY MODE

FIGURE 2.3
The large dashed box represents the gameplay mode.

The concept of the gameplay mode is central to the process of designing video games.

> **GAMEPLAY MODES** *consist of the particular subset of a game's total gameplay that is available at any one time in the game, plus the user interface that presents that subset of the gameplay to the player.*

A game can be in only one gameplay mode at a time. When either the gameplay available to the player or the user interface (or both) changes significantly, the game has left one mode and entered another. A change to the user interface qualifies as a change of mode because such changes redirect the player's focus of attention and cause him to start thinking about different challenges. Also, if the mapping between the controls on the input device and the actions in the game changes sharply, the player probably thinks of it as a new mode.

Many of the earliest arcade games have only one gameplay mode. In *Asteroids,* for example, you fly a spaceship around a field of asteroids, trying to avoid being hit by one and shooting at them to break them up and disintegrate them. The camera model and the interaction model never change, nor does the function of the controls. On the other hand, in *Pac-Man* you are chased by dangerous ghosts until you eat a large dot on the playfield. For a short period after that, the ghosts are vulnerable and they run away from you. Because this represents a significant change to the gameplay (and is a key part of the game's strategy), it can be considered a new gameplay mode even though the user interface does not change. The definition of what makes one mode different from another is not strict, but when the player feels that something about the game has changed significantly, then it has probably moved into a new mode. Mini-games are also new gameplay modes.

GAMEPLAY MODES IN AMERICAN FOOTBALL

Video games about American football have many rapid and complex mode switches, especially when you're playing the offensive team; that is, the team that has the ball. The mapping between the buttons on the controller and the actions they produce in the game changes on a second-by-second basis. Here is the sequence necessary to select and execute a pass play in *Madden NFL:*

1. Choose the offensive formation you want to use on the next play from a menu.

2. Choose the play you want to call from another menu.

3. Take control of the quarterback. Call signals at the line of scrimmage. During this period only one man, who is not the quarterback, may move under the player's control. Snap the ball to the quarterback.

4. Drop back from the line of scrimmage and look for an open receiver. Choose one and press the appropriate button to pass the ball to the chosen receiver.

5. Take control of the chosen receiver and run to the place where the ball will come down. Press the appropriate button to try to catch the ball.

6. Assuming you catch the ball, run toward the goal line. At this point you may not throw the ball again.

This process requires six different gameplay modes in the space of about 45 seconds.

Figures 2.4 and **2.5** are screen shots from *Empire: Total War* illustrating two different modes. Note that the on-screen indicators and menu items are entirely different in the two modes. The first, a turn-based campaign mode, shows an aerial perspective of a landscape. The player uses this mode for building cities, raising armies, and other strategic activities. The second, for fighting sea battles in real time, shows ship-to-ship combat. You cannot manage the entire empire from sea battle mode; you can only fight other ships such as the ones visible in the picture. The sea battle mode is essentially tactical.

FIGURE 2.4
Campaign mode in
Empire: Total War

FIGURE 2.5
Sea battle mode in
Empire: Total War

TIP If a player can take an action that influences the core mechanics—even if that influence is deferred—the game is in a gameplay mode. If he cannot, the game is in a shell menu or shell screen.

Not all gameplay modes offer challenges that the player must meet immediately. A strategy menu in a sports game is a gameplay mode because the player must choose the best strategy to help her win the game even though play is temporarily suspended while the player uses the menu. A character creation screen in a role-playing game or an inventory management screen in an adventure game both qualify as gameplay modes. A player's actions there influence the challenges she faces when she returns to regular play.

Shell Menus and Screens

Whenever the player is taking actions that influence the game world, that is, actually playing the game, the game is in a gameplay mode. However, most games also have several other modes in which the player *cannot* affect the game world but can make other changes. These modes are collectively called *shell menus* because the player usually encounters them before and after playing the game itself (they are a "shell" around the game, outside the magic circle). Examples of the kinds of activities available in a shell menu include loading and saving the game, setting the audio volume and screen resolution, and reconfiguring the input devices for the player's convenience. A pause menu in a game is also a shell menu unless it lets the player take some action that affects the game world (such as making strategic adjustments in a sports game), in which case it is a gameplay mode. Noninteractive sequences such as title screens or credits screens are called *shell screens*.

The Game Structure

NOTE A video game is always in either a gameplay mode or a shell menu or screen.

The gameplay modes and shell menus of the game, and the relationships among them, collectively make up the structure of the game. For example, in a car racing game, driving the car into the pit causes the game to switch from the driving mode to the pit stop mode. When the work of the pit crew is finished, the game switches back to the driving mode. Pressing the Start button on the controller while driving brings up a pause menu, and so on. You need to document these details for the rest of the development team.

To document the structure, you can begin by making a list of all the modes and menus in the game. You must also include a description of *when* and *why* the game switches from one mode or menu to another: What event, or menu selection, causes it to change? Each mode or menu description should include a list of other modes and menus it can switch to and, for each possible switch, a notation about what causes it.

You can document the relationships among all the modes and menus by simply writing them all down, but the result won't be easy to follow. A better approach is to document the structure of a game with a *flowboard,* a hybrid of a flowchart and a storyboard. This type of diagram is described in the section "Flowboard," later in this chapter.

Normally, a game begins with one or more title screens that run by themselves, and after that it moves among its shell menus in response to player actions. During actual play, a game changes from one gameplay mode to another in response to player actions, or automatically as the circumstances of the game require. For example, in a soccer game, certain violations of the rules result in a penalty kick, in which a single athlete on one team tries to kick the ball past the opposing team's goalie and into the goal and the other athletes on both teams play no role. This is clearly a gameplay mode different from normal play. The game enters the penalty kick mode not in response to a specific player choice but because a rule has been violated.

Stages of the Design Process

Now that you have learned about the player-centric approach to game design and the key components and structure of a video game, you are ready to start thinking about how to go about designing one. Unfortunately, there are so many kinds of video games in the world that it is impossible to define a simple step-by-step process that produces a single design document all ready for people to turn into content and code. Furthermore, unless a game is very small, it is not possible to create a complete design and then code it up afterward. That is how the game industry built games in the 1980s, but experience has shown that large games must be designed and constructed in an iterative process, with repeated playtesting and tuning, and occasional modifications to the design, throughout development. However, not all parts of the design process can be revisited. Some, such as the choice of concept, audience, and genre, should be decided once at the beginning and should not change thereafter. Therefore the process is divided into three major parts:

- The *concept stage,* which you perform first and whose results do not change

- The *elaboration stage,* in which you add most of the design details and refine your decisions through prototyping and playtesting

- The *tuning stage,* at which point no new features may be added, but you can make small adjustments to polish the game

This book uses the term *elaboration stage* rather than *development stage* because the latter runs the risk of being confused with *game development.* **Figure 2.6** shows the three stages of the design process.

CONCEPT STAGE　　　**ELABORATION STAGE**　　　**TUNING STAGE**

FIGURE 2.6
Three stages of the design process

Once you have a game concept, a role, and an audience in mind, it's time to begin thinking about how you will fulfill your player's dream. What is the essence of the experience that you are going to offer? What kinds of challenges does the player expect to face, and what kinds of actions does she expect to perform? Deciding what it means to fulfill the dream is the first step on the road to defining the gameplay itself.

DESIGN RULE Concept Elements Are Permanent

You must not make changes to the concept elements of your game—the game concept, audience, player's role, and dream that it fulfills—once you have started into the elaboration stage of design.

The Elaboration Stage

Once you have made the fundamental decisions about your game in the concept stage, it's time to move into the elaboration stage of design. At this point, your design work begins to move from the general to the specific, from the theoretical to the concrete. In the elaboration stage, you normally begin working with a small development team to construct a prototype of the game. If you are planning to incorporate radically new ideas or new technology, your team may also build a test bed or technical demonstration to try them out. From this point on, you may take your design ideas and have the development team implement them in the prototype to see how they work in practice. Based on what you learn, you can then go back and refine them.

At some point during the elaboration stage, your game (you hope!) gets the green light from a funding agency and proceeds to full production.

THE DANGER OF IRRESOLUTION

The transition from the concept to the elaboration stage of design is a critical time. At this point, the most important decisions are "set in stone," so to speak; the foundations are poured. Some designers are reluctant to make this transition; they say they're "keeping their options open." They're afraid that they might have made a bad decision or that they might have overlooked something. The consequences of this irresolution are usually disastrous. If the most critical details are still shifting as the game goes into full production, the development team is never entirely sure what it's trying to build. The designer keeps coming around and asking for changes that require huge revisions to the code and content. Production becomes slow and inefficient. It's a sure sign of a lack of vision and confidence. Projects that get into this quagmire are usually cancelled rather than completed.

When you begin the elaboration stage, if you have a team of several people, it becomes possible to begin working on the design tasks in parallel. Once you all agree upon the fundamentals of the game, each designer can start work on a particular area of responsibility.

This process of iterative refinement is not an excuse to introduce major changes into the game late in its development, nor to tweak it endlessly without ever declaring it finished. Your goal is to build and ship a completed product.

PROTOTYPING

A prototype is a simplified, but testable, version of your game. Designers make prototypes to try out game features before they spend the time and money to implement them in the actual game; they also use them for playtesting with their audience to see if the game is enjoyable. In their book *Game Mechanics: Advanced Game Design*, Joris Dormans and Ernest Adams identified three common types used by game developers: software prototypes, paper prototypes, and physical prototypes (Adams and Dormans, 2012 , pp. 15–21). We'll look at them briefly here; for further discussion, consult *Game Mechanics: Advanced Game Design*.

To build a **software prototype**, you create software that isn't as complete as your full game in order to try out some aspect of it. Tools such as Game Maker can make this much easier than doing it from scratch. You can also build software in development environments that provide a lot of features for you, such as Unity, Adobe Flash, or HTML 5. Of course, to be able to do this, you have to be a programmer or work with one.

Writing software allows you to create a *high-fidelity* prototype, one that fairly closely resembles the real game (though software prototypes can also be low-fidelity). It takes longer to make a software prototype than the other kinds, but it produces a result that can be easy to translate into the real thing. However, a word of warning: Do not assume that you will use the software you create for the prototype in the final game. The whole point of making a prototype is to be able to do it quickly, without worrying about the quality of the code or the artwork.

Also, you don't have to implement all aspects of your game in the same software prototype. For example, you might implement part of the internal economy of the game in a prototype with almost no graphics, and try out the graphics engine and user interface in a different prototype that contains no working mechanics.

To make and try out a version of your game cheaply and quickly, consider making a **paper prototype**, a tabletop version of the game—a board game, card game, or some other non-computerized implementation. You can play the game with your design team, and try it out on friends who represent your target audience, too. Paper prototyping doesn't work well for physics-based games or games that need a lot of number crunching, but it is very popular with designers as a way to test features like combat models, puzzles, and player interactions in multiplayer games.

NOTE Plan to throw away all sound, art, and code created for a prototype. That way your artists, audio people, and programmers can work quickly without worrying about having to debug their content later. Trying to build production-quality assets during preproduction just slows down the process.

Even if part of the game is physics-based, you can still make a paper prototype to test out other parts.

As a game designer, you should always have some dice, counters or tokens (such as poker chips), graph paper, blank cards, and a notebook nearby. With these tools you can rapidly design a paper version of a video game and try it out with friends. The great advantage of paper prototyping is that it enables you to change the rules of your game quickly and try them out again.

In a **physical prototype**, you enact the player's role in real life. This might mean trying out combat moves in an environment that resembles the one you plan to build in your game, or playing a game that involves physics, such as throwing objects. Obviously you really can't jump as high as Mario, but you can use your body and the laws of physics to experiment with possible player actions in the game and figure out what animations may be needed to implement the video game. A physical prototype is also a natural precursor to doing motion capture. As you play, take notes (or have someone else do it) to see what kinds of actions the player uses most often. Physical prototypes complement paper prototypes well. If you're making a game that has a strategic and a tactical element, you can prototype the strategic part on paper, and the tactical part by moving around.

DEFINING THE PRIMARY GAMEPLAY MODE

The first task after you have locked down your concept is to define the primary gameplay mode of the game, the mode in which the player spends the majority of his time. Most games have one gameplay mode that is clearly the primary one. In a car racing game, it's driving the car. Tuning up the car in the shop is a secondary mode. In war games, the primary gameplay mode is usually tactical—fighting battles. War games often have a strategic mode as well, in which the player plans battles or chooses areas to conquer on a map, but he generally spends much less time doing that than he does fighting.

At this point it's not necessary to define every detail. The main things to work on are the components that make up the mode: the perspective in which the player views the game world, the interaction model in which he influences the game world, the challenges the world presents to him in that mode, and the actions available to him to overcome those challenges. Get those decisions down on paper, and then you can move on to the details of exactly how this is to happen.

DESIGNING THE PROTAGONIST

If your game is to have a single main character who is the protagonist (whether or not the interaction model is avatar-based), it is essential that you design this character early on. You want the player to like and to identify with the protagonist, to care about what happens to her. If the perspective you chose for the primary gameplay mode was anything other than first person, the player is going to spend a lot of time looking at this character, so it's important that she be fun to watch. You must think about how she looks and also about how she behaves: What actions she is capable of, what emotions her face and body language can register, and what kind of language and vocabulary she uses. Chapter 10, "Character Development," discusses these issues in depth.

DEFINING THE GAME WORLD

The game world is where your game takes place, and defining it can be an enormous task. If the game world is based on the real world (as in a flight simulator, for example), then you can use photographs and maps of real places in order to create its appearance. But if it's a fantasy or science fiction world, you have to rely on your imagination. And establishing the look and feel is only part of the task. There are many dimensions to a game world: physical, temporal, environmental, emotional, and ethical. All these qualities exist to serve and support the gameplay of your game, but they also entertain in their own right. Chapter 8 addresses these issues.

DESIGNING THE CORE MECHANICS

Once you have a sense of the kinds of challenges and actions that you want to include in the primary gameplay mode, you can begin thinking about how the core mechanics create those challenges and implement the actions. For example, if you plan to challenge the player to accumulate money, you have to define where the money comes from and what the player has to do to get hold of it. If you challenge the player to play a sport, you must think about all the athletic characteristics—speed, strength, acceleration, accuracy, and so on—that sport requires. If your challenges involve symbolic rather than numeric relationships, as in a puzzle game, you have to think about what those symbols are and how they are manipulated. Chapter 14 explains how to create this critical part of your game.

CREATING ADDITIONAL MODES

As you decide upon your game concept, you may realize that you need more than one gameplay mode—for example, you want to include separate strategic and tactical modes in a war game or manage income and expenditures in a business simulation. Or you may discover that you need additional modes while you are defining the primary gameplay mode and core mechanics. Now that you're in the elaboration stage, design the additional modes: their perspective, interaction model, and gameplay. You must also document what causes your game to move from mode to mode—the structure of your game, as described earlier in this chapter.

Do not create additional modes unnecessarily. Every extra mode requires more design work, more artwork, more programming, and more testing. It also complicates your game. Each mode should add to the player's entertainment and serve an important purpose that the game genuinely needs.

CHAPTER 2

DESIGNING LEVELS

Level design is the process of constructing the experience that the game offers directly to the player, using the components provided by the game design: the characters, challenges, actions, game world, core mechanics, and storyline if there is one. These components don't have to be completely finished for level design to begin, but enough must be in place for a level designer to have something to work with. In the early part of the elaboration stage, the level designers work to create a typical level. This level should not be the first one that the *player* encounters because the first level in the game is atypical, as the player is still learning to play the game—usually a tutorial level. Rather, the first level that the level designers work on should be one from further along in the game, in which most of the intended gameplay is present.

Creating a working playable level is an important milestone in the development of a game because it means that testers can begin playtesting it. See Chapter 16, "General Principles of Level Design," for an overview of the level design process.

WRITING THE STORY

Small video games seldom bother with a story, but large ones usually include a story of some kind. Stories help to keep the player interested and involved. They give him a reason to go on to the next level, to see what happens next. A story may be integrated with the gameplay in a number of different ways. Your story may occur within the levels as the player plays, or it may simply be a transition mechanism between the levels—a reward for completing a level. The story may be embedded, with prewritten narrative chunks, or emergent, arising out of the core mechanics. It may be linear and independent of the player's actions, or it may go in different directions based on the player's choices. Chapter 11 addresses all these issues in detail. However you choose to do it, you define the story during the elaboration stage, usually in close conjunction with level design.

BUILD, TEST, AND ITERATE

The great game designer Mark Cerny (*Spyro the Dragon, Jak and Daxter*) asserts that during the preproduction process of development, you should build, test, and then throw away no fewer than four different prototypes of your game. This may be extreme, but the underlying principle is correct. Video games must be prototyped before they can be built for real, and they must be tested at every step along the way. Each new idea must be constructed and tried out, preferably in a quick-and-dirty fashion first, before it is incorporated into the completed product. Cerny also argues that none of the materials you create for prototyping should ever find their way into the final product—or at least, that you should never count on it. By having a firm rule to this effect, you free your programmers and artists to work quickly to build the test bed, secure in the knowledge that they won't have to debug it later. If they're trying to build maintainable code or final-quality artwork during the pre-production stage of development, the testing process takes far longer than it should.

Once development shifts from preproduction to production, the team begins to work on material that *will* go out to the customer, and it has to be built with special care. However, you still can't design something, hand off your design to the programmers, and forget it. Everything you design must be built, tested, and refined as you go. This is why in modern game development testers are brought in right from the beginning of a project rather than at the end as they used to be.

As a designer, you won't have much control over the process of building the game unless you happen to be the project leader as well. During this stage you will be working closely with other members of the team and doing anything that is necessary to help them: refining the game mechanics, testing the user interface, planning levels, and many other tasks. For example, you probably won't have specified all the details of all the characters or units that might appear in your game during the concept phase, so you will continue to do this during development. If the game uses a lot of spoken word audio, you may be writing this material and attending recording sessions. You will also be answering a lot of questions from the other developers, particularly the programmers, about how things are supposed to work. Above all, however, you will be playtesting the game—even when only a small part of it is finished—to be sure that it does what you intend for it to do, and that members of the intended audience respond to it as you expected.

GAME DEVELOPMENT/SCRUM MANAGEMENT PROCESS

In the last few years, many game development teams both large and small have begun to implement a project management process called *Scrum*. (Scrum is not an acronym; the term is borrowed from the sport of rugby.) The Scrum process helps a team organize and track its progress toward completing some body of work, usually creating a new product. In the Scrum process, the team creates and tests updated, working versions of their product in short iterations called *sprints*. Each sprint lasts from one to four weeks. The team constantly examines and adjusts their progress so as to efficiently achieve both their interim and final goals. This enables them to identify and fix problems early on. In addition, the team holds a very brief meeting every day, and all problems must be revealed—nothing is held back. When a team is committed to the Scrum methodology, the managers have a clear picture of what is going on at all times, which helps them make sure the work is finished on time.

This book is about game design, not game development, so it does not discuss project management or Scrum in more detail. Also, Scrum is intended more for actually building products, especially software, than for design. However, you should certainly learn about it if you aspire to become a commercial game developer. For additional information, read the book *Agile Project Management with Scrum*, by Ken Schwaber (Schwaber, 2004). You'll find many more Scrum resources on the Internet.

For more information about the details of managing game development, see *Game Architecture and Design* (Rollings and Morris, 2003).

The Tuning Stage

When you went from the concept stage to the elaboration stage, you locked down the game concept—the foundations of the game. During the elaboration stage, you fleshed out the concept and added new features as necessary. At some point, however, a time comes when the entire design must be locked—that is, no more features may be added to the game—and you enter the tuning stage. This transition is sometimes called *feature lock*. There's no good way to know exactly when this is. It's usually dictated by the schedule. If it is going to take all the remaining time left to complete and debug the game as the design stands, then clearly you can't add anything more to the design without making the project late! However, that is more of a reactive than a proactive approach to the issue. You should really lock the design at the point at which you feel that it is complete and harmonious, even if there is time for more design work.

Once you have locked the design, you still have work to do. During the tuning stage, you can make small adjustments to the levels and core mechanics of the game as long as you don't introduce any new features. Most of your work at this time consists of fine-tuning the balance of the game, a subject that we discuss in more detail in Chapter 15, "Game Balancing." This stage, more than any other, is what makes the difference between a merely good game and a truly great one. Tune and polish your game until it's perfect. Polishing is a subtractive process, not an additive one. You're not putting on new bells and whistles; instead you're removing imperfections and making the game shine.

Game Design Team Roles

A large video game is almost always designed by a team. Unlike Hollywood, in which guilds and unions define the job roles, the game industry's job titles and responsibilities are not standardized from one company to another. Companies tend to give people titles and tasks in accordance with their abilities and, more important, the needs of a project. However, over the years a few roles have evolved whose responsibilities are largely similar regardless of what game or project they are part of.

TIP Small indie developers are unlikely to have different people in all these jobs, but somebody still has to do all the work! Even if your team consists of only three people, you will need to figure out who will perform the roles listed here.

■ **Lead Designer.** This person oversees the overall design of the game and is responsible for making sure that it is complete and coherent. She is the "keeper of the vision" at the highest and most abstract level. She also evangelizes the game to others both inside and outside the company and is often called upon to serve as a spokesperson for the project. Not all the lead designer's work is creative. As the head of a team, she trades away creativity for authority, and her primary role is to make sure that the design work is getting done and the other team members are doing their jobs properly. A project has only one lead designer.

■ **General Game Designer.** A game designer who doesn't have a specialized role like the ones that follow is usually responsible for a little bit of everything, but in particular defining the gameplay—the challenges the player will face and the actions that he can take to overcome those challenges. This may include thinking up and describing a great many game elements: enemies, friendly non-player characters, types of units, and so on. It can also involve designing level layouts in a general way, and planning the player's progression through the game. Small teams seldom have specialist game designers; everyone is a generalist.

▧ **Mechanics Designer.** The mechanics designer defines and documents how the game actually works as a system: its core mechanics. She builds the mathematical model at the heart of the game, from vehicle physics to hand-to-hand combat. Mechanics designers also conduct background research and assemble data that the game may need, especially if it is based on a real-world activity like a sport.

▧ **Level Designer/World Builder.** Level designers take the essential components of the game provided by the other designers—the user interface, core mechanics, and gameplay—and use those components to design and construct the individual levels that the player will play through in the course of a game. On large games, level designers frequently need to build 3D models and program in scripting languages. As a result, level design is now a specialized skill, or set of skills, and is considered just as important as game design. A project usually has several level designers reporting either to a lead level designer or to the lead designer.

▧ **User Interface Designer.** If a project includes user interface design as a separate role, it's performed by one or more people responsible for designing the layout of the screen in the various gameplay modes of the game and for defining the function of the input devices. In large, complex games, this can be a full-time task. An otherwise brilliant game can be ruined by a bad user interface, so it is a good idea to have a specialist on board. (See **Figure 2.7** for a notorious example.) Large developers are increasingly turning to usability experts from other software industries to help them test and refine their interfaces.

FIGURE 2.7
Trespasser: Jurassic Park was an innovative game ruined by an awkward and buggy user interface.

■ **Writer.** Writers are responsible for creating the instructional or fictional content of the game: introductory material, back story, dialogue, cut-scenes (noninteractive narrative video clips), and so on. Writers do not, generally speaking, do technical writing—that is the responsibility of the game designers. Few games require a full-time writer; the work is often subcontracted to a freelancer or done by one of the other designers.

Four other positions have a large amount of creative influence on a game, although they do not normally report to the lead designer. Rather, they are people with whom a game designer can expect to have a lot of interaction over the course of a project.

■ **Art Director.** The art director, who may also be called the lead artist, manages production of all the visual assets in the game: models, textures, sprites, animations, user interface elements, and so on. The art director also plays a major role in creating and enforcing the visual style of the game. Within the team hierarchy, the art director is usually at the same level as the lead designer, so it is imperative that the two of them have a good working relationship and similar goals for the project.

■ **Audio Director.** Like the art director, the audio director of a game oversees production of all the audible assets in the game: music, ambient sounds, effects, and dialogue or narration. Typically there is not as much of this material as there is of artwork, so the audio director may be working on several projects at once. Audio is critical to creating a mood for the game, and the lead designer and audio director work together to establish what kinds of sounds are needed to produce it.

■ **Lead Programmer.** The lead programmer oversees the coding team and is responsible for the technical design of the game, as well as the quality of the software. If there are any ambiguities or gaps in your design documents—and you can't possibly document everything—the lead programmer will come and ask you to resolve them. Dealing with the technical constraints of your hardware will require a lot of communication, too. The programmers may find that you have designed something that is too big or too complicated to implement, and you'll need to work it out with them. Except for minor matters, you should include the lead programmer in any discussions you have with coders, because the way that you decide to resolve a problem may influence their schedule or workflow.

■ **Producer or Project Manager** (or both). Job roles in the game industry are not standardized, but typically a producer has overall responsibility for the game as a commercial product, and in addition to thinking about development, he also works with marketing, public relations, and community managers (if any) to help build excitement about the game before release. Producers usually expect to have a fair amount of creative input into the design, and they expect veto power over expensive or unworkable suggestions. The producer may also track the day-to-day progress of development, making sure that tasks are getting completed and that nobody is stuck waiting for something else to happen; on a large enough team, he may delegate this job to a project manager. The other leads also work with the project manager on this task.

DESIGN RULE Don't Design by Committee

Do not treat the design work as a democratic process in which each person's opinion has equal value ("design by committee"). One person must have the authority to make final decisions, and the others must acknowledge this person's authority.

GAME IDEA VERSUS DESIGN DECISION

Here's a game idea: "Dragons should protect their eggs."

Here's a design decision: "Whenever they have eggs in their nests, female dragons do not move beyond visual range from the nest. If an enemy approaches within 50 meters of the nest, the dragon abandons any other activity and returns to the nest to defend the eggs. She does not leave the nest until no enemy has been within the 50-meter radius for at least 30 seconds. She defends the eggs to her death."

See the difference? This is what creating design documents is about.

Game Design Documents

In the course of designing a game, you may need to produce a variety of documents to tell others about your game. Exactly what documents you write and what the documents are for will vary from project to project, but they usually follow a common thread.

Why Do We Need Documents?

Beginning game programmers often make the mistake of thinking up a game and then diving in and starting to program it right away. In modern commercial game development, however, this kind of ad hoc approach is disastrous. Different projects require different degrees of formality, but unless you have a very small team making a very small game, you'll almost certainly need to make a written record of what you plan to do. Here, from most to least important, are five reasons that game designers write design documents:

1. Design documents are a record of decisions made; they create a paper trail. A lot of game design decisions are made in meetings or over lunch. If you don't make a note of what you decided on, there's a good chance that different people will remember it differently, and you'll waste time arguing about it later. If a week or two has gone by since the previous meeting, a whole team may have spent all that time working based on an incorrect assumption.

2. Design documents turn generalities into particulars. In the process of writing a document, your mind will naturally turn vague ideas into specific plans. It's one thing to say "Harpies will be flying creatures" in a meeting, but that's nowhere near enough to build from. What the programmers need are *details:* How high can they fly? How fast do they fly? Are they affected by the weather?

3. Design documents communicate your intentions to the rest of the team and let them plan their tasks. This isn't so important with small teams working on small games, but with a big game like *Madden NFL* or the *Battlefield* series, the development team can easily have 100 people or more, perhaps working in different offices in different parts of the world. You can't spend all your time talking to them on the phone. You have to get your plans to them in written form, so they can figure out how much time and staff will be needed to implement them.

4. Design documents are sometimes the basis for contractual obligations. Most development contracts include a milestone schedule that dictates when the developer will produce certain deliverables. You can't create a schedule until you know what features will be in the game, and you can't know that until you've designed at least part of it, including some kind of a written list of features to build the schedule from. It's in your best interest to make that feature list as clear and unambiguous as possible.

5. Funding agencies (publishers and others) want design documents as evidence that you know what you're doing. Not many of the people who pay for game development are willing to simply hand over a stack of cash to someone—they want to see evidence of competence, and to know what they're going to get for their money. Good design documents help to sell your team and your ideas.

It's far easier and cheaper to correct a design error before writing any code or creating any artwork. For a PC or console title, wise developers allot anywhere from one to six months for pure design work before starting on development, usually in combination with some prototyping work for testing gameplay ideas.

Types of Design Documents

This section is a short introduction to the various types of documents a game designer might create: the high concept, game treatment, character design, world design, and story or level progression documents, as well as the flowboard and the game script. Each of these is defined in the following sections. This isn't an exhaustive list, nor does every project need all the items on the list. Rather, these are some of the most common ones.

The high concept and game treatment documents are sales tools, designed to help communicate the game concept to a funding agency such as a publisher. They are usually written in a format such as Microsoft Word or PowerPoint and are distributed as files. The other documents used to be written in a word processor as well, but it is increasingly common in the game industry to create them as pages on an

TIP Some people learn best by reading, others by listening. For the benefit of the latter, schedule meetings as necessary to go through your design decisions and introduce them to your team. This will also give them the chance to ask questions about details that may be unclear or incomplete.

internal company website or wiki, or in Google Docs. As long as you can keep them secure, using one of these methods is a good way of documenting a game design so that all the members of the team can access it, and you can update it easily. Once the wiki software is installed on the company server, the whole team can edit the content using only a browser. Be sure you have revision control and backups so that you can revert to a previous edition if someone deletes a page by accident.

You can find samples (or pointers to samples) of design documents on the book's companion website at www.peachpit.com/fgd3.

HIGH CONCEPT DOCUMENT

The *high concept document* is not a document from which to build the game. Just as the purpose of a résumé is to get you a job interview, the purpose of a high concept document is to get you a hearing from someone, a producer or publishing executive. It puts your key ideas down on paper in a bite-size chunk that he can read in a few minutes. Like a résumé, it should be short—not more than two to four pages long.

You might also want to distribute your high concept document to your sales and marketing team so they have some advance description of what you are making. Finally, it's worthwhile to write high concept documents for yourself, to record ideas that you might want to work on in the future.

GAME TREATMENT DOCUMENT

A *game treatment document* presents the game in a broad outline to someone who's already interested in it and wants to hear more about it. Like a high concept document, it's primarily a sales tool, although you can also use it to establish a concise vision of the game for your entire development team. The treatment is designed both to satisfy initial curiosity and to stimulate real enthusiasm for the game. When you give a presentation about your game to a potential publisher, you should hand her the game treatment at the end so she has something to take away and look at, something that floats around her office and reminds her of your game. Your goal at this point is to get funding, either to create a more thorough design or a prototype or (preferably!) to develop the entire game.

The game treatment is still a simple document—almost a brochure that sums up the basic ideas in the game. A good way of picturing what to write in a treatment is to imagine that you are making a website to help sell your game; then throw in some business and development details for good measure.

CHARACTER DESIGN DOCUMENT

A *character design document* is specifically intended to record the design of one character who appears in your game, most often an avatar. Its primary purpose is to show the character's appearance and above all his *moveset*—a list of animations that documents how he moves, both voluntarily and involuntarily. It should

TIP If you're working as an independent developer on a comparatively small game, you probably won't need to write all these documents. It's still a good idea to create a written record of planning decisions that you have made, however, just as an author works from a book outline.

include plenty of concept art of the character in different poses and with different facial expressions. In addition, it should include background information about the character that helps inform future decisions: his history, values, likes and dislikes, strengths and weaknesses, and so on. Chapter 10 discusses character design in detail.

WORLD DESIGN DOCUMENT

The *world design document* is the basis for building all the art and audio that portray your game world. It's not a precise list of everything in the game but, rather, background information about the kinds of things the world contains. If you have a large landscape or cityscape, for example, the world design document should include a map. You need not supply every detail, just a general overview. The level designers and artists use this information to create the actual content. Be sure also to note the sources of ambient sounds in the world so the audio designers can build them in at the appropriate locations.

The world design document should also document the "feel" of the world, its aesthetic style and emotional tone. If you want to arouse particular emotions through images and music, indicate how you will do so here.

USER INTERFACE DESIGN DOCUMENT

The user interface creates the player's actual experience of the game via graphics, audio, text, and software. You need to document the UI particularly clearly, because the whole development team will be working on it. For each gameplay mode and all the shell screens, you must describe the layout of the screen, the behavior of the virtual camera, the functions of the input devices, and any audible feedback the game will provide. The document should include aesthetic, technical, and usability considerations. Any text that appears as part of the user interface should also be detailed in an on-screen text document, described momentarilty.

FLOWBOARD

A *flowboard* is, as the name suggests, a cross between a flowchart and a storyboard. Storyboards are linear documents used by filmmakers to plan a series of shots; flowcharts are used by programmers (though rarely nowadays) to document an algorithm. A flowboard combines these two ideas to document the structure of a game.

NOTE Some people call this document a wireframe instead of a flowboard, but this creates ambiguity with wireframe graphics. We'll continue to use flowboard.

Although you can create a flowboard in an editor such as Microsoft Visio, it's actually quicker and easier to make one on several index cards or sheets of paper and stick them on a large blank wall. Use each sheet to document one gameplay mode or shell menu. On each page, write the name of the mode clearly at the top. Then, in the center of the page, draw a quick sketch of the screen as it appears in the mode, showing the perspective that the camera model implements and the user interface items that appear on it. Leave plenty of space around the edges. Off to the sides of the sketch, document the menu items and inputs available to the player and what they do. You can also list the challenges that arise in that mode, although that's less important—the key thing is to indicate the player actions that are available. Then draw arrows leading to the other gameplay modes or shell menus and indicate under what circumstances the game makes a transition from the current mode to the next one. By creating one mode per page and putting them up on the wall, you allow everyone in the office to see the structure of the game. You can also easily make revisions by adding new sheets and marking up the existing ones.

STORY AND LEVEL PROGRESSION DOCUMENT

This document records the large-scale story of your game, if it has one, and the way the levels progress from one to the next. If you're making a small game with only one level (such as a board game in computerized form) or a game with no story, you need not create this document. However, if the game has more than one level, or the player experiences a distinct sense of progress throughout the game, then you need such a document. You're not trying to record everything that can happen in the game, but rather a general outline of the player's experience from beginning to end. If the game's story branches based upon the player's actions, this is the place to document it and indicate what decisions cause the game to take one path rather than another. Here you indicate *how* the player experiences the story: whether it's told via cut-scenes, mission briefings, dialogue, or other narrative elements.

Bear in mind that the story or level progression is not the same as the game's structure. An entire story can take place in only one gameplay mode; likewise, a game can have many different gameplay modes but no story at all. Although the game changes from mode to mode over time, and the story also progresses over time, the two are not necessarily related.

ON-SCREEN TEXT AND AUDIO DIALOG SCRIPT

This may be one, or, if your game is very large, two separate documents. To localize your game for foreign languages, you need to keep a record of all the on-screen text that appears in it, both as part of the user interface and in other roles such as written dialogue or narration. It is imperative that you keep this up to date as you make changes throughout the development process, because it will go off to the localization contractors for translation about the time that the game reaches alpha testing. If you use any recorded voices in your game, you'll also need to write the lines of dialogue that your actors will read, and these, too, will need to go to the localization contractors. For audio recording scripts it's a good idea to print them in large type with widely separated lines so the actors can read them easily—recording booths tend to be rather dim, and you don't want to make your voice talent stop to peer at the pages.

THE GAME SCRIPT

Back when games were smaller, it was common to incorporate all the preceding documents except for the high concept and treatment into a single massive tome, the game script (or "bible"). As games have gotten larger, the industry has tended

TIP The game structure and the game story or level progression are not the same thing! Don't confuse them. The structure defines the relationships among the gameplay modes, documenting when and why the game changes from mode to mode. The story or level progression describes how the player experiences a sense of progress from the beginning of the game to the end.

NOTE Don't confuse the game script with the on-screen text or audio recording scripts. The game script tells the programmers how the game will work.

to break out the character, world, and story documentation into individual documents to make them more manageable. The game script documents a key area not covered by the other documents: the rules and core mechanics of the game.

As a good rule of thumb, the game script should enable you to play the game. That is, it should specify the rules of play in enough detail that you could, in theory, play the game without the use of a computer—maybe as a (complicated) board game or tabletop role-playing game. This doesn't mean you should actually sit down and play it as such, but it should theoretically be possible to do so, based solely on the game script document. Sitting down and playing paper versions of game ideas is a very inexpensive way of getting valuable feedback on your game design. For designers without huge teams and equally huge budgets, paper-play testing is an invaluable tool.

The game script does not include the technical design, though it may include the target machine and minimum technical specifications. It should not address how to build or implement the game software. The technical design document, if there is one, is usually based on the game script and is written by the lead programmer or technical director for the game. Technical design is beyond the scope of this book. If you want to know more about technical design, read *Game Architecture and Design* (Rollings and Morris, 2003).

> **NOTE** Imagination does not consist only of the ability to invent new things. It's also valuable to be able to look at an old idea and breathe new life into it with a fresh approach. J.K. Rowling does this brilliantly in her Harry Potter novels. She still has witches and wizards flying on broomsticks, but she invented the sport of Quidditch, which is played while flying on them.

The Anatomy of a Game Designer

Like all crafts, game design requires both talent and skill. Talent is innate, but skill is learned. Effective game designers possess a wide base of skills. The following sections discuss some of the most useful skills for the professional game designer. Don't be discouraged if you don't have all of them. It's a wish list—the characteristics of a hypothetical "ideal designer."

Imagination

A game exists in an artificial universe, a make-believe place governed by make-believe rules. Imagination is essential to creating this place. It comes in various forms:

■ **Visual and auditory imagination** enables you to think of new buildings, trees, animals, creatures, clothing, and people—how they look and sound.

■ **Dramatic imagination** is required for the development of good characters, plots, scenes, motivations, emotions, climaxes, and conclusions.

■ **Conceptual imagination** is about relationships between ideas, their interactions, and dependencies.

■ **Lateral thinking** is the process of looking for alternative answers, taking an unexpected route to solve a problem.

▩ **Deduction** is the process of reasoning from a creative decision you've made to its possible consequences. Deduction isn't ordinarily thought of as imagination, but the conclusions you arrive at produce new material for your game.

Technical Awareness

Technical awareness is a general understanding of how computer programs, particularly games, actually work. You don't have to be a software engineer, but it is extremely valuable to have had a little programming experience. Level designers, in particular, often need to be able to program in simple scripting languages. Get to know the technical capabilities of your target platform. You must also be aware of its limitations so that you don't create unworkable designs. For example, many low-end mobile phones don't have enough processing power to do 3D rendering.

Analytical Competence

Analytical competence is the ability to study and dissect something: an idea, a problem, or an entire game design. No design is perfect from the start; game design is a process of iterative refinement. Consequently, you must be able to recognize the good and bad parts of a design for what they are.

One example of an analytical task is detecting overly-strong (or overly-weak) strategies at the design phase and weeding them out before they get into the code, as in the infamous *Red Alert* "tank rush." In *Command & Conquer: Red Alert,* tanks on the Soviet side are so much more effective than any other unit that an experienced player can dedicate all production to building tanks and then storm the opposition base before the enemy has a chance to get a production line set up.

Mathematical Competence

Designers must have basic math skills, including trigonometry and the simpler principles of probability. Balancing games that feature complex internal economies, such as business simulations or real-time strategy games, can require you to spend a lot of time looking at numbers. You don't need a Ph.D. in mathematics, but you should be comfortable with the subject.

Aesthetic Competence

Although you need not be an artist, you should have a general aesthetic competence and some sense of style. Far too many games are visual clones of one another, depending on stereotypes and clichés rather than real imagination. It's up to you (along with your lead artist) to set the visual tone of the game and to create a consistent, harmonious look.

Expand your aesthetic horizons as much as you can. Learn a little about the fundamentals of art: the principles of composition, and which colors coordinate and which clash. Find out about famous art movements—Art Nouveau, Surrealism, Impressionism—and how they changed the way we see things. Watch movies that are famous for their visual style, such as *Metropolis* or *Blade Runner*. Then move on to the more practical arts: architecture, interior decoration, industrial design. The more aesthetic experience you have, the more likely you are to produce an artistically innovative product.

General Knowledge and the Ability to Research

The most imaginative game designers are those who have been broadly educated and are interested in a wide variety of things. It helps to be well versed in such topics as history, literature, art, science, and political affairs. More important, you must know how to research the subject of your game. It's tempting just to use a search engine on the Internet, but that's not very efficient because the information it presents is haphazard and disorganized and might not be reliable. An encyclopedia—a real one, not Wikipedia—is a better place to start for any given subject. From there, you can increase your knowledge of a particular area by moving on to more specialized books or TV documentaries.

Writing Skills

A professional game designer actually spends much of her time writing, so a designer *must* have good writing skills. This means being clear, concise, accurate, and unambiguous. Apart from having to write several detailed documents for each design, you might be expected to produce the story narrative or dialogue—especially if the budget won't stretch to include a scriptwriter.

Design writing comes in several forms:

▪ **Technical writing** is the process of documenting the design in preparation for development. The essential mechanisms of the game have to be answered unambiguously and precisely.

▪ **Fiction writing** (narrative) creates the story of the game as a whole—a critical part of the design process if the game has a strong storyline. Some of this material may appear in the finished product as text or voiceover narration. The game's manual, if there is one, often includes fictional material as well.

▪ **Dialogue writing** (drama) is needed for audio voiceovers and cinematic material. Dialogue conveys character, and it also can form part of the plot. A class in playwriting or screenwriting teaches you a lot about writing dialogue.

A designer must be able to convey the details of the design to the rest of the team, create the textual and spoken material that appears in the game, and help sell the idea to a publisher. Good writing skills are essential to accomplish these things successfully.

Drawing Skills

Some skill at basic drawing and sketching is highly valuable, although not absolutely required for a designer if you have a concept artist to work with. The vast majority of computer games rely heavily on visual content, and drawings are essential when you're pitching a product to a third party. Game-publishing executives are interested in a hot concept, a hot market, or a hot license, but like many people only pictures really excite them. The images remain in their memories long after they forget the details.

The Ability to Synthesize

Synthesis, in this context, means bringing together different ideas and constructing something new from them. Different people on the development team and at the publishing company have concerns about their own areas of expertise (programming, art, music, and so on), and their opinions pull and push the design in different directions. A professional game designer must be able to synthesize a consistent, holistic vision of a game from this variety of opinions. As the designer, you may be tempted to seek sole ownership of the vision and insist that things must be exactly as you imagined them. You must resist the temptation to do that, for two reasons:

▪ First, you must allow your team some ownership of the vision as well, or its members won't have any motivation or enthusiasm for the project. No one builds computer games solely for the money; we're all here so that we can contribute creatively.

▪ Second, a designer who can't deliver in a team environment, no matter how visionary she may be, doesn't stay employed for long. You must be able to work successfully with other people.

Game design always requires compromise, both with team members and with circumstances. At a large company, you may be given a task that limits you to designing a genre clone or a heavily restricted licensed property. Unless you are an independent, you will almost certainly be told, rather than get to choose, the target hardware upon which your game will run. Your project always has a desired budget and schedule that it is expected to meet. A professional designer must be able to work within these constraints and to make the compromises necessary to do so.

Summary

This chapter puts forward the view that game design is not an arcane art but rather a craft, just like any other, that can be learned with application.

Video games are not created by a mysterious, hit-or-miss process. Instead, they are recreational experiences that the designer provides to the players through rules and a presentation layer. A game is designed by creating a concept and identifying an audience in the concept stage, fleshing out the details and turning abstract ideas into concrete plans in the elaboration stage, and adjusting the fine points in the tuning stage. All video games have a structure, made up of gameplay modes and shell menus, that you must document so your teams know what they are building and how it fits together. In the course of this process, you use a wide variety of skills to create a wide variety of documents for your team. And at all times, you should seek to create an integrated, coherent experience for your player that meets your most important obligation: to entertain her.

Design Practice EXERCISES

In these exercises, you document existing games for practice. Your instructor may require that you do so with particular games that he is familiar with, and he sets the expected scope of the work—the amount of material he wants to see. Use a document template from the companion website or one supplied by your instructor.

1. Document the primary gameplay mode of a reasonably simple game that you like. Be sure to include a sketch of the screen, including the camera model and user interface; a list of all the buttons and menu items available in that mode; and a list of the other modes that this mode can switch to. Describe the challenges and actions that make up the mode.

2. Take a classic, well-known arcade game with a small number of gameplay modes and shell menus and create a flowboard for it. (As you cannot hand in an entire wall of pages, create a miniature version with two or three gameplay modes per sheet.)

3. Document the level progression of a well-known game that you have played all the way through, such as *StarCraft* or *Fallout 3*. (If the game does not have explicit levels, as in *Half-Life,* document major areas or sections of the game.) Describe the game world in each level and the types of challenges that it presents. If the levels are integrated into a story, explain how each level supports or relates to the story.

4. Research one of the following art or design styles from history and write a short paper to explain how it might help to establish an emotional tone in a video game: Impressionism, Constructivism, Symbolism, Pop Art, Art Deco, Art Nouveau. Back up your argument with examples from famous paintings or other works in that style.

Design Practice QUESTIONS

1. What are the strengths and weaknesses of player-centric game design? In what ways might player-centric game design conflict with other requirements imposed on the game or with the desires of the game designer?

2. Do you feel that the list of qualities in an ideal game designer is complete? What other qualities might you add? Are there any that you would remove?

3. The list of members of a design team does not include a lead programmer. Should it? Suggest some arguments for and against.

CHAPTER 3

The Major Genres

Developers, sellers, and players of video games classify them into genres so that they can easily describe what kind of gameplay a game offers without having to describe it in detail. Over the years, a number of standard game genres has evolved, although there are many more games that either don't fit into any of them or are hybrids of more than one genre. The classifications change from time to time as well, and some genres exist only on particular platforms. In this short chapter, we'll take a look at the major game genres, concentrating on the traditional ones from the PC and console game markets.

What Is a Genre?

In describing movies or books, the term *genre* refers to the content of the work. Historical fiction, romance fiction, spy fiction, and so on are different genres of popular fiction. With video games, however, *genre* refers to the types of challenges that a game offers. In games, the genres are independent of the content. Shooter games are one genre; they are set in the Old West, in a fantasy world, or in outer space, and they are still all shooter games.

> **GENRES** *are categories of games characterized by particular kinds of challenge, regardless of setting or game-world content.*

The earliest video and computer games usually ran on hardware so limited that they could offer only one kind of gameplay, and the genre boundaries were fairly strict. Arcade games such as *Asteroids* were pure action games, while computer games like *Super Star Trek* were pure strategy games. Many newer games blend elements of more than one genre. Sometimes they do this in a single gameplay mode. For example, *Deus Ex* combined both the resource management and character growth challenges of role-playing games (RPGs) with the action challenges of shooters, an unusual pairing at the time that it was released. Others implement more than one gameplay mode with different kinds of challenge in each. *Weird Worlds: Return to Infinite Space* provides a high-level turn-based mode that includes exploration and resource management challenges, and a low-level real-time combat mode with challenges that are all about tactics and timing.

It is increasingly difficult to classify games unequivocally into one genre or another, especially with smaller browser-based and mobile-phone games. The explosion of creativity that accompanied the arrival of these two platforms has meant that many games, such as *World of Goo* (**Figure 3.1**), don't belong clearly to one traditional genre. However, even the Google Play store for Android applications classifies games by genre.

FIGURE 3.1
World of Goo combines construction, puzzle solving, and unusual physical mechanics.

Subgenres

Game genres are sometimes so general that it's useful to subdivide them into smaller groups, or *subgenres,* to better understand what the gameplay of a game will be like. First-person shooters, for example, come in many varieties: arena games, meant for high-speed multiplayer competition *(Team Fortress 2* is a good example); tactical shooters, in which stealth and ammunition management play large roles; open-world games such as the *Battlefield* series; and rail shooters that are set indoors and limit the player's movement to a largely linear path. Likewise, automobile-racing games can be grouped into those that offer combat between the cars and those that don't.

These classifications change constantly according to the whims of developers, the gaming press, and of course the players themselves. As a designer who may be choosing a genre for your game, you should study the existing games that resemble the one you want to make and the things that people have said about it to get a better grasp of where your game will fall in the marketplace.

The Classic Game Genres

Here you'll find a brief introduction to the classic game genres, along with a screen shot that provides an illustrative example. If you want to learn more about a particular game genre, Peachpit Press offers a series of companion e-books, each entitled *Fundamentals of <genre name> Design,* that discusses how to design each one in detail.

Table 1.1 in Chapter 1, "Games and Video Games," listed types of challenges that games use to entertain people. Be sure you're familiar with it, because the following sections use its terminology.

Shooter Games

In *shooters,* the player takes action at a distance, using a ranged weapon. Therefore aiming is a key skill, particularly if the game provides limited ammunition. In a shooting game, the player must focus attention on two places at once: the area around the avatar, and the target or targets. Shooters can be subdivided into 2D shooters and 3D shooters, of which by far the most famous are the first-person shooters.

2D SHOOTERS

The action in 2D shooters takes place in an environment viewed from a top-down or side-view perspective (see **Figure 3.2**), or occasionally from a fixed first-person perspective in which the player faces oncoming or pop-up targets. Enemies shoot at the avatar, which can be a character or a vehicle, or approach to attack at close quarters. In many of these games, the player is under attack by overwhelming numbers of enemies and must shoot them as fast as possible; such games are often called *shoot-'em-ups.* The player is usually armed with one or more weapons, and some weapons may be better suited to particular enemies than others. It is rare for a 2D shooter to keep track of ammunition (except for particularly powerful types of weapons); instead, the player fires frenetically and indiscriminately. The weapons seldom damage anything except legitimate targets.

FIGURE 3.2
Awesomenauts,
a multiplayer
2D shooter

3D SHOOTERS

3D shooting games, such as those in the *Halo* and *Crysis* series, have become so successful that to a great many younger gamers they are the epitome of the entire medium. 3D shooters are more realistic than 2D shooters, often presenting familiar, or at least recognizable, worlds (see **Figure 3.3**). In first-person shooters, the physics of the game is reasonably like that of the real world. Gravity works correctly (for the most part), sound diminishes with distance, objects cast shadows, and collisions are modeled with a fair level of accuracy.

3D shooters use either a first-person perspective (the *first-person shooter* or *FPS*) or a third-person perspective, and many now offer both. The first-person perspective is sometimes reserved for the view through a rifle's scope or sights and usually cannot be used while the avatar is moving.

FIGURE 3.3
Crysis 3, a 3D shooter with a particularly rich environment

Action and Arcade Games

Action games include physical challenges. They may also incorporate puzzles, races, and a variety of conflict challenges, typically among a small number of characters. Action games often contain simple economic challenges as well, usually involving collecting objects. They seldom include strategic or conceptual challenges. Arcade games are action games designed around a business model of earning money through the player putting in coins. They are generally unwinnable, and simply get harder and harder until the player is certain to lose—though often they can put in more coins to continue play.

Action games may be further subdivided into a variety of subgenres. Two of the best known are *platform games* and *fighting games,* but these are far from the only ones.

PLATFORM GAMES

Platform games, or *platformers*, are cartoonish games in which an avatar moves through a vertically exaggerated environment, jumping on and off platforms at different heights, while avoiding obstacles and battling enemies (see **Figure 3.4**). The avatar has a supernatural jumping ability and can't be harmed by falling long distances (unless he falls onto something dangerous or into a bottomless chasm, both common features of platform games). Most of the player's actions consist of jumping, augmented by special moves such as flip-moves or wall jumps, and by objects in the environment such as bouncy platforms and wind gusts. Platform games use unrealistic physics; usually the avatar can change directions in midair.

FIGURE 3.4
Spelunky, a 2D platform game

FIGHTING GAMES

Fighting games have little in common with other action games because they do not involve exploration, shooting, or puzzle solving. They still qualify as action games because they place great demands on a player's physical skills: reaction time and timing. These games simulate hand-to-hand combat, usually using highly exaggerated moves modeled vaguely on Asian martial arts techniques (see **Figure 3.5**). (Serious boxing games belong more to the sports genre than to the action genre, because they try to model the techniques of boxing realistically.) Fighting games may be further subdivided into those in which characters fight in one-on-one bouts *(arena games)* and mêlée games in which one or two characters fight large numbers of opponents. (The latter are sometimes called *beat-'em-ups* or *brawlers*.) Fighting games also use hand-to-hand weapons such as swords and staves and a limited number of ranged weapons.

FIGURE 3.5
Skullgirls, a cartoonish fighting game

Strategy Games

Strategy games include strategic (naturally), tactical, and sometimes logistical challenges. They may also offer economic and exploration challenges to lengthen the game and give it more variety (see **Figure 3.6**). Once in a while, they also have a physical challenge thrown in for spice, but this often annoys strategically minded players.

FIGURE 3.6
Napoleon: Total War, a real-time strategy game

Strategy games challenge the player to achieve victory through planning, and specifically through planning a series of actions taken against one or more opponents.

This definition distinguishes strategy games from puzzle games that call for planning in the absence of conflict, and from competitive construction and management simulations that require planning but not direct action against an opponent. Strategy games often include the reduction of enemy forces as a key goal, so most strategy games are war games in greater or lesser degrees of abstraction. Checkers (draughts), for example, is an abstract war game; Risk is slightly less abstract; and *Axis and Allies,* a board game about World War II, is fairly representational.

Strategy games fall into two main subgenres: classical turn-based games and real-time strategy games. Pure strategy games (those that contain only conflict challenges, with no economic or physical challenges) tend to be turn-based rather than operating in real time.

Role-Playing Games

Role-playing games (RPGs) allow players to interact with a game world in a wider variety of ways than most other genres do and to play a richer role than many games allow. Most RPGs also offer an experience impossible in the real world: a sense of growing from an ordinary person into a superhero with amazing powers. Other genres usually provide players with these powers immediately, but in an RPG, the player earns them through successful play and gets to choose which particular abilities she wants to cultivate.

The essential parts of a computer role-playing game (CRPG) are the quest or story of the game (see **Figure 3.7**) and character growth. The quest usually requires some combat, and the rules of the game are designed to support it. The rules also define how character growth occurs. A successful CRPG depends on a captivating story and a rewarding character-growth path.

FIGURE 3.7
The Elder Scrolls V: Skyrim, seen from a first-person viewpoint

Most role-playing games involve tactical, logistical, and exploration challenges. They also include economic challenges such as collecting loot and trading it in for better weapons. They sometimes include puzzles and conceptual challenges. Older CRPGs never included action elements; they implemented combat via turn-based choices for the player to make. (*Puzzle Quest* still works this way.) Modern CRPGs have started to include physical challenges as part of their combat model, but these are seldom as difficult as in fighting games, for example.

CRPGs have elements in common with many other genres; it is the way in which they implement them and the combinations in which they occur that set them apart. Because CRPGs include so many types of challenges, it's not unusual for people to make hybrids.

Sports Games

Sports games create a special challenge for the game designer. So many people play or watch sports that they come to a video game with high expectations about what the game will be like. A designer must learn to meet those expectations. Sports games are one of the most popular genres in all of video gaming, and a well-tuned game can turn into a highly enjoyable—and profitable—product line.

Unlike most other games, which take place in a world the player knows little about, sports games simulate a world the player knows a lot about: sporting events as they are in real life. No one has ever really led an army of elves into combat, and only a small number of people know how it feels to fly an F-16 fighter jet, but a great many people know what professional football looks like and how the game is played. Sports games encourage direct comparison with the real world (see **Figure 3.8**).

FIGURE 3.8
Pro Evolution Soccer 2011

Not all sports games are ultrarealistic, of course. Some, such as Electronic Arts' old Sega Genesis game *Mutant League Football,* are fantasy games even though they are based on real sports. Others, such as Midway's *NFL Blitz* football series, simplify a sport and deliberately make it more extreme for dramatic purposes. Skateboarding games often fall into this category as well.

Most sports games concentrate on simulating actual matches, but many also include a number of management functions as well, such as the challenges of managing a team or an athlete's career. A few sports games implement only this aspect of the sport and don't allow the player to control individual athletes in matches. Occasionally called *manager games,* these are particularly popular in Europe.

Vehicle Simulations

Vehicle simulations create the feeling of driving or flying a vehicle, real or imaginary. In simulations of real vehicles, one of the chief goals is verisimilitude, an (apparently!) close relationship to reality (see **Figure 3.9**). You can expect your players to know a lot about these machines and to want an experience that is at least visually similar to that of really controlling one. If you're designing an imaginary vehicle, you're free to create any kind of driving experience that you like without being restricted by such things as gravity, g-forces, fuel capacity, and so on. Your game really needs just to create the feeling of movement; you can place whatever limitations you like on that movement.

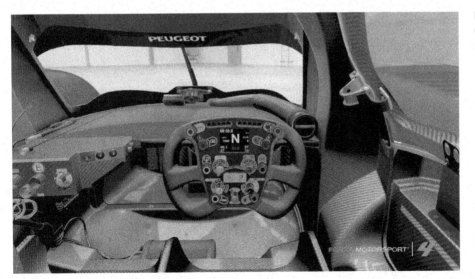

FIGURE 3.9
Cockpit view of *Forza Motorsport 4*

The biggest subgenres of vehicle simulations are flight simulators and driving simulators, although there are many more for boats and even trains. Flight simulators fall into two general categories: civilian and military. Driving simulators also tend to fall into two categories: organized racing and imaginary racing. Organized racing simulators try to reproduce the experience of driving a racing car or motorcycle in a real-world racing class, such as IndyCar. Some driving simulations implement combat between the cars, a further subgenre.

Construction and Simulation Games

Construction and simulation games, also called construction and management simulations (CMSs), offer players the chance to build things, such as anthills or cities, while operating within economic constraints (see **Figure 3.10**). These are games about processes. The player's goal is not to defeat an enemy but to create something within the context of an ongoing process. The better the player understands and controls the process, the more success she has at building. CMSs typically include both a free-form construction mode, in which the player can build things any way she likes, and prebuilt scenarios for her to manage. Most CMSs offer two sets of tools: one for building and one for managing. The actual process of building is usually an easy point-and-click mechanism, but managing can be tricky indeed.

FIGURE 3.10
FarmVille, a hugely successful browser-based CMS with an isometric camera model

These games primarily offer economic and conceptual challenges. Only rarely do they involve conflict or exploration, and they almost never include physical challenges.

Adventure Games

Adventure games are quite different from most other games on the market. An adventure game isn't a competition or a simulation. An adventure game doesn't offer a process to manage or an opponent to defeat through strategy and tactics. Instead, an adventure game is an interactive story about a character whom the player controls (see **Figure 3.11**). This character is the player's avatar, but he's more than merely a representative of the player. He is a fictional person in his own right, a protagonist, the hero of the story. Although both adventure games and role-playing games possess this quality, RPGs normally offer a heavily numbers-based character-growth system (levels, weapons, skills, and so on), while adventure games do not—their character growth is dramatic, not numeric.

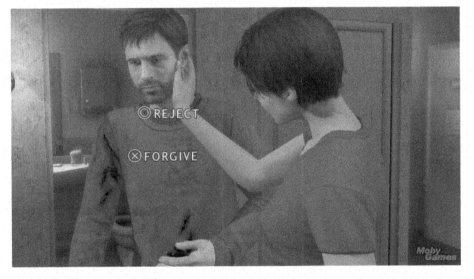

FIGURE 3.11
Heavy Rain

As the designer of an adventure game, it's your job to bring not just a story but a world to life—a world in which a story is taking place. Your talents at creating places, characters, plots, dialogue, and puzzles will be tested as in no other genre. Adventure games chiefly provide exploration and puzzle solving. Sometimes they contain conceptual challenges as well. Pure adventure games may include physical challenges, but only rarely.

Puzzle Games

In puzzle games, puzzle solving is the primary activity, though puzzles may occur within a story line or lead up to some larger goal. That doesn't mean that you can offer a random collection of puzzles and call it a game; puzzle games usually provide a series of related challenges, variations on a theme. The types of puzzles offered include recognizing patterns, making logical deductions, or understanding a process. In most cases, the puzzles give the player clues that have to be unraveled or solved somehow to meet the victory condition. Physics-based puzzle games like *Angry Birds* or *Cut the Rope* (**Figure 3.12**) are exceptions; they generally have to be solved by trial and error. A hidden-object game also qualifies as a sort of puzzle game, although its challenge is purely to look closely at a complicated scene.

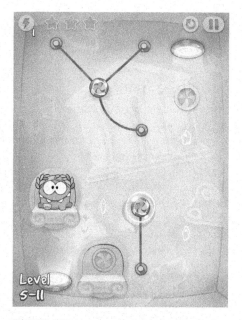

FIGURE 3.12 *Cut the Rope: Time Travel*

The number of puzzle games on the market has exploded since about 2000, when web- and smartphone-based gaming began to take off. They are a large part of the casual market and need not be really challenging to be fun and successful. For example, *Bejeweled* requires the player to match three jewels to remove them from a grid but contains so large an element of chance as new jewels appear that it requires very little brainwork. Puzzle games offer logic challenges and conceptual challenges almost exclusively, although occasionally they include time pressure or an action element. They often also offer multiple solutions.

Summary

You now know the major genres and subgenres used by the game industry. These are not all that exist, only the best-known and best-selling examples. Genres are not meant to constrain your imagination, but they provide a framework for design, a sort of scaffold upon which to build your game without inventing everything from scratch—which lowers some of the risk in designing a new game. Designing a game within a well-known genre also helps you to explain your game concisely to funding agencies, retailers, and players. Chapter 4, "Understanding Your Player," discusses players and their attitudes to games in more detail.

Design Practice EXERCISES

1. Genre classifications vary considerably. Try looking at those from MobyGames (www.mobygames.com/browse/games), Yahoo! Games (http://games.yahoo.com), and the Android or iOS app stores for mobile phones. Which genres are present or absent in the different locations? What accounts for the differences?

2. Which genres do you like, which are you indifferent to, and which do you actively dislike? What differentiates them? Do you feel this says something about you as a player? Talk to someone else you know who has different tastes and think about what might make their preferences different from yours.

Design Practice QUESTIONS

Choosing a genre for your game (or deciding that it does not belong in any genre) is part of defining your game's concept, a process that Chapter 7, "Game Concepts," discusses in detail. When you're thinking about it, consider the following questions:

1. Do the challenges and actions that you want to offer your player suggest that it belongs in a particular genre? Are there certain actions that the player will probably be performing most of the time, such as driving, that would tend to put it in a certain genre?

2. If you sell your game via either a game store or an online shop or portal, there is a good chance that that organization will want to categorize your game in a genre. Try looking at different outlets such as Yahoo! Games or the Apple App Store to see where you think your game would go.

3. Try describing your game to someone you think is a potential player, *without* naming any particular genre. Ask them which genre they think it belongs to. Do you agree?

CHAPTER 4

Understanding Your Player

The player-centric approach that this book teaches demands, above all else, that you understand your player, not merely as part of an audience of consumers, but as an individual who has an emotional connection to your game and, indirectly, to you. We often think that we know what players want from games, but much of this knowledge is intuitive and based on what *we* want from games as players. In this chapter, you'll learn about the characteristics of certain kinds of players. We'll begin with a way of looking at what kinds of feelings different players like to experience as they play. Next we'll examine several familiar demographics: men and women, boys and girls, dedicated ("hardcore") players, and casual ones. All this information will help you define what kinds of people you want to entertain and, in consequence, what kind of game you should build to entertain them.

VandenBerghe's Five Domains of Play

Jason VandenBerghe is a Creative Director at Ubisoft, and he has been studying issues of player motivation for several years. In his lecture "The 5 Domains of Play: Applying Psychology's Big 5 Motivation Domains to Games," delivered at the 2012 Game Developers' Conference (VandenBerghe, 2012), VandenBerghe proposed a way of understanding different kinds of players and why they choose the games that they do. You can apply this as part of the player-centric approach to game design by thinking about your representative player in these terms. In the next few sections we'll take a look at VandenBerghe's five domains of play.

The Five-Factor Model

VandenBerghe's work is based on a well-known psychological model of human personality traits called the Five Factor Model. This concept, also known as "The Big Five," explains personality traits in terms of five nonoverlapping domains: *openness to new experiences, conscientiousness, extraversion, agreeableness,* and *neuroticism* (which is defined as a tendency to experience negative emotions). The names of these traits produce a convenient acronym: OCEAN.

NOTE This is only a brief introduction to the subject of personality modeling. There are many books and scholarly articles available if you want to study it more closely. The book *Personality Traits*, by Gerald Matthews et al. (Matthews, 2009), looks into the theory of personality traits and the history of efforts to define them, including The Big Five.

The opposite ends of these scales are resistance to new experiences, lack of conscientiousness, introversion, disagreeableness, and stability. After thousands of surveys, the model has proven to be remarkably stable across ages and cultures.

These traits produce observable patterns of motivation and behavior: People who are open to new experiences seek them out; people who are agreeable seek social harmony; and so on. Based on his understanding of the Five Factor Model, VandenBerghe proposed that we play games to satisfy the same motivations that we feel in real life, and this is particularly true if we are unable to satisfy them in real life. Play gives us an outlet.

The Five Domains of Play

VandenBerghe correlated the five traits of the Five Factor Model with five domains of play that might fulfill them—which can also be thought of as aspects of a game that players might be motivated to seek out. Here are his five domains of play and what they mean for understanding a player.

■ **Novelty.** This correlates with the first trait, openness to experience. Players who seek novelty like games that include a lot of variety and unexpected elements. People who don't like novelty seek familiarity instead: games that offer them a comforting sameness. These players might prefer *Words with Friends* to a science fiction extravaganza set in a strange world with strange rules.

■ **Challenge.** VandenBerghe correlates a desire for challenge—and perhaps more specifically effort and control—with the trait of conscientiousness. High-challenge players prefer games that are difficult and require precision to win. Their conscientiousness drives them to act, to accomplish things, and perhaps to try to complete everything in a game. Low-challenge players like sandbox games and others in which the player is free to fool around without being required to achieve something.

■ **Stimulation.** Particularly via social engagement, this naturally correlates with extraversion. These players enjoy party games and others that involve interacting with other players. Those who prefer to avoid stimulation prefer games they can play alone, games that let them be the only real person in the game world.

■ **Harmony.** Chapter 1, "Games and Video Games," described harmony as a quality of a game, the feeling that all parts of the game belong to a single, coherent whole. In this case, however, VandenBerghe is referring to *social* harmony and correlates this motivation with the personality trait of agreeableness. He sees cooperative games such as *Little Big Planet* as good examples of games that offer social harmony, and strictly competitive games, such as the *Street Fighter* series, as ones that offer this quality's opposite, conflict.

■ **Threat.** This domain is the most peculiar one because players' reactions to it are the opposite of what you might expect. The game quality of threat (an element of danger, or frightening content—anything that is likely to generate unpleasant emotions) is popular with people who have high neuroticism scores in OCEAN tests.

In other words, people who have a tendency to experience negative emotions actually seek out those emotions. He includes players of the survival horror genre in this category.

In his talk at the Game Developers' Conference, VandenBerghe further subdivided each of these domains into six "facets." For example, threat is really composed of six other qualities of games: tension, provocation, gloom, humiliation, addiction, and danger. However, there isn't room to discuss all 30 facets of games here. To learn more about them, please download his slides at www.darklorde.com/2012/03/the-5-domains-of-play-slides.

Bear in mind that these are not binary, on-off qualities. They are continuums, sliding scales. What's more, they don't describe what players *always* like; our moods change. Sometimes we might want high-energy action, and at other times we might like a slower-moving adventure game with lots to look at.

VandenBerghe's point, and mine, is that by keeping these qualities of games in mind—these domains of play that people seek out—we can decide as designers how we want to entertain them: what experiences our games will provide.

Another Domain: Attitudes to Storytelling

One question that VandenBerghe didn't address, but that makes a big difference among players, is how they feel about stories in games. Some are dogmatically opposed to the inclusion of story-like material in a game. They dislike any narrative content such as cut-scenes, and they think of the game primarily as a system of rules that they must learn to master. The story merely interferes with their enjoyment of this process. These players prefer tactical or strategic immersion in the game (as we explained in the section called "Immersion" in Chapter 1). They have no interest in narrative immersion. To them, the non-player characters (NPCs) in the game are not people to be interacted with but symbols to be manipulated. These players prefer games of pure action or strategy, or multiplayer games that make no effort to tell a story because the main point of the game is to interact with the other players. Some genres are more suited to storytelling than others, too. Sports games, for example, gain little from the inclusion of storytelling.

For other players, the story is not only part of the game, it is the main reason for playing the game. They believe in its characters and are concerned about what happens to them. The events in the game are a part of a plot to which they are contributing as active participants. They may even care less about the gameplay than they do about the story, using cheats or walkthroughs to find out what happens without having to overcome all the challenges themselves.

Few players are this extreme, however. Most enjoy a certain amount of storytelling in a game, so long as it is coherent with the gameplay and doesn't slow them down. At the very least they find a little framing narrative to be useful in establishing context: setting the scene and explaining who the protagonist is, what she is trying to achieve, and why.

As you think about your plans for the game and your target audience, keep in mind that some audiences loves stories passionately, some hate them utterly, and many like a dash of storytelling with their gameplay. Decide which audience you want to serve, then check out Chapter 11, "Storytelling," which discusses how to include stories in games in detail.

Demographic Categories

As we saw in the previous section, the kinds of experiences that players like to have vary considerably, which accounts for the wide variety of games there are in the world. There are also significant differences among players by age and sex. The next few sections will explore these different demographic categories.

Men and Women

But what if the player is female?

—Sheri Graner Ray, *Gender Inclusive Game Design*

Women represent a large portion of the gamer market, a fact that runs counter to many stereotypes about video games. Audience research shows that in the United States, more adult women (31 percent) than teenage boys (19 percent) play video games, a statistic that may surprise you (Entertainment Software Association, 2013).

Men and women don't differ nearly as much as pop psychology would like us to believe. Few individuals conform completely to traditional stereotypes of masculinity and femininity, and men's and women's interests overlap considerably. In *Gender Blending: Confronting the Limits of Duality*, Holly Devor (Devor, 1989) quoted studies showing that as many as 50 percent of heterosexual women identified themselves as having been tomboys as children. Unfortunately, far too many game designers (and product designers in general) treat men and women as entirely different species with little in common.

GENDER INCLUSIVENESS

To attract women players, you don't have to make the game about stereotypically feminine interests such as fashion or shopping, any more than you have to make games about monster truck rallies to attract men. Rather, to make a game of interest to both sexes, you need to avoid including material that discourages one group or the other from playing. To make a game that both sexes will play, don't build content that will limit the interest of, or offend, either sex.

The biggest turnoffs for women are usually:

- Hypersexualized female avatars and other characters.

- Repetitive, monotonous play.

- Play without a meaningful goal. Simply racking up the highest score isn't enough.

- The solitary nature of single-player play. If you're making a single-player game, there is nothing you can do about this; it's just something to be aware of.

A number of people in the game industry are working to encourage the creation of more large games with adventurous female protagonists (like Lara Croft or Jade from *Beyond Good and Evil*). These efforts have met with a rather noisy backlash from a minority of men who, for reasons of their own, don't want such games to exist. You may safely ignore them; their assertions that men won't play games with female protagonists are simply not true, and in any case, it's not necessary to cater to men to make a popular game. If a game is good, they'll play it.

A FEW GENERALITIES

Having warned you not to treat men and women as polar opposites, this section offers a small number of generalities about how male and female play patterns tend to differ among Western men and women (the only group for which much research exists). These observations may not apply to women in Japan, China, Korea, or India—all important new markets for games.

- **Men and women like to learn differently.** Women generally like to know what will be expected of them before they proceed rather than be thrown into the deep end to sink or swim. The learn-by-dying approach of old arcade games—which still persists in many mobile games—is not popular with many female players. Be sure to include tutorial levels at the beginning to introduce the game to your player.

- **Men and women have different attitudes toward risk.** In a game, men are generally willing to experiment even if it means losing frequently. Women will often consolidate and preserve their achievements to avoid losing them again, even if a riskier strategy might reap larger rewards.

- **Women are more interested in people than things and like to socialize as part of their play experience.** This explains why online games are more successful than single-player games among female players: Online games allow the players to socialize. Facebook games, which encourage players to invite their friends to play, share resources, and compare achievements, have proven to be extremely popular with women even though generally they don't permit the same kind of multiplayer play that a persistent world does.

- **Men and women have different conflict resolution styles.** Women prefer that violence have a justification; fighting for its own sake is of little interest to them. They are not opposed to violence per se, but they like the violence to be given a

NOTE For further reading, check out *Gender Inclusive Game Design* by Sheri Graner Ray (Ray, 2003). She discusses these issues in considerable detail.

NOTE In the real world, women assume a large part of the responsibility for maintaining the social fabric, keeping people connected across families and communities. Social networks and even online video games have become part of how they do this.

CHAPTER 4

context, such as a story. Women also like to use lateral thinking to find alternatives to brute-force approaches. Fighting games, war games, and shooters are more popular with men than they are with women. On the other hand, role-playing games (RPGs) *are* popular with women even though they include a lot of combat because the combat has a purpose and is part of a larger aim, not an end in itself.

- **Women enjoy mental challenges and finding elegant solutions to problems.** This is reflected by the popularity of puzzle games among women.

- **Women like to customize their avatars.** Men often treat their avatar characters as puppets rather than people, someone simply to be controlled for the sake of winning the game. Women tend to identify with their avatars more. A woman uses the avatar as a means of self-expression and likes to be able to make the avatar look like herself or a fantasy version of herself. (These attitudes vary somewhat by age and game genre, however. Male players can spend a great deal of time tweaking their characters in an RPG, because that's the point of the game.)

- **Men have more leisure time and money to spend on gaming.** Particularly as they grow into young adulthood, male players are likely to treat gaming as a serious hobby—or drop it altogether in favor of something else. Men are generally more willing to spend $60 on a video game on the first day of its release than women are. The new casual business models (see Chapter 6, "Making Money from Your Game") have proven to be enormously popular with women because they don't require the player to risk a lot of money up front, and permit them to pay for a game in small transactions. Men are also more likely to devote large blocks of time to gaming. Women's time tends to be more fractured, especially if they have children, and they are much more likely to play for half an hour to two hours than they are to play for five hours at a time. Some women will play just a much time per week as men do, just in smaller chunks. This is something to keep in mind if you make a game that has a long distance between the save points. Many social network games allow players to stop at any point without losing any progress.

DESIGN RULE Women Are a Market, Not a Genre

Do not try to design a "women's game" simply by creating features that address these generalities. Rather, design an intrinsically interesting game and bear these issues in mind as you consider the effect that your design decisions will have on your potential customer base.

Again, remember that these are generalities. There are plenty of devoted female players who buy expensive console games, and there are plenty of male players who are parents of young children and have just enough time for an inexpensive puzzle game a couple of times a day. The main reason to be aware of these factors is not so that you can make a game "for women" or "for men," but so that you will know whether your game is likely to attract large numbers of women or men—or to discourage them from playing.

MALE AND FEMALE PLAYERS AND CHARACTERS

Early in the history of video games, some designers were concerned that male players (who used to make up the majority of the market) would be unwilling to play with female avatars: Men might find identifying with a female character somehow threatening. Lara Croft (**Figure 4.1**) demonstrated that this is not a problem, at least as long as the character is acting in a role that men are comfortable with. Lara engages in traditionally masculine activities, so men are happy to enter the game as Lara. They might be less comfortable with an avatar who engaged in more traditionally feminine activities.

FIGURE 4.1
Lara Croft (seen here in *Tomb Raider: Underworld*) is adventurous but hypersexualized.

Women, of course, are expected to identify with male heroes routinely, a state of affairs predating computer games. Until recently, few books, movies, TV shows, or video games about adventurous activities featured female heroes, and they're still very much in the minority. Women justifiably get tired of playing male heroes, and they appreciate the opportunity to play as female characters. At the same time, however, women aren't that interested in playing male-fantasy characters like Rayne from the *BloodRayne* series; such characters are so extreme that it discourages identification with them. Heather from *Silent Hill 3* (**Figure 4.2**) provides a better example; she looks like a real woman, not a walking lingerie advertisement.

FIGURE 4.2
Heather, from *Silent Hill 3*, looks like a real person.

TIP Many designers in the game industry are interested in creating new female adventure heroes to meet the demand from women who like to play AAA games but are tired of the same old male protagonists. For inspiring stories of real-life women, see the Facebook or Pinterest pages called *Heroic Women to Inspire Game Designers.*

In general, male players don't actually identify with their avatars as much as female players do. Men are more willing to take the default avatar provided by the game and happily run with it. Women tend to see an avatar as an extension of their own personalities and an opportunity for self-expression (or, in a game with a story, as a character to care about). One of the best things you can do to make your game more attractive to female players is to permit them to customize the avatar—to choose his or her clothes, accessories, and weapons (if any). RPGs, especially online ones, offer some of the most powerful customization features.

When possible, it's nice to give the player a choice of male or female avatars. This requires some care to do well, however. A woman is not just a man with a different body; to do it properly you should also rewrite the dialogue to make sure that when a female avatar speaks, she sounds like a woman speaking, not just a woman reading lines written for a man. Men and women have different communication styles.

Boys and Girls

Video games for children differ from those for adults, just as books and television shows for them do. Nor is there one single type of game appropriate for children—their motor and cognitive skills change throughout childhood. Here are the commonly recognized age categories:

- Preschool and kindergarten (ages 3 to 6)

- Early elementary (ages 5 to 8)

- Upper elementary (ages 7 to 12, the tweens)

- Middle and high school (13 and up, the teens)

- Late teens to mid-20s. Although these people are no longer children, their brains are still developing.

TIP If you want to learn more about childhood development, study the work of psychologist Jean Piaget. His theories of cognitive development have been hugely influential on education and many other fields.

Each of these groups has, on the whole, its own interests and abilities, reflecting that their brains and physiology are different than adults'. As with gender, any general guidelines here have plenty of individual exceptions. The key is to remember, as researchers Piaget and Montessori have illustrated, it is an error to see children as less skilled, less knowledgeable, mini-adults.

In western cultures children tend to aspire to adulthood and its privileges, and avoid anything made for an age group younger than themselves. As a general rule, entertainment made for children of a certain age group will actually feature characters older than the players. The opposite is true in other cultures, such as in Japan.

If you're planning to make games for children, consider the following issues.

Hand-eye coordination. Young children's motor skills are poorly developed at first, while those of teenagers and twentysomethings are at their peak; these skills decrease again further into adulthood. You must be aware of these differences in hand-eye coordination skill and take them into account when designing for children.

Logic development. Children enjoy puzzles just as adults do, but for younger children, the puzzles should reflect their development of logical reasoning, which comes to a peak between the ages of 6 and 7, depending on the child. A puzzle game aimed at this age or below can accommodate the range of abilities by offering several difficulty levels (which you should verify by play-testing). When such puzzles are compared to those for an adult, the number of elements involved must be fewer, and the chain of reasoning required must be shorter in order for the puzzle to provide the same amount of engagement for the child.

Systematic thinking. Children start to develop systematic thinking between the ages of 12 and 14. Keep this in mind before you add complex systems to games aimed at ages younger than this. A simple systems optimization problem that you may find easy is something that a child this age is just beginning to explore.

CHAPTER 4

- **Immediate versus long-term goals.** Games for older players often require the player to go through many steps before she reaches a long-term objective. Children are more focused on the moment-to-moment process and game play, and appreciate feedback more frequently. You don't have to have a saccharine character say "Good job!" every single time they do something right, but the priority should be on the moment-to-moment experience and less on overarching goals.

- **Visual design.** Young children don't have as much experience as adults do at filtering out irrelevant details, so keep the user interfaces in games for children simple and focused; make them deep rather than broad.

- **Linguistic complexity.** Don't talk down to children, but use age-appropriate vocabulary and syntax. Long sentences full of words that they don't know turn off kids. Short sentences made up of carefully chosen words can still express quite sophisticated ideas; for an example, read Saint-Exupéry's *The Little Prince*.

- **Experimentation.** Children have an endless capacity for experimenting, and they tend to want to jump in and try everything, which means they are clicking on everything they see. This allows you as a designer to focus on creating game worlds that reward this type of exploration.

- **Reading.** Children, especially young ones, have a limited reading ability, and even well into their teens some prefer not to spend a lot of time reading. You can use voiceover narration for important information and count on children to use their imaginations to fill in many story details that you might need to explain to an adult.

NOTE For further reading on the Kisses of Death, consult Carolyn Handler Miller's book *Digital Storytelling, Second Edition: A Creator's Guide to Interactive Entertainment* (Miller, 2008).

- **Appropriate content.** This tricky area actually has as much to do with what parents want for their children than what the children want for themselves. Children's entertainment needs to address children's concerns, whereas sexuality and high finance are not relevant to their world. This is one of the reasons the early Harry Potter books are so brilliant; they capture children's concerns perfectly. Kids easily identify with Harry's feelings of alienation, being misunderstood by his family, and his sense of latent but untapped promise. Even the emphasis on food in the early books is significant; for younger children, food is a major interest and a big part of their daily routine. A great way to remember themes of childhood is to read popular literature aimed at the age you are creating a game for.

Carolyn Handler Miller, a longtime developer of entertainment for children, has devised a list of "Seven Kisses of Death," features that drive away children rather than appealing to them. The Kisses of Death are widely held misconceptions about what children like, generally founded on what adults *want* them to like.

- **Death Kiss #1: Kids love anything sweet.** Kids love *some* things that are sweet, some of the time, but not anything and not all the time. Think about the Warner Brothers cartoons: wisecracking Bugs Bunny; Sylvester the Cat's endless efforts to eat Tweety Bird; Wile E. Coyote's similarly endless efforts to kill the Roadrunner;

homicidal Yosemite Sam and rabbit-cidal Elmer Fudd. Kids love these cartoons—which actually include a sneaky moral about violence redounding upon the violent—but there's nothing remotely sweet about them.

■ **Death Kiss #2: Give them what's good for them.** Kids are forever being told what's good for them. They're made to eat food they don't like; they're made to go to school; they're made to do chores, learn to play the piano, and a million other things supposedly meant to build their characters or strengthen their bodies or minds. Most of this is reasonable and necessary, but not in an entertainment context. How would you, as an adult, like to be fed a dose of propaganda with every book and TV show you saw? You wouldn't, and neither do kids. When they want to relax and have fun, they don't want a dose of medicine with it.

■ **Death Kiss #3: You've just got to amuse them.** This is the opposite of Death Kiss #2; it cynically assumes that kids are less discriminating than adults, so any old fluff will do. It won't. Kids can't tell the difference between good acting and bad acting, and they aren't experienced enough to recognize clichéd plot lines, but they won't put up with just anything. Walt Disney realized this, and so do the writers and animators who continue his work; Disney movies are multilayered even though they are for children. So, too, are the best children's books. Meaningful content will keep a child's attention longer than trivial content.

■ **Death Kiss #4: Always play it safe!** This is a variant of the "sweet" Death Kiss. Some people, in an effort to avoid violent or controversial content, go overboard and try to eliminate anything that might frighten or disturb a child or even raise her pulse. This inevitably results in bland, dull entertainment. Again, look at Disney films for good counter-examples: Dumbo's separation from his mother; Snow White's terrified flight through the forest; the outright murder of Simba's father in *The Lion King*. These are not happy things, and that's OK. Gerard Jones argues in his important treatment of the subject *Killing Monsters: Why Children Need Fantasy, Super Heroes, and Make-Believe Violence* (Jones, 2002) that learning to deal with threatening situations constitutes an important part of growing up.

■ **Death Kiss #5: All kids are created equal.** There's no such thing as a single children's market. Kids' interests and abilities change too quickly to lump them all into a single category. If you're planning to make a game for ages 6 to 10 and the publishers decide they want a game for ages 8 to 12, you'll have to redesign the game. One-size-fits-all definitely doesn't work with kids.

■ **Death Kiss #6: Explain everything.** Kids are much happier with trial-and-error than adults are, and they don't want long introductions explaining how to play the game. They want to dive in and play. Above all, avoid talking heads with a lot of jabber. Adults naturally tend to assume that kids need things explained to them, but it's not true of video game worlds in which they can't hurt themselves or anything else. Keep exposition—and especially anything that smacks of teaching them—to a minimum.

■ **Death Kiss #7: Be sure your characters are wholesome!** Wholesome equals boring. We wouldn't put up with bland white-bread characters in our entertainment; why should we make children do so? You don't have to introduce serial killers, but create real characters with their own personal foibles. *Sesame Street* famously offered a variety of characters, many specifically designed to represent moods or attitudes familiar to young children: greedy, grouchy, helpful, and so on.

Games for Girls

The game industry has always been overwhelmingly dominated by white men, and male developers have tended to design games that they themselves would like (or would have liked when they were boys). Whether for societal or genetic reasons, boys' and girls' interests diverge more widely from one another than men's and women's do; on their respective bell-shaped curves, the means are farther apart. At certain ages, many boys and girls may flatly reject things (clothing, toys, or other symbols) associated with the opposite sex.

For most of the game industry's history, no one made an effort to design games specifically for girls or even tried to think much about what kinds of games girls would like. It was a catch-22 situation: If you proposed a game for girls to a publisher, you would be met with the reply, "Girls don't play video games." But, of course, the reason girls didn't play video games was that there weren't many games they liked to play—or at least that was the general perception. (Further research showed that this was an unfounded stereotype; far more girls played games than people realized, even though no one was considering their interests.)

In the mid-1990s, a number of people realized that girls represented an untapped market, and several companies grew up to exploit it. Unfortunately, many of these early efforts were graphically poor and offered less value for the money than most other games. Girls want, and deserve, games just as good as those made for boys. More recently, several companies have started making games for girls again with more success. In the late 2000s the most notable was Ubisoft's *Imagine* series of games, inspired by the unexpected breakout success of *Imagine: Fashion Designer*. The subsequent series and its competitors covered a huge range of subjects as Ubisoft and other publishers sought to find out what this unexpected market wanted to play. Some of the most successful games are based on popular toy and book characters, some of which pre-date the *Imagine* era (for instance, Barbie, Bratz, and Nancy Drew), and all have earned huge success.

If you're interested in making games for this market, remember that the audience is *girls*, not women. Adult women are naturally more diverse than children and have a wider variety of interests. Don't assume that what applies to women also applies to girls generally.

MATTEL'S APPROACH

If you want to make games specifically for girls, as opposed to games that appeal to children of both sexes, you have to ask yourself what especially interests girls—and, perhaps more important, what does *not* interest girls. One way to assess this is to examine what girl consumers buy, read, and watch. As an example, you need look no farther than Mattel, manufacturer of *Barbie,* the single most famous toy for girls in the world. Mattel's great success developing games for girls results from its understanding of its target market. (Mattel doesn't publish software itself anymore; instead, it licenses its brands to others.)

Barbie's success derives partly from the proven, time-tested formula she follows and partly from a well-targeted market: Mattel aims *Barbie* at a core age group from 4 to 8 years old. After that, girls' interests change, and Mattel does not try for a one-size-fits-all approach. The company has no social agenda and makes no claim of political correctness.

JESYCA DURCHIN'S ADVICE

Jesyca Durchin owns the consulting company Nena Media (www.nenamedia.com), which creates media content for young girls, and she is a former executive producer for Mattel. At the 2000 Game Developers' Conference, she gave an extremely useful summary (Durchin, 2000) of what she had learned about how girls in this age group play games.

Girls Have a Wide Variety of Interests

It is vital to identify what type of girl is interested in your type of game. Girls are much more fragmented in their interests than boys. Girls change more rapidly, and their emotional and intellectual growth happens differently. A girl has different needs in her playtime almost every year of her childhood—loosely defined as being between ages 4 and 14.

Hinge Interactivity on Proven Play Patterns

A play pattern is a traditional and almost instinctual way a child approaches an object or an activity to entertain herself. Traditionally girls value the following:

- Fashion play
- Glamour play
- Nurture play
- Action/twitch play
- Collection play
- Adventure play
- Communication/social play

continues on next page

As well as exercising their own imaginations, girls like to reproduce daily life in play. Barbie is a vehicle for projecting adult activities into a child's world. Don't be afraid of open-ended or non-goal-oriented play.

Here are a few more observations:

- **Girls like *stuff*.** Stuff is what the girl can collect, display, or take away from the product. It is incredibly important for the girl to feel there is a reason for her to play. In some ways, collecting stuff replaces the concept of scoring in traditional boy's software. Collecting each one of a variety of shells, for example, is more interesting than trying to achieve a high, but abstract, numerical score.

- **Create environments that are attractive to girls.** Girls like environments that are reality-based but are either beautiful or make sense to the story line. Symmetry and color coherency are important to girls. Not everything has to be pink, purple, and pretty, but each environment should give the girl the feeling of being in another place. Girls (and boys) are highly imaginative, and they create alternative story lines in their own heads. Be aware that the girl's imagination influences her view of your environment.

- **Girls appreciate sensual interfaces.** Girls tend to respond more positively to what is sometimes referred to as the sensual interface. They need colorful, sound-driven interfaces that "feel" good. The interface needs to feel magical and needs to have what I call the *brrrring* factor. Don't give girls a group of identical gray pushbuttons, no matter how logically organized they may be; give them buttons that ring and change shape and color.

- **Extend the play from existing toys or media into software.** Branding is becoming more and more important in the business of software. It is doubly important in the girl's software business because girls are still just getting involved in viewing the computer as an entertainment tool. Branding is important to rising above all the muck.

- **Don't be ashamed of your work.** If you're embarrassed by what you're doing, it will show. Do it wholeheartedly or don't do it at all. Girls can tell if you're ashamed of making games for them. If you're uncomfortable using terms like "hair play" or "relationship games," don't bother.

KAYE ELLING'S FIVE CS

Kaye Elling was creative manager at Blitz Games on the *Bratz* series, and in 2006, she gave an insightful lecture called "Inclusive Games Design" at the Animex festival in the UK (Elling, 2006). Elling proposed five characteristics of games, all beginning with the letter C, that designers should strive for to make them more inclusive and accessible to girls.

- **Characterization.** As Chapter 10, "Character Development," discusses, women (and girls) see avatars as someone who represents themselves rather than someone they simply control. Therefore, an avatar has to be someone girls can identify with, and to have no qualities they find distasteful.

- **Context.** Environments matter to girls, and they will be repulsed by environments that they find ugly or hostile. This advice concurs with Jesyca Durchin's thoughts in the sidebar "Jesyca Durchin's Advice."

- **Control.** Girls like to feel as if they are in control of the game, rather than that it is in control of them. The risk-and-reward style of gameplay appeals less to girls because they don't enjoy taking risks as much as boys do. They also dislike mechanics that harshly punish failure, because those mechanics discourage experimentation.

- **Customization.** Girls customize their mobile phones and other accessories more than boys do, so it makes sense that they would want to customize their games as well—especially their avatars. *Bratz: Rock Angelz* offered 686 different items of clothing, makeup, jewelry, and so on. The more desirable ones are unlockable rewards the player can earn for completing mini-games.

- **Creativity.** Creative play is a big part of what makes *The Sims* successful with girls and women. Creativity gives players a chance to express themselves and show off what they made to others. It's not confined to girl games by any means; even in *Halo 2* players can design unique clan badges.

TIP *Puzzle Quest* is a Nintendo DS RPG that works very well for both boys and girls. Players can choose a male or female avatar, and combat is characterized as puzzle-solving. When the player loses a battle, his avatar is not killed, but simply runs away and can try again later.

A FEW MISCONCEPTIONS

Because people see fewer girls than boys playing hardcore games, they tend to jump to conclusions about what girls want. This section corrects a few of these misconceptions.

- **Girls don't like computer games because computers are techie.** This is patently false. Although most girls and women generally are less fascinated by the technical details of computers than are boys and men, that doesn't discourage them from playing computer games any more than automotive specifications discourage them from driving cars.

- **Girls don't like violence.** No, what girls don't like is nonstop, meaningless violence. It's not so much that they're repulsed by it as that they're bored by it. It doesn't stimulate their imaginations. If you've seen one explosion, you've seen them all. Elling also points out that when violence is casual, sadistic, or excessively gory, it becomes brutality, and girls do not like brutality. When violence is defensive, provoked, or cartoony, it is more acceptable (Elling, 2006).

- **Girls want everything to be happy and sweet.** Not true. If you read books written specifically for girls, you'll see that they're not just saccharine from one end to the other. Girls like stories filled with mystery, suspense, even danger—but again, it has to be meaningful, not just random or pointless.

■ **Girls don't like to be scared.** This is only partially true. Jesyca Durchin makes a useful distinction between *spooky* and *scary.* Girls like things that are spooky but not scary. The abandoned house or the carnival at night is spooky. Walking through dark streets with a murderer on the loose is scary. *Spooky* is about the possibility of being startled or frightened; *scary* is about the possibility of being hurt or killed.

A FINAL NOTE ON GAMES FOR GIRLS

Bear in mind that these are generalities. The characteristics described previously do not appeal to all girls, but they certainly appeal to many. You should take them into consideration if you're trying to make a game for girls.

Some developers, both male and female, find the idea of making games about hair, clothing, and makeup repulsive; they feel that this perpetuates a stereotype of femininity. Although there's some merit in that argument, a vastly larger number of games perpetuate a much more unfortunate stereotype of masculinity: They depict men (and reward players) who are violent, greedy, wanton, and monomaniacal. To condemn games for girls on the basis that they reflect social stereotypes is to establish an unfair double standard.

Gamer Dedication

In the previous edition of this book, this section was called "Core Versus Casual," but in the past few years these terms have begun to lose their meaning. The game industry used to assume that there was a binary distinction between hardcore, deeply committed gamers and more casual ones. With the arrival of games built around social networks, it has become clear that this is not a binary distinction but a continuum called *gamer dedication.* You can measure gamer dedication by a variety of metrics. Barry Ip and I proposed a list of these metrics in our article "From Casual to Core: A Statistical Mechanism for Studying Gamer Dedication" (Ip, 2002). Some of them were borrowed from Scott Kim's Game Developers' Conference presentation "Designing Web Games that Make Business Sense" (Kim, 2001). Even though these are older articles, their content is fundamental enough to still be relevant today.

The 15 measurable qualities of dedicated gamers that Ip and I proposed are as follows:

1. **Technologically savvy.** Highly dedicated gamers are more familiar with the latest releases and developments and show greater interest in new gaming-related technologies.

2. **Have the latest high-end gear.** Dedicated gamers will acquire the latest consoles, PC hardware, and mobile devices to keep up to date with the most recent trends. They are more likely to own, or have owned, a wide variety of older game platforms.

3. **Willingness to pay.** Enthusiasts are more inclined to spend money on games and games-related products. Conversely, casual gamers are more inclined to wait for price discounts and special offers before committing to a purchase.

4. Prefer violent/action games. Kim suggested that hardcore gamers prefer games that show comparatively violent and action-intensive content.

5. Prefer games that have depth and complexity. Dedicated gamers prefer games that deliver greater complexity and that require a longer time to master, regardless of their themes.

6. Play games over many long sessions. Dedicated gamers are likely to devote considerably more time to playing games in a single session.

7. Hunger for gaming-related information. Devouring everything from the latest news, previews, and reviews, to interviews with industry experts, the hardcore gamer actively seeks gaming-related information through the Internet, game magazines, and books, such as strategy guides.

8. Discuss games with friends online. Dedicated gamers like to discuss gaming with others and to visit game-related Internet forums or chat rooms regularly.

9. Play for the exhilaration of defeating (or completing) the game. A dedicated gamer will play persistently for the enjoyment and exhilaration of defeating the game and is likely to be more forgiving of aesthetic flaws such as poor acting or a trivial plot.

10. Much more tolerant of frustration. Hardcore gamers are much more tolerant of difficult games or games that might frustrate them in some way. Casual gamers are more likely to abandon such games.

11. Engaged in competition with himself, the game, and other players. Hardcore gamers want to feel the satisfaction and reward of competing and improving their skills against other players and/or computer-controlled opponents. Less dedicated gamers would not, for example, be inclined to play endlessly to reduce their lap-times in *Gran Turismo* by a fraction of a second, or have the patience to learn every combination attack in *Street Fighter,* or even to achieve a higher score.

12. Age at which first started playing games. If players started playing at a young age, and have since been regular gamers, then this would indicate those who are more experienced and knowledgeable. Gamers who start playing later in life are seldom as dedicated.

13. Comparative knowledge of the industry. Dedicated gamers are likely to show broader knowledge and awareness of industry activities and trends, new technologies, and game development methods. Less dedicated players may keep track of upcoming releases and game reviews, but not events such as industry layoffs or mergers.

14. Early adoption. Dedicated gamers are the ones who attend midnight release events or take extra steps to get hold of games before their official release dates through gray-market imports.

CHAPTER 4

15. Desire to modify or extend games in a creative way. Hardcore gamers frequently modify commercial games in a variety of ways. These can range from simple changes such as giving characters new skins to change their appearance to programming "aim-bots," separate pieces of software that work in concert with an existing game to give the player an unfair advantage over others. Casual gamers seldom take the time to make these kinds of modifications; they tend to play the game as-is out of the box.

Of course, how much weight you give to each of these factors is up to you. The purpose of the original article was to suggest ways of measuring these for research purposes. As a designer, however, you really need to know only the ways in which gamers exhibit their dedication. For example, if you know that dedicated gamers seek out information about a game while it is still in development, you can set up developer blogs or give out press releases to help reach that market.

In reality, of course, there are as many types of gamer as there are games; everyone has a reason for playing computer games. But if you design a game specifically for one end of the dedication continuum, you probably won't sell to many people at the other end. A few very well-designed games manage to appeal to both: *GoldenEye*, for example, can be played happily by both core and casual gamers. Core gamers can set the game at the highest difficulty level and drive themselves crazy trying to cut 15 seconds off the last time it took them to play a mission. Casual gamers can set the game at the easiest level and blast away, enjoying the game's smooth controls and visual detail. *Rock Band* is another good example.

The Dangers of Binary Thinking

You can't make a game for everyone, so your target audience is necessarily a subset of all possible players, a subset determined by your answers to the questions "Who will enjoy this game?" and "What kinds of challenges do they like?" As you answer these questions, you may be tempted to assume that the people in one category (adult men, for example) are a special audience that has nothing in common with people in other categories (adult women, children, teenagers, and so on). This is *binary thinking:* You assume that if group A likes a thing, everyone outside that group *won't* like it. It's unsound reasoning and may actually cause you to lose part of your potential customer base, as the following sections demonstrate.

Reasoning Statistically about Player Groups

Suppose you ask a group of players to rate their level of interest in a particular game on a scale of 0 to 10, with 0 representing no interest at all and 10 being fanatical enthusiasm. A few people will be at the extremes and the majority somewhere in the middle. If you graph the responses of men and women separately, you may find for a given game that the two groups have different arithmetic means; that is, the centers of their bell-shaped curves fall at different places on the graph.

Figure 4.3 shows this phenomenon. For the hypothetical game in question, men's mean level of interest is at about 5.5, while women's mean level of interest is at 4.5.

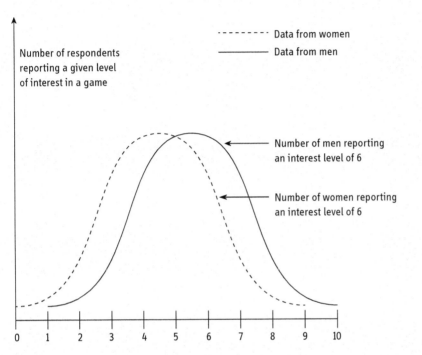

FIGURE 4.3
Reported level of interest in a game on a 0–10 scale

Note that while the graph does support the statement, "Men have a higher level of interest in this game than women do," in fact, a large area of overlap indicates that a significant portion of the women surveyed are interested in the game as well. Furthermore, the number of women reporting an interest level of 6 is about two-thirds that of the number of men reporting the same interest level. In other words, two-fifths of all the people reporting an interest level of 6 are women—far too many to simply ignore.

This is only a hypothetical example. With some games, the level of overlap may be small, and there is no point in trying to reach out to an audience that simply isn't there. A game for five-year-olds won't appeal to many 15-year-olds. The point, however, is that for most ordinary games there is *some* overlap among different populations. (For example, many Disney movies made for children include more sophisticated content that only adults would notice or find funny, thereby giving the film a broad appeal.) It is foolish to ignore, or worse yet, to offend a minority audience simply because it is in the minority, without knowing how many people fall into that category. If you ignore or repel a significant minority, you're throwing money away.

Strive for Inclusiveness, Not Universality

You cannot make a game that appeals to everyone by throwing in a hodgepodge of features because group A likes some of them and group B likes others. If you do, you will produce a game that has too many features and no harmony. For instance, you can't make a game that appeals to action fans, to strategy fans, and to fans of management simulations by combining kung fu, chess, and *Monopoly*—the result would be a mess that appeals to none of them. On the other hand, you can include a story line in a fighting game so long as the story line doesn't interfere with the gameplay. The story line adds depth to the game without driving away its key market of fighting-game enthusiasts, and it might attract the interest of people who otherwise wouldn't pay any attention to a fighting game. *Heavenly Sword* and *God of War* are good examples.

Certain groups are turned off by particular content or features. For example, women don't much care for material that portrays them as brainless sex objects; parents won't buy games for their kids if the games are nothing but blood and gore; members of minority races (and many in the majority too) are naturally offended by racist content. These are the most obvious examples, but there are more subtle ones as well. Women are generally more sensitive to the aesthetics of a game than men are, and they are less likely to buy a game with ugly artwork. Some players have no interest in narrative material and are put off if they are forced to watch it in a genre that doesn't normally include narratives. (This is why the story line in the kung fu game, mentioned earlier, shouldn't interfere with the gameplay.) These examples illustrate the effects of *exclusionary material*—content or features that serve to drive players away from a game that they otherwise might like. Your goal should be to make the best game that you can about your chosen subject, while avoiding exclusionary material that unnecessarily hurts its appeal.

> **DESIGN RULE** Keep Exclusionary Material Out of Your Game
>
> To reach a large audience while still creating a harmonious, coherent game, don't try to attract everyone by adding unrelated features. Instead, work to avoid repelling people who might otherwise be attracted.

Summary

The point of this chapter was to teach you about different kinds of players and what they want, and don't want, from their gameplaying experiences. You learned about Jason VandenBerghe's five domains of play: novelty, challenge, stimulation, social harmony, and threat; and a sixth one, storytelling. Then we looked at a few demographic categories, men and women and boys and girls, with a special focus on what it takes to make games for girls. We examined ways to think about gamer dedication and how that might affect your choice of target audience. The chapter ended with a discussion of the dangers of binary thinking, and the suggestion that you should strive for inclusiveness, not universality. In the next chapter we'll examine the different game platforms that you can design for.

Design Practice EXERCISES

1. Take a Big Five personality test at any of the many online sites that offer it. (Simply search for "big five personality test" or visit www.outofservice.com/bigfive.) Look at the results that it gives you and ask yourself how well they match your preferred domains of play. Do the same with several friends—the more, the better. Write a short paper using this data to explain whether the results you got tend to confirm or to rebut Jason VandenBerghe's hypothesis, or to produce inconclusive results.

2. Examine a currently popular AAA console game (or your instructor may assign you one) and document any exclusionary material that you think it contains—content that would tend to discourage a particular demographic from purchasing it.

3. Examine a number of games that are apparently marketed to a specific demographic such as girls or very young children. Document the design features that they seem to have in common. Be sure to address both the *types* of challenges they include (use the list in Table 1.1) and the details of their aesthetics—color palettes, typefaces, and screen layouts, for example.

Design Practice QUESTIONS

Choosing a target audience for your game (or deciding that it does not belong in any genre) is part of defining your game's concept, a process that Chapter 7, "Game Concepts," discusses in detail. When you're thinking about it, consider the following questions:

1. Which of the domains of play do you think you will be offering, and what will that say about the audience that you hope to attract?

2. What age range is your game aimed at? The answer to this question will strongly influence many things about the game: its challenges, its user interface design, its pacing, its aesthetics, and so on.

3. Do you want to be gender inclusive, or do you want to appeal to one particular sex, bearing in mind that this may limit your game's appeal to the other? If the latter, what content and features do you plan to include that you think will appeal specifically to your chosen audience?

4. How dedicated will you want your target audience to be? Requiring long play sessions, for example, will exclude some players who don't have the time for it. Go through the list of factors that make up player dedication and ask yourself if you are expecting them from your players—and if so, how you plan to meet *their* expectations of your game.

CHAPTER 5

Understanding Your Machine

When you first start fleshing out your game concept, you should concentrate on the dream, the player's role, and the target audience. However, a game concept is not complete without a statement about which machine (or machines) the game runs on. All machines have features and performance characteristics—input and output devices, processor speed, storage space—that define the scope of the game. You need to know the strengths and weaknesses of the different types of machines. The differences go far beyond hardware, however. So far as design (rather than programming) is concerned, the most important things you need to know about these machines are related to who buys them and, above all, how they use them. Some genres of games are better suited to one kind of machine than another. The physical positioning and configuration of the device plays an enormous role in determining what games will be suitable for it.

Different machines also tend to imply particular distribution channels (how the player obtains the game) and business models for selling games to your customers (retail, subscription, free-to-play, and so on). For example, games for the Apple iPhone are available only by download from the Apple's App Store, while blockbuster console titles are normally sold in retail stores. We'll address those issues in Chapter 6, "Making Money from Your Game."

There isn't room in this book to go into the exact hardware specifications of the many different kinds of game machines available, and even if there were, the information would be out of date in a few months. Instead, this short chapter will examine three broad categories of game machines: home game consoles, personal computers, and portable devices. We'll end with a look at some more specialized gear.

Home Game Consoles

Use the term *video game* and most people will think of home game consoles, even today when games have become at least as popular on mobile phones as they are on consoles. In this section, we'll look at how people use consoles and how that affects the games that we make for them.

Typical Use

A home game console is usually set up in the living room or a bedroom. The player sits or stands holding a dedicated controller 3 to 10 feet away from the television that serves as its display. Although modern high-definition digital televisions are a great improvement over the analog sets that the early consoles used, the player is still too far from the screen to see small details or to read fine print conveniently. This means that games designed for the home console machine cannot be as intricate as the personal computer games can. The graphics have to be simpler and bolder.

Because several people see the display at once, and because all consoles allow for at least two controllers, console machines are excellent for multiplayer local games in which all players look at the same screen. They're ideal for party games, dance games, sports games, and any form in which players take turns while others watch, such as *Wii Sports: Bowling*. On the other hand, console games are not so good for games that require individual players to have secret knowledge, because every player can see what every other player is doing on the screen. Also, because they're set up in a private house, players can use them for a long time with (comparatively) few distractions, so games can be designed and paced with this in mind. Mobile games, in contrast, need to be played for minutes, not hours.

Home consoles are dedicated gaming machines. They have no other function as computers; a few efforts were made to make them more general-purpose by adding keyboards—these never really caught on. Although it is possible to surf the web on them, the lack of a keyboard and the poor quality of their pointing devices limits what you can do with them. Console machines are aimed at dedicated hobbyists and children (or their parents, who actually buy them)—people who are prepared to spend a great deal of time playing games.

Input Devices

In a console game, the control method and user interface must be manageable with the controller provided. A mouse can point much more precisely than most console controllers. Still, you are guaranteed that every machine ships with a standardized controller, which means you don't have to do the configuration testing that games for the PC sometimes require. Generally speaking, hardware developers create a much larger variety of input devices for console machines—steering wheels, guitars, conga drums, fishing rods, balance boards, and so on—than they do for the PC. Because the console manufacturers rigorously test any device with their logo on it, you can be confident that these devices are compatible with their machines.

In 2006 Nintendo dramatically challenged existing conventions by introducing the Wii with its revolutionary motion-sensitive controller. Many casual players find the vast array of buttons and joysticks on the traditional game controller daunting. The Wii has made video games intuitive and easy to learn, with the result that Wii machines are being used in all sorts of unexpected ways—as therapy for injured, disabled, and elderly people, for example.

The Kinect motion-capture device for the Microsoft Xbox represents another major step, although so far it has had less impact than the Wii did. It, too, is designed to be used in a room with some dedicated open space for play such as a living room or den. This makes the Kinect an excellent choice for any game requiring a lot of physical activity. (Chapter 12, "Creating the User Experience," discusses the Kinect in much more detail.)

Business Considerations

Home consoles tend to have graphics display hardware of comparable power to the graphics hardware in personal computers, but they have slower central processing units and less RAM than personal computers possess. Because consoles sell for $200 to $400 once they have been available for a year or so, the manufacturer has to cut the hardware design to the bone to keep the cost down. This means that, as computing devices, the most expensive console is always less powerful than the most expensive personal computer, and more difficult to program. On the other hand, their low price and ease of maintenance means that far more consoles are in players' hands, which creates a larger market for their games.

The home console differs from the personal computer in another important way. Console manufacturers won't let just anyone make a game for their machine. You have to have a license from the manufacturer and their approval for your game idea—and they tend to be reluctant to approve anything controversial (though what was controversial 20 years ago now seems tame, thanks to shifting public tastes). Once the game is ready, you also have to submit it to the manufacturer for extensive testing before releasing it. Console manufacturers are very anxious that all games played on their systems should be trouble-free and easy to use. They are very protective of their brand's reputation. When developing for personal computers, you aren't constrained this way. You can create any game you want, without anyone's permission, on any subject you like. Obviously some publishers (or distribution channels like the App Store) won't publish games that they feel might be offensive or illegal, and many countries have censorship laws that explicitly prohibit certain content. But the PC is an open platform; you can build games for personal computers without being bound by any contractual limitations.

A related complication is that unlike a PC, the internal workings of a console machine are a trade secret. To get a license to develop for one, you must sign a nondisclosure agreement with the manufacturer in which you promise that you will not reveal any of the details to anyone else, a factor that makes it more difficult to get help. In order to build a game for console machines, you must also have a hardware device called a *development kit* or *dev kit*. You must purchase this device from the manufacturer of the console, and it can be extremely expensive. By contrast, anyone who owns a PC can program a PC—it does not require any special hardware to get a program into it.

In the last few years, a partial convergence has taken place between the home console and the PC. Consoles now routinely include disk drives that enable the player to

NOTE The Ouya, a so-called microconsole that runs the Android operating system, is an exception to the rule that console development requires an expensive dev kit. Anyone who owns an Ouya can program games for one, and the device is also easy to open and modify. However, the device has received only lukewarm reviews, and it is too early to tell whether it will be a game-changer or a dud. Microsoft supported dev-kit-free development for the Xbox for a few years via their XNA framework, but later abandoned it.

store far more data than before, and they all include networking capability as well. Networked play is now commonplace on console machines, and the availability of downloadable games on such services as Xbox LIVE is placing considerable pressure on the traditional retail business model.

THE GENERAL-PURPOSE SET-TOP BOX: A MARKETING DEAD END

Over the years various companies have tried to develop a device rather like a console that will serve as a means of delivering gameplay, reference information, multimedia software, and educational products—in effect combining the functions of a game console and a personal computer, along with television-related functions such as video recording. These devices are usually referred to as *set-top boxes*, meaning a box that sits on top of a television set. (This is now an anachronism, as you cannot perch a device on top of a flat-screen TV.) The idea was to provide an inexpensive computer aimed primarily at consuming media rather than doing work.

Two examples were the Phillips CD-I Player and the 3DO Interactive Multiplayer, both of which came out in the early 1990s. Neither was a success in the marketplace. Their marketing campaigns emphasized their utility for reference and multimedia software, but these functions were provided at less cost by the World Wide Web. Eventually the 3DO Company gave up on marketing the Multiplayer as a general-purpose device and concentrated solely on games, but it was too late. In time, they sold off the intellectual property rights to the hardware and simply became a game publisher. They went out of business in 2003.

If anything can be said to have inherited the mantle of the set-top box, it is the Apple iPad. Although inconvenient for typing on, and not really designed for more than one person to use at a time, it is an excellent inexpensive device for gaming and consuming entertainment and educational media—the original vision for set-top boxes.

Personal Computers

Personal computers appeared in the marketplace shortly after home game consoles did, and although they seemed to be general-purpose computing devices, the early ones were too underpowered to be that useful for home office or business use. However, they were immediately successful as gaming platforms, and the Commodore 64, Atari ST, Amiga, and other personal computers were wildly popular among gamers and early computer hobbyists, most especially because their owners could develop their own games for them. Magazines devoted to these machines routinely printed source code of games for people to type in, play, and modify. But they didn't achieve acceptance beyond the hobbyist community until IBM introduced the IBM PC in 1981.

Throughout this book you'll see many references to PCs. The IBM PC and its clones, running the Windows operating system, are by far the most popular personal computers for gaming. However, when you see the term *PC,* you shouldn't assume that it means only IBM PC clones running Windows, nor desktop machines, since PCs can be laptops or tablet devices. Developers also make games for the Macintosh and for machines running the Linux operating system, and these qualify as PCs too. For our purposes, what really characterizes a PC is the presence of a keyboard and mouse. (Tablet PCs are really portable devices and are covered in that section.)

Typical Use

A personal computer is likely to be set up away from the communal living space, on a desk. It's designed to be operated by one person while she is sitting. In this case, the player has a keyboard, a mouse, possibly a joystick, and (more rarely) a dedicated game controller such as those for console machines. The player sits 12 to 18 inches away from a high-resolution display. This high resolution means that the game can have subtle, detailed graphics. The mouse allows precision pointing and a more complex user interface. The keyboard enables the player to enter text conveniently.

The player's close proximity to the screen creates an immersive experience. Some players even add extra screens to the left and right of the main screen to display parts of the game world in their peripheral vision; this can help them see opponents better in racing games and in multiplayer battles online. It also contributes to their feeling of immersion in the game world.

The personal computer is quite awkward for more than one person to use at a time. The controls of a PC are all designed for one individual, and even the furniture it usually sits on—a desk—is intended for solitary use. Even laptops, which are more portable, are still inconvenient to use anywhere but on a desk, and that's why they are included here rather than in the later section on portable devices.

Input Devices

The keyboard and mouse are unique to the PC and laptop experience. With its 101 keys, the keyboard allows user interfaces to employ many, many buttons, and complex computer role-playing games (RPGs) such as *The Lord of the Rings Online* make heavy use of this feature. The keyboard enables the player to enter text conveniently and send chat messages to other players over a network, something that is much less convenient with console machines.

Business Considerations

The great advantage of PC development is that anyone can program one; you don't have to get a license from the manufacturer or buy an expensive development station. Consequently, personal computers are at the cutting edge of innovation in computer gaming. They're the platform of choice for interactive art and other experimental forms of interactive entertainment. Mobile devices are similarly easy and inexpensive to develop for, but they haven't achieved the same level of acceptance as platforms for artistic expression that PCs have. This may soon change, however.

The great bane of PC development is that no two machines are alike. Because they're customizable, millions of configurations are possible. In the early days of the game industry, this was a real nightmare for programmers. Fortunately, the Windows and Macintosh operating systems, and middleware solutions like Unity, have solved many of these problems by isolating the programs from the hardware. Still, games tend to require more from the machine than other applications do, and configuration conflicts still occur.

PC games may be divided into two general and quite different categories: stand-alone games, which the player installs on his machine like any other program, and browser-based games that run inside a web browser.

STAND-ALONE GAMES

A stand-alone PC game can use the full power of the PC, assuming the player isn't running any other applications at the same time. Of all games played on consumer equipment, stand-alone PC games can be the most visually spectacular. Home game consoles are sold in distinct hardware "generations," and a given manufacturer's console won't change until the next generation. In contrast, personal computers evolve constantly, so game developers can take advantage of the latest hardware innovations. Crytek's *Crysis* is a good example of a game that requires a very powerful machine for a player to enjoy it fully.

This doesn't mean that stand-alone PC games always demand high-end equipment, or that they should; it only means that if you want to develop for the highest-end gear, you should build stand-alone PC games. That choice usually limits the size of your market to the truly dedicated hobbyist gamer who will have purchased the latest PC technology. On the other hand, many stand-alone games are aimed at the middle of the range and do very well.

BROWSER-BASED GAMES

Browser-based games are a rapidly growing sector of the game market. They have one huge advantage over stand-alone games: Because they run in a web browser, they are somewhat isolated from the machine's hardware. A browser-based game can run on a Windows PC, Macintosh, or Linux machine with no modifications. This advantage comes at a price, however; browser-based games cannot take full advantage of the machine's capabilities. Most browser-based games—and there are thousands—are 2D games aimed at the casual player. They are often written in Java or Adobe's ActionScript language, which works with Flash Player.

Beginning with browser-based games is an excellent way to get started building small games, because you don't have to know much about the machine's hardware and the game will be more portable between platforms.

Portable Devices

Portable devices are a hugely popular and inexpensive form of entertainment. They began as dedicated handheld devices that could play only a few built-in games (sometimes only one), and were primarily regarded as toys for children. Since then, they have branched out and out, widening their demographics to adults and becoming moderately powerful and flexible computing devices. Their CPUs are slower than their console counterparts but still have enough power to run sophisticated games. The Sony PSP represented a huge jump in the power and display quality of dedicated handheld game machines.

Mobile phones and other networked devices such as the Nintendo DS have a distinct advantage over traditional game handhelds: They permit portable networked play. Players can compete against others while riding on trains or waiting for an appointment. Setting up a networked game on mobile phones usually requires having a deal for data transmission services with a cellular service provider. Also, unlike dedicated game machines, for the most part, phones do not require a license from the hardware manufacturer. Anyone can write a program for a mobile phone.

Typical Use

A portable device is designed to be carried around and used by one person. Such devices range in size from quite small mobile phones up to tablet computers that can be nearly the size of a laptop. A key distinction among use cases is whether the device will fit into a pocket. If it does, it can go almost anywhere; if it doesn't, the user has to have a purse, briefcase, or backpack to put it in. A few intermediate-sized devices that will fit only into a large pocket also exist; these are known by the rather unfortunate name *phablet*. The Samsung Galaxy Note series are phablets.

Because the user holds a portable device in her hands, her eyes are about a foot from the screen—closer than with any other device. However, screen size is a critical limitation and unfortunately, it is different on just about every make and model of device. Screen resolution varies considerably as well. This means that user interface elements have to be very simple and clear—even simpler than in a console game, which displays on a large TV screen.

Because portable devices are frequently used in public, every game must include a way to turn off the sound, even though the device itself also includes a master volume control. Players sometimes want to leave the master volume for their device on so they can hear notifications of incoming text messages or phone calls, but turn off the game sound so they don't annoy the people around them.

Battery life also affects the typical use of portable devices. Games tend to be CPU- and graphics-intensive applications. You cannot expect a player to play for long periods without being able to save the game as you can on other machines, because at any moment he may have to take an incoming phone call or power down the device to save the battery.

Input Devices

One peculiarity of portable devices is that the user must support the device's weight while she uses it. Holding it up can sometimes interfere with its usability. Players using console controllers also have to hold them up, but because most console controllers don't have screens in them (the Wii U's GamePad is an exception), a controller can be better designed to fit the hands. Also, the consequences of dropping an ordinary controller are less dire. Portable devices tend to be fragile.

Handheld machines support few add-on features; the input and output devices are usually fixed. These machines have a smaller number of buttons (if any at all, in the case of smartphones) than a console controller does. However, unlike either consoles or PCs, portable devices frequently include global positioning systems, enabling you to create augmented reality games that are played by moving around in the real world. The Nintendo DS and 3DS series are unique among dedicated game handhelds in that they have two screens, one of which is touch-sensitive and can be used with a stylus.

Dedicated Game Handhelds

The cheapest handheld machines offer a fixed set of built-in games, but the more versatile handhelds accept games stored on cartridges, and the PSP supports a small optical disk. Cartridges store much less data than the CD-ROMs or DVD discs that home consoles and computers use. Designing for a cartridge places severe limits on the amount of video, audio, graphics, and animation you can include in the game. Because they're solid-state electronics, though, the data on a cartridge is available instantly. There's no delay in loading data, as there is with optical media devices, and little danger that the cartridge will be damaged.

The handheld game market is potentially lucrative, but creating a game for one tests your skills as a designer. With less storage space, you have to rely on gameplay rather than content to provide the entertainment. The normal way people play these games is for a few minutes at a time, not an hour or so, and they might be interrupted at any time; your game must be designed to meet these expectations. As with home console machines, to develop for dedicated handheld game machines, you must have a license from the manufacturer. Games for dedicated game handhelds still tend to be sold at retail, although there is a growing digital distribution option.

Mobile Phones and Wireless Devices

Mobile phones now have enough computing power to play decent games. The worst thing about developing for a wide range of mobile phones is the lack of standardization. The screens are all different sizes and color depths; the processors are different; the operating systems are different. Even the layout of the buttons is nonstandard, making it difficult to be certain what user interface design is convenient across a range of phones. Expect to do a lot of compatibility testing on different hardware if you develop for mobile phones.

Unlike dedicated game handhelds, mobile phones and tablets sell their games in a number of different ways. Some are simply for sale for a flat fee, usually for far, far less money than console games cost. Some are sold as time-based subscriptions. Many are given away free and then paid for through what are called *in-app purchases (IAPs)*—small payments that allow a player to continue to buy items, play past a certain point, or play more frequently. (This is usually known as the *free-to-play* model and is discussed at greater length in Chapter 6.)

As we noted earlier, home game consoles are closed systems, and developing for them normally requires a license from the manufacturer; PCs are open systems that anyone can develop for. Mobile phones are split on this issue. Apple does not require a license to develop a game (or any other application) for their devices, but they do insist that the games be distributed only through their App Store. They also exercise (sometimes rather capricious) editorial control over what content they will permit in games, as well as books, music, and other content that they sell through iTunes. However, this control does not take the form of prior restraint as it sometimes does on consoles. Developers occasionally put a product on the App Store for sale and only later discover that it has been taken down.

Google's Play store for Android devices also exercises editorial control over the content that it permits. However, it is not necessary to distribute your game via the Play store at all. If you want to avoid compliance with Google's policies, your players with Android phones can download the installation file directly from a website, or receive it as an attachment to an e-mail message. This is not ideal from a marketing perspective, because most casual users will look for games on the Play store and nowhere else, and they must have enabled their phone to accept applications from unknown sources.

It has become so easy to develop games for mobile phones that there is a huge glut on the market, and many developers never make a profit. On the other hand, those that are lucky enough to make a hit can earn spectacular amounts of money. *Angry Birds* is one such, but it's worth remembering that Rovio made 51 games that were not so successful first.

Other Devices

Games show up on all sorts of other devices these days. The more specialized the device, the more important it is to understand clearly its technical limitations and its audience.

Airlines are starting to build video games into their seats; these games tend to be aimed at children or the casual market. Video gambling machines, too, enjoy growing popularity. Because they are heavily regulated and not sold to consumers, they really constitute an industry unto themselves, but video gambling games require programmers and artists just like any other computer game. And, of course, arcade machines, although not as popular as they once were, still provide employment to game developers. Finally, there are large location-based entertainment systems such as ride simulators in theme parks. Instead of providing an actual thrill ride, these devices use seats on platforms moved by pistons, combined with a large-screen display, to create an illusion of movement. The customers can participate in the experience with input devices attached to their seats.

Because these devices occupy niche markets and often have peculiar design restrictions, this book doesn't address them in detail.

Summary

In this chapter we looked at three broad categories of game devices: home game consoles, personal computers, and portable devices. Each has its own strengths and weaknesses, and the convergence among them will never be total. Consoles are best used in the living room, where there is some controlled physical space to play in; PCs are best used on a desk by one person; portable devices trade off game complexity for convenience and ease of development. When you think about what machine to put your game on, bear these characteristics in mind.

Design Practice EXERCISES

1. Certain genres are more often found on one kind of machine than on another. Write an essay explaining which machine each genre works best on and why. How do the machine's features and the way that it is used in the home or in the hand facilitate or hinder the gameplay in each genre?

2. Visit a retail store and look at the shelves, and then go to an online app store. Note the genres you observe in each place and count the number of games available. What is different about the games or genres available for the different machines?

CHAPTER 6

Making Money from Your Game

If you make a game to give away, or as an art project or a student project, then you can follow your heart and make whatever game you can afford to build. However, if you're making a game for sale, it will have to appeal to your target audience, and that will influence your design decisions. Even more importantly, *how* and *where* you sell your game will affect your decisions. In this chapter, we'll present an overview of the different ways that you can make money from your game, and how different monetization schemes (ways of making money) will affect the way you design your game. First we'll look at direct payment models, in which customers simply buy the game, and then at indirect models, in which they pay in other ways. We'll also consider ways you can still make money even though you give the game away free of charge. The chapter ends with a brief discussion of world markets.

Direct Payment Models

The direct payment model, in which players simply purchase a game, either as a whole or over time, is the oldest. With retail sales or digital distribution, players simply buy your game outright. Three other approaches are subscription-based sales (players subscribe to your game as a service rather than buying it as a product), episodic delivery (players buy episodes of your game as they become available), and crowdfunding (players pay for your game in advance as a way of funding its development). We'll look at all of them.

Retail Sales

The traditional distribution and sales model for video games is the retail model, and although it is in decline for PC games, it remains strong for console games. It's not used for mobile phone games at all, although it is for dedicated handhelds. The reason that the retail model remains popular for certain kinds of games can be summed up in one word: Christmas. People like to buy, and to receive, physical objects as Christmas presents, and the conventional game industry is still heavily dependent on the Christmas retail buying season for its annual revenue. This model works well for large studios making large games, but not for small independents because they have limited access to shelf space and marketing.

The key drawback to retail sales is that you must have a publisher or distributor to get your game onto the store shelves. Retailers, and especially large retail chains like Wal-Mart, make deals only with suppliers they know, and especially suppliers who will devote a lot of money to marketing their product.

Normally a publisher will either develop a game in-house or will contract with a development studio to develop it for them. Either way, they finance development of the game, and they're also responsible for marketing it, which costs still more money. The marketing for retail games can easily cost three to ten times as much as the development costs. These costs tend to make publishers conservative—they're interested only in publishing games that have a good chance of earning back the money invested in them. Many games don't turn a profit, so the hit games subsidize the others.

NOTE Occasionally, but very rarely, a development company will have enough (or can raise enough) money to design and build a large game without any support from the publisher. This means that they get a much better deal from the publisher, and the publisher has little leverage over them to insist that the game be made the publisher's way. This happened when GSC Game World made *S.T.A.L.K.E.R.: Shadow of Chernobyl* for THQ (a publisher that is now defunct).

Publishers almost never accept submissions from people they've never heard of; even more important to them than the quality of the game idea is the reliability of the developer. They like to work with people who they have worked with before, people who have a track record for delivery. Electronic Arts made a business out of finding good developers, publishing their games for several years, and then buying them up outright and turning them into an in-house development team. This was a way of rewarding the owners of good development companies, while gaining control over their intellectual property.

Once the game is built, the publisher pays to have it manufactured, and they market it to the world. If it's a console or dedicated handheld game, the hardware company (Nintendo, Sony, and so on) does the manufacturing at a large price per disk or cartridge, which is how those companies make most of their money. If it's a PC game, the manufacturing is fairly inexpensive.

In the retail sales model, the publisher sells the game at wholesale to the retailer. Typically the retailer marks up the wholesale price by anywhere from 25 percent to 100 percent and sells it to the consumer. The publisher pays the developer a *royalty* of 10 to 15 percent of what the publisher nets after subtracting the manufacturing costs. In other words, if a customer pays $50 for a game, and the publisher has a $10 profit after paying for manufacturing, the developer gets $1.00 to $1.50...at most. This is a gross oversimplification of a very complicated business, but it gives you a general idea of how it works. As you can see, it's not very much per copy, but with a blockbuster like *Grand Theft Auto V,* a developer can still earn tens or even hundreds of millions of dollars.

From a design standpoint, the chief constraint on a game distributed at retail is publisher conservatism, and a major reason for this conservatism is inventory risk—the chance that a publisher will pay to manufacture more copies than the market wants to buy and get stuck with them. These games simply must sell well; there's no room for niche market games that appeal to only a few people. The retailers can't afford to have their limited store shelves occupied by stock the consumer doesn't want, and the publishers can't afford to manufacture a lot of games that nobody will buy. If a publisher is financing your company to build a game for them, even if the game was originally your idea, you can expect them to want a lot of input into its design.

Digital Distribution

Distributing games electronically over the Internet gets rid of inventory risk and cuts out the retailers, which offers game developers (and publishers, if there is a publisher) far more freedom and flexibility. There's no retailer taking a cut, and if no publisher financed the development or marketing, they don't get a cut either. Instead, the organization that actually does the distribution takes a percentage. For example, if you sell a game on Steam, the Apple App Store, or Xbox Live Marketplace, those organizations will take a certain amount per copy sold. It is difficult to discover exactly how much, because these organizations are reluctant to discuss it, but estimates are generally around 30 percent, leaving the remaining 70 percent to go directly to the developer.

That may sound very good, but this kind of electronic distribution has two serious disadvantages. First, if there is no publisher, you have to market the game yourself, and as we have already seen, the marketing can be extremely expensive. Most small developers count on building buzz through word-of-mouth, developer diaries, a presence on social networks, and other inexpensive methods that they hope will go viral. This is great if it works, but it doesn't have the impact that television advertising does. Without any marketing, your game simply disappears into the vast pile of anonymous games that fill the App Store.

The second disadvantage is that the prices are far lower. The online customer simply isn't prepared to pay $50 for a video game; for that amount of money, they expect to get a physical object. Most App Store games cost between one and five dollars. Once you deduct your marketing costs, even with a 70 percent cut, the revenue you can expect per unit sold is less than you might make at retail unless you have the great good luck to create a hit.

However, this model gives you much more freedom as a designer than the retail model does. Normally these distribution portals don't care too much what you do as long as it doesn't offend them; if you want to make a game for a niche market, that's OK, because they don't have to deal with physical copies, that is, inventory.

Subscriptions

In the subscription model, players pay you a fee, usually monthly, for access to games that you provide via your own servers. This used to be the standard model for massively multiplayer online games (MMOGs), but it is gradually being replaced by the indirect payment models described in the next section. Subscription models obviously make sense only if you are selling access to game content that changes periodically, or to a game that works more as an ongoing service than as a single entertainment experience (such as an adventure game). Subscription-based games need access to a server to be played.

The subscription model actively discourages some players, who don't like the idea of having to continue to pay again and again to play a game. It also means that you have to live up to your obligation to provide an enjoyable experience on a continuing basis to earn subsequent payments. Under the retail and electronic distribution models, players pay once, and your responsibility to them ends with delivery of the product, apart from customer service to help users who have problems.

Episodic Delivery

Many developers have expressed an interest in trying to find a way to deliver game software in episodes, like a television show. There have been several efforts to do so over the years: *Majestic, Kentucky Route Zero,* and *The Walking Dead* are all episodic games. Instead of paying every month as with a subscription, customers pay for each new episode as it becomes available.

Episodic games are not the same as sequels in a franchise. Ordinarily the story in a sequel is different from its predecessor or, if the game has no story (as in long-running sports franchises), the technology and features are different. Episodic games, by contrast, are really one big game distributed in pieces over time (although they sometimes include technology updates as well). Because you make and release only one episode at a time, the game gets quickly to market and you can benefit from consumer feedback about one episode before you begin the next one.

Episodic delivery allows you to charge the player a smaller price per episode than a full online sale would cost, which makes the game more attractive to players. If the game is entertaining enough, this builds customer loyalty and encourages them to continue buying episodes, which means they can end up spending more than they ordinarily would on a single sale.

The disadvantages of episodic delivery are that you still have to have all the core mechanics and user interface (UI) software written prior to delivering the first episode, which can be expensive. If interest in the game tails off after a few episodes, you may find that your revenue stream is not great enough to finish the game in the way that you planned, and you have to shorten the story line or leave out features that you had already promised to your customers.

As a designer, delivering your game episodically means that it must be designed to be episodic in the first place. This works well for games with stories, but less well for games that cannot easily be broken up into episodes, such as sandbox games or sports games.

Crowdfunding

You don't necessarily have to wait until your game is finished to get money for it; you can fund its development by asking people to pay you in advance, a process called *crowdfunding*. Normally you do this through an online system that takes a percentage of the money you earn. Kickstarter and Indiegogo are the two best-known examples.

A number of crowdfunded games have been hugely successful at raising money. The Double Fine studio asked for $400,000 and got $3,336,371 for a new game, which caused game developers to take this model seriously for the first time. Several other games have now surpassed this record.

Crowdfunding may sound easy, but it requires a lot of preparation to run a successful campaign. You will need to create high-quality videos of your work and to give regular updates to your funders. It works best for people who already have a positive reputation in the industry. Players are unlikely to donate money to people they've never heard of. Most crowdfunding is not a form of investment, but simply a form of preordering: Players get a copy of the game once it comes out, along with extras if they pay more.

As a means of raising money, crowdfunding doesn't affect your design decisions much. Naturally, your game must sound exciting to your potential donors, but you are free of pressures from publishers and retailers because you deliver the game directly to the people who gave you money. This model is particularly popular with developers with niche market projects who don't necessarily want to reach the widest population possible, but to target dedicated fans. The game that Double Fine is developing will be a point-and-click adventure, a genre that is not broadly popular but has passionate support among its players.

Indirect Payment Models

The recent explosion in the popularity of video games can be attributed to several factors—the new emphasis on casual games, the arrival of smartphones, and the fact that middleware now makes it easier than ever to develop games. More important than any of these, however, has been the shift to indirect payment models. Asking a player to pay between $20 and $75 in advance for the game—the traditional model—represents a serious barrier to less dedicated players. By allowing them to pay a little at a time, or only for the parts of the game that they want to pay for, we make it easier to attract them to our games. However, most of these models work only with games that are delivered online, either with a continuous or a periodic connection to a server operated by the development company.

The state of this business is still in flux, and that includes its terminology. Don't be surprised if you hear these terms used differently by different people. When in doubt, ask for clarification.

Freemium Games

In the *freemium* (*free+premium*) model, a business gives away a partially functional version of its software but allows customers to purchase upgrades that render it more useful. (If the free version of the software is too weak to be good for much, it is derogatorily called *crippleware*.) The first products to be widely successful under the freemium model were antivirus suites.

In the case of games, you give away the game but offer premium items for sale within the game (called in-app purchases or IAPs) that make the game more fun or interesting. This usually takes the form of *downloadable content* (DLC). Downloadable content can consist of all kinds of things: extra levels, new clothing for an avatar character, additional game modes, and new objects in the game, such as weapons or powerups. Dance games often offer additional music as downloadable content, which helps to keep the experience fresh if the players are getting tired of the music that came with the original game.

The chief criticism of the freemium model, from a player's perspective, occurs when the game isn't any fun without buying the premium content—the game equivalent of crippleware. Naturally, as a designer, you want people to pay you, but you also have to make your game enjoyable enough that they *want* to pay you.

PAY-TO-WIN: A BAD IDEA

The majority of freemium games are single-player or multiplayer cooperative experiences. However, you can also make multiplayer competitive or team-based games in which players purchase premium items. If these items are not merely cosmetic, but confer an actual gameplay advantage in competition with others, the game is described as *pay-to-win*. Rich players can simply buy better weapons, armor, or other items than poorer players, and so they beat them by spending real-world money. In other words, they are altering the mechanics of the game in their favor.

This design produces a lucrative (for the publisher) arms race among players who try to outspend each other to gain a competitive advantage, but it is bad sportsmanship and violates an essential rule of multiplayer competitive play: The game must be fair. Tiger Woods, no matter how rich he is, cannot simply buy a tee 50 yards closer to the hole that his competitors cannot use. It is essential to golf that all golfers play on the same course. Video games can be asymmetric, with different players playing by different rules for one reason or another, but they still must be fair and give all the players an equal chance of winning (except for differences in talent or experience), regardless of how much money they have. Many players find pay-to-win designs highly objectionable.

The freemium model affects game design because rather than designing one single experience, you have to design an experience that can be upgraded through purchases—and you have to make sure that these purchases are desirable enough that you can earn a living from your game. Many of the games that use this model are endless online games in which players keep advancing forever, buying more and more premium items. Freemium games rely heavily on statistics collected from players to find out how often they are logging in, how long they are playing, and above all, what they are buying. Designers then use these statistics to tune the game in an effort to provide more of what players are enjoying, and thus generate more revenue. Traditional game designers tend to find this data-driven design rather soulless, since the games it creates are less a product of creative vision than of numerical analysis.

Free-to-Play

In *free-to-play* games, players get a version of the game that is free but is designed to encourage them to pay a subscription or some other kind of fee. A common design allows players to play completely free of charge forever, but advancement in the game is very slow, and players must log off periodically and come back later to continue. Paying a fee removes this limitation. Another approach puts free players on one set of servers and paying players on another. The servers for paying players are much less crowded, so the player experiences better performance from the game.

Many free-to-play games are designed to offer the player a small amount of advancement in the game at frequent intervals in response to fairly trivial player activities—sometimes this means the player doesn't have to do anything more than click a button to advance, as in *Mafia Wars*. This setup always gives the player something easy to do. Although keeping the player occupied may sound desirable as a game design principle, it can be overdone or so extreme that the player feels like an animal being trained to press a button on cue in exchange for a reward.

The free-to-play model is closely related to the freemium model, and many free-to-play games also include premiums that players can buy.

Advertising and Sponsorships

You can earn revenue by selling advertising alongside your game. Advertising that appears beside your game on the player's screen does not intrude too much, and you earn money for each person who sees, or clicks on, one of the ads. This model is normally used for online games and, if successful, can even enable you to give away the game for free and make all the money from the ads. Many of the games on Facebook and Yahoo! work this way. Some developers also sell an ad-free version of the same game to players who don't like the advertisements and are willing to pay not to see them.

You can also have advertisements appear within your game; you do this by selling sponsorships to companies that want to have their message in your game world. If your game is a standalone game sold at retail or online, the sponsor simply pays you based on the number of copies that you sell; if the game is an online game delivered via a server, they will pay you per view or per click as is done when the advertising appears alongside the game.

Sponsorships are most common in sports games and vehicle simulations that emulate a real-world sport or car race. Since the real-world events have advertising signage, it's only natural that the video game should too. Obviously this doesn't work in games set in fantasy worlds or the ancient past, where advertising would be out of place.

The design implications of advertising, and especially of sponsorship, are that your game content must not upset your sponsors. With sports games this is unlikely to be a problem, but it is something to bear in mind.

Commissioned Games

The final category is the commissioned or sponsored game, in which you get paid to build a game for someone else, but you don't get any royalties for sales. The only money you see is what you get paid to build the game in the first place, which means that you must build your profit margin into the price you charge to do the work. This model is normally used when a charity or government agency wants to give away a game for free for some reason—often for an educational or informative purpose.

With a commissioned game, naturally you must work closely with your client to make the game that they want. Of all the business models described here, this one constrains the designer the most, because it is really the client's game and not the designer's. However, it can be a lot of fun to work with such clients and make a game that pleases them, especially if you also believe in the message they want to deliver with their game.

World Markets

The appetite for video games is growing all over the world, but different regions like different kinds of things and have different amounts of money to spend. In this section, we'll look very briefly at various world markets, including both traditional and emerging markets.

Traditional Markets

The traditional markets for video games are, not surprisingly, in the developed and high-tech world. Even these, however, are quite distinct. They include

▪ **The English-speaking world.** The U.S. is the largest market for video games in the world, and the vast majority of games, no matter where they are developed, are aimed at this market. (Games made by the Japanese for their own large market are a notable exception.) Americans like happy endings; they prefer to see virtue rewarded. Grim Kafka-esque stories are not popular except among a subcategory of disaffected youth. Games with military themes also sell well generally in the U.S., but as the country that invented video games, with a large, diverse population, almost any kind of game can be developed for this audience. The United Kingdom, English-speaking Canada, Australia, and New Zealand all have a similar per capita demand for games and generally, their audiences have similar tastes in game genres, but of course these are smaller overall markets due to their smaller populations. These markets also tend to be more cynical, however, and they find the flag-waving military games made for the American market rather self-righteous.

▪ **Continental Europe.** European demand for games is similar to the American demand, but Europe is more complicated to develop for because each nation has its own language, and tastes in games vary somewhat among them. Many Northern Europeans (Nordic countries and the Netherlands) are happy to buy games in English because they routinely learn English in school. The largest markets, however, including France and Germany, prefer games in their own language. In general, Europeans like darker stories and regard some games made for Americans as rather saccharine. They are much less concerned by nudity and sexual themes than Americans are and are more disturbed by violence. Also, as a result of their experience with Nazi Germany, Europeans are suspicious of overt displays of patriotism. A uniform labeling standard called Pan European Game Information (PEGI) is emerging so that developers don't have to submit their games to be rated to authorities in each country. However, Germany, Finland, and some others still retain their own rating systems. European countries have no strong tradition of freedom of expression in commercial entertainment, and many countries exercise outright censorship, especially Germany, which prohibits any Nazi symbols.

▪ **Japan.** The Land of the Rising Sun is unique among video-game-playing countries. Some of the most successful game characters and franchises (*Mario, Zelda, Final Fantasy, Metal Gear Solid,* and so on) come from Japan, yet these games make few concessions to Western tastes. Rather, Western gamers have come to appreciate Japanese games just as they are. The converse is not the same, however; the Japanese do not play many Western games, and it is almost impossible for a Western game company to work in Japan without a Japanese partner. Japan has a large and highly successful game industry of its own, and in addition to the worldwide hits just mentioned, the game industry in Japan makes many, many games that they never export because the Japanese consider them too distinctly Japanese to be popular elsewhere. Namco did not originally intend to publish *Katamari Damacy* in the West, but the response of western reviewers was so positive that they changed their minds. Dating simulations, a kind of role-playing game (RPG) about dating rather than combat, are another example of games that are seldom exported to the West. Romantic and explicit sexual content are far more acceptable in Japan than they are in the West.

■ **South Korea.** Korean demand for games is not as great as that of Japan and, as a more socially conservative country, erotic content is less acceptable. The most distinctive feature of Korean gaming is how Koreans like to play: in public spaces. Role-playing and real-time strategy games and especially massively multiplayer online role-playing games (MMORPGs) are particularly popular, and these are played in a *PC bang* (literally, "PC room")—a large commercial space outfitted with many desks and LAN-connected PCs, rather like an Internet café only much bigger. Professional gaming is also more popular in South Korea than anywhere else. Large prizes are offered and top players practice for several hours every day. Despite its age, *StarCraft* is a favorite game for professional competitions.

Emerging Markets

These markets are ones to watch over the next 20 years or so, as their populations and economic fortunes rise. They're listed here in the order in which we expect them to take up gaming on a large scale.

■ **China.** Although China is not as economically advanced as the rest of the Far East, its sheer population makes it one to watch in the future. Software piracy is rampant in China, so developers have turned to selling online games that use a subscription or freemium model; as a result, China now contributes one third of the worldwide online gaming revenue. Video game consoles were banned as harmful to youth education until 2013, and it remains to be seen if sales will be significant now that they're allowed. Because few Chinese can afford personal computers, Internet cafés are popular. The Chinese government is cautiously supportive of gaming, but is suspicious of anything that could be interpreted as criticism of the authorities or their policies. Censorship is absolute, and the Internet firewall that prevents access to many Western websites makes it complicated for Western companies to do business there; most online games played by the Chinese are domestically produced.

■ **India.** With a population close to that of China and a growing middle class, India is the next country to watch as an emerging market. However, despite these indicators, the country is unlikely to take up PC and console games in large numbers soon. Despite having a similar population, India has only a little over one-fourth as many PCs as China does. In India, there is a strong emphasis on education, which makes parents reluctant to buy consoles. Consequently, the Indian gaming revolution, when it comes, will almost certainly be on mobile phones. At the moment only 10 percent of India's 400 million mobile phones are smartphones capable of playing games, but we can expect this to change over the next few years. India's middle class is also English speaking, which will make it easier to make games for that market. However, Indians are very socially conservative (couples do not kiss in public), which will restrict the kinds of games that will be acceptable to them.

▦ **Mexico, Central, and South America.** This region has a rapidly growing enthusiasm for games, but of course it has a far smaller population than either of the two preceding countries. Brazil is an emerging economic powerhouse, and the Mexican retail video game industry is now larger than the movies and music industries combined, and it is still growing rapidly. The other nations in the region vary considerably, but all except Brazil (the national language in Brazil is Portuguese) are Spanish speaking, which makes localization easier (although local idioms can still trip up the incautious translator).

▦ **The Islamic world.** Certain parts of the Islamic world (Saudi Arabia, the Emirates) are very wealthy and can easily afford video games, while others (Sudan, Palestine) are severely disadvantaged. These markets will continue to grow in the future, though much more slowly than India and China. The real obstacle to acceptance of video games is cultural. Muslim countries have no history of video gaming and are unlikely to want games made for the West. Their social conservatism, even greater than that of India, means that great care must be taken not to offend local sensibilities. Contrary to stereotype, most of the Muslim world does not speak Arabic (the largest Muslim country in the world is Indonesia), but there is a band of Arabic-speakers from North Africa to Iraq that will make it easier to localize games for those countries (with the same caveat about local idiom that applies to all the Hispanic countries). In other respects—varying local cultures and tastes—the Islamic world resembles Europe, thus complicating development.

▦ **Sub-Saharan Africa.** This region will be the last to get into video gaming for both financial and cultural reasons. These nations speak hundreds of different languages and localizing for them will be extremely difficult; in addition, they have less money available for luxury entertainment like video gaming, and no history of involvement with high technology. South Africa is an exception, although its middle class is not yet large enough overall to represent an important market.

Summary

This chapter didn't teach you much about *how* to design games, but it showed you how your design decisions can be influenced by how you make money from your game and where you choose to sell it. You now know something about both the traditional direct payment models and the new indirect ones. You also have learned which markets around the world are large and stable and which are growing, either rapidly or slowly. This information will help you as you begin to create your game concept, which is the subject of the next chapter.

Design Practice QUESTIONS

1. Who will finance the development of your game? A publisher, an investor, a client, yourself, or someone else? How do you expect this relationship (if it's not yourself) to affect your design choices?

2. Who is going to market your game? If the answer is "I am," what are your plans to do so and what resources (money and staff) have you allocated to it?

3. How do you hope to make money from your game? Via a direct payment model or an indirect payment one?

4. If your answer to question 3 was a direct payment model, which one? If you plan to use a subscription model or episodic delivery, do you have the resources to make a game that you will regularly update?

5. If your answer to question 3 was an indirect payment model, which one? If you plan to use a freemium model, have you thought of some premium items that you can sell for money in your game?

6. Do you know in what markets you hope to sell your game? Are you familiar enough with its tastes and barriers to entry?

CHAPTER 7

Game Concepts

Designing a video game begins with an idea. This chapter discusses how to turn that idea into a *game concept*, a more fleshed-out version of the idea that you can use as the basis for further discussion and development. Creating a game concept is what you do in the first stage of game design. Your goal at this point should be to write the high concept document that Chapter 2, "Designing and Developing Games," discussed. To do this, you don't have to have all the details worked out yet, but you do need to understand clearly what your game is about. You also need to know the answers to essential questions about your intended player, machine, and target audience, as well as how you plan to make money with your game (if you do). You learned how to think through these issues in the last four chapters. Now you'll put it all together.

Getting an Idea

You can find game ideas almost anywhere, but only if you're looking for them. Creativity is an active, not a passive, process. Look everywhere; some of the most unexpected things can hide a game idea. *BioShock*, for instance, is a satire on the philosophy of Ayn Rand that asks the question, "What might happen in a libertarian utopia that allowed completely unregulated biological experimentation?," whereas *Angry Birds* is much simpler: It's just a physics-based game designed around a slingshot. There have been slingshots in games before, but none so cleverly realized.

One idea isn't enough. It's a common misconception that a brilliant game idea will make you a fortune. In fact, this occurs extremely rarely. Even if you think you have the game idea of the century, you should always look out for more. Make a note of each one and go on. If one seems especially promising, then start to expand and refine it, but don't let that prevent you from thinking about other games as well.

Dreams of Doing

A lot of games are light entertainment, designed to while away a few minutes with a puzzle or a simple challenge. But larger, richer games begin with a dream. If you've ever thought to yourself, "I wish I could… " or "Imagine what it would be like to…," then you've taken an important step on the road to creating a video game. Computers can create almost any sort of visual and auditory experience you can imagine, even experiences that are physically impossible in the real world. The design of a game begins with the question, "What dream am I going to fulfill?"

Perhaps it's a dream of exploring a dungeon infested with monsters. Perhaps it's a dream of coaching a football team. Or perhaps it's a dream of being a fashion designer. Video games allow players to have experiences that are difficult, expensive, or even impossible in the real world. Before you do anything else, you must dream the dream. Understand it. Feel it. Know who else dreams it and why.

Dreams from Other Media

Books, movies, television, and other entertainment media can be great sources of inspiration for game ideas, so long as the ideas include plenty of activity. People dream of being Spider-Man, Harry Potter, or Nancy Drew, and all these characters have video games about them. But games don't have to have licenses from famous books or TV shows just to take inspiration from them. For instance, the game *Grand Theft Auto: Vice City* borrows from the TV show *Miami Vice* (**Figure 7.1**), and the game *No One Lives Forever* is a parody of James Bond movies. Any story containing exciting action with something important at stake can form the kernel of a game. Think over the books you've read and the movies you've seen, and ask yourself whether any of the activities in them could serve as the basis for a game.

FIGURE 7.1
Grand Theft Auto: Vice City was inspired by another medium— television.

NOTE Licenses and intellectual property law are beyond the scope of this book. Generally speaking, however, you cannot use the names, artwork, audio, text, or any other material copied directly from another game or any other medium. In the United States, parody is a protected form of free speech, but your parody must be visibly distinct from the original, must actually have the function of commenting on the original, and must not be libelous or intended to inflict emotional distress. Laws in other jurisdictions vary. Be cautious: If you are in any doubt whether your content violates someone else's intellectual property rights, change it!

You can't, of course, steal other people's intellectual property. Even if the *Pirates of the Caribbean* ride at Disneyland seems like the basis for a great game, you can't make it without a license from Disney. But you can certainly make a lighthearted game about pirates—as LucasArts did with its *Monkey Island* series.

You should also look beyond the usual science fiction and fantasy genres and beyond the usual sources like novels and movies. How about poetry? Beowulf's epic battle with the monster Grendel and then his even more terrible battle with Grendel's mother in a cave at the bottom of a lake sound like the basis for a game. Alfred, Lord Tennyson's "The Charge of the Light Brigade" might make you wonder about cavalry tactics. Would a game based on cavalry warfare be interesting to anyone? It's worth thinking about.

Game ideas can crop up in all sorts of unlikely places. The smash-hit game franchise *The Sims* was partly inspired by a nonfiction book by Christopher Alexander called *A Pattern Language* (Alexander, 1977), which is about the way people's lives are affected by the design of their houses. Just as great scientists look at even the most common things in the world—light, air, gravity—and ask how they work, great game designers are always looking at the world and wondering what parts of it they can make into a game. The trick to finding original ideas, beyond the elf-and-wizard combinations that have been done so often, is to develop a game designer's instincts, to look for the fun and challenge even in things that don't sound like games at all.

Game Ideas from Other Games

When you play a lot of games, you develop a sense of how they work and what their good and bad points are. Playing games is a valuable experience for a game designer. It gives you insight and lets you compare and contrast the features of different games.

Sometimes new game ideas are motivated by a desire to improve an existing game. We think, "If I had designed this game, I would have…." To learn from other games, you have to pay attention as you play. Don't just play them for fun; look at them seriously and think about how they work. Take notes, especially of things that you like or don't like and of features that seem to work particularly well or not well at all. How do resources flow into the game? How do they flow out? How much of your success comes from luck? How much comes from skill?

If you are inspired by an existing game, try to bring something new to it. *BioShock* and *Half-Life* weren't just shooters; they were shooters that offered something distinctly different from the ones that came before them. If pursued exclusively, imitation produces similarity and, ultimately, mediocrity. The greatest games break new ground. They're unlike anything seen on the store shelves before.

How to Brainstorm

In the previous few sections, we looked at ways that you can generate ideas as an individual, but a great many games are designed by groups of people. *Brainstorming* is a way for several people to generate large numbers of ideas without (initially) concerning themselves about quality. You all get together in one room and think of ideas rapidly without judging their value, usually for a limited amount of time. The four principles of brainstorming are

■ **Focus on quantity.** The greater the number of ideas generated, the greater the chance of producing an interesting or useful one. Don't stop to discuss an idea, simply record it and move on.

■ **Withhold criticism.** Debating the value of an idea slows down the process, and if people feel that they will be criticized, they will be more reluctant to generate ideas.

■ **Welcome unusual ideas.** Part of the point of brainstorming is not only to find ideas, but to find ones that you might never have considered otherwise. This is particularly important for creative endeavors like game design.

■ **Combine and improve ideas.** Ideas don't have to be unique. Rather like a jam session in music, the participants can build upon each others' suggestions, adding features or combining them to make new ones.

To hold a brainstorming session, you need a room where people can sit comfortably and a person who writes down the ideas (or a way to record everyone's suggestions). Try to avoid including more than about 12 people, and appoint a leader (this might be the person taking notes) who can make sure the discussion doesn't drift off-topic.

Brainstorming can go wrong, or at least be disappointingly unproductive, in various ways. Don't let one person dominate the conversation to the point that others feel intimidated. Also, don't let anyone spend a long time explaining their idea—this might cause others to forget ideas of their own. In order to discourage side conversations or criticism, you might want to impose a rule like that used in government meetings, that all remarks must be addressed to the chair.

After the brainstorming session is over, then you can start debating the merits of particular ideas. There's more than one way to brainstorm; the Wikipedia article on the subject lists a number of variants.

Communicating Your Idea to Others

If your game is in a well-known genre and setting (for example, a World War II flight simulator), you can be pretty certain that a number of people will be interested in playing your game right away. But if your game is in a new setting (a futuristic city of your imagination, for example)—and especially if you are introducing a new genre—you have to be very careful and thorough in communicating your dream to others. Here are two of the first questions a publishing executive is going to ask you: "Why would people want to play this game?" and "What's going to make someone buy this game instead of another?"

So what does it mean to entertain someone? Many people think entertainment is synonymous with having fun, but even that isn't completely straightforward. People have fun in all kinds of ways. Some of those ways involve hard manual labor, such as gardening or building a new deck. Some of them involve frustration, such as solving a puzzle. Some, such as athletic competitions, even involve pain. One person's entertainment is another person's insufferable boredom. To build a game that entertains, you must know *who* it will entertain and *how*. Chapter 1, "Games and Video Games," discussed a variety of ways in which video games entertain people, and Chapter 4, "Understanding Your Player," looked at different kinds of players. Keep them in mind as your work takes you from dream to game.

TIP Publishers will ask you what other games your game competes with. Be sure you study the market so you know what's already out there and how your game will be different and better.

From Idea to Game Concept

Chapter 2 described a game concept as "a general idea of how you intend to entertain someone through gameplay." That description was accurate enough for an overview, but to discuss game concepts in detail, we need a more complete explanation.

A *game concept* is a description of a game that is detailed enough that a group can begin discussing it as a potential commercial product—a piece of software that the public might want to buy. It should include, at a minimum, the following key points:

▪ *A high concept statement,* which is a two- or three-sentence description of what the game is about. Here's a high concept statement for a game about street football: "The game at its grittiest. No pads, no helmets, no refs, no field. Just you and the guys, a ball, and a lot of concrete."

▪ *The player's role(s)* in the game, if the game is representational enough to have roles. If the player will have an avatar, describe the avatar character briefly.

▪ *A proposed primary gameplay mode,* including camera model, interaction model, and general types of challenges the player(s) will experience in that mode.

▪ *The genre* of the game or, if you think it is a hybrid, which features it will incorporate from the different genres to which it belongs. If it is an entirely new kind of game, include an explanation of why its gameplay doesn't fit into any existing genre.

▨ *A description of the target audience* for the game and perhaps the expected rating that it will get. Chapter 4 looks at different kinds of players and the styles of play that they like.

▨ *The name of the machine* on which the game will run and details of any special equipment or features the game will utilize (for example, a camera or dance mat). Chapter 5, "Understanding Your Machine," discusses the variety of game machines available.

▨ *A brief statement of how you expect to make money* with your game, if you intend to sell it commercially. Chapter 6, "Making Money from Your Game," describes the different places around the world where you can sell games and looks at business models for making money with games.

▨ *Any licensed characters or other intellectual property* that the game may be based on, such as a sports league or a movie hero.

▨ *The competition modes* that the game will support: single-, dual-, or multiplayer; competitive or cooperative.

▨ *A general summary* of how the game will progress from beginning to end, including a few ideas for levels or missions and a synopsis of the storyline, if the game has one. Do *not* spend too much time on the story. Many game developers spend too much time on the story and not enough on the gameplay.

▨ *A short description* of the game world.

TIP A good way to describe the progress of the game in a high concept document is to include a section called "The First Five Minutes of Play." This gives people a clear picture of what it will be like to begin playing your game.

You should put all these items into a high concept document. This chapter discusses how to think about these issues, except for a few that are self-explanatory or were covered in earlier chapters. You can see a sample high concept document on the companion website.

In a commercial environment, whoever funds your game (most often a publisher) wants to see several additional details: the game's potential competition, the *unique selling points* (often abbreviated USPs) that make your game stand out in the marketplace, and possible marketing strategies and related merchandising opportunities.

As you can see, a game concept is much more than an idea. It is an idea that you have thought about and begun to develop. A game concept contains enough detail that you can begin discussing how it will feel to play the game and what further design work you need to create the game.

The Player's Role

To understand your game and to explain it to others, you must know what the player will do and, in a sense, what the player will *be* in the game world—what her role is. These are the first questions you face in creating your game concept.

WHAT IS THE PLAYER GOING TO DO?

It's sometimes tempting to start thinking about a game in terms of its setting or its characters. For example, "Wouldn't it be fun to play a game set in ancient Rome?" or "Wouldn't it be fun to play a game as Indiana Jones?" These are reasonable ideas, and of course many games have been made from both of them. However, you cannot make a game from a setting or character alone. The first step toward turning the idea into a game concept is to answer the question, "What is the player going to do?"

This is *the* single most important question you can ask yourself at the concept stage. You don't have to assign activities to input devices yet ("the X button kicks and the O button punches"), but you do have to know the activities that you want to offer the player—the verbs of the game. For games in some genres, the answer is simple and obvious: Drive a race car or fight in a boxing match. For games in other genres, such as role-playing games, the question may have many answers: explore, fight, cast spells, collect objects, buy and sell, talk to dragons.

Video games allow someone to play—that is, to *act*. The player has purchased the game in order to *do* something, not just to see, hear, or read something. Interactivity is the *raison d'être* of all gaming; it is what sets gaming apart from presentational forms of entertainment such as books and movies. The correct answer to the question, "Wouldn't it be fun to play a game set in ancient Rome?" is another question: "Yes, it would. What kinds of things could a player do in ancient Rome?" The more precise you are, the better. Avoid generalities such as "the player builds a city," and think of the exact verbs to assign to the input devices: buy land, sell land, construct a road, and so on.

> ### DESIGN RULE Think About Player Actions First
>
> Do not start designing the story, avatar, game world, artwork, or anything else until you have answered the question, "What is the player going to do?"

DEFINING THE ROLE

Playing a game, especially a board game or a computer game, often involves playing a *role* of some sort. In *Monopoly*, the role is a real estate tycoon. In the *Harry Potter* games, the role is, naturally, Harry Potter. Defining the player's role in the game world is a key part of defining your game's concept. If the player's role is difficult to describe, it may be difficult for the player to grasp as well, and that may indicate conceptual problems with the game. This doesn't mean that the role always has to be simple or that the player sticks to just one role per game. In many sports games, for example, the player can be an athlete, a coach, or the general manager. In team games, the player often switches from one athlete to another as play progresses.

TIP The easier it is to explain the player's role, the easier it is for the publisher, the retailer, and the customer to understand it... and to decide to spend money on it.

Shifting roles work well in a sports game because the game's audience understands them, but if your game takes place in a less familiar world with less familiar objectives, you must make the roles especially clear. If the player's role changes from time to time—especially involuntarily—the player must know why it changed and how to adapt to the new circumstances.

If you explain the player's role clearly, it helps him understand what he's trying to achieve and what rules govern the game. In *America's Army,* for instance, the player takes on the role of a real-world soldier. Real soldiers can't just shoot anything that moves; they have to obey rules of engagement. By telling the player that the role is based on reality rather than fantasy, the game designer ensures that the player knows his actions will have to be more cautious than in the usual frenetic shooter game.

In defining the player's role, you face the question of how realistic you want your game to be. At the concept stage, you need not—and should not—start defining the details of the core mechanics and the presentation layer, but you should have a general idea of whether you want your game to be abstract or representational. Other considerations, such as the target audience (discussed in the section "Defining Your Target Audience," later in this chapter) may influence that decision.

Genres and Hybrids

If you're a student or an independent developer, we recommend that the first thing that you do in designing a game is define the player's role and think about the actions that will be available to that player. This allows you maximum flexibility to create any sort of game that you like. However, if you're working for a large conventional publisher, they will probably want you to make a game that fits within an existing genre. The more money the publisher spends to develop a game, the more conservative they tend to be.

NOTE In addition, e-books will be available for purchase from the Peachpit website that each discuss one genre in detail. They are all named *Fundamentals of <genre name> Design.*

Working with a well-known genre such as a shooter or a racing game gives you a shortcut through the early design process. Because conventional genres are defined in terms of their challenges, they naturally have a fairly standard set of actions that players will expect to find in them as well. Chapter 3, "The Major Genres," introduced them.

Some games cross genres, combining features not typically found together. By far the most successful hybrid is the *action-adventure,* as seen in the more recent *Legend of Zelda* games. (The earlier 2D *Zelda* games were almost entirely action games.) Action-adventures are still mostly action, but they include a story and puzzles that give them some of the qualities of adventure games. Games that offer a major gameplay mode in one genre, but one or more mini-games in another, are increasingly popular. For example, *Puzzle Quest* (**Figure 7.2**) was a successful hybrid, a simple role-playing game that used the match-three gameplay of many casual games to implement combat.

Crossing genres is more work for the design and development teams and not without its risks. Rather than appealing to two groups, you might end up appealing to neither. Many players (and game reviewers) prefer particular genres and don't want to be confronted by challenges of a kind that they normally avoid. If you plan to do something unusual, be sure to playtest your idea early with people who represent your intended audience.

FIGURE 7.2
Puzzle Quest

However, you should not allow the standard genres to circumscribe your creativity—especially at the concept stage. If you have a wholly new, never-before-seen type of game in mind, design it as you envision it; don't try to shoehorn it into a genre to which it doesn't belong. A game needs to be true to itself, so a truly hybrid game may need to mix challenges that aren't typically presented together. But don't mix characteristics of different genres without good reason; a game should cross genres only if it genuinely needs to as part of the gameplay. A flight simulator with a logic puzzle inserted in the middle of the game just to make the game different from other flight simulators will only annoy flight sim fans.

NOTE Occasionally two people on a design team want their game to belong to different genres, and they compromise by including challenges from both. Conflicting visions are a poor reason to create a hybrid game, and the result will lack harmony.

Defining Your Target Audience

Many game designers make the mistake of thinking that all players enjoy the same things that the designer enjoys, so the designer has only to examine her own experience to know how to make a game entertaining. This is dangerous hubris. We make video games to entertain an audience. You must think about who your audience is and what *they* like. Chapter 4 and Chapter 6 address some of the issues you will encounter.

CHAPTER 7

Unless you have been commissioned by a single individual, you design a game for a class of people, not for one person. At this early stage, you must think about your audience broadly, as a group of people you hope will enjoy your game. When a publisher asks, "Who will buy this game?," think carefully about the answer. What characteristics are your players likely to have in common? What things set them apart from other gamers? What challenges do they enjoy? More important, what challenges do they *not* enjoy? What interests them, bores them, frustrates them, excites them, frightens them, and offends them? Know the answers to these questions, and keep the answers close at hand as you design your game. If you don't already know your audience well, talk to some players who belong to this group and watch them play other games that are similar to the one you want to build.

THE PLAYER-CENTRIC PHILOSOPHY AND THE TARGET AUDIENCE

As Chapter 2 explained, the player-centric philosophy of game design requires that you think about how your design decisions affect a representative player's experience of the game. This approach ensures that your decisions serve the player's interests first, especially in the later stages of development when you are often tempted to make decisions based on cost or convenience.

A game concept is not complete without a statement describing its intended audience.

Defining a target audience is not the same as player-centric design. You can apply the player-centric approach only *after* you have defined the target audience. You must begin by asking yourself the question, "Who am I trying to entertain?" Once you have that answer, you can use it to apply the player-centric approach to other design issues, asking yourself, "Does this feature entertain a representative player from my target audience?"

Progression Considerations

If your game will be a long one, the player will need a sense of progress through it. At this stage of game design, you must decide what will provide that sense of progress: levels, a story, or both. Will your game be so large that it should be divided into levels? Will your levels be unrelated and all available to the player at any time, or will they be organized into a sequential or branching configuration, in which completing a level makes the next one available? What types of conditions will determine when a player has completed a level? The genre that you have chosen will help you to determine your answers.

The other question is whether you want a story. Stories give games a dramatic context and goal. Some genres, such as sports and puzzle games, don't usually include stories because their context is self-explanatory. In other genres, such as role-playing and adventure games, the story is a large part of the game's entertainment.

Representational games frequently provide a story; abstract games generally don't, although *Ms. Pac-Man* was an exception in a small way. Stories about abstract characters are seldom very involving.

If you do choose to have a story in your game, you don't have to know exactly what narrative content you want to include at the concept-formation stage. All you need to know is whether you want a story and, if so, what its overall direction will be. You should be able to summarize it in a sentence or two; for example: "When Moses Oyeleye, a college student in America, inherits his father's farm in Nigeria, he finds himself in violent conflict with local bandits, the police, and Western oil companies. He has to battle to save his family and his birthright." Errors in the storyline are much easier to correct than errors in the gameplay, and gamers will forgive story errors more quickly as well. Make sure you understand your game first; then build your story into it.

> ### DESIGN RULE The Story Comes Later
>
> Do not spend a lot of time devising a story at the concept stage. This is a cardinal error frequently made by people who are more used to presentational media such as books and film. You *must* concentrate most of your efforts on the gameplay at this point.

Summary

In this chapter, you learned what a game concept is and what decisions you have to make to create a high concept document. You should now understand the importance of defining the player's role. You also learned how to use game genres and how to think about choosing a target audience.

Creating a game concept is like designing the framework of a building: It gives you the general outlines but not the details. The remainder of the book is dedicated to creating those details.

Design Practice EXERCISES

1. Create a high concept document for one of your favorite games or one that your instructor assigns.

2. Write a short paper contrasting the player's roles in a *Tomb Raider* game and a *Civilization* game.

3. Think of a hybrid game that you have played (or your instructor will assign one). Write an essay describing what worked and what didn't in combining the two different kinds of gameplay.

Design Practice QUESTIONS

Once you have a game idea in mind, these are the questions you must ask yourself in order to turn it into a fully fledged game concept. You don't have to be precise or detailed, but you should have a general answer for all of them.

1. Write a high concept statement: a few sentences that give a general flavor of the game. You can reference other games, movies, books, or any other media if your game contains similar characters, actions, or ideas.

2. What is the player's role? Is the player pretending to be someone or something, and if so, what? Is there more than one role? How does the player's role help to define the gameplay?

3. Does the game have an avatar or other key character? Describe him/her/it.

4. What is the nature of the gameplay, in general terms? What kinds of challenges will the player face? What kinds of actions will the player take to overcome them?

5. What is the player's interaction model? Omnipresent? Through an avatar? Something else? Some combination?

6. What is the game's primary camera model? How will the player view the game's world on the screen? Will there be more than one perspective?

7. Does the game fall into an existing genre? If so, which one?

8. Is the game competitive, cooperative, team-based, or single-player? If multiple players are allowed, are they using the same machine with separate controls or different machines over a network?

9. Why would anyone want to play this game? Who is the game's target audience? What characteristics distinguish them from the mass of players in general?

10. What machine or machines is the game intended to run on? Can it make use of, or will it require, any particular hardware such as dance mats or a camera?

11. What is the game's setting? Where does it take place?

12. Will the game be broken into levels? What might be the victory condition for a typical level?

13. Does the game have a narrative or story as it goes along? Summarize the plot in a sentence or two.

CHAPTER 8

Game Worlds

Games entertain through gameplay, but many also entertain by taking the player away to an imaginary place—a *game world*. (This book uses the terms *world*, *setting*, and *game setting* interchangeably with *game world*.) The gameplay in most single-player video games appears to the player as interactions between himself and the game world. This chapter defines a game world and introduces the various dimensions that describe a game world: the physical, temporal, environmental, emotional, and ethical dimensions, as well as a quality called *realism*.

What Is a Game World?

A game world is an artificial universe, an imaginary place in which the events of the game occur. When the player enters the magic circle and pretends to be somewhere else, the game world is the place she pretends to be.

Not all games have a game world. A real-world sport like football takes place in a real location, not an imaginary one. Playing football still requires pretending because the players assign an artificial importance to otherwise trivial actions, but the pretending doesn't create a game world. Many abstract games, such as tic-tac-toe, have a board but not a world—there is no imaginary element in playing the game. *Stratego* has a more elaborate world: The board is printed to look like a landscape, and the pieces are illustrated with little pictures, encouraging us to pretend that they are colonels, sergeants, and scouts in an army. *Stratego* could be played entirely abstractly, using only numbers and a bare grid for a board, but the setting makes it more interesting. Except for a few abstract games like *Vib Ribbon*, video games normally have rich game worlds realized through art, animation, music, and sound effects.

ARTWORK IS NOT ENOUGH

When defining your game world, it will be tempting to start drawing pictures right away, especially if you're artistically inclined anyway. That's good in the early stages of design; you will need concept art to pitch your game. But don't make the mistake of thinking that nice drawings are enough. Your game world must support and work with the core mechanics and gameplay of your game. To make the world serve the game well, you must design it carefully. Otherwise you may forget to address an important issue until late in the development process, when it's expensive to make changes.

Most video games present their game world with pictures and sound: art, animation, music, and audio effects. Not all game worlds have a visible or audible component, however. In interactive fiction, the player creates the images and sounds of the world in his imagination when he reads the text on the screen. Designing such a world is a matter of using your literary skills to describe it in words.

Game worlds are much more than the sum of the pictures and sounds that portray them. A game world can have a culture, a style, a set of moral values, and other qualities that you'll look at in this chapter. The game world also has a relationship to reality, whether it is highly abstract, with little connection to the world of every-day things, or highly representational, attempting to be as similar to the real world as possible.

The Purposes of a Game World

Games entertain by several means: gameplay, novelty, social interaction (if it is a multiplayer game), and so on. In a game such as chess, almost all the entertainment value is in the gameplay; few people think of chess as a game about medieval warfare. In atmospheric games such as the *Silent Hill* series, the world is essential to the fantasy. Without the world, the game would not exist, and if it had a different world, it would be a different game. One of the purposes of a game world is simply to entertain in its own right: to offer the player a place to explore and an environment to interact with.

As a general rule, the more that a player concentrates on a game's core mechanics, the less the game world matters to her. Mastering the mechanics requires a kind of abstract thought, and fantasy can be a distraction. Serious chess players don't think of the pieces as representing actual kings and queens and knights. When players become highly skilled at a game such as *Team Fortress 2*, they no longer think about where they are or why they're there; they think only about hiding, moving, shooting, ambushing, obtaining ammunition, and so on. However, this kind of abstract play, ignoring a game's world, usually occurs only among the most experienced and analytical of players. To someone who's playing a game for the first time, the world is vital to creating and sustaining her interest.

The other purpose of a game's world is to sell the game in the first place. It's not the game's mechanics that make a customer pick up a box in a store, but the fantasy it offers: who she'll be, where she'll be, and what she'll be doing there if she plays that game.

The Dimensions of a Game World

Many different properties define a game's world. Some, such as the size of the world, are quantitative and can be given numerical values. Others, such as the world's mood, are qualitative and can only be described with words. Certain properties are related to one another, and these groups of related properties are the *dimensions* of the game world. To fully define your world and its setting, you need to consider each of these dimensions and answer certain questions about them.

The Physical Dimension

Video game worlds are almost always implemented as some sort of simulated physical space. The player moves his avatar in and around this space or manipulates other pieces or characters in it. The physical properties of this space determine a great deal about the gameplay. Three of these properties are spatial dimensionality, scale, and boundaries.

SPATIAL DIMENSIONALITY

One of the first questions to ask yourself is how many spatial dimensions your physical space will have. It is essential to understand that the dimensionality of the game's physical space is not the same as how the game *displays* that space (the camera model) or how it implements the space in the software. How to implement the space and how to display it are separate but related questions. The former has to do with technical design, and the latter has to do with user interface design. Ultimately, all spaces must be displayed on the two-dimensional surface of the monitor screen unless you are devising an alternative reality game, or a game for 3D virtual reality gear like the Oculus Rift.

These are the typical dimensionalities found in video games:

■ **2D.** Thanks to the explosion in casual and mobile gaming, most of the video games in the world still have only two dimensions. This design is especially noticeable in 2D side-scrolling games such as *Prince of Persia Classic,* a remake of the original *Prince of Persia* (see **Figure 8.1**). The prince can run left and right and jump up and down, but he cannot move toward the player (out of the screen) or away from him (into the screen). Two-dimensional worlds have one huge advantage when you're thinking about how to display them: The two dimensions of the world directly correspond to the two dimensions of the monitor screen, so you don't have to worry about conveying a sense of depth to the player. Some games with 2D game worlds still use 3D engines to display the world so that objects appear three-dimensional even though the gameplay does not use the third dimension.

NOTE Even text adventures and point-and-click adventures have a physical dimension. The player moves from one location, usually called a room even if it's described as outdoors, to another. The connections between the rooms are abstractions, however, and don't have to make physical sense, which makes it possible to create illogical spaces in these kinds of worlds. Teleportation, such as Portal offers, also permits designers to make use of unrealistic spaces.

■ **2.5D,** typically pronounced "two-and-a-half D." This refers to game worlds that appear to be three-dimensional spaces, but in reality, consist of a series of 2D layers, one above the other. *StarCraft,* a war game, shows plateaus and lowlands, as well as aircraft that pass over obstacles and ground units. The player can place objects and move them horizontally within a layer with a fine degree of precision, but vertically an object must be in one plane or another; there is no in-between. Flying objects can't move up and down in the air; they're simply in the air layer as **Figure 8.2** depicts.

▦ **3D.** Three true dimensions. Thanks to 3D hardware accelerators and middleware engines like Unity, 3D spaces are now easy to implement on hardware that supports them. They give the player a much greater sense of being inside a space (building, cave, spacecraft, or whatever) than 2D spaces ever can. With a 2D world, the player feels as if he is looking at it; with a 3D world, he feels as if he is in it. 3D worlds are great for games with exploration challenges or vehicle simulations such as *Need for Speed: Most Wanted* (see **Figure 8.3**). Most large games for personal computers and consoles now use three dimensions.

FIGURE 8.3
Need for Speed: Most Wanted, a fully 3D environment

▦ **4D.** If you want to include a fourth dimension for some reason (not counting time), implement it as an alternate version of the 3D game world rather than an actual four-dimensional space. In other words, create two (or more) three-dimensional spaces that look similar but offer different experiences as the avatar moves among them. For example, the *Legacy of Kain* series presents two versions of the same 3D world, the spectral realm and the material realm, with different gameplay modes for each. The landscape is the same in both, but the material realm is lit by white light whereas the spectral realm is lit by blue light, and the architecture is distorted in the spectral realm (see **Figure 8.4**). The actions available to the player are different in each realm. The realms look similar but are functionally different places governed by different laws. In the movie version of *The Lord of the Rings*, the world that Frodo inhabits while he is wearing the Ring can be thought of as an alternate plane of reality as well, overlapping the real world but appearing and behaving differently.

FIGURE 8.4

Legacy of Kain: Soul Reaver's material (top) and spectral (bottom) realms, showing the same environment. Notice how the architecture is twisted in the spectral realm.

TIP   Make sure all the dimensions will contribute meaningfully. Many games that work extremely well in two dimensions don't work well in three. *Lemmings* was a hit 2D game, but *Lemmings 3D* was nowhere near as successful because it was much more difficult to play. The addition of a third dimension detracted from the player's enjoyment rather than added to it.

When you first think about the dimensionality of your game space, don't immediately assume that you want it to be three-dimensional because 3D seems more real or makes the best use of your machine's hardware. As with everything else you design, the dimensionality of your physical space must serve the entertainment value of the game.

SCALE

Scale refers to both the *absolute* size of the physical space represented, as measured in units meaningful in the game world (meters, miles, or light-years, for instance), and the *relative* sizes of objects in the game. If a game doesn't correspond to anything in the real world, the sizes of objects in its game world don't really matter. You can adjust them to suit the game's needs any way you like. But if you are designing a game that represents (if only partially) the real world, you'll have to address the question of how big everything should be to both look real and play well. Some distortion is often necessary for the sake of gameplay, especially in war games; the trick is to distort the scale without harming the player's suspension of disbelief too much.

In a sports game, a driving game, a flight simulator, or any other kind of game in which the player expects a high degree of verisimilitude, you have little choice but to scale things to their actual sizes. Similarly, you should scale most of the objects in first-person games accurately. Because the player's perspective is that of a person walking through the space, objects need to look right for their surrounding area. You might want to slightly exaggerate the size of critical objects such as keys, weapons, or treasure to make them more visible.

If you're designing a game with an aerial or isometric perspective, you will probably need to distort the scale of things somewhat. For example, in modern mechanized warfare, ground battles can easily take place over a 20-mile front, with weapons that can fire that far or farther. If you were to map an area this size onto a computer screen, an individual soldier or even a tank would be smaller than a single pixel—completely invisible. Although the display will normally be zoomed in on one small area of the whole map, the scale of objects will have to be somewhat exaggerated so that the objects are clearly identifiable on the screen.

Similarly, games often distort the relative heights of people and the buildings or hills in their environment so that the player can see everything clearly. The buildings are often only a little taller than the people who walk past them. (See **Figure 8.5** for an example.) Because the vertical dimension is seldom critical to the gameplay in products such as war games and role-playing games, it doesn't matter if heights are not accurate, so long as the distortion doesn't harm the player's immersion.

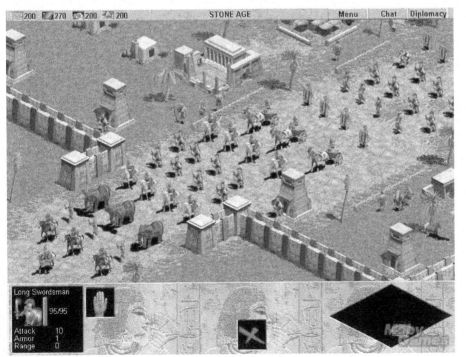

FIGURE 8.5
In *Age of Empires*, the buildings are only a little taller than the people.

Designers often make another scale distortion between indoor and outdoor locations. When a character walks through a town, the player wants the character to get there reasonably quickly. When the character steps inside a building, however, and needs to negotiate doors and furniture, you should expand the scale to show these additional details. If you use the same animation for a character walking indoors and outdoors, this will give the impression that the character walks much faster outdoors than indoors. However, this seldom bothers players—they'd much rather have the game proceed quickly than have their avatar take hours to get anywhere, even if that would be more accurate.

This brings up one final distortion, which is also affected by the game's notion of time (see the section "The Temporal Dimension," later in this chapter), and that is the relative speeds of moving objects. In the real world, a supersonic jet fighter can fly more than a hundred times faster than an infantry soldier can walk on the ground. If you're designing a game that includes both infantry soldiers and jet fighters, you're going to have a problem. If the scale of the battlefield is suitable for jets, it will take infantry weeks to walk across; if it's suitable for infantry, a jet could pass over it in the blink of an eye. One solution is to do what the real military does and implement transport vehicles for ground troops. Another is simply to accept a certain amount of distortion and create jets that fly only four or five times as fast as people walk (*StarCraft* uses this trick). As long as the jet is the fastest thing in the game, it doesn't really matter how much faster it is; the strike-and-retreat tactic that jets are good at will still work. Setting these values is all part of balancing the game, as Chapter 13, "Gameplay," discusses in more detail.

BOUNDARIES

In board games, the edge of the board is the edge of the game world. With procedural rendering, we can create unlimited game worlds, but normally we establish artificial boundaries to avoid overwhelming the player or letting her go into regions where no gameplay has been implemented. Computer games are usually more immersive than board games, and they often try to disguise or explain away the fact that the world is limited to help maintain the player's immersion.

In some cases, the boundaries of a game world arise naturally, and we don't have to disguise or explain them. Sports games take place only in a stadium or an arena, and no one expects or wants them to include the larger world. In most driving games, the car is restricted to a track or a road, and this, too, is reasonable enough.

Setting a game underground or indoors helps to create natural boundaries for the game world. Everyone expects indoor regions to be of a limited size, with walls that define the edges. The problem occurs when games move outdoors, where players expect large, open spaces without sharply defined edges. A common solution in this case is to set the game on an island surrounded by water or have the outdoor setting be surrounded by some other kind of impassable terrain: mountains, swamps, or deserts. These boundaries establish both a credible and a visually distinctive "edge of the world." *World of Warcraft* uses dangerous enemies to keep players out of regions where they should not go, another believable approach.

In flight simulators, setting the boundaries of the world creates even more problems. Most flight simulators restrict the player to a particular area of the real world. Because there are no walls in the air, there's nothing to stop the plane from flying up to the edge of the game world; when the player arrives there he can clearly see that there's nothing beyond. In some games, the plane just stops there, hovering in midair, and won't go any farther. In *Battlefield 1942*, the game tells the player that he has left the scene of the action and forcibly returns him to the runway.

A common solution to the edge-of-the-world problem is to allow the flat world to "wrap" at the top, bottom, and sides. Although the world is implemented as a rectangular space in the software, objects that cross one edge appear at the opposite edge—they wrap around the world. If the object remains centered on the screen and the world appears to move beneath it, you can create the impression that the world is spherical. Maxis's *Spore* actually displays the world as a sphere on the screen (see **Figure 8.6**).

FIGURE 8.6
Parts of *Spore* are set on a genuinely spherical world.

Finally, you can solve the problem of boundaries by requiring the player to move among defined locations. For example, you might let a player fly from planet to planet in the solar system by clicking on the planet she wants to go to. The player cannot go beyond the boundary of the solar system because there are no planets in interstellar space. The user interface for movement creates a natural limit that requires no further explanation.

The Temporal Dimension

The *temporal dimension* of a game world defines the way that time is treated in that world and the ways in which it differs from time in the real world.

In many turn-based and action games, the world doesn't include a concept of time passing: days and nights or seasons and years. Everything in the world idles or runs in a continuous loop until the player interacts with the game in some way. Occasionally, the player is put under pressure by being given a limited amount of real-world time to accomplish something, but this usually applies to only a single challenge and is not part of a larger notion of time in the game.

In some games, time is implemented as part of the game world but not part of the gameplay. The passage of time creates atmosphere and gives the game visual variety, but it doesn't change the game's challenges and actions. This usually feels rather artificial. If the player can do exactly the same things at night that she can during the day and no one ever seems to sleep, then there's little point in making the distinction. For time to really support the fantasy, it must affect the experience in ways besides the purely visual.

Minecraft is a good example of a game in which time is meaningful. Many of the enemies in *Minecraft* are inactive during the daytime. It's also darker and hard to see at night. In the underground portions of the game, day and night have less meaning, as you would expect.

VARIABLE TIME

NOTE Bullet time or hero time, as seen in *Max Payne* and many other games, is another example of variable time. When the player engages in combat, the game automatically goes into a super slow-motion mode.

In games that do implement time as a significant element of the gameplay, time in the game world usually runs much faster than in reality. Time in games also jumps (as it does in books and movies), skipping periods when nothing interesting is happening. Most war games, for example, don't bother to implement nighttime or require that soldiers get any rest. In reality, soldier fatigue is a critical consideration in warfare, but because sleeping soldiers don't make exciting viewing and certainly aren't very interactive, most games just skip sleep periods. Allowing soldiers to fight continuously without a pause permits the player to play continuously without a pause also.

The Sims, a game about managing a household, handles this problem a different way. The simulated characters require rest and sleep for their health, so *The Sims* depicts day and night accurately. However, when all the characters go to sleep, the game speeds up considerably, letting hours go by in a few seconds. As soon as anyone wakes up, time slows down again.

The Sims is a rather unusual game in that time management is one of the most important challenges. The player is under constant pressure to have his characters accomplish all their chores and get time for sleep, relaxation, and personal development as well. The game runs something like 48 times as fast as real life, so it takes about 20 minutes of real time to play through the 16 hours of game-world daytime. However, the characters don't move 48 times as fast. Their actions look pretty normal, about as they would in real time. As a result, it takes them 15 minutes according to the game's clock just to go out and pick up the newspaper. This contributes to the sense of time pressure. Because the characters do everything slowly (in game terms), they often don't get a chance to water their flowers, which consequently die.

ANOMALOUS TIME

In *The Settlers: Rise of an Empire*, a complex economic simulation, a tree can grow from a sapling to full size in about the same length of time that it takes for an iron foundry to smelt four or five bars of iron. This is *anomalous time:* time that seems to move at different speeds in different parts of the game. Blue Byte, the developer of *The Settlers*, tuned the length of time it takes to do each of the many tasks in the game to make sure that the game as a whole would run smoothly. As a result, *The Settlers* is very well balanced at some cost to realism. However, *The Settlers* doesn't give the player a clock in the game world. There's no way to compare game time to real time, so in effect, the game world has no obvious time scale (see **Figure 8.7**).

FIGURE 8.7

Activities in *The Settlers: Rise of an Empire* take anomalous lengths of time, but the user interface does not include a clock.

Another example of anomalous time appears in *Age of Empires,* in which tasks that should take less than a day in real time (gathering berries from a bush, for example) seem to take years in game time according to the game clock. *Age of Empires* does have a time scale, visible on the game clock, but not everything in the world makes sense on that time scale. The players simply have to accept these actions as symbolic rather than real. As designers, we have to make them work in the context of the game world without disrupting the fantasy. As long as the symbolic actions (gathering berries or growing trees) don't have to be coordinated with real-time actions (warfare) but remain essentially independent processes, it doesn't matter if they operate on an anomalous time scale.

LETTING THE PLAYER ADJUST TIME

In sports games and vehicle simulations, game time usually runs at the same speed as real time. A football game is, by definition, an hour long, but because the clock stops all the time, the actual elapsed time of a football game is closer to three hours. All serious computerized football games simulate this accurately. Verisimilitude is a key requirement of most sports games; if a game does not accurately simulate the real sport, the league might not approve of it, and its competitors are bound to point out the flaw. However, most such games also allow the players to shorten the game by playing 5- or 10-minute quarters instead of 15-minute quarters because most people don't want to devote a full three hours to playing a simulated football game. This is also a useful feature in testing; it takes far too long to test the product if you have to play a full-length game every time.

Flight simulators also usually run in real time, but there are often long periods of flying straight and level during which nothing of interest is going on. To shorten these periods, many games offer a way to speed up time in the game world by two, four, or eight times—in effect, make everything in the game world go faster than real time. When the plane approaches its destination, the player can return the game to normal speed and play in real time. *The Elder Scrolls V: Skyrim* also allowed the player to change the speed of game time.

The Environmental Dimension

The environmental dimension describes the world's appearance and its atmosphere. You've seen that the physical dimension defines the properties of the game's space; the environmental dimension is about what's in that space. The environmental characteristics of the game world form the basis for creating its art and audio. We'll look at two particular properties: the cultural context of the world and the physical surroundings.

CULTURAL CONTEXT

The cultural context of a game refers to its culture in the anthropological sense: the beliefs, attitudes, and values that the people in the game world hold, as well as their political and religious institutions, social organization, and so on—in short, the way those people live. These characteristics are reflected in the manufactured items that appear in the game: clothing, furniture, architecture, landscaping, and every other man-made object in the world. The culture influences not only what appears and what doesn't appear (a game set in a realistic ancient Egypt obviously shouldn't include firearms), but also how everything looks—including the user interface. *Cleopatra: Queen of the Nile* is an excellent example of a game's culture harmonizing with its user interface; see **Figure 8.8**. The way objects appear is affected not only by their function in the world, but also by the aesthetic sensibilities of the people who constructed them; for example, a Maori shield looks entirely different from a medieval European shield.

FIGURE 8.8
The cultural context of *Cleopatra: Queen of the Nile* influences everything on the screen, including the icons and text.

The cultural context also includes the game's backstory. The *backstory* of a game is the imaginary history, either large-scale (nations, wars, natural disasters) or small-scale (personal events and interactions), that preceded the time when the game takes place. This prior history helps to establish why the culture is the way it is. A warlike people should have a history of warfare; a mercantile people should have a history of trading. In designing the backstory, don't go into too much depth too early, however. As Chapter 7, "Game Concepts," warned, the story must serve the game, not the other way around. Sometimes designers create a backstory purely to inspire the development team, without planning to build it into the game.

For most game worlds, it's not necessary to define the culture or cultures in great detail. A game set in your own culture can simply use the things that you see around you. The *SimCity* series, for example, is clearly set in present-day America (few European cities are so rectilinear), and it looks like it. But when your game's culture does not resemble your own, you need to think about how it is different, and how you will convey that to the player.

THE PHYSICAL WORLD

The physical aspects of the game world—its environment and contents—define what the game actually looks and sounds like. This is a part of game design in which it's most helpful to be an artist or to work closely with one. In the early stages of design, you don't need to make drawings of every single thing that can appear in the game world (although sooner or later someone will have to do just that). For the time being, create *concept sketches:* pencil or pen-and-ink drawings of key visual elements in the game. Depending on what your game is about, this can include buildings, vehicles, clothing, weaponry, furniture, decorations, works of art, jewelry, religious or magical items, logos or emblems, and on and on. See *Grim Fandango* (**Figure 8.9**) for a particularly distinctive example. The game's culture influences constructed artifacts in particular. A powerful and highly religious people are likely to have large symbols of their spirituality: stone temples or cathedrals. A warlike nomadic people have animals or vehicles to carry their gear and weapons they can use on the move. (Note that these might be future nomads, driving robo-camels.)

Nor should you neglect the natural world. Games set in urban or indoor environments consisting entirely of manufactured objects feel sterile. Think about birds and animals, plants and trees, earth, rocks, hills, and even the sky. Consider the climate: Is it hot or cold, wet or dry? Is the land fertile or barren, flat or mountainous? These qualities, all parts of a real place, are opportunities to create a visually rich and distinctive environment.

If your world is chiefly indoors, of course, you don't have to think about nature much unless your character passes a window, but there are many other issues to think about instead. Where does the light come from? What are the walls, floors, and ceilings made of, and how are they decorated? Why is this building here? Do the rooms have a specific purpose, and if so, what? How can you tell the purpose of a room from its contents? Does the building have multiple stories? How does the player get from one floor to another?

The physical world includes sounds as well as sights: music; ambient environmental sounds; the particular noises made by people, animals, machinery, and vehicles. If you think about the sounds things make at the same time that you think about how they look, this helps you create a coherent world. Suppose you're inventing a six-legged reptilian saddle animal with clawed feet rather than hooves. How does that creature sound as it moves? Its scales might rattle a bit. Its feet are not going to make the characteristic clip-clop sound of a shod horse. With six legs, it will probably have some rather odd gaits, and those should be reflected in the sound it makes.

FIGURE 8.9
Grim Fandango combines Aztec, Art Deco, and Mexican Day of the Dead themes.

The physical surroundings play a big role in setting the tone and mood of the game as it is played, whether it's the lighthearted cheerfulness of *Mario* or the grim realities of Dubai destroyed by a sandstorm in *Spec Ops: The Line* (see **Figure 8.10**). The sound, and especially the music, will contribute greatly to this. Think hard about the kind of music you want, and consider what genres will be appropriate. Stanley Kubrick listened to hundreds of records to select the music for *2001: A Space Odyssey*, and he astonished the world with his choice of "The Blue Danube" for the shuttle docking sequence. You have a similar opportunity when you design your game.

FIGURE 8.10
A city destroyed by a sandstorm in *Spec Ops: The Line*

DETAIL

Every designer must decide how much detail the game world needs—that is to say, how richly textured the world will be and how accurately modeled its characteristics will be. Technical limitations and time constraints will necessarily restrict your ambitions. No football game goes to the extent of modeling each fan in the stadium, and few flight simulators model all the physical characteristics of their aircraft. Detail helps to support the fantasy, but it always costs—in development time and in memory or storage space on the player's machine. In an adventure game, it should, in principle, be possible to pick up everything in the world; in practice, this usually isn't technically practical. And there's a good reason not to allow the player to pick up anything even if it is feasible: It's confusing. The player knows that if he can pick up an object, it must be important for some reason; if he can't pick it up, it isn't important.

The camera model you choose, and the way that the player moves through the world, may influence your decisions about the level of detail. For example, in a small stadium such as the Wimbledon tennis courts, the athletes may be conscious of specific people in the crowd, so it makes sense to model them in some detail. In motorsports, however, the spectators will flash past in a blur, and there's no point in putting much effort into their appearance.

Here's a good rule of thumb for determining the level of detail your game will contain: Include as much detail as you can to help the game's immersiveness, *up to* the point at which it begins to harm the gameplay. If the player must struggle to look after everything you've given him, the game probably has too much detail. (This is one of the reasons war games tend to have hundreds rather than hundreds of thousands of units. The player in a war game can't delegate tasks to intelligent subordinates, so the numbers have to be kept down to a size that she can reasonably manage.) A spectacularly detailed game that's no fun to play doesn't sell many copies.

DEFINING A STYLE

In describing how your world is going to look, you are defining a visual style for your game that will influence a great many other things as well: the character design, the user interface, perhaps the manual, and even the design of the box and the advertising. You actually have two tasks to take on here: defining the style of things *in* your world (that is, its intrinsic style), and also defining the style of the artwork that will *depict* your world. They aren't the same. For example, you can describe a world whose architectural style is inspired by Buddhist temples but draw it to look like a *film noir* movie. Or you could have medieval towns with half-timbered houses but depict them in a slightly fuzzy, Impressionistic style. You must choose both your content and the way in which you will present that content.

Both decisions will significantly influence the player's experience of the game, jointly creating a distinct atmosphere. In general, the style of depiction tends to superimpose its mood on the style of the object depicted. For example, a Greek temple might be architecturally elegant, but if its style of drawing suggests a Looney Tunes cartoon, players will expect something wacky and outrageous to take place there. The drawing style imposes its own atmosphere over the temple, no matter how majestic it is. For one example, take a look at *Naruto: Ultimate Ninja Storm* (see **Figure 8.11**). All the locations in *Naruto* are rendered in a flat-shaded style reminiscent of the comic book that inspired the game.

FIGURE 8.11
Naruto overlays the architecture of a modern Japanese city, and many other places, with a comic book style.

Unless you're the lead artist for your game as well as its designer, you probably shouldn't—or won't be allowed to—define the style by yourself. Your art team will have ideas of its own, and you should listen to those suggestions. The marketing department might insist on having a say as well. It's important, however, that you try to keep the style harmonious and consistent throughout your game. Too many games have been published in which different sections had wildly differing art styles because no one held and enforced a single overall vision.

OVERUSED SETTINGS

All too often, games borrow settings from one another or from common settings found in the movies, books, or television. A huge number of games are set in science fiction and fantasy worlds, especially the quasi-medieval, sword-and-sorcery fantasy inspired by J. R. R. Tolkien and *Dungeons & Dragons*, popular with the young people who used to be the primary—indeed, almost the only—market for computer games. But a more diverse audience plays games nowadays, and they want new worlds to play in. You should look beyond these hoary old staples of gaming. *Interstate '76* was inspired by 1970s TV shows. It includes cars, clothing, music, and language from that era, all highly distinctive and evocative of a particular culture. *Interstate '76* had great gameplay, but what really set it apart from its competitors was that it looked and sounded like nothing else on the market.

TIP The choice of art style can have a significant effect on how long it takes to make the game's artwork, another reason to consult closely with the lead artist. If your game is not heavily dependent on a particular style, you might save time and money by using a different one.

NOTE If you use other cultures that you aren't familiar with in your game, be sure to check with people who are part of that culture to make sure that your portrayal isn't offensive. The Activision game *Gun*, set in the American Old West, provoked serious controversy with its portrayals of Native Americans.

Especially if you are going to do science fiction or fantasy, try to make your game's setting distinctively different. At present, real spacecraft built by the United States or Russia look extremely functional, but as spacecraft become more common, and especially as we start to see personal spacecraft, we should expect them to exhibit stylistic variation as well. This is an area in which you have tremendous freedom to innovate.

The same goes for fantasy. Forget the same old elves, dwarves, wizards, and dragons (**Figure 8.12**). Look to other cultures for your heroes and villains. Right now about the only non-Western culture portrayed with any frequency in games is Japanese (feudal, present-day, and future) because the Japanese make a lot of games and their style has found some acceptance in the West as well. But there are many more sources of inspiration around the world, and most are untapped. Around AD 1200, while the rulers of Europe were still holed up in cramped, drafty castles, Islamic culture reached a pinnacle of grace and elegance, building magnificent palaces filled with the riches of the Orient and majestic mosques of inlaid stone. Yet this proud and beautiful civilization seldom appears in computer games because Western game designers haven't bothered to learn about it or don't even know it existed. Set your fantasy in Valhalla, in Russia under Peter the Great, in the arctic tundra, at Angkor Wat, on Easter Island, or at Machu Picchu.

FIGURE 8.12
Yet another quasi-medieval setting:
Armies of Exigo

SOURCES OF INSPIRATION

Art and architecture, history and anthropology, literature and religion, clothing fashions, and product design are all great sources of cultural material. Artistic and architectural movements, in particular, offer tremendous riches: Art Nouveau, Art Deco, Palladian, Brutalism. If you haven't heard of one of these, go look it up now. Browse the web or the art, architecture, and design sections of a bookstore or public library for pictures of interesting objects, buildings, and clothing. Carry a digital camera around and take pictures of things that attract your eye; then post the pictures around your workspace to inspire yourself and your coworkers. Collect graphic scrap from anywhere that you find it. Try old copies of *National Geographic*. Visit museums of art, design, and natural history if you can get to them; one of the greatest resources of all is travel, if you can afford it. A good game designer is always on the lookout for new ideas, even when he's ostensibly on vacation.

It's tempting to borrow from our closest visual neighbor, the movies, because the moviemakers have already done the visual design work for us. *Blade Runner* introduced the decaying urban future; *Alien* gave us disgustingly biological aliens rather than little green men. The problem with these looks is that they've already been borrowed many, many times. You can use them as a quick-and-dirty backdrop if you don't want to put much effort into developing your world, and players will instantly recognize the world and know what the game is about. But to stand out from the crowd, consider other genres. *Film noir*, the Marx Brothers, John Wayne westerns, war movies from the World War II era, costume dramas of all periods—from the silliness of *One Million Years B.C.* to the Regency elegance of *Pride and Prejudice*, they're all grist for the mill.

Television goes through its own distinct phases, and because it's even more fashion-driven than the movies, it is ripe for parody. The comedies of the 1950s and 1960s and the nighttime soaps of the 1970s and 1980s all had characteristic looks that seem laughable today but that are immediately familiar to most adult Americans. This is not without risk; if you make explicit references to American popular culture, non-Americans and children might not get the references. If your gameplay is good enough, though, it shouldn't matter.

Comic books and illustrated children's books also have visually distinctive styles and can serve as sources of inspiration, particularly if you're making a 2D game. A number of games have been made from children's books, copying their art styles; one of the best was *The Fantastic Flying Books of Mr. Morris Lessmore*.

The Emotional Dimension

The emotional dimension of a game world defines not only the emotions of the people in the world but, more important, the emotions that you, as a designer, hope to arouse in the player. For much of their history, games have been seen only as light entertainment without much emotional impact, and most casual games are still like that. But games such as *The Walking Dead* and *Journey* have proven that it's possible to create emotionally rich games. Multiplayer games evoke the widest variety of emotions, because the players are socializing with real people and making friends (and, alas, enemies) as they play. Single-player games have to influence players' emotions with storytelling and gameplay. Action and strategy games are usually limited to a narrow emotional dimension, but other games that rely more heavily on story and characters can offer emotional content that deeply affects the player. Greater emotional variety enables us to reach the players who value it.

INFLUENCING THE PLAYER'S FEELINGS

Games are intrinsically good at evoking feelings related to the player's efforts to achieve something. They can create "the thrill of victory and the agony of defeat," as the old ABC *Wide World of Sports* introduction used to say. Use the elements of risk and reward—a price for failure and a prize for success—to further heighten these emotions. Games can also produce frustration as a by-product of their challenges, but this isn't a good thing; some players tolerate frustration poorly and stop playing if it gets too high. To reduce frustration, build games with player-settable difficulty levels and make sure the easy level is genuinely easy. Excitement and anticipation, too, play large roles in many games. If you can devise a close contest or a series of stimulating challenges, you will generate these kinds of emotions. Construction and management simulations, whose challenges are usually financial, arouse the player's feelings of ambition, greed, and desire for power or control. They also offer the emotional rewards of creative play. Give the player a way to amass a fortune, then let her spend it to build things of her own design. The *SimCity* and various *Tycoon* games (*RollerCoaster Tycoon, Railroad Tycoon,* and so on), do this well. Artificial life games and god games such as *Spore* or *The Sims* let the player control the lives of autonomous people and creatures for better or worse, satisfying a desire to be omnipotent over a world of beings subject to the player's will. (This may not be a very admirable fantasy, but it's one that a lot of people enjoy having fulfilled.)

To create suspense, surprise, and fear, use the time-honored techniques of horror films: darkness, sudden noises, disgusting imagery, and things that jump out at the player unexpectedly. Don't overdo it, however. A gore-fest becomes tedious after a while, and Alfred Hitchcock demonstrated that the shock is all the greater when it occurs infrequently. For suspense to work well, the player needs to feel vulnerable and unprepared. Don't arm him too heavily; the world's a lot less scary when you're carrying a rocket launcher around. *Survival horror* is a popular subgenre of action game, as seen in the *Silent Hill* and *Resident Evil* series, that uses these approaches.

Another class of emotions is produced by interactions between characters and the player's identification with one of them. Love, grief, shame, jealousy, and outrage are all emotions that can result from such interactions. (See **Figure 8.13** for a famous example.) To evoke them, you'll have to use storytelling techniques, creating characters that the player cares about and believes in and credible relationships between them. Once you get the player to identify with someone, threaten that character or place obstacles in his path in a way that holds the player's interest.

This is the essence of dramatic tension, whether you're watching Greek tragedy or reading *Harry Potter*. Something important must be at stake. The problem need not necessarily be physical danger; it can also be a social, emotional, or economic risk. The young women in Jane Austen's novels were not in imminent peril of death or starvation, but it was essential to their family's social standing and financial future for them to make good marriages. The conflict between their personal desires and their family obligations provides the tension in the novels.

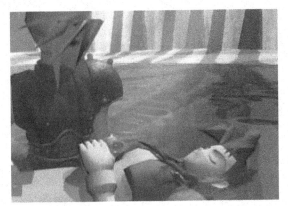

FIGURE 8.13
The death of Aeris,
from *Final Fantasy VII*

You can further influence the player's feelings by giving her difficult moral choices to make, with varying consequences depending on her decision. *BioShock* is one of the best-known recent examples; as the player, you have the choice of whether to kill or to save creatures called Little Sisters (there are short- and long-term advantages to either strategy), and the ending of the game is different depending on what you choose to do.

A good many games set the danger at hyperbolic levels with extreme claims such as "The fate of the universe rests in your hands!" This kind of hyperbole appeals to young people, who often feel powerless and have fantasies about being powerful. To adults, it just sounds a bit silly. At the end of *Casablanca*, Rick said, "The problems of three little people don't amount to a hill of beans in this crazy world," but he was wrong. The whole movie, a movie still popular over a half century after its first release, is about the problems of those three little people. For the duration of the film, these problems hold us entranced. It isn't necessary for the fate of the world to be at stake; it is the fates of Rick, Ilsa, and Victor that tug at our hearts.

DESIGN RULE Avoid Implausible Extremes

Don't make your game about the fate of the world if you are serious about producing emotional resonance with your audience; the fate of the world is too big to grasp. Make your game about the fate of people instead.

Finally, research shows that players value amusement highly. Comedy works best in adventure games, which tend to have more detailed characters than other genres, although role-playing games occasionally include funny moments or unexpected wisecracks from non-player characters. If your game is about an unrelentingly serious subject, you might want to include moments of comic relief just to lighten the tone from time to time. These have to be handled carefully, however, or they will seem inappropriate.

THE LIMITATIONS OF FUN

Weaver's Law: The quality of an entertainment is inversely proportional to the awareness of time engaged in it.

—CHRIS WEAVER, FOUNDER OF BETHESDA SOFTWORKS

Most people think that the purpose of playing games is to have fun, but *fun* is a rather limiting term. It tends to suggest excitement and pleasure, either a physical pleasure such as riding a roller coaster, a social pleasure such as joking around with friends, or an intellectual pleasure such as playing cards or a board game. The problem with striving for fun is that it tends to limit the emotional range of games. Suspense, excitement, exhilaration, surprise, and various forms of pleasure fall within the definition of fun, but not pity, jealousy, anger, sorrow, guilt, outrage, or despair.

Games don't only provide fun; they provide entertainment just as books, movies, and television do. You can entertain people in all sorts of ways. Movies with sad endings aren't fun in the conventional sense, but they're still entertaining. The potential of our medium to explore emotions and the human condition is much greater than the term *fun game* allows for; *Journey* is a highly popular example of a game that succeeded at moving beyond simple fun.

All that said, however, bear in mind that most publishers and players want fun. Too many inexperienced designers are actually more interested in showing how clever they are than in making sure the player has a good time; they place their own creative agenda before the player's enjoyment. As a designer, you must master the ability to create fun—light enjoyment—before you move on to more complex emotional issues. Addressing unpleasant or painful emotions successfully is a greater aesthetic challenge and may limit your audience somewhat.

YOU CAN'T PAINT EMOTION BY NUMBERS

The idea that games should include more emotional content and should inspire more emotions in players has been gaining ground in the game industry for several years. Unfortunately, this has produced a tendency to look for quick and easy ways to do it, mostly by relying on clichés. The young man whose family is killed and who is obsessed by his desire for revenge or the beautiful princess who needs to be rescued both belong more to fairy tales than to modern fiction. That may be all right if your game aspires to nothing more, but it won't do if you're trying to create an experience with any subtlety. Contrast, for example, the simple themes of the early animation films and the more psychologically rich stories in the recent Pixar films.

Beware of books or articles that offer simple formulas for emotional manipulation: "If you want to make the player feel X, just do Y to the protagonist." An imaginative and novel approach to influencing the players' feelings requires the talents of a skilled storyteller. Paint-by-numbers emotional content has all the sensitivity and nuance of paint-by-numbers art.

The Ethical Dimension

The ethical dimension of a game world defines what right and wrong mean within the context of that world. At first glance, this might seem kind of silly—it's only a game, so there's no need to talk about ethics. But most games that have a setting, a fantasy component, also have an ethical system that defines how the player is supposed to behave. As a designer, you are the god of the game's world, and you establish its morality. When you tell a player that he must perform certain actions to win the game, you are defining those actions as good or desirable. Likewise, when you say that the player must avoid certain actions, you are defining them as bad or undesirable. The players who come into the world must adopt your standards or they will lose the game.

In some respects, the morality of a game world is part of its culture and history, which are part of the environmental dimension, but because the ethical dimension poses special design problems, it needs a separate discussion. The ethics of most game worlds deviate somewhat from those of the real world—sometimes they're entirely reversed. Games allow, even require, you to do things that you can't do in the real world. The range of actions that the game world permits is typically narrower than in the real world (you can fly your F-15 fighter jet all you want, but you can't get out of the plane), but often the permitted actions are quite extreme: killing people, stealing things, and so on.

MORAL DECISION-MAKING

On the whole, most games have simple ethics: clobber the bad guys, protect the good guys. It's not subtle but it's perfectly functional; that's how you play checkers. Not many games explore the ethical dimension in any depth. A few include explicit moral choices, but unfortunately, these tend to be namby-pamby, consistently rewarding good behavior and punishing bad behavior. Such preachy material turns off even children, not to mention adults. But you can build a richer, more involving game by giving the player tough moral choices to make. Ethical ambiguity and difficult decisions are at the heart of many great stories and, indeed, much of life. Should you send a platoon of soldiers to certain death to save a battalion of others? How would you feel if you were in the platoon?

NOTE Serious games often address serious subjects, and while they are challenging and enjoyable, they often require players to confront difficult subjects such as abuse, illness, or the real costs of war or famine. Such games are seldom bestsellers; they are designed to inform rather than to make a lot of money.

CHAPTER 8

THE PECULIAR MORALITY OF AMERICA'S ARMY

America's Army, a team-based multiplayer first-person shooter (FPS) game distributed free by the U.S. Army, is intended to serve as an education and recruiting tool, teaching players how real soldiers are supposed to fight (**Figure 8.14**). It differs from most FPS games in two significant ways. First, it requires that the player act in conformance with the actual disciplinary requirements of the Army, so it detects and punishes dishonorable behavior. The Army is anxious to make the point that soldiering comes with serious moral responsibilities. Second, and rather strangely, all sides in a firefight see themselves as U.S. soldiers, and they see the enemy as rather generic terrorists. The Army did not want to give any player the chance to shoot at American soldiers, even though they are obviously shooting at one another. So a player sees himself and his teammates as U.S. soldiers carrying M-16 rifles, but his opponents see him and his teammates as terrorists carrying AK-47s. In other words, everyone perceives himself as a good guy and his opponent as a bad guy, and the game's graphics literally present two different versions of reality to each team. By avoiding a politically unacceptable design (letting players shoot at American soldiers in a game made by the U.S. Army), they created a moral equivalence: The question of who is in the right is purely a matter of perspective. *America's Army*'s trick of displaying different versions of the game world to different players may be unique among video games.

FIGURE 8.14 Our guys get the drop on somebody who also thinks he's one of our guys.

In many role-playing games, you can choose to play as an evil character who steals and kills indiscriminately, but other characters will refuse to cooperate with you and might even attack you on sight. It's easier to get money by robbing others than by working for it, but you may pay a price for that behavior in other ways. Rather than impose a rule that says, "Immoral behavior is forbidden," the game implements a rule that says, "You are free to make your own moral choices, but be prepared to live with the consequences." This is a more adult approach to the issue than simply punishing bad behavior. Be aware, however, many countries' video game rating systems take a game's ethics into account. If you do permit immoral behavior in your game, it will probably get a rating indicating that it is not for children.

You must be sure to explain the ethical dimension of your game clearly in its introductory material or in mission briefings. For example, some games that have hostage-rescue scenarios make the death of a hostage a loss condition: If a hostage dies, the player loses. This means that the player has to be extra careful not to kill any hostages, even at the risk of his own avatar's life. In other games, the only loss condition is the avatar's death. In this case, many players shoot with complete abandon, killing hostages and their captors indiscriminately. In real life, of course, the truth is somewhere in between. Police officers who accidentally shoot a hostage are seldom prosecuted unless they've been grossly negligent, but it doesn't do their careers any good. You can emulate this by penalizing the player somehow. To be fair to the player, however, you need to make this clear at the outset.

The ethical dimension of multiplayer games, whether online or local, is an enormous and separate problem. Chapter 17, "Design Issues for Online Gaming," discusses this issue at length.

A WORD ABOUT GAME VIOLENCE

It's not part of this book's mission to debate, much less offer an answer for, the problem of whether violent video games cause violent behavior in children or adults. This is a psychological question that only prolonged and careful study can resolve. Unfortunately, a good many people on both sides of the issue seem to have made up their minds already, and arguments continue to rage in government and the media, supported for the most part by very few facts.

For you, as a designer, however, consider these suggestions. The essence of many games is conflict, and conflict is often represented as violence in varying degrees of realism. Chess is a war game in which pieces are killed—removed from the board— but nobody objects to the violence of chess; it's entirely abstract. Football is a violent contact sport in which real people get injured all the time, but there are no serious efforts to ban football, either. The only way to remove violence from gameplay is to prohibit most of the games in the world because most contain violence in some more-or-less abstract form. The issue is not violence, per se, but how violence is portrayed and the circumstances under which violence is acceptable.

NOTE *Call of Duty: Modern Warfare 2* included a level in which the player had to decide whether or not to kill civilians in order to protect his cover as he tried to infiltrate a terrorist cell. Even though the game was rated for adults, the player was given a choice, and the entire level was optional, the game caused a huge outcry. Many people are still uncomfortable with this kind of material.

CHAPTER 8

Games get into political trouble when they have a close visual similarity to the real world but an ethical dimension that is strongly divergent from the real world. The game *Kingpin* encourages the player to beat prostitutes to death with a crowbar, with bloodily realistic graphics. Not surprisingly, it has earned a lot of criticism. On the other hand, *Space Invaders* involves shooting hundreds of aliens, but it is so visually abstract that nobody minds. In other words, the more a game resembles reality visually, the more its ethical dimension should resemble reality as well, or it's likely to make people upset. If you want to make a game in which you encourage the player to shoot anything that moves, you're most likely to stay out of trouble if those targets are nonhuman and just quietly disappear rather than break apart into bloody chunks. Tie your ethical realism to your visual realism.

Computer games are about bringing fantasies to life, enabling people to do things in make-believe that they couldn't possibly do in the real world. But make-believe is a dangerous game when it's played by people for whom the line between fantasy and reality is not clear. Young children (those under about age eight) don't know much about the real world; they don't know what is possible and what isn't, what is fantasy and what is reality. An important part of raising children is teaching them this difference. But until they've learned it, it's best to make sure that any violence in young children's games is suitably proportionate to their age. Graphic, realistic violence can be terrifying to children who have not yet learned to process it and is best avoided. For a detailed and insightful discussion of how children come to terms with violence, read *Killing Monsters: Why Children Need Fantasy, Super Heroes, and Make-Believe Violence* by Gerard Jones (Jones, 2002). Ultimately, the violence in a game should serve the gameplay and the game's audience. If it doesn't, then it's gratuitous and you should consider doing without it.

Realism

NOTE If you're mathematically inclined, think of realism as a vector over every aspect of the game, with values ranging from 0, entirely abstract, to 1, entirely realistic. However, no value ever equals 1 because nothing about a game is ever entirely realistic—if it were, it would be life, not a game.

Chapter 2, "Designing and Developing Games," introduces the concept of *realism* in the context of a discussion about core mechanics. All games, no matter how realistic, require some abstraction and simplification of the real world. Even the multimillion-dollar flight simulators used for training commercial pilots are incapable of turning the cockpit completely upside down. This event is so rare (we hope) in passenger aircraft that it's not worth the extra money it would take to simulate it.

The degree of realism of any aspect of a game appears on a continuum of possibilities from highly representational at one end to highly abstract at the other. Players and game reviewers often talk about realism as a quality of an entire game, but in fact, the level of realism differs in individual components of the game. Many games have highly realistic graphics but unrealistic physics. A good many first-person shooters accurately model the performance characteristics of a variety of weapons—their rate of fire, size of ammunition clips, accuracy, and so on—but allow the player to carry about 10 of them at once with no reduction in speed or mobility.

Therefore, realism is not a single dimension of a game world, but a multivariate quality that applies to all parts of the game and everything in it.

The representational/abstract dichotomy is mostly useful as a starting point when you're thinking about what kind of a game you want to create. On the one hand, if you're designing a cartoony action game such as *Ratchet & Clank,* you know that it's going to be mostly abstract. As you design elements of the game, you'll need to ask yourself how much realism you want to include. Can your avatar be hurt when she falls long distances? Is there a limit to how much she can carry at once? Do Newtonian physics apply to her, or can she change directions in midair?

On the other hand, if you're designing a game that people will expect to be representational—a vehicle or sports simulation, for example—then you have to think about it from the other direction. What aspects of the real world are you going to remove? Most modern fighter aircraft have literally hundreds of controls; that's why only a special group of people can be fighter pilots. To make a fighter simulation accessible to the general public, you'll have to simplify a lot of those controls. Similarly, a fighter jet's engine is so powerful that certain maneuvers can knock the pilot unconscious or even rip the plane apart. Are you going to simulate these limitations accurately, or make the game a little more abstract by not requiring the player to think about them?

Once again: Every design decision you make must serve the entertainment value of the game. In addition, every design decision must serve your goals for the game's overall degree of realism. Some genres demand more realism than others. It's up to you to establish how much realism you want and in what areas. You must also make sure that your decisions about realism don't destroy the game's harmony and balance. During the design process, you must continually monitor your decisions to see if they are meeting your goals.

Summary

At this point, you should know when and where your game takes place. You will have answered a huge number of questions about what your world looks like, what it sounds like, who lives there, and how they behave. If you've done it thoroughly, your game world will be one in which a player can immerse himself, a consistent fantasy that he can believe in and enjoy being part of. The next step is to figure out what's going to happen there.

Design Practice EXERCISES

1. Imagine that you could use any content you liked in a game without regard for copyright. Choose one of the following game genres and then select a painter, photographer, or filmmaker, and a composer or musician, whose work you would like

to use to create the appropriate emotional tone for your game. Create a short pre-sentation (PowerPoint or similar) that shows how the images and music work together for your purpose. The genres are action (survival horror subgenre), real-time strategy (modern warfare), or children's nonviolent adventure game.

2. Write an essay discussing two contrasting systems of morality in games you have played or in two games assigned by your instructor. What actions does each game reward, and what actions does it punish? Address the relationship between moral behavior in the two game worlds and moral behavior in the real world.

Design Practice QUESTIONS

Ask yourself the questions about each of the following game world dimensions.

PHYSICAL DIMENSION

1. Does my game require a physical dimension? What is it used for? Is it an essential part of gameplay or merely cosmetic?

2. Leaving aside issues of implementation or display, how many imaginary spatial dimensions does my game require? If there are three or more, can objects move continuously through the third and higher dimensions, or are these dimensions partitioned into discrete "layers" or zones?

3. How big is my game world, in light-years or inches? Is accuracy of scale critical, as in a football game, or not, as in a cartoon-like action game?

4. Will my game need more than one scale, for indoor versus outdoor areas, for example? How many will it actually require?

5. How am I going to handle the relative sizes of objects and people? What about their relative speeds of movement?

6. How is my world bounded? Am I going to make an effort to disguise the "edge of the world," and if so, with what? What happens if the player tries to go beyond it?

TEMPORAL DIMENSION

1. Is time a meaningful element of my game? Does the passage of time change anything in the game world even if the player does nothing, or does the world simply sit still and wait for the player to do something?

2. If time does change the world, what effects does it have? Does food decay, and do light bulbs burn out?

3. How does time affect the player's avatar? Does she get hungry or tired?

4. What is the actual purpose of including time in my game? Is it only a part of the atmosphere, or is it an essential part of the gameplay?

5. Is there a time scale for my game? Do I need to have measurable quantities of time, such as hours, days, and years, or can I just let time go by without bothering to measure it? Does the player need a clock to keep track of time?

6. Are there periods of time that I'm going to skip or do without? Is this going to be visible to the player, or will it happen seamlessly?

7. Do I need to implement day and night? If I do, what will make night different from day? Will it merely look different, or will it have other effects as well? What about seasons?

8. Will any of the time in my game need to be anomalous? If so, why? Will that bother the player? Do I need to explain it away, and if so, how?

9. Should the player be allowed to adjust time in any way? Why, how, and when?

ENVIRONMENTAL DIMENSION

1. Is my game world set in a particular historical period or geographic location? When and where? Is it an alternate reality, and if so, what makes it different from ours?

2. Are there any people in my game world? What are they like? Do they have a complex, highly organized society or a simple, tribal one? How do they govern themselves? How is this social structure reflected in their physical surroundings? Are there different classes of people, guilds, or specialized occupations?

3. What do my people value? Trade, martial prowess, imperialism, peace? What kinds of lives do they lead in pursuit of these ends? Are they hunters, nomadic, agrarian, industrialized, even postindustrial? How does this affect their buildings and clothing?

4. Are my people superstitious or religious? Do they have institutions or religious practices that will be visible in the game? Are there religious buildings? Do the people carry charms or display spiritual emblems?

5. What are my people's aesthetics like? Are they flamboyant or reserved, chaotic or orderly, bright or subtle? What colors do they like? Do they prefer straight lines or curves?

6. If there aren't any people in the game, what are there instead, and what do they look like and how do they behave?

7. Does my game take place indoors or outdoors, or both? If indoors, what are the furnishings and interior decor like? If outdoors, what is the geography and architecture like?

8. What are the style and mood of my game? How am I going to create them with art, sound, and music?

9. How much detail can I afford in my game? Will it be rich and varied or sparse and uncluttered? How does this affect the way the game is played?

EMOTIONAL DIMENSION

1. Does my game have a significant emotional dimension? What emotions will my game world include?

2. How does emotion serve the entertainment value of my game? Is it a key element of the plot? Does it motivate characters in the game or the player himself?

3. What emotions will I try to inspire in the player? How will I do this? What will be at stake?

ETHICAL DIMENSION

1. What constitutes right and wrong in my game? What player actions do I reward and what do I punish?

2. How will I explain the ethical dimensions of the world to the player? What tells her how to behave and what is expected of her?

3. If my game world includes conflict or competition, is it represented as violence or as something else (racing to a finish, winning an economic competition, outmaneuvering the other side)?

4. What range of choices am I offering my player? Are there both violent and nonviolent ways to accomplish something? Is the player rewarded in any way for minimizing casualties, or is he punished for ignoring them?

5. In many games, the end—winning the game—justifies any means that the game allows. Do I want to define the victory conditions in such a way that not all means are acceptable?

6. Are any other ethical questions present in my game world? Can my player lie, cheat, steal, break promises, or double-cross anyone? Can she abuse, torture, or enslave anyone? Are there positive or negative consequences for these actions?

7. Does my world contain any ethical ambiguities or moral dilemmas? How does making one choice over another affect the player, the plot, and the gameplay?

8. How realistic is my portrayal of violence? Does the realism appropriately serve the entertainment value of the game?

CHAPTER 9

Creative and Expressive Play

Playing any game involves an element of self-expression because the decisions a player makes reflect his play style: cautious or reckless, aggressive or defensive, and so on. Video games can let players express themselves in the ways traditional games always have and in a variety of other ways as well. This chapter examines several types of creative and expressive play that you can build into a game: self-defining play, in which players modify the avatar that represents them in the game; constrained creative play, in which players may exercise their creativity but only within certain limits; freeform, or unconstrained, creative play; and storytelling and role-playing, in which players interact with other players in a dramatic context. We end the chapter by briefly discussing some features you may wish to include that allow players to modify your game for their own entertainment: level editors, mods, and bots.

Self-Defining Play

When a player selects a token to represent herself in *Monopoly,* she chooses an avatar and so engages in an act of self-definition. Many games allow the player to choose an avatar from a number of different ones available and to customize the avatar in various ways. Because the avatar represents the player in the game world, these activities are called *self-defining play.* Players greatly enjoy defining themselves, choosing an avatar that either resembles them physically (if it's a human character) or that is a fantasy figure with whom they identify. It isn't just a question of choosing an avatar, however; players also enjoy customizing their avatar as well.

Forms of Personality Expression

Self-defining play gives the player an opportunity to project his personality into the game world, and explore alternate identities, by means other than gameplay choices. It takes several forms:

■ **Avatar selection** allows the player to choose from a number of predefined avatars, usually at the beginning of the game. These avatars are most often humanoid characters, but in driving and flying games, they're vehicles. Many driving games start the player with a small selection of cars, motorcycles, or whatever vehicles are involved and make new choices available as the player's performance improves. You can let the player purchase a new car with winnings earned in previous races, for example. The right to choose a new and more powerful avatar serves as a reward to some players.

▨ **Avatar customization** allows the player to modify the appearance or abilities of an avatar that the game supplies by modifying its features. In role-playing games (RPGs), this often takes the form of giving the avatar new skills, clothing, weapons, and armor. In driving games, the customizable features may include the paint color of the car and its engine, transmission, tires, and brakes. Customization can occur both at the beginning of the game and through upgrades awarded or purchased as the game goes on. In this way, a player creates a unique character of her own design. Customization can be purely cosmetic or visual, as with the Nintendo Mii characters, or it can include choices about the character's attributes that may have an effect on gameplay. Younger children pay more attention to visuals than to attributes, as they are not yet used to thinking about games as systems.

▨ **Avatar construction** gives the player the greatest freedom of all; he can construct his avatar from the ground up, choosing every detail from a set of available options. Usually offered in RPGs, avatar construction allows the player to choose such features as the sex, body type, skin color, and clothing of the avatar, as well as the avatar's strength, intelligence, dexterity, and other functional qualities. The online RPG *Lord of the Rings Online* offers a particularly extensive avatar construction feature, as does the single-player RPG *The Elder Scrolls IV: Oblivion* for the PC. Some, such as *Second Life* and *Minecraft,* even let the player import his own graphics for avatars or clothing.

Understanding Attributes

The qualities that a player modifies when constructing or customizing an avatar are called *attributes.* Chapter 14, "Core Mechanics," discusses attributes in more detail, but for now, it's enough to know that an attribute is any quality that helps to describe something else. *Hair color* is an attribute of a person. *Maximum airspeed* is an attribute of an aircraft. The computer can represent an attribute as a numeric value (such as maximum airspeed) or a symbolic value (such as hair color). All attributes in a video game must be characterized in one of these two ways. Even if you create an attribute intended to describe something that we normally think of as unquantifiable, like smell, ultimately it will come down to either a numeric or a symbolic value.

You can divide attributes in a game into those that affect the gameplay, which are called *functional attributes,* and those that don't affect the gameplay, which are called *cosmetic attributes.* (Some designers prefer the term *aesthetic attributes,* but the meaning is the same.) The next two sections examine these types more closely.

FUNCTIONAL ATTRIBUTES

Functional attributes influence the gameplay through interactions with the core mechanics. Functional attributes can be further divided into *characterization attributes,* which define fundamental aspects of a character and change slowly or not at all, and *status attributes,* which give the current status of the character and may change frequently. For example, *maximum airspeed* is a characterization attribute of an aircraft, while *current airspeed* is a status attribute. For the purposes of creative play, we're interested in the characterization attributes.

You have probably heard of the six characterization attributes used in *Dungeons & Dragons:* strength, dexterity, intelligence, wisdom, charisma, and constitution. Each of these attributes affects a character's ability to perform certain actions in the game: fight, cast magic spells, charm others, withstand poisons, and many other tasks. When a *Dungeons & Dragons* player creates a character, she receives a certain number of points (usually obtained by rolling dice) to distribute among these attributes. How she distributes them—giving more to dexterity and less to intelligence, for instance—establishes the character's strengths and weaknesses. These strengths and weaknesses, in turn, determine how the player must play with the character to be successful in the game: taking advantage of the strengths and avoiding situations in which the weaknesses render the player vulnerable.

When a player sets the characterization attributes of her character, the player defines herself in a creative way. Hardcore players, whose main interest is in winning, tend to look for the setting that gives them the greatest advantage in the game—that is, to optimize the attributes' influence on the core mechanics. Casual players either don't worry about the assignments much, or they select settings that allow for interesting role-playing. A character who is highly charismatic but physically weak, for example, has to be played quite differently from a conventional warrior.

If you allow players to assign any legitimate value to their functional attributes, some players will set up their attributes in the best possible configuration, and the game will be very easy for them. You may want to prevent this to keep the game challenging. Consider the following approaches:

▪ Give players a fixed or random number of points to assign among all their attributes, as in *Dungeons & Dragons.* This allows them to make interesting choices and create an avatar who reflects their own personality or fantasies without unbalancing the game. If you generate a random number of points for the player, use a nonuniform distribution as *Dungeons & Dragons* does in order to avoid producing unusually strong or weak characters. See "Random Numbers and the Gaussian Curve" in Chapter 14.

▪ Include a set of default, or recommended, settings so players who want to get started quickly can do so without spending a lot of time setting attributes. This is especially valuable for players who don't understand how the attributes affect the gameplay anyway. They will find it frustrating to be required to set attributes when

NOTE If the player's choice of avatar or attribute settings will have an effect on the gameplay, you must make the consequences of those choices reasonably clear to the player. If you require the player to make this decision before play begins, either all choices must provide a reasonable chance of winning (even if the fastest way to win varies from one choice to another), or you should clearly mark the choices that make the gameplay easier or harder. Don't force your players to choose an avatar or set its attributes without telling them how those decisions will affect their chances of winning.

all they want to do is get into the game and start playing. They will appreciate being given a reasonable default. This is sometimes called a *quick start* mode.

■ Allow players to *earn* the right to set their character's functional attributes any way they like by completing the game with constrained attributes first. You can also offer this right explicitly as a cheat feature of the game, so players will know they're getting an unusual advantage.

Dungeons & Dragons provides one of the most familiar examples of player-adjustable functional attributes, but many, many games use them. First-person shooters typically give the player a choice of weapons, and when a player chooses a sniper rifle over a submachine gun, she is saying something important about the way she will play the game.

COSMETIC ATTRIBUTES

Cosmetic attributes don't have any effect on the player's ability to perform actions or overcome challenges; that is, they're not part of the core mechanics of the game. Cosmetic attributes exist to let the player define himself in the game world, to bring his own personal style to the avatar. The paint color of a racing car has no effect on the car's performance characteristics, but the player is apt to enjoy the game more if he can choose a color that he likes. One cosmetic attribute—shape—differentiates the tokens in *Monopoly*.

In multiplayer video games, cosmetic attributes can play a more important role because other players rely on visual appearances to make decisions. A few years ago, some bright player in a first-person shooter game got the idea to design an avatar that looked exactly like a crate. The other players assumed that they were looking at an actual crate, so they ignored it and then were surprised when they were shot by someone in a room that apparently contained only a crate. In online RPGs, players also use cosmetic attributes to identify themselves as members of a particular clan or group.

Cosmetic attributes make a game more fun at a low implementation cost. Because they don't affect the gameplay, they don't have to be tested and balanced as thoroughly as a functional attribute. Just be sure that your cosmetic attributes really *are* cosmetic. Avatar body size may sound like a cosmetic attribute, but if you later decide to take it into account when performing combat calculations (bigger people make bigger targets, for instance), then size becomes a functional attribute after all.

Typical cosmetic attributes for human characters include headgear, clothing, shoes, jewelry, hair color, eye color, skin color, and body type or size. Players typically customize paint color and decals or insignia of vehicles.

SHOULD SEX BE A FUNCTIONAL ATTRIBUTE OR A COSMETIC ATTRIBUTE?

Should the sex of an avatar have an effect on gameplay? Because men generally have more upper-body strength than women do and women are generally more dexterous than men are, you may be tempted to build these qualities directly into your core mechanics: to restrict the strength of female avatars and to restrict the dexterity of male ones.

However, unless you're making an extremely realistic simulation game, it's better not to associate bonuses or penalties with one sex or the other. First, although men as a group are *generally* stronger than women, it is not true that all men are stronger than all women. Women who exercise are often stronger than men who don't, and men who play the piano are usually more dexterous than women who don't. There are always exceptions and overlaps.

Second, video games provide a form of escapism. Players like to imagine themselves doing things that they can't do in the real world. If you impose real-world rules on what is meant to be their fantasy experience, you take some of the fun out of it.

It's better to allow the players to construct their avatars to suit their own styles of play rather than to establish an arbitrary standard connected to sex. Leave sex as a cosmetic attribute and let the players adjust their functional attributes, such as strength and dexterity, independently.

Creative Play

Many games offer the player the chance to design or build something. In the *Caesar* series, it's a Roman city; in *Spore,* it's a creature; in *Minecraft,* it's a landscape. People enjoy designing and building things, and this kind of play is the main point of construction and management simulations.

If you offer creative play, you should allow players to save their creations at any time and reload them to continue working on them. You should also let players print out their creations, take screenshots, copy them to other players' machines, and upload them to websites. Sharing creations contributes to the fun.

Computerized creative play falls into two categories, constrained creative play and freeform creative play. A computerized game necessarily restricts creative play to whatever domain the game supports—painting, composing music, animation, and so on. In freeform creative play, few or no rules limit what the player can do within the confines of the game world, although play remains constrained by the domain, the set of actions that the user interface offers, and the machine's physical limitations.

Constrained Creative Play

If the player may create only within artificial constraints imposed by the rules, her activity is called *constrained creative play*. Constraining creativity may sound undesirable, but it really just provides a structure for the player's creativity. This type of gameplay grows out of some familiar ideas: the expressive power offered by creativity tools; the growth in the number of actions available to a player as games progress; and the fact that players must overcome challenges in order to succeed. These may be combined in various ways, as the next two sections discuss.

PLAY LIMITED BY AN ECONOMY

In *SimCity,* the player can't build a whole city immediately; it costs money to zone each empty plot of land, and he can use only the money he has available. As his city prospers, he earns more money and so can establish new neighborhoods. Once he gets enough money, new features such as stadiums and airports, which were too expensive in the early stages of the game, become available to him. As long as the player continues to produce economic growth, he can make his city ever larger and add more and more facilities.

Construction and management simulations routinely implement this system of structuring the player's creativity. The player must successfully manage an economy to construct larger creations and also to get additional creative power. This is a system closely related to that found in RPGs, in which players must gain experience to learn new magic spells, and to that found in strategy games, in which players must harvest resources to perform the research necessary to get better weapons. In those genres, the economy of the game limits the player's ability to have adventures and fight wars; in creativity games, the economy limits the player's ability to create. The primary challenge in such games is successful economic management, with creative power serving as the reward for success.

This system rewards skill, granting players more exciting and powerful tools once they master the tools they already have. Educational software also uses this mechanism.

CREATING TO PHYSICAL STANDARDS

Another approach to constrained creative play gives players all the tools and resources they would like but requires them to construct an object that meets certain requirements, usually having to do with making the object perform a function. For example, *Spore* from Maxis lets players design and build virtual creatures that then interact with creatures created by other players. The player gets a set of standard parts including arms and legs, eyes and ears, and weapons such as claws. Once the player constructs a creature, she turns it loose in the game world to fight or socialize with other creatures, and she can add additional features as she earns "DNA points." Although *Spore* can animate almost anything no matter how odd-looking, it does impose some physical standards: Every creature must have a backbone and be a land animal. The game offers no way to create a creature with an exoskeleton, like an insect, or no skeleton at all, like an octopus.

The *RollerCoaster Tycoon* series requires the player to construct roller coasters in a theme park. The roller coaster must be designed in such a way that it doesn't crash or make the (virtual) riders sick but is still exciting to ride. *RollerCoaster Tycoon* combines the challenge of meeting physical standards with an economic challenge: Each element of the theme park costs money, and the player must stay within a budget.

Whenever you require the player to build to a standard and test his construction, when he fails he needs to know why—otherwise he can't learn the principles upon which you based the standards. *RollerCoaster Tycoon 2* includes a feature to show the player how high and how steep the different segments of the coaster are, so he can figure it out with a little experimentation. See **Figure 9.1**.

The physical standards of a game do not need to conform to the conventional laws of physics, however. The physics of *Minecraft* are so rich that players can build incredible things in the game world, up to and including working computers. But *Minecraft*'s physical laws are quite different from those of the real world.

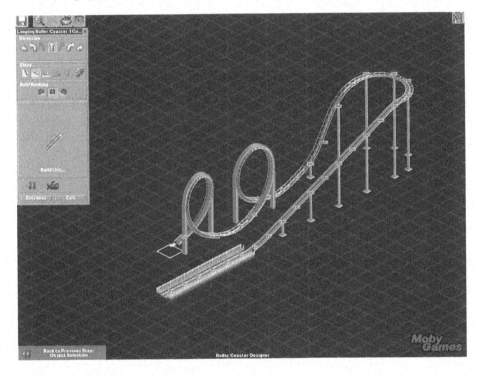

FIGURE 9.1
RollerCoaster Tycoon 2's coaster-design screen.

CREATING TO AESTHETIC STANDARDS

With an adequate physics simulation, any game can test a player's creativity against a physical standard. An architecture game can test a building both for structural integrity and also for usability—rooms with no way to get into them are useless.

Aesthetics present a much larger problem, because they don't consist of a set of universal laws in the way that physics does. To test the aesthetic quality of a player's creations, you have to set some standards of your own. Consider some of the following options:

NOTE Ubisoft's *Imagine: Fashion Designer* implements the fixed-rule mechanic but does so badly. The player designs clothing for a NPC "client." Unfortunately, the game offers no way for the player to find out exactly what the client wants. If the client refuses to accept a design, he doesn't say why, so the player has to find out by trial and error—a serious design flaw.

▪ **Test against a fixed (but hidden) set of rules that you establish.** A game about clothing design could include well-known rules about color combinations, not mixing stripes with polka dots, and using fabric textures that harmonize and complement each other. This system rewards players who know the rules and conform to them. It's good for teaching the basics, but it doesn't encourage brilliant but unconventional combinations. Nintendo's *Style Savvy* for the 3DS improves on this by giving the player non-player character (NPC) customers to make clothes for, but instead of using a single set of rules, each customer has personal preferences within certain broad categories (princess, punk, Goth, contemporary, and so on). The customer explains in general terms what she wants and the player proposes an outfit. If the outfit isn't acceptable to the customer, she gives hints about what she might like better. In effect, each customer is a puzzle to be solved. Better solutions (happier customers) produce repeat business, so the player comes to know the customers well.

▪ **Create a system of trends that the player can research.** If you want to make a game in which creative challenges change over time, such as the way fashion trends change from year to year, design a system in which the standard against which you measure the player's work fluctuates. Each attribute of the player's product could be tested against a trend with its own rate of variation, so—using the clothing example again—hemlines might move up and down over a 10-year period, and preferred fabrics might change from synthetics to natural fibers over a 20-year period. The periodicity should never be completely regular or predictable, however. The trend information should be hidden from the player but partially accessible via a research process. When I ran a series of game design workshops on this theme, participants suggested several options for doing this research. The player, in the role of a fashion designer, could attend parties within the game and listen to computer-generated gossip, some of which would include clues about current trends; he could read automatically created fashion magazines and newspapers for clues; or he could even break into other fashion designers' workshops to find out about their works in progress.

▪ **Allow the public to vote online.** You can let the players upload their creations to a website and let the community vote on them. For example, *The Sims 2: H&M Fashion Runway* allows players to vote on clothing created in *The Sims 2*. This system relieves the computer of the responsibility for determining the aesthetic quality of the player's creations, but it significantly lengthens the time scale of the game—the player may have to wait hours or days until the votes come in, unless the game has a large player base. You will also have to build a secure system that rewards players for voting and prevents vote rigging.

Freeform Creative Play and Sandbox Mode

If a game lets the player use all the facilities that it offers without any restrictions on the amount of time or resources available (other than those imposed by techno-logical limitations), then it supports *freeform creative play*. Many games that normally offer constrained creative play also include a special mode that removes ordinary constraints. This mode is called the *sandbox mode*. Sandbox mode lets the player do whatever she wants but usually doesn't offer the same rewards as the constrained mode—and may not offer any rewards at all. In this mode, the game resembles a tool more than a conventional video game.

The first *RollerCoaster Tycoon* game did not include a sandbox mode, and reviews of the game cited it as a deficiency. The developers added a sandbox mode to the later editions. Generally speaking, if you are making a game that offers creative play, you should include a sandbox mode if you can. Players enjoy them, and because sandbox modes don't interact much (if at all) with the game's core mechanics, they are fairly easy to tune.

One interesting, though very early, form of freeform creative play appeared in *Pinball Construction Set*. This game let players build and play their own virtual pinball machines. A more recent example, and certainly the most successful of all time, is the Creative mode of *Minecraft*. Players have an infinite number of blocks to build with and can fly through the air, so their construction activities are largely unconstrained. *LittleBigPlanet* allows players to create and share whole levels and a great deal of other content besides, and Microsoft's forthcoming *Project Spark* apparently plans to let players build entire video games.

FIGURE 9.2
Draw Something

Creative play isn't restricted to sandbox modes within a complicated world, though. *Draw Something* (**Figure 9.2**) is an enormously popular two-player mobile game in which one player draws a picture that represents a word he has been given by the game, and the other player has to identify the word by looking at the picture. The player doing the drawing can draw anything he likes (although his choices of colors is initially limited).

Other Forms of Expression

This sections covers forms of creative play that don't involve making something substantive (like building a virtual city or drawing a picture). Two of the major forms of expression commonly found as gameplay are role-playing and storytelling.

Role-Playing

The term *role-playing* is rather overloaded in gaming, because it can mean everything from genuine acting in an improvisational drama to simply playing a video game with *Dungeons & Dragons*-style rules. For the purposes of this chapter, role-playing means controlling an avatar character in such a way that it exhibits some of the behaviors or personality characteristics of real people.

To offer a player opportunities to act as a character, you have to first design the avatar that she will play with and decide to what extent the player can modify it. We already covered that in the section "Self-Defining Play" earlier in this chapter, and there's a great deal more in Chapter 10, "Character Development." In the process of doing this, you also have to decide what means you will give the player to make the avatar seem like a person and not just a puppet.

Actors portray characters through their voice, movements, and facial expressions. In presentational entertainment, these details are normally worked out in advance with a director, but in video games they are improvised, and of course everything has to be mediated through the game's user interface. Here are some features you might consider implementing:

- **Mood indicators.** At the moment most games don't give the player any way to change the facial expression of an avatar. A mood indicator is an icon that the player can select that allows her to indicate her avatar's state of mind in a crude sort of way. The game engine can detect the mood and have NPCs react appropriately; in a multiplayer game, other players can see it.

- **Emotes.** Massively multiplayer online role-playing games (MMORPGs) usually offer *emotes,* special animations the player can trigger to indicate an emotional state, but of course these don't have the subtlety of real body language. The dances available in *World of Warcraft* are one example. Emotes are usually used to entertain other players rather than to influence the game engine.

- **Dialogue choices.** One of the most common ways of letting players enact a character is to offer them several different ways to say the same thing in a conversation with an NPC. You can give the player aggressive, courteous, or humorous ways of replying to another character. The player's choice affects the character's attitude and may open up, or close off, different lines of conversation; it may also influence the game engine by changing the NPC's attitude toward the player.

These are just a few suggestions for ways to let the player express herself beyond choosing physical actions in the game. Role-playing allows the player to feel like she is someone else, a powerful kind of entertainment and personal self-expression.

Storytelling Play

Some players enjoy creating stories of their own, using features provided by a game, which they can then distribute online for others to read. *The Movies,* by Lionhead Software, stands as the most ambitious project of this kind to date. The purpose of the game is to let people make their own movies and share them online. *The Movies* also allows players to export movies so they can edit their films using external tools such as Adobe Premiere Pro. *The Movies* offers more expressive power than any other storytelling game yet made, but it does require a lot of effort from the players. If you want to make a game with similar features, you will have to work with the programmers to design a system that allows players to set up cameras in the game world, record the images and sounds generated by the game engine, and edit them.

The independent designer Jason Rohrer used another approach in his game *Sleep Is Death.* This game is designed for two players, the storyteller and the story-player. The teller creates a storylike experience in real time for the player and has to react to the player's actions. It has something in common with tabletop role-playing in that respect, but it avoids all the number crunching and the emphasis on quests and magical items. The game is small and the graphics are retro, but *Sleep Is Death* got very good reviews from a number of game publications and is well worth your time to investigate.

But you don't have to build a complex storytelling mechanism for someone to play with. *The Sims* proved to be a huge success with a much simpler system: Players can create characters and construct houses for them to live in, and then initiate events by giving commands to the characters. *The Sims* also lets players capture screen shots from the game, put captions under them, organize them into storyboards, and upload them to a website for others to see. Telling stories this way requires much less complex software than *The Movies* uses, and the players don't have to know how to edit video.

An even easier solution involves generating a log of the player's activities in text form. She can then edit this log any way she likes, turning her raw game actions and dialogue into narrative form.

Game Modifications

To give your players the utmost creative freedom with your game, you can permit them to modify the game itself—to redesign it themselves. Game modifications, or *mods,* are extremely popular with the dedicated gamer community and almost an obligatory feature of any large multiplayer networked game (though not persistent worlds, because in those games the company must maintain control of the game world).

Providing the player with mod-building tools also makes good business sense. Your game's original content can keep people interested for only a certain amount of time, but if people can build mods that use your game engine (as they can with the *Unreal* and *Half-Life 2* engines), people will continue to buy your game just to be able to play the mods.

Allowing for mods is more of a programmer's problem than a designer's problem, so this book does not discuss them in much detail.

DANGERS OF ALLOWING MODS

Mods bring with them certain risks. When you allow players to modify your game, you risk the possibility that they will create a mod that includes material you would never use yourself: pornographic or racist content, for example. You could find people distributing a highly offensive variant of your game, but one that still displays your company's name and logo when it starts up. The public might be sophisticated enough to realize that a game designer shouldn't be held responsible for the contents of homemade mods, but then again it might not be. The general public doesn't know much about video game development, and the politicians who seek to regulate video games know even less.

There are also questions about the intellectual property ownership of game mods. The game's publisher will probably assume, not unreasonably, that it owns the game and any modification of the game as well; it certainly can't afford to let control of the game pass to someone else. On the other hand, players who mod games extensively may feel as if they are entitled to own the fruits of their own labor. This isn't really a design issue, but if you're planning to allow mods to your game, you may want to discuss it with the lawyers who draw up the game's licensing terms.

Level Editors

A level editor allows players to construct their own levels for a game. Some level editors permit players to define only a new landscape; others allow them to define new characters as well; and a few go so far as to permit rebuilding the entire game. Generally, however, a good level editor lets the player construct a completely new landscape, place challenges in it, and write scripts that the game engine can operate. If you work on a large game for commercial sale, your team will almost certainly include tools programmers who will build a level editor for the level designers to use. To make the level editor available to the players, rather than useful only as an in-house tool, you must make sure it is as robust and well-designed as the game software itself. Two superb level editors that you should study are the 2D *StarCraft* Campaign Editor, which is included with *StarCraft,* and the Hammer 3D editor that comes with *Half-Life 2*. *Minecraft*'s world-building tools are worth a look, too. For further reading about level editors and other design tools, see Richard Rouse's article "Designing Design Tools" in the *Gamasutra* developers' webzine (Rouse, 2000).

Bots

A *bot* is an artificially intelligent opponent that the player can program for himself. (*Bot* also has a secondary meaning: a program that help players cheat at multiplayer networked games. This section is about the other kind.) By building bots, players can create tougher and smarter opponents than those that normally ship with the game (usually a first-person shooter). Some players use bots as sparring partners for practice before playing against real people in online tournaments. *Quake III Arena* contains a great deal of support for bots, and a number of third-party tools have been built to help players create them.

Summary

Players love to express themselves and to build things. This chapter looked at options for self-expression through avatar selection, customization, and creation. It also examined both freeform and constrained creative play, and discussed some of the different kinds of constraints that you may impose on a player's creativity to produce challenges. We noted some options for permitting storytelling play and ended with a brief discussion about allowing players to modify your game. With these tools in hand, you should be able to add support for creative play to your game.

Design Practice EXERCISES

1. Using a game that you are familiar with and that permits avatar customization or construction (or one that your instructor assigns), identify and document those functional and cosmetic attributes of the avatar that the player may modify. In the case of the functional attributes, indicate how they affect the gameplay.

2. Think of an idea for a game that permits the player to construct something you have not seen in commercial games (no cities, buildings, or vehicles). Assume that you will constrain the player's abilities via an economy but allow him to earn new tools and features for his construction over time. Design a set of elementary parts from which the item may be constructed, and specify a price for each part. Include a number of upgrades—more expensive parts that replace cheaper versions. Write a short paper explaining the domain in which the player will be creating, and supply your list of parts, giving them in the order in which the player will earn the ability to buy them (cheapest to most expensive). Also indicate in a general way how the player can use the item he constructs to earn money. Your instructor will inform you of the scope of the exercise.

3. Choose a domain in which the player must construct something to meet an aesthetic standard for which a known set of aesthetic rules exists in the real world, such as architecture, clothing design, music, interior decoration, landscaping, or a domain that your instructor assigns. Research your chosen domain to learn its aesthetic rules. (Because many such rules change over time, you may choose a period from history if you can find adequate documentation.) Be careful not to confuse rules about usability with those about aesthetics. Write a short paper explaining your domain, including the range of choices that the player may make in constructing something, and document the aesthetic rules. Provide references to your sources.

Design Practice QUESTIONS

1. What features do you want to include to allow the player to define herself in the game: avatar selection, customization, or creation from the ground up? What attributes can she change, if any?

2. How will you make clear to the player the possible consequences of his avatar customization decisions so that he can make informed choices? Where will you provide this information?

3. If you offer creative play, what will its domain be? What limitations will the machine impose?

4. Do you plan to offer constrained creative play? If so, what will be the constraining factor or factors—economics, physics, or aesthetics? Will the game provide a growth path to gradually free the player of constraints? In the case of aesthetics, how will you implement an aesthetic judgment mechanism, and how will the results of that judgment become clear to the player? Will aesthetically successful (however you determine that) creations earn more money, win prizes, produce points, or gain some other reward?

5. Will you offer freeform creative play? If so, will it be part of ordinary play, or will it be a separate sandbox mode? If you do offer freeform creative play, can the player's creations affect the gameplay?

6. Does your game include features for role-playing or storytelling play? What will they be? How can you seamlessly integrate such features into the rest of the game?

7. Do you plan to allow mods? What will you let players modify? Can they create new levels, bots, or narrative material? What tools will you want to ship to support these activities?

8. How will you create a sense of community between the players and allow them to share their creations with others?

CHAPTER 10

Character Development

It is our choices, Harry, that show what we truly are, far more than our abilities.

—J. K. ROWLING, *HARRY POTTER AND THE CHAMBER OF SECRETS*

Characters play a key role in entertaining us in many video games. The character that we play and those we interact with help make the game world believable to us. Not all games need characters, but they add life and warmth to a game, and they're essential to any game that includes a story.

This chapter looks at how to design compelling and believable characters. We'll start by examining the characteristics of the avatar character, both player-designed and built-in. Next we'll look at the issues inherent in gender-specific character design, paying attention to the common game stereotypes you should avoid. We'll also look at the attributes associated with characters—visual, behavioral, and audible— and how you can use them to design your own characters. We'll also talk about the difference between art-driven character design and story-driven character design, and why you might prefer one over the other. A section on the importance of good audio design for your characters concludes the chapter.

The Goals of Character Design

In many genres, games structure gameplay around characters. Action games (especially the fighting and platform subgenres), adventure games, action-adventure hybrids, and role-playing games all use characters extensively to entertain. Players need well-designed characters to identify with and care about—heroes to cheer and villains to boo. The best games also include complex characters who aren't heroes or villains but fall somewhere in between, characters designed to intrigue the player or make the player think. If characters aren't interesting or appealing, the game is less enjoyable.

Many factors combine to determine the degree to which a character appeals to people. A character need not be attractive in the conventional sense of being pleasant to look at, but he must be competently constructed—well drawn or well described. His various attributes should work together harmoniously; his body, clothing, voice, animations, facial expressions, and other characteristics should all join to express him and his role clearly to the player. (However, disharmonious elements can be introduced for humor's sake, as with the cute but foul-mouthed squirrel in the *Conker* series.) Characters should be distinctive rather than derivative. Even a stereotypical character should have something that sets him apart from others of the same type.

A good character should also be credible. Players come to know a character through her appearance and actions, and if that character then does something at odds with her apparent persona, players won't believe it. An evil demon from the underworld can't be seen worrying about orphans. For that matter, neither can James Bond. Simple characters must be consistent. Richer characters, with more human frailties, may be more inconsistent, but even so, players must feel that the character holds certain core values that she will not violate.

Avatar characters have an extra burden: The player must want to step into their shoes, to identify with them, and to play as them. The next section discusses avatars in more detail.

TIP A good character is the most financially valuable part of any video game's intellectual property.

Important business considerations enter into character design as well. Customers identify many games by their key characters; that's why so many games take their name directly from their characters, from *Pac-Man* to the latest in the *Ratchet & Clank* series. Good characters occupy what the marketing people call *mindshare*, consumer awareness of a product or brand. You can use the character in a book, movie, or TV series; you can sell clothes and toys based on a character; you can use a character to advertise other products. It's more difficult to license a game's world or its gameplay than its characters.

The goal of character design, then, is to create characters that people *find appealing* (even if the character is a villain, like Darth Vader), that people can *believe in*, and that the player can *identify with* (particularly in the case of avatar characters). If possible, the character should do these things well enough, and be distinctive enough, to be highly memorable to the players.

The Relationship Between Player and Avatar

Lara Croft is attractive because of, not despite of, her glossy blankness—that hyper-perfect, shiny, computer look. She is an abstraction, an animated conglomeration of sexual and attitudinal signs—breasts, hotpants, shades, thigh holsters—whose very blankness encourages the viewer's psychological projection. Beyond the bare facts of her biography, her perfect vacuity means we can make Lara Croft into whoever we want her to be.

—STEVEN POOLE, "LARA'S STORY"

The game industry uses the term *avatar* to refer to a character in a game who serves as a protagonist under the player's control. Most action and action-adventure games provide exactly one avatar. Many role-playing games allow the player to manage a party of characters and switch control from one to another, but if winning a role-playing game is contingent upon the survival of a particular member of the party, then that character is often the player's avatar (though some games require that more than one character survive). The player usually sees the avatar onscreen more than any other character (except in first-person games). Displaying the avatar requires the largest number of animations, which must also be the smoothest animations, or you risk distracting the player. People are very sensitive to the movement of human beings, and flaws in the animation will break their immersion. The avatar's movements must be attractive, not clumsy, unless clumsiness is part of the avatar's character.

The nature of the player's relationship with the avatar varies considerably from game to game. Whether the player designed the avatar himself, whether the game displays the avatar as a visible and audible presence, how the player controls the avatar's movements, and many other factors influence that relationship.

Player-Designed Avatar Characters

Whereas most games have an established character as the player's avatar, role-playing games, especially multiplayer online ones, almost always give players considerable freedom to design an avatar to their own specifications. They can choose the avatar's race, sex, body type, hair, clothing, and other physical attributes, as well as a large number of other details, such as strength and dexterity, that have a direct effect on the way the avatar performs in challenging situations.

Figure 10.1 shows an example character creation screen from *The Lord of the Rings Online*. In such games, the avatar is a sort of mask the player wears, a persona she adopts for the purposes of the game. Because the player herself designs the avatar, the avatar has no personality other than what the player chooses to create. In such games, then, your task as a game designer is not to create avatars for the players but to provide the necessary tools to allow players to create avatars for themselves. This feature is especially useful (and most commonly found) in multiplayer online games in which players interact socially with one another through their avatars. The more opportunities for personal expression you can offer, the more the players will enjoy exercising their creativity. This is particularly true for children and younger people, who are at an age at which playing with identity is a part of their own development.

FIGURE 10.1
The Lord of the Rings Online gives the player many options for designing her own avatar.

Specific and Nonspecific Avatars

In games in which the player does *not* get to design or choose an avatar but must use one supplied by the game, the relationship between the player and the avatar varies depending on how completely you, the designer, specified the avatar's appearance and other qualities.

The earliest adventure games, which were text-based, were written as if the player *himself* inhabited the game world. However, because the game didn't know anything about the player, it couldn't depict him or say much about him. Such avatars were *nonspecific*—that is, the designer didn't specify anything about them.

The nonspecific avatar does not belong entirely to the past, however. Gordon Freeman, the hero of *Half-Life,* does not speak and is never even seen in the game (although he does appear on the box). The designers did this deliberately; *Half-Life,* a first-person shooter in a world with no mirrors, offers Gordon as an empty shell for the player to inhabit.

However, many game designers find this model too limiting. They want to develop games in which the avatar has a personality of his own and is someone who belongs in the game world rather than just being a visitor there. It's awkward to write a story around a character whose personality the designer knows nothing about. Besides, designers often want to show the avatar on the screen. As soon as you depict a person visually, he begins to exhibit some individuality.

Modern games with strong storylines use detailed characters who have histories and personalities of their own. Max Payne, the lead character in the series of the same name, comes equipped with a past and a number of personal relationships that affect his life. Nancy Drew from the many *Nancy Drew* games (and of course all the books that preceded them) is another good example. These are *specific* avatars, and the player's relationship with them is more complex than it is with a nonspecific avatar. With a specific avatar, the player's relationship to her is more like that of the reader's relationship to the protagonist of a novel. The reader is not the protagonist, but the reader does identify with her. The difference is that in a game, the player can help and guide the protagonist rather than just read about her. But—at least in some games—the specific avatar is also free to reject the player's guidance. If the player asks April Ryan (from The *Longest Journey)* to do something dangerous, she refuses with comments such as, "That doesn't seem like a good idea." Specific avatars sometimes have minds of their own.

Between the two extremes of nonspecific and specific avatars lies a middle ground in which the avatar is only partially characterized—specified to a certain degree but not fully detailed. For many games, especially those *without* strong stories, it's better to create the avatar as a sort of cartoonish figure (even if he's depicted realistically). Many avatars in action games fit this description. Mario isn't a real plumber; he's a cartoon plumber in the same way that Bugs Bunny is a cartoon rabbit rather than a real one. Lara Croft, too, has more looks than personality; she's a stand-in for the player, not a three-dimensional human being. Generally speaking, the more perfectly photorealistic characters are, the more the players will tend to regard them as being someone other than themselves, independent human beings, and expect them to behave as such. This isn't always a good thing, as it causes players to exercise more critical judgment than we might want them to. Nobody objects to a cartoon plumber jumping on cartoon turtles, but they probably would if both Mario and the turtles were photorealistic.

The Effects of Different Control Mechanisms

The way a player feels about an avatar depends somewhat on how the player controls the avatar in the game. In the case of Nancy Drew and the avatars in all other point-and-click adventure and computer role-playing games, the player's control is *indirect;* he doesn't steer the avatar around but points to where he wants the avatar to go, and the avatar walks there of her own accord. The player feels more like a disembodied guide and friend than a personal inhabitant of the game world. This is also how units move in strategy games: The player doesn't steer them; the player gives them orders.

Lara Croft and Mario, in contrast, are under *direct* control: The player steers their bodies through the game world, running, swimming, jumping, and fighting as necessary. The player becomes them and revels in the abilities that they have that she does not. But she doesn't worry too much about their feelings. That's partly because Lara and Mario are only partially specified, but it's also because exercising so much control makes them more like puppets than people.

Designing Your Avatar Character

As you design the avatar for your game, think about how you want the player to relate to him. Do you want an entirely nonspecific avatar, really no more than a control mechanism for the player; a partially-specified avatar, which the player sees and knows a little about, but who doesn't have an inner life; or a fully specified avatar, separate from the player, an individual with a personality of his own? The more detail you supply, the more independent your avatar will be. Consider psychological and social detail as well as visual detail. How much will he talk? The more he talks, the more we know about him; the more we know, the more he becomes differentiated from us. Gordon Freeman never talks; Mario and Lara Croft don't talk much; April Ryan talks a lot. Gordon *is* the player; Mario and Lara are representatives of the player; April is a person in her own right.

Also think about how the player will control your avatar: directly or indirectly? Your decision will have a profound effect on the player's identification with the avatar. With indirect control, the avatar is distinctly *someone else,* with a mind of his own; with direct control, the avatar is to some degree an extension of the player himself. Your job is to find the right balance for each particular game, to create an avatar whose characteristics serve your goals for the player-avatar relationship. The player will see the avatar all the time; it must be a character the player can identify

NOTE If you are making a game based on a licensed character such as a Marvel hero or a Disney princess, you won't make these decisions. The player will already have a relationship with the avatar through her relationship with the character in other media.

with and must possess qualities he is likely to appreciate, such as bravery, intelligence, decency, and a sense of humor.

The worst decision you can make is to create an avatar with qualities that players actively dislike. Squall Leonhart, the protagonist of *Final Fantasy VIII,* seemed at first to be self-absorbed and obnoxious, and those players who weren't willing to put up with his attitude stopped playing the game. This is one reason designers make games with only semispecific characters. Link, from the *Zelda* series, is a semispecific character (though perhaps a little more detailed than Mario). We don't know enough about Link to form much of an opinion of his character, either positive or negative.

Visual Appearances

In modern video games, almost all the characters have a visible manifestation in the game. The exceptions are nonspecific avatars who view the world only in the first-person perspective (like Gordon Freeman) and disembodied characters who sometimes speak to the character (via headphones, telepathy, or other means) but are never seen. In all other cases, you will need to display your characters, and the way those characters look will have an enormous effect on the way players feel about them.

Many designers, especially those who are visually inclined, start to create a character by thinking about her visual appearance first. If the character doesn't exhibit a complex personality and she doesn't change much during the course of the game— either behaviorally or visually—then this is often the best way to do it. Such an approach is called *art-driven character design.* It works well for games with fairly simple, cartoonlike characters. Art-driven design also makes a lot of sense if you hope to exploit the character in a number of other media besides video games, such as comic books and toys.

Story-driven character design, an alternative to art-driven, is defined in the following section. You will use both visual and behavioral design techniques when creating your character, but you will probably find that you prefer either the art-driven or the story-driven approach. This may depend on the genre of game that you are making.

Character Physical Types

We'll begin with the basic body types of game characters and some of the ways that they may be depicted.

HUMANOIDS, NONHUMANOIDS, AND HYBRIDS

Characters in video games fall into three general categories: human or humanoid; nonhumanoid; and hybrids. (A small number of characters appear as disembodied voices or animate objects, but they aren't included here because this section is specifically about visual design.) Humanoid characters have two arms, two legs, and one head, and their bodies and faces are organized like a human's. The more you deviate from this arrangement, the less human a character seems. Truly human characters can have either realistic human proportions or exaggerated ones in a cartoon style, but if you use cartoon proportions, you should use a cartoon drawing style as well. A photorealistic human with exaggerated proportions will read as disturbingly deformed.

Nonhumanoid characters include those shaped like vehicles or machines (often indicated by the presence of metal and wheels), animals, or monsters. In the *Star Wars* universe, R2-D2 is clearly a machine, albeit one with endearing qualities. R2 has three legs with wheels on the bottom, a variety of mechanical appendages, and a head, but no real face. The Daleks of *Doctor Who* are also machines, at least as seen from the outside, for similar reasons. Animals, even imaginary ones, look organic; the presence of wings or more than two legs distinguishes them from humanoids. Skin covered with fur, scales, or feathers further sets them apart. Many video game characters, such as Crash Bandicoot, have animal-like heads but humanoid bodies; they're still classified as humanoids rather than animals. Designers often modify the faces of animal-like humanoids, shortening the muzzle and bringing the eyes to the front, to make them more like humans as well.

Monsters are distinguished by such characteristics as significantly asymmetric bodies, a different facial arrangement (eyes below the nose or jaws that move sideways, for example), and extreme proportions. Many of their qualities are borrowed from orders of animals that humans in some societies find frightening or repulsive: reptiles, insects, and the more bizarre sea creatures. Claws, fangs, oozing slime, and an armor-like exoskeleton all add to a monster's appearance of alienness and danger. The creature from the *Alien* movies exhibited all of these distinguishing features.

Hybrids include beings such as mermaids or human/machine combinations. Davros, the creator of the Daleks, has a humanoid torso and head but a mechanical bottom half. The Borg from *Star Trek* and C-3PO from *Star Wars* read as humanoids rather than true hybrids, however, because they still follow the rules for humans: two arms, two legs, and one head in the appropriate configuration. Cylons, from the popular *Battlestar Galactica* series, are hybrid machines/humans. In the latest incarnation of this show, they push the boundaries of how visuals can deceive the viewer as to what is human and what is not.

CARTOONLIKE QUALITIES

Relatively few art-driven characters are drawn with ordinary proportions or with photorealistic features. Rather, they are exaggerated in various ways that should be familiar to you from comic books and cartoons. These exaggerations serve as convenient symbols to indicate a character stereotype. Four of the most common are *cool, tough, cute,* and *goofy*. A character isn't always limited to one of these qualities, however; he can sometimes shift from one to another as circumstances require.

CHAPTER 10

▪ **Cool** characters never get too upset about anything. The essence of cool is detachment. If something irritates them, it's only for a moment. A rebellious attitude toward authority often accompanies cool. Cool characters often wear sunglasses and their body language is languid; when not doing anything else, they slouch. Frequently clever or wisecracking, cool characters may, depending on the situation, use their wits rather than brute force to overcome an obstacle. Ratchet, from the *Ratchet & Clank* series, exemplifies the cool character. Though cool characters are often drawn as insouciant when standing still, their game actions (jumping, running) are usually fast and focused.

▪ **Tough** characters exemplify physical aggression. Often male—although Lara Croft would be classed as a tough character—they are frequently drawn with exaggerated height and bulk. They use large, expansive gestures and tend to talk with their fists. Tough characters are frequently *hypersexualized* as well (see the next section). Ryu, from the *Street Fighter* series, is a tough character. Yosemite Sam is a tough character whose small stature leavens his toughness with a comic quality. The birds in *Angry Birds* are also tough but funny—they're just birds, after all. Animations for tough characters are usually big and abrupt, fast moving, and aggressive. Postures that lean forward, implying motion and action even where there is none, are common.

▪ **Cute** characters are drawn with the proportions of human babies or baby animals: large eyes and oversized heads. They have rounded rather than angular bodies, dress in light colors, and have a general demeanor of cheerfulness, although they may exhibit moments of irritation or determination. Mario is the ultimate cute video game character. Animations of cute characters usually allow characters to achieve things that they physically could not accomplish in the real world: jumping wide gaps, climbing long ropes, firing weapons larger than themselves. They usually look innocent and detached.

▪ **Goofy** characters have slightly odd proportions and funny looking, inefficient walks and other movements. Their behavior is largely comedic. Like cool characters, they are seldom upset by anything for long, but their physical awkwardness means that they are definitely not cool. The Disney character named Goofy is a perfect example; among video games, Crash Bandicoot is a goofy character. Animations for a goofy character in a game sometimes include the goofiness, as long as it doesn't affect the player's experience of the play. Tripping while running can be humorous, but if the character dies because of the visual joke, the player won't appreciate it. Instead, save the humor for cut-scenes or idle moments where there is no game impact.

These are, of course, far from all the cartoonlike character types possible; consider the mock-heroism of Dudley Do-Right and George of the Jungle, the twisted evil of the witch in *Snow White,* and so on. **Figure 10.2** shows a variety of cartoonlike characters.

FIGURE 10.2
Several cartoon characters from video games and other media

Note that for the most part, these are Western classifications. Art styles vary wildly among different cultures, particularly for characters. Japanese animation often uses large eyes and tiny mouths for characters, but the mouths sometimes swell to huge sizes when they shout, which looks grotesque to Americans. The animé style also sometimes gives cute childlike faces to sexually provocative women, producing somewhat disturbing results—to Western eyes, at least. European cartoon characters often seem slightly grotesque to Americans, too. Asterix and Tintin, two exceptions, enjoy huge worldwide success. If you want your game to sell in a number of different countries, study those countries' native cartoon and comic styles closely to make sure you don't violate local expectations. For example, in the West, cartoon characters often have only four fingers and nobody really notices it, but Crash Bandicoot's four fingers seem like a mutation to the Japanese. When the game is localized for Japan, Crash's artwork has to be changed to give him five fingers.

The design of art-driven characters depends considerably on the target audience. For example, the adjectives *cute* and *scary* mean different things to a five-year-old and a 25-year-old. *Doom*-style monsters certainly won't go down well in a Mario-esque adventure.

Conker's Bad Fur Day presented an interesting twist on this rule. Rare, the game's developer, transplanted their cute children's characters into a game for adults (or rather, adolescent boys), full of bad language and vulgar jokes. But it's a one-way transformation; you wouldn't want to insert the jokes into a game genuinely intended for children.

COOL WITHOUT ATTITUDE

Kids hate goody-two-shoes characters just as much as parents dislike characters with foul attitudes—but just because a character doesn't cop an attitude with authority figures doesn't make him a goody-two-shoes. The *Scooby Doo* kids provide a pretty good example of characters who retain their appeal with kids despite not being rebellious. Kids like to identify with the characters' intelligence, bravery, and resourcefulness. Scooby is funny, too, because despite his large size, he is a coward. But because he's a dog and not a child, Scooby doesn't get picked on or treated with contempt for being scared. This is a very clever piece of character design: Children know that no matter how scary the situation is, Scooby is even more scared than they are, so they can feel virtuous for being braver than he is.

HYPERSEXUALIZED CHARACTERS

Hypersexualization refers to the practice of exaggerating the sexual attributes of men and women in order to make them more sexually appealing, at least to teenagers. Male characters get extra-broad chests and shoulders, huge muscles, prominent jaws, and oversized hands and feet. Female characters get enormous breasts, extremely narrow waists, and wide hips. Skimpy clothing lets them display their physical attributes as much as possible, and sexually suggestive poses further drive the point home (as if there were any doubt). Both sexes boast unrealistic height, with heads that seem disproportionately small and with extra-long legs. High heels often further exaggerate women's height.

Kratos, from the *God of War* games, typifies the hypersexualized male character, as do most of the male characters in fighting games. Lara Croft is the best-known example of a hypersexualized female character among the hundreds populating any number of video games. Comic book superheroes (male and female) are also traditionally hypersexualized, a quality that got comic books into trouble with the U.S. Congress in the 1950s.

Such characters obviously sell well to young men and teenage boys, but by now these images are clichéd. So many stereotypical he-men and babes have been created over the years that it's difficult to tell them apart, and any new game that relies on such images runs the risk of being lumped in with all the others. Using such characters may actually obscure any technological or game design advances you have made. Finally, hypersexualized characters really appeal only to a puerile audience. They actively discourage older players, who've seen it all before, and female players. Strip clubs are male preserves; a character that looks as if she just stepped out of one sends clear signals that female players are not wanted or welcome. (To give her her due, Lara Croft's hiking boots, backpack, and khaki clothing do set her apart from the common run of women clad in chain-mail bikinis or skintight leather.)

NOTE In 1954, American psychiatrist Frederic Wertham published a book titled *Seduction of the Innocent* in which he alleged the bulging muscles and tight clothing of comic-book superheroes promoted homosexuality, and that Wonder Woman's strength and independence meant that she must be a lesbian. Following Congressional investigations, the American comics industry self-censored its products for many years.

In short, avoid hypersexualizing characters just for their titillation value. It limits your market and seldom adds much. You might get away with it if it's intentionally done for laughs; putting Cate Archer into a 1960s retro catsuit worked out well for the designers of *No One Lives Forever* because of the game's humorous context. But *No One Lives Forever* was also an excellent game in its own right. Big breasts won't sell a poor game, as the developers of *Space Bunnies Must Die!* discovered.

Clothing, Weapons, Symbolic Objects, and Names

When designing ordinary human beings, body shape is only the beginning. In the real world, we have only a limited ability to change our bodies, so instead we express our personal style through things that we hang on the outside of our bodies: clothing and accessories. In a video game, the player can more easily see who is whom—especially important in situations requiring snap decisions, like a shooter game—if characters' clothing and props uniquely identify them. Indiana Jones wears a certain hat and khaki clothes, and he carries a bullwhip. Darth Vader's flowing black cape, forbidding helmet, and even the sound of his breathing instantly set him apart from everyone else in the *Star Wars* universe. Crucial for avatars, this rule applies to a lesser extent to minor characters.

A character's choice of weapons tells a lot about him, too. On the one hand, a meat cleaver or an axe is a tool repurposed for use as a weapon, so it suggests crude and bloody violence. On the other hand, a rapier's thin elegance suggests a dueling aristocrat. Indiana Jones can use his bullwhip to get himself out of all kinds of scrapes; it's a symbol of his resourcefulness. That he generally prefers the nonlethal bullwhip and carries a pistol only as a backup (in the movies, anyway) sends the message that he'd rather not kill if he doesn't have to.

Hairstyles and jewelry tend to remain the same in games with specific avatars even when the avatar's clothing changes. Both function as good identifiers if you make them visible and distinctive enough. Jewelry, in particular, has a long history of magic, meaning, or mysticism: Consider the significance of wedding rings, military medals, the crucifixes of Christianity, and the steel bracelets of the Sikhs. If you want a magical power or status transferred to another character, you can easily do it by transferring a crown, ring or chain of gold, or gems. You don't necessarily have to give jewelry a meaning; as long as it's visually distinctive, it will help to identify the character and define her style.

> ### DESIGN RULE Don't Add Too Much Detail
>
> Don't overwork a character by adding too many distinctive visual features. Two or three is usually enough—more than that and she will start to look ridiculous.

You can also give your characters distinctive names and ethnicities if appropriate. Consider how the men of Sergeant Rock's Easy Company in the old DC Comics World War II series reflected the ethnic diversity of America with names such as Dino Manelli, Izzy Cohen, and "Reb" Farmer—not to mention the square-jawed American hero, Sgt. Frank Rock.

There is a flip side to using such obvious names. Naming your characters in such a fashion lends them a cartoonlike style. This may be exactly what you need for some games, but for others, it is not necessarily such a good fit. If realism is your aim, for instance, then such an unrealistic collection of names, each obviously chosen to represent an ethnicity or a stereotypical group, cheapens the final result.

Names do not have to spell out explicitly the character's persona. The name of Sylvester Boots, the hero of *Anachronox,* says little or nothing about his personality, though his nickname, Sly, is altogether more revealing. Lara Croft's name, although it does not immediately seem to indicate anything about the character, does (to English sensibilities, at least) imply a degree of upper-class Englishness.

CONCEPT ART AND MODEL SHEETS

Concept art consists of drawings made early in the design process to give people an idea of what something in the game will look like—most often, a character. Many people involved in the game design, development, and production process will need such pictures. This includes everyone from the programmers (who might need to see a vehicle before they can correctly model its performance characteristics in software) to the marketing department (who will want to know what images they can use to help sell the game). By creating a number of different versions of a character, you can compare their different qualities and choose the one you like the best to be implemented by the game's modeling and animation teams.

Concept art shouldn't take too long to draw—minutes, not hours. The object isn't to produce final artwork; the concept drawings shouldn't end up in the final product at all. Rather, its purpose is to explain and inspire.

Figure 10.3 shows a character drawn by artist Björn Hurri. Told only to draw an imaginary Mongol horsewoman as the hero of an action-adventure game, and without any reference materials, he made a number of key decisions about her age, features, clothing, and weapons, all of which are visible in the picture. Her emotional temperament comes through in the image as well—this is not a woman to be trifled with. Good concept art like this definitely bears out the old adage that a picture is worth a thousand words.

Another visualization tool that you should consider using is the *model sheet,* a traditional animator's device. A model sheet shows a number of different poses for a single character all on one page, representing different emotions and attitudes through his or her facial expression and body language. This lets you compare one with another and gives you more of an overall feel for the character than a single image can do. **Figure 10.4** is a model sheet from *The Act,* a coin-op game by Cecropia, Inc. that uses hand-drawn animation.

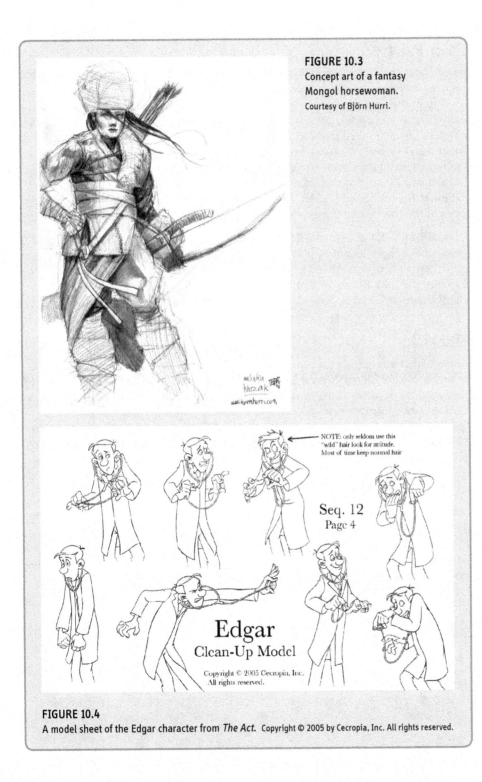

FIGURE 10.3
Concept art of a fantasy
Mongol horsewoman.
Courtesy of Björn Hurri.

FIGURE 10.4
A model sheet of the Edgar character from *The Act*. Copyright © 2005 by Cecropia, Inc. All rights reserved.

Color Palette

As you work on your character's appearance, also think about creating a color palette for her—specifically, for her clothing. People in games seldom change clothes, which saves money on art development and helps to keep them visually distinctive. In the early *Tomb Raider* games, Lara Croft wore a teal-colored shirt unique to her; no other object or character used that color. If you spotted teal, you'd found Lara. Comic-book superheroes furnish another particularly strong example. Superman wears a lot of red in his cape, boots, and shorts; blue in his suit; and a small amount of yellow in his belt and *S* logo. Batman wears dark blue, black, and again a small amount of yellow as the background to his logo. Characters can share a palette if the proportions of the colors vary from individual to individual.

Choose your color palette to reflect your character's attitudes and emotional temperament. As upholder of "truth, justice, and the American way," Superman's colors are bright and cheery; the red and blue of his uniform recall the American flag. Batman, the Dark Knight of Gotham City—a much grittier, more run-down place than Superman's Metropolis—dresses in more somber colors.

Sidekicks

Hero characters are sometimes accompanied by sidekicks. A tough hero may travel with a cute sidekick (or vice versa) to provide some variety and comic relief. The cheerful look of Miles "Tails" Prower, the two-tailed fox who accompanies Sonic the Hedgehog, complements Sonic's expression of determination and mischief. Sidekicks appear in many action games: *Jak and Daxter, Ratchet & Clank,* and so on. Link from the *Zelda* series has had various sidekicks. Banjo and Kazooie were, in *Banjo-Kazooie,* really only one avatar; they could only work together (Kazooie rode around inside Banjo's backpack). Later in the series, they began to operate independently some of the time.

Sidekicks offer several benefits. They allow you to give the player additional moves and other actions that would not be believable in a single character; they extend the emotional range of the game by showing the player a character with a different personality from the hero; and they can give the player information she wouldn't necessarily get any other way. Link's fairy in *The Legend of Zelda: Ocarina of Time,* for example, doesn't do very much, but she offers valuable advice at key points in the game.

Additional Visual Design Resources

This is not a book about drawing or modeling, so it can't address the actual techniques of creating character artwork. However, these crafts are an essential part of the process of character design, especially if you prefer the art-driven approach. If you would like to know more, consult *Digital Modeling,* by William Vaughan (Vaughan, 2012), and *Digital Character Animation 3,* by George Maestri (Maestri, 2006).

You don't have to purchase expensive software to learn to draw and model characters. There are many free tools available. Among the best are GIMP, the GNU Image Manipulation Program, for editing bitmap pictures; Inkscape, for editing vector graphics (line drawings); and Blender, a 3D modeling tool that approaches the quality of some packages costing thousands of dollars. Sculptris is useful for sculpture. You can also download student editions of the industry-standard Maya and 3ds Max applications from Autodesk. Although the student versions of these commercial tools may be restricted in some ways, it will be useful to learn how to use them if you want to get a job doing 3D modeling.

Character Depth

The visual appearance of a character makes the most immediate impact on the player, and you can convey a lot of information about the character through his appearance, but you can't convey everything. Nor does his appearance necessarily determine what role he will play in a story, how he will behave in different situations, or how he will interact with the game's core mechanics. To address those issues, you have to give your attention to deeper questions about who the character is and how he behaves.

If you begin your character design with the character's role, personality, and behavior rather than his appearance, you are doing *story-driven character design*. In story-driven design, you decide these things first, and only then let the artists begin to develop a physical appearance for the character. Artists often like to work from a detailed description; it helps them to understand and visualize the character.

Even games that you would not expect to have fully developed characters can gain much by including them. Konami's game *Powerful Golf* for the Nintendo DS, shown in **Figure 10.5**, has customizable characters, a story, and a variety of mini-games. The addition of these elements makes it more than a simple sports game. The player chooses a character and begins to identify with her even though the artwork is very abstract. This creates a greater sense of immersion in the game. The player chooses her own friends—or enemies—from the other characters at will, and her choices do affect the gameplay.

CHAPTER 10

Interaction between characters is one of the most interesting aspects of stories— sometimes more so than the actual plot. Although a plot details the path of a story (which is covered in the next chapter), the characters' interactions add the flavor and subtlety that differentiate a well-crafted story from a fifth-grade English composition assignment.

FIGURE 10.5
Powerful Golf is a sports game that includes real character development.

Role, Attitudes, and Values

Every character in a story plays a role, just as every character in a movie plays a role, even if only as an extra. The moment a character appears for any reason, the audience needs to know something about him. For minor characters, appearance and voice may convey all the information the audience needs—we don't need a detailed biography of the coffee-shop waitress who appears for only 30 seconds.

Major characters need richer personalities, however, and to design them, you will have to envision the character in your head and then answer a large number of questions about them. In his 2001 article "Building Character: An Analysis of Character Creation," designer Steve Meretzky recommends that you create a character background paper, or *backgrounder,* for each one. You don't necessarily have to write it in narrative form; lists of qualities will do. The main thing is to get the information down on paper so that it's documented somewhere. Meretzky suggests that you consider the following:

Where was the character born?

What was his family life like as a kid?

What was his education?

Where does he live now?

Describe his job.

Describe his finances.

Describe his taste in clothes, books, movies, etc.

What are his favorite foods?

What are his favorite activities?

What are his hobbies?

Describe any particular personality traits and how they manifest.

Is he shy or outgoing? Greedy or giving?

Does he have quirks?

Does he have superstitions?

Does he have phobias?

What were the traumatic moments in his life?

What were his biggest triumphs?

Describe his important past romances.

Describe his current romantic involvement or involvements.

How does he treat friends? Lovers? Bosses? Servants?

Describe his political beliefs, past and present.

Describe his religious beliefs, past and present.

What are his interesting or important possessions?

Does he have any pets?

Does he have unusual talents?

What's the best thing that could happen to him?

The worst thing?

Does he drink tea or coffee?

Obviously, this list is intended primarily for documenting ordinary humans, not sentient robo-camels or creatures of the underworld; if you set your game in the realm of fantasy, you'll have to adjust the list of considerations as necessary. But in all cases, your goal is to become the world expert on this character, to know everything worth knowing about him. Try to imagine how he will behave in a variety of situations.

Once you know the answers to these questions, you can begin to think about how they will manifest themselves in your game's story. If your character is slightly dishonest, say—a small-time crook but not a villain—how will you make this clear to the player? One of the cardinal rules of fiction writing is that you should show— rather than tell—things about the characters to the reader. This goes double for video games, in which players expect to be interacting most of the time and show little tolerance for expository material. How, then, will you show your characters' personalities? Consider these three factors: *appearance, language,* and *behavior.* The earlier section "Visual Appearances" deals with the first of these; the later section "Audio Design" addresses language. Appearance and language quickly and directly establish character but may produce stereotypes if you're not careful. The third factor, behavior, is the most subtle way of conveying character to the audience. Appearances can be deceiving, and deeds matter more than words. But establishing character through behavior takes longer; you must give the player the opportunity to observe a character's actions. What will your character do, what events might he get caught up in that will cause him to display his true nature?

Attributes

Chapter 9, "Creative and Expressive Play," first introduced attributes, and this section discusses attributes of characters. Attributes are the data values that describe a character in some way: her location, state of health, property, emotional condition, relationships with others, and so on. Functional attributes form part of the game's core mechanics, but deciding on appropriate values is also a part of character design.

As we saw in Chapter 9, status attributes change frequently and by large amounts, and characterization attributes change infrequently and by only small amounts or not at all. Characterization attributes define the bedrock details of a character's personality, which—unless the character is mentally ill—shouldn't change much. In the *Dungeons & Dragons* universe, hit points (or health) is a status attribute; it changes moment by moment during a fight. Constitution is a characterization attribute referring to the character's overall degree of hardiness and resistance to injury or poison; it changes rarely or not at all.

In the past, most video games limited characters' attributes to physical details such as their health and inventory. In recent years, more games have made an effort to model social relationships and emotional states. The standout example of the latter is *The Sims,* a game simulating the behavior of people living in a suburban neighborhood. A set of characterization attributes for each character (called a *sim)* determines, in part, its affinity for other sims; those with conflicting qualities won't get along well if forced to interact. The original version of the game called those attributes neat, outgoing, active, playful, and nice. Status attributes named hunger, comfort, hygiene, bladder, energy, fun, social, and room represented sims' personal needs, which could be met by directing them to perform appropriate activities (such as visiting a neighbor or taking a shower) or by improving their surroundings. An overall happiness value went up or down depending on whether the sim's needs were being met. Few games had ever bothered to measure their characters' happiness before, but this mechanic is now commonplace in games about pets and other kinds of nurturing games.

The Sims' model was simple but more sophisticated than anything that had yet been tried. As games get more complex and their stories get richer, undoubtedly there will be much more detailed models of human emotional states and relationships.

NOTE Books and movies about small groups of people sometimes manage to achieve a thorough realization of the entire cast of characters; see the movie *The Big Chill* or read Gabriel García Márquez's novel *One Hundred Years of Solitude* for examples.

Defining your characters' attributes is part of character design, but the attributes that a character needs depend entirely upon the genre and the nature of the gameplay. The *Fundamentals* e-books that are companion volumes to this book discuss the character attributes appropriate in each genre.

Character Dimensionality

In everyday language, people often speak disparagingly of characters in books and movies as being two-dimensional. By this they mean that the character isn't very interesting, doesn't grow or change, doesn't feel fully human, or adheres to a stereotype without any nuances. This criticism usually applies to heroes and villains; it's not realistic to expect everyone who appears in a story to be a fully rounded character with his own quirks and foibles.

This book proposes a slightly more formal use of the idea of character dimensionality, which may help you define characters for computer games. Characters may be classified into four groups: zero-, one-, two-, and three-dimensional. A character's degree of emotional sophistication and the ways in which her behavior changes in response to emotional changes determine her degree of dimensionality. Here we'll examine each group in terms of the kinds of characters found in *The Lord of the Rings,* simply because that story is so well known.

■ **Zero-dimensional** characters exhibit only discrete emotional states. A zero-dimensional character may exhibit any number of such states, but there is no continuum of states; that is, the character's emotional state never moves smoothly from one state into another or shows evidence of being in two states at the same time; there is no such thing as "mixed feelings." The nameless orcs in *The Lord of the Rings* feel only two emotions: hate and fear. The orcs hate the heroes and attack whenever they feel they outnumber their enemies, and they fear the heroes and run away whenever they feel vulnerable or outnumbered. This minimal level of emotional variability is typical of the enemies in a simple shooter or action game (see **Figure 10.6**).

HATE **FEAR**

FIGURE 10.6 Zero-dimensional characters have binary emotional states with no mixed feelings. They may have more than two.

The emotional simplicity of zero-dimensional characters can make them comic. The characters in classic Warner Brothers cartoons—Bugs Bunny, Sylvester, and so on—change almost instantaneously from one extreme emotion to another.

■ **One-dimensional** characters have only a single variable to characterize a changing feeling or attitude; in other respects their character is largely fixed. In *The Lord of the Rings,* the dwarf Gimli is hostile and suspicious toward elves at first, but over time his respect for the elf Legolas grows until they are boon companions. His other attitudes don't change much. The movies make him a more one-dimensional character than the book does (see **Figure 10.7**).

FIGURE 10.7
One-dimensional characters have a single variable that describes an emotion that changes over time.

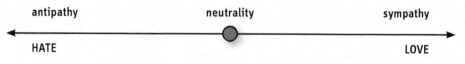

Two-dimensional characters are described by multiple variables that express their impulses, but those impulses don't conflict. Such variables are called orthogonal; that is, they describe completely different domains, which permits no emotional ambiguity. In *The Lord of the Rings*, Denethor is a two-dimensional character. He has a variety of strong emotions—pride, contempt, despair—but he never faces a moral dilemma. His senses of duty and tradition trump all other considerations, even when they are wildly inappropriate (see **Figure 10.8**).

FIGURE 10.8
Two-dimensional characters have multiple, nonconflicting impulses.

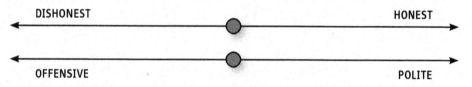

Three-dimensional characters have multiple emotional states that can produce conflicting impulses. This state of affairs distresses and confuses them, sometimes causing them to behave in inconsistent ways. Most of the major characters in *The Lord of the Rings* are three-dimensional, especially those who are tempted by the Ring. Frodo and, above all, Gollum are three-dimensional; Gollum's conflicting desires have driven him mad (see **Figure 10.9**).

FIGURE 10.9
Three-dimensional characters can have conflicting impulses that produce inconsistent behavior.

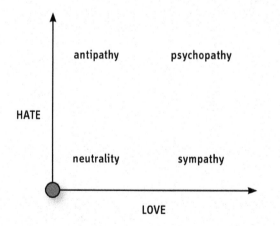

If you plan to allow conflicting emotional states to exist in a character, then you must decide how this conflict manifests itself so that the player perceives it. At any given time, one state will dominate, but if the character really is of two minds about something, his behavior may become erratic as one emotion dominates and then another. For example, a person doing something he really doesn't want to do may be visibly reluctant, change his mind in the middle, or even subconsciously take some action that sabotages his own efforts. There isn't space to discuss this issue in depth here, but you will have to think long and hard about how to portray your characters' mixed feelings, and you should also discuss the problem with both your programmers (who will have to implement the necessary algorithms) and your artists (who will have to create animations showing, for example, reluctance or uncertainty).

Both the game industry and the playing public would benefit from more games with three-dimensional characters. April Ryan in *The Longest Journey* and The Nameless One in *Planescape: Torment* both face a number of moral dilemmas and questions about what it means to be who they are. This kind of writing helps to improve the public perception of our medium as an art form worthy of serious consideration.

Character Growth

If a game aspires to be more than a simple adventure, and if it seeks to have a meaningful story and not just a series of exciting episodes, then it must include character growth of some kind.

The way in which character growth takes place varies by genre. Action games typically restrict growth to new moves and new powerups; the character's mental state does not change. Adventure games, which depend on strong characters and plots, allow for a more literary type of change: personal and emotional growth, unrelated to gameplay. Role-playing games focus on character growth as one of the game's top-level challenges. Role-playing games offer several dimensions for growth: personal, if the story is rich enough; skills, such as the ability to use magic or weapons; and strength, intelligence, or any number of such character attributes.

To build character growth into your game, you'll have to decide *which* characters will grow (most often the hero, if there is one) and *how* they will grow. Physically? Intellectually? Morally? Emotionally? Games use physical growth, in abilities and powers, more than any other kind of growth because it is easy to implement and show to the player.

Then ask yourself how you will implement this growth within the game—through changes in numeric or symbolic attributes, or through changes in the plot of the story, or some other means? How will growth affect the gameplay, if at all? Finally, how will it be represented to the player? Some of your options include displaying numbers on the screen to show the growth (the crudest method), changing the character's appearance, changing the actions available to the player if the character is an avatar, and showing that the character has matured by changing her language and behavior (a more subtle method).

NOTE The psychologist Carl Jung originated the concept of character archetypes, and although his work is increasingly out of fashion in psychological circles, students of the humanities and literature still find it useful.

Character Archetypes

In his book *The Hero with a Thousand Faces* (Campbell, 1972), folklore scholar Joseph Campbell identified a pattern that many stories follow, which he called the *Hero's Journey*. Stories that follow this pattern frequently include archetypal characters—that is, characters of types that have been fundamental to storytelling since the days of

TIP Using character archetypes, like working within a well-known game genre, can shorten the design process and take advantage of the fact that the player already understands what they mean. However, character archetypes may not translate well across cultures.

myth, that are found in the stories of virtually all cultures, and that may even be fundamental to the human psyche. These characters assist or impede the hero in various ways on his journey. In *Banjo-Kazooie,* for example, Bottles the mole teaches the protagonists (and thereby the player) a number of things they need to know to fulfill their quest, so he fits neatly into the archetype of the *mentor* character.

There isn't room to discuss each of Campbell's character archetypes here, but Christopher Vogler's book *The Writer's Journey* (Vogler, 1998) gives a condensed treatment of Joseph Campbell's work for screenwriters and discusses archetypes in depth. For how to make the best use of characters who represent these archetypes in your own games, refer to *The Writer's Journey.*

You should not implement character archetypes slavishly, nor must a game have all or even any of them. Video games do not necessarily have to be heroic journeys, and good characters don't have to fit into neat little boxes.

Audio Design

Audio design, both sound effects and language, is also a part of character design. You will need to work with your team's audio director—and sometimes defer to her experience—to find the right effects and voice for your character.

Sound Effects and Music

The sounds a character makes tell us something about his personality, even if he doesn't speak. Sounds—anything from a gunshot, to a shouted "Hi-yah!" accompanying a karate chop, to a verbal "Aye, aye, sir"—confirm acceptance of the player's command. Sounds also signal injury, damage, or death. The sound of a punch that we're all familiar with from the movies is in fact quite unrealistic, but we're used to it and we know what that *THWAP!* means when we hear it. Likewise, drowning people don't really go "glug glug glug," but that's what games have taught us to expect. Much of sound design involves meeting psychological expectations. Deep sounds suggest slow and strong characters; high sounds suggest light and fast ones. The tone of the sound a thing makes should confirm and harmonize with its visual texture: Metallic objects make metallic sounds. As usual, however, incongruity can be funny, so you can mismatch sounds and visuals on purpose for comedic effect. As you define your character's movements and behaviors, think about what sounds should be associated with him.

As the audio gear in computers and home consoles has improved, game developers have begun to create musical themes associated with specific characters, just as the movies have for decades. John Williams is a master at creating themes for film characters and situations. Everyone remembers the themes from *Star Wars:* the Imperial March that accompanies Darth Vader, with its harsh, discordant trumpets; Princess Leia's love theme; the main title theme that represents the Rebel Alliance generally.

Even Jabba the Hutt has a theme. This book can't teach you music composition, but you should be aware of certain common techniques. Evil or bizarre characters often get themes in a minor key; good or heroic ones get themes in a major key. Instruments playing in unison, especially to a monotonous rhythm, suggest enforced conformity, another characteristic of the Imperial March. These are, of course, traditional Western notions; music for an Indian audience would be different. However, Western dominance of the video game industry has meant that even games made in Japan follow similar rules. The music from the *Final Fantasy* series has become particularly popular.

If you're involved in designing the game sounds and their technical implementation, be sure that you keep music, sound effects, and dialogue or spoken narration in separate sound files that the game mixes together during playback. This is important for two reasons. First, if the game is ever localized into another language, it will be necessary to replace the spoken audio. If the dialogue is already mixed into the music, the sound files in the new language will have to be remixed with the music before they can be added to the game. It's much easier just to drop in a new file of spoken audio and let the game mix it.

Second, the music and sound effects should have separate volume controls in the game for the benefit of the hearing-impaired. Players with a condition called tinnitus find that music prevents them from hearing the sound effects properly, which makes it more difficult to play the game. Keep the two separate so the players can turn off the music if they need to. For more on music and sound effects in video games, read *Game Sound: An Introduction to the History, Theory, and Practice of Video Game Music and Sound Design,* by Karen Collins (Collins, 2008).

TIP In addition to separate volume controls, an overall mute button is useful too, especially on mobile devices. Many people playing video games in public prefer to keep the sound off entirely so as not to annoy those around them.

Voice and Language

The way a character speaks conveys an enormous amount of information. This breaks down into various elements:

- **Vocabulary** indicates the age, social class, and level of education of the character. People who don't read much seldom employ big vocabularies. Teenagers always use a slang vocabulary of their own in order to exclude adults. Beware, however: If you use too much current slang, your game will sound dated six months after publication. Conversely, period slang can help set a game in a different time—calling a gun a roscoe promptly suggests the hardboiled detective fiction of the 1930s and 1940s. In all cases, a light touch is best unless you're deliberately trying to be funny.

- **Grammar and sentence construction** also convey information about education and class; bad grammar reveals bad schooling. Although it's not really valid, we associate articulateness and long, complex sentences with intelligence.

- **Accent** initially tells us something about a person's place of origin and social class. City people and country people speak differently the world over. Accent is also, unfortunately, thought of as an indicator of intelligence. (This can backfire;

smart lawyers from the American South occasionally play up their southern accents to fool their northern opponents into thinking they're not as bright as they really are.) Avoid the "dumb redneck" stereotype; it is offensive.

▣ **Delivery** refers to the speed and tone of the person's speech. Slow speech is— again, mistakenly—often associated with a lack of intelligence, unless the speaker is an Eastern mystic, in which case slow speech can be mistaken for wisdom. Try to steer clear of stereotypes. Speed and tone can still work for you, indicating your characters' excitement, boredom, anxiety, or suspicion. The speaker's tone conveys an attitude or emotional state: friendly, hostile, cynical, guarded, and so on.

▣ **Vocal quirks** include things like a stutter (Porky Pig), lisp (Sylvester the cat), and catchphrases that identify a character ("Eh... what's up, doc?" from Bugs Bunny).

Consider how *The Simpsons* defines its characters' education, intelligence, and interests through language. Homer's limited vocabulary and simple sentences show that he's not well educated; the kinds of things he says indicate that his interests are chiefly food and beer. Marge's middle-sized vocabulary goes with her middle-class outlook on life; from her statements we see that she's concerned with work, friends, and her children. Lisa is the scholar of the family, interested in reading, writing, and music; she has an unusually rich vocabulary for her age and speaks in long, complex sentences. Bart's use of language varies considerably based on his situation, from moronically crude when he's playing a practical joke to quite sophisticated when he's making an ironic observation. Bart is a carefree hedonist but self-aware enough to know it and even comment on it. He's a postmodern sort of character.

StarCraft, which draws on a variety of American accents to create several different types of characters, exhibits some of the most interesting uses of language in games in recent years. Although designers did include the regrettable redneck Southerner stereotype, they also included the southern aristocrat and western sheriff speech patterns for Arcturus Mengsk and Jim Raynor, respectively; the laconic, monosyllabic diction of airline pilots for the Wraith pilots; a cheerful, competent midwestern waitress's voice for the pilots of the troop transports; and a sort of anarchic, gonzo biker lingo for the Vulture riders. This gave the game a great deal of character and flavor that it would have otherwise lacked if it had used bland, undifferentiated voices.

NOTE To make games accessible to the hearing-impaired, dialogue should be available in both audible and text form (subtitles). However, subtitles can't convey accents, so you may need to use carefully chosen slang or dialect terms to help indicate characters' origins. Use a light touch with this, however! Reading a lot of slang or dialect quickly becomes irritating.

Summary

Character creation is an important part of computer game design. Games have come far since the rudimentary characters of their early days, and character design continues to become increasingly sophisticated. For many games, simple, iconic characters will do. However, as our medium continues to mature, more games need rich and deep characters as well. Whether a player defines the avatar she uses in the game or a designer creates a complete character for her to use, the designer has to make characters belong in the game world they inhabit, making them complete, compelling, and believable.

Design Practice EXERCISES

1. Design a human, two-dimensional character for a computer game in three different versions: child, teenager, and adult. The design must include several distinct attributes (visual or personal) that signify the character's age and level of maturity at each stage. Make the character's emotional temperament different at each stage and suggest some events that might have happened to the character that would account for the change. Your instructor will give you the scope of the assignment; we recommend two to five pages.

2. Choose a game that you've never played whose box displays a cartoonlike avatar character. What does the character's general appearance tell you? What attributes does the character possess that make players want to play? What kind of player is the character designed to appeal to? Is there anything you'd like to add, and if so, why? Is there anything you want to remove? Why?

3. Think of someone you know: a friend, family member, or even yourself. Think about the qualities that are the most dominant characteristics of this person's personality—his key attributes, if he were a game character—and write those down. Then imagine the person in one of the following scenarios:

- The person is wrongfully accused of a serious crime—murder or armed robbery, for example.

- Earth is invaded by an enormous alien armada whose objective is to blast everyone to bits.

- The person wakes up from sleep to find himself in another body in another place, but with the same personality.

Write a short essay addressing the following questions. What would your chosen person do in these situations? Situations like these are extremely unusual, but what if they happened? Would an ordinary person like the one you've chosen be a compelling and appealing character?

4. Try designing two characters whose strengths and weaknesses complement each other, so that while they seem very unalike, they actually work together quite well. (Consider the characters Banjo and Kazooie or Ratchet and Clank as examples.) Choose a game genre and design characters and attributes suitable for that genre. Show how their qualities complement each other when the characters are together but leave each character vulnerable to the game's dangers when they are apart.

Design Practice QUESTIONS

As you begin the task of developing characters for a game, consider the following questions:

1. Are the game's characters primarily art-based or story-based?

2. What style is your art-based character drawn in: cartoon, comic-book superhero, realistic, gothic? Will your character be exaggerated in some way: cute, tough, or otherwise?

3. Do your art-based characters depend upon visual stereotypes for instant identification, or are they more subtle than that? If they are more subtle, how does their appearance support their role in the game?

4. Can the player tell by looking at a character how that character is likely to act? Are there reasons in the story or gameplay for wanting a character's behavior to be predictable from her appearance, or is there a reason to make the character ambiguous?

5. If the game offers an avatar, does the avatar come with a sidekick? What does the sidekick offer the player—information, advice, physical assistance? How will the sidekick complement the avatar? How will the player be able to visually distinguish between the two of them at a glance?

6. With a story-based character, how will you convey the character's personality and attitudes to the player—through narration, dialogue, gameplay, backstory, or other means?

7. What about the avatar will intrigue and interest the player?

8. What about the avatar will encourage the player to like him?

9. How will the avatar change and grow throughout the game? Physically, emotionally, intellectually? Or will she remain essentially static?

10. Do the characters correspond to any of Campbell's mythic archetypes? Or do they have less archetypal, more complex roles to play, and if so, what are they?

11. What sorts of sounds will each character in your game make? What sorts of music are appropriate for them? How will your choices of sounds and music support the way you want the player to feel about each character?

12. How do the character's grammar, vocabulary, tone of voice, and speech patterns contribute to the player's understanding of the character?

CHAPTER 11

Storytelling

Storytelling is a feature of daily experience. We do it without thinking about it when we recount some experience we have had or make up a story for our children. We also consume stories continually—fictional ones through novels, movies, plays, and television; nonfictional ones through books, documentaries, and the news media.

Video games often include fictional stories that go beyond the events of the games themselves. Game designers add stories to enhance a game's entertainment value, to keep the player interested in a long game, and to help sell the game to prospective customers.

This chapter looks at how to weave a story into a game. It focuses mostly on games that rely heavily on stories, though the chapter covers stories within all genres. We'll examine what makes a good story and how to keep the stories from overwhelming the gameplay of a video game. You'll learn the terms *interactive story* and *narrative*, and then we'll discuss linear and nonlinear storytelling and mechanisms you can use to advance the plot. Then we'll address *scripted conversations*, which allow the player to participate in dialogue with non-player characters (NPCs). The chapter concludes with the topic of episodic storytelling in games, which digital distribution has helped to make possible.

Why Put Stories in Games?

Game designers, game theorists, and players have debated the subject of stories in games for many years, disputing issues such as whether stories belong in games at all and, if so, what these stories should be like and how they should work (see "The Great Debate" sidebar). Many players want a story along with their gameplay, and some game genres—role-playing games (RPGs), action-adventures, and above all adventure games—definitely require one.

Reasons to Include a Story

Whether a story will improve a game depends on the genre and how rich a story you want to tell. Although a story won't help in all cases, here are four good reasons for including a story in your game:

■ **Stories can add significantly to the entertainment that a game offers.** Without a story, a game is a competition: exciting, but artificial. A story gives the competition a context, and it facilitates the essential act of pretending that all games require. A story provides greater emotional satisfaction by providing a sense of progress toward a dramatically meaningful, rather than an abstract, goal.

- **Stories attract a wider audience.** The added entertainment value of a story will, in turn, attract more people to a game. Many players need a story to motivate them to play; if the game offers only challenges and no story, they won't buy it. Although adding a story makes game development cost more, it also makes the game appeal to more people. On the other hand, players who don't need a story are free to ignore it—provided that the story is not intrusive.

- **Stories help keep players interested in long games.** Simple, quick games such as *Bejeweled* don't need a story and would probably feel a bit odd if one were tacked on; that would be like adding a story onto a game of checkers or tic-tac-toe. In a short game, getting a high score provides all the reward the player needs. But in a long game—one that lasts for many hours or even days—simply racking up points isn't enough reason for most players to carry on. Furthermore, stories offer novelty. A long game needs variety, or it begins to feel repetitive and boring; a compelling story provides that variety.

- **Stories help sell the game.** Gameplay, as an active process, isn't always easy to explain in words or static pictures on a poster or a website. But you can depict characters and situations from your game's story and even print part of the story itself in advertising materials.

THE GREAT DEBATE

Among theoreticians, interactive storytelling is the single most hotly debated issue in all of game design. What does *interactive storytelling* actually mean? Is such a thing possible? Should we do it? *How* should we do it? What are we trying to achieve by doing it? How can we determine if we're doing it well? And the problem gets worse: The game industry doesn't even know what to *call* it. *Interactive storytelling, interactive narrative, interactive drama, interactive fiction,* and *storyplaying* have all been proposed. In the 1990s, the academic community began to consider the issue and drew its own battle lines. The narratologists (people who study narrative) conducted fierce and often impenetrable arguments with the ludologists (people who study games and play) in the learned pages of scholarly journals. Search Google Scholar for "interactive narrative" and you will be overwhelmed by a confusing tide of conflicting verbiage.

For the most part, these arguments have not had any effect on the game industry. Your chief concern is to build a game. Use the principle of player-centric design and don't worry about theoretical arguments. Build a story into your game if you believe it will help to entertain the player, and don't build one in if it won't.

This book can't teach you the fundamentals of good storytelling; you can choose from many hundreds of books and classes on creative writing for that. Instead, we'll look at the ways that stories may be incorporated into video games and how interactive stories differ from traditional ones. Designing characters, an important part of any kind of storytelling, is covered in depth in Chapter 10, "Character Development."

Figuring Out What You Want to Achieve

There isn't one right way to include a story in a game; how you do it depends on what kind of entertainment experience you want to deliver and what kind of player you want to serve. Many game developers don't stop to think about exactly *why* they want a story in the game or what it will do for the player.

The type of game you choose to build will determine whether it needs a story and, if so, how long and how rich that story should be. A simple game such as *Space Invaders* requires only a one-line backstory and nothing else: "Aliens are invading Earth and *only you* can stop them." Indeed, such a game should *not* include any more story than that; a story only distracts the player from the frenetic gameplay. At the other end of the spectrum, adventure games such as *Heavy Rain* and *The Walking Dead* offer stories as involved as any novel. These games cannot exist without their stories; the story offers up to half the entertainment in the game.

CHAPTER 11

HOW TO WRITE A REQUIREMENTS SPECIFICATION FOR YOUR STORY

I recommend that you write a *requirements specification* for your interactive story: a document that describes how the story will operate within the game and what it is supposed to accomplish. Requirements specifications are commonplace in other forms of engineering but are seldom found in game development. It may sound odd to write a specification document for something that we think of as a creative endeavor, but in a video game, the story is part of a larger system: a piece of entertainment software. The process of writing a requirements specification will help you figure out what you want to achieve.

As part of my Ph.D. thesis I created a template and guide to writing a requirements specification. This document provides you with a template that you can use, as well as a guide and questions to consider as you decide what you want to do. In addition to interactive storytelling, it also addresses some issues about designing your avatar character.

You can download it in Word 2003 DOC format, OpenOffice ODT format, or Adobe Reader PDF format at the following links:

http://www.designersnotebook.com/public/storytelling_reqspec_template_1_0.doc

http://www.designersnotebook.com/public/storytelling_reqspec_template_1_0.odt

http://www.designersnotebook.com/public/storytelling_reqspec_template_1_0.pdf

NOTE There is no single "right" way to design an interactive story. Each approach has strengths and weaknesses. Choose the one that best serves the player's entertainment.

A few games allow the storytelling to overshadow the gameplay and give the player little to do. This was a common mistake when the industry first began to make video games based on movie or book franchises. Critics and players uniformly considered them poor games because they violated the design rule that *Gameplay Comes First.* A designer must always keep that design rule in mind, no matter where the original story came from.

The following factors affect how much and what kind of a story a game should include, and you should take them into account when you make your decision:

- **Length.** As the previous section said, the longer a game, the more it benefits from a story. A story can tie the disparate events of a longer game into a single continuous experience and keep the player's interest.

- **Characters.** If the game focuses on individual people (or at least, characters the player can identify with, whether human or not), then it can benefit from a story. If the game revolves around large numbers of fairly anonymous people—such as the visitors in *Theme Park*—then adding a story won't be easy.

- **Degree of realism.** Abstract games don't lend themselves to storytelling; representational ones often do. You may find it difficult to write a compelling story about a purely artificial set of relationships and problems, while you find that a realistic game can often benefit from a story. This rule does not hold in all cases: Highly realistic vehicle simulators and sports games usually don't include stories because the premise of the game doesn't require one; on the other hand, *Ms. Pac-Man,* an abstract game, did tell a cute little story because the game included characters.

- **Emotional richness.** Ordinary single-player gameplay seldom inspires more than a few emotions: pleasure in success; frustration at failure; determination, perhaps; and occasionally an aha! moment when the player figures out a puzzle. Deeper emotions can come only when the player identifies with characters and their problems, which happens within a well-written story. If you want to inspire a greater variety of emotions, you need to write a story to do it.

You may also want to include a story to set your game apart from games using similar gameplay mechanics. The gameplay of *Spec Ops: The Line* is similar to that of most other first-person shooters, but the story sets it apart.

Key Concepts

Before we look at the design processes required to put a story into your game, you need to understand a number of key concepts, because they come up again and again throughout the discussion.

Story

In the loosest definition, a *story* is an account of a series of events, either historical or fictitious. On that basis, a few people would say that every game contains a story because the action of the game can be described afterward. Although theoretically correct, this position isn't very useful to a game designer. The description of a *Tetris* game would make a supremely uninteresting story and is not worth telling. If you're going to incorporate stories into games, they should be *good* stories.

REQUIREMENTS OF GOOD STORIES

For the purpose of putting good stories into games, we need to expand the original definition beyond "an account of a series of events." A minimally acceptable story, then, must be *credible, coherent,* and *dramatically meaningful.* It must not be *repetitive* or *arbitrary.*

You can be the last member of the human race left alive, or you can invent a time machine, but not both.

—Ken Perlin, professor at New York University

Credible simply means that people can believe in the story and the characters, although in the case of fiction, they may have to suspend some disbelief to make belief possible. Many fantasy and science fiction stories are incredible in real-world terms but are believable once the reader accepts their premises. Even fantasy and science fiction stories mustn't push it too far, as the quotation from Ken Perlin illustrates. They must also offer characters that the audience can sympathize with, identify with, or recognize as convincing. If a character isn't believable, the story is flawed. Humorous stories, such as the tall tales about Paul Bunyan, don't have to be as credible as serious ones. Different audiences also tolerate varying levels of credibility, so you should test your story on several people to see if they find it believable.

Coherent means that the events in a story must not be irrelevant or arbitrary but must harmonize to create a pleasing whole. Even if some events are not related by cause and effect or some events just add color, all events still have to belong in the story. A story about the Apollo space program that includes events from the first-century Roman invasion of Judea is incoherent because the Roman invasion of Judea has no connection at all with the Apollo program. On the other hand, if the story of the Apollo program includes a scene of Galileo building his telescope, that can be harmonious because Galileo's use of the telescope to study the heavens represents an important milestone in astronomy that ultimately led to the moon landings.

Arbitrary or seemingly random content destroys coherence and credibility. A few writers can get away with including material that doesn't appear to belong in their story if they are trying to make a surrealist or absurdist point. It requires tremendous skill to do this well, and it is very uncommon in video games. If you include an arbitrary event in your game, your player is likely to interpret it as nonsense.

NOTE A good story must, at minimum, be a credible and coherent account of dramatically meaningful events, without undue repetition or arbitrary content.

Repetition harms player immersion in a story, at least to modern ears. If you write a story in which a detective has to go knock on a witness's door four separate times before he finds anyone home, the reader is going to get bored after the second or third time he has to do this. Even if your story is an account of real events, you would normally condense these visits by writing, "He had to visit several times before he found anyone home." This process is called *dramatic compression.* Children are more tolerant of repetition in stories than adults are, because they are still learning how to predict consequences from actions.

To be *dramatically meaningful,* the story's events have to involve something, or preferably someone, the listener cares about. The story must be constructed in such a way that it encourages the listener to take an interest in, and preferably identify with, one or more of the story's characters. When a game tells a story, the dramatically meaningful events may be explicitly planned by the writer, or they may arise naturally out of the process of playing. Either way, all events must contribute to the player's involvement in the story as she identifies with characters and becomes interested in what happens to those characters. See the "Dramatic Tension and Gameplay Tension" section, later in this chapter.

INTERACTIVE STORIES

In English, stories—even those set in the future—are normally written using the past tense. An interactive story, on the other hand, takes place now, with the player in the middle of the series of events, moving forward through those events. Furthermore, the player's actions form part of the story itself, which makes an interactive story very different from a story presented to a passive audience. In fact, an interactive story includes three kinds of events:

- **Player events** are actions performed directly by the player. In addition to giving the player actions to perform as part of gameplay—actions intended to overcome challenges—you can give the player additional actions to perform as part of the story. Role-playing by talking to other characters, for example, might serve the needs of the story even if overcoming the game's challenges does not require talking. If the player's actions can affect the plot of the story and change its future, they're called *dramatic actions.* Some player actions are not dramatic, however: Some player events aimed at overcoming challenges may not affect the plot.

- **In-game events** are events initiated by the core mechanics of the game. These events may be responses to the player's actions (such as a trap that snaps when the player steps on a particular stone) or independent of the player's actions (such as a simulated guard character checking to see that the castle doors are locked). The player might be able to intentionally cause these events to occur, to change the way they occur, or to prevent them entirely—which is part of what makes the story interactive.

▪ **Narrative events** are events whose content the player cannot change, although he may be able to change whether they occur or not. A narrative event narrates some action to the player; he does not interact with it. Narrative events are described in the "Narrative" section, which follows this one.

With this in mind, consider the following formal definition of an *interactive story*.

> **INTERACTIVE STORIES** *are stories the player interacts with by contributing actions to them. A story may be interactive even if the player's actions cannot change the direction of the plot line.*

This definition of an interactive story differs from those put forth by many other designers, who often assert that if the player's actions do not change the direction of the plot line (that is, the plot is *linear*), the story is not interactive. The power to change the direction of the player's path through the plot, and perhaps the story's future events—is called *agency*. Some designers feel that if a game with a story does not offer the player agency, it can't be said to be truly interactive. This is a misconception, because it ignores the role of the player's own actions in forming her experience of the game. A player still feels as if she is interacting with a story even if her actions do not change future events. The player contributes to the sequence of events, and that is what matters.

Consider a situation in which a player must find a way to get past a security guard to enter a building. You can give the player several ways to accomplish this: through violence, or trickery, or patience—waiting until the security guard goes off shift. No matter which approach the player chooses, he still enters the building through the same door and encounters the same things on the other side. If his decision does not actually affect the future events of the story, he has no agency. But his decision about how to get through the door contributes to the plot; his own actions are part of his experience of the game. This is how a story can be linear and still be interactive.

We discuss the distinction between stories that cannot be changed and those that can be changed in the sections "Linear Stories" and "Nonlinear Stories," later in this chapter.

Notice that the definition does not say anything about quality. Remember that to be a *good* story, a story's events must be credible, coherent, and dramatically meaningful. The player's actions constitute events in the story, so the more that those actions are credible, coherent, and dramatically meaningful events, the better the story will be. (Even an action that is not a *dramatic action*—one that changes the plot, as explained earlier—can still be *dramatically meaningful*; that is, it can be about something the player cares about.) When designing an interactive story, you shouldn't give the player things to do that don't credibly belong in the story; the result will be incoherent. In the *Grand Theft Auto* series, the player can't set up a charity for the homeless, and in the *Police Quest* series she can't steal cars.

In most games with an interactive story, the player's actions move an avatar through the plot. When the player overcomes a challenge, the game responds with the next event in the story. If the player doesn't overcome a challenge, either the story comes to a premature end (as it would when, say, the avatar dies in the attempt) or the story simply fails to advance—the player doesn't see future story events until she manages to get past the specific obstacle. However, there are exceptions to this arrangement; in some games the story progresses whether or not the player meets the game's challenges. The section "Mechanisms for Advancing the Plot" addresses this issue in detail later.

Narrative

The definition of *narrative* is open to debate, but this book uses a definition that conforms pretty closely to the one used by theorists of storytelling. Narrative consists of the *text* or the *discourse* produced by the act of narration. In an interactive story, narrative is the part of the story that you, the designer, narrate to your player—as opposed to those actions that the player performs, or those events that the core mechanics create.

> **NARRATIVE** *refers to story events that are narrated—that is, told or shown—by the game to the player. Narrative consists of the noninteractive, presentational part of the story.*

THE ROLE OF NARRATIVE

The primary function of narrative in a video game is to present events over which the player has no control. Typically these events consist of things that happen to the avatar that the player cannot prevent and events that happen when the avatar is not present but that we still want the player to see or to know about. Scenes depicting success or failure are usually narrative events.

Narrative also lets you show the player a prologue to the game or the current level if you want to do so. It not only introduces the player to the situation in the game—the game's main challenge—but also to the game world itself. When a football game shows the athletes running onto the field at the beginning of the game, that's a narrative event that the player can't change. It simply creates context. Although the sights and sounds of your game—the graphics and audio—create the immediate physical embodiment of your game's world (*how* the world looks), they can't explain its history and culture (*why* it looks that way). If you don't design that culture and history, the game world will feel like a theme park: all false fronts and a thin veneer over the game's mechanics. To establish a feeling of richness and depth, you must create a background, and you can reveal some of that through narration. Narrative very often serves as a reward when the player achieves a major goal of the game—he gets to see a movie or read more of the story he's playing through. Players who don't like stories in games usually ignore these narrative moments, but many players enjoy them a great deal.

COMMONLY USED NARRATIVE BLOCKS

Many video games use blocks of narrative material—brief episodes of noninteractive content—to tell parts of the story. Designers commonly use a narrative block as an opening sequence to introduce the story at the beginning of the game; as an ending sequence to wrap up the story when the player completes the game; as an interlevel sequence that often takes the form of a briefing about what the player will encounter in the next level (or chapter or mission); or in the form of *cut-scenes,* short noninteractive sequences presented during play that interrupt it momentarily.

The game *Half-Life,* for example, begins with a movie in which Gordon Freeman, the player's avatar, takes a tram ride through the Black Mesa research complex while a voice explains why he is there. This opening sequence introduces the game world and sets the stage for the experience to follow.

Narrative blocks presented between levels tend to last from 30 seconds to 4 or 5 minutes. Those at the beginning and end of the game are sometimes longer still, because they provide important narrative bookends to the entire experience. In *Halo 2,* the introduction scene is more than 5 minutes long.

Cut-scenes during play, on the other hand, should be shorter because they interrupt the flow and rhythm of the player's actions. Players who like fast-moving genres, such as real-time strategy games or action-adventures, are annoyed if you keep them listening or watching for too long without giving them something to do. Players of slower-moving games such as adventure games or RPGs tolerate long cut-scenes better.

> ### DESIGN RULE Noninteractive Sequences Must Be Interruptible
>
> All narrative material *must* be interruptible by the player. Provide a button that allows players to skip the sequence and go on to whatever follows, even if the sequence contains important information that players need to know to win the game. A player who has played the game before already knows what the narrative contains.

FORMS OF NARRATIVE

Narrative in a video game can take many forms. A prerendered movie, a cut-scene displayed by the graphics engine, scrolling text that introduces a mission, voice-over commentary that explains the backstory of the game, or even a long monologue by a character can all be considered narrative elements of the game.

There's one exception to the definition of narrative. A single, prerecorded line of dialogue spoken by a game character might be considered to be narrative because the player can't change it as it is being played back. However, dialogue in games usually occurs in an interactive context, with the player choosing a line for her character to say, and the game choosing an appropriate line in response, based on what the player's avatar said. This kind of interactive dialogue is not narrative because the player actually takes part in it. A long, *noninteractive* dialogue between NPCs, on the other hand, qualifies as narrative.

BALANCING NARRATIVE AND GAMEPLAY

Because playing games is an active process and watching a narrative is a passive one, the player notices the difference between them. A simple arcade game such as *Tempest* presents no narrative—it is entirely gameplay. A novel or a movie offers no gameplay—it is entirely narrative. The more narrative you include, the more you are asking the player to sit doing nothing, simply observing your story.

TIP Just as children are more tolerant of repetition in stories, they are also more tolerant of video games that give them little feeling of power over the direction of the story.

But players don't play games in order to watch movies; they play in order to act. Any game that includes narrative elements must find an appropriate balance between the player's desire to act and the designer's need to narrate. If you offer too much narrative and too little gameplay, players will feel that your game gives bad value for the money they paid. Players pay for the opportunity to act out a fantasy. If most of your game's content is noninteractive, they'll feel cheated—they won't get the experience that they paid for.

Too much narrative also tends to make the game feel as if it's on rails, the player's actions serving only to move the game toward a predestined conclusion. Unless you've written a game with multiple endings, the conclusion *is* predestined, but you want to make the player feel as if he actively participates in the story. When the designer takes over too much of the telling, the player feels as if he's being led by the nose. He doesn't have the freedom to play the game in his own way, to create his own experience for himself.

> ## DESIGN RULE Do Not Seize Control of the Avatar
>
> When you create your game's narrative segments, try to avoid seizing control of the player's avatar, and above all, do not make the avatar do something that the player might not choose to do. In too many games, the narrative suddenly takes over and makes the avatar get into a fight, walk into danger unnecessarily, or say something stupid that the player would never choose to say. It is fair to change the world around the avatar in response to the player's actions; it is less fair to take away control of the avatar from the player.

The *raison d'être* of all computer gaming is *interactivity:* giving the player something to do. The trick, then, is to provide enough narrative to enrich the game world and motivate the player, but not so much as to inhibit her freedom to meet the game's challenges in whatever way she chooses. Consider this paraphrase of the words of the wizard Gandalf in *The Lord of the Rings:* "We cannot choose the times in which we live. All we can decide is what to do with the time that is given us." The player cannot decide the world in which she plays; that is for you to determine. But she must have the freedom to act within that world, or there is no point in playing.

Dramatic Tension and Gameplay Tension

Many designers are led astray by a false analogy between two superficially similar concepts, *dramatic tension* and *gameplay tension*. This section defines these terms, discusses their roles in entertaining the player, and explains why you shouldn't confuse them.

DRAMATIC TENSION

When a reader reads (or a viewer watches) a story, she feels *dramatic tension*, the sense that something important is at stake coupled with a desire to know what happens next. (Screenwriters call this *conflict*, but game developers, who use *conflict* to refer to the opposition of hostile forces in a game, prefer *dramatic tension*, which is more accurate in any case.) Dramatic tension is the essence of storytelling, whatever the medium. *Cliffhangers*—exciting situations at the ends of book chapters or TV shows that remain unresolved until the next chapter or episode—increase the audience's sense of dramatic tension and ensure they stick around to see the situation resolve. At the climactic event in a story, the action turns, so instead of the tension mounting, it begins to fall.

GAMEPLAY TENSION

When a player plays a game, he feels *gameplay tension;* again, he has a sense that something important is at stake and a desire to know what happens next. But gameplay tension arises from a different source than dramatic tension does; it comes from the player's desire to overcome a challenge and his uncertainty about whether he will succeed or fail. In multiplayer games, the player's uncertainty about what his opponents will do next also creates gameplay tension.

THE FALSE ANALOGY

Game designers have tended to perceive an analogy between dramatic tension and gameplay tension, as if the two terms simply denoted the same feeling. However, the analogy is a false one. Dramatic tension depends on the player's identification with a character (or several of them) and curiosity about what will happen to that character. Gameplay tension does not require any characters. For instance, a darts player feels gameplay tension in wondering whether she can hit the bull's-eye; but this situation would provide dramatic tension only if the outcome mattered to a character in the context of a story.

A key difference between dramatic tension and gameplay tension lies in the differing abilities of these feelings to persist in the face of arbitrary or repetitive content, as described in the section "Requirements of Good Stories."

Dramatic tension, and reader interest in the dramatic subject, fades in the presence of arbitrary or repetitive content. Gameplay tension, on the other hand, easily tolerates arbitrary and random and repetitive content for much longer. Poker and *Tetris* include a lot of randomness and repetition, yet they retain their gameplay tension.

Consider the following dialogue from the British television science fiction comedy *Red Dwarf*. Arnold Rimmer, who is sitting around one evening with his roommate, Dave Lister, recounts every detail of a game of *Risk*, die-roll by die-roll, that he played 10 years earlier. Lister asks him repeatedly to shut up, and Rimmer can't understand why.

RIMMER: But I thought that was because I hadn't got to the really interesting bit.

LISTER: What really interesting bit?

RIMMER: Ah well, that was about two hours later, after he'd thrown a three and a two and I'd thrown a four and a one. I picked up the dice…

LISTER: Hang on Rimmer, hang on… the really interesting bit is exactly the same as the dull bit.

RIMMER: You don't know what I did with the dice though, do you? For all you know, I could have jammed them up his nostrils, head-butted him on the nose and they could have blasted out of his ears. That would've been quite interesting.

LISTER: OK, Rimmer. What did you do with the dice?

RIMMER: I threw a five and a two.

LISTER: And that's the really interesting bit?

RIMMER: Well, it was interesting to me, it got me into Irkutsk.

—*RED DWARF* SERIES 4, EPISODE 6, "MELTDOWN"

Two lines in this exchange illustrate the point quite clearly. Lister says, "The really interesting bit is exactly the same as the dull bit," and later Rimmer says, "Well, it was interesting to me, it got me into Irkutsk." Like *Tetris*, *Risk* is full of repetition and randomness. Rimmer believes that it's interesting because he confuses the gameplay tension that he felt—will I conquer Irkutsk?—with dramatic tension.

DESIGN RULE Randomness and Repetition Destroy Dramatic Tension

The narrative events in a game's story must not occur randomly or arbitrarily, nor should the narrative repeat itself, even if the play itself is repetitive.

The Storytelling Engine

To design a game that includes a story, you must interweave the gameplay—the actions taken to overcome the game's challenges—with the narrative events of the story. Narrative events must be interspersed among the gameplay events in such a way that all events feel related to each other and part of a single sequence that entertains the player. If the gameplay concerns exactly the same subject matter as the narrative—and it should, in order to present a coherent and harmonious whole—then the entire experience, play and narrative together, will feel like one continuous story.

The storytelling engine does the weaving. Chapter 2, "Designing and Developing Games," introduced the storytelling engine briefly as the third major component of a video game along with the core mechanics and the user interface. Unlike the other two, the storytelling engine is optional; if the game doesn't tell a story, it doesn't have a storytelling engine.

Just as the core mechanics generate the gameplay, the storytelling engine manages the interweaving of narrative events into the game. The core mechanics oversee the player's progress through the game's challenges; the storytelling engine oversees the player's progress through the game's story. The storytelling engine and core mechanics must work together to create a single, seamless experience.

Figure 11.1 illustrates the relationship between the storytelling engine, core mechanics, user interface, and player. Notice that Figure 11.1 resembles Figure 2.1 from Chapter 2, which showed how the core mechanics produce and manage gameplay. Figure 11.1 shows how both the core mechanics and storytelling engine together produce the experience of interacting with a story.

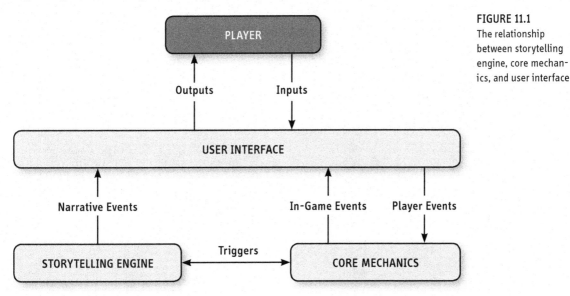

FIGURE 11.1
The relationship between storytelling engine, core mechanics, and user interface

CHAPTER 11

As the section "Interactive Stories" explained earlier, an interactive story contains three types of events: player events, in-game events, and narrative events. The core mechanics manage the player events and in-game events, as the figure shows. The storytelling engine manages the narrative events. However, the storytelling engine does more than just play movies or cut-scenes; it also keeps track of the progress of the story and determines what part of the plot should come next.

In Figure 11.1, notice that a double-headed arrow labeled Triggers connects the storytelling engine to the core mechanics. At times, the core mechanics may determine that the interaction should stop and the storytelling engine should present some narrative—for instance, when a player completes a level. The core mechanics send a message to the storytelling engine saying that the player finished the level, and the storytelling engine should now display any interlevel narrative events. Likewise, the storytelling engine can send a trigger back to the core mechanics when a narrative event finishes (or when the player interrupts a narrative event), telling the core mechanics to resume play. This is the simplest and, in small games, the most common kind of storytelling engine. The system that displays the cut-scenes between levels of *Angry Birds* is one such.

In a more complicated system, the storytelling engine doesn't sit idle during play. As the player progresses, the mechanics continually send triggers to the storytelling engine—that way, the storytelling engine can keep up with what's going on. If, for example, the player makes a key decision that will affect the story later on, the core mechanics inform the storytelling engine of the decision.

Similarly, during play, the storytelling engine can determine that the story has reached a critical plot point and can trigger the core mechanics to cause changes to the internal economy of the game. Suppose the story says, "When the avatar reaches the bridge, he will be attacked by a highwayman in a cut-scene and robbed of all his property." The core mechanics, tracking the player's progress through the game world, sends a message to the storytelling engine, "The avatar has reached the bridge." The storytelling engine detects that this is a key point, halts play, and displays a cut-scene showing the robbery. Then it transmits a message back to the core mechanics saying, "Transfer the avatar's inventory to the highwayman and resume play."

Normally, the level designers do the work that actually implements such events in the game. Among the level designer's tools for level-building will be a mechanism for detecting the avatar's position and for triggering both the cut-scene and the transfer of the avatar's property. At the moment, a development company cannot license a storytelling engine from a middleware company the way it can license a graphics engine or a physics engine, but that may change. Still, at a conceptual level, it will help you to design the story and its interaction with the gameplay if you think of these events in terms of triggers sent between the two separate components, the core mechanics and the storytelling engine.

As you can see, the storytelling engine plays a critical role in weaving the gameplay and narrative together to create the whole experience. The rest of this chapter refers to the storytelling engine frequently.

Linear Stories

From the earliest days of computer gaming, designers have been intrigued by the idea of agency: letting the player influence the plot and change the outcome. Game developers refer to stories that the player cannot change as *linear stories* and those that the player can change as *nonlinear stories*. The next section addresses nonlinear stories.

A linear story in a video game looks similar to a linear story in any other medium— the player cannot change the plot or the ending of the story. In a game, however, the player still faces challenges as she goes through the story, and in fact the challenges form part of the story itself. Thus, a linear story in a game is still an interactive story, but the player's interactions are limited to contributing actions. Still, many games use this format. Consider *Half-Life* and *StarCraft:* Both tell linear stories, the outcome of which the player cannot change, but the player performs many actions as part of the story along the way. The narrative blocks between missions in *StarCraft* become a reward for completing the mission.

Creating linear stories offers many advantages, which explains why, after a flurry of experimentation with nonlinear ones in the 1990s, the game industry largely returned to this practice. Linear stories do have disadvantages as well, however. Here are some of the pros and cons to consider when designing your own story.

▪ **Linear stories require less content than nonlinear ones.** If a player can only ever experience one fixed sequence of events, you need to create material only for those events. Developing the game using a linear story requires less time and money.

▪ **The storytelling engine is simpler.** The storytelling engine managing a linear story has to keep track of only a single sequence of plot events. Because the player cannot change the course of events, the storytelling engine doesn't need to record critical decisions that the player makes: There aren't any. The storytelling engine will be easier to implement and test if you use a linear story. Testing the storytelling engine can take up a significant amount of time, and many developers fail to plan for it.

▪ **Linear stories are less prone to bugs and absurdities.** If the sequence of events remains the same regardless of players' actions, you can guarantee that the story makes sense. On the other hand, if you allow the sequence of events to vary—that is, you present a nonlinear story—you introduce the risk of error. The storytelling engine must guarantee that the events make sense. If the player wrecks a car during play in a game with a nonlinear story, the storytelling engine must ensure that the game does not present any subsequent gameplay or narrative material that shows the car undamaged. If you're not careful, you can introduce what the film industry calls *continuity errors:* things that look different from the way they should look, given the events of preceding scenes, because narrative material can't change to keep up with game events. Linear stories don't incur this risk. If a car is wrecked as part of the story, it stays wrecked; if it mustn't be wrecked, then you must not give the player any way to wreck it.

■ **Linear stories deny the player agency.** The player may have freedom to do a lot of things in the game, but none of it influences the story apart from causing it to progress. As the previous consideration said, if the story requires a functional car throughout, then the gameplay cannot allow the player to wreck the car. The section "Endings," later in this chapter, discusses this issue in more depth.

■ **Linear stories are capable of greater emotional power.** From a creative standpoint, this is one of their greatest advantages. The section "Emotional Limits of Nonlinear Stories," later in this chapter, explains this point in more detail.

Note that if you want to tell a strictly linear story, that decision will have consequences for any story you plan to treat as a journey (as many stories in games are). See the section "The Story as a Journey," later in this chapter.

Nonlinear Stories

If you allow the player to influence future events and change the direction of the story, then the story is nonlinear. This chapter examines two of the most common structures for nonlinear stories—*branching stories* and *foldback stories*—in detail in the next two sections. A third approach, *emergent storytelling,* is more of a research problem than a standard industry mechanism, and we'll discuss it briefly. After that we'll look at a new hybrid technique that shows great promise for the future of interactive storytelling. Finally, we'll study an important issue for any teller of nonlinear stories: How many endings should the story have?

Branching Stories

A *branching story* allows the player to experience the story differently each time he plays the game. The story offers not one plot line but many that split off from each other at different points. As the designer, you decide on the different possible plot lines and how they relate to each other. During play, the storytelling engine keeps track of which plot line the player is following at any given time. When the story reaches a *branch point*—a place where the current plot line subdivides—the core mechanics must send a trigger to the storytelling engine to tell it which of the possible branches of the story the player will follow next.

Game events—either player events or in-game events generated by the core mechanics (such as an action taken by an AI-driven NPC)—determine which branch the story will take. Player events that influence the direction of the story fall into two categories: efforts to overcome a challenge or decisions that the story asks the player to make. Branch points connected with player decisions have one branch for each option that you offer to the player. Typically, branch points associated with challenges have only two branches leading on from the branch point, one for success and one for failure, though you can also create different numbers of branches for different degrees of success if you want to. We'll consider the emotional consequences of branches based on challenges versus those based on choices in the later section "Endings."

IMMEDIATE, DEFERRED, AND CUMULATIVE INFLUENCE

If an event in the game causes the plot to branch right away, that event has an *immediate* influence on the story. This is the most common kind of branch and the easiest to implement. The player makes an irrevocable decision—which road to take, for example—and the story promptly reflects her choice.

However, sometimes the player can make a decision early in the game that influences a branch point much later, in which case that decision has *deferred* influence. Or she can make a whole series of decisions throughout the game that cumulatively affect a branch point, such that her actions and decisions, when taken together, have *cumulative* influence.

If you use deferred or cumulative influence, you must make it clear to the player what the possible consequences of her decisions will be. It's unfair to give the player a choice early in the game without warning her that this choice will have long-term repercussions, and then change the direction of the story hours or days later based on that choice. Furthermore, if she wants to change her mind, she has to reload the game all the way back at the point where she first made the choice, choose differently, and then play all the way through the game again. (That's assuming she still has a save point there to reload from.) And she can do this only if she realizes how her decisions affected the current branch, which may not be obvious.

For example, if you allow a player to choose right at the beginning of a role-playing game whether she will play as a healer character or a fighter character, you should tell her that such an important choice will have significant deferred consequences throughout the game.

Many RPGs use cumulative influence to build up a sort of reputation for the player. The game keeps track of the player's behavior over time, and if the player consistently performs evil deeds, the NPCs in the game begin to treat her as an evil character. Again, you should warn the player that her cumulative behavior will have consequences later in the game.

TIP To lessen the frustration a player can feel when a decision has a deferred or cumulative effect that he does not like, allow the player to save the game multiple times. This way he can save the game prior to making critical decisions. This is normal practice in computer role-playing games.

Trivial decisions—which color hat will I wear?—should have only trivial consequences. If a trivial decision has a profound consequence, the player will feel cheated: She didn't know that the decision mattered and had no reason to expect it to matter. Attaching important consequences to trivial decisions violates the requirement that stories be credible and dramatically meaningful. *The Hitchhiker's Guide to the Galaxy,* a text adventure game, did this for comedic and ironic purposes, but most players and critics judged it to be an unreasonably difficult game for exactly this reason: The player couldn't predict what the consequences of her actions would be.

> ### DESIGN RULE Be Clear About Consequences
>
> Give players a reasonable amount of information about the possible consequences of their decisions, especially if the decision's consequences are deferred, so they can make informed choices. Don't tie important consequences to what seem to be trivial decisions.

THE BRANCHING STORY STRUCTURE

A diagram of a branching story looks somewhat like a tree, although by convention the root—the beginning of the story—appears at the top, so that the tree branches out as it goes down the page and the story goes forward in time. **Figure 11.2** shows a small part of the structure of a branching story.

FIGURE 11.2
Part of the structure of a branching story

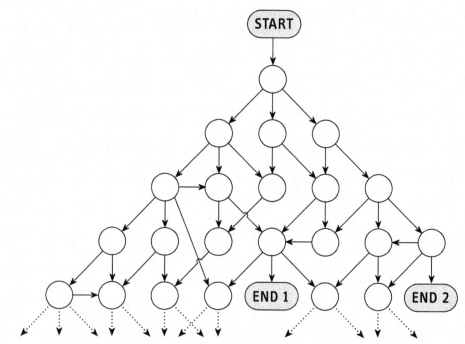

Each of the circles in the figure represents a branch point and each arrow represents a branch, that is, the player's movement along a plot line to the next branch point. The storytelling engine keeps track of the player's position in the story at any given moment.

As you look at Figure 11.2, be sure to note the following:

▦ The branch points don't always have the same number of branches leading away from them. A story can branch in any number of directions at any given point.

▦ The branches go down or sideways, but they never go back up again. The diagram depicts the possible progress of a story, and stories always move forward in time, never backward. In the course of playing a single game, the plot never follows the same branch or passes through the same branch point twice. This enforces the rule that stories must not contain identical repeating events and helps avoid the risk of continuity errors, as discussed earlier.

▦ Unlike branches on a real tree, different branches can merge; that is, different plot lines can converge. Many branch points can be reached by more than one path.

▦ The diagram depicts two possible endings that may be reached by different paths. The complete diagram would show additional endings farther down.

▦ The diagram shows only one start point, but in fact a story could have several start points if the player made a key decision before the story actually began. The player might select one of several different characters to be his avatar, and that choice could determine where the story begins. Or the storytelling engine could choose from among several designated start points at random just to make the beginning different each time the player plays the game.

The branching story mechanism is the classic method for creating interactive stories that give players lots of agency. Branching plot lines let you tell a story in which the player's actions strongly affect the plot, and he can see the effect of his actions if he plays the game more than once and makes different decisions the second time through.

DISADVANTAGES OF THE BRANCHING STORY

Be aware of the following three serious disadvantages of the branching story mechanism before you decide to use that structure for your game's story.

▦ **Branching stories are extremely expensive to implement.** Each branch and each branch point require their own content. In Figure 11.2, a player can experience at most six branch points in playing from the top to the bottom of the figure—not very many. That represents six player choices or challenges. After six choices—for example, to take the left fork of the road, to enter the building, to go upstairs instead of down, to talk to the old woman, to accept a letter she offers, to leave the room— the player has barely started the game. Yet even this simplified example involves 21 branch points and 35 different branches, each of which requires its own story content: gameplay and narrative material. If none of the branches merged again, there would be even more. This rapid growth in the number of branches is called the *combinatorial explosion*. (*Combinatorics* is the field of mathematics that studies the number of possible combinations of a set of things—in this case, a set of branch points in a branching story.) As a result, most modern games don't actually include much branching, and they often include long periods during which the player plays but doesn't change the story. *Wing Commander*, a space combat simulator, contained a branching story, but it branched only between missions, not during them. Eventually, the *Wing Commander* series abandoned branching storylines entirely because they proved to be too expensive.

▪ **Every critical event** (those that affect the entire remainder of the plot) **has to branch into its own unique section of the tree.** Suppose a character can live or die at a particular branch point. If he dies, he must never be seen again, which means none of the plot lines from his death onward can include him. His death requires an entirely separate part of the tree that can never merge back into the rest—otherwise, he might reappear after the player knows that he's dead. If this happens with two characters, the game requires four separate versions of the story: a version in which both live; a version in which both die; a version in which A lives and B dies; and a version in which B lives and A dies. Again, the number of possible combinations explodes.

▪ **The player must play the game repeatedly if she wants to see all the content.** If the storyline branches based on how well the player meets the game's challenges and she's very successful, then the next time she plays she has to play badly on purpose to learn the dramatic consequences of her failure! A lot of players would consider this to be absurd. They paid a great deal of money for the content in the game, and the only way to see it all is to play badly part of the time. This factor further contributed to the industry's abandoning stories that branch frequently.

If you want to make a branching story, you will have to plan out the structure in the concept stage of design. You should not actually write the story at that point in the design process, but you won't be able to plan a budget or schedule for your game unless you know how much content it will require, and a branching story's resource requirements expand very rapidly.

If you find that these drawbacks discourage you from using a branching structure, you can choose the compromise that the game industry most often uses when it creates nonlinear stories today: the foldback story.

Foldback Stories

Foldback stories represent a compromise between branching stories and linear ones. In a foldback story, the plot branches a number of times but eventually *folds back* to a single, inevitable event before branching again and folding back again to another inevitable event. (These are also sometimes called *multilinear* stories.) This may happen several times before the end of the story. See **Figure 11.3** for a simplified example. *The Secret of Monkey Island* follows this format, as do many of the traditional graphic adventure games.

Most foldback stories have one ending, as shown in the figure, but this isn't a requirement. You can construct a foldback story that branches outward to multiple endings from its last inevitable event.

Foldback stories offer players agency but in more limited amounts. The player believes that his decisions control the course of events, and they do at times, but he cannot avoid certain events no matter what he does. He may not notice this the first time that he plays and may think that the story reflects his own choices at all times. If he plays the game more than once, however, he will suspect that some events are inevitable and that the apparent control he enjoyed on the first play-through was limited. This is not necessarily a bad thing and can be useful to you as a storyteller. There's no reason why an interactive story must offer the player a way to avoid *any* event that he doesn't want to experience. After all, stories have always included the occasional event that the protagonist can do nothing about. If Scarlett O'Hara could have prevented Atlanta from being burned in *Gone with the Wind,* the story would have had a very different outcome and lost much of its emotional power. It's reasonable to use inevitable events to establish plot-critical situations that the player cannot reasonably expect to prevent or change.

The foldback story is the standard structure used by modern games to allow the player some agency without the cost and complexity of a branching story. Developers routinely construct the interactive stories in adventure games and RPGs as foldback stories. Of all forms of nonlinear interactive storytelling, it is the easiest to devise and the most commercially successful.

If you want to create a foldback story, you should choose critical turning points in the plot to be the inevitable events. They need not always be large-scale events like the burning of Atlanta. They simply should be events that change things forever and from which there is no turning back. The hero facing her final challenge, for instance, or the death of an important character, both work well as inevitable events. Obi-Wan Kenobi's death, in *Star Wars IV: A New Hope,* works well as an inevitable event.

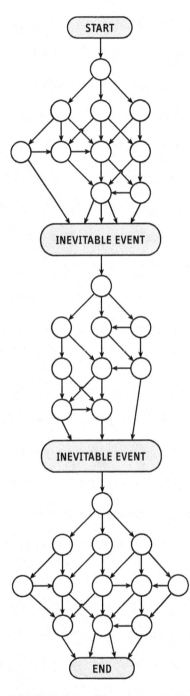

FIGURE 11.3 Simplified structure of a foldback story

CHAPTER 11

Emergent Narrative

Emergent narrative, a term introduced by designer Marc LeBlanc in his lecture "Formal Design Tools" at the 2000 Game Developers' Conference, refers to storytelling produced entirely by player actions and in-game events (LeBlanc, 2000). Emergent narrative storytelling does not contain narrative blocks (which he calls *embedded narrative*) created by a writer. The story *emerges* from the act of playing. There is no separate storytelling engine and no preplanned story structure, either linear or branching; in principle, anything can happen at any time so long as the core mechanics permit it.

Playing *The Sims* can create emergent narratives because the game simulates the activities of a group of characters and contains no prewritten narrative blocks. However, *The Sims* is not really a device for telling stories to the player because it gives the player so much control that he doesn't feel as if he's *interacting* with a story, but rather that he's *creating* a story. The game is more of an authoring tool. (See Chapter 9, "Creative and Expressive Play," for further discussion of player storytelling as a form of creative play.)

The chief benefit of emergent narrative is that the sequence of events is not fixed by a linear or branching structure, so the player enjoys more agency. He can bring about any situation that the core mechanics will let him create. However, the player can control the story's events only to the extent that he can control the core mechanics through his play. If the designer sets up the core mechanics in such a way as to force a particular situation on the player, his experience can be just as restricted as in a foldback story.

LeBlanc himself points out that emergent narrative is not without its problems. For one thing, it requires that the core mechanics be able to generate credible, coherent, and dramatically meaningful stories automatically—an extremely tall order. Core mechanics are defined in terms of mathematical relationships rather than human ones; how can they produce reasonable human behavior? How can you make them generate emotionally satisfying stories algorithmically? At the moment, with the field in its infancy, nobody knows. Furthermore, the core mechanics must limit repetition and randomness, and at the moment, the core mechanics of most games produce a lot of both. Finally, emergent narrative seems to offer nothing for conventionally trained writers to do, and it might not be wise to give up on ordinary writers just yet, given the millennia of storytelling experience they represent.

The industry does not yet have any software that generates stories good enough for commercial entertainment products. At the moment, emergent narrative remains an experimental technique, part of an AI research field known as *automated storytelling,* which offers great potential for the future. Multiplayer games, however, can generate emergent narratives more easily because they rely on the storytelling skills of the human participants—provided that the participants cooperate! *Journey, World of Warcraft,* and *Minecraft* all offer situations in which story-like experiences can emerge.

CHARACTER-AGNOSTIC PLOTS AND *KING OF DRAGON PASS*

In most role-playing games, the player gets to design her avatar from scratch at the beginning of the game—to choose the avatar's race, sex, profession, and many other details. The game's plot, therefore, must be *character-agnostic*, which is to say, the details of the plot do not depend on the character. Such plots have some of the same problems as plots created for nonspecific avatars, which were introduced in Chapter 10. However, there is a difference. Nonspecific avatars have *no* details the designer can work with. When a player creates an avatar, she creates those details, and the core mechanics and storytelling engine can work with them.

The plots of the stories in most RPGs aren't very sophisticated, so for the most part this doesn't matter much. The player completes a quest, usually by killing a lot of monsters, and the plot moves forward. It may branch one way if the player is choosing to role-play as an evil character, and another if she is good; but it's usually a large foldback story that ends up in the same place regardless.

The game *King of Dragon Pass*, published in 1999 by A-Sharp, is an important exception that deserves more attention than it received. The game is set in Glorantha, the magical world of the *RuneQuest* tabletop RPG games. Superficially, *King of Dragon Pass* appears to be a sort of management simulation. The player spends much of her time managing food production and looking after her tribe. What sets *King of Dragon Pass* apart, however, is its storytelling mechanism.

The goal of the game is to become king of an entire region known as Dragon Pass through a combination of economic growth, warfare, and diplomacy. The player leads her tribe assisted by a Council of Elders, consisting of seven NPCs. Each Elder has his or her own appearance, personality, and other attributes, and the player may call on any of them for advice when a critical situation arises that demands a decision. The advice the player gets naturally depends on the personal characteristics of the Elder that the player asks—some Elders are aggressive, some timid, some diplomatic, and so on. The player may also send Elders on missions of one kind and another, and the outcome of the mission may depend on which Elder the player sends. Sending a warmonger on a diplomatic mission can have disastrous consequences; sending a skilled negotiator on a purchasing mission can be highly profitable.

Ordinary RPGs treat the story as a journey, and their character-agnostic plot situations are normally associated with a particular location. If the player avoids visiting the location, she never experiences the situation. Also, most of the situations in ordinary RPGs must be resolved through combat, so no matter who the player has in her party, she has to fight her way out of it one way or another.

continues on next page

CHAPTER 11

CHARACTER-AGNOSTIC PLOTS AND
KING OF DRAGON PASS *continued*

King of Dragon Pass is different because instead of the player going to find adventure, the adventures come to her. The player does not have an avatar who moves around, but events happen to her all the same. The game maintains a huge database of character-agnostic situations and a separate database of Elders (and potential replacement Elders). Situations arise either at random or in response to earlier events. When a situation occurs that requires an Elder's attention, the player must choose which Elder will deal with it. The storytelling engine reads the Elder's attributes and computes an outcome from them. It narrates this outcome to the player and, if appropriate, triggers another situation that was caused by the first one. (The database of situations in *King of Dragon Pass* does not look like an ordinary story; rather, it is code written in a special programming language devised just for this purpose.)

This design has two benefits. First, because each situation is character-agnostic, an Elder may die with no harm to the story. That NPC simply gets removed from the database of Elders and cannot take part in any future events. There is no problem of a combinatorial explosion.

Second, and even more important, the outcome of a situation not only changes global status attributes such as the state of the tribe, it can also change the attributes of the Elder who was involved. The player's choice of Elder influences the outcome of the situation, and the situation in turn may affect the Elder's personality: making a callow young man more wise or humbling an arrogant warrior. This, then, may influence subsequent situations that the Elder is involved in. Just as in presentational fiction, there is an interplay between characters and events that changes both.

As a result, the game can be very different every time the player plays. The Elders she chooses to surround herself with can produce much more varied results than we see in the usual RPG. The player must be a good judge of character to know which Elders to use for what missions. For this reason, *King of Dragon Pass* might best be characterized as a *leadership simulator*—but so far, it is the only one of its kind.

Endings

Readers find the ending of a story one of its most critical emotional moments. Storytellers craft their endings to evoke specific feelings in the audience—sometimes even in the very last sentence. But an interactive story can have multiple endings. How many endings should your story have?

Include multiple endings if you want to give the player an outcome that reflects the dramatic actions he took throughout the story—those actions that actually matter to the story, as opposed to actions irrelevant to the drama, such as reorganizing his inventory or buying nicer clothing. However, the player's desire for an outcome that reflects his actions varies somewhat depending on what those actions were. Players' dramatic actions in a game may be divided into those taken to surmount a *challenge* and those in which the player makes a *choice*.

PREMATURE ENDINGS DON'T COUNT!

By *ending* we mean a true conclusion to the story, not a premature ending caused by the player failing to meet a challenge. Although dying in the middle of a long RPG does amount to losing the game, it's not really the end of the story, but simply an interruption in the player's experience of that story. The player will undoubtedly restart the game and continue if she finds playing the game a compelling experience. Premature endings should be quick because they're only temporary, so don't squander resources creating a lot of narrative material to accompany premature avatar death. Nor should you make the player wait a long time to get started again. Many modern games don't even require the player to reload the game after a premature ending; they reload automatically for her, restarting near where she left off. Other games simply don't let the avatar die at all to avoid the whole issue.

CHALLENGES AND CHOICES

Ordinary competitive games, those without stories at all, still offer more than one ending: The player wins or he loses, depending on how well he played. So if the player meets your game's challenges well, you might want the story to end well; if he meets them badly, you might let the story end badly. Just as the final score of an ordinary competitive game reflects the player's skill in a numeric way, so the outcome of the story can reflect the player's skill in a dramatic way. In general, players expect that if they meet all the game's challenges and make it to the end, the story will end in some reasonably positive way, reflecting the skill that got the player successfully to the end. If bad play produces a *premature* ending, you don't have to create a full-fledged conclusion for it. When a game's dramatic actions consist mostly of those taken to overcome challenges, players usually tolerate stories that offer only one ending.

If, on the other hand, the different possible endings reflect the player's *dramatic choices*—critical decisions the player made in the course of the interactive story—rather than his ability to overcome challenges, then the player will definitely expect his choices to affect the outcome of the story. If the game tells him that a choice is important and he finds out that it really wasn't, it will be distinctly disappointing. You may wish to create a number of endings to show the consequences of the player's dramatic choices. Games that include a lot of decision-making—especially moral choices, which feel dramatically important—should be nonlinear and offer multiple endings.

WHEN TO USE MULTIPLE ENDINGS

Devise multiple endings for your story if—and only if—each one will wrap up the story in a way both dramatically meaningful and emotionally consistent with the player's choices and play. If you gave the player a lot of dramatic freedom, or if it is important that the ending reflect the skill with which she played, then you should give her whatever ending her actions earn. You may have to create several endings, depending on how many critical choices you gave the player.

For a more detailed discussion, see the Designer's Notebook column "How Many Endings Does a Game Need?" (Adams, 2004).

Granularity

Granularity, in the context of games that tell a story, refers to the frequency with which the game presents elements of the narrative to the player. Consider *StarCraft,* which tells a long story that runs throughout all 30 missions available in the game but generally presents narrative (in the form of conversations among the major characters of the story) only between the missions. Because the missions take anywhere from 20 minutes to over an hour to complete, the game presents narrative blocks rather infrequently, so we can say that the storytelling in *StarCraft* exhibits *coarse granularity.* The *Wing Commander* series of games also tells a story between missions and so also illustrates coarse granularity.

LucasArts' famous adventure games—*The Secret of Monkey Island* and the *Indiana Jones* series—offer the player a small amount of narrative every time he solves a puzzle. This can happen as frequently as every 4 or 5 minutes, so the storytelling in these games shows *fine granularity.* LucasArts' games also use shorter narrative blocks, generally in the form of cut-scenes or spoken exposition.

There's no fixed standard for what constitutes coarse or fine granularity; you will find the terms mostly useful for comparing the relative granularity of one game to another.

In theory, the storytelling in a game may have *infinitesimal granularity*—that is, an interweaving of story and gameplay with such fine granularity that the player, unaware of narrative events as separate from the rest of the game, sees the game as one seamless interactive experience. Game developers have long attempted to achieve this quality for interactive storytelling with varying degrees of success. Generally, games come closest to reaching this goal if all story events pertain to the avatar and his actions (as in *Half-Life,* for instance) rather than if the story includes other events that the player must simply sit and watch.

Note that different authors use *granularity* to refer to a variety of different game design concepts: how frequently the player may take action; the degree to which the game reflects the player's achievements through point-scoring; and so on. Because of this ambiguity, this book uses the term only with respect to interactive storytelling.

Mechanisms for Advancing the Plot

In presentational media, the reader advances through the plot of a story at the rate at which she reads or the display mechanism displays. In a video game, the storytelling engine causes the plot to advance, but not at a fixed rate and not always triggered by the same mechanisms each time it advances. Different games use different triggers to tell the storytelling engine to move forward. In some games, succeeding or failing at a challenge triggers plot advancement. In others, the avatar's journey through the game world makes the story advance; in such games, entering a room or area may act as the trigger. In a very few games, the passage of time alone makes the plot advance, rather than anything the player does. The next three sections look at these mechanisms more closely. Each approach brings with it strengths and weaknesses, and you have to choose the one that works best for the story that you want to present.

The Story as a Series of Challenges or Choices

In a good many games, the plot advances only when the player meets challenges or makes decisions. In a war game or a vehicle simulator, completing a mission or level might advance the plot. This system works well for games that involve no travel at all or those in which travel itself doesn't affect the plot. In a combat flight simulator, the player can fly all over the sky, but none of that travel influences the story. What affects the story is shooting down enemy planes or being shot down by them.

Phoenix Wright: Ace Attorney, an adventure game for the Nintendo DS, also uses this mechanism. All game and story events take place in restricted areas—the courthouse and a small number of other locations. Solving puzzles in the different rooms causes the plot to advance.

Sometimes the trigger for advancing the story isn't surmounting a challenge but making a choice or decision. Role-playing games often give the player important decisions to make, such as whether or not to join a particular guild, the consequences of which significantly affect the story. Once the player makes a decision—and decisions are often irreversible—the plot advances.

If you require the player to succeed at challenges to advance the plot, the storytelling will be jerky, with sudden stops and starts. The player will sense that the story stalls every time she's stymied by a challenge, then starts up again when she meets the challenge. That doesn't matter much in coarse-grained stories—the player only expects storytelling at long intervals anyway—but in fine-grained ones it feels rather mechanical.

Adventure games and RPGs use this approach, but they combine it with avatar travel as a means of triggering plot advances, somewhat reducing the mechanistic feel of the plot advancement. They treat the story as a journey, which is the next topic.

The Story as a Journey

If your game involves an avatar on a journey—that is, a game in which much of the activity involves moving the avatar from place to place in the game world—you may choose to have the avatar's movements trigger the storytelling engine to advance the plot. Games that use this approach almost always set up obstacles to travel so the avatar cannot move through the game world freely, but so she must overcome the obstacles to reach new areas. In effect, then, the story as a journey consists of a series of challenges and sometimes choices—as we've discussed—but it adds a travel element: The avatar's arrival in an area can trigger a plot advancement all by itself, without any challenge or choice being involved.

Presenting a story as a journey offers the following benefits:

■ **It automatically provides novelty.** Because the player continually sees new things as he moves through the world, the experience remains fresh and interesting. The game gets the novelty that it needs to keep the player's interest from the visual appearance of the world, so you don't have to write as much novel dramatic material.

■ **It allows the player to control the pace.** Most games allow the player freedom to decide when to move and when to stand still. Unless the gameplay imposes a time limit, the player remains free to control the pace of the story—to stop and think about the characters and the game world and to explore without time pressure. The story progresses only when the player triggers that progress by moving.

Many games use not merely a journey but specifically the Hero's Journey story structure identified by folklorist Joseph Campbell. Some designers find the Hero's Journey's mix of challenges and travel particularly well suited to single-player, avatar-based game designs. For more information on the Hero's Journey, read Campbell's *The Hero with a Thousand Faces* (Campbell, 1972) and Christopher Vogler's discussion specifically for writers, *The Writer's Journey* (Vogler, 1998).

If you treat the story as a journey and you make it a linear story, although the player might be able to move her avatar backward through the game world, no more dramatic events can occur in areas she's already visited. For this reason, many adventure games periodically require the player to pass through *one-way doors*— travel mechanisms that cannot be reversed, though they may take the form of something other than actual doors. In *The Secret of Monkey Island,* the hero gets off a ship and onto an island by shooting himself out of a cannon. Once off the ship, there is no way back. The mechanism guarantees that the plot moves forward, along with the avatar.

Computer RPGs routinely treat stories as journeys but use highly nonlinear stories. The party can explore a large area, generally choosing any direction at will (though the game includes mechanisms for keeping the party out of regions that it isn't yet strong enough to tackle). Most of them also allow the player to replay chapters or levels to gain more experience points. Doing this naturally disrupts the player's perception of the game as a continuous story, however, which is why it is optional.

The Story as a Drama

A small number of games treat the story as a drama that progresses at its own pace, advancing with the passage of time itself. The story takes place in *real time*. In this case, the core mechanics don't send triggers to the storytelling engine to advance the plot; rather, the storytelling engine advances the plot on its own and sends triggers to the core mechanics to indicate when it's time to offer some gameplay.

The game *Night Trap* operates as a drama. The story unfolds continuously, whether or not the player takes any action. Set at a party in a suburban house, the game assigns the player the goal of protecting partying teenagers from a group of invading monsters. The house is conveniently fitted with a security system consisting of closed-circuit cameras and various traps that, when the player sets them off, catch and contain any monster nearby. The player watches the different rooms on the security cameras, and sets off the traps if a monster appears and tries to harm one of the teenagers who, in typical horror-movie fashion, are extraordinarily oblivious to it all. *Night Trap* requires the player to switch his view from camera to camera, following the various events of the party and looking out for the monsters. If the player does nothing and a monster drags away one of the kids, the player loses points.

Night Trap consists almost entirely of storytelling; the player's only action is to switch from one camera to another or to trigger a trap. Because the story progresses whether or not the player does anything, each game always takes the same amount of time to play.

The more recent, noncommercial game *Façade* also presents a story as a drama. In *Façade,* the player visits a couple of old friends and quickly realizes that their marriage is in trouble. The player can help them work through their problems—or not—by engaging in dialogue with them. The entire game takes place in the couple's apartment, and like *Night Trap,* the story progresses even if the player does nothing. But the player's actions during the game profoundly affect both the direction that the story takes and its ending.

Emotional Limits of Interactive Stories

Video games that don't include a story—that is, games that primarily entertain via the challenge and achievement of gameplay—don't try to arouse complex emotions in their audiences. They limit themselves to the thrill of victory and the agony of defeat, or perhaps to the frustration of repeated failure. But with a story, you can create other kinds of feelings as well. By crafting characters that the audience cares about and subtle relationships among those characters, you have a chance to make your audience feel (in sympathy with the characters) betrayal by a lover, satisfaction at justice done, or a protective instinct for a child.

However, the nature of the interactive medium imposes some limits on what you can do. This section looks at the emotional limitations of nonlinear stories and of avatar-based interaction models.

Emotional Limits of Nonlinear Stories

When you tell a nonlinear story, you give the player the freedom to make choices that significantly affect the relationships among the characters, which may include decisions that feel emotionally wrong—or at least that don't conform to what you, as a storyteller, would like the player to do. Suppose that you tell a story based on Shakespeare's *Hamlet,* but you give the player controlling Hamlet a number of options. In the play, Hamlet discovers that his mother and his uncle have conspired to kill his father, the king of Denmark, and usurp the throne. Hamlet's father's ghost appears to him and demands that Hamlet seek revenge, but Hamlet is unsure of what to do.

In your game, the player, acting as Hamlet, could simply run away and never come back; he could ignore his father's ghost and forgive his mother and uncle; he could try to assassinate his uncle and assume the throne himself; or he could just kill himself. None of these outcomes is quite as interesting as what Shakespeare actually wrote; in fact, some of them would bring the story to a bland and unsatisfactory conclusion.

By offering the player the power to change the course of the story—or at least to change the ending—you agree to accept the player's decisions, even decisions that are not ideal in ordinary storytelling terms. You cannot guarantee that the player will experience the most emotionally powerful resolution you feel that your story offers unless you confine the player to a single resolution (and even then, the player may prefer a different ending because individual taste varies).

Designers often restrict otherwise nonlinear stories to a single ending simply to guarantee that the players experience the emotionally meaningful outcome the designer planned. That means that the player's agency is limited. Players tolerate this in exchange for a satisfying ending, so long as you don't promise them that their choices will change an ending which, in fact, is fixed from the start.

Emotional Limits of Avatar-Based Games

An avatar-based game is analogous to a story written in the first person. Reading a first-person story, the audience can be fairly confident that regardless of what happens in the story, the narrator must have survived to write the story afterward. This isn't absolutely always the case—the narrators in the novel *A Game of Thrones* are periodically killed off and replaced by new narrators. This isn't the norm for first-person stories, however, nor for avatar-based games. Because avatars often begin the game with a fixed number of lives, players know that an avatar should survive to the end of the game. Over the years, the avatar's premature death has come to signify the player's failure to meet a challenge rather than being an actual element of the story, so the death of the avatar carries almost no emotional impact. The player simply reloads the game and tries again.

TIP Many of the traditional rules for writing good stories in noninteractive media don't apply to interactive media. A new medium requires new rules. Be wary of slavishly applying principles from other forms (such as Aristotle's principles for drama or Robert McKee's observations about screenwriting) to interactive stories. If it doesn't work for you, throw it out!

If you really want to affect the player's feelings with the death of a character, your game should kill not the avatar, but one of the avatar's friends. Two famous examples occur in the games *Planetfall* and *Final Fantasy VII*. In *Planetfall,* the player's sidekick, a wisecracking robot, sacrificed himself at a critical moment to allow the player to go on. Players often cite this as the first really emotionally meaningful moment in a computer game. In *Final Fantasy VII,* the villain kills Aeris Gainsborough, the player's ally. Nothing the player does can prevent this, and players often mention this death, too, as a particularly emotional moment in a game.

Party-based interaction models offer you more freedom to kill off members of the cast than avatar-based ones because the other members of the party remain to carry the story along. Two different television shows serve as good examples. *The Fugitive* could not have tolerated the death of Dr. Kimble, the hero of the show— equivalent to the avatar in an avatar-based game. On the other hand, the long-running *Law and Order* series about New York detectives and prosecutors has an ensemble cast with no single hero. Over the many years that it has aired, the entire cast has changed as one character or another has come and gone. The show continues to run because its central premise doesn't depend on any single individual.

Scripted Conversations and Dialogue Trees

Natural language refers to ordinary language as spoken or written by human beings. Computer scientists devised the term to contrast ordinary human language with *computer* (or *programming*) *languages*. The extremely difficult problem of making computers understand and react appropriately to natural language—whether the language occurs as conversation or instruction—has puzzled artificial intelligence researchers for decades. Recent research efforts have been fruitful enough to produce simple question-answering systems like Apple's Siri, but the state of natural language comprehension is still not good enough for a video game to implement a real conversation.

Game designers would like to be able to include natural language in games without trying to solve a decades-old research problem. We want the player to be able to engage in conversations with NPCs, especially in storytelling games. A *scripted conversation* allows us to approximate this. (Note that level design makes use of a technique often called "scripting" or "scripted events," which is a different, unrelated phenomenon.)

When entering a scripted conversation, either because the player chooses to speak to an NPC or an NPC chooses to speak to the player, the game enters a new gameplay mode created specifically for the purpose. All other actions normally become unavailable. The player doesn't speak or type his dialogue, but instead chooses a prewritten line of dialogue from a menu (see **Figure 11.4**). When the player chooses a line of dialogue, the game plays or prints an appropriate response from the NPC, after which the system gives the player a new menu of lines to choose from (some of which may be left over from the previous menu). This process goes back and forth until either the NPC refuses to speak to the player any longer or the player chooses to end the conversation.

In Figure 11.4, which was adapted from *Neverwinter Nights 2,* the player's character, Joshua, is talking with a character named Zaxis. The upper window displays the last few exchanges from the conversation. The lower window displays Zaxis's most recent remark, plus a list of lines for the player to choose from. Notice that each option is accompanied by a manner of speaking: diplomacy, bluff, intimidate, and so on. This lets the player have some idea of the tone of voice his avatar would use if the words were spoken aloud. Different approaches might work better with some NPCs than with others.

As the NPC says phrases the player hasn't heard before, the player may ask for elaboration, end the conversation, or switch the subject to a different topic. Offering the useful option, "Tell me again about…," enables the player to return to an earlier point in the conversation and go through the NPC's responses again if he didn't pay close enough attention the first time. To end the conversation, the player chooses a line clearly intended as a farewell message ("Thanks for your help. Maybe I'll talk to you again later."), or occasionally an NPC may cut off the conversation with a line such as "I don't have anything else to tell you" or "I won't talk to you if you're going to be rude."

Structure of a Dialogue Tree

Scripted conversations may be designed using a *dialogue tree,* a branching data structure a little like the branching story tree. In a branching story tree, each branch point, or *node,* represents a place where the plot divides based on some factor— usually a player decision. In a dialogue tree, each node represents a place where a conversation may branch, based on the player's decision about what he wants to say. Unlike a branching story, the arrows in a dialogue tree can go backward as well as forward because players sometimes want to repeat parts of their conversations.

Each node contains a menu of *exchanges,* and each exchange includes one line of dialogue available to the player and the NPC's response to that line. From each exchange, an arrow points to the next node in the tree—that is, the menu of dialogue options that the player will see next. In a scripted conversation, the computer displays all the dialogue options in the current menu to the player, and waits for the player to choose one. When the player makes a selection, the computer plays back the NPC's response, then follows the arrow to the next menu and displays the dialogue options there. The conversation passes through menu after menu as the conversation progresses.

In addition to letting the player discuss a variety of topics with a given NPC, the menu system allows the player to choose from a variety of different attitudes in which she says essentially the same thing, enabling her to project herself into the game as, for example, aggressive, deferential, formal, or flippant. The NPC can then respond to each phrase differently, in whatever way his personality dictates. An easygoing character might find a flippant response amusing and may choose to reveal more information to the player, while a powerful character who brooks no nonsense might be offended by wisecracks and refuse to talk to the player any more. (If you take this approach and the NPC's information is vital to the plot, make sure that either the powerful NPC gets over his snit after a while or there's some other way for the player to obtain the information.)

Figure 11.5 illustrates a brief conversation in which the player is acting as a police detective, interviewing someone who may have witnessed (or possibly committed) a crime. The conversation begins at the first menu, and in that menu the player has a choice of four approaches to the witness: polite, neutral, direct, or accusatory. Each approach produces a response from the witness, which then leads on to another menu of things for the player to say. Each menu has its own name.

In this example, the witness is rather uncouth, but is prepared to help the player as long as the player is not too hostile to him. If the player takes a strongly aggressive approach, the witness demands to see a lawyer, which ends the conversation. In this case, the player will not learn some of the information that the witness has, so the player will either have to reinterview the witness later or find it out some other way.

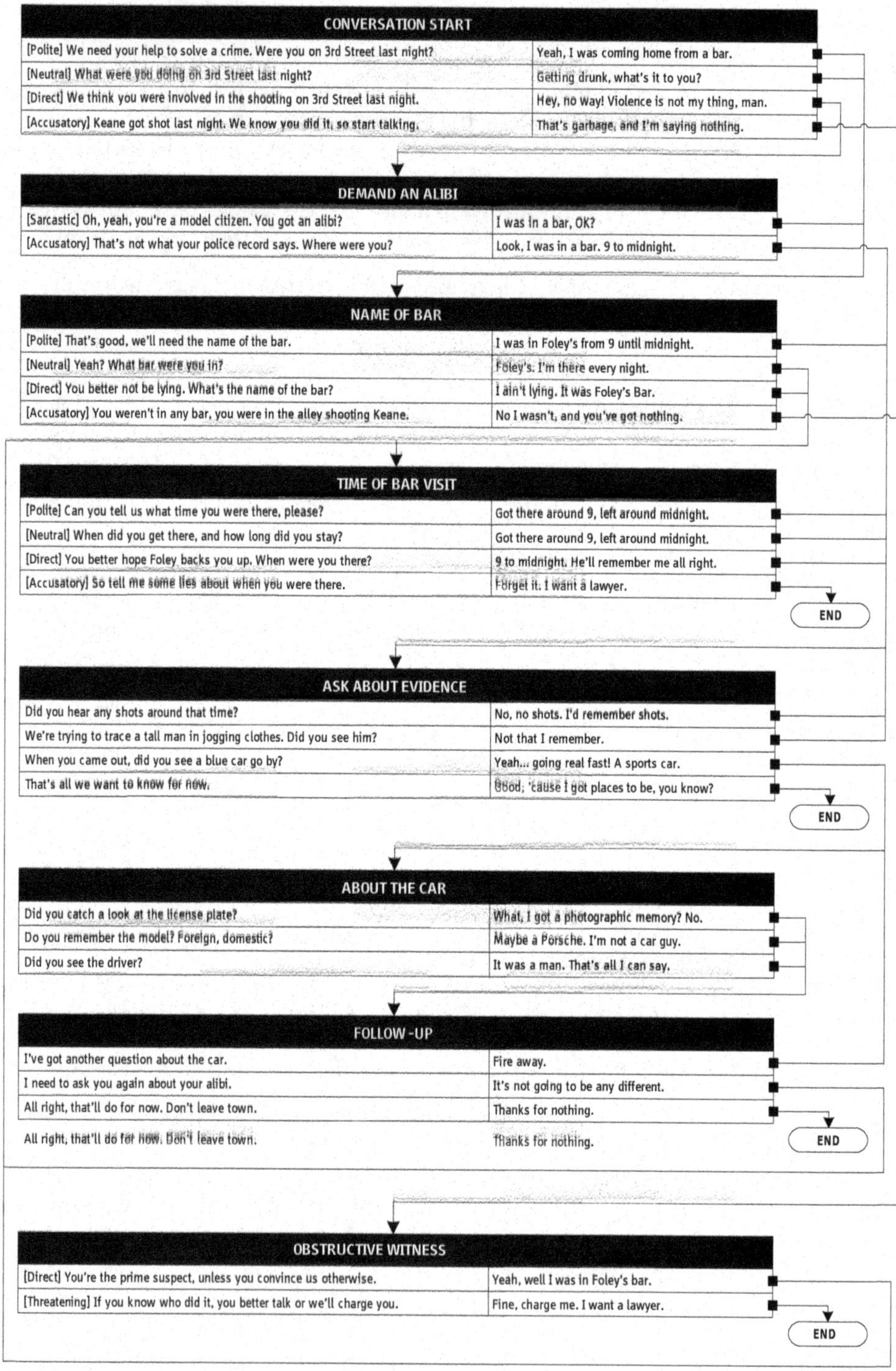

FIGURE 11.5
A small dialogue tree

CONVERSATION START

[Polite] We need your help to solve a crime. Were you on 3rd Street last night?	Yeah, I was coming home from a bar.
[Neutral] What were you doing on 3rd Street last night?	Getting drunk, what's it to you?
[Direct] We think you were involved in the shooting on 3rd Street last night.	Hey, no way! Violence is not my thing, man.
[Accusatory] Keane got shot last night. We know you did it, so start talking.	That's garbage, and I'm saying nothing.

DEMAND AN ALIBI

[Sarcastic] Oh, yeah, you're a model citizen. You got an alibi?	I was in a bar, OK?
[Accusatory] That's not what your police record says. Where were you?	Look, I was in a bar. 9 to midnight.

NAME OF BAR

[Polite] That's good, we'll need the name of the bar.	I was in Foley's from 9 until midnight.
[Neutral] Yeah? What bar were you in?	Foley's. I'm there every night.
[Direct] You better not be lying. What's the name of the bar?	I ain't lying. It was Foley's Bar.
[Accusatory] You weren't in any bar, you were in the alley shooting Keane.	No I wasn't, and you've got nothing.

TIME OF BAR VISIT

[Polite] Can you tell us what time you were there, please?	Got there around 9, left around midnight.
[Neutral] When did you get there, and how long did you stay?	Got there around 9, left around midnight.
[Direct] You better hope Foley backs you up. When were you there?	9 to midnight. He'll remember me all right.
[Accusatory] So tell me some lies about when you were there.	Forget it. I want a lawyer.

END

ASK ABOUT EVIDENCE

Did you hear any shots around that time?	No, no shots. I'd remember shots.
We're trying to trace a tall man in jogging clothes. Did you see him?	Not that I remember.
When you came out, did you see a blue car go by?	Yeah... going real fast! A sports car.
That's all we want to know for now.	Good, 'cause I got places to be, you know?

END

ABOUT THE CAR

Did you catch a look at the license plate?	What, I got a photographic memory? No.
Do you remember the model? Foreign, domestic?	Maybe a Porsche. I'm not a car guy.
Did you see the driver?	It was a man. That's all I can say.

FOLLOW-UP

I've got another question about the car.	Fire away.
I need to ask you again about your alibi.	It's not going to be any different.
All right, that'll do for now. Don't leave town.	Thanks for nothing.
All right, that'll do for now. Don't leave town.	Thanks for nothing.

END

OBSTRUCTIVE WITNESS

[Direct] You're the prime suspect, unless you convince us otherwise.	Yeah, well I was in Foley's bar.
[Threatening] If you know who did it, you better talk or we'll charge you.	Fine, charge me. I want a lawyer.

END

Figure 11.5 includes several features that are particularly worth noting:

■ Not all the menus in the figure let the player ask the same question in different tones. Some give the player a choice of questions to ask about different subjects. The menu "Ask About Evidence," for example, lets the player ask about gunshots, a car, or a man in jogging clothes. If the witness doesn't know anything about one of these subjects, the arrow leads back to the same menu again so the player can ask about a different subject.

■ Although all the witness responses in the menu "About the Car" lead to the same place (the "Follow-Up" menu), each one still provides the player with some different information.

■ Not all questions produce unique answers. In the "Time of Bar Visit" menu, the polite and neutral approaches both elicit the same answer from the witness. This is perfectly allowable if there's no particular reason to differentiate them.

Finally, note that in Figure 11.5, the maximum number of exchanges the player can have, without repetition, is eight. As with branching stories, if the menus continue to branch without folding back, you will soon get a combinatorial explosion of menus. In practice, they frequently converge or link back to previous menus.

Unfortunately, there is no industry standard system of notation or scripting for designing dialogue trees. Instead of creating a diagram with arrows as in Figure 11.5, you may find it easier to write your dialogue in a text file, and instead of drawing arrows, simply write "Go to Menu [menu name]" to indicate which menu should follow a given response. If such factors will affect your dialogue, you should sit down with your programmers and devise a system of notation that will be easy for you to create and easy for them to understand; they have to understand all the factors and when those factors come into play so they can write the software that actually implements the system. When you do this, be sure you devise a test plan for the system too, to ensure that it cannot produce nonsensical conversations.

Design Issues for Dialogue Trees

When you create a dialogue tree, you must be sure that every possible pathway through the tree produces a credible conversation. If the tree is large, verifying this can be a tedious and time-consuming job. If any of the arrows go back to an earlier point in the conversation, you may find that you have to rewrite some dialogue to make sure that it works both for the first time through the tree and also for subsequent times through. In the sample dialogue tree, one aspect definitely is not credible: The player can ask the same question in the "Ask About Evidence" menu again and again, and the witness will always give exactly the same response without complaining. This is a weakness of scripted conversations, but it is so common that it has almost become a gaming convention. Players are usually willing to overlook it.

CONDITIONAL BRANCHES AND EXCHANGES

Dialogue trees are seldom actually as simple as the sample dialogue tree makes them look. Figure 11.5 shows a purely fixed conversation whose content is not influenced by the core mechanics: Each player input produces exactly one response from the witness. But sometimes you want other factors to determine what choices the player has and how the NPCs respond. An NPC's response won't necessarily be rigidly connected with a player's menu choice. Some other factor, such as the level of the avatar's charisma attribute, may influence the NPC's reply. In order to specify this in the tree, you must include a way of indicating conditional branching: some text that reads (for example), "If the avatar's charisma is greater than 12, give response A; otherwise give response B." Likewise, role-playing games that include a diplomacy skill or a negotiation skill may give players with high skill levels extra menu items so that they can say things that unskilled characters cannot. To specify this in the tree, you would have to indicate the presence of conditional exchanges, such as "If the avatar's diplomacy attribute is greater than 10, also include…" and specify an exchange that only diplomatic avatars will get to use.

TOOLS FOR DESIGNING DIALOGUE TREES

As you saw in Figure 11.5, it can be difficult to document dialogue trees in a static medium like a diagram. Various tools exist to help you design a dialogue tree on a computer, but not all of them are free:

- *articy:draft* (pronounced "artsy draft"), from Nevigo, is commercial game design software that permits you to document interactive stories and dialogue trees as well as characters, objects, and locations. Its nested structure allows for complex systems that remain clear on the screen. It is available only for Windows. articy:draft can export its content to XML files for your programming team to use, and with the extra-cost articy:access middleware, your articy:draft designs can be incorporated directly into a game.

- *Chat Mapper* is not as powerful as articy:draft, but it also permits you to build dialogue trees in a graphical user interface and export them in various formats, including a script suitable for voice talent to use. It's commercial software and runs under Windows. A limited version is available free.

- *Twine* is a free graphical tool for making hypertext games and dialogue trees. It runs on both OS X and Windows. Twine's simple format makes it accessible to nonprogrammers.

- *Scapple*, from Literature and Latte, is an inexpensive tool for documenting relationships among ideas, although it is not really designed for game development. It runs on OS X and is in the process of being ported to Windows.

- *Scrivener*, also from Literature and Latte, is a powerful commercial writer's tool that helps you keep many kinds of ideas, file pictures, and other content organized, and actually write your text. However, it's not specifically designed for dialogue trees.

Again, a diagram with arrows may or may not be the best way to document a scripted conversation with conditional content. Many developers use spreadsheets to document scripted conversations because a spreadsheet program makes it easy to add rows and columns as necessary while keeping the document looking tidy, and using multiple sheets gives even more flexibility. If you have any programming experience, you may find it easiest to write pseudo-code. Discuss it with the programmers, because whatever approach you choose, it is essential that they understand it in order to produce the correct results.

ANOTHER APPROACH

A completely different approach is to think of the conversation mechanism not as a sort of flowchart (as in Figure 11.5), but as a flexible list of options to which different exchanges may be added or deleted at different times. In this approach, instead of creating menus of exchanges, you write each exchange separately, as an individual item, and give it its own name or number. Remember that an exchange consists of a player dialogue choice and a response from the NPC that the avatar is talking to. After each exchange, instead of drawing arrows leading to a new menu, you would indicate which new exchanges should be added to the current list, and which should be deleted. This way you can easily add certain exchanges that remain in the conversation permanently, without having to document them in each new menu. For example, you can add a "That's all I wanted to know" exchange, which ends the conversation, to the menu at the very beginning, and never delete it no matter what else is said. That would enable the player to end the conversation at any point. Once a subject has been raised for the first time, you could add a "Tell me again about..." exchange to the menu, and until it is deleted, the player could always ask to hear about that subject again.

Here's how the first few lines of the conversation in the sample dialogue tree would look using this approach. A conversation-ending dialogue option, which was not in Figure 11.5, has been included; it is exchange 5.

Beginning Action: Add exchanges 1, 2, 3, 4, and 5 to the menu.

Exchange 1:
Player: [Polite] "We need your help to solve a crime. Were you on 3rd Street last night?"
Response: "Yeah, I was coming home from a bar."
Action: Delete exchanges 1, 2, 3, and 4. Add exchanges 6, 7, 8, and 9.

Exchange 2:
Player: [Neutral] "What were you doing on 3rd Street last night?"
Response: "Getting drunk, what's it to you?"
Action: Delete exchanges 1, 2, 3, and 4. Add exchanges 6, 7, 8, and 9.

Exchange 3:
Player: [Direct] "We think you were involved in the shooting on 3rd Street last night."
Response: "Hey, no way! Violence is not my thing, man."
Action: Delete exchanges 1, 2, 3, and 4. Add exchanges 10 and 11.

Exchange 4:
Player: [Accusatory] "Keane got shot last night. We know you did it, so start talking."
Response: "That's garbage, and I'm saying nothing."
Action: Delete exchanges 1, 2, 3, and 4. Add exchanges 12 and 13.

Exchange 5:
Player: "That's all we need. You can go."
Response: "About time."
Action: END.

Exchange 6:
Player: [Polite] "That's good, we'll need the name of the bar."
Response: "I was in Foley's from 9 until midnight."
Action: Delete exchanges 6, 7, 8, and 9. Add... [exchanges from the "Ask About Evidence" menu].

Exchange 7:
Player: [Neutral] "Yeah? What bar were you in?"
Response: "Foley's. I'm there every night."
Action: Delete exchanges 6, 7, 8, and 9. Add... [exchanges from the "Time of Bar Visit" menu].

Exchange 8:
Player: [Direct] "You better not be lying. What's the name of the bar?"
Response: "I ain't lying. It was Foley's Bar."
Action: Delete exchanges 6, 7, 8, and 9. Add... [exchanges from the "Time of Bar Visit" menu].

Exchange 9:
Player: [Accusatory] "You weren't in any bar, you were in the alley shooting Keane."
Response: "No I wasn't, and you've got nothing."
Action: Delete exchanges 6, 7, 8, and 9. Add exchanges 12 and 13.

Exchange 10:
Player: [Sarcastic] "Oh, yeah, you're a model citizen. You got an alibi?"
Response: "I was in a bar, OK?"
Action: Delete exchanges 10 and 11. Add exchanges 6, 7, 8, and 9.

Exchange 11:
Player: [Accusatory] "That's not what your police record says. Where were you?"
Response: "Look, I was in a bar. 9 to midnight."
Action: Delete exchanges 10 and 11. Add... [exchanges from the "Ask About Evidence" menu].

Exchange 12:
Player: [Direct] "You're the prime suspect, unless you convince us otherwise."
Response: "Yeah, well I was in Foley's Bar."
Action: Delete exchanges 12 and 13. Add... [exchanges from the "Time of Bar Visit" menu].

Exchange 13:
Player: [Threatening] "If you know who did it, you better talk or we'll charge you."
Response: "Fine, charge me. I want a lawyer."
Action: END.

.
.
.

This approach saves you a lot of duplicated effort if there are dialogue options that you want to occur every time the game waits for input, such as the "I'm finished talking" option. You simply specify when they are added to the menu, and they remain in the menu until they are deleted. It also lets you document conditional responses, or conditional exchanges, easily by including *if* statements in the Response and Action lines.

The system is also powerful, because each exchange is a separate item that you can add to the menu any time you want to, instead of being part of a fixed collection of exchanges as in Figure 11.5. However, with this power, as always, comes some risk. It's much harder to read than a diagram like Figure 11.5, and it doesn't document exactly what's on the screen at any given point. In order to find out what options the player has at any point, you have to work your way through the whole conversation, keeping track of which items are added and deleted as you go.

Benefits of Scripted Conversations

Although scripted conversation forces the player to say only the lines available in the script, it produces a sequence of plausible remarks and replies. It also gives you a way to illustrate both the avatar's and the NPC's personality through something other than their appearance. You can write their lines in such a way that you give them distinct personalities of their own. For instance, Guybrush Threepwood, the hero of the *Monkey Island* games, uses phrases that reveal him as a wise guy who seldom takes anything seriously. The character's vocabulary, grammar, dialect, and—if the game features recorded audio—tone of voice and accent provide important cues.

The scripted conversation is not merely a mechanism for giving the player information, however. It's a real part of the story, and the player's choices can have a distinct effect on the progress of the game. If an NPC asks the player to entrust him with a valuable secret, then the player's decision, whether to tell or not to tell, could have far-reaching consequences. The player has to choose responses based on her assessment of the NPC's character—to which you, the designer, must provide clues.

For a more detailed discussion of different ways of designing scripted conversations, read Chapter 14, "Dialogue Engines," of the book *Game Writing: Narrative Skills for Videogames,* edited by Chris Bateman (Bateman, 2006). Bateman points out that large dialogue trees can be unwieldy to work with, and he proposes some simpler alternatives. He is undoubtedly correct, but for complex conversations about a variety of subjects, the dialogue tree offers you the most comprehensive scripting power.

When to Write the Story

A strict design rule, which first appeared in Chapter 7, "Game Concepts," specifies that you must not write the story during the concept stage of design but only later during the elaboration stage. During the concept stage, your job is to define the player's role and the kinds of gameplay that he will experience in that role. You may make a list of episodes or levels that you would like to include in the game during the concept stage, and you can think about what the player may do in each level, but you must not write the whole story yet. (To reiterate, you will need to lay out the *structure* of a branching story before you try to compute the budget for the entire project, but you should not actually write the story itself.)

We want you to wait to write the story because, until you know what gameplay the game will offer, you do not know what kinds of challenges the player will face and what sorts of actions she will be permitted to take. Even more important, you don't yet know what sorts of actions she *won't* be able to take. It's easy to write a story that includes too many different kinds of actions—actions that the programmers may not have time to implement in software. If you've written a story that includes the player's avatar riding a horse as well as traveling on foot and only later decide not to implement horseback riding for technical reasons, you've wasted a lot of time.

The task of writing the story falls into the second major stage of game design, the elaboration stage. You should begin writing *after* you define the game's primary gameplay mode, and preferably after you define all the major gameplay modes you will offer, because the details of those modes will tell you what sorts of actions the player can take and under what circumstances. In reality, writing the story will be an iterative process that takes place in conjunction with level design because level design creates the moment-by-moment sequence of experiences that the player can go through. If a game presents narrative only between levels, you can write a story with large granularity, in pieces after completing the design of each level, or even after all the levels are designed. But if narrative events can occur within a level, then you must write the story as you design the levels.

Other Considerations

This section wraps up the discussion of interactive stories by addressing the frustrated author syndrome and episodic delivery, and includes a few thoughts about how the industry may tell stories in the future.

The Frustrated Author Syndrome

Game designers who would really rather be authors in noninteractive media—would-be movie directors, for example—often make a couple of key mistakes when writing interactive stories. First, they tend to write linear stories while pretending to themselves and to the players that the story offers more agency than it really does, promising a big role for the player and then actually giving her almost none at all. The game *Critical Path* illustrates this problem; its introduction suggests that the player gets to do all kinds of exciting things when in fact its story is so rigidly linear that the avatar dies every time the player deviates from the storyline in any way. (Rumors say that the developers named the game *Critical Path* in an effort to justify this weakness.)

Players see the second symptom of frustrated author syndrome as they sit through large quantities of narrative when they would really rather be playing. Although an excellent game in other respects, *The Longest Journey* included one scene that consisted of 20 minutes of nonstop monologue by a NPC. That would be a long soliloquy even for Shakespeare! The game's designer, Ragnar Tørnquist, who originally trained as a screenwriter, admitted afterward that this was an error. Never forget that players come to play—to *do* something. Almost any sophisticated story requires some narrative, but you must parcel out narrative in reasonably sized blocks. Players won't want to sit through much more than 3 or 4 minutes of narration at a time, and many will get frustrated long before the 3-minute mark.

> **DESIGN RULE** Be a Game Designer, Not a Filmmaker
>
> Don't design a game to show off your skills as a film director or an author. Design a game to entertain by giving the player things to do. Always give the player more gameplay than narration. The player, not the story, is the star of the show.

Episodic Delivery

Most of our discussion so far has concentrated on individual stories that come to a definite end. However, you may want to exploit the popularity of a hit game by producing one or more sequels, a situation now so commonplace that this section addresses designing for it intentionally. The game industry has expressed much interest in the business opportunities that episodic delivery might offer, selling players entertainment a few hours at a time instead of in a single large chunk, as games sold at retail do now.

There are three main formats for delivering multipart stories, as the following sections reveal. The television industry has more experience at delivering multipart stories than the game industry does, so we use familiar TV terms to help illustrate these three formats.

UNLIMITED SERIES

An *unlimited series* comprises a set of episodes, each consisting of a self-contained story in which the plot is both introduced and resolved. A single theme or context runs through the entire series but not a single plot; in fact, the stories exist so independently of each other that you can view episodes in any order and the story still makes sense. American evening TV dramas used this format almost exclusively up through the early 1980s: In each episode of *Columbo,* Columbo solved exactly one crime. Viewers can watch each episode individually with little disadvantage. A consistent world and an overarching theme tie the series together. Because each episode offers a self-contained story, the producers can create as many episodes as they want (see **Figure 11.6**).

FIGURE 11.6
The structure of an
unlimited series

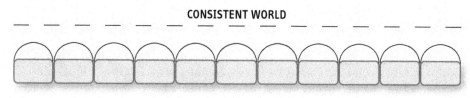

CONSISTENT WORLD

EPISODES   Each episode deals with opening and resolving one major plot strand.

The majority of games and their sequels use the unlimited series format. Each game in the series contains a complete story set against a consistent world. Sometimes the publicity materials claim that sequels carry on the story from the previous game, but often the connection between them is flimsy; in any case the player gets a thorough introduction, so even if he didn't play the previous game, he can still enjoy the current one.

SERIALS

A *serial* consists of a (theoretically) infinite sequence of episodes. In a serial, plot lines extend over several episodes, developing simultaneously but at different rates so that only rarely does any plot begin and end within a single episode. Consequently, the episodes are not self-contained, and if you see an isolated episode without seeing what went before, you won't know what's going on. To maintain interest, each episode generally ends at a critical point in a major plot strand, creating a cliffhanger that the writers hope will create a strong desire to see the next episode. Soap operas depend on this format.

Serials rely on a large cast of characters who come together in smaller groups to play out each of several different (and often unrelated) plot lines, of which some, at any one time, may be beginning, coming to a climactic point, or ending. With no single overarching plot, events usually center on a group of people in a specific location or on a small group of families. Serials lack the grand sense of resolution that the Hero's Journey provides. Instead, they offer opportunities to observe different characters interacting under a variety of stresses. The cliffhanger at the end of each episode may involve some shocking revelation or event that leaves us wondering how a key character will react to the news or the change in situation.

It's a fair bet that you will see efforts to create interactive serials over the next few years, because the game industry would like to find a way to get players hooked on a story—and therefore paying to play it, episode after episode—in the same way that TV viewers seem hooked on serial dramas. Each episode of such an interactive serial can't be a multihour blockbuster of the sort that the video game industry makes today; these games take too long to build. TV soap operas typically lower their production values and deliver short episodes frequently rather than long episodes infrequently, and you would expect interactive serials to work the same way. **Figure 11.7** depicts the structure of a serial.

FIGURE 11.7
The structure of
a serial

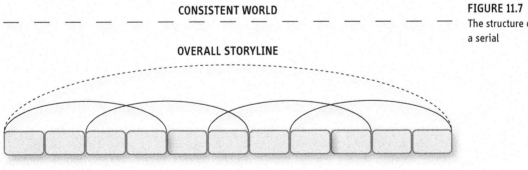

CONSISTENT WORLD

OVERALL STORYLINE

EPISODES

Plot strands overlap episodes.

LIMITED SERIES

A *limited series* includes features of both the unlimited series and the serial. The limited series often combines single-episode plot lines, begun and resolved within one episode, with other plot lines that carry over from one episode to another. Unlike the unlimited series or the serial, however, a limited series also maintains one overarching plot line that runs throughout all episodes and eventually comes to a definite end, which is what makes the series limited. The TV show *Babylon 5* was a limited series. *Kentucky Route Zero* is a video game example.

Unlike the serial, the limited series format doesn't rely heavily on cliffhangers to create interest in the subsequent episodes. Instead, the overall plot line provides the driving interest, and the cliffhanger becomes only a secondary means of keeping the viewer's interest (see **Figure 11.8**).

FIGURE 11.8
The structure of a limited series

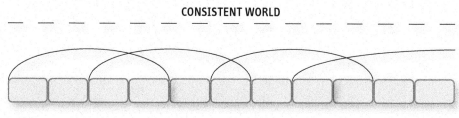

CONSISTENT WORLD

EPISODES   Plot is continuous. Strands overlap. Episodes end on a cliffhanger.

POTENTIAL AND LIMITS OF EPISODIC DELIVERY

The industry already makes games in the unlimited series format, but it may start making games in the limited series format as well to encourage players to buy the whole set. Developing games as limited series will require more money and planning but may prove to be worth it for a game that a publisher can be certain will be a hit. The *Harry Potter* series of games, based on the books and movies, will probably prove to be a limited series: When the overarching story ends, the series of games will end just as the author planned for the series of books to end. The speed of change of technology may prove a problem, in that the later games may not be able to rely on the earlier games' code without appearing dated. Rewriting the software in the middle of the series would cancel out the cost savings generated by planning the whole series at the beginning. If the industry can find a way to make content quickly and cheaply on a continuing basis, you may eventually see interactive serials, with no fixed episode count and a constantly evolving story. Running such games in web browsers over the Internet makes the most sense because the web offers cheaper development and delivery compared to standalone games. If the prediction proves true and publishers develop limited serial games for the web, then to be profitable, those games may need to use an advertising-based business model; few players will pay for web-based games because there are so many free ones available.

Currently, most efforts to develop content on a continuing basis involve maintenance and expansion of *persistent worlds*—massively multiplayer online games (MMOGs) rather than episodically delivered serials. The MMOGs use a subscription business model, and once proprietors recoup the extremely high level of investment required to set up such a game, they can be extremely profitable.

If you're working on a PC or console game, we don't recommend that you leave its story unfinished intentionally. It's too much of a disappointment to play for hours only to find that you must buy another game to find out how the story ends; critics roasted the few games that took that approach. A long game should end with its major problem resolved, either for good or ill. If you want to leave room for a sequel, the sequel should be about a *different* problem that arose during the course of the first story. *Star Wars IV: A New Hope* serves as a perfect example: The story ended with the heroes destroying the Death Star (the movie's major problem), but with Darth Vader (a character introduced during the story) escaping to cause trouble later on. The story in *StarCraft* ended with the destruction of the Overmind (its major problem), but with Sarah Kerrigan, a key character, having apparently turned traitor and gone on to lead a renegade faction against the heroes of the first story. Unless your story is quite explicitly part of a multipart story and you can guarantee that all parts will eventually be told, players deserve some resolution at the end of a game—especially a long game. The unsatisfactory ending of *Mass Effect 3* caused so much outrage among players that BioWare, the developers, released a free extension to the game to address their concerns.

Summary

Most video games will benefit from the addition of a good story, one that is credible, coherent, and dramatically meaningful. A designer should not attempt to write a movie or a novel when making the video game story, however; she should remember that interactivity is the reason people play games. Whether you decide to make a linear, nonlinear, or a foldback, multiple-ending story for your game will depend on the gameplay and genre you've designed in the concept phase. For more engaging gameplay, deeper emotional response from the player, and greater satisfaction upon completing the game, designers should work on a good story that maintains player interest, that shows character growth, that balances narrative elements with gameplay, and that, above all else, remains enjoyable to play.

Design Practice EXERCISES

1. Game writers often find themselves asked to write content with very limited information, and they have to make it up as best they can. This is an exercise about writing dialogue in such a situation. Assume the following scenario: An adventurer arrives at an old ruin. The main entry gate is guarded by a huge stone golem that

has to be convinced to let the adventurer pass through. The player might take three different approaches to the conversation at hand: *intimidation, admiration,* or *subterfuge.* Write a scripted conversation for this situation in which, at each menu, the player has a choice of three options corresponding to each of the three approaches. Your conversation must include no fewer than four exchanges, counting introducing and parting dialogue lines. If the player chooses a consistent approach throughout the conversation, the golem opens the gate; if the player does not, the golem refuses and the conversation ends.

2. This exercise is a case study. Choose a game that you have played through (or one that your instructor assigns) that contains a story. Analyze the story according to the principles introduced in this chapter and write an essay (your instructor will inform you of the required length) addressing the following questions. Is it a linear or a nonlinear story, and if nonlinear, what story structure does it use? Does it have more than one ending? What is its granularity? What kinds of narrative does the story use (cut-scenes, scrolling text, voice-over narration, and so on)? What proportion of the player's actions are dramatically meaningful versus dramatically irrelevant? Considering all the player actions, in-game events, and narrative events, do you feel it is a good story according to the requirements for credibility, coherency, and dramatic meaningfulness? Why or why not? Does the story evoke any emotions other than those associated with victory and defeat? If so, give an example.

3. Pick a linear story of your own choice from a book or a movie and write a half-page summary of the plot (don't start with *War and Peace*). Then make a nonlinear story out of it by introducing no fewer than three branch points into the story at what you consider to be key moments in the plot—points at which an event could have occurred differently or one of the characters could have taken a different action from the one portrayed by the original story. (Each branch point may have as few as two options, but you can include more if you like.) Draw a diagram of the result and show the options at each branch you introduce. The diagram should include the original plot as well. Write a brief summary of the consequences of the alternate branches arising from taking a different path. If you want, you can fold back the story to a single ending, or leave it branching with multiple endings. If you include multiple endings, be sure they follow credibly as a result of the particular path taken through the branching storyline you created.

Design Practice QUESTIONS

These questions are a shortened form of the questions available in the "How to Write a Requirements Specification for Your Story" sidebar in the section "Figuring Out What You Want to Achieve," earlier in this chapter.

1. How do the actions that you make available to the player work with the story in your game such that the story remains credible, coherent, and dramatically meaningful?

2. How will you design your gameplay to be sure that the player does not experience so much randomness or repetition that it harms the dramatic tension of your story?

3. Will the story in your game be linear or nonlinear?

4. If your story is nonlinear, will the story branch or fold back? What kinds of things will cause it to branch: challenges, choices, or both? Will you allow deferred or cumulative influences, or will all influences be immediate?

5. If the story folds back, how many inevitable events will it have? What will they be like?

6. How many endings will your story have? How does each ending reflect the player's play and/or choices throughout the game?

7. What will be the size of your game's granularity? How and when are narrative events interwoven with game events and player actions?

8. What mechanism will you use to advance the plot? Travel, events, time, or some combination?

9. Can the story begin at the beginning of the game, or would the game benefit from a prologue as well?

10. Will the game include narrative (that is, noninteractive) material? What role will it play—an introduction, mission briefing, transitional material, a conclusion, or character definition? Is the narrative essential for the player to understand and play the game?

11. What form will the narrative material take? Pages in the manual? Scrolling text in the program? Movies? Cut-scenes? Voice-over narration? Monologues by characters?

12. What actions might the player take that are story actions but not efforts to overcome challenges? Conversations? Construction? Exploration?

13. Will the game include scripted conversations? Between the player and which characters? For what purpose?

14. Will the story be multipart? If so, how will the plot lines be handled: as an unlimited series, a limited series, or a serial?

CHAPTER 12

Creating the User Experience

A player experiences a video game through its input and output devices, as well as (possibly) through interactions with other players in the same room. The software, art, and audio assets that present the game to the player and interpret his inputs are collectively called the user interface (UI). Designing the player's experience via the UI is one of the game designer's most important jobs. It has an enormous effect on whether the player perceives the game as satisfying or disappointing, elegant or graceless, fun or frustrating.

These days we tend to describe this process as user *experience* design rather than simply user *interface* design to emphasize that our goal is to entertain the player, not simply to build screens and menus. The player-centric approach has a profound influence on user experience design, because it is here that your decisions are most critical to how the player feels about your game. You must subject each design decision you make to the test: How does this make your player feel? Does it help to entertain her?

In this chapter, you'll learn the general principles of user experience design and a process for designing your interface, along with some ideas about how to manage its complexity. We'll then look at two key concepts related to game interfaces: *interaction models* and *camera models*. After that we'll delve into specifics, examining some of the most widely used visual and audio elements in video game UI and analyzing the functionality of various types of input devices. Because the overwhelming majority of video games include some notion of moving characters or vehicles around the game world, we'll consider a variety of navigation mechanisms as they are implemented in different camera models and with different input devices. The chapter concludes with a few observations on how to make your game customizable.

What Is the User Interface?

As you saw in Figure 2.1, the user interface lies between the player and the internals of the game. The UI knows all about any supported input and output hardware. It translates the player's input—the button-presses (or other actions) in the real world—into actions in the game world according to the *interaction model* (see Chapter 1, "Games and Video Games"), passing on those actions to the core mechanics, and it presents the internal data that the player needs in each situation in visible and audible forms.

NOTE To see representative examples of screen layouts suitable for different game genres, read the companion e-books that discuss the genres.

NOTE At first glance, it may seem that this chapter uses the terms *user interface* and *user experience* interchangeably. They aren't the same. The *experience* is something that happens inside the player's head. The *interface* is a part of the game software; it mediates between the core mechanics and the player, and creates the player's experience.

NOTE When you design the core mechanics, you should avoid making choices that depend on the performance characteristics of particular input/output (I/O) devices. Let the UI manage the hardware, and keep the internals of the game hardware-independent. If you later port the game to another machine, you will have to redesign only the UI, not the core mechanics.

This chapter refers to the outputs as the *visual elements* and *audio elements* of the UI and to the inputs as the *control elements*. When the game gives important information to the player about his activities, the state of the game world, or the state of his avatar (such as the amount of health or money he has), we say that it gives *feedback* to the player—that is, it informs him of the effects of his actions. The visual and audio elements of the UI that provide this information are called *feedback elements*.

TERMINOLOGY ISSUES

Unfortunately the term *button* is overloaded: Sometimes it refers to a button on an input device that the player can physically press, and other times it refers to a visual element on the screen that the player can click or tap. To disambiguate the two, this chapter always refers to physical buttons on an input device as *controller buttons* and those on the screen, activated by the mouse or a tap, as *screen buttons*. *Keys* refers to keys on a computer keyboard (or the on-screen keyboard mobile phones use). Keys are generally interchangeable with controller buttons because they both transmit the same type of data.

Menus and screen buttons appear on the screen as visual elements, but clicking or tapping them sends a message to the internals of the game, which makes them control elements as well. Furthermore, the appearance of a screen button may change in response to a click, making it a mechanism for giving information as well as for exercising control. Your experience with computers should allow you to tell from context what these terms refer to when you encounter them in this text.

Any discussion of UI design runs into a chicken-and-egg problem: You can't learn how to design a good UI without already knowing the names of common visual elements such as power bars and gauges, and this chapter can't introduce the common visual elements without making references to how they're used. So, to address the most critical information first, we'll start with the principles of interface design. If you encounter a reference to an interface element you've never heard of, see the section "Visual Elements," later in the chapter, for an explanation.

Dozens, perhaps hundreds, of published books address UI design, and this chapter does not try to duplicate all that material. The following sections concentrate specifically on UIs for games, how they interact with the game's mechanics, and how they create the entertainment experience for the player. If you want to read more about UIs in general, see *The Elements of User Experience: User-Centered Design for the Web and Beyond, 2nd Edition* by Jesse James Garrett (Garrett, 2010).

Player-Centric Interface Design

A game's user interface plays a more complex role than does the UI of most other kinds of programs. Most computer programs are tools, so their interfaces allow the user to enter and create data, to control processes, and to see the results. A video game, on the other hand, exists to entertain and, although its UI must be easy to learn and use, it doesn't tell the player everything that's happening inside the game, nor does it give the player maximum control over the game. It mediates between the internals and the player, creating an experience for the player that feels like gameplay and storytelling.

The player-centric approach taught in this book applies to user experience design, as it does to all aspects of designing a game. Therefore, the discussion is tightly focused on what the player needs to play the game well and how to create as smooth and enjoyable an experience as possible.

About Innovation in Interface Design

Although innovation is a good thing in almost all aspects of game design—theme, game worlds, storytelling, art, sound, and of course gameplay—do *not* innovate unnecessarily when designing a new interface. This is especially true of button assignments on controllers and keyboards. Over the years, most genres have evolved a practical set of feedback elements and control mechanisms suited to their gameplay, and these have now become standardized conventions that players know so well that they are part of their muscle memory. Learn these conventions by playing other games in your chosen genre and adopt whichever of them is appropriate for your game. Pay special attention to games that are widely admired as the best of their kind. Their UI probably helped them secure that reputation.

> **DESIGN RULE** Do *Not* Innovate Unnecessarily in UI Design
>
> If a convention exists, use it—or as much of it as works with your game. If you force the player to learn an unfamiliar UI when a perfectly good one already exists, you will frustrate her and she will dislike the game no matter what other good qualities it has.

If you do choose to offer a new UI for a familiar problem, build a tutorial level and play-test it thoroughly with both novice and experienced players. If testing shows that your new system is not a *substantial* improvement over the traditional approach, go back to what works. Also be sure to allow the player to customize the interface in case he doesn't like it. The section "Allowing for Customization," near the end of this chapter, addresses this further.

Some General Principles

The following general principles for UI design apply to all games regardless of genre:

■ **Be consistent.** This applies to both aesthetic and functional issues; your game should be stylistically as well as operationally consistent. If you offer the same action in several different gameplay modes, assign that action to the same controller button or menu item in each mode. The names for things that appear in indicators, menus, and the main view should be identical in each location. Your use of color, capitalization, typeface, and layout should be consistent throughout related areas of the game.

■ **Give good feedback.** When the player interacts with the game, he expects the game to react—at least with an acknowledgment—immediately. When the player presses any screen button, the game should produce an audible response even if the button is inactive at the time. An active button's appearance should change either momentarily or permanently to acknowledge the player's click.

■ **Remember that the player is the one in control.** Players want to feel in charge of the game—at least in regard to control of their avatars. Don't seize control of the avatar and make him do something the player may not want. The player can accept random, uncontrollable events that you may want to create in the game world or as part of the behavior of non-player characters (NPCs), but don't make the avatar do random things the user didn't ask him to do.

■ **Limit the number of steps required to take an action.** Set a maximum of three controller-button presses to initiate any special move unless you need combo moves for a fighting game. It's a nuisance to have to press several buttons just to give one command, especially if the player has to give it often. Similarly, don't require the player to go through menu after menu to find a commonly used command. (See "Depth Versus Breadth," later in the chapter, for further discussion.)

■ **Permit easy reversal of actions.** If a player makes a mistake, allow him to undo the action unless that would affect the game balance adversely. Puzzle games that involve manipulating items such as cards or tiles should keep an undo/redo list and let the player go backward and forward through it, though you can set a limit on how many moves backward and forward the game permits.

■ **Minimize physical stress.** Video games famously cause tired thumbs, and unfortunately, repetitive stress injuries from overused hands can seriously debilitate players. Assign common and rapid actions to the most easily accessible controller buttons. Not only do you reduce the chance of injuring your player, but you allow him to play longer and to enjoy it more.

■ **Don't strain the player's short-term memory.** Don't require the player to remember too many things at once; provide a way for him to look up information that he needs. Display information that he needs constantly in a permanent feedback element on the screen.

- **Group related screen-based controls and feedback mechanisms on the screen.** That way, the player can take in the information he needs in a single glance rather than having to look all over the screen to gather the information he needs to make a decision.

- **Provide shortcuts for experienced players.** Once players become experienced with your game, they won't want to go through multiple layers of menus to find the command they need. Provide shortcut keys to perform the most commonly used actions from the game's menus, and include a key-reassignment feature. See the section "Allowing for Customization," at the end of the chapter.

What the Player Needs to Know

Players naturally need to know what's happening in the game world, but they also need to know what they should do next, and most critically, they need information about whether their efforts are succeeding or failing, taking them closer to victory or closer to defeat. In this section, you learn about the information that the game must present *to* the player to enable her to play the game. In keeping with a player-centric view of game design, think of these items as questions the player would ask.

- **Where am I?** Provide the player with a view of the game world. This visual element is called the *main view*. If she can't see the whole world at one time (she usually can't), also give her a map or a mini-map that enables her to orient herself with respect to parts of the world that she can't currently see. You should also provide audio feedback from the world: ambient sounds that tell her something about her environment.

- **What am I actually doing right now?** To tell the player what she's doing, show her avatar, party, units, or whatever she's controlling in the game world so that she can see it (or them) moving, fighting, resting, and so on. If the game uses a first-person perspective, you can't show the player's avatar, so show her something from which she can infer what her avatar is doing: If her avatar climbs a ladder, the player sees the ladder moving downward as she goes up. Here again, give audio feedback: Riding a horse should produce a clip-clop sound; walking or running should produce footsteps at an appropriate pace. Less concrete activities, such as designating an area in which a building will be constructed, should also produce visible and audible effects: Display a glow on the ground and play a definitive *clunk* or similar sound.

- **What challenges am I facing?** Display the game's challenges, puzzles, combat, or whatever they may be—directly in the main view of the game world. Some challenges make noise: Monsters roar and boxers grunt. To show conceptual or economic challenges, you may need text to explain the challenge, for example, "You must assemble all the clues and solve the mystery by midnight."

- **Did my action succeed or fail?** Show animations and indicators that display the consequences of actions: The player punches the bad guy and the bad guy falls down; the player sells a building and the money appears in her inventory.

Accompany these consequences with suitable audio feedback for both success and failure: a whack sound if the player's punch lands and a whiff sound if the player's punch misses; a *ka-ching!* when the money comes in. Naturally, some actions will have deferred consequences. Investing in a factory may not produce visible effects in a game for several minutes, but the player still needs some kind of feedback element to show whether the factory is being productive or not.

▪ **Do I have what I need to play successfully?** The player must know what resources she can control and expend. Display indicators for each: ammunition, money, energy, and so on.

▪ **Am I in danger of losing the game?** Show indicators for health points, power, time remaining in a timed challenge, or any other resource that must not be allowed to reach zero. Use audio signals—alarms or vocal warnings—to alert the player when one of these commodities nears a critical level.

▪ **Am I making progress?** Show indicators for the score, the percentage of a task completed, or the fact that the player passed a checkpoint.

▪ **What should I do next?** Unless your game provides only a sandbox-type game world in which the player can run around and do anything she likes in any order, players need guidance about what to do. You don't need to hold their hands every step of the way, but you do need to make sure they always have an idea of what the next action could or should be. Adventure games sometimes maintain a list of people for the avatar to talk to or subjects to ask NPCs about. Road races over unfamiliar territory often include signs warning of curves ahead.

▪ **How did I do?** Give the player emotional rewards for success and (to a lesser extent) disincentives for failure through text messages, animations, and sounds. Tell her clearly when she's doing well or badly and when she has won or lost. When she completes a level, give her a debriefing: a score screen, a summary of her activities, or some narrative.

> ## DESIGN RULE Do *Not* Taunt the Player
>
> A few designers think it's funny to taunt or insult the player for losing. This is mean-spirited and violates a central principle of player-centric game design: the duty to empathize. The player will feel bad about losing anyway. Don't make it worse.

What the Player Wants to Do

Just as the player needs to know things, the player wants to do things. You can offer him many things to do depending upon the game's genre and the current state of the game, but some actions crop up so commonly as to seem almost universal. Here are some extremely common actions.

▦ **Move.** The vast majority of video games include travel through the game world as a basic player action. How you implement movement depends on your chosen camera and interaction models. You have so many different options that a whole section, "Navigation Mechanisms," addresses movement later in this chapter.

▦ **Look around.** In most games, the player cannot see the whole game world at one time. In addition to moving through the world, he needs a way of adjusting his view of the world. In avatar-based games, he can do this through the navigation mechanism (see "Navigation Mechanisms"). In games using multipresent and other interaction models that provide aerial perspectives, give him a set of controls that allow him to move the virtual camera to see different parts of the world.

▦ **Interact physically with non-player characters.** In games involving combat, this usually means attacking NPCs, but interaction can also mean giving them items from the inventory, carrying or healing them, and many other kinds of interactions.

▦ **Pick up portable objects and put them down.** If your game includes portable objects, implement a mechanism for picking them up and putting them down. This can mean anything from picking up a chess piece and putting it down elsewhere on the board to a full-blown inventory system in a role-playing game (RPG) in which the player can pick up objects in the environment, add them to the inventory, give them to other characters, buy them, sell them, or discard them again. Be sure to include checks to prevent items from being put down in inappropriate places (such as making an illegal move in chess). Some games do not permit players to put objects down, in order to prevent the players from leaving critical objects behind.

▦ **Manipulate objects.** Many objects in the environment can be manipulated in place but not picked up, such as light switches in a room, or puzzle pieces in a puzzle game. For an avatar-based game, design a mechanism that works whenever the avatar is close enough to the object to press it, turn it, or whatever might be necessary. In other interaction models, let the player interact more directly with fixed objects by clicking them. You can simplify this process by giving fixed objects a limited number of states through which they may be rotated: a light switch is on or off; curtains are fully open, halfway open, or closed.

▦ **Construct and demolish objects.** Any game that allows the player to build things needs suitable control mechanisms for choosing something to build or materials to build with, selecting a place to build, and demolishing or disassembling already-built objects. It also requires feedback mechanisms to indicate where the player may and may not build, what materials he has available, and, if appropriate, what it will cost. You should also include controls for allowing him to see the structure in progress from a variety of angles. For further discussion of construction mechanisms, see the companion e-book *Fundamentals of Construction and Simulation Game Design*.

▦ **Conduct negotiations and financial transactions, and set numeric values.** In complex simulations, players sometimes need to deal with numbers directly, especially when managing quantities of intangible resources such as money.

Conventional UIs for desktop applications employ many ways of obtaining a number from the user—typed characters, scrolling list boxes, sliders, and so on. Unfortunately, most of these prosaic mechanisms harm the player's fantasy unless he is playing a game set in the modern world. If you need to let the player manipulate raw numbers, try to find a way—perhaps with appropriate artwork and consistent typefaces—to make it fit into your game's cultural style.

▪ **Give orders to units or characters.** Players need to give orders to units or characters in many types of games. Typically this requires a two- or three-step process: designating the unit to receive the order, giving the order, and optionally giving the object of the order, or *target*. Orders take the form of verbs, such as *attack, hug, open,* or *unload,* and targets take the form of direct objects for the verbs, such as *thug, doll, crate,* or *truck,* indicating what the unit should attack, hug, open, or unload.

▪ **Conduct conversations with non-player characters.** Video games almost always implement dialogue with NPCs as *scripted conversations* conducted through a series of menus on the screen. See "Scripted Conversations and Dialogue Trees" in Chapter 11, "Storytelling."

▪ **Customize a character or vehicle.** If your game permits the player to customize his character or vehicle, you will have to provide a suitable gameplay mode or shell menu. The player may want to customize visible attributes of avatar characters, such as hair, clothing, and body type, as well as invisible ones, such as dexterity. Players like to specify the color of the vehicles they drive, and they need a way to adjust a racing car's mechanical attributes because this directly affects its performance.

▪ **Talk to friends** in networked multiplayer games. Multiplayer online games must give players opportunities to socialize. Build these mechanisms through chat systems and online bulletin boards or forums.

▪ **Pause the game.** With the exception of arcade games, any single-player game must allow the player to pause the action temporarily.

▪ **Set game options.** Outside the game world, the player may want to set the game's difficulty level, customize the control assignments (see "Allowing for Customization," later in this chapter), or adjust other features such as the behavior of the camera. Build shell menus to allow the player to do this.

▪ **Save the game.** All but the shortest games must give the player a way to stop the game and continue from the same point when the player next starts up the game software. See "Saving the Game" in Chapter 13, "Gameplay."

▪ **End the game.** Don't forget to include a way to quit!

The Design Process

You will recall from Chapter 2, "Designing and Developing Games," that the game design process takes place in three stages: concept, elaboration, and tuning. Designing the user interface takes place early during the elaboration stage. There's no point in designing it any earlier; if you do so before the end of the concept phase, the overall design may change dramatically and your early UI work will be wasted.

This section outlines the steps of the UI design process. You can find definitions for many of the components you will use for your game's UI later in this chapter.

Define the Gameplay Modes First

A gameplay mode consists of a camera model, an interaction model, and the gameplay (challenges and actions) available. During the concept stage, define, in general terms, what gameplay modes the game will have. At the beginning of the elaboration stage, start to design the gameplay modes in detail.

Your first job will be to design the *primary gameplay mode,* the one in which the player spends the majority of her time. See the sections "Interaction Models" and "Camera Models," later in this chapter, for details about each of them. Once you have chosen the camera model, interaction model, and gameplay for the primary gameplay mode, you can begin to create the details of the UI for that mode.

When you have designed the primary gameplay mode, move on to the other modes that you think your game will need. Plan the structure of the game using a flowboard, as described in Chapter 2. In addition to gameplay activities, don't forget story-related activities. Design modes that deliver narrative content and engage in dialogue if your game supports these. Be sure to include a way to interrupt narrative and get back to gameplay and a pause menu (if it's a real-time game) so the player can answer the telephone.

Typically gameplay modes do not use completely different user interfaces but share a number of UI features, so it's best to define all the modes before you begin UI work. If your game provides a small number of gameplay modes (say, five or fewer), you can start work on the UIs as soon as you decide what purpose each mode serves and what the player will do there. However, if the game provides a large number of modes, then you should wait until *after* you have planned the structure of the game and you understand how the game moves from mode to mode.

Once you have the list of gameplay modes, start to think about what visual elements and controls each will need. Using graph paper or a diagramming tool such as Microsoft Visio, make a flowchart of the progression of menus, dialog boxes, and other UI elements that you intend to use in each mode. Also document what the input devices will do in each.

NOTE In a large development team, the lead designer and the user interface designer(s) are normally different people. For simplicity's sake, this chapter assumes you will do both jobs.

CHAPTER 12

Occasionally gameplay modes can share a single UI when the modes differ only in the challenges they offer. If you want to allow the player to control the change from one mode to another, your user interface must offer commands to accomplish these mode changes.

Steps in designing a game's UI include, for each mode, designing a screen layout, selecting the visual elements that will tell the player what she needs to know, and defining the inputs to make the game do what she wants to do. We'll take up these topics in turn. The remainder of this discussion assumes that you're working on the UI for the most important mode—the primary gameplay mode—although this advice applies equally to any mode.

BUILD A PROTOTYPE UI

Experienced designers always build and test a prototype of their user interfaces before designing the final specifications. When you have the names and functions of your UI elements for a mode worked out, you can begin to build a prototype using placeholder artwork and sounds so that you can see how your design functions. Don't spend a lot of time creating artwork or audio on the assumption that you'll use it in the final product; you may have to throw it away if your plans change.

Plenty of good tools allow interface prototyping, including graphics and sound, with minimal programming. You can make very simple prototypes in Microsoft PowerPoint using the hyperlink feature to switch between slides. Adobe Flash offers more power, and if you can do a little programming, other game-making tools such as those from Blitz Research Ltd (www.blitzbasic.com) will let you construct a prototype interface. For mobile phone games, you can make paper prototypes on index cards and try "playing" them to see how they feel.

Your prototype won't be a playable game but will display menus and screen buttons and react to signals from input devices. It should respond to these as accurately as possible given that no actual game software supports it. If a menu item should cause a switch to a new gameplay mode, build that in. If a controller button should shoot a laser, build the prototype so that at least it makes a *zap* noise to acknowledge the button press.

As you work and add additional gameplay modes to the prototype, keep testing to see if it does what you want. Don't try to build it all at once; build a little at a time, test, tune, and add some more. The finished prototype will be invaluable to the programming and art teams that will build the real interface. And again, don't innovate unless you have to. Borrow from the best.

Choosing a Screen Layout

Once you have a clear understanding of what the player does in the primary (or any) mode and you've chosen an interaction model and a camera model, you must then choose the general screen layout and the visual elements that it will include.

The main view of the game world should be the largest visual element on the screen, and you must decide whether it will occupy a subset of the screen—a window—or whether it will occupy the entire screen and be partially obscured by overlays. See "Main View," later in the chapter, for more information about your options.

You will need to find a balance between the amount of screen space that you devote to the main view and the amount that you devote to feedback elements and on-screen controls. Fortunately this seldom presents a problem in personal computer and console games, which use high-resolution screens. It remains a bigger challenge for handheld devices and mobile phones, which can have diverse screen sizes and shapes.

Telling the Player What He Needs to Know

What, apart from the current view of the game world, does the player need to see or to know about? What critical resources does he need to be aware of at all times, and what's the best way to make that information available to him? Select the data from your core mechanics that you want to show, and choose the feedback elements most suited to display those kinds of data using the list in "Feedback Elements," later in this chapter, as a guide. Also ask yourself what warnings the player may need and then decide how to give both visual and audible cues. Use the general list from "What the Player Needs to Know" earlier in this chapter, but remember that the gameplay you offer might dictate a slightly different list. Your game may include unique attributes that have never been used before, which require new types of feedback elements. For example, a game about clothing design might include an attribute called *originality,* and you could display the level of *originality* with a set of iconic images of T-shirts, ranging from plain white (unoriginal) to something outrageously tie-dyed (very original).

Once you have defined the critical information, move on to the optional information. What additional data might the player request? A map? A different viewpoint of the game world? Think about what feedback elements would best help him obtain needed information and how to organize access to such features.

Throughout this process, keep the general principles of good UI design in mind; test your design against the general principles listed in "Some General Principles," earlier in this chapter.

NOTE Sometimes motion-sensitive input devices such as the Wii controller and the Kinect permit better mappings than traditional controllers offer, and sometimes worse. For example, if the player wants the avatar to jump in the game, the Kinect can detect the player physically jumping in her living room. On the other hand, turning does not work so well; if she physically turns in the living room, she will no longer be facing the screen. Again, study other games to see how they handle these issues.

Letting the Player Do What She Wants to Do

Now you can begin devising an appropriate control mechanism to initiate every action the player can take that affects the game (whether within the game world or outside of it, such as saving the game). Refer to the list provided earlier in "What the Player Wants to Do" to get started.

What key actions will the player take to overcome challenges? Refer to the companion e-books for special UI concerns for each genre. What actions unrelated to challenges might she need: Move the camera, participate in the story, express herself, or talk to other players online? Create visual and audible feedback for the actions to let the player know if these succeeded or failed.

You'll need to map the input devices to the player's actions, based on the interaction model you have chosen (see "Interaction Models," later in this chapter). Games vary too much to tell you exactly how to achieve a good mapping; study other games in the same genre to see how they use on-screen buttons and menus or the physical buttons, joysticks, and other gadgets on control devices. Use the latter for player actions for which you want to give the player the feeling that she's acting directly in the game without mediation by menus. Whenever possible, borrow tried-and-true techniques to keep it all as familiar as possible.

Work on one gameplay mode at a time, and every time you move to a new gameplay mode, be sure to note the actions it has in common with other modes and keep the control mechanisms consistent.

Shell Menus

Shell menus allow the player to start, configure, and otherwise manage the operation of the game before and after play. The screens and menus of the shell interface should allow the player to configure the video and audio settings and the game controls (see "Allowing for Customization," later in the chapter), to join in multiplayer games over a network, to save and load games, and to shut down the game software.

The player should not have to spend much time in the shell menus. Provide a way to let players get right into the action with one or two clicks of a button.

A surprising number of games include awkward and ugly shell menus because designers assumed that creating these screens could wait until the last minute. Remember, the shell interface is the first thing your player will see when he starts up the game. You don't want to make a bad impression before the player even gets into the game world.

Managing Complexity

As game machines become more powerful, games themselves become increasingly complex with correspondingly complex UIs. Without a scheme for managing this complexity, you can end up with a game that players find extremely difficult to play—either because no one can remember all the options (as with some flight simulators) or because so many icons and controls crammed onto the screen (as in some badly designed strategy games) leave little room for the main view of the game world. Here you learn some options for managing your game's complexity.

Simplify the Game

This option should be your first resort. If your game is too complex, make it simpler. You may do this in two ways: with *abstraction* and *automation.*

ABSTRACTION

When you *abstract* some aspect of a complicated system, you remove a more accurate and detailed version of that aspect or function and replace it with a less accurate and detailed version or no version at all. This makes the game less realistic but easier to play. If the abstracted feature required UI control or feedback mechanisms, you may save yourself the trouble of designing them.

Many driving games don't simulate fuel consumption; the developers abstracted this idea out of the game. They don't pretend that the car runs by magic—the player can still hear the engine—but they just don't address the question. Consequently, the user interface needs no fuel gauge and no way to put fuel in the car. The player doesn't have to think about these things, which makes the game easier to play.

AUTOMATION

When you *automate* a process, you remove it from the player's control and let the computer handle it for her. When the game requires a choice of action, the computer chooses. Note that this isn't the same as abstraction because the underlying process remains part of the core mechanics; you just don't bother the player about it. The computer can take over the process entirely, in which case, again, you can save the time you would have spent on designing the UI, or you can build the manual controls into the game but keep them hidden unless the player chooses to take over manual control (usually through an option in a shell menu). Racing games often automate the process of shifting gears so it just happens by itself; the player doesn't have to think about it.

If you let the player choose between automated or manual control over a game feature, you can refer to the two options as *beginner's mode* and *expert mode* in the menu where she makes the choice. You might want to reward the player for choosing the more complex task. For example, you can make automated gear-shifting slightly less efficient than expert manual gear-shifting, so the player who gets really good at manual shifting gets a benefit. If the automated task is perfectly efficient, the player has no incentive to learn the manual task.

Depth Versus Breadth

The more options you offer the player at one time, the more you risk scaring off a player who finds complex user interfaces intimidating. A UI that provides a large number of options simultaneously is said to be a *broad* interface. If you offer only a few options at a time and require the player to make several selections in a row to get to the one he wants, the UI is said to be *deep*.

Broad interfaces permit the player to search the whole interface by looking for what he wants, but finding the one item of current interest in that broad array takes time. Once the player learns where to find the buttons or dials, he can usually find them again quickly. Players who invest the (sometimes considerable) training time find using a broad interface to be efficient; they can quickly issue the commands they want. The cockpit of a commercial passenger aircraft qualifies as an enormously broad interface; with such a huge array of instruments, the pilot can place his hand on any button he needs almost instantly, which makes flying safer. On the other hand, pilots must train for years to learn them all.

Normally, deep interfaces offer all their choices through a hierarchical series of menus or dialog boxes. The user can quickly see what each menu offers. He can't know in advance what sequence of menu choices he must make to find the option he wants, so the menus must be named and organized coherently to guide him. Even once he learns to find a particular option, he still has to go through the sequence of menus to get to it each time. On the other hand, using a well-designed deep interface takes almost no training, and some players simply prefer them no matter how experienced they become.

It's a good idea to offer both a deep and a broad interface at the same time: deep for the new players, broad for the experienced ones. You can do this on the PC by assigning shortcut keys to frequently used functions. The large number of keys on a PC keyboard enables you to construct a broad interface easily. Console machines, with fewer controller buttons available and no mouse for pointing to screen elements, offer fewer options for creating broad interfaces.

If you can offer only one interface, try to make the breadth and depth of your interface roughly equal; but avoid making anything more than three or four levels deep if you can help it. When deciding how to structure menus, categorize the options by frequency of access. The most frequently accessed elements should be one or two steps away from the player at most. The least frequently accessed elements can be farther down the hierarchy.

Context-Sensitive Interfaces

A context-sensitive interface reduces complexity by showing the player only the options that she may actually use at the moment. Menu options that make no sense in the current context simply do not display. Microsoft Windows takes a middle path, continuing to show unavailable menu options in gray, while active menu items display in black. This reduces the user's confusion somewhat because she doesn't wonder why an option that she saw a few minutes ago has disappeared.

Graphic adventures, RPGs, and other mouse-controlled games often use a context-sensitive pointer. The pointer changes form when pointed at an object with which it can interact. When pointing to a tree, for instance, it may change to the shape of an axe to indicate that pressing the mouse button will cause the tree to be cut down. The player learns the various things the mouse can do by pointing it at different objects in the game world and seeing how it changes.

Avoiding Obscurity

A UI can function correctly and be pretty to look at, but when the player can't actually tell what the buttons and menus do, the interface is said to be *obscure*. Several factors in the UI design process tend to produce obscurity, and you should be on the lookout for them:

▪ **Artistic overenthusiasm.** Naturally, artists want to make a UI as pleasing and harmonious as they can. Unfortunately, sometimes they produce UI elements that, while attractive, convey no meaning.

▪ **The pressure to reduce UI screen usage.** Using an icon instead of a text label on a screen button saves space, and so does using a small icon instead of a large one. But icons can't convey complicated messages as well as text can, and small, simple icons are necessarily less visually distinctive than large, complex ones. When you reduce the amount of space required by your UI, be sure you don't do so to the point of making its functions obscure.

▪ **Developer familiarity with the material.** *You* know what your icons mean and how they work—you created them. That means you're not the best judge of how clear they will be to others. Always test your UI on someone unfamiliar with your game. See whether your test subjects can figure out for themselves how things work. If it requires a lot of experimentation, your UI is too obscure.

Interaction Models

Chapter 2 defined the *interaction model* as the relationship between the player's inputs via the input devices and the resulting actions in the game world. You create the game's interaction model by deciding how the player's controller-button presses and other real-world actions will be interpreted as game world activities by the core mechanics. The functional capabilities of the various input devices available will influence your decisions (see "Input Devices," later in the chapter). There isn't room here to discuss button assignments in detail, so you should play other games in your genre to find examples that work well.

In practice, interaction models fall into several well-known types:

- *Avatar-based,* in which the player's actions consist mostly of controlling a single character—his avatar—in the game world (Mario, for example). The player acts upon the world through the avatar and, more importantly, generally can influence only the region of the game world that the avatar currently inhabits. An avatar is analogous to the human body: To do something in our world, we have to take our bodies physically to the place where we want to do it. That doesn't mean an avatar must be human or even humanoid; a vehicle can be an avatar. To implement this mode, therefore, many of your button-assignment decisions will center on navigation (see "Navigation Mechanisms," later in the chapter).

- *Multipresent* (or *omnipresent*), in which the player can act upon several different parts of the game world at a time. For him to do so, you must give him a camera model that permits him to see the various areas that he can change; typically, an aerial perspective. Chess uses a multipresent interaction model; ordinarily the player may move any of his pieces (which can legally move) on any turn. Implementing this mode requires providing ways for the player to select and pick up objects or give orders to units.

- In the *party-based* interaction model, most commonly found in RPGs, small groups of characters generally remain together. In this model, you will probably want to use point-and-click navigation and an aerial perspective.

- In the *contestant* model, the player answers questions and makes decisions, as if he is a contestant in a TV game show. Navigation will not be necessary; you will simply assign different decision options to different buttons.

- The *desktop* model mimics a computer (or a real) desktop and ordinarily is found only in games that represent some kind of office activity, such as business simulations.

A coherent design that follows common industry practice will probably fit into one of these familiar models. You can create others if your game really requires them, but if you do so, you may need to design more detailed tutorial levels to teach your player the controls.

Camera Models

Old computer games used to treat the game screen as if it were a game board in a tabletop game. Today we use a cinematic analogy and talk about the main view on the screen as if it displays the output of a camera looking at the game world. This is the source of the terms *virtual camera* and *camera model.*

To define the camera model, you will make a number of design decisions about how you want the player to view the game world, what the camera focuses on, and how the camera behaves. Certain camera models work best with particular interaction models; the next few sections introduce the most common camera models and discuss the appropriate interaction models for them.

FILMMAKING TERMINOLOGY

The game industry has adopted a number of terms from filmmaking to describe certain kinds of camera movements. When a camera moves forward or back through the environment, it is said to *dolly,* as in *the camera dollies to follow the avatar.* When it moves laterally, as it would to keep the avatar in view in a side-scrolling game, it *trucks.* When it moves vertically, it *cranes.* When a camera swivels about its vertical axis but does not move, it *pans.* When it swivels to look up or down, it *tilts.* When it rotates around an imaginary axis running lengthwise through the lens, it is said to *roll.* Games almost never roll their cameras except in flight simulators; as in movies, normally the player expects the horizon to be level.

The 3D Versus 2D Question

A question you must decide early on is whether your game should use a 3D or a 2D graphics display engine. Although your game world may be fully three-dimensional, you might want to use a 2D engine to display it for either aesthetic or technical reasons. If a game uses 2D graphics, the first-person and third-person perspectives will not be available; those camera models require a 3D engine.

Virtually all large games running on powerful game hardware such as a personal computer or home game console employ 3D. (Small games and those played within a web browser often use 2D graphics.) With modern hardware now standard, whether you use 2D or 3D is really a question of the aesthetic effect you are trying to achieve, the skills of your art team, and the time you have available. 2D graphics can produce a more hand-painted look, which is preferable for some games. 3D art and animation can also take a lot longer to do. As a general rule, use 3D if and *only* if you have the tools, the skills, and the time to do it well. If you do *not* have the more complex tools and the specialized skills to get good results, you should not try it. Good-looking 2D graphics are always preferable to bad-looking 3D graphics.

NOTE A 2D engine can produce a limited sort of first-person 3D effect by showing 2D objects (called *sprites)* that get larger and larger as they approach the avatar. Usually this makes them look pixelated, which is undesirable unless you have intentionally chosen a retro visual style.

Although it may take the player a while to detect weak AI or bad writing in a game, bad graphics show up from the first moment.

This question becomes critical for games on low-end mobile phones. With no 3D graphics acceleration hardware, if these devices display 3D graphics, they must do it with software rendering—a complex task that burdens the slow processors that run these gadgets. Think twice before committing yourself (and your programming team) to providing 3D graphics on such platforms. Here, above all, heed the warning that if you cannot do it well, don't do it at all.

First-Person Perspective

In the *first-person perspective,* used only in avatar-based gameplay modes, the camera takes the position of the avatar's own eyes and is fixed with respect to the avatar. Therefore, usually the player doesn't see the avatar's body, though the game may display handheld weapons, if any, and occasionally the avatar's hands. The first-person perspective also works well to display the point of view of a vehicle's driver: It shows the terrain ahead as well as the vehicle's instrument panel but not the driver herself. It conveys an impression of speed and helps immerse the player in the game world. First-person perspective also removes any need for the player to adjust the camera and, therefore, any need for you to design UI for camera adjustment. To look around, the player simply moves the avatar.

ADVANTAGES OF THE FIRST-PERSON PERSPECTIVE

Note the following benefits of the first-person perspective compared with the third-person perspective:

▦ Your game doesn't display the avatar routinely, so the artists don't have to develop a large number of animations, or possibly any image at all, of the avatar. This can cut development costs significantly because you need animations only for those rare situations in which the player can see the avatar: cut-scenes, or if the avatar steps in front of a mirror.

▦ You won't need to design AI to control the camera. The camera looks exactly where the player tells it to look.

▦ The players find it easier to aim ranged weapons at approaching enemies in the first-person perspective for two reasons. First, the player can see clearly because the avatar's body does not block his view; second, the player's viewpoint corresponds exactly with the avatar's, and therefore, the player does not have to correct for differences between his own perspective and the avatar's.

▦ The players may find interacting with the environment easier. Many games require the player to maneuver the avatar precisely before allowing him to climb stairs, pick up objects, go through doorways, and so forth. The first-person perspective makes it easy for the player to position the avatar accurately with respect to objects.

DISADVANTAGES OF THE FIRST-PERSON PERSPECTIVE

Some of the disadvantages of the first-person perspective (as compared with third-person) include these:

▨ Because the player cannot see the avatar, the player doesn't have the pleasure of watching her or customizing her clothing or gear, both of which form a large part of the entertainment in many games. Players enjoy discovering a new animation as the avatar performs an action for the first time.

▨ Being unable to see the avatar's body language and facial expressions (puzzlement, fear, caution, aggression, and so on) reduces the player's sense of her as a distinct character with a personality and a current mood. The avatar's personality must be expressed in other ways: through her scripted interactions with other characters, hints to the player, or when she talks to herself.

▨ The first-person perspective denies the designer the opportunity to use cinematic camera angles for dramatic effect. Camera angles create visual interest for the player, and some games rely on them heavily: *Resident Evil,* for example, and *Grim Fandango.*

▨ The first-person perspective makes certain types of gymnastic moves more difficult. A player trying to jump across a chasm by running up to its edge and pressing the jump button at the last instant finds it much easier to judge the timing if the avatar is visible on screen. In the first person, the edge of the chasm disappears off the bottom of the screen during the approach, making it difficult to know exactly when the player should press the button.

▨ Rapid movements, especially turning or rhythmic rising and falling motions, can create motion sickness in viewers. A few games tried to simulate the motion of walking by swaying the camera as the avatar moves; this also tends to induce motion sickness.

Third-Person Perspective

Games with avatar-based interaction models can also use the *third-person perspective.* The most common camera model in modern 3D action and action-adventure games with strongly characterized avatars has the great advantage of letting the player see the avatar, and the disadvantage that it requires much more work to implement. Normally the camera follows the avatar at a fixed distance, remaining behind and slightly above her as she runs around in the world; this makes it so the player can see way beyond the avatar into the distance.

The standard third-person perspective depends on an assumption that threats to the avatar will come from in front of her. Now some games include fighting in the style of martial-arts movies, in which enemies can surround the avatar; consider recent games in the *Prince of Persia* series. To permit the player to see both the avatar and the enemies, the camera must crane up and tilt down to show the fight from a raised perspective.

Designing the camera behavior for the third-person perspective poses a number of challenges, discussed in the next few sections.

CAMERA BEHAVIOR WHEN THE AVATAR TURNS

So long as the avatar moves forward, away from the camera, the camera dollies to follow; you should find this behavior easy to implement. When the avatar turns, however, you have several options:

▨ The camera keeps itself continuously oriented behind the avatar, as in the *chase view* in flight simulators (see the companion e-book *Fundamentals of Vehicle Simulation Design*). The camera always points in the direction in which the avatar looks, allowing the player to always see where the avatar is going, which is useful in high-speed or high-threat environments. Unfortunately, the player never sees the avatar's side or front, only her back, which takes some of the fun out of watching the avatar. Also, a human avatar can change directions rapidly (unlike a vehicle), and the camera must sweep around quickly to remain behind her, which can give the player motion sickness.

▨ The camera reorients itself behind the avatar somewhat more slowly, beginning a few seconds after the avatar makes her turn. This option enables the player to see the avatar's side for a few seconds until the camera reorients itself. Fewer players will find such images dizzying. *Super Mario 64*, one of the first, and best, 3D console games, adopted this approach.

▨ The camera reorients itself behind the avatar only after she stops moving. Although this is the least-intrusive way to reorient the camera, it does mean that if the player instructs the moving avatar to turn and run back the way she came, she runs directly toward the camera, which does not reorient itself; instead it simply dollies away from her to keep her in view. The player cannot see any obstacles or enemies in the avatar's way because they appear to be behind the camera (until the instant before she runs into them). *Toy Story 2: Buzz Lightyear to the Rescue* uses this option; the effect, while somewhat peculiar, works well in the game's largely nonthreatening environment.

If you plan for the camera to reorient itself automatically, you can give the player control over how quickly the reorientation occurs by switching between *active camera mode* and *passive camera mode*. In active mode, the camera either remains oriented behind the avatar at all times or reorients itself quickly; in passive mode, it either orients itself slowly or only when the avatar stops moving.

INTRUDING LANDSCAPE OBJECTS

What happens when the player maneuvers the avatar to stand with his back to a wall? The camera cannot retain its normal distance from the avatar; if it did, it would take up a position on the other side of the wall. Many kinds of objects in the landscape can intrude between the avatar and the camera, blocking the player's view of him and everything else.

If you choose a third-person perspective, consider one of the following solutions:

- Place the camera as normal but render the wall (and any other object in the landscape that may come between the camera and the avatar) semitransparent. This allows the player to see the world from his usual position but makes him aware of the presence of the intruding object.

- Place the camera immediately behind the avatar, between him and the wall, but crane it upward somewhat and tilt it down, so the player sees the area immediately in front of the avatar from a raised point of view.

- Orient the camera immediately behind the avatar's head and render his head semitransparent until he moves so as to permit a normal camera position. The player remains aware of his position but can still see what is in front of him.

When the player moves the avatar so that an object no longer intrudes, return the camera smoothly to its normal orientation and make the object suitably opaque again, as appropriate.

PLAYER ADJUSTMENTS TO THE CAMERA

In third-person games, occasionally players need to adjust the position of the camera manually to get a better look at the game world without moving the avatar. If you want to implement this, assign two buttons, usually on the left and right sides of the controller, to control manual camera movement (on tablet devices you can use screen buttons or detect a left-right swipe movement). The buttons should make the camera circle around the avatar to the left or right, keeping her in focus in the middle of the screen. This enables the player to see the environment around the avatar and also to see the avatar herself from different angles.

Toy Story 2: Buzz Lightyear to the Rescue uses a different adjustment: The left and right buttons cause the avatar to pivot in position while the camera sweeps around to remain behind her back. This changes the direction the avatar faces, moves the camera, and helps line up the avatar for jumps.

Allowing the player to adjust the camera can help with the problem of intruding landscape items, but it is not a real solution; the player would prefer that the camera handle the situation automatically.

Aerial Perspectives

Games with party-based or multipresent interaction models need a camera model that allows the player to see a large part of the game world and several different characters or units at once. Normally such games use an aerial perspective, which gives priority to the game world in general rather than to one particular character.

In games with multipresent interaction models, you must provide a way for the player to scroll the main game view around to see any part of the world that he wants (although parts of it may be hidden by the *fog of war;* see the companion e-book *Fundamentals of Strategy Game Design*). With party-based interaction models, you may reasonably restrict the player's ability to move the camera so that it cannot move away from the region of the game world where the party is.

TOP-DOWN PERSPECTIVE

The *top-down perspective* shows the game world from directly overhead with the camera pointing straight down. In this respect, it resembles a map, so players find the display familiar. It's easy to implement using 2D graphics, which keeps its use common on smaller devices, but its many disadvantages have led designers to use other methods on more powerful machines.

For one thing, this perspective enables the player to see only the roofs of buildings and the tops of people's heads. To give a slightly better sense of what a building looks like, artists often draw them *cheated*—that is, at a slight angle even though that isn't how buildings appear from directly above (see **Figure 12.1**).

FIGURE 12.1
Cheated perspective in the very first *SimCity*

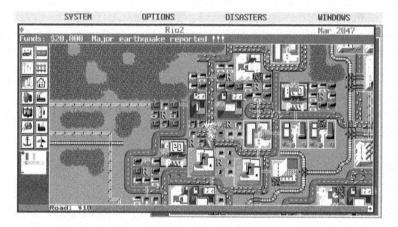

The top-down perspective also distances the player from the events below. He feels remote from the action and less attached to its outcomes. It makes a game world feel like a simulation rather than a place that could be real.

Now designers of computer and console games usually reserve this perspective for showing maps, although it is still common on smaller devices and some web-based games. *Flight Control,* for example, is a hugely popular top-down game for the iPhone.

ISOMETRIC PERSPECTIVE

The *isometric perspective* is often used to display 2D outdoor scenes that include limited vertical elements such as houses, trees, or small hills. Whereas the top-down perspective looks straight down at the landscape from an elevated position, the isometric perspective looks across the landscape from a somewhat lower elevation, with the camera tilted down about 30 degrees from the horizontal. If the game world is rectilinear, as they usually are in games that use the isometric perspective, normally the camera is positioned at a 45-degree angle from the north-south axis of the landscape. This permits players to see the sides of buildings in the landscape, as well as the roof. See Figure 8.5 for a typical example. In the main view, a mixed troop of soldiers marches out through a gap in a city wall. You can see two sides and the roofs of various buildings around the soldiers.

Normally, a 2D display engine draws the isometric perspective using interchangeable tiles of a fixed size. As a result, the isometric perspective distorts reality somewhat because objects that are farther from the camera are not smaller on the screen. However, the camera does not display much of the landscape at one time, so players don't mind the slight distortion. The player can truck or dolly the camera above the landscape but cannot pan, tilt, or roll it. You can also allow the player to shift the camera orientation to one of the other ordinal points of the compass to see other sides of objects in the game world. If you want to provide this feature, the artists will have to draw four sets of tiles, one for each possible camera orientation. You can also let the player choose an altitude from which to view the world, but the artists will have to draw multiple sets of tiles at different scales.

The isometric perspective brings the player closer to the action than the top-down perspective and allows him to see the sides of buildings as well as the roofs, so the player feels more involved with the world. It also enables him to see the bodies of people more clearly. Real-time strategy games and construction and management simulations, both of which normally use multipresent interaction models, routinely display the isometric perspective or its modern 3D alternative, the free-roaming camera. Some role-playing games that use a party-based interaction model still employ the isometric perspective.

FREE-ROAMING CAMERA

For aerial perspectives today, designers favor the *free-roaming camera,* a 3D camera model that evolved from the isometric perspective and is made possible by modern 3D graphics engines. It allows the player considerably more control over the camera; she can crane it to choose a wide or a close-in view; and she can tilt and pan in any direction at any angle, unlike the fixed camera angle of the isometric perspective. The free-roaming camera also displays the world in true perspective: Objects farther away seem smaller.

In spite of its flexibility, there are various disadvantages to the free-roaming camera. Because the player can move the camera anywhere, you have to create enough artwork to make sure she always has something to look at no matter where the camera is pointed, and much of it will be art that the gameplay itself does not really need. It can also be tricky to correctly determine the difficulty of the game in a given area when you don't know what the player is actually looking at. Finally, of course, you have to implement all the controls for moving the camera and teach the player how to use them.

CHAPTER 12

CONTEXT-SENSITIVE CAMERA MODELS

Context-sensitive camera models require 3D graphics and are normally used with avatar-based or party-based interaction models. In a context-sensitive model, the camera moves intelligently to follow the action, displaying it from whatever angle best suits the action at any time. You must define the behavior of the camera for each location in the game world and for each possible situation in which the avatar or party may find themselves.

Journey implements a context-sensitive model, using different camera positions in different regions of the world to show off the landscape and the action to the best advantage. This makes *Journey* an unusually beautiful game. Context-sensitive models allow the designer to act as a cinematographer to create a rich visual experience for the player. Seeing game events this way feels a bit like watching a movie because the designer intentionally composed the view for each location.

This approach brings with it two disadvantages. First, composing a view for each location in the game world requires you and your programmers to do a lot more work than is needed to implement other camera models. Second, a camera that moves of its own accord can be disorienting in high-speed action situations. When the player tries to control events at speed, he needs a predictable viewpoint from which to do so. The context-sensitive perspective suits slower-moving games quite well and frenetic ones less well. Some games, such as those in the survival horror series *Silent Hill*, use a context-sensitive perspective when the avatar explores but switch to a third-person or other more fixed perspective when she gets into fights.

LIMIT CAMERA MOVEMENT DURING FRENETIC ACTION

In the early *Resident Evil* games, sometimes the camera jumped to a different point of view without warning, right when the player was in the middle of a fight. This disoriented the player and upset his understanding of the relationship between the controls and the screen, often causing him to lose the fight. Don't move the camera in unexpected ways during high-speed action. Use a fixed, or at least a predictable, perspective.

Other 2D Display Options

This section lists a few approaches to 2D displays that are now seldom used in large commercial games on PCs and consoles but are still widely found in web-based games and on smaller devices. Modern games that intentionally opt for a retro feel, such as *Alien Hominid* and *Strange Adventures in Infinite Space,* also use 2D approaches.

- **Single-screen.** The display shows the entire world on one screen, normally from a top-down perspective with cheated objects. The camera never moves. *Robotron: 2084* and *Pac-Man* provide classic examples. When zoomed all the way out, *Angry Birds* is also a single-screen game.

- **Side-scrolling.** The world of a side-scroller—familiar from an entire generation of games—consists of a long 2D strip in which the avatar moves left and right (mostly right), with a limited ability to move up and down. The player sees the game world from the side as the camera tracks the avatar.

- **Top-scrolling.** In this variant of the top-down perspective, the landscape scrolls beneath the avatar (often a flying vehicle). (Sometimes the landscape scrolls by at a fixed rate that the player cannot change; this is called *forced-scrolling*.) This forces the player to continually face new challenges as they appear at the top of the screen.

- **Painted backgrounds.** Many graphical adventure games display the game world in a series of 2D painted backgrounds rather like a stage set. The avatar and other characters appear in front of the backgrounds. The artists can paint these backgrounds from a variety of viewpoints, making such games more visually interesting than side-scrolling and top-scrolling games, constrained only by the fact that the same avatar graphics and animations have to look right in all of them. Some use a 2D/3D combination model in which the background is 2D but the character animations are rendered with a 3D engine in front of the background. (See **Figure 12.2** for an example.)

FIGURE 12.2
A Vampyre Story used 2D painted backdrops but a 3D engine to render the characters.

Visual Elements

Whichever interaction model and camera model your game offers, you'll need to supply information that the player needs to know by using the visual elements discussed in this section.

Main View

TIP If you need to display text in an overlay, as many RPGs do, use opaque or nearly opaque overlays so little of the background is visible through them. Text in a semitransparent overlay is hard to read because the image underneath confuses the text. Players find it irritating to read text with graphics underneath it, especially moving graphics.

The player's main view of the game world should be the largest element on the screen. You must decide whether the main view will appear in a window within the screen with other user interface elements around it, or whether the view will occupy the whole screen and the other UI elements will appear on top of it. We'll look at these options next. (See also "Choosing a Screen Layout," earlier in the chapter.)

WINDOWED VIEWS

In a windowed view, the oldest and easiest design choice—the main view—takes up only part of the screen, with the rest of the screen showing panels displaying feedback and control mechanisms. You find this view most frequently in games with complicated UIs such as construction and management simulations, RPGs, and strategy games, because they require so many on-screen controls (see Figure 8.8 for a typical example). Using a windowed view does not mean that feedback elements never obscure the main view, only that they need to do so less often because most of them are around the edges.

The windowed view really does make the player feel as if she's observing the game world through a window, so it harms immersion somewhat. It looks rather like a computer desktop UI, and you see this approach more often in PC games than in console games. The loss of immersion matters less when the game requires a great deal of control over a complex internal economy and the player needs access to all those controls at all times.

FULL-SCREEN VIEWS WITH A HEAD-UP DISPLAY

If you want to create a greater sense of immersion than the windowed view offers, you can have the main view fill all or almost all of the screen and superimpose graphical elements, such as indicators or a score, on top of it. You can think of these elements as resting on an imaginary glass screen between the player and the main view. Borrowing from the design of displays in military aircraft, this virtual screen of indicators is called a *head-up display* (HUD). Sometimes individual HUD elements are called *overlays*.

Overlays may be either opaque, completely obscuring the main view behind them, or semitransparent. Semitransparent overlays let the player see partially through them (see **Figure 12.3** for an example). Semitransparent overlays feel less intrusive than opaque ones and work well for things such as instruments in the *cockpit-removed view* in a flight simulator. However, the bleed-through of graphic material from behind these overlays can confuse the information that the overlay presents. Be sure your overlay isn't *too* transparent.

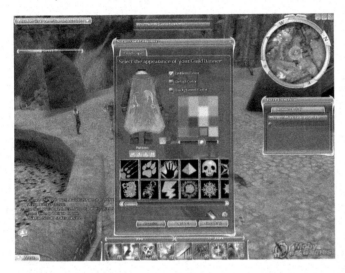

FIGURE 12.3
A semitransparent overlay in *Guild Wars*. The people and landscape are visible through the overlay.

Be careful about using too many overlays, or your HUD will become cluttered and confusing. Games with a great deal of information to present often let players turn individual HUD elements on or off and even reposition them. *The Lord of the Rings Online* includes this feature. It also allows players to hide the entire HUD with a single key press, allowing them to view the main view without any intruding items.

Feedback Elements

Feedback elements communicate details about the game's inner states—its core mechanics—to the player. They tell the player what is going on, how she is doing, what options she has selected, and what activities she has set in motion.

INDICATORS

Indicators inform the player about the status of a resource, graphically and at a glance. This section uses common examples from everyday life as illustrations. The meaning of an indicator's readout comes from labels or from context; the indicator itself provides a value for anything you like. Still, some indicators suit certain types of data better than others. Choose indicators that fit the theme of your game and ones that don't introduce anachronisms; a digital readout or an analog clock face both would be shockingly out of place in a medieval fantasy.

Indicators fall into three categories: general numeric, for large numbers or numbers with fractional values; small-integer numeric, for integers from 0 to 5; and symbolic, for binary, tri-state, and other symbolic values. Here are some of the most common kinds of indicators, with their types.

▨ **Digits.** General numeric. (A car's odometer.) Unambiguous and space-efficient, a digital readout can display large numbers in a small screen area. Digits can't be read easily at a glance; however, *171* can look a lot like *111* if you have only a tenth of a second to check the display during an attack. Worse, many types of data the player needs—health, energy, and armor strength—can't be communicated appropriately to the player by a number; no one actually thinks, "I feel exactly 37 points strong at the moment." Use digits to display the player's score and amounts of things for which you would normally use digits in the real world: money, ammunition, volumes of supplies, and so on. Don't use digits for quantities that should feel imprecise, such as popularity.

▨ **Needle gauge.** General numeric. (A car's speedometer.) Vehicle simulations use duplicates of the real thing—speedometers, tachometers, oil pressure levels, and so on—but few other games require needle gauges. Generally easy to read at a glance, they take up a large amount of screen space to deliver a small amount of information. You can put two needles on the same gauge if you make them different colors or different lengths and they both reflect data of the same kind; an analog clock is a two-needle gauge (or a three-needle gauge if another hand indicates seconds). Use needle gauges in mechanical contexts.

▨ **Power bar.** General numeric. (On an analog thermometer, the column of colored fluid indicating temperature.) A power bar is a long, narrow colored rectangle that becomes shorter or longer as the value that it represents changes, usually to indicate the health of a character or time remaining in a timed task. (The name is conventional; power bars are not limited to displaying power.) When the value reaches zero, the bar disappears (though a framework around the bar may remain). If shown horizontally, zero is at the left and the maximum at the right; if shown vertically, zero is at the bottom and the maximum is at the top. The chief benefit of power bars is that the player can read the approximate level of the value at a glance. Unlike a thermometer, they rarely carry gradations. You can superimpose a second semi-transparent bar of a different color on top of the first one if you need to show two numbers in the same space. Many power bars are drawn in green when full and change color to yellow and red as the value indicated reaches critically low levels to help warn the player. Power bars are moderately space efficient and, being thematically neutral, appear in all sorts of contexts. You can make themed power bars; a medieval fantasy game might measure time with a graduated candle or an hourglass.

■ **Small multiples.** Small-integer numeric. (On a mobile phone, the bars indicating signal strength.) A small picture, repeated multiple times, can indicate the number of something available or remaining. Traditionally, small multiples are used to represent lives remaining in action games; often they appear as an image or silhouette of the avatar. Nowadays designers use them for things the avatar can carry, such as grenades or healing potions, although you should limit the maximum number to about five; beyond that the player can't take in the number of objects at a glance and must stop to count the pictures. To make this method thematically appropriate for your game, simply choose an appropriate small picture.

■ **Colored lights.** Symbolic. (In a car, various lights on the instrument panel.) Lights are highly space efficient, taking up just a few pixels, but they can't display much data; normally they indicate binary (on/off) values with two colors, or tri-state values with three colors (off/low/high). Above three values, players tend to forget what the individual colors mean, and bright colors are not thematically appropriate in some contexts. Use a suitable palette of colors.

■ **Icons.** Symbolic. (In a car, the symbols indicating the heating and air conditioning status.) Icons convey information in a small space, but you must make them obvious and unambiguous. Don't use them for numerical quantities but for symbolic data that record a small number of possible options. For example, you can indicate the current season with a snowflake, a flower, the sun, and a dried leaf. This will be clear to people living in the temperate parts of the world where these symbols are well known, but it will work less well in cultures where snow doesn't fall. The player can quickly identify icons once she learns what they mean, and you can help her learn by using a *tooltip,* a small balloon of text that appears momentarily when the mouse pointer touches an icon for a few seconds without clicking it. Don't use icons if you need large numbers of them (players forget what they mean) or if they refer to abstract ideas not easily represented by pictures. In those cases, use them with text alongside, or use text instead. Make your icons thematically appropriate by drawing pictures that look as if they belong in your game world. The icons in *Cleopatra: Queen of the Nile,* set in ancient Egypt, are excellent (see Figure 8.8).

■ **Text indicators.** Symbolic. Text represents abstract ideas well, an advantage over other kinds of indicators. In *Civilization III,* for example, an advisor character can offer the suggestion, "I recommend researching Nationalism." Finding an icon to represent nationalism or feudalism or communism, also options in the game, poses a problem. On the other hand, some people find text boring, and two words can look alike if they're both rendered in the same color on the same color background. The worst problem with text, however, is that it must be localized for each language that you want to support. (See "Text," later in this chapter.)

The books of Dr. Edward Tufte, particularly *The Visual Display of Quantitative Information* (Tufte, 2001), give some of the best advice anywhere about conveying data to the player efficiently and readably.

NOTE You can see an example of using text with icons in Microsoft Word's ribbon interface, introduced in Word 2007. Earlier versions of Word used a toolbar with dozens of icons whose meaning was often obscure.

CHAPTER 2

MINI-MAPS

A *mini-map,* also sometimes called a *radar screen,* displays a miniature version of the game world, or a portion of it, from a top-down perspective. The mini-map shows an area larger than that shown by the main view, so the player can orient himself with respect to the rest of the world. To help him do this, designers generally use one of two display conventions: *world-oriented* or *character-oriented* mini-maps.

▓ The world-oriented map displays the entire game world with north at the top, just like a paper map, regardless of the main view's current orientation. An indicator within the mini-map marks that part of the game world currently visible in the main view. (See Figure 8.2 for an example. The small rectangle on the mini-map indicates which part of the world is currently showing in the main view.) In a multipresent game, you can use the world-oriented map as a camera control device: If the player clicks the map, the camera jumps to the location clicked.

▓ The character-oriented map displays the game world around the avatar, placing him at the center of the map facing the top of the screen. If the player turns the avatar to face in a new direction in the game world, the landscape, rather than the avatar, rotates in the map. These mini-maps don't show the whole game world, only a limited area around the avatar, and as the avatar moves, they change accordingly. They're often round and for this reason are sometimes called radar screens. Because the landscape rotates in the map, sometimes character-oriented mini-maps include an indicator pointing north, making the map double as a compass.

Because the mini-map must be small (usually 5 to 10 percent of the screen area), it shows only major geographic features and minimal non–mission-critical data. Key characters or buildings typically appear as colored dots. Areas of the game world hidden by the fog of war are hidden in the mini-map also.

A mini-map helps the player orient himself and warns him of challenges not visible in the main view, such as nearby enemies in a strategy or action game or a problem developing in a construction and management simulation. Mini-maps typically show up in a corner of the screen. You can find them in virtually any game that uses aerial perspectives and many others as well—especially racing games in which the player needs to know where he is with respect to the whole track, and where his opponents are. Figures 8.2, 8.5, 8.6, and 8.8 all contain mini-maps.

COLOR

You can always double the amount of data shown in a numeric indicator by having the color of the indicator itself represent a second value. You might, for example, represent the speed of an engine with a needle gauge, and the temperature of that engine by changing the color of the needle from black to red as it gets hotter. Colors work best to display information that falls into broad categories and doesn't require precision within those categories. Consider the green/yellow/red spectrum used for safety/caution/danger: It doesn't display a precise level of safety but conveys the general level at a glance. (However, note the warnings about color-blind players in the section "Accessibility Issues," later in this chapter.)

Colors are also useful for differentiating groups of opponents, and you can apply them to uniforms and other insignia. This is especially handy if the shapes or images of the actual units are identical regardless of which side they're on... as any chess player knows! *Halo*'s Red and Blue teams are another good example.

You can also use color as a feedback element by placing a transparent color filter over the entire screen. Some first-person shooters turn the whole screen reddish for a few frames to indicate that the avatar has been hit.

Character Portraits

A *character portrait*, normally appearing in a small window, displays the face of someone in the game world—either the avatar, a member of the player's party in a party-based game, or a character the player speaks to. If the main view uses an aerial perspective, it's hard for the player to see the faces of characters in the game, so a character portrait gives the player a better idea of the person he's dealing with. Use character portraits to build identification between your player and his avatar or party members and to convey more about the personalities of NPCs. An animated portrait can also function as a feedback element to give the player information; *Doom* famously uses a portrait of the avatar as a feedback element, signaling declining health by having the avatar appear bloodier and bloodier. This portrait also allows the player to see his avatar even though he is playing a first-person shooter.

Screen Buttons and Menus

Screen buttons and menus enable the player to control processes too complex to manage with controller buttons alone. They work best with the mouse as a pointing device but can also be used with a D-pad (directional pad, the oldest form of directional control mechanism on game machines) or joystick. Because a console doesn't have a mouse, console games use screen buttons and menus less than do PC games, one of several reasons why console games tend to be less complex than PC games.

Screen buttons and menus should be so familiar to you from your experience with personal computers that there is no need to discuss them in detail here, though you should keep a couple of key issues in mind. First, putting too many buttons and menus on the screen confuses players and makes your game less accessible to casual players (see "Managing Complexity," earlier in the chapter). Second, unless you use the desktop model, try to avoid making your buttons and menus look too much like an ordinary personal computer interface. The more your game looks like any other Windows or Macintosh application, the more it harms the player's immersion in the game. Make your screen-based controls fit your overall visual theme.

Text

Most games contain a fair amount of text, even action games in which the player doesn't normally expect to do much reading. Text appears as a feedback element in its own right, or as a label for menu items, screen buttons, and to indicate the meaning of other kinds of feedback elements (a needle gauge might be labeled *Voltage,* for example). You may also use text for narration, dialogue (including subtitles), a journal kept by the avatar, detailed information about items such as weapons and vehicles, shell menus, and as part of the game world itself, on posters and billboards.

LOCALIZATION

Localization refers to the process of preparing a game for sale in a country other than the one for which you originally designed the game. Localizing a game often requires a great many changes to the software and content of the game, including translating all the text and voiceover in the game into the target market's preferred language. To make the game easily localizable, you should store all the game's text in text files and never embed text in a picture (or in the code). Editing a text file is trivial; editing a picture is not.

> ### DESIGN RULE Keep Text Separate from Other Content
>
> *Never* have the programmers build text into the program code. *Never* build text that the player is expected to read into an image such as a texture or a shell screen background. Store all text in one or more text files.
>
> The only exception to this rule applies to text used purely as decoration when you don't expect the player to read it or understand what it says. A billboard seen in a game set in New York should be in English and remain in English even after localization *if* the billboard text doesn't constitute a crucial clue.

Note that a word and its translation may differ in length in different languages, so that a very short menu item in English can turn into a very long menu item in, say, German. When you design your UI, don't crowd the text elements too close together; the translations may require the extra space.

TYPEFACES AND FORMATTING

Make your text easily readable. The minimum height for text displayed on a screen should be about 12 pixels; if you make the characters any smaller, they became less legible. If the game will be localized to display non-Roman text such as Japanese, 12 pixels is the bare minimum, and 16 pixels is distinctly preferable.

If you're going to display a lot of text, learn the rules of good typesetting and use typefaces (fonts) that have been designed specifically for reading on a computer screen, such as Verdana. Use mixed uppercase and lowercase letters for any block of text more than three or four words long. Players find text set entirely in uppercase letters difficult to read; besides, it looks like SHOUTING, creating a sense of urgency you might not want. (On the other hand, in situations that *do* require urgency, such as a warning message reading *DANGER*, uppercase letters work well.)

Choose your typefaces with care so that they harmonize both with the theme of your game and with each other. Avoid using too many different typefaces, which looks amateurish. Be aware of the difference between *display fonts* (intended for headlines) such as Impact, and ordinary *serif* and *sans serif* fonts (intended for blocks of text) such as Times or Arial, respectively.

Avoid *monospaced* (also called *fixed width*) fonts, such as Courier, in favor of proportional fonts, such as Times, unless you need to display a table in which letters must line up in columns. For other uses, fixed-width fonts waste space and look old-fashioned and unattractive.

TIP Although computers often come with a variety of free fonts, remember that many typefaces must be licensed. Before you release a commercial game, be sure you have the rights to the fonts that you are planning to use.

Audio Elements

This chapter has already mentioned sound briefly, but this section presents more detail, addressing several topics: sound effects, ambient sounds, music, dialogue, and voiceover narration. Many professional development teams create a sound design document separately from their other game design documentation to help focus their attention on the task.

Your programming team should keep music, sound effects, and recorded speech in separate files, and play them back through separate channels on the machine. Always include a facility that allows the player to adjust the volume level of the music independently from the volume level of the other audio effects—including turning off one or the other completely. Many players tire of hearing the music but still want to hear the sound effects and other sounds. Bear in mind that not all your players will have perfect hearing, and the more control you can give them, the better. See the section "Accessibility Issues," later in this chapter.

TIP If your game includes repeated sounds (such as the multiple gunshots of a machine gun), don't simply play the same sound effect over and over—it sounds fake and will quickly become boring. If your machine's audio hardware supports it, vary the pitch randomly up or down by about 5 percent each time the effect is played. If your hardware can't do that, use multiple different sound samples and mix them up randomly when playing them back.

Sound Effects

The most common use of sound in a game is for sound effects. These sounds correspond to the actions and events of the game world—for example, a burst of gunfire or the squealing of tires as a car slides around a corner. In the real world, sound often presents the first warning of approaching danger, so use sound as an indicator that something needs the player's attention. Suspense movies do this well, and you can borrow techniques from them: Play the sound of footsteps or the sound of a gun being cocked before the player can see it. You can also use sound to provide feedback about aspects of the game under the player's control, such as judging when to change gears in a racing game by listening to the pitch of the engine.

You should also include sound effects as audible feedback in your UI, not just in the game world. At the very minimum, make sure the screen buttons make an audible *click* when pressed, but try to find interface effects that harmonize with the theme of your game world as well. Avoid long or unpleasant sounds, however; if the player hears them every time he presses a button, they can quickly become annoying—and this is especially true of speech used to confirm a button press.

Be sure to support audio feedback from the UI with visual feedback too so that when players hear a click or beep or buzz, the visual feedback directs them to the issue that generated the audible signal. We interpret events that we can see more easily than with audio alone.

Vibration

Many modern controllers include a vibration feature, which you can use to provide sensory feedback (often called *rumble*) about game events. Although rumble is not technically an audio element, the player can usually hear it as well as feel it.

Normally you can control two aspects of the vibration: intensity and duration. Be sure to scale these appropriately to the game world phenomenon that they're associated with. Rumble can be very startling when it's unexpected, which makes it an excellent feature for survival horror and stealth games. Don't use rumble constantly, or the player will learn to ignore it. Also, if you use rumble too much, the player's hands will begin to tingle unpleasantly.

It's best to use rumble when something big happens, such as an explosion, or when something bad happens, such as when the player's racing car scrapes the wall of the racetrack.

Ambient Sounds

Just as the main view gives the player visual feedback about where she is, ambient sounds give her aural feedback. Traffic sounds tell her that she's in an urban street; cries of monkeys and exotic birds suggest a jungle. Anything that ordinarily makes distinctive sounds in the real world, such as a fountain or a jackhammer, should make the same sound in your game.

A first- or third-person game should definitely use *positional audio* if the platform's audio devices support it. Positional audio refers to a system in which different speakers present sounds at different volume levels, allowing you to position the point sources of sound in the three-dimensional space of the world. Some personal computers support as many as seven speakers, but even a two-speaker stereo can help a player detect where a sound is coming from. Correctly positioning sound sources in the 3D space helps the player orient herself and find things that she may be searching for, such as a river, an animal, or another member of the party.

Don't overuse ambient sounds, especially in games that mostly feature mental challenges. A cacophonous environment isn't conducive to thought. Your ambient sounds must also work with the music you choose, which the next section addresses. You may also be limited by the capabilities of your audio hardware, because some machines support only a small number of channels for simultaneous playback; when playing all the sound effects, you may not have channels left to use for ambient sounds.

Music

Music helps to set the tone and establish the pace of your game. Think about what kind of music will harmonize with the world and the gameplay that you're planning. Music sends strong cultural messages, and those must also fit thematically with the rest of the game. A pentatonic scale composition for the *shamisen* (a traditional Japanese lute) might work well in a medieval Japanese adventure game, but it would certainly sound out of place in a futuristic high-tech game. You will probably collaborate with an audio director to choose or compose music for the game. Many larger commercial games now use licensed music from famous bands. Increasing numbers of games are built directly around music; see for examples *Rock Band, Dance Central,* and *Elite Beat Agents.*

The music doesn't have to support the game world at every moment; you can choose music to create a contrasting effect at times. The introductory movie for *StarCraft* uses classical opera as its theme, set against scenes in which admirals calmly discuss the war situation as they prepare to abandon the men on the planet below to their fate. The choice of music accentuates the contrast between the opulence and calm of the admiral's bridge and the hell of war on the surface. In a simpler example, the tempo of the music in certain levels of *Sonic the Hedgehog* is out of sync with the pace of the level, which, in a subtle way, makes the game harder to play. Don't overuse these techniques, however; the rarer they are, the more effective they are.

In the real world, few pieces of music last as long as an hour, but players may hear the same music for several hours at a stretch in a game. Whatever you choose, be sure it can tolerate repetition. Avoid background music with a wide dynamic range; the louder parts will become intrusive and remind the player that the music repeats itself.

For some years, the game industry has experimented with the difficult problem of writing music that changes dynamically in response to current game situations, a technique called *adaptive music.* Adaptive music must follow and even anticipate unpredictable situations. Creating adaptive music remains an experimental technique for the moment. On the other hand, game musicians have become extraordinarily skilled at *layering*—writing separate but harmonizing pieces of music that the audio engine delivers simultaneously by mixing them together at different levels of volume. The engine determines which piece should be most clearly heard depending on what happens in the game.

TIP If you would like to know more, read *Audio for Games: Planning, Process, and Production,* by Alexander Brandon (Brandon, 2004), and *The Fat Man on Game Audio: Tasty Morsels of Sonic Goodness,* by George "The Fat Man" Sanger (Sanger, 2003).

TIP In a long game, make sure the music in the game is not all in the same key, or it will seem repetitive (even if the melody itself is not repetitive). Bands and orchestras planning a concert avoid playing too many pieces in the same key for just this reason.

Dialogue and Voiceover Narration

Just about any kind of game can use spoken material to provide information, whether it's narration, dialogue, commentary in sports games, units responding to orders in strategy games, and so on. From a user interface standpoint, you should be aware of two key things that set spoken words apart from other forms of audio feedback:

TIP For more information on writing for games, read *Game Writing: Narrative Skills for Videogames*, edited by Chris Bateman (Bateman, 2006).

■ **Repetitive spoken content rapidly becomes tiresome.** The longer the sentence, the worse the problem. To solve this, write and record multiple versions for each line that is likely to be repeated. You may frequently repeat short clips such as "Aye aye, sir" and "Strike three!" (though you should still record several variants), but if you want to deliver a longer sentence such as, "Sire, your peasants are revolting!" you must either have a large number of variants available or, better yet, play the sentence only once when the problem first occurs and then use visual feedback for as long as the problem continues.

■ **Writing and acting *must be* good.** You cannot emphasize this enough to your writers and audio people. The quality of writing in the vast majority of games ranges from terrible to barely passable, and the voice acting is frequently worse than the writing. Players tolerate a sound effect that's not quite right, but an actor who can't act instantly destroys immersion. Don't use actors whose voices don't work thematically with the material, either. You wouldn't use the voice of an Englishman in a game set in the Old West, so don't use an American in a game set in medieval times. The American accent didn't exist then. Don't try to get an actor to fake a foreign accent, either; hire a native speaker.

Input Devices

So far, this book has placed little emphasis on the game machine's hardware, because the variety and rapid evolution of processors, display screens, data storage, and audio devices makes it impossible to address the topic comprehensively. In the case of input devices, however, certain standards have evolved. It is critically important that you understand the capabilities, strengths, and weaknesses of the various devices because they constitute the means by which your player will actually project his commands into the game. Designing for them well makes the difference between seamless gameplay and a frustrating experience.

This section concentrates on the most common types of input devices for mobile, PC, and console games—the sorts normally shipped with the machine. It doesn't address extra-cost items such as flight control yokes, steering wheels, rudder pedals, dance mats, fishing rods, and conga drums. If you build a game that requires these items, you limit the size of your market to a specialist audience, and there isn't room to discuss such issues in a work on general game design. You should design for the default control devices shipped with a machine if at all possible. Support extra-cost devices only if using them significantly enhances the player's experience, or if you are intentionally designing a technology-driven game to exploit the device.

For most of their history, input devices for personal computers differed greatly from those of game consoles, so the two were best discussed separately. Console games never used analog joysticks; PC games never used D-pads. Now, both types of machines can use either, so we'll look at the various input devices independently of the platforms.

Terminology

The following discussion uses the game industry's standard terminology for the kinds of data that control devices send to the processor as the result of player inputs. You may find some familiar terms that nevertheless require explanation, because the game industry uses those terms in ways that may differ from what you're used to.

Most input devices—the mouse being a notable exception—default to a neutral position. To send a signal to the game, the user must push, pull, grasp, or press the device to deflect it, and a spring-loaded mechanism returns it to the neutral position when the player releases the device. Joysticks and D-pads return to center; buttons and keys return to the off state.

A device that can return only two specific signals is called a *binary device,* the signals generally being interpreted as off and on. Another common kind of input device transmits a value from a range of many possible values and the industry, for historical reasons, calls these *analog devices.* Any game control device can be classed as either analog or binary, although all the technology is digital.

Don't confuse the type of data (binary or analog) with the *dimensionality* of the device. A one-dimensional device transmits one datum, a two-dimensional device transmits two data, and so on, regardless of whether they transmit binary or analog data.

A device that returns data about its current position as measured from the neutral position provides *absolute* values. Such a device—a joystick, for example—can travel only a limited distance in any direction, and so it transmits values in a range from zero to its maximum. Likewise, a touch screen returns the absolute position of the region(s) being touched.

Other devices offer effectively unlimited travel and have no neutral position. These return *relative* values, that is, the relative distance that the device has traveled from its previous position. Mouse wheels and trackballs are examples; the player may rotate them indefinitely.

NOTE Some devices built for non-gaming applications need to measure acceleration in only one or two dimensions, so they contain simpler accelerometers. However, motion-sensitive gaming devices routinely use accelerometers capable of measuring acceleration in all three spatial dimensions so they can detect movement in every direction. They provide three acceleration data at a time.

Three-Dimensional Input Devices

A three-dimensional device delivers three data values simultaneously. Such devices were once rare but are now nearly standard in smartphones and console controllers.

ACCELEROMETERS

An *accelerometer* is not a switch or button that the player manipulates directly. It is an electronic device that measures the rate of acceleration it experiences. Game hardware manufacturers build accelerometers into controllers such as the Wii Remote so the player can wave the controller around rather than simply hold it and press buttons. With the data from multiple accelerometers, you can compute how far and how fast the player moves the remote, and in what direction. The Nintendo Wii Remote and Nunchuck, and the Apple iPhone, are the best-known devices that use accelerometers in gaming, but most smartphones and handheld game platforms now include three-axis accelerometers.

When an accelerometer is at rest with respect to the Earth (sitting still on a table, for example), it reports the force of gravity. This means that you can also use an accelerometer as a tilt sensor. If the acceleration of gravity appears to change direction, it means the device has been tilted with respect to the ground. You can also detect if the player has turned it upside down: The direction of the acceleration of gravity will be reversed.

An accelerometer returns absolute acceleration information. If it were in zero gravity and undergoing no acceleration, it would return zero in all three dimensions.

GLOBAL POSITIONING SYSTEMS

Global positioning systems have become commonplace in smartphones and tablets, and it won't be long before they are ubiquitous in all portable devices. A GPS returns the device's latitude and longitude on the surface of the Earth, as well as the altitude above sea level. The player uses a GPS as input to a game by moving the GPS around in the environment. The UK-based art collective Blast Theory has constructed several augmented reality games that use global positioning systems. Players travel around a cityscape on foot, carrying a GPS-enabled device that helps them play the game.

GPS devices return absolute positional information. By taking measurements over time, you can use this data to compute the player's speed and direction.

GPS devices have two significant drawbacks at the moment. First, because they need to receive data from satellites orbiting the Earth, they work only in areas where they can easily receive the satellites' transmissions—usually outdoors. Second, the current generation of GPS technology is accurate only to within several meters, so they're useful only on a large scale. The European Galileo satellite navigation system is designed to be accurate to the 1-meter range.

A REVOLUTIONARY DEVICE: THE NINTENDO WII REMOTE

No piece of hardware has changed the landscape of console video gaming as dramatically as the Nintendo Wii and its motion-sensitive controller, the Wii Remote (often shortened to *Wiimote*). It implements a number of significant innovations:

- A three-dimensional accelerometer reports how the player is moving the remote.

- An infrared transmitter positioned near the player's TV and an infrared camera in the Wii Remote allow a Wii game to compute the remote's position relative to the TV. Wii games know where the remote is in the room, and approximately where it is pointing. As a pointing device, it is not as precise as a mouse, however.

- The remote contains a speaker, so it can make appropriate sounds (golf club, tennis racket, gun) right in the player's hand.

- The relatively small number of buttons on the Wii Remote (as compared to traditional controllers such as the Sony SIXAXIS) makes the remote much less daunting to inexperienced players.

- Because the remote uses Bluetooth wireless to communicate with the computer, players can move around with it as much as they like (as long as they don't move too far from the Wii). This allows for much more active games than the traditional wired controller does.

- The Wii Remote contains a small amount of memory, which lets players store data (such as avatar attributes) in the remote itself. A player can use his Wii Remote on another player's Wii machine, and the data he stored will be available to the game.

The Wii Remote also includes several conventional controller features: a D-pad, a trigger, several buttons, and a vibration feature. The Nunchuck, an additional device for the player's other hand, provides another accelerometer, an analog joystick, and two more buttons. An accessory for the Wii Remote, the Wii Motion Plus, adds a gyroscope-based angular rate sensor to the basic remote. This device provides information about the way the remote turns as it moves and makes it more accurate.

continues on next page

CHAPTER 12

No less important than the Wii Remote's innovations are the games that support it. Nintendo deliberately made the *Wii Sports* games that ship with the Wii easy to learn and very forgiving. In the tennis game, for example, the player's avatar automatically runs to where the ball will land. All the player has to do is wave the controller to deliver a forehand or a backhand. The ease of playing these games has made them accessible to many people who would never have considered playing video games before. Wii consoles have been installed in nursing homes, because the motion-based interaction encourages elderly people to exercise. They're also being used as physical therapy for people recovering from injuries. Playing a Wii game is much more appealing than doing repetitive exercises.

The Wii Remote works very well in games that map a player's physical activity directly onto the avatar's activity in the game world, such as action, sports, and driving games. It is less successful with games that traditionally use a mouse, such as role-playing, strategy, and construction and management games. If you want your players to control your game with the Wii Remote (which works with PCs as well as the Wii itself), you should design the game for the Wii Remote from the beginning.

Two-Dimensional Input Devices

Two-dimensional input devices allow the player to send two data values to the game at one time from a single device.

DIRECTIONAL PADS (D-PADS)

D-pads are the oldest form of directional control mechanism on game machines and are still offered by many smaller handheld machines. Console and PC controllers often supply a D-pad in addition to a joystick to provide backward compatibility with older software.

A D-pad is a circular or cross-shaped input device on a game controller constructed with binary switches at the top, bottom, left, and right edges. The D-pad rocks slightly over its central point and, when pressed at any edge, turns on either one switch or, if the player presses two adjacent switches at once, two. Therefore, it can send directional information to the game in eight possible directions: up, down, left, and right with each of the individual sensors, and upper-left, upper-right, lower-left, and lower-right when the player triggers two sensors together. (In **Figure 12.4**, the cross-shaped device on the upper-left face of the controller is a D-pad.)

FIGURE 12.4
The Sony SIXAXIS controller

The D-pad gives the player a crude level of control over a vehicle or avatar; she is able to make the vehicle move in any of the eight major directions but not in any other. You should use D-pads for directional control only if you have no better device available. D-pads do remain useful alongside a joystick; you can assign functions to the D-pad that require less subtle control, such as scrolling the main view window in one of the eight directions, which leaves the joystick free for such tasks as avatar navigation control.

JOYSTICKS

A *joystick* is a single vertical stick anchored at the bottom that can be tilted a limited amount in any direction. The joystick is spring-loaded and returns to its central position if the player lets go of it. When the game software checks the position of the joystick, it returns two absolute data: an X-value indicating tilt to the left or right, and a Y-value indicating the tilt forward or back.

A joystick offers a finer degree of control than a D-pad does. The Sony SIXAXIS controller in Figure 12.4 features two small joysticks (the circular objects at the bottom) as well as a D-pad.

Joysticks make ideal steering controls for vehicles—which, of course, is how they began, as steering for aircraft. To return to a default activity—flying straight and level, for instance—the player only has to allow the joystick to return to the neutral position. Since joysticks may travel only a limited amount in any direction, they allow the player to set a direction and a *rate* of movement. The UI interprets the degree of tilt as indicating the rate. For instance, moving a joystick to the left causes an airplane to roll to the left; moving it farther left causes the airplane to roll faster.

Joysticks don't work well for precise pointing because when the player lets go, the joystick returns to center, which naturally causes it to point somewhere else. To allow the player to point a cursor at an object *and leave it there* while she does something else, use a mouse. Efforts to port mouse-based games to console machines, substituting a joystick for the mouse, have an extremely poor success rate.

NOTE Modern joysticks built for use with combat flight simulators may include a large number of other controller buttons as well. All these ultimately amount either to binary buttons or sliders. This section is concerned only with the tilting action of the basic device.

CHAPTER 12

THE MOUSE (OR TRACKBALL)

We're all familiar with a mouse from our experiences with personal computers. A mouse returns two data values that consist of X- and Y-values, but these are *relative* data, indicating how far the player moved the mouse relative to its previous location. For high precision, the computer *polls* (checks) the mouse for updated data many times a second. A mouse offers more precise positioning than a joystick and unlimited travel in any direction on the two-dimensional plane in which it operates. This unlimited relative movement makes a mouse ideal for controlling things that can rotate indefinitely in place, so first-person PC games virtually always use a mouse to control the direction in which the avatar looks. Because it stays where it is put, a mouse is invaluable for interfaces in which the player needs to let go of the pointing device to do something else.

Note that when a mouse is used specifically to control a cursor on the screen, its driver software converts the mouse's native relative data into absolute data for the cursor position. This choice of either absolute or relative modes lends the mouse great flexibility.

A mouse wheel constitutes a separate knob with unlimited movement that also functions as a controller button when pressed. Not all mice come with mouse wheels, however, so you cannot count on players having them. If you support the mouse wheel, supply alternative controls.

The mouse's lack of a neutral position makes it weak as a steering mechanism for vehicles that need a default behavior, such as driving straight or flying straight and level. The player must find the vehicle's straight or level position herself rather than allowing the device to snap back into neutral. You may want to designate an extra controller button that returns the vehicle to its default state if the mouse will be your primary control option.

Designers find that a mouse is generally a more flexible input device than a joystick, but players find it more tiring to use for long periods.

TOUCH-SENSITIVE DEVICES

Most smartphones and all tablets, as well as Nintendo DS devices, offer the player a touch-sensitive screen, and laptop personal computers usually come with a touch pad below the keyboard. These devices return absolute analog X and Y positions to indicate where they are touched, as a mouse cursor does. Unlike a mouse, you can make a touch-sensitive device's cursor return to a neutral position whenever you detect that the player has stopped touching the device. Touch-sensitive screens may be manipulated by the fingers or sometimes by a stylus; usually touch pads cannot detect a stylus and must be touched with the fingers, which tends to make fingers sore after long use.

Early touch-sensitive screens could detect only one touch at a time, but the *multitouch* interface is now standard, which allows the user to touch it in several locations at once. This is likely to become increasingly common on new handheld devices. The problem of sore fingers after extended play remains.

One-Dimensional Input Devices

One-dimensional input devices send a single value to the game. Ordinary controller buttons and keys send binary values; knobs, sliders, and pressure-sensitive buttons send analog values.

CONTROLLER BUTTONS AND KEYS

A controller button or a keyboard key sends a single binary value at a time: on when pressed and off when released. Despite this simplicity, you can use buttons and keys in a variety of ways:

▪ **One-shot actions.** Treat the on signal as a trigger, a message to the game to perform some action immediately (ignoring the off signal). The action occurs only once, when the player presses the button; to perform it twice, he must press the button again. You might use this to let players fire a handgun, firing once each time they hit the button.

▪ **Repeating actions.** The on signal tells the game to begin some action and to repeat it until it receives the off signal from the same button at a repetition rate determined by the software. You could let the players fire a machine gun continuously from button press to button release.

▪ **Continuous actions.** The button's on signal initiates a continuous action, and its off signal ends it. Golf games use this to give a player control over how hard the golfer swings the club; the player presses the button to start the golfer's backswing and releases the button to begin the swing itself; the longer the backswing, the harder the golfer hits the ball. Some football games allow the player to tap the button quickly to throw a short pass or to hold it down for a moment before release to throw a long pass, with the length of time between a button's on and off signals determining the distance thrown.

Console game controllers feature anywhere from one to about ten buttons. Buttons on the top face of the controller, to be pressed with the thumbs, are known as *face buttons*. Others, known as *shoulder buttons*, appear on the part of the controller facing away from the player, under the index fingers. Faced with large numbers of buttons, the player can find it quite difficult to remember what they all do. Here, as elsewhere, be sure to maintain consistency from one gameplay mode to another, and if an industry standard has evolved for your game's genre, do not depart from it without good reason.

Personal computer keyboards have 110 keys, allowing for very broad user interfaces indeed. Be sure to assign actions to keys in such a way that the letter printed on the key becomes a mnemonic for the action, for example, F for flaps or B for brakes. If you implement the feature, players themselves can assign actions to keys, so they don't have to select those functions with mouse clicks.

KNOBS, SLIDERS, AND PRESSURE-SENSITIVE BUTTONS

You rarely find knobs (also sometimes called *Pong paddles* for historical reasons) nowadays, although the mouse wheel functions as a knob. Limited-travel knobs can move only so far, like a volume knob on a stereo, and return an absolute value. Unlimited-travel knobs, including the mouse wheel, may be spun continuously and return relative data. Knobs are generally not self-centering; they stay where the user puts them. Knobs, especially large ones, offer fine unidimensional control.

A slider is a small handle that moves along a slot in the controller, which constrains its travel. It returns an absolute position and stays where the player puts it. You find sliders usually used as adjuncts to joysticks for flight simulators; the slider controls the throttle for the engine, letting the player set his speed and leave it there.

A few controllers, such as the Nintendo GameCube controller, include analog pressure-sensitive buttons that, instead of transmitting a binary on or off value, send a number that indicates how hard the player presses. This gives the player a finer degree of control than an ordinary binary controller button. The trigger buttons on the Xbox controller also return analog values. You can think of them as spring-loaded sliders that return to a zero point when released.

COMPASSES

Like global positioning systems, compasses are mostly useful for augmented reality games played outdoors. A digital compass returns a single numeric value, the direction in degrees that a handheld device is facing with respect to true north. If the player holding it turns the device in a different direction, the compass detects it. Most smartphones now include a compass.

THE KINECT: A DIFFERENT APPROACH TO INPUT

Microsoft's Kinect device, which now routinely ships with the Xbox console, offers a completely different approach to collecting data from the player as input to video games. Instead of transmitting button presses or joystick positions, the Kinect uses cameras and infrared sensors to detect the positions of parts of the players' bodies in three-dimensional space. The device has considerable intelligence built into its software so that it can assemble this data without placing a burden on the CPU of the Xbox itself. (Developers can also read raw data streams directly from its cameras if desired.) It is capable of recognizing six separate players, and can track the movements of two of them, even if one player is partially in front of the other.

continues on next page

TIP Don't try to convert a game designed for a knob to work with a joystick. The joystick's combination of limited travel and self-centering contradicts the game's original design. The arcade game Tempest used a large, heavy knob that could be spun continuously; when ported to a console machine with a joystick, players enjoyed the game less despite the improved graphics.

The Kinect's internal model of a human body consists of twenty separate body parts organized in a hierarchy starting from the pelvis (the initial point of reference) out to the extremities. This is called *skeletal tracking*. The Kinect can provide information about the rotation angle of each bone relative to the next higher bone in the hierarchy. For example, the hand is relative to the wrist, the wrist is relative to the elbow, and so on back to the spine and then the pelvis.

The idea behind the Kinect is to enable controller-free gameplay, using only gestures and voice commands (the Kinect also includes an array of microphones). This has the advantage that it isn't as daunting to novice players as a controller is, and the physical activity of the player can be mapped directly to the actions of a humanoid avatar. It's ideal for dance games, for example. Compared to the Wii remote, the Kinect knows a great deal more about the player's movements. The Wii remote, via its accelerometers, knows only about its *own* movements; if it's in the player's hand, it can't transmit any information about what his feet are doing.

Although it is a technical marvel, the Kinect has not proven to be as revolutionary as the Wii remote was. Its chief drawback is its lack of tactile feedback. When a player presses a controller button, he can feel the button depress; he has an immediate sensation that he has done something. The Kinect only shows the results of the player's gestures on the screen. The player can feel his hands moving, but he cannot feel the resistance to their movement that a spring-loaded button provides.

It's possible to use a Kinect in conjunction with an ordinary Xbox controller, but this isn't very satisfactory in practice. An Xbox controller is designed to be held in two hands. Moving around with your hands close together is awkward and doesn't permit a large range of gestures.

The original version of the Kinect is not very precise, although Microsoft has announced that the newest version will be able to recognize faces and individual finger positions. But any kind of gestural interface can produce fatigue with long use. In dance and other exercise games, physical exertion is part of the point, but in something like a shooter, or even more, a strategy game, the player may make hundreds of actions. It's not reasonable to expect a player to wave his arms around continuously for several hours. Gestural interfaces like those shown in the movie *Minority Report* may look innovative and clever, but they aren't practical for long-term use.

All this isn't meant to suggest that you shouldn't develop for the Kinect. It's a wonderful technological achievement and, if exploited properly, can offer the player fun and intuitive game experiences. But the device isn't suitable for all genres. It's more like a specialized controller than an ordinary one; it's optimized for dance and other athletic activities, not for bidding in an auction or giving orders to units. If you want to develop a game for the Kinect, develop *around* the Kinect's strengths to get the best use out of it.

CHAPTER 12

Navigation Mechanisms

Navigation mechanisms allow the player to tell a character, vehicle, or other mobile unit how to move. This section uses the term *avatar* to refer to anything that the player controls directly, including vehicles. It also uses the word *steering* to describe the act of controlling both vehicles and characters directly, even though the idea of steering a walking character may sound a little odd. UI designers usually find creating vehicle navigation systems easier than creating ones for characters because input devices more closely resemble a vehicle's controls than they do an avatar's body.

A navigation mechanism establishes a relationship between the way the player moves the controls and the way the avatar responds on the screen. The player learns this relationship and uses it until it becomes automatic. When a player gives movement commands, the avatar must respond in a consistent and predictable way. Anything that disrupts the player's understanding of the control relationship, such as a sudden change of camera angles, may cause the player to make a steering error.

This section assumes that players steer using a joystick except where otherwise indicated; for most purposes, you may consider a joystick interchangeable with a D-pad but know that it offers finer control. Joystick directions are referred to as up (forward or away from the player), down (toward the player), left, and right. Steering wheels for cars or control yokes for aircraft aren't covered here because they should be self-explanatory.

The two most common steering mechanisms are screen-oriented and avatar-oriented, and the next few sections will discuss them in detail. If the player designates a point in the landscape and the character or vehicle moves to that target without further player control, the game uses *point-and-click navigation.*

Screen-Oriented Steering

In *screen-oriented steering,* when the player moves the joystick up, the avatar moves toward the top of the screen. As a very general rule, you should use screen-oriented steering when your chosen camera model is fixed or free-roaming and does not follow an avatar. Implementation details vary somewhat, however, so this section documents several major variants.

TOP-DOWN AND ISOMETRIC PERSPECTIVES

In a *top-down* or *isometric perspective* in which the player sees the avatar from above, moving the joystick up, down, left, or right causes the avatar to instantly turn and face the corresponding edge of the screen, and then move in that direction. Classic arcade games that used a top-down perspective, such as *Gauntlet,* use this simplest of all steering methods.

2D SIDE-SCROLLING GAMES

In traditional side-scrollers, the joystick controls left and right movement as it does for the top-down perspective. If the avatar walks rather than flies, then the player controls the avatar's vertical jumps to platforms using a separate controller button. Moving the joystick up can augment the effect of the jump button; moving the joystick down may remain undefined; and because the game world is 2D, the avatar cannot move away from or toward the player.

3D GAMES

Three-dimensional games usually use avatar-oriented rather than screen-oriented steering to provide a consistent set of controls regardless of camera angle, but rare exceptions do exist. *Crash Bandicoot* provides the best-known example. When the player pushes the joystick up, the avatar moves toward the top of the screen, which is also forward into the 3D environment, away from the player. Moving the joystick down makes the avatar turn to face the player and move toward him through the 3D environment. Pushing the joystick left or right makes the avatar turn to face and then move in that direction.

Unlike avatar-oriented steering, in this model, left and right cause the avatar to *move* in those directions while the camera continues to face forward and to show the avatar from the side. In this respect, *Crash Bandicoot* feels rather like a side-scroller with an additional dimension. In avatar-oriented steering, addressed next, left and right cause the avatar to *turn and face* in those directions *but not to move* while the camera swings around to remain behind him.

Avatar-Oriented Steering

In *avatar-oriented steering,* the only suitable model for first-person games, pushing the joystick up causes the avatar to move forward in whatever direction she currently faces, regardless of her orientation to the screen. However, implementation of avatar-oriented steering varies somewhat from one device to another, so the following sections treat these devices individually.

Avatar-oriented steering remains consistent regardless of the camera model, but it works best with models that follow the avatar. It presents a slight disadvantage in games using aerial perspectives: Avatar-oriented steering can be rather disorienting when the avatar faces the bottom of the screen, yet the player must push the joystick up to make the avatar walk down to the bottom of the screen. Both *Resident Evil* and *Grim Fandango* used fixed cameras but avatar-oriented steering, which made them more difficult to play than they should have been.

JOYSTICK AND D-PAD CONTROLS

As stated earlier, pushing the joystick up makes the avatar move forward in whatever direction he faces. Pulling the joystick down makes the avatar move backward away from the direction he faces, while continuing to face the original direction; that is, he walks backward. In some vehicle simulators, *down* applies the brakes rather than reversing the direction of movement, and the player must press a separate controller button to put the vehicle in reverse. Pushing the joystick to the left or right makes the avatar turn to face toward the left or right or turns the wheels of a vehicle. The avatar does not move in the environment if the joystick moves directly to left or right; the player must push the joystick diagonally to get forward (or backward) motion in addition to a change of direction. This feels more natural with vehicles than it does with characters.

MOUSE-BASED CONTROL

With mouse-based navigation, now standard for first-person PC games, the mouse controls only the direction in which the avatar faces, and the player uses the keyboard to make the avatar move. Moving the mouse left or right causes the avatar to turn in place, to the left or the right, and to a degree in proportion to the distance the mouse moves. Up and down mouse movements tilt the camera up or down, which becomes important if the player wants the avatar to climb or descend, but these commands do not move the avatar. Considerably more flexible than a joystick-based system, mouse-based navigation allows the player to look around without moving the character.

Keys on the PC's keyboard control movement. The standard arrangement for players who use their right hands for the mouse and left hands for the keyboard uses W to produce forward movement in the direction the avatar currently faces; movement continues as long as the player holds down the key. S works similarly for moving backward (or applying the brakes). A and D produce movement at right angles to the direction the avatar faces, left or right respectively, thus producing the feeling of sliding sideways while facing forward. This sideways movement is often called *strafing*. Left-handed players usually use the arrow keys or the I, J, K, and L keys, whose layout mimics the W, A, S, and D keys.

Flying

Flying presents a further complication because it involves moving through three dimensions, whereas a two-dimensional input device such as a joystick offers control in only two dimensions. Control over movement in the third dimension must be handled by a separate mechanism, either extra controller buttons or an additional joystick. How you implement this depends on the nature of the aircraft itself, generally using the mechanisms in real aircraft as your model. Navigational controls in modern flying games are almost always intended for the first-person perspective from inside the cockpit. (See the companion e-book *Fundamentals of Vehicle Simulation Design* for further details.)

FIXED-WING AIRCRAFT

The player maneuvers the aircraft using the joystick to *pitch* (the equivalent of a camera's tilt) or roll the aircraft, and the engine pulls the plane in the direction the nose faces. A throttle control, generally a slider or keys that increase and decrease the engine speed by fixed increments, sets the rate of forward movement. When flying straight and level, forward on the joystick pushes the nose down, producing descent, and back pulls the nose up, causing it to climb. Left on the joystick causes the plane to roll to the left while remaining on the same course; right rolls it to the right in the same manner. To turn in the horizontal plane, the pilot rolls the aircraft in the desired direction and pulls the joystick back at the same time, so the nose follows the direction of the roll, producing a banked turn. When the joystick returns to center, the plane should fly straight and level at a speed determined by the throttle.

HELICOPTERS

Game user interfaces typically simplify helicopter navigation, which is more complicated than flying fixed-wing aircraft. The joystick controls turning and forward or backward movement, and a slider control or keys cause the helicopter to ascend or descend. Left on the joystick causes the helicopter to turn counterclockwise about its vertical axis but not to actually go in that direction unless it is also moving forward. Right causes the equivalent rotation to the right. Forward propels the helicopter forward, and back the reverse. When the joystick returns to center, the helicopter should gradually slow down through air friction until it remains hovering above a fixed point in the landscape.

NOTE Real helicopters can also travel sideways while facing forward (what's called *strafing* in shooter games); to implement this would require extra controls, which few games do.

SPACECRAFT

Most designers treat spacecraft as they would fixed-wing aircraft, although in one variant left or right on the joystick causes the vehicle to *yaw* (the equivalent of panning a camera), turning about its vertical axis to face in a different direction, rather than rolling.

Point-and-Click Navigation

Aerial or context-sensitive camera models in which the player can clearly see his avatar, party, or units as well as a good deal of the surrounding environment can use point-and-click navigation (which also applies to touch screens). In a game with a multipresent or party-based interaction model, the player first chooses which unit or units should move (unnecessary in an avatar-based model), then in all cases the player selects a destination in the environment, and the unit or avatar moves to that location automatically using a *pathfinding* algorithm (an artificial intelligence technique to avoid obstacles). Typically the player can select one of two speeds: When the player selects a location, the avatar walks to it, but if he holds down a special key while selecting the location, the avatar runs rather than walks.

NOTE Many smaller games don't use a full pathfinding algorithm; they just move the avatar along a straight path to the place where the player clicked or touched, stopping at any obstacles. The player must guide the avatar around the obstruction by hand. This approach is more suitable for small projects, because pathfinding algorithms can be difficult to implement.

This technique is most often used in real-time strategy and party-based role-playing games in which many units may need to be given their own paths and the player does not have time to control them all precisely. If a unit cannot get to the location the player designated, that unit either goes as far as it can and then stops or, upon receipt of the command, warns the player that it cannot proceed to an inaccessible destination.

Using point-and-click navigation, the player can indicate precisely where he wants the unit to end up without concerning himself about avoiding obstacles, a convenience in cluttered environments where the player may not clearly see which objects actually block the path. It is also helpful in context-sensitive camera models because the player cannot always see clearly how the avatar should get from one place to another and often has no freedom to move the camera.

At times, it can be a disadvantage that the player cannot control the path that the unit takes, so allow the player to designate intermediate points, called *waypoints*, that the unit must pass through one by one on its way to the final destination. Waypoints enable the player to plot a route for the unit and so exercise some control over how the units get to where they are going.

Accessibility Issues

Although it took them a while to get around to it, Microsoft now leads the world in making their operating system and office products available to people with disabilities of various kinds. The game industry, regrettably, remains far behind. Its origins in arcade and twitch gaming have produced an unquestioned assumption that games are only for people with excellent eyesight and good hand-eye coordination. But many people who don't possess these abilities also would like to play games, and you should consider ways to make your game more accessible to them.

Impairments fall into four general categories: visual, auditory, mobility, and cognitive. We can't address all these in detail here, but you can do a number of fairly simple things to make your game much more accessible to impaired players. There is a large amount of literature on the subject of design for the disabled if you want to study it further. You can find many more resources at the websites listed in the sidebar "Accessibility Resources." The International Game Developers' Association's Top Ten list of things that you can do to assist disabled players is particularly useful; you can find it at wiki.igda.org/Top_Ten.

Vision-Impaired Players

Vision impairments fall into several subcategories that require slightly different adjustments. In any case, you should provide audio cues to go with visual cues. Very few events in a video game should be silent ones. When a player selects a unit, have the unit acknowledge its selection with a sound. When the player gives an order, presses a button, or chooses a menu item, be sure to indicate it with an audible cue. These cues can be quite subtle; there's no need to ring loud bells, but make sure the player hears something, even if only a little *tick* sound.

PLAYERS WITH LOW VISION

You can help some players with cataracts and similar conditions by giving them brighter, more high-contrast images. Most likely, these players will already have turned up the brightness and contrast on their monitors, but your game can augment this further by letting players adjust the contrast in your game, assuming that you have a display engine powerful enough to support this feature. Also, make the textures in your game available for modification. Vision-impaired players can then edit your textures to meet their own needs.

Be sure to include enough contrast in your UI elements as well as your game world. Don't try to be cool by using black-on-black or gray-on-gray menus or indicators.

Increasing brightness or contrast alone is not enough to help people with certain low-vision conditions such as macular degeneration. If you really want to make a game that vision-impaired players can see well, you will need to do further research. Institutions such as Lighthouse International and the Wilmer Eye Institute at Johns Hopkins University (both in the USA) may be able to direct you to additional resources.

PLAYERS WHO NEED MAGNIFICATION

Many vision-impaired players simply need everything to be a bit larger. Older players provide a good example; after about age 45, most people need reading glasses—but even reading glasses aren't much help with tiny type. Tiny type is a bad idea in any case, especially if players have to read it under time pressure.

You can meet the needs of these people in three ways. First, if possible, allow players to change the font size of text that appears in your game, the way web browsers do. Second, support multiple monitor resolutions in your game. Let players who really need to see things in larger scale set their monitors to 640×480. If you have a complicated UI, this may be rather tricky, but if it is, perhaps you should revisit the design of your interface and see if you can do without some of those screen elements. If you have a broad interface, consider making it deeper.

Finally, you can provide a magnifying glass feature that the player can move around over the screen to magnify different areas. The device probably won't be usable in action scenarios, but at least it's trivial to implement. *Strange Adventures in Infinite Space* includes a magnifying glass and switchable menu sizes, both of which are very helpful.

COLOR-BLIND PLAYERS

Color blindness is a sex-linked genetic disorder primarily affecting men. Total color blindness is quite rare, but one milder form (*deuteranomaly*) affects about 6 percent of the male population. People with this disorder have reduced sensitivity to different shades of green; they appear more like yellow. (So-called red–green color blindness is actually a misnomer for several related conditions.)

This issue matters most in UI design. If you create identical objects distinguishable only by their color, and you use similar shades of yellow and green, you risk confusing the color-blind player. Vehicles or characters in a strategy game whose appearance is identical except for their color would be an example. Also be careful with indicators, such as colored lights, that turn yellow or green. Color-blind drivers can tell the difference between yellow and green traffic lights because the yellow and green lights are separate lights, so even if the driver can't see a difference, he can tell whether the signal is yellow or green by its position (the middle light is always the yellow light). You can adopt this convention too: make more than one light, with the yellow light in a predictable location. If you don't have room and have to make do with a single light, use colors other than yellow and green, such as black and white or black and green.

You can test the appearance of your artwork to players with different forms of color blindness at the Vischeck website, www.vischeck.com.

Hearing-Impaired Players

To help support hearing-impaired players, consider the following:

 Display visible cues for audible events. If a car scrapes along a railing, show sparks; when a gun fires, show a muzzle flash. Naturally, you can't do this in some circumstances. In horror games, scary sounds often come from unseen sources, and that aspect is critical to creating the desired emotional effect. But for games that aren't in the horror genre—which means most of them—you should be able to design for hearing-impaired players by including visual cues for the most critical audible events.

 Offer two separate volume controls, one for music and one for sound effects. Be sure the player can mute either one entirely. Hearing-impaired people often complain that they cannot filter out background sounds from foreground ones, so conversation becomes impossible in noisy environments. In a video game, music can prevent them from hearing important sound effects. If you can, separate spoken dialogue into a third category and let the players control its volume level, too. Make these controls easily accessible from a pause menu—don't require the player to save the game and return to a shell menu to adjust them.

 Use the rumble (vibration) feature of the controller if the controller includes one. If you do this, players will be able to feel events even if they cannot hear them. Also allow the player to turn off vibration—not all of them like it.

Supply optional subtitles for dialogue and sound effects. (This feature is also called *closed captioning*.) It is very inexpensive to implement and enormously help-ful to hearing-impaired players. The biggest drawback of subtitles is that you must leave space for them on the screen. *Half-Life 2* includes closed captioning and uses different colors to indicate different speakers.

For more information on accommodating hearing-impaired players, visit Deafgamers.com at www.deafgamers.com.

Mobility Impairments

The best thing you can do for mobility-impaired players is to reduce the time pressure required to accomplish tasks. Many people with physical impairments can manage well enough given time, but they don't always get the time. If it's feasible, include a switch that lets the player adjust the speed of the game. There's no such thing as *too slow.*

Keep your control set simple. *Strange Attractors,* one of the finalists at the Independent Game Festival in 2006, uses a single button for player control. *Weird Worlds: Return to Infinite Space* uses a purely mouse-based interface. Researchers are also working on ways to adapt games and game controllers to what is called single-switch opera-tion; see "Accessibility Resources," later in this section, for more details. Obviously not all games can make do with so few controls, but even if you're not specifically designing for the mobility-impaired, you will find it a useful exercise to ask your-self how well a mobility-impaired person would do trying to use your interface. If your answer is "not that well," perhaps you should revisit your interface's design.

If you implement fidgets for characters while they're not doing anything, don't include any that make fun of the player for being slow. (Sonic, in *Sonic the Hedgehog,* used to fold his arms, tap his foot, and look irritated if the player didn't do anything for a certain length of time.) Use animations that don't appear to pass judgment.

Older Players

Be aware of the changing demographic of game players. As the gamer market ages, older people play games more frequently, particularly casual web-based games. Frequently, older players have some or all of the previously mentioned accessibility problems, yet they still want to play games. A needlessly complex interface or exclu-sionary design may cost you market share. For more information about the special needs of older people, look at the Spry Foundation's publications at www.spry.org.

ACCESSIBILITY RESOURCES

For additional information on accessibility issues and video games, please visit the following websites:

- IGDA Accessibility SIG: wiki.igda.org/Game_Accessibility_SIG

- Game Accessibility.Com: www.game-accessibility.com

- UK Accessibility Site Article on Games: www.bbc.co.uk/ouch/features/accessible_gaming.shtml

- The OneSwitch Organization: www.oneswitch.org.uk

- Accessibility Top Ten List: wiki.igda.org/Top_Ten

- Physical Barriers in Video Games article: www.oneswitch.org.uk/2/ARTICLES/physical-barriers.htm

- Examples of games with a wide variety of control mechanisms: www.ics.forth.gr/hci/ua-games/games.html

- Games playable by sound alone, for vision-impaired players: www.audiogames.net

Allowing for Customization

One of the most useful, and at the same time easiest to design, features you can offer your player is to allow her to customize her input devices to suit herself. Normally you handle this via a shell menu, although a few PC games store the information in a text file that the player can edit. These are two of the most commonly offered customizations:

▓ **Swap left and right mouse buttons** (or handedness on touch screen devices). If the mouse has more than one button, left-handed and right-handed players may need different button assignments. Swapping two buttons takes little trouble, so don't make players go through a function-reassignment process just for this; give them a feature that allows them to simply reverse the current assignments. Swapping handedness on touch screen devices will be more complicated, however, as you will have to have a mirror image of your user interface if the player is expected to tap screen buttons. Comparatively few games do this, but it would be welcome to left-handed players.

▓ **Swap the up and down directions of the mouse or joystick in first-person 3D games.** Some players like to push the mouse or joystick up to make their avatar look up (an idea borrowed from screen-oriented steering in 2D games); others like to pull it down to look up (an idea borrowed from airplane joysticks). Let the player play as she prefers.

The term *degrees of freedom* refers to the number of possible dimensions that an input device can move through. An ordinary key or button has one degree of freedom: It can move only up and down. A joystick or mouse has two degrees of freedom: It can move up and down, left and right. The Wii Remote has three degrees of freedom. If two devices, both binary or both analog (see the discussion in "Input Devices," earlier), have the same degree of freedom, generally you can let the player interchange them, although there will be practical difficulties if one device is self-centering and the other is not, or if one allows unlimited travel and the other does not. When exchanging assignments between two devices not identical in every way, some functionality or convenience is almost always lost.

Almost all games assign some of their player actions to particular keys or buttons. Your game should include a *key reassignment* shell menu that allows players to assign actions to the keys they prefer. If your game includes menus, also allow the player to assign menu items to keys so she can select them quickly without using the mouse. You may need to enforce some requirements: If the game requires a particular action to be playable (for example, the fire-weapon action in a shooter game), warn the player if she tries to exit the shell menu with the action still unassigned.

When implementing a shell menu for key reassignment, show *all* the current assignments, *all* the game features not currently assigned to keys, and *all* the currently unassigned keys *on the same screen*. Don't force the player to flip from screen to screen to reassign keys.

Be sure to save the player's customizations between games so that she doesn't have to set them up every time she plays. If you want to be especially helpful, let players save different setups in separate, named profiles so that each player can have her own set of customizations. Include a *restore defaults* option so the player can return her customizations to the original factory settings.

Summary

When game reviewers praise a game highly, they cite its user interface more often than any other aspect of the game as the feature that makes the game great. The gameplay may be innovative, the artwork breathtaking, and the story moving, but a smooth and intuitive UI improves the player's perception of the game like nothing else.

In this chapter, you learned about interaction models and camera models, two concepts central to game UIs. Now you know some ways to manage the complexity of an interface, and you are familiar with a number of visual and audio elements that games use. You also studied input devices and navigation mechanisms in detail.

If you tune and polish your interface to peak perfection, your players will notice it immediately. Give it that effort, and your work will be well justified.

Design Practice EXERCISES

1. Design and draw one icon for each of the following functions in a game:

- Build (makes a unit build a certain structure)

- Repair (makes a unit repair a certain structure)

- Attack (makes a unit attack a certain enemy unit)

- Move (moves a unit to a certain position)

- Hide (makes a unit hide to be less visible to enemy units)

Briefly explain the design choices you made for each icon. All icons should be for the same game, so make them consistent to a game genre of your choice.

2. In this exercise, you will practice designing user interfaces for two different gameplay modes, each of which has different indicators. Using the following descriptions of the modes, decide how best to display the functions to the player and sketch a small screen mock-up showing how these indicators can be positioned on the screen. Briefly explain your design decisions.

In the primary gameplay mode, the avatar can move around in the game world and do different things such as attacking, talking to NPCs, and so on. The mode is avatar-based in the third-person perspective.

Functions/indicators:

- Character's health

- Character's position in the game world

- Currently chosen weapon

- Waypoint to the next mission

- Character visibility to enemies (indicate that, if the character stands in shadows or in darkness, he is less visible to enemies)

In the secondary gameplay mode, the player enters vehicle races that include shooting at other vehicles driven by NPCs. The perspective is first person.

Functions/indicators:

- Vehicle health

- Vehicle speed

- Primary weapon ammo left

- Type of secondary weapon mounted, if present (if not present, so indicate)

- Position in race

- Laps remaining in race

3. In this exercise, you design the same UI, once for breadth and once for depth. Make the broad UI no more than two levels deep at any point. Make the deep UI at least three levels deep at one point, offering no more than three options at the top level. Present the UIs by making flowcharts showing the different levels of interaction or how you group different functions. Include all the following functions. Briefly explain your design decisions.

Attack	Research	Save current game
Defend	Build barracks	Load game
Guard	Build headquarters	Quit game
Patrol	Build hospital	Change video settings
Move	Destroy	Change sound settings
Set waypoint	Repair	Change control settings
Choose weapon	Harvest	

4. A game intended for a console needs to have its functions mapped to a game pad with a limited number of buttons. Make a button layout that supports all the actions in the primary gameplay mode (described in the following list). Discuss the pros and cons of your button layout.

NOTE This is the button layout of the Sony PSP controller, excluding the start and select buttons.

The game pad has the following button layout:

- A D-pad
- One analog joystick
- Four face buttons
- Two shoulder buttons

The main gameplay mode has the following actions:

Normal	Jump	Strafe right
Hard attack	Crouch	Rotate left
High attack (attack upward)	Move forward	Rotate right
Low attack (attack downward)	Move backward	Choose weapon
Block attack	Strafe left	Use health pack

5. Select one of the newer input devices (touch screen, Wii remote, Kinect, or one that your instructor assigns) and recommend some conventions based on initial games or apps that are using it. Do conventions already exist? Are there aspects that are being experimented with? If you made a game, which conventions would you select and which would you make optional?

Design Practice QUESTIONS

1. Does the gameplay require a pointing or steering device? Should these be analog or will a D-pad suffice? What do they actually do in the context of the game?

2. Does the function of one or more buttons on the controller change within a single gameplay mode? If so, what visual cues let the player know this is taking place?

3. If the player has an avatar (whether a person, creature, or vehicle), how do the movements and other behaviors of the avatar map to the machine's input devices? Define the steering mechanism.

4. How will the major elements of your screen be laid out? Will the game use a windowed view, opaque overlays, semitransparent overlays, or a combination?

5. What camera model will the main view use? What interaction model does the gameplay mode use? Is it one of the common ones or something new? How does the camera model support the interaction model?

6. Does the game's genre, if it has one, help to determine the UI? What standards already exist that the player may be expecting the game to follow? Do you intend to break these expectations, and if so, how will you inform the player of that?

7. Does the game include menus? What is the menu structure? Is it broad and shallow (quick to use but hard to learn) or narrow and deep (easy to learn but slow to use)?

8. Does the game include text on the screen? Does it need provisions for localization?

9. What icons does the game use? Are they visually distinct from one another and quickly identifiable? Are they culturally universal?

10. Does the player need to know numeric values (score, speed, health)? Can these be presented through nonnumeric means (power bars, needle gauges, small multiples), or should they be shown as digits? If shown as digits, how can they be presented in such a way that they don't harm suspension of disbelief? Will you label the value and if so, how?

11. What symbolic values does the player need to know (safe/danger, locked/unlocked/open)? By what means will you convey both the value and its label?

12. Will it be possible for the player to control the game's camera? Will it be necessary for the player to do so in order to play the game? What camera controls will be available? Will they be available at all times or from a separate menu or other mechanism?

13. What is the aesthetic style of the game? How do the interface elements blend in and support that style?

14. How will audio support the player's interaction with the game? What audio cues will accompany player actions? Will the game include audio advice or dialogue?

15. How does music support the UI and the game generally? Does it create an emotional tone or set a pace? Can it adapt to changing circumstances?

CHAPTER 13

Gameplay

Chapter 1, "Games and Video Games," defined gameplay as consisting of the challenges and actions that a game offers: challenges for the player to overcome and actions that let her overcome them. Games also include actions unrelated to gameplay, but the essence of gameplay remains the relationship between the challenges and the actions available to surmount them.

This chapter begins by discussing how we make games fun, setting out some things you need to be aware of and principles you need to observe. Next we'll look at some important ideas related to gameplay: the hierarchy of challenges and the concepts of skill, stress, and difficulty. The bulk of the chapter consists of a long list of types of challenges that video games offer, with some observations about how you might present them, mistakes you should avoid, and how you can adjust their difficulty. Next we'll turn to actions, listing a number of common types found in games. Finally, we'll examine the questions of if, when, and how to save the game.

Making Games Fun

As Chapter 1 asserted, the game designer's primary goal is to provide entertainment, and gameplay is the primary means by which games entertain; without gameplay, an activity may be fun, but it is not a game. *Entertainment* is a richer and more manifold idea than *fun* is. Nevertheless, most games concentrate on delivering fun rather than offering moving, thought-provoking, or enlightening entertainment. How, then, do we provide fun?

Execution Matters More Than Innovation

Genius is one percent inspiration, ninety-nine percent perspiration.

—THOMAS EDISON (ATTRIBUTED)

For games, the proportions are a little different from Edison's proportions for genius, but the idea is the same. Most of what makes a game fun has nothing to do with imagination or creativity. The vast majority of things that make a game *not* fun—boring or frustrating or irritating or simply ugly and awkward—result from bad execution rather than a bad idea. A surprising amount of the job of making a game fun, therefore, simply consists of avoiding those things that reduce fun. Here's a list, from most to least important, showing how the different aspects of game development contribute to fun:

■ **Avoiding elementary errors is the most important thing you can do.** Bad programming, bad music and sound, bad art, bad user interfaces, and bad game design all ruin the player's fun. Find and fix those bugs!

■ **Tuning and polishing are the second-most important aspects of making a game fun.** This means paying attention to detail, getting everything perfect. Dedicated tuning sets a good game apart from a mediocre one.

■ **Imaginative variations on the game's premise contribute to the player's fun.** Take the basic elements of the game and construct an enjoyable experience out of them. Level designers do most of this work.

■ **True design innovation is perhaps five percent of the source of a game's fun.** Design innovation encompasses the game's original idea and subsequent creative decisions that you make.

The smallest and most mysterious part of the fun in a game emerges from an unpredictable, unanalyzable, unnamable quality—call it luck, magic, or stardust. You can't make it happen, so you might as well not worry about it. But when you can feel it's there, be careful about making changes to your design from that point on. Whatever it is, it's fragile.

So innovation by the game designer contributes only a small part of the fun of the game. That may make it sound as if there's not a lot of point in game design. But to build a game, someone must design it and design it well. Most game design decisions give little room for innovation, but they're still necessary. A brilliant architect may design a wonderful new building, but it still needs heat and light and plumbing, and in fact, the majority of the work required to design that building goes into creating those mundane but essential details. The same is true of game design.

Finding the Fun Factor

There's no formula for making your game fun, nothing that anyone can set out as a reliable pattern and tell you that, if you just slide in a really cool monster here and a fabulously imaginative weapon there, the resulting game is guaranteed to be fun every time. But there is a set of principles to keep in mind as you design and build your game; without them, you risk producing a game that's no fun.

■ **Gameplay comes first.** Before all other considerations, create your game to give people fun things to do. A good many games aren't fun because the designers spent more time thinking about their graphics or their story than they did thinking about creating gameplay.

■ **Get a feature right or leave it out.** It is far worse to ship a game with a broken feature than to ship a game with a missing feature. Shipping without a feature looks to players like a design decision; a debatable decision, possibly, but at least a deliberate choice. Shipping with a broken feature tells players for certain that your team is incompetent. Broken features destroy fun.

■ **Design around the player.** Everything in this book is based on player-centric game design, as Chapter 2, "Designing and Developing Games," explains in detail. You must examine *every* decision from the player's point of view. Games that lose sight of the player lose sight of the fun.

■ **Know your target audience.** Different groups of players want different things. You don't necessarily have to aim for the mass market, and in fact it's much harder to make a game that appeals broadly than it is to make a game that appeals to a niche market you know well. But whatever group you choose, find out what they want and what they think is fun, and then provide it. Don't assume that you already know it. Play-test with representative members of your audience regularly.

■ **Abstract or automate parts of the simulation that** aren't **fun.** If you model your game on the real world, leave out the parts that aren't fun. But remember your audience: To somebody who just wants a chance to drive a fast car, changing the tires isn't fun, but to a hardcore racing fan, changing the tires *is* fun and a critical part of the experience. If—and only if—you have the time and resources, you may include two modes. Otherwise, choose one market and optimize the fun for the members of that market.

■ **Be true to your vision.** If you envision the perfect sailing simulation, don't add powerboat racing as well because you feel that adding features might attract a larger market. Instead, adding powerboats will distract you from your original goal and cut in half the resources you were planning to use to perfect the sailing simulation. Both halves will be inferior to what the whole could have been. You will lose the fun, and without it you won't get the bigger market anyway.

■ **Strive for harmony, elegance, and beauty.** A lack of aesthetic perfection doesn't take *all* the fun out of a game, but the absence of these qualities appreciably diminishes it. And a game that is already fun is even *more* fun if it's beautiful to look at, to listen to, and to play with.

NOTE There is a tension between staying true to your vision and providing what your audience wants—or says that it wants. At larger publishers, marketing people are notorious for asking developers to add features because the marketers think those features will increase sales, whether or not they really work with the game's premise. If you're an independent developer, you'll probably do your own market research by looking at Internet forums and game reviews. This is useful material, but don't overestimate its importance.

The Hierarchy of Challenges

When you're up to your ___ in alligators, it's hard to remember that your original objective was to drain the swamp.

—U<small>NATTRIBUTED</small>

In all but the smallest games, the player faces several challenges at a time, organized in a *hierarchy of challenges.* Ultimately, she wants to complete the game. To accomplish that, she must complete the current mission. Completing the mission requires completing a *sub-mission,* of which the current mission probably has several. At the lowest level, she wants to deal with the challenge that immediately faces her: the enemies threatening her at the moment, perhaps, or the locked door for which she needs the right spell. These lowest-level challenges are called *atomic challenges* (*atomic* in the sense of *indivisible*). Atomic challenges make up sub-missions, sub-missions make up missions, and missions make up the ultimate goal: completing the game.

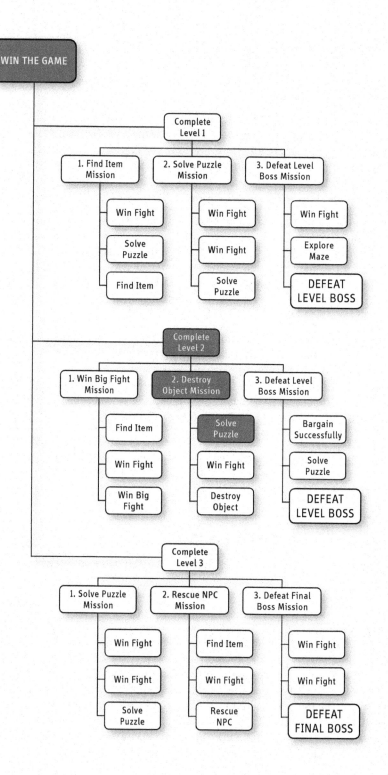

Figure 13.1 illustrates this idea. It displays the hierarchy of challenges for a (very) small action-adventure game. The entire game consists of three missions or game levels; each level consists of three sub-missions, the last of which pits the player against a level boss. Each sub-mission consists of three atomic challenges, of which the final one (in bold text) completes the sub-mission. The gray boxes indicate the challenges the player faces simultaneously at one particular moment in the middle of level 2. At the atomic level, you find him trying to solve a puzzle; doing so will help him to—or allow him to proceed to—destroy the critical object, all of which contributes to succeeding in the Destroy Object sub-mission, which itself makes up a part of winning level 2. Ultimately, he hopes to win the entire game.

To design your game, you create this hierarchy and decide what challenges the player will face. During play, the player focuses most of her attention on the atomic challenges immediately facing her, but the other, higher-level challenges will always be in the back of her mind. Her awareness of the higher-level challenges creates anticipation that plays an important role both in entertaining her and in guiding her to victory. The remainder of this section discusses how the hierarchy affects the player's experience and what that means for game design.

Informing the Player about Challenges

Video games normally tell the player directly about some challenges, called *explicit challenges,* and leave him to discover others on his own, which are called *implicit challenges.* In general, games give the player explicit instructions about the topmost and bottommost levels of the hierarchy but leave it to him to figure out how to approach the intermediate levels. The topmost level includes the victory condition for the entire game, and games tend to present their overall victory condition explicitly. They may also state an explicit victory condition for each level. Normally, the game's *tutorial levels* teach the player explicitly how to meet the atomic challenges. (For more on tutorial levels, see the discussion on that topic in Chapter 16, "General Principles of Level Design.") Unless you provide completely self-explanatory gameplay *and controls,* you should always include one or more tutorial levels in your game, or an explanation of the controls and how to use them to meet atomic challenges.

You should always tell the player about the victory condition, otherwise he won't know what he's trying to accomplish. You don't have to tell the complete truth, however. In storytelling games, you usually want to keep the outcome a surprise. Many stories start by telling the player one thing, but plot twists along the way deepen and complicate matters. He may change or meet a goal only to find it replaced by another, more important goal. Detective stories, in particular, are famous for this. (Don't do it more than three or four times in any one story, though, or the player will start to become irritated about being repeatedly lied to.) Be sure that the player gets whatever information he needs to *think* he clearly knows the victory condition so he's never left without any motivation.

CHAPTER 13

NOTE Game designer Ben Cousins proposed this notion of a hierarchy, but in a slightly different form. For more information on Cousins' original scheme, see the sidebar "Cousins' Hierarchy," later in this chapter.

TIP Make the victory condition and the atomic challenges explicit. Be sure the player always has some overarching goal in mind toward which she works. Never leave her without a reason for continuing to play.

The Intermediate Challenges

Most designs leave intermediate-level challenges implicit. If you give the player nothing to do except follow explicit instructions, it doesn't feel like a game; it feels like a test. Part of the player's fun lies in figuring out—whether through exploration, through events in the story, or by observing the game's internal economy—what she's supposed to do. Armed with the knowledge of both the victory condition at the top and the right way to meet the atomic challenges at the bottom, she has the tools to figure out the intermediate challenges—if you have constructed them coherently. For example, in *Angry Birds,* the player knows that she is supposed to destroy all the pigs (the victory condition for a level) and that launching a bird accurately into the defenses will destroy them (the atomic challenge). The intermediate challenge of *Angry Birds* is to figure out exactly *where* to launch the birds to destroy the defenses most efficiently. (See the section "Avoid Conceptual Non Sequiturs" in Chapter 16 for an example of how *not* to construct an intermediate-level challenge.)

> ### DESIGN RULE Reward Victory No Matter How the Player Achieves It
>
> Players will think of things to try that you might not have anticipated; even if you've given them multiple ways to win, they may find another way entirely. If the player achieves the victory condition, even in a completely unexpected way, he deserves credit for it. Don't test to see if he got there in one of the ways that you intended; just test to see if he got there. Of course, the game should prevent any form of cheating that it can reasonably control—but finding an unusual way to win is not cheating as long as it is equally available to all players.

For a good many games, overcoming the intermediate-level challenges requires only that the player meet all the lowest-level ones in sequence. That's how most action games work, and what Figure 13.1 illustrates. If the player beats all the enemies and gets past all the obstacles, she finishes the level. If she finishes all the levels, she wins the game.

In more complex games, the player may have a choice of ways to approach an intermediate-level challenge. Suppose the explicit top-level challenge—the victory condition—in a war game consists of defeating all the enemy units, and the atomic challenge consists of destroying one enemy unit. The simple and obvious strategy is apparently to destroy all the enemy units one by one, but the player isn't likely to get that chance. Most war games include a production system for generating new units, so even if the player can kill off enemy units one by one, his opponent can probably produce new ones faster than he can destroy them. Disrupting the enemy's production system is often an effective strategy, while protecting his own production system ensures that he can eventually overwhelm the enemy with superior numbers. Neither the specification of the victory condition nor the atomic challenges explicitly includes the intermediate-level challenge of *disrupt the enemy's production system,* and protecting his own production system doesn't destroy enemy units at all. The player must figure out what he should do by observing and deducing and, by planning and experimenting, find ways to accomplish his goals. Observing, deducing, planning, and experimenting all add to the fun.

You construct these implicit, intermediate challenges for the player to figure out. The conventions of the genre you choose guide you, but keep in mind that the most interesting games offer multiple ways to win. To give your player a richer experience, design your game so that she can win in a variety of ways—so that meeting *different* intermediate challenges will still get her to victory. Different strategies may be better or worse, but if you permit only one right way to win, you don't reward the player's lateral thinking skills. The game becomes an exercise in reading the designer's mind.

Figure 13.2 illustrates the idea of offering multiple ways to win a war game. The victory condition is to capture the flag. The hierarchy is organized as before, except that the dotted lines indicate a *choice of possible approaches* rather than a *sequence of required sub-missions,* as in Figure 13.1. The gray boxes indicate the challenges in the player's mind at one particular moment—in this case, we assume that he chose to use a stealth approach and sent units out to scout.

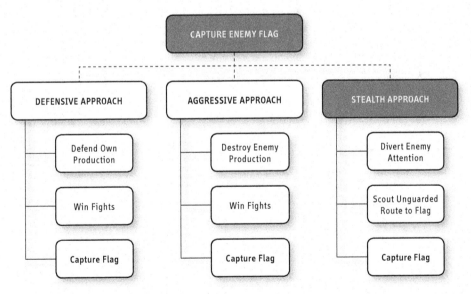

FIGURE 13.2
A hierarchy of challenges with multiple options

Simultaneous Atomic Challenges

Although the player simultaneously faces several challenges in the hierarchy, she pays less attention, on a moment-by-moment basis, to those challenges that are further up in the hierarchy. But games can also present several atomic challenges at once.

These divide the player's attention. If she can deal with them one at a time at her own pace (as in a turn-based game), then they're not really different from sequential challenges; but if she has to surmount them all in a limited amount of time, then adding simultaneous challenges makes the game more stressful. (Stress is discussed in the next section, "Skill, Stress, and Absolute Difficulty.")

COUSINS' HIERARCHY

In an article for *Develop* magazine, Ben Cousins suggested thinking of gameplay as a hierarchy (Cousins, 2004). This book adopts his idea but modifies it somewhat and uses different terminology. For example, Cousins referred to *atoms of interaction* rather than *atomic challenges.*

Cousins studied the game *Super Mario Sunshine* by making a video recording of the screen while he played, and then examining the results in a video editor, which enabled him to identify the atoms of interaction in the game. By thinking about what he was trying to accomplish at each moment as he played, he found that he could organize the gameplay into a five-level hierarchy with "complete the whole game" as the topmost interaction, "complete the current game level" as the second level of the hierarchy, and so on down to individual atoms of interaction at the bottom level.

Cousins studied an action game; action games typically require players to use specific low-level actions to meet low-level challenges (to get across the chasm, jump). In other genres, however, there isn't a one-to-one mapping between challenges and actions even at the atomic level. Some challenges may be overcome by several different kinds of actions; overcoming others requires complex sequences of actions. Accordingly, actions don't appear in the hierarchy, only challenges.

You should try Cousins' technique of analyzing the way that games organize their gameplay by examining them second by second in a video editor; it's a valuable technique for understanding gameplay.

An early and still common way of creating simultaneous atomic challenges, typical of side-scrolling shooter games, consists of bombarding the player with enemies. Each enemy represents a significant risk, and the player must defeat each one while fending off the others. A player who works quickly can generally defeat these added enemies one at a time while keeping the others at bay.

Other games present more complex and interrelated simultaneous challenges. In its default mode, *SimCity* imposes no victory condition; its highest-level challenge is to achieve economic growth so the player can expand his city. (Expanding the city itself isn't a challenge, just a series of choices available so long as the player brings in enough money to keep going.) The player doesn't attain economic growth unless he can provide a balanced supply of services to the city. The city needs police protection *and* power *and* hospitals *and* water and so on, all at the same time; each represents an atomic challenge, and the player must meet all these simultaneously. The complex juggling of competing needs requires regular attention and frequent action. Furthermore, unlike fighting enemies, the player can never finish balancing the services; the juggling act never stops.

It's part of your job to design the hierarchy of challenges and decide how many of them the player will face at once, both vertically up the hierarchy and at the bottom of the hierarchy. The more simultaneous atomic challenges she will face under time pressure, the more stressful the game will be. The more different levels of challenge she will have to think about at once—especially if she can't simply achieve the higher ones by addressing the lower ones in sequence—the more complex and mentally challenging the game will be—which may or may not be fun for a particular audience.

Skill, Stress, and Absolute Difficulty

Chapter 15, "Game Balancing," addresses gameplay difficulty in detail, but this chapter introduces some important concepts because the terms involved come up in a discussion of different types of gameplay later in this chapter. Although these are not industry standard terms, you should find them useful.

This chapter is concerned with controlling the absolute difficulty of the challenges that you will present to the player. Two different factors determine the absolute difficulty of a challenge: *intrinsic skill required* and *stress.* Chapter 15 addresses additional factors that affect the player's perceptions about how easy or hard the game is.

Intrinsic Skill

The *intrinsic skill required* by a challenge is defined as the level of skill needed to surmount the challenge *if the player had an unlimited amount of time in which to do it* (regardless of the player's actual abilities). You can compute the intrinsic skill required for a challenge by taking the conditions of the challenge and leaving out any element of time pressure. How you measure the skill level of a challenge varies with the type of challenge and can involve physical tasks, mental tasks, or both. Consider three examples:

▓ An archer aiming at a target requires a certain level of skill to hit the target. It takes more skill to hit the target if you move the target farther away or make it smaller. The archer gets an unlimited amount of time to aim. Even if he takes more time, it does not change the skill required.

▓ Sudoku puzzles printed in the newspaper often include a rating that indicates whether they are easy or hard to solve. The player may take as long as she wants to solve the puzzle, so the rating reflects an intrinsic quality of the puzzle—how many clues the player gets—rather than the effect of a time limit.

▓ A trivia game requires the player to have certain factual knowledge. Some questions are about familiar facts and some are about obscure facts. The skill level required by a question doesn't change if you give the player more time to answer.

Some challenges *must* include time pressure by the way they are defined—a test of the player's reaction time, for example. The carnival game *Whac-a-Mole* tests hand-eye coordination combined with time pressure; it wouldn't be much of a challenge if a healthy adult player had all the time in the world to do it.

Stress

If a challenge includes time pressure, a new factor comes into play: *stress*. Stress measures how a player perceives the effect of time pressure on his ability to meet a challenge requiring a given level of intrinsic skill. The shorter the time limit, the more stressful the situation. Succeeding in a stressful game requires both quick reflexes and a quick mind. The challenges of *Tetris* do not require a great deal of intrinsic skill—if the player had plenty of time to think about the task, it would be easy to keep the blocks from piling up—but *Tetris* is stressful because the player must complete the task under time pressure. Golf, on the other hand, demands skill without being stressful—at least, in the sense of heavy time pressure. It would be considerably more stressful if the rules imposed more time pressure.

Tetris gives the player a short amount of time to complete a series of tasks one by one, but you can also create stress by giving the player many different tasks to perform at once. Classic arcade action games such as *Tempest* attacked the player with a dozen or more enemies at once, and the player had to prioritize and defeat them all in a limited amount of time.

Games often create physical stress on the player's body. Time pressure requires players to use their eyes and hands more quickly; it makes them stiffen their muscles, and it raises their heart rates and adrenaline levels. Many people love this sensation, but not all do, so you must play-test with representative members of your target audience to be sure your game's pace is acceptable to them. As a general rule, even for the most skilled of players you should modulate the pacing of your game to give them time to rest at intervals. Chapter 16 discusses this in more detail in the section "Vary the Pacing."

NOTE The absolute difficulty of a challenge consists of a combination of the intrinsic skill required to meet the challenge without time pressure and the stress added by time pressure.

Absolute Difficulty

Absolute difficulty refers to intrinsic skill required and stressfulness put together. When a game offers multiple difficulty levels, the easy mode both demands less skill and exerts less stress than the hard mode. Some players like a challenge that demands a lot of skill but they can't tolerate much stress. If they know they have plenty of time to prepare for a challenge, they're perfectly happy for the challenge to require great skill. Others thrive on stress but don't have much skill. Simple, high-speed games like *Tetris* and *Collapse!* suit them best. **Figure 13.3** shows a graph of the relationship of intrinsic skill and stress in various games or tasks. The higher the task ranks on both scales, the greater its difficulty.

When you're deciding how difficult you want your game to be, think about both skill levels and stress, and keep your target audience in mind. Teenagers and young adults handle stress better than either children or older adults because teenagers and young adults have the best vision and motor skills. When you allow the player to set a difficulty level for the game, try to preserve an inverse relationship between skill level and stress at that particular level of difficulty. If a challenge requires more skill, give the player longer to perform it, and vice versa.

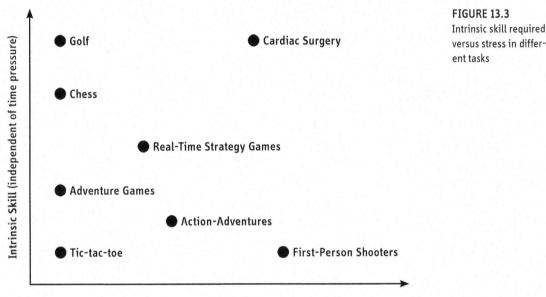

FIGURE 13.3
Intrinsic skill required versus stress in different tasks

Commonly Used Challenges

This section presents categories of commonly used challenges you should understand. Because games can set a top-of-the-hierarchy challenge of just about anything—take on the role of Jason and win the golden fleece, use your zombie army to drive the werewolves out of your ancestral home, capture a giant squid from the ocean depths, win a rodeo competition—this book can't discuss all the possible top-of-the-hierarchy goals. The discussion here focuses on lower-level challenges, many of which could be classified as atomic challenges.

These categories may help you to think about the kinds of traditional challenges you'd like to include in your game, but you're free to design any type of challenge you can imagine if you can make it workable. Players always appreciate innovative challenges; a beautiful setting or interesting overall concept gets you only so far. Gameplay is in the challenges.

This section includes observations from time to time about ways to make a particular type of challenge easier or harder. Most of these comments concentrate on making them easier because novice game developers frequently make their games too hard without realizing it.

Physical Coordination Challenges

Physical coordination challenges test a player's physical abilities, most commonly hand-eye coordination. One of the earliest coin-op video games, *Pong*, required only this one skill to win. Physical coordination challenges remain a basic component of arcade gaming and a significant part of most video games to this day. They fall into several subcategories, which the following sections discuss.

The absolute difficulty of a physical coordination challenge most frequently relates to the amount of time pressure the player is under; to make such a challenge easier, simply give the player more time. Each subcategory addresses exceptions when they occur.

SPEED AND REACTION TIME

Speed challenges test the player's ability to make rapid inputs on the controls, and reaction time challenges test his ability to react quickly to events. Usually both of these appear in combination with other types of challenges, most often other coordination challenges. You can expect to find speed and reaction time challenges in platform games, shooters, and fast puzzle games such as *Tetris*. From the frenetic button-banging of Konami's 1983 arcade game *Track & Field* (two buttons controlled an athlete's legs; the player pressed them alternately to make the athlete run) to the modern-day frenzy of the latest *Team Fortress* game, speed and reaction time challenges perennially please those who have the reflexes for them.

ACCURACY AND PRECISION

Steering and shooting comprise the majority of tests of accuracy or precision, though you can devise many more. Steering includes navigating characters as well as vehicles. Usually found in action and action-adventure games, sports games, and vehicle simulations, accuracy and precision challenges increasingly feature in role-playing games (RPGs), such as the *Fable* series, which include a combat element. Brain-training games, which are intended to sharpen a player's mental and motor skills, often include accuracy and precision challenges to test the player's hand-eye coordination. Because brain-training games are not usually aimed at conventional gamers, the challenges are seldom characterized as steering or shooting.

Accuracy challenges need not take place within time limits. In a sport such as archery, athletes may take as long as they want to line up a shot, but they still face a considerable challenge. To make an accuracy challenge easier or harder, adjust the degree to which the physics engine in the game forgives errors in the inputs. For example, the player of an archery game ordinarily needs to position the joystick or mouse within a particular range of values to hit the bull's-eye; you can make the game easier by widening that range. First-person shooters sometimes include an auto-aiming feature to assist the player as well.

INTUITIVE UNDERSTANDING OF PHYSICS

Vehicle simulations require more than just an ability to steer a vehicle; they also require an intuitive understanding of the physics of the game world. Players must learn, usually through experience, a car's braking distance, acceleration rate, at what rate it may take a turn without sliding off the road, and so on. Similarly, *Angry Birds* requires the players to develop an intuitive understanding of elementary ballistics. Learning and internalizing these features of the game world constitute another challenge. These appear under physical coordination challenges because the player tends to develop a visceral rather than an intellectual understanding of these aspects of the game world (darts players don't need to know calculus), which finds its expression in successful physical coordination.

You can help the player develop an intuitive understanding of the game's physics. First, make sure the physics remains consistent. The physics engine must be reliable and produce predictable results. Programmers handle the physics engine, but you should at least specify the limits of the game physics—how high and far a character can jump, for example. Second, the simpler the physical model of the world, the easier it will be for the player to develop that intuitive understanding. Sports games often simplify their physics to help the player. For example, many sports games don't implement the physical property of inertia for an athlete running under the player's control because the player wants to be able to turn her player instantaneously and will find it harder to get used to the game if she cannot. Flight simulators, too, model the physics of flight with greater and lesser degrees of accuracy depending on how easy the designer wants to make it for the player to understand how the airplane behaves.

TIMING AND RHYTHM

Side-scrolling action games rely heavily on timing challenges, in which the player learns to dodge swinging blades and attack predictable enemies. Rhythm challenges, tests of the player's ability to press the right button or perform the correct move at the right time, feature in dance games such as *Dance Dance Revolution* and other music-based games such as *Donkey Konga* and *Guitar Hero*. The popularity of rhythm-based games resulted in a significant aftermarket in specialty input devices such as dance mats and electronic conga drums.

TIP Players' ability to pick out the beat from a piece of music varies considerably. Be sure to include visual cues about the beat as well as audible ones. *Elite Beat Agents* for the Nintendo DS does this well.

COMBINATION MOVES

Many fighting games require complex sequences of joystick moves and controller-button presses that, once mastered, allow the player's avatar to perform some especially powerful feat. Executing a combo move requires speed, timing, and a good memory, too: The player has to remember the button sequence and produce it perfectly at just the right time. You can make combination moves easier by shortening them, requiring fewer presses.

Logic and Mathematical Challenges

Logical and mathematical reasoning has been part of gameplay since the dawn of human history. Logic provides the basis for strategic thinking in any turn-based game of perfect information and many other games in which the player can make precise deductions from reliable data. This section is confined to logic *puzzles*. The "Strategy" section, later in the chapter, deals with strategic thinking.

Mathematics underlies all games in which chance plays a role or the player does *not* have reliable data and so must reason from probabilities. Such games present explicit mathematical challenges to the player: If he doesn't compute the odds when playing poker, or at least know the odds and reason correctly given what he knows, he's much more likely to lose.

In the broadest sense, any game that includes numeric relationships offers a mathematical challenge, because the player must learn how those relationships work. Much of the time, games present mathematical challenges implicitly, couching numeric relationships in other terms: physics, strategy, or economics.

FORMAL LOGIC PUZZLES

NOTE The *Professor Layton* games for the Nintendo DS contain a wide variety of formal logic puzzles and serve as an excellent example of the form.

A puzzle is a mental challenge with at least one specific solution. *Formal logic* means classic deductive logic in which the definition of the puzzle contains, or explains, everything the player needs to know to solve the puzzle. A formal logic puzzle can be solved by reasoning power alone. It shouldn't require any outside knowledge. Many other types of puzzles require logic too, but they also expect the player to supply some additional information.

A logic puzzle typically presents the player with a collection of objects related in ways that are consistent but not directly obvious. To solve the puzzle, the player must put the objects into a specified configuration. The player manipulates the objects and receives feedback about their relationships, which she eventually comes to understand by observation and deduction. *Rubik's Cube*, a classic logic puzzle with a simple mechanism, consists of so many cubes that move in ways so intricately interrelated that it is quite difficult to solve.

Adventure games often present logic puzzles as combination locks or other machinery that the player must learn to manipulate because those devices make sense in the fantasy world in which the game exists. Other puzzle-based games don't try to be realistic but concentrate on offering an interesting variety of challenges.

To adjust the difficulty of a logic challenge, raise or lower the number of objects to be manipulated and the number of possible ways in which the player can manipulate them. A *Rubik's Cube* with four tiles per side (a 2×2×2 cube) instead of nine (3×3×3) would be far easier to solve. You can also modulate the difficulty of the challenge by allowing multiple solutions to a puzzle with differing numbers of points, or some other reward, granted for the solution. Many casual games use a three-star system, offering one, two, or three stars depending on which solution the player found.

Players normally get all the time they need to solve puzzles. Because different people bring differing amounts of logic ability to the task, requiring players to solve a puzzle within a time limit might make the game impossible for some. Exceptions to this rule can sometimes succeed; *ChuChu Rocket!* offers both a time-limited multiplayer mode and an untimed mode.

A few games do not make the correct solution clear at the outset of the puzzle. The player not only has to understand how the puzzle works, but he also has to guess at the solution he must try to achieve. This is bad game design: It forces the player to solve the puzzle by trial and error alone because there's no way to tell when he's on the right track. In order to open the stone sarcophagus at the end of *Infidel*, the player had to find the one correct combination of objects out of 24 possible combinations. The game gave no hints about which combination opened the box; the player simply had to try them all.

DESIGN RULE Avoid Trial-and-Error Solutions

Solving most logic puzzles requires a certain amount of experimentation, but the player must be able to make deductions from her experiments. Do not make puzzles that can be solved *only* by trial and error, without any clues about what the correct solution state is.

MATHEMATICAL CHALLENGES

Entertainment games don't usually test the player's mathematical abilities explicitly, but often they do require the player to reason about probabilities. Many games such as poker and craps include an element of chance or require the player to make educated guesses about situations of which he has only an imperfect knowledge. Video games have long been used to teach mathematics as well, with varying success. Too many such games are simply disguised math drills with little to interest the player, but clever mathematics-based puzzles such as those in *Wuzzit Trouble* (see **Figure 13.4**) challenge the player's arithmetical thinking in an engaging context.

FIGURE 13.4
Wuzzit Trouble

Races and Time Pressure

In a race, the player attempts to accomplish something before someone else does, whether that involves a physical race through space or a race to create a structure, to accumulate something, or to do practically anything as long as the game can distinguish which player finishes first. Normally we think of races as peaceful, involving competition without conflict, but races can be combined with fighting and many other kinds of challenges.

Time pressure discourages careful strategic thought and instead encourages direct, brute-force solutions. With only 15 seconds to get through a host of enemies and disarm a bomb, the player won't stop to pick off enemy units one by one with sniping shots; she's going to mow them down and charge through the gap, even if that means taking a lot of damage.

Time pressure increases the stress on a player and changes the feeling of the gameplay considerably, sometimes for better and sometimes for worse. In something like a car racing game, time pressure is an essential part of the experience, but use caution in adding time pressure to challenges that aren't ordinarily based on time constraints. You will deter some players entirely and make the challenge more difficult in any case. To keep the absolute difficulty level constant, whenever you increase the time pressure on a player, you should also reduce the amount of intrinsic skill required.

Factual Knowledge Challenges

Direct tests of the player's knowledge of factual information generally occur only in trivia and quiz games. In any other type of game, you must either present all the factual knowledge required to win the game somewhere *in* the game (or the manual) or make it clear in the game's marketing materials that players will need some factual knowledge. It's not fair to require the player to come up with some obscure fact from the real world in order to make progress through the game; doing so also detracts from full immersion.

Note the difference between factual knowledge challenges and conceptual reasoning challenges (discussed in the section "Conceptual Reasoning and Lateral Thinking Puzzles," later in this chapter). If an adventure game features a puzzle the player can't solve without knowing that helium balloons rise or that metal objects conduct electricity, such a puzzle is a conceptual reasoning challenge, not a factual knowledge challenge.

Memory Challenges

Memory challenges test the player's ability to recall things that he has seen or heard in the game. Adventure games and RPGs often make use of memory challenges. Players can defeat memory challenges by taking notes, so you may want to impose a limit on the length of time you give them to memorize material they must recall. To make a memory challenge easier, give them longer to memorize it and ask that they recall it soon after memorizing it rather than much later.

Memory challenges often form one component of exploration challenges. In Raven's *Star Trek Voyager: Elite Force*, for example, the player must remember the layout of complex tunnels onboard the Borg cube.

NOTE *Trivial Pursuit*, the popular board game that tests players' factual knowledge in several different domains, also runs as a video game on a variety of platforms. You Don't Know Jack is a popular series of trivia video games that was first published in 1995 and continues today as a Facebook game.

> **DESIGN RULE** Make It Clear When Factual Knowledge Is Required
>
> If your game requires factual knowledge from outside the game world to win, you must make this clear to the player in advance.

Pattern Recognition Challenges

Pattern recognition challenges test the player's ability to spot visible or audible patterns, or patterns of change and behavior. One of the most common instances of a pattern recognition appears in visual match-3 games such as *Bejeweled, Puzzle Quest,* and *Candy Crush Saga.* But this challenge is not restricted to spotting patterns of items on a grid. In many action games, a large number of identical enemies, each of which behaves in a predictable way, confronts the player. The player can try alternative strategies until she finds one effective against that enemy, then use that strategy to vanquish any number of enemies that attack using the same pattern. To make things harder and more interesting, the boss enemy at the end of a level usually has a different and more complex pattern of behavior from the smaller enemies that preceded it.

Visual clues often figure in pattern recognition challenges. In the original *Doom,* the player could find secret doorways by searching for areas of wall that looked slightly different from the norm. *Brain Spa,* a brain-training game, requires the player to match pairs of similar-looking objects while under time pressure.

To make pattern recognition challenges easier, make the patterns shorter, simpler, and more obvious. To make them harder, make the patterns longer, more intricate, and more subtle. Many games also make pattern recognition easier by flashing a hint on the screen after a short delay.

Exploration Challenges

Exploration is often its own reward. Players enjoy moving into new areas and seeing new things, but exploration cannot be free of challenge or it becomes merely sightseeing. Design obstacles that make the players earn their freedom to explore.

SPATIAL AWARENESS CHALLENGES

The most basic form of exploration challenge simply requires the player to learn her way around an unfamiliar and complicated space. In the old text adventure games, this was particularly difficult because the games lacked visual cues, but even modern 3D environments can be made so tangled that they're hard to navigate. Unfamiliar architecture also challenges the player; navigation is easier when things look the way she expects them to look. *Descent* required the player to move around a warren of similar corridors inside an asteroid and complicated matters further by setting the environment in zero gravity, so the player perceived no obvious *up* or *down* to help her orient herself.

To make spatial awareness challenges easier, give the player a map that always shows his location precisely within the game world. If you want to give the player a map but also make it slightly more difficult, give him a map of the game world that doesn't include his location, so he has to determine his location from landmarks.

LOCKED DOORS

Locked door is a generic term for any obstacle that prevents the player from proceeding through the game until she learns the trick for disabling it. A sheet of ice covering a cave entrance that melts if you build a fire constitutes a locked door for game design purposes. Assuming, for discussion only, you want an actual door, you can require that the player find a key elsewhere and bring it back, find and manipulate a hidden control that opens the door, solve a puzzle built into the door, discover a magic word that opens the door, defeat the doorkeeper in a test of skill, or perform some other task—just make sure you offer an interesting and fresh challenge.

Avoid using an unmarked switch far from the door. *Doom* featured these, and they weren't much fun. When the player arrived at a locked door and saw no means of opening it or any clue, he had to search the entire world pressing unmarked switches at random; then he had to return to see whether one of the switches had opened the door. Worse yet, in a few cases, the switch *did* open the door, but only for a little while. If the player didn't get back to the door in time, he found it locked again and assumed that switch must not be the right one.

TRAPS

A *trap* is a device that harms the player's avatar when triggered—possibly killing her or causing damage—and, in any case, discourages her from going that way or using that move again. Similar to a locked door with higher stakes, a trap poses an actual threat. Traps can take a variety of forms:

▪ Some fire once and then are harmless.

▪ Others fire and require a certain rearming time before they can fire again.

▪ Still others respond to particular conditions but not to others, like a metal detector at an airport, and the player must learn what triggers the trap and how to avoid triggering it.

A player may simply withstand some traps that don't do too much damage; he may disarm or circumvent other traps. A trap the player can find only by falling into it is really just the designer's way of slowing down the player; if you make these, don't make many of them because the player can find them only by trial and error, and they become frustrating after a while. For players, the real fun comes in outwitting traps: finding and disabling them without getting caught. This gives players a pleasurable feeling of having outfoxed the game.

MAZES AND ILLOGICAL SPACES

A *maze* is an area in which every place looks alike, or mostly alike; to get out, the player must discover how the rooms or passages relate to each other, usually by wandering around. Good designers implement mazes as logic or pattern-recognition puzzles in which the player can deduce the organization of the mazes from clues found in the rooms. Poor mazes offer no clues and make the player find the way out by trial and error. Mazes are now considered rather old-fashioned and difficult to justify in the context of a story, but they can still be fun to solve if you make them truly clever and attractive.

In illogical spaces, areas do not relate to each other in a way that the player might reasonably expect. In text adventures, a player sometimes finds that going north from area A takes her to area B, but going south from area B does not take her back to area A. Illogical spaces require the player to keep a map, because she can't rely on her common sense to learn her way around. Now also considered outdated, and more difficult to implement with today's 3D engines, illogical space challenges still crop up from time to time. If you use them, do so sparingly, and only if you can explain their presence: "Beware! There is a rip in the fabric of space-time!"

TELEPORTERS

Teleporters superseded illogical spaces in the game designer's toolkit. A *teleporter* is any mechanism that suddenly transports the player from where he is to someplace else, often without warning if the designer created no visual representation for the teleporter device. Several hidden teleporters in an area can make exploration diffi-cult. Teleporters can further complicate matters by not always working the same way, teleporting the player to one place the first time they are used but to some other place the second time, and so on. You can also use one-way teleporters if you want to leave the player with no way to get back.

To make the exploration challenge created by teleporters easier, make the teleporter predictable and reversible, so the player can return at will to where he came from. The *Portal* games are excellent examples of games that make use of teleporting, not as a hidden and unexpected challenge but as an action that permits the player to overcome other challenges. A good many games also include teleporters not as a challenge but as a visible and optional feature to let the player jump across large distances that he has already explored.

FINDING HIDDEN OBJECTS

Many games require the player to find an object hidden somewhere in their simulated space, often in areas that are difficult to get to. Sometimes the objects are hidden in reasonable places that the player can deduce from clues; sometimes they are in obscure ones. The player not only has to learn her way around, she has to keep a sharp lookout for whatever she needs. A number of puzzle games use a variant of the "find the hidden object" challenge in which the player doesn't move through a simulated space, but simply looks at a picture of a room with dozens of objects in it, trying to find the ones required, sometimes against a time limit. This works well in games for casual players who want an uncomplicated point-and-click puzzle.

Easter eggs are a specialized variant of hidden objects. They're items, or sometimes hidden regions or game features, that are fun to discover but not actually needed to win the game—a bonus such as special clothing for the avatar or an extra-powerful weapon. Players love finding Easter eggs. You should hide them in particularly obscure locations. Be cautious about the content, however. Sometimes Easter eggs have been used as a way to include offensive content in a game or material that is incompatible with the game's rating. This can result in extremely expensive legal action against the publisher and developer... which means you.

Conflict

A *conflict challenge* is one requiring the direct opposition of forces, some of which are under player control. If one player must beat the others by opposing or impeding them directly, the challenge qualifies as conflict, even without combat or violence. Checkers has no bloodshed but still presents conflict challenges. Classic activities to overcome conflict challenges include taking away another player's resources and impeding another player's ability to act.

CONFLICT CHALLENGES VERSUS CONFLICT OF INTEREST

Formal *game theory* is a field of mathematics that studies situations that contain a *conflict of interest*. By that definition, any game in which players are rivals for victory contains conflict. However, in pole-vaulting, darts, and many other games, that opposition applies only at the top of the challenge hierarchy. At lower levels, the players do not (and sometimes are forbidden to) impede each other directly. Even in *Monopoly*, the rules provide no means by which players may choose to target each other for hostile action. Such games may contain a conflict of interest but no conflict challenges. The players must achieve their top-level goal not through the direct opposition of forces but through vaulting over the higher bar, throwing darts more accurately, or whatever other atomic challenges the game specifies.

The asymmetric board game Fox and Geese, introduced in Chapter 1, gives the two players different conflict challenges. The fox tries to eat the geese by jumping over them on the board (taking away the other player's resources). The geese try to trap the fox while moving in configurations that prevent the fox from jumping over them (preventing the enemy from acting).

Create interesting conflict challenges by varying such factors as these:

▨ The scale of the action (from individuals to whole armies)

▨ The speed at which the conflict takes place (from turn-based, allowing the players all the time they want, to frenetic activity as in action games)

▨ The complexity of the victory conditions (from simple survival to complex missions with goals and subgoals)

Many action games focus on the immediate, visceral excitement of personal conflict. The player generally controls an avatar that battles directly against one or more opponents, often at high speeds.

Conflict challenges can be broken down into strategy, tactics, logistics, and other components.

STRATEGY

Strategy means planning, including taking advantage of your situation and resources, anticipating your opponent's moves, and knowing and minimizing your weaknesses. A strategic challenge requires the player to carefully consider the game (a process called *situational analysis*) and devise a plan of action. In a turn-based game of *perfect information* (one that contains no element of chance or hidden information), players may use *pure strategy* to choose their moves by analyzing possible future states of the game. Chess is a classic game of perfect information. (In formal game theory, *pure strategy* has a special meaning, but we'll use the term in an informal sense to distinguish it from *applied strategy.*)

Succeeding in a game of pure strategy requires a talent for systematic reasoning that does not emerge until early adolescence and that relatively few people possess in a high degree. Computer game developers usually aim to attract a broad audience, so few of them offer these kinds of challenges. Instead, they hide information from the player and include elements of chance, making situational analysis to some extent a matter of guesswork and of weighing probabilities rather than a matter of logic. Such games call for applied strategy. Real-time strategy (RTS) games normally require applied strategy and offer economic and exploration challenges as well, making RTS games accessible to players with less skill at logic and providing other ways to win besides strategy alone.

TACTICS

Tactics involve executing a plan, accomplishing the goals that strategy calls for. Tactics also require responding to unexpected events or conditions: new information or bad luck. A player might have a strategy for defeating his opponents in poker, but he uses tactics to decide how to play each particular hand.

You can design a purely tactical game with no strategy. A small-squad combat game in which the soldiers continually move into unknown territory contains no opportunities for strategy—a player can't plan if she doesn't know where she's going or what she's up against—but contains many opportunities for tactics, such as keeping soldiers covered, taking advantage of their particular skills, and so on.

LOGISTICS

The business of supporting troops in the field and bringing fresh troops to the front lines is called *logistics*. Most war games don't bother with logistical challenges such as transporting food and fuel to where the troops can use them; players tend to find combat entertaining but find logistics a boring distraction from the combat.

Modern RTS games routinely include one important logistical challenge: weapons production. Unlike war board games in which the players often start with a fixed number of troops, RTSs require the players to produce weapons and to research new types of weapons using a limited amount of raw material. The players must construct and defend the production facilities themselves. Adding this new logistical challenge to what was formerly a purely combat-oriented genre changed the face of war gaming.

In RPGs, the limited size of the characters' inventories presents another logistical challenge: requiring players to decide what to carry and what to leave behind. Equipping and balancing a party of heterogeneous characters with all that they need to face a dangerous adventure occupies a significant amount of the player's time.

SURVIVAL AND REDUCTION OF ENEMY FORCES

The fundamental challenge in any game based on conflict is survival. The player must preserve the effective playing time—the lives—of her units, or she cannot achieve the victory condition. In a few games, survival itself constitutes the victory condition regardless of other achievements, but in most, survival is necessary, but not sufficient, to win.

The converse of the survival challenge is the challenge to reduce enemy forces. To design such a challenge, you must create rules that determine how a unit may be removed from the game. Chess and checkers provide examples of such rules: *capture by replacement* and *capture by jumping,* respectively. War games implement simulated combat using complex mathematical models and track the health of each unit, which may be reduced by repeated attacks until reduction to zero destroys the unit.

DEFENDING VULNERABLE ITEMS OR UNITS

The player may be called upon to defend other units or items, especially items that cannot defend themselves. In chess, all units protect the king. To meet such a challenge requires that the player know not only the capabilities and vulnerabilities of his units, but also those of the entity he must protect. He must be prepared to sacrifice some units to protect the vital one.

Many multiplayer war games such as the *Battlefield* series implement a capture-the-flag victory condition, in which teams must defend their own flags and capture the enemies'.

STEALTH

The ability to move undetected, an extremely valuable capacity in almost any kind of conflict, especially if the player takes the side of the underdog, can form a challenge in its own right. Games occasionally pose challenges in which the victory condition cannot be achieved through combat but must be achieved through stealth. *Thief: The Dark Project* was designed entirely around this premise. It required players to achieve their missions by stealth as much as possible and to avoid discovery or combat if they could.

Stealth poses a considerable problem in the design of artificial opponents for war games. In a game with no stealth, the AI-driven opponent has access to the complete state of the game world; to include stealth, you must restrict the opponent's knowledge, limit its attention, and leave it ignorant of whole regions of the game world. You decide what the AI opponent does and doesn't know and define what steps it takes, if any, to gain further information.

Economic Challenges

An *economy* is a system in which resources move either physically from place to place or conceptually from owner to owner. This doesn't necessarily mean money; any quantifiable substance that can be created, moved, stored, earned, exchanged, or destroyed can form the basis of an economy. Most games contain an economy of some sort. Even a first-person shooter boasts a simple economy in which the player obtains ammunition by finding it or taking it from dead opponents and consumes it by firing her weapons. Health points are also part of the economy, being consumed by hits and restored by medical kits. You can make the game easier or harder by adjusting the amount of ammunition and number of medical kits so that a player running short of firepower or health must manage her resources carefully.

The behavior of resources, as defined by the core mechanics of the game, creates economic challenges. Construction and management simulations frequently require the player to manage a complex economy in which processes produce and consume resources at various rates, and playing the game successfully requires an intuitive grasp of the mathematics involved. *SimCity 4* (**Figure 13.5**) gives the player access to quite a lot of numerical information. Such games tend to have flattened challenge hierarchies in which the atomic challenges appear similar to the overall goal of the game. Other games, such as first-person shooters, combine economic challenges with others such as conflict and exploration. Chapter 14, "Core Mechanics," addresses the internal economies of games at length.

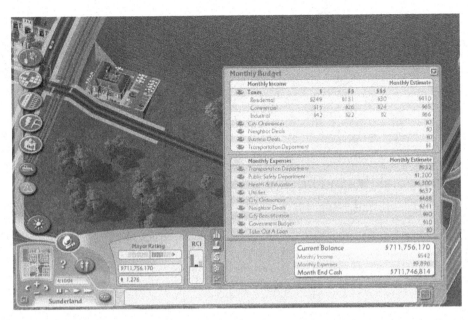

FIGURE 13.5
Detail from *SimCity 4*, showing the city's monthly budget

ACCUMULATING RESOURCES

Many games challenge the player to accumulate something: wealth, points, or anything else deemed valuable. Acquisition of this kind underlies *Monopoly* and many other games in which the top-level challenge is to accumulate more money, plutonium, or widgets than other players. The game challenges the player to understand the mechanisms of wealth creation and to use them to his own advantage. In the case of *Monopoly,* the player learns to mortgage low-rent properties and use the cash to purchase high-rent ones because high-rent properties produce more in the long run.

ACHIEVING BALANCE

Requiring your players to achieve balance in an economy gives them a more interesting challenge than simply accumulating points, especially if you give them many different kinds of resources to manage. Players in *The Settlers* games juggle quantities of raw materials and goods that obey complex rules of interaction: Wheat goes to the mill to become flour, which goes to the bakery to become bread; bread feeds miners who dig coal and iron ore, which goes to the smelter to become iron bars, which then go to the blacksmith to become weapons; and so on. Produce too little of a vital item and the whole economy grinds to a halt; produce too much and it piles up, taking up space and wasting time and resources that could be better used elsewhere.

CARING FOR LIVING THINGS

A peculiar sort of economic challenge involves looking after a person or creature, or a small number of them, as in *The Sims* and *Spore*. (*Spore* expands to whole populations in its later stages.) The game challenges the player to meet the needs of each individual and possibly improve its development. Because the game measures and tracks these needs via numeric terms, and the player must meet them from limited resources, these qualify as economic challenges. *Nintendogs* and other pet simulations are good examples too.

Conceptual Reasoning and Lateral Thinking Puzzles

Conceptual reasoning puzzles and *lateral thinking puzzles* are in the same section because they both require *extrinsic knowledge,* that is, knowledge from outside the domain of the challenge itself. This sets them apart from formal logic puzzles in which all the knowledge required to solve the puzzle must be contained within its definition. Lateral thinking puzzles and conceptual reasoning puzzles may still require the use of logical thinking, however.

CONCEPTUAL REASONING

Conceptual reasoning puzzles require the player to use her reasoning power and knowledge of the puzzle's subject matter to arrive at a solution to a problem. In one round of the online multiplayer game *Strike a Match,* a number of words or phrases appear, and as they do, the player must find conceptually related pairs: if *Kong* appears, should the player watch out for a match with *King* (a movie) or *Hong* (a place) or *Donkey* (a video game)?

Another sort of conceptual challenge occurs in mystery or detective games in which the player must examine the evidence and deduce which of a number of suspects committed the crime and how. In the game *Law and Order,* based on the television series of the same name, players follow clues, ignore red herrings, and arrive at a theory of the crime, assembling the relevant evidence to demonstrate proof. In order to succeed, however, the players must have some familiarity with police forensic techniques as well as an understanding of human motivations for committing crimes. These details are extrinsic knowledge, not spelled out as part of the definition of the puzzle.

You may find designing conceptual reasoning challenges a lot of fun because they offer a lot of scope to the designer, but you'll work harder when creating these than putting together simpler trials such as physical or exploration challenges.

LATERAL THINKING

Lateral thinking puzzles are related to conceptual reasoning puzzles, but they add a twist: The terms of the puzzle make it clear to the player that what seems to be the obvious or most probable solution is incorrect (or the necessary elements to achieve the obvious solution are unavailable). The player must think of alternatives instead. A classic test of lateral thinking—and one used to demonstrate that chimpanzees possess this faculty—requires the subject to get an item down from a high place without using a ladder. Deprived of the obvious solution, he must find some other approach, such as putting a chair on top of a table, climbing up on the table, and then climbing up on the chair. Because chairs do not ordinarily belong on tables, and neither chairs nor tables are intended for climbing, the test requires the subject to transcend his everyday understanding of the functions of objects.

Lateral thinking puzzles often require the player to use extrinsic knowledge gained in real life, but to use it in unexpected ways. In *Escape from Monkey Island,* the player has to put a deflated inner tube onto a strange-looking cactus to make a giant slingshot (or catapult), which requires knowing that inner tubes are stretchy. Adventure games frequently include lateral thinking puzzles. You must be careful not to make the solution too obscure or to rely on information that goes beyond common knowledge; you can expect the average adult player to know that wood floats, but you cannot expect the player to know that cork comes from the bark of certain species of Mediterranean oak tree (that challenge belongs in a trivia game). Provide hints or clues to help a player who gets stuck. In general, the more realistic the game, the more it may rely on extrinsic knowledge because players know that they can count on their real-world experience as being meaningful in the game world. In a highly abstract or highly surreal game, the player won't expect common-sense experience to be of any use. Such games may still include lateral thinking puzzles, but you must provide the knowledge the player needs to solve them within the game.

Actions

As Chapter 12, "Creating the User Experience," explains, the user interface links the input devices in the real world to actions that take place in the game world. *Actions,* in this sense, refer to events in the game world caused directly by the user interface interpreting a player input. If the player presses a button on a game controller and the user interface maps that button to striking a cue ball in a game of pool, striking the cue ball constitutes an action. If the cue ball knocks another ball into a pocket, that is an event, but not an action; the movement of the other ball is a *consequence* of the player's action.

Actions are the verbs of the game, and the way in which the player usually thinks about his play: "I run, I jump, I punch, I buy, I build." On arcade machines, each input device is usually labeled with a verb: Fire, Boost, and so on. When you define the player's role in the concept stage of game design, you should make a list of some of these verbs. If the player's role is to be a cowboy, what does a cowboy do? Don't think in high-level terms ("protect the cattle") but in terms of verbs that might be assigned to input devices ("spur the horse," "fire his gun," "sell a cow," and so on.)

NO HIERARCHY OF ACTIONS

Challenges are explained in terms of a hierarchy because that hierarchy remains in the player's mind throughout the game, a collection of goals that she works to achieve. You might think, then, that there should be an equivalent hierarchy of actions—that if the game presents the high-level challenge "try to defeat the boss monster," there should be a high-level action called "defeat the boss monster."

Actions aren't in a hierarchy because a hierarchy of actions doesn't benefit either you or the player. Making up an artificial high-level action (defeat the boss monster) to go with a high-level challenge isn't terribly useful. If you tell the player, "To defeat the boss monster, perform the 'defeat the boss monster' action," she hasn't learned anything. There's no such button on the controller, so what good does it do her?

Instead, actions are defined in low-level terms, as events resulting directly from the player's use of the control devices. In fact, a game's tutorial levels often teach players how to defeat monsters not in terms of game actions but in terms of real-world button-presses. Tutorials say, "Attack monsters using your punch, kick, and throw shuriken buttons." It's up to the player to figure out how to combine these to defeat the boss monster.

Actions for Gameplay

Most of the actions that a player takes in a game are intended to meet the challenges that he faces. This book cannot possibly provide a list of all the kinds of gameplay-related actions that players can perform in game worlds; they vary from the simple and concrete, such as *fire weapon*, to those as complex and abstract as *send covert operatives to arouse antigovernment sentiment in a hostile nation*—which the player could do in *Balance of Power* by choosing a single item on a menu. Study other games in the genre you have chosen to see what actions they support.

The interaction model that you have chosen for a particular gameplay mode determines a lot about the kinds of actions available in that mode. If you use an avatar-based interaction model, then the actions available to the player, for the most part, consist of influencing the game world through the avatar. In games using a multipresent model, the player acts indirectly by issuing commands to units, which themselves act within the game world (as in real-time strategy games), or acts directly on features of the world itself (as in construction and management simulations and god games such as *Pocket God*).

Don't expect a one-to-one mapping between actions and challenges; many games include a large number of types of challenges but only a small number of actions, leaving the player to figure out how to use the actions in various combinations to surmount each challenge. Puzzles frequently do this. Faced with a scrambled *Rubik's Cube*, the player can take only one action: She can rotate one face of the cube 90 degrees. The solution to the puzzle consists entirely of making similar rotations.

Games offer many challenges but limited numbers of actions for two reasons. First, if you give the player a large number of actions to choose from, you must also provide a large user interface, which can be confusing to the player and increase the difficulty of learning the game. Massively multiplayer online role-playing games (MMORPGs) such as *World of Warcraft* often include complex screen overlays that can be daunting to a novice. (If you implement a context-sensitive interface that chooses the correct action for the user based on context, you don't give the player the freedom to try interesting combinations.) Second, a large number of actions usually requires a large number of animations to display them all. This makes the game expensive to develop.

Many great games implement only a small number of actions but still let the player use them to overcome a wide variety of challenges. If you are imaginative enough, the challenges will be so interesting that the player will never notice.

DEFINING YOUR ACTIONS

To define the actions that you'll implement, begin by thinking about the player's role in the game. At the concept stage of your project, you asked, "What is the player going to do?" You should have some general answers to that question. Now it's time to go into detail for each gameplay mode. Begin with the primary mode. If you wrote, "In the primary gameplay mode, the player will drive a car," think about exactly what actions that driving entails. Pressing the accelerator, turning the steering wheel, and braking, of course, but what else? Shifting the gears? Turning on the lights? Using the handbrake? Some of the actions you decide on may have to do with challenges; others will simply be another part of the role.

Next, look at the challenges you designed for the primary gameplay mode. Begin with the atomic challenges you plan to offer; for each atomic challenge, write down how you expect the player to overcome it. Your answers will probably consist of individual actions or small combinations of actions. Ben Cousins has argued that game designers should spend most of their effort defining and refining the way that actions overcome atomic challenges because the player spends most of his time performing those actions (Cousins, 2004); this is excellent advice.

After you define the actions that will meet the atomic challenges, consider the intermediate and higher-level challenges in the gameplay mode. Can they all be met with the actions you've defined, or will they require additional ones? Add those to the list.

Finally, consider actions unrelated to gameplay that you may want to make available to the player. You may already have some that come with the player's role, but you may want to include others for other reasons. See the list in the next section for some ideas.

Once you have been through this process for the primary gameplay mode, do it all again for each of the other modes. When you believe you have comprehensive lists of all the actions that you want to include in each mode, you're ready to start defining the user interfaces for the different modes: assigning actions to control mechanisms (see Chapter 12).

Actions That Serve Other Functions

Games include many actions that allow the player to interact with the game world but not engage in gameplay. Games also offer actions that aren't specifically play activities, but they give the player control over various aspects of the game. The following list describes a number of types of non–challenge-related actions.

▪ **Unstructured play.** You will almost certainly want to include some fun-to-perform actions that don't address any challenge. Players often move their avatars around the game world for the sheer fun of movement or to see a new area even if it offers no challenges; this is referred to as *sightseeing.* You may want to include actions just because they're part of the role. In most driving games, honking the horn accomplishes nothing, but if you couldn't honk the horn, the game would feel incomplete.

▪ **Actions for creation and self-expression.** See Chapter 9, "Creative and Expressive Play," for a discussion of actions allowing players to create and customize things, including avatars. Much of the activity in construction and management simulations consists of creative play rather than gameplay, although the player's actions are often constrained by limitations imposed by the game's internal economy.

▪ **Actions for socialization.** Players in multiplayer games, especially online games, need ways to talk to each other, to form groups, to compare scores, and to take part in other community activities. (See Chapter 17, "Design Issues for Online Gaming.")

▪ **Actions to participate in the story.** Participating in interactive dialogue, interacting with non-player characters (NPCs), or making decisions that affect the plot all constitute actions that allow the player to participate in a story, even if those actions don't address a challenge directly. The more of them you offer, the more your player feels she is taking part in a story.

▪ **Actions to control the game software.** The player takes many actions to control the game software, such as adjusting the virtual camera, pausing and saving the game, choosing a difficulty level, and setting the audio volume. Some such actions may affect the game's challenges (setting the difficulty level certainly does), but the player doesn't take them specifically to *address* a challenge.

Saving the Game

Saving a game takes a snapshot of a game world and all its important particulars at a given instant and stores them away so that the player can load the same data later, return to that instant, and play the game from that point. Saving and restoring a game is technologically easy (though some devices have limited save space), and it's essential for testing and debugging, so it's often slapped in as a feature without much thought about its effect on gameplay. As designers, though, it's our job to think about anything that affects gameplay or the player's experience of the game.

Saving a game stores not only the player's location in the game but also any customizations she might have made along the way. In *Michelle Kwan Figure Skating*, for example, the player could customize the skater's body type, skin tone, hair color and style, and costume. She could even load in a picture of her own face. The more freedom you give the player to customize the game or the avatar, the more data must be saved. Until recently, this limited the richness of games for console machines, but now console machines routinely come with enough storage to save a lot of customization data.

Reasons for Saving a Game

Reasons for saving a player's game or allowing him to save it include these:

▪ **Allowing the player to leave the game and return to it later.** This is the most important reason for saving the game. In a large game, it's an essential feature. It's not realistic and not fair to the player to expect him to dedicate the computer or console machine to a 40-hour game from start to finish with no break.

▪ **Letting the player recover from disastrous mistakes.** In practice, this usually means the death of the avatar. Arcade games, which offer no save-game feature, traditionally give the player a number of lives and chances to earn more along the way. Until recently, console action games have tended to follow the same scheme. Richer games, such as role-playing or adventure games, usually give the player only one life but allow him to reload a saved game if his avatar dies or he realizes that he cannot possibly win the current game.

▪ **Encouraging the player to explore alternate strategies.** In turn-based strategic games, saving the game allows the player to learn the game by trying alternative approaches. If one approach doesn't seem to work, he can go back to the point at which he committed himself and try another approach.

Consequences for Immersion and Storytelling

Saving a game is not always beneficial to the player's experience. The act of saving a game takes place outside the game world and, as a consequence, stopping play to save the game harms the player's immersion. If a game tries to create the illusion that the player inhabits a fantasy world, the act of saving destroys the illusion. One of the most significant characteristics of real life is that you cannot return to the past to correct your errors; the moment you allow a player to repeat the past, you acknowledge the unreality of the game world.

The essence of a story is dramatic tension, and dramatic tension requires that something be at stake. Reloading a game with a branching story line affects the player's experience of the story because if she can alter the future by returning to the past and making a different decision, nothing really hangs in the balance. Real-world decisions bring permanent consequences; you can modify some in the future, but the original decision cannot be unmade. But when a player follows first one branch of a branching storyline and then goes back in time and follows another branch, she experiences the story in an unnatural way. The consequences of her actions lose their meaning, and her sense of dramatic tension is either reduced or destroyed completely. What is a benefit to strategic games—the chance to try alternate strategies—presents problems for storytelling.

Nevertheless, the arguments for saving outweigh these disadvantages. If the player destroys his immersion by repeatedly reloading the game, that is his choice and not the fault of the game designer or the story. As Chapter 11, "Storytelling," pointed out, a weakness of branching storylines is that they require the player to play the game again if he wants to see plot lines that he missed on his first play-through. Allowing the player to save and reload makes that easier for him. He may always choose not to reload if he doesn't want to.

Ways of Saving a Game

Over the years, designers have devised a variety of different ways to save a game, each with its own pros and cons for immersion and gameplay.

TIP Level access codes used to be called *passwords* in older games, but modern games will assume that *password* refers to a login password. Calling them *level access codes* avoids this confusion.

LEVEL ACCESS CODES

If your game runs on a device with no storage at all (a rarity nowadays), you can't save the game in the middle of a level, but you can let the player restart the last level attempted. Each time the player completes a level, give her a unique code that unlocks the next level. At start-up, ask if she wants to enter a code; if she does so correctly, load the level that it unlocks. She can go directly to that level without having to replay all the earlier ones. This method also allows her to go back and replay any completed level if she wants to.

SAVE TO A FILE OR SAVE SLOT

The player may interrupt play and save the current state of the game either to an individual file on the machine's storage device or, more usually, to one of a series of named *save slots* within a single file that is managed by the game program. (If you allow the player to save to individual files, he can save as many times as he wants; if you provide save slots, you can limit the number of slots so the player can save only that many times.) When the player wants to begin the saved game, he tells the program to load it from the directory of files or slots. This allows the player to keep several different copies, saved at different points, and to name them so that he can remember which one is which.

Unfortunately, although this is the most common way of saving, it's also the method most harmful to the game's immersiveness. The user interface for managing the files or save slots necessarily looks like an operating system's file-management tool, not like a part of the fantasy world that the game depicts. You can harmonize this procedure better with appropriate graphics, but saving almost always takes the player out of the game world. Some games salvage the immersion to some degree by calling the file system the player's *journal* and making it look as if the saved games are kept in a book.

QUICK-SAVE

Fast-moving games in which the player's avatar stays in more or less constant danger (such as first-person shooters) frequently offer a quick-save feature. The player presses a single button to save the game instantly at any time, without ever leaving the game world. The screen displays the words "Quick saved" for a moment, but otherwise the player's immersion in the world remains undisturbed. The player can reload the game just as swiftly by pressing a quick-load button. The game returns immediately to its state at the last quick-save, without going out of the game world to a file-management screen.

Disadvantages of quick-save arise because saving so quickly usually means the player doesn't want to take the time, and isn't offered the chance, to designate a file or slot. Normally such games offer only one slot, although some let players designate a numbered slot by entering a digit after they press the quick-save button. Players remember which slot is which when quick-loading. Quick-save sacrifices flexibility to retain immersion and speed.

AUTOMATIC SAVE AND CHECKPOINTS

Many games automatically save the state of the game when the player exits, so players can leave and return at any time without explicitly saving. This harms the player's immersion least of all, but if the player has recently experienced a disaster, she has no way to recover from it. More often, games save whenever the player passes a checkpoint, which may or may not be visible to her. Checkpoint saving is less disruptive than quick-saving because the player never has to do anything. The player *can* go back and undo a disaster, provided that the disaster happened after the most recent checkpoint. But it means that the player can't choose to save whenever she wants or choose to restart at some earlier point. If the checkpoints occur infrequently, she might lose a great deal of progress in the event of a disaster. Although it's better for immersion from the player-centric standpoint, automatic checkpoint saving is inferior to quick-saving. With quick-save, the player always has the option *not* to save if for some reason she enjoys the risk of having to go back a long way. With automatic checkpoints, she has no choice.

If you implement automatic save or checkpoints at particular times or locations in the game world, you must choose them with great care and play-test them thoroughly. It's easy to create annoying situations without realizing it. Here are a few mistakes to avoid:

■ Be sure the player *can* save the game after fine-tuning features of the avatar (such as making adjustments to a car in a racing game or a character in an RPG). If the last checkpoint is before the player makes the changes, her changes will be lost if she has to restore from the checkpoint.

■ If the player is just about to lose the game and the game auto-saves into a single slot, whenever the player reloads the game, she will immediately lose again. The only remedy is to start over from the beginning. To avoid this, either offer multiple save points and let the player choose one upon reloading, or be sure that the game only saves when the avatar is in a place of safety and the player has a reasonable chance of continuing the game after a reload. If the game involves battle, you may want to put some health-restoring items near the save point, too. Respawning with low health right before an inevitable battle is a common player complaint.

■ Place checkpoints *before* any critical moments, such as big decisions the player must make or fights she may be about to enter. If the player has to reload, she needs the opportunity to change her mind (make a different choice or select different weapons before the fight, for example).

■ Place checkpoints *after* any long, noninteractive content such as cinematics, noninteractive dialogue, or long travel that the player must pass through before encountering another challenge. Players often complain about respawning at a point at which their only option is to walk or drive for a long time before they can continue play.

A few games offer optional checkpoint saving in which the player may choose to save or not every time he reaches a checkpoint. This gives him a little more control but still doesn't allow him to save at will, which is preferable.

To Save or Not to Save

A few designers don't allow players to save their games within certain regions of the game or even to save at all. If the player can save and reload where she wants and without limit, she can solve puzzles or overcome other obstacles by trial and error rather than by skill, or she can use the saving system to avoid undesirable random events; if something bad happens by chance, the player can reload the game repeatedly until the undesirable event doesn't occur. This reduces the game's difficulty, and some designers argue against allowing players to save on that basis.

That, however, is lazy game design. Preventing the player from saving adds difficulty without adding fun. If you really want to make the game harder, devise harder challenges. Forcing the player to replay an entire level because he made a mistake near the end wastes his time and condemns him to frustration and boredom—and that certainly is not player-centric game design.

You may not like it if a player repeatedly reloads a game to avoid a random event or to solve some problem by trial and error rather than skill, but the player doesn't play (or buy) the game to make you feel good. She might need to save the game for perfectly legitimate reasons. The notion that saving makes a game too easy assumes that the player is your opponent, a violation of the player-centric principle. Most games now recognize that players want—and sometimes need—to cheat by offering cheat codes anyway.

> **DESIGN RULE** Allow the Player to Save and Reload the Game
>
> Unless your game is extremely short or your device has no data storage, allow the player to save and reload the game. His right to exit the game without losing the benefit of his achievements supersedes all other considerations.

It's the player's machine; it's not fair to penalize him just because he has to go to the bathroom or because it's now his little brother's turn to play. Choose which mechanism works best for your game, weighing the advantages and disadvantages of each, but do let the player save the game, and preferably, whenever and wherever he wants to. It does no harm to your game to give the player the freedom to choose when he wants to save—or whether he wants to save at all. The player has a fundamental right to be able to stop playing without losing what he has accomplished.

Summary

Gameplay is the heart of a game's entertainment, the reason players buy and play games. This chapter began with some principles to keep in mind to make gameplay fun. Next we examined the *hierarchy of challenges,* the fact that a player experiences several challenges at once, and defined the concept of atomic challenges. We noted the difference between the *intrinsic skill* required by a challenge and the *stress* that time pressure puts on a player and how these two elements combine to create *difficulty.*

Gameplay itself took up most of the chapter, with definitions and discussions of the many types of challenges that video games employ and various ways of adjusting their difficulty level. From challenges, we turned to the actions that you can offer the player, which include actions not related directly to gameplay. Finally we looked at the pros and cons of different ways of saving the game, an important feature for any game more than a few minutes long.

Armed with this information and with a little research, you should be able to analyze the gameplay of most of the video games currently for sale, and to design others using similar kinds of challenges and actions.

Design Practice EXERCISES

1. Write the rules for a simple, single-player, puzzle game like *Bejeweled* but make up your own mechanics for earning points. Document all the challenges and actions of the game. You must create at least 10 different *kinds* of atomic challenges. Indicate what action the player should use to surmount each challenge and what reward the player gets for doing so. You must also create and document at least four actions that are not intended to meet challenges but serve some other purpose. You do not have to design a user interface in detail but may find it helpful to make and submit a quick sketch of the screen and the layout of the controls.

2. Choose an action or action-adventure game you are familiar with (or your instructor will assign one). Document the challenge hierarchy of the first level in the game that is *not* a tutorial level, diagramming it as in Figure 13.1. (If the level includes more than 50 sequential atomic challenges, you may stop after 50, but be sure to include any level bosses or major challenges that occur at the end of the level.) If you have the necessary software, play partway through the level, take a screen shot, and indicate on your diagram what challenges you were facing at that moment, similar to the gray boxes in Figure 13.1. If you faced simultaneous challenges, indicate that also. Submit the screen shot along with your diagram.

3. Think of a game you are familiar with that permits the player to achieve victory by different strategies, similar to Figure 13.2. Write a short essay documenting each approach and how the hierarchy of challenges (including the intermediate challenges) differs in each one. If one strategy seems more likely to achieve victory than another, say so and indicate why. Your instructor will give you the scope of the assignment.

4. Choose a single or multiplayer RPG that you are familiar with (or your instructor will assign one). Identify all the actions it affords. (You may find the game's manual helpful.) Divide the actions into those intended to meet challenges, those that participate in the story, those that facilitate socializing with other players (if any), housekeeping operations such as inventory management, and those that control the software itself. If another category suggests itself, document it. Also note any actions that fall into more than one category and indicate why. The size of the game that you or your instructor selects will determine the scope of the assignment.

5. Choose ten different types of challenges from among the ones listed in the section "Commonly Used Challenges" in this chapter. For each type, devise one example challenge and *two* example actions that overcome it (this may rule out some types). Describe the challenge and the two actions in a paragraph, ten paragraphs in all.

Design Practice QUESTIONS

1. What types of challenges do you want to include in your game? Do you want to challenge the player's physical abilities, her mental abilities, or both?

2. Game genres are defined in part by the nature of the challenges they offer. What does your choice of genre imply for the gameplay? Do you intend to include any cross-genre elements, challenges that are not normally found in your chosen genre?

3. What is your game's hierarchy of challenges? How many levels do you expect it to have? What challenges are typical of each level?

4. What are your game's atomic challenges? Do you plan to make the player face more than one atomic challenge at a time? Are they all independent, like battling enemies one at a time, or are they interrelated, like balancing an economy? If they are interrelated, how?

5. Does the player have a choice of approaches to victory? Can he decide on one strategy over another? Can he ignore some challenges, face others, and still achieve a higher-level goal? Or must he simply face all the game's challenges in sequence?

6. Does the game include implicit challenges (those that emerge from the design) as well as explicit challenges (those that you specify)?

7. Do you intend to offer settable difficulty levels for your game? What levels of intrinsic skill and stress will each challenge require?

8. What actions will you implement to meet your challenges? Can the player surmount a large number of challenges with a small number of actions? What is the mapping of actions to challenges?

9. What other actions will you implement for other purposes? What are those purposes—unstructured play, creativity and self-expression, socialization, story participation, or controlling the game software?

10. What save mechanism do you plan to implement?

CHAPTER 14

Core Mechanics

The core mechanics of a game determine how that game actually operates: what its rules are and how the player interacts with them. This chapter begins by defining the core mechanics and explaining their role in creating the entertainment experience. You'll learn about the five types of mechanics most commonly found in video games: physics, internal economies, progression mechanisms, tactical maneuvering, and social interaction.

After discussing the general features of core mechanics, we'll examine internal economies in some detail and then look at how designers use mechanics to create gameplay by implementing both challenges and actions. After becoming familiar with all these aspects of core mechanics, you'll learn an approach for designing them, which involves reexamining your early design work and rendering it specific and concrete. We wrap up the chapter by briefly discussing random numbers and how to use them in games.

For a much more in-depth study of mechanics, please read Peachpit Press's *Game Mechanics: Advanced Game Design* by Ernest Adams and Joris Dormans (Adams, 2012).

What Are the Core Mechanics?

Isn't the greatest rule of all the rules simply to please?

—Molière

You first read about core mechanics in Chapter 2, "Designing and Developing Games." There you learned that the core mechanics are the heart of the game, generating the gameplay and implementing the rules. This chapter examines the core mechanics in further detail and offers a formal definition:

> **CORE MECHANICS** *consist of the data and the algorithms that precisely define the game's central rules and internal operations.*

Turning Rules into Core Mechanics

In the early stages of design, you may have only a hazy idea of the details of your game's rules. Early on, you may say, "Players will be penalized for taking too long to get through the swamp" or "Players will have only a limited amount of time to get through the swamp." Neither of these descriptions supplies enough information from which to build a game. For example, what is the penalty? And how long does the player have?

When you design the core mechanics, you define the rules precisely and completely. That same rule in the core mechanics might read something like this: "When the avatar enters the swamp, the black toadstools begin to emit a poison gas that the player can see filling the screen. It starts at the bottom and rises at a rate of 1 game-world inch every 3 seconds; by the end of 3 minutes, the gas reaches the height of the avatar's face, and if at that time the avatar is still in the swamp, the avatar dies. If the avatar returns to the swamp later, the gas is gone but the process starts over again from the beginning." In this example, the clauses beginning with *when* and *if* refer to algorithms, and *1 game-world inch every 3 seconds* and *3 minutes* are examples of data that also form a part of the rule.

THE RULES AND CORE MECHANICS OF *MONOPOLY*

The rules of *Monopoly*, the ones that Parker Brothers ships with the game, take up less than three full pages. However, the rules printed on the paper are not sufficient to build a computer game: They don't include complete documentation of all the data necessary to play. To properly specify the core mechanics of *Monopoly*, you would have to include not only the printed rules but the prices of each of the properties on the board, the different amounts of rent that may be collected at each location (including special mechanics for the utilities and railroads), the layout of the board, and the effects of all the Chance and Community Chest cards. A full specification of the core mechanics of *Monopoly* is considerably more detailed than the general rules.

Five Types of Mechanics

In our book *Game Mechanics: Advanced Game Design,* mentioned earlier, Joris Dormans and I identify five major types of game mechanics:

▪ **Physics,** the science of motion and force. We won't discuss physics much in this chapter because the concepts involved should be familiar to you already. Most video games that use physics implement some form of Newtonian mechanics, although often they simplify them or change them to make the game more enjoyable. If a game contains really outlandish distortions of ordinary physical behavior (such as balls that bounce higher and higher each time they hit the ground), we call that *cartoon physics.*

▪ **Internal economies.** An economy is a set of rules that governs the creation, consumption, and exchange of quantifiable resources of some kind. These resources can be *tangible,* such as gold coins, or *intangible,* such as popularity. Because internal economies are at the heart of almost all video games, we'll look into them closely.

▧ **Progression mechanisms.** These mechanics govern the player's progress through a series of challenges, each of which often has only one solution, in a sequence that is largely the same each time the game is played. (This includes fold-back storylines.) Frequently the progression takes the form of the player moving an avatar through a simulated enclosed environment (such as a building that may be controlled by locks and keys), or through a virtual path such as a sequence of levels.

▧ **Tactical maneuvering** takes place in largely open or semi-open spaces. Chess, *Go,* and computer games such as the *Total War* series use the mechanics of tactical maneuvering. Even a game with simple rules like chess can provide remarkably sophisticated gameplay. The rules must state which advantages each type of unit may gain from being in a particular location relative to another unit.

▧ **Social interaction.** This doesn't refer simply to players talking to one another, but to rules that control the relationships among players. These can include rules about forming and breaking alliances, the nature of team play, and so on.

In this chapter we will address all of these except physics, which for the most part is more of a programming and tuning challenge than a design one. Be aware that these aren't entirely separate fields, and many games include elements of more than one kind of mechanics. Massively multiplayer online games (MMOGs) can include all of them. We'll devote the most attention to internal economies because they are the most basic and appear in the greatest number of games.

Where Are the Core Mechanics?

Unlike the art or audio that goes into a video game, the core mechanics are an abstraction, and you can't just point to a file and say, "That's where the mechanics are." Rather, they're *implemented* in some way, and that will change as your project goes through the different stages of the design and development process. First you document the algorithms in ordinary language in a design document. Later you may build a spreadsheet that contains the algorithms and data and tweak them there. Or you might make a paper prototype that allows you to play the game to see if the mechanics you defined produce the game experience you want to offer.

Eventually the core mechanics should be so precisely stated that the programmers can write code using your design document or your spreadsheet as specifications. The algorithms of the core mechanics become the algorithms in the programmers' code, and the data required by the core mechanics reside in files that the game software can read. At this point, if you want to change the mechanics, you ask the programmers to change the code. You should also change the design documents to reflect the changes to the code. In short, the core mechanics are wherever your team considers their *official* implementation to be: in the design documents, the spreadsheets, or the code and data files.

If you apply player-centric design principles, all the core mechanics work together to provide a good game experience even though players may not know what core

TIP Although it may seem like there is no need to update the design documents once the code has been written, the testing team will still need an accurate description of what the game is supposed to do so they can design a test plan. You don't have to update your design documents for every little tweak, but if you make a significant change to the mechanics, you should record it.

mechanics are and might only infer the functionality of the core mechanics from the way the game behaves.

You don't have to know how to program to design the core mechanics, but you must be generally familiar with algorithmic processes. The section "Mechanics," later in this chapter, addresses this in more detail.

> ## DESIGN RULE Design the Game, Not the Software
>
> The *game engine* is the part of the software that implements the game's rules. Although the core mechanics spell out the rules of the game in detail so that in practice they specify what the game engine will do, they do not dictate exactly *how* the game engine will do it. Don't worry about defining the precise algorithms the programmers should use to build the game engine. That decision is theirs to make. In short, if there is more than one way to achieve the same effect in the game, let the programmers decide which one to use.

The Core Mechanics as Processes

If you get a job in the game industry, you will hear industry professionals talk about the core mechanics as if the mechanics actively take part in the game: The core mechanics "talk to the storytelling engine" or "signal the UI." But rules can't act. You would never say of *Monopoly* that the rules do anything beyond perhaps "allow" the player to take a particular action or "specify" a penalty. So what's going on?

The relationship between the core mechanics and the game engine is extremely close, because the core mechanics specify how it will behave. So references to the core mechanics may sound like references to the engine itself. As long as you understand that the core mechanics consist of algorithms and data that precisely define the rules, it doesn't really matter. When these algorithms exist only in the core mechanics design document, they obviously can't do anything, but when the programmers turn them into code, they can.

Therefore, when you read, "The core mechanics send triggers to the storytelling engine," it's just shorthand for a longer sentence that reads, "The game engine, using algorithms specified by the core mechanics, sends triggers to the storytelling engine."

Functions of the Core Mechanics in Operation

During play, the core mechanics (as implemented by the game engine) operate behind the scenes to create and manage gameplay for the player, keep track of everything that happens in the game world, and work with the storytelling engine to help tell the story. The following list details what the core mechanics do:

- **Operate the internal economy of the game.** These are the physics, economics, progression mechanism, tactical maneuvering, and social mechanics that the game uses. This is the most important role of the core mechanics.

- **Present active challenges** to the player via the user interface (UI), as the level design specifies. Active challenges are those governed by mechanics. Passive challenges, such as a chasm that the avatar must jump over, don't have mechanics of their own. The later section "Challenges and the Core Mechanics" discusses the distinction between active and passive challenges.

- **Accept player actions** from the UI, and implement their effects upon the game world and other players.

- **Detect victory or loss** and the termination conditions of the game. More generally, the mechanics detect success or failure in all challenges in the game and apply whatever consequences the rules call for.

- **Operate the artificial intelligence** of artificial opponents.

- **Switch the game from mode to mode.** The core mechanics keep track of the current gameplay mode and, whenever a mode change occurs (either because the nature of the game requires it or the player requests it), the core mechanics switch modes and signal the user interface to update the UI accordingly.

- **Transmit triggers to the storytelling engine** when game events or player actions that influence the plot occur.

Real-Time Games Versus Turn-Based Games

Your specification of the core mechanics will read somewhat differently depending on whether your game is turn-based or takes place in real time.

Most video games operate in real time, so the core mechanics specify the parameters of a living world that operates on its own whether the player acts or not. Many of the mechanics you design will be *processes* that operate continuously or for extended periods. AI-driven characters go about their business, traps check to see if they should spring upon anyone, banks collect and pay interest, and so on. When you specify one-shot *events* rather than continuous processes, the events will often occur as a direct or indirect consequence of player actions or because some process detects a special condition, such as when a runner crosses the finish line in a race. (The later section "Mechanics" discusses events and processes in greater detail.)

In a turn-based game with no artificial opponents, the core mechanics don't do anything at all until a player takes his turn. Once he has done so, the core mechanics can compute the effects of his actions on the game world. Then the mechanics remain idle while the next player takes her turn, and so on. In some games, all the players enter their intended actions simultaneously while the mechanics remain idle; once the players finish for that turn, the core mechanics compute the effect of all players' actions.

In a turn-based game, your design for the mechanics will read like a specification for a sequence of events rather than a set of processes that operate all the time. You will state the effects of each possible action and what other computations take place as a consequence. Although you may design processes for a turn-based game, you must realize that processes do not really operate continuously; they run only between player turns. Your design for a process in a turn-based game must include points at which the process may be interrupted safely for the next player's turn.

In a turn-based game that does have artificial opponents or NPCs, the mechanics don't remain entirely idle between turns because they must compute the behavior of these characters. However, the artificial characters still act in turns, just as the player does.

Core Mechanics and Level Design

Most video games for consoles and personal computers present gameplay in separate levels (also called chapters, missions, or scenarios, depending on the genre), each with its own set of initial conditions, challenges, and termination conditions. Level designers plan, construct, and test these levels, as Chapter 16, "General Principles of Level Design," discusses.

Ordinarily, the level design specifies the type, timing, and sequence of challenges that appear during play, whereas the core mechanics specify how different challenges actually work. When a level starts up, the core mechanics read the level design data from a file, which includes the initial state of the game world for each level; the challenges, actions, and NPCs for each level; and the victory conditions for the levels (see **Figure 14.1**). If the game consists of only one level or creates randomized levels, the core mechanics must also include mechanics for setting up the level before the game first enters a gameplay mode.

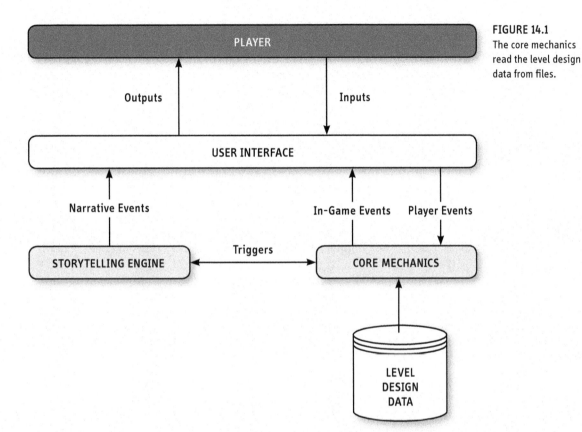

FIGURE 14.1
The core mechanics
read the level design
data from files.

Therefore, your design for the core mechanics should specify *how* challenges work
in general but not exactly *which* challenges each level will contain. As you design
the core mechanics, concentrate on those features of the game that will be needed
in more than one level, and leave special-case features found only in a particular level
to the level design stage of development. It may be that you (or the level designers)
can create code for those features using a scripting language and won't have to ask
the game's programmers to do it.

This doesn't mean that you can push all the work off onto the level designers,
though. Think of the features you create in the core mechanics as being like LEGO
blocks that the level designers will use to build their level. In a war game, the core
mechanics, not the level designs, define how all the units in the game move and
fight. Once you design all the units, the level designers can use your information
on how the units operate to construct exciting levels featuring those units.

Key Concepts

To design the core mechanics, you must document the different components that define how your game works: resources, entities, attributes, and mechanics. This section defines these terms. Although you do not have to be a programmer to design a game, you wouldn't be a game designer if you didn't intend for your ideas to turn into computer programs eventually. You will need to have at least a nodding acquaintance with how programmers think about data and the relationships between different items of data, ideas that crop up in this discussion.

Resources

NOTE Purely cosmetic items are not a resource. If you build a level full of flowers but the player can't do anything with them and nothing ever happens to them, then flowers are not a resource. The flowers set the stage and contribute aesthetically, but the core mechanics will not need to take flowers into account.

Resources refer to types of objects or materials the game can move or exchange; the game handles these as numeric quantities, performing arithmetic operations on the values. Resources do not refer to specific instances of these types of objects but to the type itself in an abstract sense. Marbles constitute a resource in your game if your player can pick up marbles, trade them, and put them down again, but the word *resource* doesn't describe a specific marble in your player's pocket or even a specific collection of marbles; it describes marbles generally. Marbles are a resource, but *the 15 marbles in the player's pocket* are an *instance* of a resource: a particular collection of marbles.

The core mechanics define the processes by which the game creates, uses, trades, and destroys resources; that is, the rules by which specific instances of resources—one lump of gold, the marbles in the player's pocket, the ammo in her inventory, the water in her reservoir—can be moved legally from place to place or from owner to owner, or can come into or go out of the game.

A resource may be of a type that can be handled as individual items, such as marbles, or of a type that cannot be divided into individual items, such as water (although water may be measured in volumetric units).

Games often treat nonphysical concepts such as *popularity* or vague concepts such as *resistance to poison* as resources, even though we don't ordinarily think of these as quantities that can be measured and even bought and sold. Part of a game designer's job involves quantifying the unquantifiable—turning such abstract qualities as *charisma* or *pugnacity* into numbers that a program can manipulate.

Entities

An *entity* is a particular instance of a resource or the state of some element of the game world. (A light may be on or off, for instance.) A building, a character, or an animal can be an entity, but perhaps less obviously a pile of gold or a vessel of water can be an entity. The state of a traffic light that at any given time might be red, green, or yellow can also be an entity.

Be sure you understand the difference between resources and entities. Remember that a resource is only a type of thing, not the thing itself. A specific airplane is an entity, but if your game includes a factory that manufactures airplanes, such that management of the supply of airplanes makes up part of the gameplay, then airplanes, as a commodity, constitute a resource even though each individual airplane remains an entity. Earlier we noted that marbles can be a resource but a marble in the player's pocket is not; now we can see that each marble in his pocket is an entity. Points in a sports game qualify as a resource, but the team's score is an entity. The score pertains only to that team, recording a number of points scored.

SIMPLE ENTITIES

The player's score or the current state of a traffic light can be completely specified by a single datum; this is called a *simple entity*. The single value stored in this datum can be numeric, such as a score, or symbolic, such as the possible states of a traffic light: red, green, or yellow. The later section "Numeric and Symbolic Relationships" discusses the differences between numeric and symbolic values.

Once you decide to add a symbolic entity, such as a traffic light, to the game world, you will need to define it in the core mechanics as a simple entity, specifying its initial state and providing a list of all its possible states. For a numeric entity, you'll need to define an initial quantity and the range of possible legal values. In the tuning stage of design, you will spend a great deal of time adjusting these values, so don't worry too much about getting them exactly right at first.

COMPOUND ENTITIES

It may take more than one data value to describe an entity. In a flying game in which characterizing the wind requires stating both its speed and its direction, the wind is a *compound entity*. Each of these values is called an *attribute*.

An *attribute* is an entity that belongs to, and therefore helps to describe, another entity. To describe the wind, you need to know the values of its speed attribute and its direction attribute. You can specify the wind's speed with a numeric value and its direction with a symbolic value (one of a set that includes *northwesterly, westerly, southwesterly,* and so on). In this case, each attribute of our overall entity (the wind) is itself a simple entity, but this is not always, and not even usually, the case. Attributes themselves may be compound entities. In a sports game, a team has attributes such as its name, hometown, and statistics, as well as its collection of athletes, each of whom is an entity with his own attributes such as speed and agility. In a driving game, the car the player drives is a compound entity with attributes that describe its performance characteristics. In a business simulation, factories are compound entities with attributes for rates of production, stock on hand, and so forth. Most of the entities you will define for any game, other than the most elementary of games, will be compound entities. **Figure 14.2** shows an example of three types of entities: one simple, one compound containing only simple attributes, and one compound containing both simple attributes and another compound entity. The gray boxes are only labels to aid understanding; their contents are not stored as data.

FIGURE 14.2

Examples of three different entities

A Simple
Numeric Entity

Points Scored
1,755,245

A Compound Entity
with Two Attributes

Wind	
Speed	35
Direction	Northwest

A Compound Entity Containing Another
Compound Entity as an Attribute

Avatar	
Name	Voldarok
Money	25
Health	117
Race	Elf
Location	Feasting Hall
Inventory	
# Items	5
Item 1	Sword
Item 2	Shield
Item 3	Food
Item 4	Helmet
Item 5	Armor

Both Chapter 9, "Creative and Expressive Play," and Chapter 10, "Character Development," discuss attributes at some length, so that information is not repeated here. Be aware, however, that you don't use attributes only for characters. *Any* entity in the game may have attributes that describe it: Vehicles have performance characteristics, factories have production rates, and so on.

As with any simple entity, you should choose an initial quantity or state for an attribute when you decide to include the attribute in your game.

IF YOU HAPPEN TO BE A PROGRAMMER...

If you are a programmer, you may have noticed that entities sound a lot like *objects* in object-oriented programming: They include variables for storing numeric and symbolic values, and may be made up of other entities in the same way that programming objects may be made up of other objects. And like *classes* of objects in programming, entities have associated mechanics (though programmers would call them *functions* or *methods*) for manipulating these data.

For most practical purposes, you can treat entities and programming objects as identical, and if you happen to program as well as design your game, you will certainly implement entities as objects in your code. This book uses the term *entity* rather than *object* because we normally use *object* in the everyday sense to refer to some physical item in the game world.

UNIQUE ENTITIES

If your game contains exactly one entity of a particular type, then that is a *unique entity*. In most adventure games, the objects that the avatar can pick up are unique entities. The avatar itself in most games is a unique entity because there is usually only one avatar. In a football game, the football is a unique entity, because there may never be two footballs in play at any one time.

Note that the airplanes mentioned in the previous section are not unique entities because there can be more than one of them, and they can be bought and sold in groups.

DEFINING ENTITIES FOR YOUR GAME

As you specify your core mechanics, you will need to define entities for any character, object, or substance that the game needs to manipulate and for any value that the game needs to remember. In the case of items such as footballs, vehicles, money, and health, determining what attributes each entity requires will probably seem obvious—although defining their mechanics won't always be simple. You may also need to create entities that hold quantities or other information that the user interface will display. Every indicator in the user interface needs an entity that reflects the indicator's state or appearance.

Suppose you want to warn the player when a valuable resource, such as fuel in a car's gas tank, reaches critically low levels. Normally you would put a needle gauge in the UI to show the fuel level, and you may want to add a warning light to draw the player's attention to the gauge. The light can be either on or off. To support the light, you need to define an entity called *fuel warning* that can exist in two states. During play, the UI checks the state of the fuel warning entity to display the appropriate image of the light. You also need to create a mechanic (discussed in the next section, "Mechanics") to define precisely what conditions change the state of the fuel warning entity.

You may wonder why you should create an additional entity and mechanic for the state of the warning light rather than have the UI software check the fuel level and decide for itself whether to turn on the warning light. Professionals keep the mechanics in one part of the design and the UI in another. That way, the UI designer doesn't have to worry about underlying mechanics; she can concentrate on screen layouts and usability considerations, and if you want to adjust the point at which the light comes on during the tuning stage of design, you can do so without interfering with the user interface itself.

Mechanics

Mechanics document how the game world and everything in it behave. Mechanics state the relationships among entities, the events and processes that take place among the resources and entities of the game, and the conditions that trigger events and processes. The mechanics describe the overall rules of the game but also the behavior of particular entities, from something as simple as a light switch up to the AI of a very smart NPC. The earlier section "Functions of the Core Mechanics in Operation" gave a list of the kinds of things mechanics do in a game.

Some core mechanics operate throughout the game, while others apply only in particular gameplay modes and not in others. A mechanic that operates throughout the game is called a *global mechanic*. Any game with more than one gameplay mode needs at least one global mechanic that governs when the game changes from mode to mode and an entity that records what mode it is in.

RELATIONSHIPS AMONG ENTITIES

If the value of one entity depends upon the value or state of one or more other entities, you need to specify the *relationship* between the entities involved. In the case of numeric entities, you express the relationship mathematically. For example, many role-playing games (RPGs) define character levels in terms of experience points earned; when a character earns a certain amount of experience, his level goes up. The formula may be given by a simple equation, such as `character level = experience points × 1000`, or a more complicated equation, or it may require looking up the value in a table. If the nature of this relationship remains constant throughout the game, you need not worry about specifying *when* it should actually be computed; let the programmers decide that. Just specify the relationship itself.

EVENTS AND PROCESSES

When you describe an event or a process, you state that something happens: A change occurs among, or to, the entities specified in the mechanics.

An *event* is a specific change that happens once when triggered by a *condition* (defined in the next section) and doesn't happen again until triggered again. "When the player picks up a golden egg" specifies a trigger condition, and "she gets two points" defines an event.

A *process* refers to a sequence of activities that, once initiated, continues until stopped. A player action or other game event starts a process that runs until something stops it.

Both events and processes may consist of whole sequences of actions that the computer must take. When you document such a sequence, be clear about the order in which things should happen. Part of the sequence *getting dressed* might be, "First put on socks, then put on shoes." If you leave the language ambiguous and the programmer misinterprets your meaning, you will introduce a bug into the game.

NOTE Designing the core mechanics requires the greatest clarity and precision of language. Ambiguous mechanics turn into buggy code.

ANALYZING A MECHANIC

Let's go back to the sample mechanic that Chapter 2 introduced in the sidebar "Game Idea Versus Design Decision" and identify its various components. To specify the idea "Dragons should protect their eggs," we create a mechanic that reads: "Whenever they have eggs in their nests, female dragons do not move out of visual range of the nest. If an enemy approaches within 50 meters of the nest, the dragon abandons any other activity and returns to the nest to defend the eggs. She does not leave the nest until no enemy has been within the 50-meter radius for at least 30 seconds. She defends the eggs to her death."

This mechanic makes up one small part of the specification of a female dragon's artificial intelligence. It applies to all female dragons at any time, so it belongs in the core mechanics, not in the design of a level. (However, if dragons appear in only one level, this mechanic should be part of that level's design, and if the dragon is a unique entity, you should specify the mechanics relating to its behavior wherever you define what a dragon is, and nowhere else.)

Here's how this mechanic looks with the components identified:

"*Whenever* they have *eggs* in their *nests* (a condition about a relationship between a resource, eggs, and an entity, the nest, such that *eggs in nest* > 0), *female dragons* (each one an entity) do not *move* (a process) *out of visual range of the nest* (a condition placed on the movement process). If an *enemy* (an entity) *comes within 50 meters of the nest* (a condition), the dragon *abandons any other activity* (end her current process) and *returns to the nest* (a process) to *defend the eggs* (a process). She does not *leave the nest* (initiate a process) until *no enemy has been within the 50-meter radius for at least 30 seconds* (a complicated condition that prevents her from initiating the process of leaving the nest). She defends the eggs *to her death* (a condition indicating that the dragon does not initiate any other process while defending the eggs, such as running away)."

Even this, complex as it is, isn't complete. It doesn't say whether or not eggs can be destroyed or removed from the nest and, if so, what the dragon does about it. It doesn't state how *visual range* should be computed, how the dragon goes about returning to her nest, or what defending the eggs actually consists of. It also includes a negative condition ("she does not leave the nest until...") without a general rule stating when she *does* leave the nest in the first place. All that information must be included elsewhere in the definition of the dragon's AI and the definition of a nest and an egg. If you don't define these things specifically, the programmers will either come and ask you to, or they will make a guess as a placeholder, which you may need to revisit later.

CONDITIONS

Use conditions to define what causes an event to occur and what causes a process to start or stop. Conditional statements often take the form if (condition) then (execute an event, or start or stop a process); whenever (condition) take action to (execute an event, or start or stop a process); and continue (a process) until (condition). Mechanics defining victory and loss conditions conform to this style.

You can also define conditions in negative terms, such as if (condition) then do not (execute an event, or start or stop a process), although a condition in this form is incomplete. "If the mouse is wearing its cat disguise, the cat won't attack it" doesn't provide enough information because it doesn't tell the programmers when the cat *does* attack the mouse. Use this form of conditional mechanic for indicating exceptions to more general rules already specified: "When a cat sees a mouse, the cat will attack it. But if the mouse is wearing its cat disguise, the cat won't attack it."

ENTITIES WITH THEIR OWN MECHANICS

Some mechanics define the behavior of only one type of entity and nothing else in the game, in which case you should figure out the details and document the entity and its associated exclusive mechanics together. This makes it easier for the programmers to build the game and for you to find the documentation if you need to change something. This is very like object-oriented programming. In object-oriented programming, you think about the variables and the algorithms that manipulate them together as a unit.

Examples of entities with their own mechanics include symbolic entities that require special mechanics to indicate how they change state (such as a traffic light); numeric entities whose values are computed from other entities by a formula (such as the amount of damage done in an attack under *Dungeons & Dragons* rules—it is computed from several other factors, some of them random); NPCs with AI-controlled behavior (the definition of the artificial intelligence consists of mechanics); and entities that act autonomously even if their behavior doesn't really qualify as artificial intelligence, such as a trap that triggers whenever a character comes near. In the case of a triggered trap, you define its various attributes, both functional and cosmetic, and a set of mechanics that indicate exactly what sets it off and what kind of damage it does to the character who triggers it.

Numeric and Symbolic Relationships

This section discusses the differences between the numeric and symbolic relationships and how you may combine them to achieve your design goals for the core mechanics.

NUMERIC RELATIONSHIPS

A *numeric relationship* is a relationship between entities defined in terms of numbers and arithmetic operations. For example, the statement "A bakery can bake 50 loaves of bread from 1 sack of flour and 4 buckets of water" specifies a numeric relationship between water, flour, and bread. Here is another example: "The probability of an injury occurring to an athlete in a collision with another athlete is proportional to the weight difference between the two athletes and their relative speeds at the time of the collision." Although this second example leaves the precise details up to the programmer to decide, it does specify a numeric relationship: *Weights* and *speeds,* both numeric attributes of the athletes, go into computing the *probability of an injury,* a numeric entity. (Remember that an attribute is just an entity that belongs to another entity.)

Defining numeric relationships precisely requires some familiarity with algebra and arithmetic. First, you must ensure that you use robust equations; if you write that *the speed the convoy will travel* is in part a function of the quantity defined by (the weight of supplies) ÷ (number of pack horses - number of camp followers), you may very well end up with a divide-by-zero error or a negative value. Because the resulting value interacts with other parts of the mechanics, changes in the way you calculate that value will have a domino effect, ultimately influencing the gameplay itself, and you must be able to understand and predict these effects. You need to consider the full spectrum of possible values, and you may need multiple equations to cover special cases.

Numeric relationships lie at the heart of internal economies, and the later section "The Internal Economy" discusses them further.

SYMBOLIC RELATIONSHIPS

The values of symbolic entities—red, on, empty, found, and the like—cannot be added together or otherwise manipulated mathematically. You must specify all the states that a symbolic entity may represent, and the relationships among them, without equations. For instance, the red, yellow, and green states of a traffic light are not related to each other numerically; they're simply different. To use a traffic light, you must document how it gets into each of its possible states and how the light in each of those states affects the behavior of other entities. To define the behavior of an NPC driver who sees a traffic light, you would write three separate mechanics into his AI, one for each state of the light, to say how the driver reacts to seeing a red light, a yellow light, or a green light. When any entity in the game (such as a driver) interacts with a symbolic entity (such as a traffic light), you must state exactly what happens for each possible symbolic state of the entity. If you leave out one state, no interaction will occur with that state.

A binary (two-state) entity is sometimes called a *flag.* Often you will create flags in your game to document whether the avatar has entered locations, overcome specific obstacles, and so on.

NOTE Chris Crawford's *Balance of Power: International Politics as the Ultimate Global Game* (Crawford, 1986) remains one of the best books ever written on numeric relationships in the core mechanics. Although it is out of print, used copies are still available from online bookstores. The text is also available in ASCII form at www.erasmatazz.com/library/my-books/balance-of-power.html.

TIP The values of numeric entities may change according to arithmetic processes, but you must create mechanics that explicitly change symbolic entities from state to state.

This chapter doesn't discuss symbolic relationships much further because they are relatively easy to define and their results are easier to predict; numeric relationships are harder to create and tune. Although it is possible to create extremely complicated symbolic relationships (think about *Rubik's Cube*), most of the symbolic relationships in games tend to be rather simple.

INTEGRATING SYMBOLIC AND NUMERIC RELATIONSHIPS

Although you cannot perform arithmetic operations on symbolic values, you can define how symbolic entities change from state to state in terms of other numeric data. If the symbolic entity *fuel warning* can take the values on and off, you can define a mechanic for each of the states based on the quantity of fuel available: "When the amount of fuel goes below two gallons, the *fuel warning* value switches to on. When the amount of fuel rises to two gallons or more, the *fuel warning* value switches to off."

A symbolic entity can contribute to a mathematical function if you have a mechanic that associates a symbolic entity with a number. For example, the state of a car's transmission is symbolic; the transmission is either in one gear or another, and you can't add gears together. But you can make a table that shows the gear ratio of each gear and use the results to make computations about the speed of the driveshafts. For example you can specify, "In first gear, the ratio is 3.83 to 1. In second gear, the ratio is 2.01 to 1. In third gear, the ratio is 1.46 to 1. In reverse gear, the ratio is 4 to –1. The negative value causes the driveshaft to turn backward." This mechanic converts a symbolic entity (transmission state) into a numeric entity (gear ratio).

NON-CORE MECHANICS

The core mechanics are called *core* because they are at the heart of the game and they operate in every level of the game. This includes the AI that implements an artificial opponent, such as the leaders of other nations in the *Civilization* series. In contrast, mechanics that operate only on a single level of a game, or that define the AI of individual NPCs, would not be considered part of the core mechanics.

The Internal Economy

An *economy* is a system in which resources and entities are produced, consumed, and exchanged in quantifiable amounts. Most games have an internal economy, though the complexity and importance of the internal economy varies considerably from genre to genre. The companion e-book *Fundamentals of Construction and Simulation Game Design* provides more discussion of internal economies.

A game designer spends part of her time designing and tuning her game's economy, and the more complex the economy, the more time she needs to spend. This section introduces aspects of an internal economy, which it explains by referencing both a simple action game (a shooter) and a complex game (a construction and management simulation).

Sources

If a resource or entity can come into the game world having not been there before, the mechanic by which it arrives is called a *source*.

In a simple shooter, the game begins with some resources, such as enemies, already in the game world, but more enemies may appear at *spawn points*. A spawn point is a designated location where the core mechanics insert new resources into the game world and therefore into the economy. Enemies are part of the economy, a resource that is produced at spawn points and consumed by conflict with the avatar. Each spawn point is governed by a mechanic that specifies its location, what kind of resource it generates (spawn points in shooters can also produce weapons, ammunition, or health packs), and at what frequency.

Sources often produce resources automatically (or at least produce resources automatically once the player starts them going, for example, by building a factory). You will need to define a *production rate*, either fixed or variable, and different sources may produce the same resource at different rates. In *The Settlers* games, rivers produce fish at a constant rate. A mechanic also defines the maximum number of fish that may be in a river at any one time, so the river stops producing fish when it gets full.

Sources can be global mechanics: A mechanism that pays the player interest at regular intervals on the money he owns would be one example. An interest-payment mechanism applies throughout the game regardless of anything else, so it is global. Sources can also make up part of the mechanics governing the behavior of entities. In *The Settlers,* a stream that produces fish is an entity, one of whose attributes is the number of fish it contains.

Sources can be limited or unlimited. In *Monopoly,* the "Go" square constitutes an unlimited source—according to the rules, it can never run out of money. (If the bank runs low, the banker may make more money by writing on paper.) But the collection of houses and hotels stored in the bank is a limited source: Once the banker sells all the houses and hotels, no more may come into the game. The stream in *The Settlers* is an unlimited source of fish. Although it can be temporarily empty if too many fishermen are catching fish from it, it goes on producing fish until it is full, as long as the game is running.

Drains

A *drain* is a mechanic that determines the consumption of resources—that is, a rule specifying how resources permanently drop out of the game (not to be confused with a *converter,* which we'll look at next). In a shooter game, the player firing his weapon drains ammunition—that's what makes ammunition, a resource, disappear.

Being hit by an enemy shot drains health points. Enemies drain out of the game by dying when their health points reach zero. The most common drain in a construction and management simulation is *decay*—ongoing damage to the objects the player constructed, which she must spend resources to reverse or repair. (Decay is also sometimes called entropy, although technically *entropy* refers to increasing disorder rather than loss of resources.) Typical decay mechanics look something like this: "Each section of road includes a numeric attribute indicating its level of decay as a percentage, with 0 (zero) indicating that the section is new and 100 indicating that the section is fully decayed and impassable. Sections of roads begin to decay three months after they are constructed, and 3 percent is added to their level of decay every year, plus an additional 1 percent for every 100,000 car trips over the section in the course of that year. When decay reaches or exceeds 100 percent, the road section becomes impassable and it must be replaced."

Because resources are valuable, the player wants to know why a resource disappears from the world and what benefit compensates for its loss. In *Monopoly*, players get money from the bank by passing "Go"—in effect, for no reason at all—but whenever a player has to give money back to the bank, the game provides a reason: The player owes income tax, incurs a fine, or something similar. Players don't mind getting money for free, but when they have to spend it, they want to know why. Explain your drains.

Converters

NOTE A trader is different from a converter. A trader changes the ownership of things, but does not change the things themselves. A converter turns something into something else, consuming the first item and producing the second one.

A *converter* is a mechanic—and usually an entity, too—that turns one or more resources into another type of resource. In designing a converter, you must specify its production rate and the input-to-output ratio that governs the relationship of resources consumed to resources produced. *The Settlers* offers several examples. The windmill converts grain into flour at a rate of one to one, so one bag of grain produces one bag of flour. It takes 20 real-time seconds to turn one bag of grain into one bag of flour, so the rate of production of flour works out to three bags per minute. The iron smelter turns one load of ore into one iron bar, consuming one load of coal in the process. However, if fed charcoal instead of coal, the smelter requires three loads of charcoal for each iron bar because charcoal is less efficient than coal.

Traders

A *trader* mechanic governs trades of goods, generally between the player and the game. In a stock-trading game, the trader may be a faceless financial construct; in an RPG, the trader may be in the form of a blacksmith who trades in swords or something similar.

Traders cause no change in the game world other than reassignment of ownership. If you trade your old dirk and a gold coin for a new short sword, then, in theory, the game still contains that dirk, that coin, and that short sword, although all three articles have been assigned to new owners. If your game permits it, the trader can sell the old dirk to the next player who comes along.

You can also build a bargaining feature into the mechanics of a trader, such that it sells at a high price but can, via a UI mechanism designed for the purpose, lower its price after a little haggling. Your scheme might make some traders more flexible than others, thereby encouraging players to shop around for the best deal.

THE PROBLEM OF RUNAWAY PROFITS

A player must never be able to buy an item repeatedly from a trader at a low price and sell it back at a higher price unless you set limits on the process. If players can buy from and sell to traders indefinitely and rapidly, and they can sell something for more than they paid for it, they will exploit this ruthlessly, piling up huge fortunes by buying and reselling endlessly, and ignoring the rest of the game.

You can use various schemes to prevent this. You can make it impossible to make a profit by requiring all subsequent sales to be for less than the original purchase price. If you want players to be able to make a reasonable profit, place limits on the amount of buying and selling they can do: Require that they wait a while before selling an item back again, or have the trader refuse to sell items to them more than a certain number of times or refuse to buy goods back. The trader itself can have limited funds and be unable to buy if funds run out. In a multiplayer game, you can let players buy and sell at a profit to one another but not to an automated or NPC trader. Transactions among the players don't change the total amount of money in the game; but selling things back to an automated trader mechanic that has an unlimited supply of money has the potential for abuse.

Production Mechanisms

Production mechanism describes a class of mechanics that make a resource conveniently available to a player. These include sources that bring the resource directly into the player's hands, but they can also include special buildings, characters, or other facilities that gather resources from the landscape and make them available to the player. Many real-time strategy games employ special characters to perform this function. For instance, in the *Command & Conquer* series, a harvester vehicle collects a resource called tiberium and carries it to a refinery where it is converted into money that the player can use to buy weapons. The harvester is a production mechanism; the refinery is a converter.

Tangible and Intangible Resources

If a resource possesses physical properties within the game world, such as requiring storage space or transportation, the resource is said to be *tangible*. On the other hand, if it occupies no physical space and does not have to be transported, it is *intangible*.

In a shooter game, ammunition is tangible—it exists in physical form in the environment, and the avatar has to carry it around. Most construction and management simulations treat money as intangible: It exists as a meaningful resource in the game world but takes up no space and has no particular location.

A number of games treat resources in a mixed fashion, sometimes tangible and sometimes intangible. In *Age of Empires,* food and building materials have to be transported from their production points to a storage facility; during transport, these items can be stolen or destroyed by an enemy. Once stored, however, materials become intangible: They cannot be seized or destroyed even if the enemy demolishes the storage facility.

Similarly, most construction and management simulations and real-time strategy games don't require a resource to be physically transported before it can be spent or consumed; the commodity simply vanishes. When constructing a building in *Age of Empires,* the player doesn't transport the stone from the storage pit to the construction site. This takes an extra management burden off the player. The section "Logistics" in the companion e-book *Fundamentals of Strategy Game Design* discusses the gameplay implications of intangible resources at greater length.

Feedback Loops, Mutual Dependencies, and Deadlocks

A production mechanism that requires some of the resource that the mechanism itself produces constitutes a *feedback loop* in the production process. Note that this use of the term *feedback* is not related to the feedback elements discussed in Chapter 12, "Creating the User Experience." In the context of a user interface, *feedback* refers to a means of giving the player information about the effects of his actions upon the game world. In the context of an internal economy, *feedback* refers to resources that are *fed back* into a production mechanism.

So long as the mechanism has a supply of the resource to start with and the mechanism produces more than it requires, there's nothing wrong with using a feedback loop. But if for any reason the system runs out of the resource, the mechanism won't be able to produce any more. This condition, called a *deadlock,* locks up that part of the economy unless you provide some other supply of the resource—a way to *break the deadlock.*

DESIGN RULE Provide Means to Break Deadlocks

If your internal economy contains either feedback loops or mutual dependencies, be sure you include a means to break a deadlock if one occurs.

The Settlers III contains a feedback loop. The player needs stone to build a stonecutter's hut in order to house a stonecutter who produces more stone (see **Figure 14.3**). Ordinarily, the game starts with some stone already in storage, so if the player builds a stonecutter's hut right away, the stonecutter produces the stone needed for other activities. However, if the player uses up all her stored stone constructing other buildings, she might not have enough to build a stonecutter's hut, and she will be in a deadlock—hut building can't proceed without stones; stones can't be produced without a hut. *The Settlers III* provides a way to break the deadlock: The player can demolish another building and get back enough raw stone to build a stonecutter's hut after all. Note that the stonecutter's hut doesn't actually need stone to operate, but the player does need stone to build it in the first place. As long as the player builds and retains one stonecutter's hut, she shouldn't get into a deadlock.

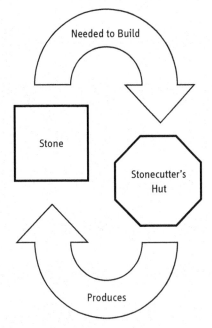

FIGURE 14.3 The feedback loop in *The Settlers III*

Two production mechanisms that each require the other's output as their input in order to work are *mutually dependent*. Again, there's a loop in the process. If the resources produced by either one are diverted elsewhere and production stops for lack of input, this, too, can produce a deadlock.

In designing your game's internal economy, you need to watch out for deadlocks, which can occur whenever there's a loop in the production process. To avoid deadlocks, either avoid such loops or provide an alternative source for one of the resources. This is the point of collecting $200 when you pass "Go" in *Monopoly*. A player who owns no properties can't earn money by collecting rent, but without rent, the player can't buy properties: a deadlock. *Monopoly* solves this by giving the players money to start with and by giving them $200 every time they pass "Go." As the game progresses, that $200 becomes less significant, but it is enough to break a deadlock.

THE MACHINATIONS DESIGN FRAMEWORK

Inspired by a previous edition of this book, the Dutch game designer and scholar Joris Dormans devised a diagramming language for describing internal economies in a visual way, which he called *Machinations*. Later he built a tool for drawing Machinations diagrams and simulating them in real time. With Machinations, you can experiment with, and tune, a game economy. The Machinations tool is available free of charge on Joris's website at www.jorisdormans.nl/machinations.

There isn't room in this introductory textbook to explain Machinations in detail, but we'll include one simple example to show what a Machinations diagram looks like (see **Figure 14.4**). A source (the triangle) generates resources at a production rate of one every second. (The asterisk by the source means that it operates automatically, without needing to be triggered by something else.) The resource travels along a *resource connection* (the solid arrow) and ends up in a *pool* (the circle). A pool is Dormans' term for what this book calls a simple entity. The pool is connected by a *state connection* (the dotted arrow) back to the resource connection. The +1 label on the state connection tells Machinations to increase the production rate of the source by one unit for each new item stored in the pool.

When you run this diagram in the Machinations tool, one resource (which would appear as a small black dot) will travel from the source into the pool in the first second of operation. Its arrival will trigger the state connection to increase the production rate of the source by one, and the number under the resource connection line will change to 2. In the next second, two resources travel from the source to the pool. Each new resource further increases the production rate: a classic positive feedback loop.

For more information about Machinations, read our book *Game Mechanics: Advanced Game Design* from Peachpit Press (Adams, 2012). It builds upon the ideas in this chapter and explains the Machinations framework in depth.

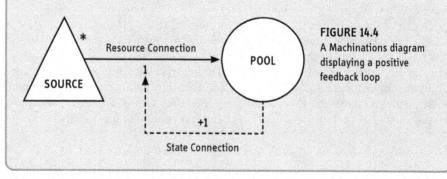

FIGURE 14.4
A Machinations diagram displaying a positive feedback loop

Static and Dynamic Equilibrium

It's possible to design a system in such a way that, left alone, it enters a state of equilibrium. Static equilibrium is a state in which the amounts of resources produced and consumed remain constantly the same: Resources flow steadily around without any significant change anywhere. Dynamic equilibrium occurs when the system fluctuates through a cycle. It's constantly changing, but it eventually returns to a starting point and begins again.

Here's an example of static equilibrium. Suppose you have a miller grinding wheat to make flour and a baker baking bread from the flour. If the bakery consumes the flour at exactly the same rate at which the mill produces it, then the amount of flour in the world at any one time will remain static. If you upset the system by stopping the bakery for a while, the flour will build up. When the bakery restarts, the amount of flour available will be static at the new level. The system returns to static equilibrium because the key factors—the production and consumption rates of the mill and the bakery—have not changed (see **Figure 14.5**).

NOTE The terms *static* and *dynamic equilibrium* are borrowed from economics. In economics, *static equilibrium* means that supply and demand for goods are balanced, and although the goods themselves move from sellers to buyers, the amount of goods being transferred does not change over time.

FIGURE 14.5
An example of static equilibrium

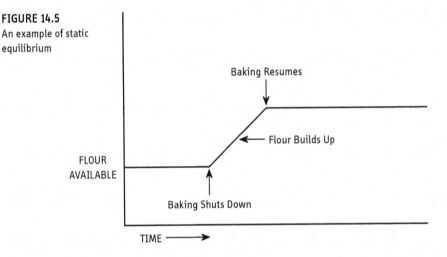

Now let's suppose that only one person does both jobs. She mills enough to bake three loaves of bread, then she bakes the three loaves, then she mills again, and so on. This is an example of dynamic equilibrium: Conditions are changing all the time, but they always return to the same state after a while because the process is cyclic. If we tell the woman to stop baking and only mill for a while, and then resume baking later, again the flour builds up. When she resumes baking, the system settles into a new state of dynamic equilibrium (see **Figure 14.6**).

FIGURE 14.6
A new state of dynamic
equilibrium

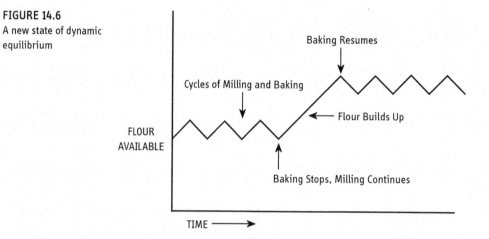

When a game such as a construction and management simulation settles into a static equilibrium, players can easily judge the effect of their actions on the system by making one small change and watching the results. This makes the game easy to learn and play. Dynamic equilibrium is more difficult for players to manage. With the system in constant flux, it's hard to tell whether the changes players see result from a purely internal process or from something they've done.

Settling into a state of equilibrium, static or dynamic, takes the pressure off the player. She can simply watch the game run for a while and make adjustments when she feels like it. Some construction and management simulations do work that way, but most give the player more of a challenge. Rather than settling into equilibrium, the designers build in a factor that requires the player to take action to prevent the system from running out of some needed resource. To use our milling–baking metaphor, perhaps the player has to take action to keep the mill supplied with wheat. If the player doesn't keep an eye on the wheat supply, both milling and baking come to a halt. In *Age of Empires*, farms produce food automatically, but after a while they stop working and the player must intervene to rebuild them. In *SimCity*, the roads wear out and the player has to repair them.

Whether your system settles into equilibrium or runs down without player action, one thing is certain: The player should always have to do something to obtain growth—she should have to press on the gas pedal of your game, as it were. If the system can grow constructively and profitably of its own accord, there's no reason for the player to interfere. This is the player's primary challenge: figuring out how to produce growth using the many (metaphorical) levers and knobs that you provide via the core mechanics. In effect, the player herself is an element of the economy, and growth depends on her active participation.

Progression Mechanics

The game scholar Jesper Juul divided the universe of games into *games of emergence* and *games of progression* (Juul, 2002). In games of emergence the game's flow of events emerge from the operation of the rules and are not preplanned by the game designer. Tabletop games such as chess or bridge belong to this category; so does *Tetris*.

Games of progression, on the other hand, contain predefined systems that cause the player to experience the game in such a way that certain events are certain to follow other events. Most frequently, this means that the player takes an avatar through a space onto which a story has been mapped. By progressing through the various parts of the game world in the correct order, the player experiences the events of the story in a way that is coherent and preserves his sense of cause and effect. Game developers usually manage this by putting the avatar in an enclosed space and further constraining his movement through the use of locked doors and one-way doors that prevent him from going backward. Role-playing and adventure games are good examples.

Usually, creating the actual progression of the game is the job of the level designer and sometimes the writer, if the game has a story. The *mechanics* of progression are the tools that the level designer uses to ensure that the game progresses in the way that the designer intends. It is up to the game designer to define what progression mechanics will be available to the level designer and writer.

Progression can be divided into three major kinds, with different design features: progress through space, progress through time, and progress through a story.

Progress Through Space

To control a player's progress through space (which usually means via an avatar), the game mechanics need to provide the following features:

■ **Constraints on movement.** These usually take the form of walls or other impenetrable barriers that the game engine enforces. It can also include limits on how high the avatar can jump.

■ **Locked doors**, which really means any kind of constraint on movement that can be removed in some way. The door could be opened in a variety of ways: The player possesses an object that opens it (a key), or does *not* possess an object that is not permitted to pass; or the player solves a puzzle or overcomes some other kind of challenge that unlocks the door.

■ **One-way doors** permit the player to pass through in one direction but not in the other. These are useful for ensuring forward movement in a story. A one-way door can be implemented as a door that is locked from one side but not the other, or it can be something as simple as a height that the player must jump down from, but cannot climb back up to.

■ **Hidden regions** are spaces that the player has to work to find. You can implement this challenge by a variety of means: requiring the player to make a particularly difficult jump or other maneuver to get into the region; requiring the player to search for hidden doors that look like normally impenetrable objects such as walls; or simply making the access to the region inconspicuous, and requiring the player to be observant.

■ **Illogical spaces and unmarked teleporters** confuse the player by upsetting his expectations about the nature of movement through space. The mechanics of teleportation are simple: The game engine simply changes the avatar character's coordinates to a new location without indicating how he got there. (Visibly marked teleporters are not challenges but convenience features that allow the player to move quickly from one location to another.) Illogical spaces, such as two rooms that both appear to be above each other, require a game engine that can appear to shift a room within the simulated game space.

Progress Through Time

Real-world time always moves forward, but game-world time can speed up, slow down, pause, and even go backward. Some of the mechanics you may want to implement include

■ **A pause feature.** This simply lets the player stop the flow of time. Most games include a pause feature that brings up a menu where the player can save or exit the game.

■ **A means of tracking time.** Many games don't keep track of time because they simply consist of a series of challenges that the player may solve at any rate he wishes, but in others (such as racing games), time is critical.

■ **Bullet time** or other means of speeding up and slowing down game-world time with respect to real-world time. This feature may or may not be under player control.

■ **Time bonuses** don't speed up time or slow it down, but they give the player more time to play than he was allotted originally.

■ **Reversing time.** Allowing the player to go back in game-world time is comparatively rare except when the player restarts a level or reloads the game from a save point. However, it is not unheard-of: *Prince of Persia: The Sands of Time* permitted the player to spend a resource called sand to go back in time and retry a failed maneuver. The most famous example, however, is a game called *Braid*, which consists almost entirely of time-based puzzles.

■ **Scripted events** can occur at particular moments in time. For example, the avatar may enter a region that becomes dangerous after a certain amount of time has passed. He must traverse the region before the timer runs out.

Progress Through a Plot

As we explained, games of progression often include a story. If the story is mapped strictly onto a physical space, then progression through the plot can be managed entirely by the means described in the section "Progress Through Space," above, but in most cases the player's experience of the plot is also affected by decisions that she makes or the quality of her play. These issues are discussed in detail in the section "Nonlinear Stories" in Chapter 11, "Storytelling." To allow for storytelling in a game, the game engine must implement the following features:

▪ **Triggers** that detect when it is time to play a narrative event such as a cut-scene. These can be set off by almost anything: particular actions by the player, the elapse of time, or the arrival of the avatar in a certain location.

▪ **A dialogue engine.** These were discussed in the section "Scripted Conversations and Dialogue Trees" in Chapter 11.

▪ **A system for tracking progress through the plot.** Normally, branching and foldback stories are implemented as directed acyclic graphs—that is, networks of events in which the player may never return to an event he has already seen, but may take different routes through the network on different plays through the game. However this is implemented in code, the system must keep track of where the player is in the plot (which may have nothing to do with where the avatar is in the game world).

▪ **A system for choosing a direction at branch points in the plot.** If the plot is nonlinear, at the branch points some system must decide which part of it the player will experience next. This decision can be based on player choices, his ability to meet challenges, or simple luck. If it is based on player choices, the system must also keep track of what player decisions affected the outcome, and whether the consequences of the player's choices were immediate, deferred, or cumulative. All these issues were described in detail in the section "Branching Stories" in Chapter 11, but if you want to include them as features of the game, you must document them as part of the game mechanics, not just the story, so the programmers will know to implement them.

Summary on Progression

Progression mechanics enable you to create sequences of events that you design, in contrast to emergent mechanics, which generate events as a product of the operation of the rules. We have suggested three kinds of progression—through space, through time, and through a plot—but the mechanics of progression can include many more features than these. For example, you can include optional sequences of challenges that grant the player extra rewards for overcoming them; balanced alternatives such as a shortcut through the environment that requires high skill versus a longer path that requires less skill; easy, medium, or difficult sequences that the player may choose among; or mutually exclusive approaches in which one player choice precludes others. The key point is that you must document the progression features that you want, and once they are in the game, it is imperative that you play-test them to be sure that they are working correctly.

Tactical Maneuvering Mechanics

Tactical maneuvering is about the challenges associated with moving units through a space, usually a space that contains other units that are both mobile and hostile. In this section we'll look briefly at the mechanics of tactical maneuvering. The companion e-book *Fundamentals of Strategy Game Design* discusses the subject in more detail.

The Goals of Tactical Maneuvering

Tactical maneuvering requires the player to travel through or to control a space, particularly to gain some kind of advantage over one or more opponents in the same space. The challenge may involve one unit (which can be an avatar) or many. There are many different possible definitions of success, which tend to influence the mechanics:

- **Eliminate enemies from the space.** This often means destroying the enemies through combat, but it can also mean pushing them out of the space and preventing them from returning.

- **Control regions of the space.** In this case *control* is often defined in terms of a zone (usually circular) around a unit that the unit is said to control, and the units may be distributed across the space to maximize their region of control. Sometimes this control isn't computed in terms of an actual area, but through control of a symbolically important point. This is usually called a *capture-the-flag* objective. Capturing all of the enemy flags is defined as victory.

- **Establish an unbroken line across a space.** In conventional ground warfare there are three particular reasons for establishing and maintaining a line: one, to ensure the supply of material (supply lines); two, to ensure that troops can retreat to a place of greater safety should it be necessary (lines of retreat); three, to prevent the ingress of hostile troops into areas that you control (the front line of battle).

- **Survive (or remain undiscovered) while traversing hostile territory.** In this case the goal is not to control space *per se*, but to elude enemies in the same space. This is the classic challenge of stealth shooters. Naturally, the inverse of this goal is to capture one or more particular enemy units.

- **Outmaneuver an opponent in a race through the space.** In racing through simple spaces, such as NASCAR's circular tracks, tactical maneuvering consists only of testing the vehicles and drivers against each other rather than against the conditions of the track, but in other kinds of racing through varying terrain, tactical maneuvering has a lot to do with making the most efficient use of the landscape itself.

In the next section, we'll look at how the nature of the space itself affects the mechanics of tactical maneuvering.

Defining Your Space

Because tactical maneuvering always involves a space, you need to understand your options for creating that space, and how your choices will affect the gameplay. In this section, we'll look at some of the major considerations for defining your space: its dimensionality, whether it is discrete or continuous, and the effect of landscape features.

DIMENSIONALITY OF THE SPACE

In Chapter 8, "Game Worlds," we saw that game worlds are typically 2D, 2.5D, or 3D, except in those few games that don't simulate a physical space at all. The vast majority of games that involve tactical maneuvering do so in 2D or 2.5D space. Three-dimensional board games such as Tri-D Chess (as seen in the original series of *Star Trek*) have never been as popular as their 2D counterparts; the complications of regular chess are quite enough to manage. *Pillars of Plato* (also known as *Score Four*) is a game of maneuver rather like a 3D version of tic-tac-toe, but the players don't have complete freedom; they must build up from ground level (see **Figure 14.7**). Fully 3D real-time maneuvering is usually confined to either aerial or space combat in tactical games. In the air, gravity plays an important role, because airborne vehicles' maneuverability is constrained by their need to maintain lift.

FIGURE 14.7
Pillars of Plato
(Photo courtesy of
Martin Stever)

If you decide to design a 3D space that allows full maneuvering without gravity (for a space combat game, for example), bear in mind that this will significantly complicate the challenge of controlling a region, because the region that a single unit controls will extend in all three dimensions and have a spherical rather than a circular boundary. Patrolling a three-dimensional spatial region is also more complicated. Aerial combat in planes concentrates on eliminating the enemy aircraft rather than holding territory, although barrage balloons were used for a brief time as a means of holding territory.

Most games of tactical maneuvering are set on the ground, however. The ground is either completely flat, like a chessboard, or varies somewhat in height; these higher regions usually provide a tactical advantage.

DISCRETE VERSUS CONTINUOUS SPACES

The oldest games of tactical maneuvering that we know use discrete spaces divided into a grid. These are convenient for games in which the nature of the maneuvering is abstract and formalized rather than realistic; chess is a perfect example. All the moves in chess are specified in terms of the grid. There are various ways to divide up a 2D space into discrete elements:

- **Rectangular grids.** The chessboard is the most famous example, of course. Rectangular grids have the advantage that they are easy to understand, to draw, and to make computations about. Their chief disadvantages are that they don't represent natural landscapes well and that diagonal movement is faster than orthogonal movement. If you allow a player to move from one square to any adjacent square in a single turn, diagonal moves go 1.414 times as far. If you disallow diagonal movement, maneuvering becomes less realistic. Chess permits a combination, depending on which piece is being moved.

- **Hex grids.** The hexagonal grid, beloved of wargamers, resolves the problems of the rectangular grid at the price of losing easy comprehensibility. All the hexes that surround a central hexagon are the same distance away, and hexagons are better at representing natural features with curved boundaries such as rivers and forests, but not so good in rectilinear spaces like cities. It also feels more natural to be able to move north, south, east, or west as on a rectangular board, and rather peculiarly constrained to be able to move east, west, northeast, northwest, southeast, and southwest on a hex grid, but not due north or south.

- **Irregular discrete spaces.** You don't have to subdivide your space into regular discrete regions such as squares or hexes. If your game of maneuvering is more about the relationships among regions rather than physical distances, they can be any shape you want. For example, the shapes of the countries in *Risk* approximate real geographical features. *Risk* doesn't model distance across a landscape; it models only a network of regions that either are, or are not, adjacent to one another. It even creates artificial adjacency where none exists on the board.

Continuous spaces, on the other hand, simulate the real world more closely—and require more CPU power to perform computations about. In practice, many video games that appear to have continuous spaces, such as *StarCraft*, actually have hidden grids to simplify the artificial intelligence required. But even some tabletop games use continuous spaces. *Regatta* is a game about yacht racing that is played directly on the table, without the use of a board.

Continuous spaces permit fine gradations of speed and angle at which units move, and as a result the units can be more similar to each other in power and ability. The stylized moves of chess on the rectangular grid tend to diversify the pieces' relative strengths and weaknesses, but the relative strengths of, say 19th-century warships are less easy to calculate. This in turn makes tactical maneuvering a more complex business.

THE EFFECTS OF LANDSCAPE FEATURES

Sea warfare is one of the classic maneuvering challenges, and is very pure because it takes place in an (almost) uniform environment—although night and weather conditions can play a role. However, many players find the maneuvering in the open sea a little too dull, so most games about sea battles, such as the multiplayer Android game *Pirates Fight,* include coastal features or islands in the sea to offer the players a more interesting place to fight.

On land, maneuvering becomes considerably more complicated. Some of the key issues to consider are

- **Altitude advantage.** In warfare, being higher up almost always confers a battle advantage, so it is worth trying to achieve—but it's also harder to get there, sometimes much harder. It can also give a player a false sense of security. You will have to determine how much of an advantage being at a higher elevation provides.

- **Protection.** Solid natural features such as hills and valleys, and man-made ones such as walls and bunkers can provide protection from both ranged and mêlée attacks, making these regions desirable to hold.

- **Concealment.** Another classic challenge of tactical maneuvering is remaining hidden from enemies. You can include the protective features mentioned above to provide concealment, as well as less sturdy elements of the landscape such as wooden buildings, hedges, woods, and even fields of corn.

- **Obstacles to movement.** Many games incorporate a model of the landscape that slows travel or halts it completely for different kinds of units. Roads naturally permit the fastest ground travel, farmland and open country the next, and woods and hills slow down travel considerably. Mountains may prevent it entirely, especially for vehicles. You can also use these obstacles to create choke points, such as mountain passes, that are traditional points of conflict when trying to control a region or prevent entry to it.

Although building these features into a *specific* landscape belongs to level design, designing the mathematical models underlying them is the job of the mechanics designer. How much protection does a brick building give from small arms fire? How much faster can a tank travel along a road than over a field? You will need to provide the answers to these questions and then play-test them extensively until the mechanics are balanced correctly.

Defining the Attributes of Units

Now that you know something about building the space through which your game's units will maneuver, we'll turn to the units themselves. This section is specifically about maneuvering, so we'll leave out such considerations as armor and weapon firepower. The companion e-book *Fundamentals of Strategy Game Design* discusses strategy game unit design in considerable detail.

The earlier section "The Goals of Tactical Maneuvering" gave you some suggestions for goals or victory conditions in a game of tactical maneuver. Which goal you choose will influence the attributes that you use to describe your avatar or units. We'll use naval warfare, in which the object is to sink or drive off enemy ships, as our baseline example because it is the least complicated.

Obviously to begin with, every unit needs a *location, coordinates* in the space, and usually a *direction* that it is facing. Before aircraft carriers, naval vessels' largest guns—and the largest *number* of guns—fired sideways, 90 degrees from their direction of movement, so the direction that a ship faced was vitally important.

In naval warfare the combatants have a clear view of the "battlefield"—the sea around them. However, their view is not unlimited, because the curvature of the Earth hides distant ships. The higher the mast of a ship, the farther the lookout can see. For each unit, therefore, you will need to define its *observation range*. Large vessels are easier to see than small ones, so you may also want to specify its *visibility*. (Obviously these considerations don't apply in games of perfect information such as chess.)

The single most critical attribute of a vessel in the open sea is its *speed*. A vessel that can run away from its enemies lives to fight another day. Large numbers of fast, light units can quickly overwhelm a heavy one with hit-and-run-away tactics.

The second most critical attribute is the *range of fire* of its longest guns. A ship with a longer range than its enemy can hit that enemy without being hit itself... until the enemy comes within its own range. The combination of superior speed *and* range is invincible, because the ship that possesses it can always stay out of harm's way while doing damage to the enemy. Not all games of maneuver include ranged firepower, but for those that do, the range has a profound effect on its tactics. If you're making a game about a unit's ability to control a certain zone around itself, this amounts to the same thing as range of fire.

Another important consideration is *maneuverability*—the rate at which a vessel can turn. Given two ships of equal speed, the one that can turn faster can run away from the one that turns slower, simply by changing direction. The slower-turning ship wastes time changing to the new course. A more maneuverable unit can also move more quickly through terrain that includes a lot of obstacles.

If you want to create an accurate simulation of real ships, you may also want to consider their *range,* which is the distance that they can travel before needing to refuel. Ultimately a vessel's ability to take part in maneuvers will be restricted by its need to travel back to port for more fuel. The farther out it goes, the farther it must travel to get back. In military parlance, when a vessel has exactly enough fuel to return directly to base, it is said to be at *bingo* fuel (this is used more often of aircraft than of ships). Such a ship is vulnerable because it cannot afford to maneuver while returning home.

Summary on Tactical Maneuvering

Maneuver is chiefly about movement and control in open or semi-open spaces. (Movement through enclosed spaces is covered in the "Progression Mechanics" section, above.) You can combine the mechanics of tactical maneuvering with other kinds of mechanics: physics, economics, or social interaction to produce all sorts of gameplay. But you need not go so far unless you want to. *Go* is a classic game of pure tactical maneuver that still requires many years of play and study to master.

Social Interaction Mechanics

Any multiplayer game naturally involves social interactions among the players, especially if they're in the same room. We can facilitate or encourage more interactions by building them into the game. With online games, in which players can't (ordinarily) see or hear each other, it becomes more important to include these mechanisms.

This is an introductory textbook, and there isn't room to examine these mechanics in detail. Instead, we've simply provided **Table 14.1**, which includes the general kinds of social mechanics you may want to design into your game. The table is subdivided into different categories of social interaction in the context of gameplay (cooperation, competition, and so on), as well as other kinds of social interactions that aren't necessarily related to gameplay, such as establishing social hierarchies.

TABLE 14.1 A Variety of Social Mechanics

COOPERATION	
MECHANIC	COMMENTS
Advising and mentoring	Can be formal or informal (through chat)
Giving	Economic function
Loaning	Economic function
Supporting or assisting	Can take many forms in different genres
Trade (obligatory reciprocity)	Economic function
Common labor for a purpose	Can take many forms
Tragedy of the commons	Occurs when people overuse a limited resource

continues on next page

TABLE 14.1 A Variety of Social Mechanics *continued*

CREATION	
MECHANIC	COMMENTS
Crowdsourcing	Good technique for serious games
User-generated content (UGC)	Many kinds of creative play
Public galleries of UGC	People love to show off what they made

COMPETITION	
MECHANIC	COMMENTS
Comparing scores	The most common winning/losing mechanic
Leader boards	Let people show off individual achievements
Tournament play	Competitive play for large numbers
Competing for renewable resources	Economic function
Competing for limited resources	Economic function
Racing	Physics function
Tug of war	Taking opponents' resources (economic)
Handicapping	Permits people of different skill to play together
Bidding and auctions	Economic function, many varieties
Deception or bluffing	Lets players misrepresent their situation
Pay-to-win	Real-world money buys in-game advantages

TEAM PLAY	
MECHANIC	COMMENTS
Group identity definition	Team names, logos, and so on
Specialized roles	Different positions in sports
Planning strategy and tactics	Coaching function, usually informal
Assembling short-term teams	Temporary alliances
Assembling long-term teams	Guilds or other types of player groups
Recruiting players	Coaching function, usually informal
Coordinating activity in real time	Coaching function, sometimes formalized
Keeping secret information	Permits teams to surprise others

AMBIGUOUS SITUATIONS	
Mechanic	Comments
Trust	Use in games of shifting alliances
Betrayal	Use in games of shifting alliances
Spying or sabotage	One player secretly undermines teammates
Vigilantism	Some people appoint themselves to be police

SOCIAL HIERARCHIES	
Mechanic	Comments
Referees or game masters	Give special players power or judgment
Choosing leaders	Can be formalized through elections
Exclusivity	Can be formalized through membership rules
Reputation and fame systems	Sometimes an economic function
Taunting	Sometimes a game feature but often informal
Griefing newcomers or others	Discussed in Chapter 17, "Design Issues for Online Gaming"

PURE SOCIALIZING	
Mechanic	Comments
Chatting	Discussed at length in Chapter 17
Performing for others	Depends heavily on available UI features
Rituals and ceremonies	A special case of performance
Role-playing in character	Improvisational drama, usually via chat
Planning social events	May be formalized via a calendar, e-mail
Personal identity definition	Discussed at length in Chapter 10
Complimenting	Can be formalized via graphical features

Many of the mechanics in the table interact with the other types of mechanics, especially economics. A social mechanic may be formalized as a part of the game with its own UI feature, or it may be purely informal and may be performed through chat or by some other means. For example, some online games offer players the chance to compliment each other by some means visible to everyone nearby, such as causing a temporary cascade of flowers to fall on them. This feature costs either game-world or real-world money to use, but it is more noticeable than simply giving a compliment in chat. The "Like" feature in Facebook has the same effect, although it doesn't cost anything.

Most of these mechanics are taken directly, or adapted, from Raph Koster's very thorough talk "Social Mechanics for Social Games" (Koster, 2011).

Table 14.1 is not by any means exhaustive. It's simply a list to get you started. How socially oriented you want your game to be, and what sort of a society it should be, is up to you—though experience has shown that it is very difficult to enforce a particular social structure or ethos.

When creating social interaction mechanics, you must take particular care that players cannot abuse or exploit vulnerable populations such as children. Chapter 17 addresses some of these issues in the section "Social Problems."

Core Mechanics and Gameplay

Figure 14.1 shows that, during play, the core mechanics present challenges to the player and accept actions from the player, both mediated by the user interface. So far, our discussion has concentrated on the core mechanics as a description of a system, without addressing the role of the player. The core mechanics manage the gameplay of the game, implementing all player actions and many challenges. This section discusses how that works.

NOTE Passive challenges do not require mechanics to operate, though level designers may want to establish a condition to detect when the challenge has been surmounted.

Challenges and the Core Mechanics

The core mechanics implement the mechanisms by which most challenges operate, and they perform tests to see whether a challenge has been surmounted. The challenges that the core mechanics present may appear at any level of the challenge hierarchy, from atomic challenges to the victory condition for the entire game. Remember that the level design actually specifies the type and placement of individual challenges for each level, but the core mechanics implement challenges, if necessary, when the player encounters them.

PASSIVE CHALLENGES

Suppose the level designers want to set up a purely static obstacle as a challenge, such as a wall that the avatar must climb over in an action game. You would not need to create an entity to represent the wall or a mechanic to present the challenge itself; the wall would simply be an unchanging feature of the landscape. The mechanics play a role in implementing the action the player takes to meet the challenge (climbing) but play no role in presenting the challenge itself. This type of challenge is called a *passive challenge.*

If the level designers need to detect that a player has conquered a passive challenge (in order to give a reward, perhaps), they design a special event that occurs when the avatar arrives on the other side of the wall—that is, when the avatar's location attributes meet a condition that the level designers establish. Otherwise, the player's presence on the other side implies success, which doesn't require any special mechanics.

ACTIVE CHALLENGES

Suppose that the level designers want to set up a more complex challenge for the player, such as a puzzle that the player manipulates to unlock a door. Your design for the core mechanics must supply the level designers with the necessary entities and mechanics to define the puzzle, allow the player to interact with it, display the consequences of her actions, and detect when the puzzle has reached its solution state. This is an *active challenge.*

NOTE Active challenges require mechanics that implement their activity.

An enemy character that the player must defeat in combat represents another active challenge. The core mechanics define the characteristics and the AI of the enemy character. The level designers place that character at a location in the landscape by setting his location attributes and perhaps some other attributes as well, such as health and ammunition. In effect, your design creates the tools and parts that the level designers use to build levels, create puzzles, position enemies, and so on. In a long game, the level designers probably reuse the same tools several times to create variants of the same challenge in different parts of the game. (This is one of the reasons why the same characters seem to appear over and over in a game: The level designers reuse the basic mechanics.)

Actions and the Core Mechanics

The challenges in a game vary from level to level in type, frequency, sequence, and other respects, but normally the actions available to the player do not change from level to level except that, in some games, more actions become available as the player progresses through the game. Consequently, the level designers play a smaller role in determining what actions are available than they do in choosing challenges for a level, though they can choose challenges that tend to require the use of some actions more than others. (Sometimes level designers also specify that familiar actions should *not* be available. See "Make Atypical Levels Optional" in Chapter 16.)

PLAYER ACTIONS TRIGGER MECHANICS

When you design the core mechanics, you must specify a mechanic that implements each action in each gameplay mode, which will either initiate an event or start or stop a process. When the user interface detects data arriving from an input device, UI routines determine what action the player desires by checking the assignment of actions to buttons (or similar control devices) established by the gameplay mode's interaction model. The UI then triggers whatever mechanic you specified for that action.

Let's look at a simple example from a first-person game. When a player presses a button assigned to the *crouch* action, the UI triggers a *crouch* mechanic that implements the action. You must define this mechanic to do two things. First, it changes a symbolic *posture* attribute of the avatar from the *walking upright* state to the *crouching* state. (This attribute may affect other mechanics—it could influence how big a target the crouching figure presents—but the *crouch* mechanic does not implement those effects itself.) Next, because all actions should be accompanied by feedback, your *crouch* mechanic lowers the value of a numeric attribute of the avatar that determines how far the avatar's head is above the ground. The graphics engine detects this and shows the first-person view from a crouching, rather than an upright, perspective.

ACTIONS ACCOMPANIED BY DATA

TIP Implement actions in the core mechanics by creating mechanics that the UI can trigger and entities that the UI can supply with data from the input devices.

More complicated actions may involve manipulation or storage of data that arrives from the UI. In such cases, you must create both an event mechanic that implements the action and an entity that stores the data. The UI sets the value of the entity for the mechanic to interpret.

Suppose that in our first-person game, the player uses a mouse to control which direction the avatar faces, and he moves the mouse to the right. This input translates into an action, causing the avatar to turn to the right. But a mouse is an analog device, not a binary one like a controller button, so in addition to the information that the mouse moved, the UI also sends data about how far it moved. This event requires a mechanic that must interpret the data and make the appropriate changes to the avatar's direction-facing attribute.

Core Mechanics Design

Entia non sunt multiplicanda praeter necessitatem. (Do not create more entities than necessary.)

—Attributed to William of Occam

Designing the core mechanics consists of identifying the key entities and mechanics in the game and writing specifications to document the nature of the entities and the functioning of the mechanics. This is the very heart of the game designer's job, and the more complex the game, the longer it takes—sometimes weeks or months. Because you can make so many kinds of games, this book can describe the process only in general terms. Use your knowledge of existing games and of your chosen genre to fill in the details.

Reading this chapter alone gives you the tools to document your core mechanics, but it doesn't contain the information necessary to create a balanced game. Don't start designing your mechanics until you have also read Chapter 15, "Game Balancing."

Goals of Core Mechanics Design

Before looking into the question of how to go about designing the core mechanics, remember what you are actually trying to achieve with your design. Never forget that your ultimate goal is to create entertainment for the player—that's the point of the quote from Molière at the beginning of the chapter. But in addition to this overarching objective, certain principles help you design an enjoyable game efficiently.

STRIVE FOR SIMPLICITY AND ELEGANCE

The most elegant games operate with the smallest number of rules. Some of the greatest games are those whose mechanics are extremely simple yet still manage to offer interesting variety. As the quote from William of Occam suggests, try to avoid making your mechanics too complex. Simple games are easier for players to learn, and that gives simple games a broader appeal than complicated ones.

You can maintain players' interest with a variety of content that explains a small number of mechanics in a large number of ways. As mentioned in the sidebar "The Rules and Core Mechanics of *Monopoly*," the general rules of *Monopoly* are simple, but the Chance and Community Chest cards create additional interest. The majority of these cards concern the transfer of money to or from the player who draws the card—a simple mechanic—but each card gives a different explanation for why the money is being transferred (such as "Income tax refund, collect $20"). The explanations are purely cosmetic, but they add variety and entertainment value. You can build similar features into your own game while still keeping the rules simple.

LOOK FOR PATTERNS, THEN GENERALIZE

Learn to recognize patterns in your ideas for your game and to convert them into generalized systems rather than trying to document dozens of individual cases. Here's an example. Suppose you decide that swamp leeches really belong in water and that a swamp leech should lose 10 points of health for every minute that it's out of the water. Later, you decide that a salamander (a mythical fire-loving creature) should lose five points of health for every minute that it's out of the fire. A pattern emerges: Certain creatures are dependent upon their native environment, and they lose health at a specified rate when they leave it. Instead of describing this mechanic over and over for each creature, explain the general case only once, for all environment-dependent creatures. Note that each creature in the game will need two attributes to support this mechanic: a symbolic attribute indicating what the creature's native environment is (water, fire, and so on, and be sure to include a special value to use if the creature is not dependent on any environment), and a numeric attribute stating the rate at which the creature loses health when out of its environment (the value should be zero if the creature is not environment-dependent). Then, as you design each creature in your game, you can decide what values these attributes should have without having to document the whole mechanism again.

By designing general patterns rather than individual cases, you can more easily understand how your game will really work, and you will also make it easier for the programmers to program it. The programmers will write general-case code that applies most of the time, rather than having to write separate subroutines for each creature. You can still create a few special cases for variety or when circumstances require it. In *Monopoly,* the rules for collecting rent on colored properties (the ones named after streets) are the general case, while the railroads and utilities are special cases that create additional interest. But try to avoid creating large numbers of special cases.

DON'T TRY TO GET EVERYTHING PERFECT ON PAPER

Unless you're designing a trivially simple game, you won't get everything perfectly right in your design documents, because you won't be able to compute the effects of all your mechanics in your head. Designing core mechanics (and just about everything else in a video game, too) requires iterative refinement. Create a first draft of your mechanics and then build a prototype that implements them, either in a paper prototype that you can play on a tabletop, in a spreadsheet, or in software. If your mechanics are primarily economic, you can also build a Machinations diagram. Test and adjust your mechanics using the prototype. If you try to get everything exactly right on paper, you won't ever get the project finished. Although this may sound odd, it is more important to be clear in your documentation than it is to be accurate. You will find it much easier to correct a mechanic that doesn't work quite the way you expected by testing a prototype than it is to try to fix it late in the development process.

FIND THE RIGHT LEVEL OF DETAIL

You can design core mechanics at any level of detail, but there are tradeoffs. If you document the core mechanics minutely, with no detail left unaddressed, the programmers can turn your mechanics directly into code very quickly. That seems like a good idea in principle, but in practice you will almost certainly be swamped with work. Designers who try to document every single thing about the core mechanics delay their projects—or cause them to be canceled.

The problem at the opposite end of the spectrum, leaving too much unclear, is almost as bad. Either the programmers will have to come and ask you for further details, which slows them down, or they will make their best guess for themselves. If you have clearly communicated your vision to them, and you see eye to eye about how the game should work in principle, then their guesses may be good ones. But in practice, the programmers will often make assumptions other than what you intended, and you'll notice the mistake in the tuning phase. It can be time consuming to go back and correct bugs introduced by ambiguous design decisions.

To find a happy medium, use traditional gaming conventions where appropriate to avoid overloading yourself. If your game features some typical scenarios and you are confident that the programmers will know what you mean, you can afford to use general language. You don't have to write, "When a car's *number of laps* attribute goes over 500, set the *eligible to win* flag to TRUE for that car. Continuously check all cars to see if the *location* attributes of the cars that are eligible to win show that they are on or beyond the finish line. Set the *winner* entity with the number of the first car whose *location* attribute meets that condition." It's okay just to say, "The first car that has completed all 500 laps and crosses the finish line is the winner," because this is a perfectly familiar situation.

The less familiar the mechanisms that you document, the more specific you need to be, especially if any of them run counter to convention. In the dart game *301*, the player *starts* with a score and *reduces* that score by the amount that he hits on the dartboard. The object of the game is to be the first to achieve a score of exactly zero. Because this runs counter to convention, it's the sort of thing you have to explain more precisely. Similarly, the mechanic that describes the behavior of female dragons in the earlier sidebar "Analyzing a Mechanic" requires more detail because female dragons are entirely imaginary; nobody can count on his existing experience with dragons to know how they should behave.

If you know how to program even a little bit, you can write *pseudo-code* to document processes that you need to explain extremely carefully. Pseudo-code includes the *if* and *while* statements that indicate conditional or repeated operations but without exact variable names or the other syntactic features of a real programming language. Pseudo-code can be handy in circumstances that call for precise explanations, which is why potential designers would benefit by taking at least one class in programming. It doesn't much matter what language you study, as long as it includes the concepts of conditional and repeated execution.

Revisit Your Earlier Design Work

To begin designing the core mechanics, go back to your earlier design work and reread it to identify entities and mechanics. Make a list of the nouns and verbs that you encounter. Whenever you come across a noun in your design documents, that noun will probably be implemented in the core mechanics as an entity, a resource, or both. Whenever you see a verb, that action will probably be implemented as a mechanic. Also watch for sentences that include the words *if, when,* and *whenever*. These designate conditions that will become part of the mechanics.

TIP It's a good idea to get feedback from your programmers early in the core mechanics design process—they may be able to spot ambiguities that you're missing or details that you have forgotten to write down.

Look particularly closely at the following items:

- **Your answers to the question, "What is the player going to do?"** The answers to this question give the player's role and some information about the challenges she will face and the actions she will perform. They will include some of the most critical nouns and verbs of all. Even if the answer is simply "fly an airplane," it contains the key verb for the whole game, *fly*, and the key noun, *airplane*.

- **Your flowboard of the game's structure.** Each gameplay mode and shell menu represents a separate state of the mechanics, so the mechanics will require a symbolic entity to keep track of the current gameplay mode during play.

- **Your list of gameplay modes and your plans for them.** Be sure to pay special attention to the challenges and actions you plan to offer the player in each mode and any UI feedback and control mechanisms you have specified.

- **The general outline of the story you want to tell**, if any. If it's a branching or foldback story, look at the structure that you made for it. Take note of the circumstances that cause it to branch. You will convert these into conditions.

- **The names of any characters** you planned for your story. Unless these characters appear only in narrative events, they will certainly be entities in the core mechanics.

- **Your general plans for each level in the game.** Unless the level designers are already at work, you won't have specific details, but you will know what kinds of things you wanted to include in each level.

- **The progression of the levels** that you want to provide, if the levels progress in a sequence. Note whether any information carries over from level to level; you will create entities to store the data.

- **Any victory or loss conditions** that you expect to use (or that you anticipate the level designers will want to establish).

- **Any non-gameplay actions** that you may wish to include, such as moving the virtual camera, pausing or saving the game, and other forms of creative play.

Certain nouns and verbs in this material may not apply to the core mechanics. If a noun describes a passive landscape feature that acts as a challenge or something purely cosmetic, you can cross it off your list. If a verb describes an activity unrelated to gameplay, such as setting the volume level of the sound effects, you can cross that off, too.

List Your Entities and Resources

Once you have your list of nouns, decide whether each represents a resource, an independent entity, an attribute of another entity—or perhaps none of the above, in which case, you can cross those off the list. Now you have a list of resources and entities. For each item on your list, consider these questions:

▪ Does the noun describe a resource—some item or substance that changes in a general way throughout the game? Or does it describe an entity, a particular value, or quantity?

▪ If the noun describes an entity, is the entity simple or compound? If simple, is it symbolic or numeric? If symbolic, what states can it take? If numeric, what is the range of numbers? What will its initial symbolic or numeric value be? These initial data form a critical part of the core mechanics that you will tune throughout the development process. Write them down in your document or in a spreadsheet.

▪ If the noun describes a compound entity, what attributes describe it? (They might be elsewhere on the list, or you might have to invent some new ones.) Add any new attributes to your definition of the compound entity and go back to the previous question to determine their qualities.

Unless a game offers only one gameplay mode and no shell menus (which would be extremely rare), it will undoubtedly require an entity to record which gameplay mode or shell menu the game occupies at any given time.

This process will give you an initial list of all the resources and entities your game features. It won't be a complete list; undoubtedly you will add more as work goes on. If your early design stated generalities but not specifics, add the details now. Suppose you wrote, "Level 5 will consist mostly of formal logic puzzles." At this point, you must define the entities that the level designers will require to build the formal logic puzzles. Will the player drag tiles, flip switches, and click on colored marbles? Then add tiles, switches, and marbles to your list of entities. Now you've got some attributes to think about: The tiles have positions, the switches have states, and the marbles have colors. Write it all down.

Add the Mechanics

With your list of entities and list of verbs, you're ready to start defining the mechanics. Again reread your earlier design work. If any sentence includes or implies the word *somehow,* now is the time to define exactly how. "The player gets money" or "gets money somehow" must turn into a precise specification of when the player's money entity increases and by what amount.

As you read, remember that mechanics consist of *relationships, events, processes,* and *conditions.*

THINK ABOUT YOUR RESOURCES

Start with any resources that you identified in the previous step and think about how they flow through the game. What sources bring them into the game? What drains remove them? Can they be traded or converted automatically into another resource? Every source, every drain, and every conversion requires mechanics that determine how a conversion operates, when, and at what rate. Also ask yourself what happens when the resource runs out. If nothing much changes, you may not need the resource. Because a resource is a general concept rather than a specific quantity like an entity, you may be able to determine a lot about a resource's mechanics just by thinking through the resource flow in the economy.

Remember that games that don't deal in numeric quantities don't have resources. Such games contain only symbolic entities.

STUDY YOUR ENTITIES

Once you have a good grasp of your resources' sources, drains, and conversions, move on to your entities. Go down your list of entities and ask the following questions about each one:

▨ Does this entity store an amount of a resource, and if so, have I already documented how it works in the previous step?

▨ What events, processes, and relationships affect the entity? What conditions apply to these events, processes, and relationships?

▨ What events, processes, and relationships does the entity contribute to? What conditions apply to them?

▨ What can the entity do by itself, if anything? Any entity that can do something by itself—whether the entity is as simple as a detector or as complicated as an NPC—requires mechanics to define what it does and how.

▨ What can the player do to the entity, if anything? If the player can manipulate the entity, he requires an action to do so, and actions require mechanics.

▨ Is this a symbolic entity? If so, it requires mechanics to control how the entity gets into each of its possible states.

Many of the verbs in your list of verbs will be associated with particular entities, so as you examine an entity, check to see which verbs apply to it and what mechanics they imply.

ANALYZE CHALLENGES AND ACTIONS

Go over the list of challenges and actions that you intend to offer in each gameplay mode. All the active challenges and each action must have an associated mechanic and possibly some associated data. (If it requires data, you should already have an entity defined for it.) How does the action affect the world? How does the challenge affect the avatar or the other entities under the player's control? Use the answers to these questions to document your mechanics.

LOOK FOR GLOBAL MECHANICS

Global mechanics operate all the time, regardless of what gameplay mode or level the game may be in. Global mechanics include those that implement actions such as pausing the game or, if the player can win or lose in more than one gameplay mode or level, detecting the victory or loss conditions. (In many games, the level designers specify a different victory condition for each level, but the loss conditions—such as running out of money or health—remain the same in every level.) Go through your list of verbs and see how many of them describe global mechanics, and then define how each works.

> ### DESIGN RULE Every Mechanic Must Be Tested
>
> As you design the core mechanics of your game, don't forget that you will have to test each of them to make sure they work the way that you intend. If you can't think of a way to test a mechanic that you have included in the game, there's a good chance that it isn't needed at all. If it *is* needed, its operation ought to be observable during play.

Random Numbers and the Bell-Shaped Curve

So many games use random numbers that, although you may not know any programming, you should understand how to use random numbers in a computer game.

When a computer generates random numbers, by convention it always does so as a real number value greater than or equal to 0 but less than 1. In statistical calculations, probabilities are always expressed as a fractional value between 0 and 1, so an event with a probability of 0.1 has 1 chance in 10, or a 10 percent chance, of occurring. To see if an event with a given probability occurs or not, the computer generates a random number, then checks to see if the random number is less than the event's probability. If so, the event happens. The random number is always less than 1, so if an event's probability is exactly 1, the event always happens. The random number is never less than 0, so if an event's probability is 0, it never happens.

For example, suppose we want to use a random number when computing whether a weapon hits the point at which it's aimed. A weapon with an accuracy rating of 0.8 hits its mark 80 percent of the time. To see whether a particular shot hits, generate a random number and compare the number to the weapon's accuracy rating. If the random number is less than the rating, the weapon hits.

Pseudo-Random Numbers

NOTE The random-number generation functions provided in the standard mathematical libraries of some programming languages do not allow the programmer to set the seed. If this is the case, the programmers should look for another library that does, or implement their own. Search the Internet for suitable examples.

Truly random numbers have to be generated by a physical process (like rolling dice), and special hardware exists that can do this using obscure electrical phenomena to supply the randomness. But for gaming purposes it's more convenient to use what are called *pseudo-random numbers* that are generated by an algorithm based on a mathematical formula. Random-number generation algorithms take an input value, called a *seed,* that determines the sequence of random numbers the algorithm produces. If the seed is identical each time the game is played, the sequence of random numbers that the algorithm generates is identical each time, too. In other words, it's as if each time you play a board game, you get the exact same sequence of die rolls that you got the last time you played. Each roll may be different from the previous roll, but the *sequence* of rolls is identical each time you play. This is why the numbers are called *pseudo-random.*

This feature is extremely useful when you're tuning the game's mechanics. When you make adjustments to the mechanics, it is difficult to determine what the effect of your change is if the operation of chance keeps changing the game. By using the same seed each time you play, you always get the same random numbers, so the effects of chance don't change from one playing to the next. The mechanics become *deterministic* and predictable. This quality is also essential for bug-fixing. If a bug happens by chance, it might not happen the next time someone plays the game, so the programmer won't be able to find it and fix it. If the game uses pseudo-random numbers, the bug should be easier to reproduce.

Naturally, in the final version of the game that the customer buys, you won't want the effects of chance to be the same on each play through. Just before the game is ready to ship, the programmers will change the code to take the seed from some random source, such as the system clock, so the player will get a different experience each time he plays.

Monte Carlo Simulation

If you have a simple deterministic mechanic that simulates some real-world effect, then it doesn't take long to see if it works correctly. For example, the gears in a car's drive train govern the relationship between the speed of a car's engine and the speed of the car's wheels. It's a fixed mathematical relationship and easy to compute. On the other hand, if you design a complicated mechanic with all sorts of factors, it may be difficult to predict how it will behave. You don't have time to test all possible outcomes to make sure they all make sense. Instead, you can do something called *Monte Carlo simulation.*

In Monte Carlo simulation, you make a large number of test runs of your system using random inputs and record the results in a file. Then you can examine the file and make sure that the outcomes reflect the behavior that you expect. Here's an example: Many sports games let the player manage a team throughout a whole season and play each match that the real team would play. The game simulates all the other matches in the league season (the ones not involving the player's team) automatically. If you don't want the machine to play each simulated match through moment by moment, which the player probably won't want to wait for, you will need to design a mechanic that fakes it with an algorithm that generates the win-loss results for all the other matches without really playing them. Your mechanic will probably be based on the attributes (such as the performance characteristics) of the athletes on the team. (The companion e-book *Fundamentals of Sports Game Design* discusses this issue in more detail.) But how can you be sure that your mechanic produces realistic results? You can try it by hand a few times, but that's not enough to constitute a serious test.

NOTE This method of simulating a process with a variety of random inputs is named after the famous casino at Monte Carlo. Gambling games all use random values (shuffled cards, thrown dice, and so on), but by repeated simulation, a casino can compute the probable profitability of a particular game.

To perform a Monte Carlo simulation, randomly generate two teams of athletes, with a variety of random attribute settings for each athlete, and then apply your mechanic to them and record which team wins. Do this repeatedly, 1000 times or so. Afterward, analyze the data from the simulations to see if any anomalies occurred. Did a weak team ever beat a strong team? Did it happen often, or was it a fluke? If it was a fluke, happening once in 1000 times, that's OK—if sports matches were completely predictable they'd be boring. But if it happened often, you know your mechanic has a problem. If you know statistical methods, you can compute the correlation between the inputs (relative team strength) and the outputs (who won) and make sure that there's a positive correlation between strength and victory.

People use Monte Carlo simulation for all sorts of things: to predict profits when people buy products at different price points, to predict the failure rate of new products, and so on. Microsoft Excel and other spreadsheet programs contain built-in tools for performing Monte Carlo simulations. If you can define your mechanic in a spreadsheet, you can use these tools easily.

Uniform Distribution

When a computer generates a pseudo-random number, ordinarily it does so with a *uniform distribution.* That means the chance of getting any one number equals the chance of getting any other number. It's like rolling a single die: There's an equal chance that a die will land on any one of its faces. That is exactly the behavior you will want whenever you ask the computer to choose among a certain number of equally probable options. For example, if you specify that four possible answers in a multiple-choice quiz game should be presented to the player in a random order, you'll want the possibilities to be mixed up so that each answer has an equal chance of being presented first, second, third, or fourth.

You can create a uniformly distributed die roll value with the following formula (and by discarding any digits after the decimal point in the result):

```
Die Roll = (Random number × Number of faces on the die) + 1
```

Nonuniform Distribution

In other circumstances, you may not want the random values to be evenly distributed but may instead want some values to occur frequently and others to occur only rarely. Suppose you're designing a game about Olympic archery. The player will compete against an artificial opponent, and you want to use a random number to decide where the artificial opponent's arrow lands. At the Olympics, the chances that an archer will hit the bull's-eye are pretty high. The chances that she'll miss the target entirely are extremely low. In specifying where the arrow lands, you won't want it to be distributed uniformly across the target, you'll want it to have a better chance of landing in the middle than anywhere else.

One of the simplest ways to achieve this result is to generate more than one uniformly distributed random number (that is, roll several dice) and add the resulting numbers together to give you a value. This does not yield a uniform distribution of values; the values tend to cluster around a central point, with few values at the extremes. For example, if you roll two six-sided dice and add them together, there are six possible ways to roll a 7, but only one possible way to roll a 2 or a 12.

The rules of *Dungeons & Dragons* specify that certain types of random numbers must be generated by rolling *three* six-sided dice and adding them together. With three dice, the chances are even higher that the result will be somewhere in the middle. There are 216 possible combinations, producing 12 possible values from 3 (1 + 1 + 1) to 18 (6 + 6 + 6). There are 27 ways to throw a 10 or an 11, but again, only one way to throw a 3 or an 18. In other words, you're 27 times as likely to roll a 10 as you are an 18.

The Bell-Shaped Curve

When you add dice together like this, the probability of each possible result forms a bell-shaped curve, a phenomenon familiar to mathematicians. **Figure 14.8** shows a graph of all the possible results when rolling three six-sided dice and adding the resulting numbers.

It's important that you realize what this means for your game. If you use this additive dice mechanism and you specify that a player must roll an 18 to succeed at a task, he has only one chance in 216 of actually rolling it. That's less than one-half of 1 percent. In other words, it will almost never happen. This system is *not the same* as rolling one die with 16 faces numbered from 3 to 18. With one such die, the chance of rolling an 18 is identical to the chance of rolling any other face, 1 in 16, or 6.25 percent. That's far more than one chance in 216.

NOTE You may also have seen this phenomenon called a *Gaussian curve.* However, a true Gaussian curve is a precise shape that adding dice together only approximates, so this edition avoids the use of that term.

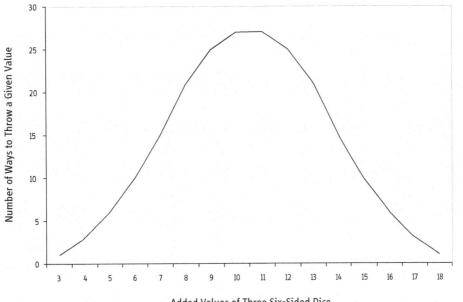

FIGURE 14.8
The bell-shaped curve representing the probability of throwing each possible value, from 3 to 18, produced by adding the results from three six-sided dice.

These curves describe many phenomena in the universe, from the pattern of water droplets falling from a central point to the intelligence levels of animals (and humans). To put it succinctly, most things lie somewhere in the middle of the curve; rare things lie in the extremes. When that's the sort of effect you want in your game design, use a sum of uniform distributions.

Summary

Now you have a clear understanding of what core mechanics are and what they do in games. Mechanics consist of algorithms and data that govern the way the game is played, and you have learned how to document them in the form of resources, simple and compound entities, and mechanics composed of events, processes, and conditions. We also examined the idea of an internal economy—a system whereby resources flow from place to place or from owner to owner, all governed by mechanics.

Be sure that you read Chapter 15 before you start designing your core mechanics.

Design Practice EXERCISES

1. Devise and document the core mechanics for a traditional analog alarm clock. The alarm clock possesses the following indicators: an hour hand, a minute hand, a hand indicating the time at which the alarm should go off, and a buzzer. It also has the following input devices: a knob to set the time, a knob to set the time at which the alarm will go off, and a two-state switch that arms the alarm when the switch is in one position and cancels it in the other. (Assume that it is an electric clock and does not need to be wound.) Explain what entities are needed inside the clock, what processes operate within it, and what conditions and mechanics govern the functioning of the alarm. (Explain the movement of the hands in terms of the passage of time not the workings of the clock.)

2. Research the history and rules of *Tetris,* and then perform the following exercises:

    a. Devise an entity that contains enough attributes to describe the tetromino (a *Tetris* block) that is currently under the player's control. Name each attribute in the entity; state whether it is symbolic or numeric; and if symbolic, list its possible values. Your entity should include one cosmetic attribute.

    b. Document the effect of each of the player actions allowed in *Tetris* on the attributes of the currently falling tetromino. Bear in mind that some actions have different effects depending on which tetromino is currently falling. Where this is the case, be sure to document the effects of the action on each different type of tetromino.

    c. Document one of the scoring systems for *Tetris* (there are several; you may choose one), indicating what condition of the play field causes the *score* numeric entity to change and by how much. Your mechanic for changing the score should include as a factor the current *game level* (another numeric entity). Also document what makes the current game-level entity change.

3. Using a real-time strategy game or construction and management simulation of your choice (or one that your instructor assigns), write a short paper describing its resources, sources, drains, converters, production mechanisms that are *not* sources (if any), and traders (if any). Note whether the game has any feedback loops or mutual dependencies; if so, indicate whether any mechanism exists to break a possible deadlock.

4. Define a mechanic for a trap that harms a character when it detects the character's presence and then must wait for a period before it can detect another character. Document the condition that triggers the trap (the nature of the sensing mechanism), the character attribute(s) that change when the trap is triggered, and the length of the reset wait period. Incorporate one or more nonuniform random numbers to determine the amount of damage done and explain how they are computed. Indicate what states the trap may be in and what causes it to change from state to

state. Include a vulnerability in the sensing mechanism that could either (a) set off the trap without harming character or (b) allow a character to move within range of the trap's sensor mechanism without setting it off. (For example, a pressure-sensor in the floor would not go off if the character weighed less than a certain amount.) Propose a means by which a clever player could exploit this vulnerability to avoid the trap.

Design Practice QUESTIONS

1. Which of the five major types of mechanics will your game use, if any? Will your game use more than one of them? If it doesn't use any of them, what will the mechanics be like instead?

2. What entities and resources will be in the game? Which resources are made up of individual entities (such as a resource of airplanes consisting of individual planes that the computer can track separately) and which are described by mass nouns (such as water, which cannot be separated into discrete objects)?

3. What unique entities will be in the game?

4. Which entities will actually include other entities as part of their definition? (Remember that an avatar may have an inventory, and an inventory contains objects.)

5. What attributes describe each of the entities that you have identified? Which attributes are numeric and which are symbolic?

6. Which entities and resources will be tangible, and which will be intangible? Will any of them change from one state to another, like the resources in *Age of Empires?*

7. What mechanics govern the relationships among the entities? Remember that any symbolic entity requires mechanics that determine how it can get into each of its possible states and how other entities interact with each possible state. Which entities have their own mechanics connected only with themselves?

8. Are there any global mechanics in the game? What mechanic governs the way the game changes from mode to mode?

9. For each entity and resource, does it come into the game world at a source, or does it start off in a game world that does not provide a source for additional entities or resources? If it does come in at a source, what mechanics control the production rate of the source?

10. For each entity and resource, does it go out of the game world at a drain, or does it all remain in the game world and never leave? If it does go out at a drain, what conditions cause it to drain?

11. What conversion processes exist in your world? What trader processes exist? Do any feedback loops or mutual dependencies exist? What means have you provided to break or prevent deadlocks?

12. Can your game get into a state of equilibrium? Static or dynamic? Does it include any form of decay or entropy that prevents states of equilibrium from forming?

13. How do mechanics create active challenges? Do you need to establish any mechanics to detect if a challenge has been surmounted?

14. How do mechanics implement actions? For each action that may arrive from the user interface, how do the core mechanics react?

15. For autonomous entities such as non-player characters, what mechanics control their behavior? What mechanics define their AI?

CHAPTER 15

Game Balancing

To be enjoyable, a game must be balanced well—it must be neither too easy nor too hard, and it must feel fair, both to players competing against each other and to the individual player on his own. In this chapter, you'll learn what qualities a well-balanced game has, and how to balance your own. We'll begin by examining dominant strategies and how to avoid them. We'll look at ways to set up and balance both transitive and intransitive relationships among player choices and how to make them simultaneously interesting and well balanced. We'll also look at ways to incorporate chance into games in such a way that the game still rewards the better player.

The bulk of the chapter examines two major issues of balance: fairness and difficulty. The meaning of *fairness* differs between player-versus-player and player-versus-environment games, and we'll address each separately. The question of difficulty applies primarily to player-versus-environment games, and this chapter will expand upon ideas in Chapter 13, "Gameplay," explaining the various factors that affect the player's perception of difficulty and how to manage those factors.

Next we'll look at the role of positive feedback in games: how to use it and how to control it. Finally, we'll briefly investigate the problems of stagnation, trivialities, and how to design your game to make the tuning stage of the process easier.

What Is a Balanced Game?

So divinely is the world organized that every one of us, in our place and time, is in balance with everything else.

—Johann Wolfgang von Goethe

As with so many other game design concepts, the conventional notion of *balance* defies formalization. In the most general sense, a balanced game is fair to the player (or players), is neither too easy nor too hard, and makes the skill of the player the most important factor in determining her success. In practice, several different game features combine to produce these qualities, and game balancing refers to a collection of design and tuning processes that create those qualities in a game under development.

The concept of balance differs considerably depending upon whether we speak of games in which a player plays against one or more opponents (either human players or artificial opponents that are implemented by software), or of games in which a player faces challenges posed by the game world without an opponent. The first type of game, in which the player faces one or more opponents (even artificial ones), is called a *player-versus-player (PvP)* game. The second type is a *player-versus-environment (PvE)* game. As you look at the techniques for balancing a game, note how they differ between PvP and PvE games.

A well-balanced game of either type, PvP or PvE, possesses the following characteristics:

▪ **The game provides meaningful choices.** If the game allows the player to choose from several possible strategies for approaching the game's challenges, no strategy should be so much more effective than the others that the player sees no point in ever using a different one. If such a *dominant strategy* exists, it indicates a poorly balanced game. The section "Avoiding Dominant Strategies," later in this chapter, discusses such strategies.

▪ **The role of chance is not so great that player skill becomes irrelevant.** This does not mean that a player cannot have bad luck, but in the long run—over the course of a long game or many short games—a better player should be more successful than a poor one. (Games for children often break this rule; for a child to have a chance to beat an adult, the game needs to include a large element of chance.)

A well-balanced PvP game also possesses the following qualities:

▪ **The players perceive the game to be fair.** As Chapter 1, "Games and Video Games," explained, the exact meaning of fairness varies among different players. The later section "Making PvP Games Fair" addresses this further.

▪ **Any player who falls behind early in the game gets a reasonable opportunity to catch up again before the game ends.** The definitions of *early in the game* and *a reasonable opportunity* vary depending on how long the designer expects a game to last. If a player falls behind in the first 10 minutes of a 2-hour game and the rules give him no chance to catch up, most players would perceive that game as unfair, and a game designer would describe that game as poorly balanced. Similarly, a game that the designer intends to last for 2 hours but that someone invariably wins in 15 minutes also gives other players no time to catch up or even to test their skill. These imbalances often indicate problems with positive feedback, a game feature that the later section "Understanding Positive Feedback" discusses.

▪ **The game seldom or never results in a stalemate, particularly among players of unequal ability.** A stalemate disappoints players because their efforts produce no victor. If stalemates occur frequently among players of unequal ability, the game violates the principle that player skill should influence the outcome more than any other factor. Chess, though a well-balanced game, can still end in a stalemate, but this seldom happens between players of unequal ability. Other games, such as backgammon, make stalemates impossible. "Understanding Positive Feedback" addresses this.

In a well-balanced PvE game, these characteristics should be evident:

▪ **The player perceives the game to be fair.** In a PvE game, the player's perception of fairness involves a number of factors and is complicated by the absence of a human or simulated opponent. The later section "Making PvE Games Fair" addresses these issues.

▪ **The game's level of difficulty must be consistent.** The *perceived difficulty* of the game's challenges (described later) remains within a reasonable range so as not to surprise the player with abrupt jumps or drops. The perceived difficulty may be low or high but should not change suddenly, especially within a single game level. The later section "Managing Difficulty" discusses this in detail.

To balance your game, you need to use certain design and tuning techniques to be sure the game exhibits these properties. The remainder of the chapter discusses these techniques.

Avoiding Dominant Strategies

A *strategy* is a plan for playing a game, usually according to a principle or approach that the player believes is likely to produce success. For instance, one player may favor an aggressive approach while another may depend on a defensive approach, but each thinks her strategy has the better chance of bringing victory. The term *dominant strategy*, which comes from formal game theory, refers to a strategy that reliably produces the best outcome a player may achieve, no matter what her opponent does. Dominant strategies are undesirable because once a player discovers one, she never has any reason to use any other strategy. It makes all other choices pointless and thus limits the fun the player can have with such a game. Still worse is a dominant strategy that one player may use but another player may not, which can occur in asymmetric games (the later section "Balancing Asymmetric Games" discusses this scenario). When that occurs, the dominant strategy not only obviates other strategies, but it makes the game unfair. Designing your game's mechanics to avoid a dominant strategy is, therefore, an essential part of game balancing.

NOTE The term *dominant strategy* doesn't mean that the player who uses it always dominates his opponent. It means that the strategy is superior to all the other strategies a player has available. A player using a dominant strategy can still lose through bad luck.

Sometimes one single choice can be a dominant strategy, if that one choice gives the player enough of an advantage. This section refers to player strategies, options, and choices interchangeably because any of these may cause one strategy to dominate all others.

Strategies that avoid loss or prevent an opponent from scoring points can also qualify as dominant. Prior to 1955, a basketball team could use endless delaying tactics to kill time on the clock to preserve their lead—a dominant strategy because it prevented the other side from getting control of the ball and scoring. Leagues implemented the shot clock to force the team with possession in such situations to shoot the ball, thus creating more opportunities for their opponents to get the ball back.

Dominant Strategies in Video Games

Video games seldom permit players to use strategies so strongly dominant that they absolutely guarantee victory; however, some PvP and PvE games do allow powerful strategies that give the player little reason to use any other. By far the best-known dominant strategy in any PvP video game is the tank rush in Westwood's *Command & Conquer: Red Alert*. An experienced player playing as the Soviet side can devote all of his energies to producing a large force of tanks in the early part of the game; he can then use those tanks to attack the nascent enemy base en masse. Against an unprepared opponent, this almost always produces a victory; an experienced opponent can prepare for the onslaught, but the tank rush remains so effective that it takes the fun out of the game. Many players add an additional rule to the game— no tank rushes allowed—just to balance this problem.

Several editions of *Madden NFL* included unstoppable offensive plays that guaranteed success against an AI-controlled opponent. Fighting games, too, are especially prone to dominant strategies. In both fighting games and football games, the large numbers of possible combinations of offensive and defensive actions makes it difficult to test them all. Badly designed characters can also result in dominant strategies; in *Super Street Fighter II Turbo,* the secret character Akuma's unbeatable attack, the air fireball, leaves the rest of the characters with no chance. Tournament matches ban the use of Akuma to ensure fair play.

The next few sections discuss ways that dominant strategies can emerge in a video game and how to avoid them or remove them by using balancing methods.

TRANSITIVE RELATIONSHIPS AMONG PLAYER OPTIONS

The term *transitive* describes a relationship among three or more entities so that if A stands in a certain relationship to B, and B stands in the same relationship to C, then A stands in the same relationship to C also. If you may correctly draw this conclusion, the relationship displays a property called *transitivity. Greater than* in arithmetic provides an example of a transitive relationship: If A is greater than B, and B is greater than C, then A is greater than C.

If a transitive relationship exists among a player's strategic options, then option A is better than option B, and option B is better than option C. Why, then, would a player ever use option C? Selecting option A becomes a dominant strategy. To use a concrete example, if you design a game so that an aggressive strategy is always better than a defensive one, and a defensive strategy is always better than a stealthy one, a smart player always chooses the aggressive strategy—it is superior to all the others.

To correct this imbalance, you may impose direct costs on using each strategy— costs that counteract the superiority of the stronger strategies and so give players a reason to consider the (formerly) weaker strategies as well. To draw an analogy, a lot of kids who would like to ride horses have to ride bikes instead because, even though horses are more fun to ride, they cost a lot of money.

Suppose you build a road-racing game in which players vie to earn the most prize money available over a series of races. You offer the player the chance to buy one of three cars made by three different manufacturers, such as Ford, Dodge, and Chevrolet. To make this a meaningful choice, you decide to create some variety among the cars so that the Ford is faster than the Dodge, and the Dodge is faster than the Chevrolet. If they all cost the same amount and their performance is identical in other ways, choosing the Ford constitutes a dominant strategy. However, if you price each car in proportion to its advantage so that the Ford costs the most and the Chevrolet costs the least, the game regains balance. Because the players' goal is to earn money, not merely to win races, the financial disadvantage of the faster car offsets its speed advantage if you set the costs correctly.

Setting up direct costs that exactly counter the advantages of certain choices does balance the game, but such a clear and obvious balancing mechanism produces a game that seems rather bland. The player can see that there's no real difference among the choices. To create a more interesting choice for the player, you can instead impose shadow costs. *Shadow cost,* a term from economic theory, refers to secondary, or hidden, costs that lie behind the apparent costs of goods or services. For our purposes, a shadow cost is one that the designer creates but doesn't warn the player about explicitly. It serves to balance the game without being blatant about the mechanisms. For instance, giving the Ford a smaller fuel tank that requires the car to stop to refuel more often in the road race could counter its speed advantage. The smaller fuel tank serves as a shadow cost that the player becomes aware of through repeated play.

You can hide a shadow cost completely by building it into the mechanics and not documenting it in the game's manual—for instance, not telling the players how big the fuel tanks in the cars are so they have to find it out through trial and error. More often, a shadow cost is available to the player but not obvious. Continuing the same example, the player might be able to learn the sizes of the fuel tanks by comparing the numbers on the fuel gauges in each car, but the instructions for the game don't draw attention to it. Another classic example is a weapon that does a great deal of damage but has a slow rate of fire. The slow rate of fire is a shadow cost that the player discovers only once she starts to use the weapon.

Players of PvE games often feel that entirely hidden shadow costs are unfair because the player cannot know what costs lurk behind the scenes or learn to compensate for them. For example, if a game reduces a character's accuracy at throwing a javelin in proportion to the weight of the character's backpack (on the theory that throwing a javelin while wearing a heavy backpack is bound to be rather uncertain) but never explains this to the player, the player can't learn to compensate for it. He finds that his accuracy worsens at times, but he can't understand why. If he does figure it out, he will probably cry foul and post a warning on an Internet gaming forum for the benefit of other players. A number of game publishers deliberately hide shadow costs from the players but reveal the costs in printed strategy guides that the player must pay extra for. This is an abusive practice.

TIP If you give a player an option that appears to be clearly superior to his other options, you can balance this by imposing a higher direct (visible) cost for choosing that option, or a shadow (hidden) cost. For example, *FarmVille* offers higher-yielding crops that appear to be superior to others, but they have to be harvested so frequently that the player seldom is able to obtain an advantage from planting them. The waste when a player cannot harvest a crop in time is a shadow cost.

CHAPTER 15

In practice, designers most often use transitive relationships to *upgrade* a player's powers during her progress through the game. The player begins with a single option, the weakest, and works her way up to better ones. In other words, she starts with the Chevrolet, then receives the Dodge as a reward for good performance, and later still receives the Ford. This creates positive feedback, which is covered in the section "Understanding Positive Feedback" later in this chapter. If you also make it possible for a player to *lose* her upgrade due to poor performance—going back to the Dodge after a bad performance in the Ford—you can create an interesting progression/regression dynamic that can lead to some taut and suspenseful gameplay. Take care to ensure that the player can reestablish her previous level once she does well again.

INTRANSITIVE RELATIONSHIPS (ROCK-PAPER-SCISSORS)

If the relationship between strategies or other player options is *intransitive,* then just because A beats B and B beats C, you can't assume that A also beats C. Game professionals use *intransitive relationship* to mean not merely a lack of transitivity but an explicit loop in which option A beats option B, B beats C, and C beats A (see **Figure 15.1**). The game rock-paper-scissors (also called scissors-paper-stone and Rochambeau) works that way: Paper beats rock, rock beats scissors, scissors beat paper. This results in a balanced, three-way intransitive relationship (although intransitive relationships are not confined to systems of only three entities).

FIGURE 15.1
A three-way intransitive relationship, with arrows indicating which option beats another

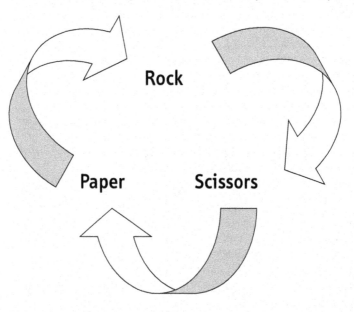

Rock

Paper   Scissors

The rock-paper-scissors (or RPS) mechanism is a classic design technique for avoiding dominant strategies and forms the basis for balancing player strategies in many games. Designer David Sirlin pointed out in his article "Rock, Paper, and Scissors in Strategy Games" that *Virtua Fighter 3* includes RPS relationships among general types of moves available to the player: Attacking moves beat throwing moves, throwing moves beat blocking moves, and blocking moves beat attacking moves (Sirlin, 2000). *The Ancient Art of War,* an early example of a video game that includes an RPS relationship, offers players three unit types: knights, archers, and barbarians. Knights have an advantage over barbarians, barbarians over archers, and archers over knights.

A direct implementation of the RPS model without any modifications fails to meet the needs of modern war games due to its simplicity. It doesn't offer any interesting choices—there's no reason to choose any one unit or strategy over any of the others. However, as Sirlin points out, you can adjust the system to produce different benefits. If you give the player different amounts of money for winning with rock, paper, or scissors, players have to think not only about which object their opponent might choose, but which choice earns the most money.

Now imagine a system in which instead of just allowing each choice to beat another in all circumstances, as in rock-paper-scissors, one choice is marginally better than others in some circumstances but not in others. You can make this adjustment in the core mechanics of your game, and it need not be a war game. For example, suppose you set up a race between a lizard, a frog, and a mouse. The lizard does best on rocky ground; the frog does best in swamps; and the mouse does best on grassy ground. If you design the mechanics such that these advantages remain slight rather than overwhelming, it will take a while for the players to learn about the system of advantages. Make the race course a complex mixture of rocks, grassland, and swamps, and give players partial but not total freedom over the routes they take. Add some shadow costs: The frog is generally slower than the others overall; the mouse has to stop for air every 15 seconds while swimming; and the lizard slows down sharply at transitions between types of ground. If you set these values carefully, your game remains balanced, and players will have some interesting decisions to make about which creature they would rather play with.

ORTHOGONAL UNIT DIFFERENTIATION

In his lecture at the 2003 Game Developers' Conference, "Orthogonal Unit Differentiation," game designer Harvey Smith argued that each type of unit a player can control in a game (a car, a soldier, an RPG character, or anything else the player can command) should be orthogonally different from all the others (Smith, 2003). By *orthogonal,* he meant that each kind of unit should be unlike the others in a different dimension, not simply more or less powerful when measuring in one dimension. The example of the Ford, Dodge, and Chevy in the preceding section differentiates between them in the same dimension—speed—so they are not orthogonally different.

To make the player's choice of units more interesting and to offer her a larger variety of strategies, Smith suggests that units should not only differ in the magnitude of their power at performing one task, as the Fords and Dodges did, but also should display entirely different qualities. Ideally, every type of unit should possess capabilities

TIP Giving players a choice of units that have different abilities also lets the player choose a unit that reflects their personal play preferences. The classic trio of tank, damage-dealer, and healer in role-playing games (RPGs) is a good example of this.

CHAPTER 15

that no other unit has, and this gives each type a distinct role to play in the game. Otherwise, there's little point in including a weaker unit in the game except as part of an upgrade path to a stronger one.

The more diverse the types of challenges in your game, the easier you will find it to create orthogonally differentiated unit types. In a realistic car racing game, all the cars face the same challenge and must be constructed to similar standards, which makes racing games a poor field for examples of orthogonal differentiation. Player success depends more on driving skill than on the attributes of their cars, which is appropriate for a racing game. In a war game, however, opportunities to create orthogonally differentiated units abound. Some units may fly or travel on water, whereas others may not; some may transport other units; some may possess ranged weapons and others only hand-to-hand weapons; and so on. You cannot directly compare the advantages of a unit that wields hand-to-hand weapons with the advantages of one that heals the wounded: These qualities make the player's choices more interesting, and success in the game consists of deploying the appropriate combination of units to defeat the enemy's forces.

Orthogonally differentiated units also help to prevent dominant strategies from arising if you define the victory condition in such a way that the player must use a variety of different units to win the game. Many inexperienced chess players rely on using the queen aggressively, wrongly believing this a dominant strategy because she is the most powerful piece on the board. In fact, each type of chess piece plays a role and they work cooperatively. The queen cannot control the board alone; she needs the help of the other pieces. The types of pieces exhibit enough diversity to keep games interesting and prevent dominant strategies.

> ### DESIGN RULE Differentiate All Your Units
>
> Every character or unit in a game must have a unique reason for existing. If a unit is simply a more powerful version of another one, make it more expensive, or make it an upgrade that is not initially available.

Dominant Strategies in PvE Games

As Chapter 13 explained, most games offer a large number of different types of challenges but a somewhat smaller number of actions with which to overcome them. One action may overcome several different types of challenges. This encourages players to experiment to find the right action or combination of actions to surmount each type of challenge, whereas offering only one unique action for each type of challenge makes for a dull game.

Implementing fewer actions does introduce a potential problem, however. By creating actions that can overcome several different kinds of challenges, you risk accidentally creating *exploits,* actions so powerful because of a weakness in the design that the player becomes unstoppable. This happens occasionally when players use an action in a way that you did not expect. For example, in an old side-scrolling space-shooter game on the Super Nintendo Entertainment System (which this book does not name to avoid embarrassing the individuals responsible), the player could, after upgrading her weapons to a certain level, make her way through the rest of the game without ever losing a life by traveling as low on the screen as possible and keeping her finger on the fire button. Although clearly unintended, this position made her invulnerable to enemy attacks.

As of yet, no one has invented a way to prevent these problems other than through play-testing, trying as many actions and as many combinations as possible on each challenge. The smaller the number of actions that you implement in your game, the less likely you are to introduce a dominant strategy by accident because you will be able to test them all rigorously. Be especially careful with powerups and special actions that give the player more power than usual; these require extra testing.

TIP Although you want to avoid exploits that make the player invulnerable, you can still include invulnerability as a reward, a cheat (you'll probably need it during play-testing anyway), or a temporary powerup.

> **DESIGN RULE** Test *Thoroughly* to Eliminate Dominant Strategies
>
> Do your best when designing a game's mechanics to avoid creating dominant strategies, but you may find some during playtesting anyway. There is no substitute for thorough testing with members of your intended audience.

Incorporating the Element of Chance

The role of chance varies enormously from game to game. Some games, such as checkers, make no use of chance at all; in others, such as craps, chance is all-important. We've seen that skill, not chance, must be the primary factor in determining the player's success (except in games for children). If chance plays a role, how can we ensure that the more skillful player wins? Here are several recommendations.

▓ **Use chance sparingly.** Design the game so that chance affects only a minority of the player actions that lead to victory, and the majority of the player's actions depend on skill. This is the simplest solution, but it's not suitable for all types of games.

If chance is to play a larger role in the game, balance its effects as follows:

▓ **Use chance in frequent challenges with small risks and rewards rather than in infrequent challenges with large risks and rewards.** Poker provides a good example. Chance plays a large role in each hand, but smart players don't bet large amounts on a single hand; they count on the cumulative effect of good play over many hands. Player skill remains the major factor that determines winners if a game includes enough hands. This approach also appears in war games, in which chance plays a role in the mechanics governing combat between individual units (although not a large role) but plays no direct role in the victory and loss conditions of the mission. The influence of chance on victory and loss occurs frequently but only on a small scale, so good luck tends to cancel out bad luck over time, leaving skill to determine long-term results.

■ **Allow the player to choose actions to use the odds to his advantage.** If the player knows the probabilities that significant events will occur, he can make decisions that he believes will be to his advantage. Even in a game in which chance plays an enormous role, such as craps, the player may choose to bet on different outcomes that he believes more or less probable. His skill in making decisions in his favor on the basis of the odds thus plays a role in determining his success. Video games seldom tell players the odds explicitly, but with experience, players come to learn the odds and make good decisions. If a player has *no* possibility of acquiring knowledge of the odds and gets no opportunity to decide whether to take a risk, chance plays too large a role.

■ **Allow the player to decide how much to risk.** Allow the player to choose how much she places at risk at frequent intervals. By offering the player this choice, you give her more control over her resources and so tend to reward skill. This again becomes critically important in gambling games, as in the game of poker. If you do not let the player choose how much to risk on any given challenge that involves chance, then the game should not risk too much on her behalf. In a war game, for example, chance typically affects the accuracy of each shot. By sending a unit into combat, the player risks a few health points on each shot and cannot choose how many points she risks. However, she almost always has the option to withdraw the unit from combat (retreat); the number of points at risk is seldom very large; and one shot typically affects only one unit.

Put simply, don't use chance to determine large issues unless the player explicitly chooses to take large risks (and has the option not to) or in short games. It's possible to lose by pure bad luck in *Minesweeper,* but the game takes so little time to play that this doesn't matter.

Making PvP Games Fair

Part of your job includes making sure that your game is fair and that players perceive it to be fair. Fairness means something different in PvP games than it does in PvE games, so we'll examine them separately. Players generally consider a PvP game to be *fair* if they believe (1) the rules give each player an equal chance of winning when play begins, and (2) the rules do not give advantage or disadvantage to players unequally during the game in ways that they cannot influence or prevent apart from the operation of chance (in moderation).

Balancing Games with Symmetry

In designing a PvP game, you must decide early on if you want the game to be symmetric or asymmetric. Chapter 1 introduced the concept of symmetry; see the section "Symmetry and Asymmetry" there for a refresher if you need one. The concept doesn't apply to PvE games; all PvE games are asymmetric because there is only one player.

You will find it easiest to create a PvP game that players perceive as fair if you make the game symmetric. Each player begins with the same resources, has the same options available to her, faces the same challenges, and tries to achieve the same victory condition. The vast majority of traditional games (chess, backgammon, *Othello*, and so on) follow this pattern. So, too, does *Monopoly*, in which each player begins with $1500 and all launch their tokens from the "Go" square. One player gets to go first, but because a random roll of the dice controls who begins the game, players accept this as fair. (See the sidebar "Who Goes First?" in Chapter 1 for further discussion.)

So long as whatever you do for one player you do for all the others, your game will remain fair, and little else needs to be said. However, video game players generally consider symmetric games rather uninteresting. Symmetric games don't allow players to control different forces and study their relative strengths and weaknesses the way asymmetric games do. Symmetric games also feel rather contrived, because little in the real world is symmetric.

In PvP games, dominant strategies occur most often under asymmetric rules (the next section addresses those issues), but a dominant strategy can also occur in symmetric games. Because all players start with symmetric attributes and positions, they all may use this superior strategy, so it does not create an unfair advantage for one player. Nevertheless, such a strategy leaves the players with only one good option, so the game isn't as fun as it could be.

Balancing Asymmetric Games

Asymmetric PvP games run a greater risk of suffering from dominant strategies because the players effectively play by different rules. In Fox and Geese, which Chapter 1 describes, one player controls a single fox on the game board while the other player controls 11 geese (see Figure 1.2). The fox may move in any direction and jump over the geese, whereas the geese may move only toward the fox. The victory condition for the fox is to jump over all the geese (removing them from the board), whereas the victory condition for the geese is to trap the fox so that it cannot move. Thus, the rules provide entirely different units, available actions, and victory conditions for each side. In designing an asymmetric game, you must test the mechanics for each type of competitor against every other possible type of competitor to make sure that none has a dominant strategy that confers an advantage over all his opponents. This lengthy and involved procedure makes it more likely that a mistake will get past your in-house testers. This is one reason for doing beta-testing with members of the public; the larger number of people testing the game increases the chance that they'll find problems.

In addition to the risk of dominant strategies emerging, players often disagree on the fairness of an asymmetric game. It becomes much harder to judge whether a game really gives all players an equal chance of winning and doesn't disadvantage any player who plays by different rules or with different resources. These arguments often result in variants—alternative versions of the rules—which arise to rectify what players see as problems. Several variants of Fox and Geese have emerged: one that puts more geese on the board, one that includes two foxes instead of one, one that lets the geese move backward as well as forward, and so forth.

CHEATING AI AND SECRET ASYMMETRY

In a single-player PvP game, the player takes on an artificial opponent and tries to defeat it in exactly the same way she would a human player. Sometimes the single-player competition mode in a PvP game is just an added feature in an otherwise multiplayer PvP game. When a game is designed this way, the player naturally tends to assume that the artificial opponent plays by the same rules that a human player would play by in its place.

Unfortunately, the AI in many games isn't good enough to beat a human opponent on equal terms. AI can beat most human players in games such as chess and checkers but has a harder time with *Go* and a very hard time with complex war games. To help the AI, designers occasionally let it cheat. Some classic cheats include allowing the AI to see units that should be hidden by the fog of war; making the AI-controlled units tougher than the player's units, while claiming that they are identical; or giving the artificial opponent a faster production rate for valuable resources than the player gets for the same resources. In effect, what the player thinks is a symmetric game is secretly asymmetric; the artificial opponent plays by different rules.

You should use this approach only as a last resort. Although it can produce a well-balanced single-player PvP game, players hate it when they discover that the AI is cheating against them (and with enough effort, they will discover it eventually). A better solution is to be open about the artificial opponent's advantages and build them into a set of different difficulty levels for the player to choose from. This allows the player to decide for herself how tough an opponent she wants to face, and the game doesn't have to pretend to be symmetric.

THE POINT ASSIGNMENT SYSTEM

You can balance a more complex asymmetric game than Fox and Geese by giving the players identical quantities of raw materials at the beginning of the game and then letting them choose what units to build using the raw materials. *Spectre* (an old Macintosh game recently rereleased for iOS devices) allows players to design a tank by assigning points to three attributes: speed, armor (defensive strength), and shot power (offensive strength). Each player gets the same number of points, so none has a built-in advantage, but each can construct a tank that matches his own preferred style of play.

The point distribution system, while generally fair, doesn't absolutely guarantee that no dominant strategy will emerge. The risk always exists that one particular combination of features may be superior to any other combination. To help prevent this, the attributes to which the player can assign points should be orthogonally related. One attribute should not affect the domain of another attribute. Having two closely related attributes, such as health and armor, undermines the point system. The player should not be able to gain the same effect by pumping points into one attribute as she can by pumping the points into another.

Also, make sure that spending a point on one attribute magnifies the unit's power in that dimension to the same degree that it magnifies powers in other dimensions if the player spends that point on any other attributes. This means that, for example, if the player can spend 10 points on strength to double the unit's strength, spending 10 points on intelligence should not multiply the unit's intelligence by 1000. If using a point on intelligence produces a significantly greater chance of winning than using it on strength, a dominant strategy will emerge: Players will always put all their points into intelligence.

THE EXAMPLE OF *STARCRAFT*

StarCraft offers the most well-balanced combination of asymmetric features in any war game available, which explains why, despite being over 15 years old, it remains a favorite at gaming tournaments. The game offers players a choice of three races called the Terran (or humans), the Protoss, and the Zerg. Each race produces flying attack units, construction units, small infantry units, and so on. Most important, building these units carries approximately equivalent costs, in terms of raw materials: A Zerg, a Protoss, and a Terran each must use similar amounts of resources to build units that provide equivalent fighting power. The capabilities of the units, however, vary from race to race; therefore, the game is asymmetric. The Terran construction unit can repair damaged units, so assigning additional construction units to a job can speed repairs. Damaged Zerg units may heal themselves without a repair unit, but only at a fixed rate. Protoss units possess both health, which cannot be replaced by any means, and shields, which the Protoss may recharge at special locations. Because Protoss units possess both health and shields, they usually cost about twice as much as their counterparts in the other races. See **Table 15.1**.

TYPE	COSTS		BENEFITS		
	Direct: Price	**Shadow: Build Time**	**Health**	**Damage**	**Range**
Zergling	25	28	35	5	1
Marine	50	24	40	6	4
Zealot	100	40	100+	16	1

TABLE 15.1
Costs and Benefits of Basic Infantry Units in *StarCraft*

StarCraft is an excellent example of a well-balanced asymmetric game and is well worth taking the time to study. Buy a strategy guide for the game and read about the attributes of the units. Notice how their costs tend to balance their abilities. The balance in *StarCraft* makes use of both direct costs (computed from the amount of raw material required to build a unit) and shadow costs—hidden weaknesses.

Balance Issues for Persistent Worlds

Persistent worlds are multiplayer online games that run continuously, offering a game world that persists even if a player is not logged in. Chapter 17, "Design Issues for Online Gaming," discusses persistent worlds, but this section addresses a couple of issues in the context of balancing.

Persistent worlds are never symmetric and are always intrinsically unbalanced because long-time players accumulate significant resources and experience that put newcomers at a disadvantage. As a result, online games *must* provide protection and encouragement for beginning players. Most now allow players to avoid PvP combat unless they specifically want to engage in it (Chapter 17 addresses this at further length), but online games must also give new players a chance to earn resources, explore areas without finding them already crowded by others, take up interesting occupations, and so on. A persistent world cannot be a zero-sum game: New resources must constantly flow into it from outside for new players to find.

The designers of persistent worlds, unlike designers of standalone games, can rebalance on the fly, changing the rules after their customers begin play. Such rule changes, while sometimes necessary, tend to cause howls of outrage from players who have optimized their play according to the existing rules and enjoy the game as it stands. Most persistent world games have had to implement rule changes this way to rectify design errors and to correct imbalances.

In spite of such changes, the persistent world *Asheron's Call* is an example of a game that remains fundamentally unbalanced in favor of magic users. Apparently that's what the magic users want, and obviously the publishers want to hold their audience. In this case, designers balance the game in such a way that the majority of players enjoy the game in the way they like to play it rather than in such a way as to make the game objectively fair. The aim of this balance involves ongoing sales and politics more than it involves equal distribution of resources or opportunities—but as a designer, you may be required to consider how market forces call for a different kind of balance.

Making PvE Games Fair

Because the challenges in PvE games come from the environment rather than from other players, making a fair game involves more than giving all players equal opportunities to succeed. In general, players expect a fair PvE game to exhibit qualities enumerated in the following list. Some may not appear to have much to do with balance, but we'll look at them here because they constitute part of a player's notion of fairness.

▦ **The game should offer the player challenges at a consistent maximum level of difficulty, with no sudden spikes.** Players regard sudden spikes in difficulty as unfair. The next section, "Managing Difficulty," is devoted to this important issue.

▦ **The player should not suddenly lose the game without warning and through no fault of his own.** So-called *learn-by-dying* designs, once commonplace, are now considered unfair unless resurrection is nearly instantaneous and without cost to the player. *The Immortal,* an old Electronic Arts game, notoriously requires the player to learn by dying. Fortunately, it allows players to restart the game indefinitely without having to start over at the beginning, but still, repeated character death isn't much fun. You can easily avoid this by providing the player with adequate warnings of dangers ahead.

▦ **A stalemate should not occur.** Stalemates can result from deadlock (see Chapter 14, "Core Mechanics") or from other combinations of circumstances that prevent the player from winning or losing. If a player fails to pick up a critical item in an adventure game and then passes through a one-way door that prevents him from retrieving the item, he's in a stalemate. He hasn't lost the game, but he can't win it either. Well-designed games don't let the player proceed without the item. Some don't let players put down items once they have picked them up, just to help avoid this problem. Study your mechanics carefully to see if the game can ever enter a state that completely precludes victory but does not meet a loss condition. If it can, you should either change that state to a loss condition or—preferably—redesign the mechanics to prevent the game from ever getting into that state.

▦ **The game doesn't ask the player to make critical decisions without adequate information.** The ZX Spectrum game *Monty on the Run* by Gremlin Graphics required the player to choose at the beginning of the game exactly five items to take with her as she tried to escape her pursuers. Unfortunately, it gave her no clues about which items she needed; she could find out only by trial and error. Give players the information they need.

▦ **All the factual knowledge required to win the game should be contained within the game.** Players should not have to do research outside the game world to win a game, with the sole exception of trivia games. Chapter 13 discusses this at greater length.

▦ **The game should not require the player to meet challenges not normally presented in the game's genre** (such as a formal logic puzzle in a flight simulator). If the game belongs to a hybrid genre, you must make this clear before the player starts to play.

Managing Difficulty

Psychologist Mihaly Csikszentmihalyi observed that people performing tasks enter an enjoyable state of peak productivity, which he calls *flow*, when (among other things) their abilities balance the difficulty of the tasks they face. If the challenges are too difficult, people become anxious; if the challenges are too easy, people become bored (Csikszentmihalyi, 1991). Csikszentmihalyi's observations apply to games as well as to other tasks. Balancing a game, then, includes managing the difficulty of its challenges to try to keep the players within the flow state—the point at which their abilities just match the problems they face. This provides another example of the player-centric approach: Your goal is not simply to set a level of difficulty, but to think about how to adjust that difficulty to maximize the player's enjoyment. See **Figure 15.2** for an illustration.

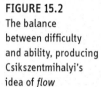

FIGURE 15.2
The balance between difficulty and ability, producing Csikszentmihalyi's idea of *flow*

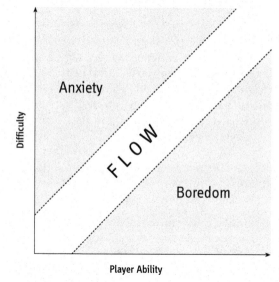

Chapter 13, in the section "Skill, Stress, and Absolute Difficulty," examined two factors, the intrinsic skill required (ISR) to overcome a challenge and the stress placed on the player by time pressure, that combine to form the *absolute difficulty* of the challenge. The remainder of this section extends the discussion of difficulty to take into account two additional factors, ultimately arriving at the idea of *perceived difficulty*—the type that matters to the player. As the preceding section explained, the perceived difficulty of a well-balanced game must remain within a certain range and not have sudden spikes or dips.

Because game challenges fall into many extremely different domains—physical coordination, factual knowledge, formal logic, pattern recognition, and so forth—there's no way to compare difficulty across these domains. Even within a given domain, such as factual knowledge challenges, it may be hard to decide when one challenge is more difficult than another; questions of fact that some audiences find hard are easy for other audiences. Most Americans would be unable to answer many factual knowledge questions about the history of Angola, and eight-year-olds would certainly struggle with complex logic puzzles. Consequently, the following discussion makes no reference to any audience or unit of measure.

Factors Outside the Designer's Control

In managing the difficulty of a game, you command a number of factors, but a few remain outside your knowledge or control. You cannot know how much time the player has already spent playing other games similar to yours—or, more accurately, facing challenges similar to those that you offer. This factor is called *previous experience*. (The experience the player gains while playing *your* game is called in-game experience.)

You also cannot know how much *native talent* the player brings to the game: hand-eye coordination, reasoning faculties, and so on. As a result, we can't include either previous experience or native talent in our calculation of perceived difficulty. We look into these factors when we come to the question of difficulty modes in the later section "Establishing Difficulty Modes."

Finally, in multiplayer games, the skill of the player's opponents plays the greatest role in determining how hard it is to beat them, and you do not control that. Consequently, you don't have to put as much effort into managing difficulty throughout the game, so long as the game is fair. You still have to set the difficulty of individual challenges posed by the environment in a multiplayer game, however. The height of the basketball hoop and the size of the rim determine how hard it is to shoot a ball through the hoop in absolute terms, but how hard it is to win the game depends on the quality of the opposing team.

OFFERING CHEATS TO THE PLAYER

Some games try to account for differences in previous experience and native talent among the players by offering so-called *cheats:* hidden options that the player may use to gain an extra advantage. Cheats originally arose as a convenience feature for game testers, allowing them to jump ahead in the game, bypass certain challenges, and so on, so that they could go quickly to the part of the game they needed to test. Eventually designers realized that players could benefit from cheats too, and they began to leave the cheats as hidden features in the shipped version of the product. This practice is now so widespread that it has become standard.

In spite of its ubiquity, however, if your design *depends* on the use of cheats, your game is poorly balanced. If a player cannot get through a game without using a cheat, the game is too hard. Instead of offering a hidden cheat that the player must search the Internet to discover, simply build in the cheat as a normal feature of the game's easiest difficulty mode and leave it out of the harder modes.

Types of Difficulty

Players care most about *perceived difficulty;* what matters is how hard the player finds surmounting a given challenge. To design a challenge at your target level of perceived difficulty, you must take into account four factors: intrinsic skill required and stress, both introduced in Chapter 13, as well as power provided and in-game experience, defined shortly. We'll also examine absolute difficulty and relative difficulty, concepts that are helpful when you are trying to gauge in advance how difficult players will find the challenges you design for them.

ABSOLUTE DIFFICULTY

To judge the *absolute difficulty* of a challenge, compare the amounts of intrinsic skill required to meet the challenges and the stress that the challenge imposes on a trivial challenge of the same type. For instance, in an action game, a trivial enemy would stand still, could not harm the avatar, and could be killed with one punch. If you design another enemy that takes more effort to kill (because it has more health points), that moves around (requiring more intrinsic skill to hit), and that hits the avatar back (thereby placing the player under time pressure—stress—to kill the enemy before the enemy kills the avatar), you can be confident you have designed an enemy more difficult to defeat, in absolute terms, than the trivial enemy that established the baseline. In effect, the absolute difficulty of a challenge equals the intrinsic skill required and the stress of the challenge *compared to the trivial case.*

You will find the concept of absolute difficulty useful when you need to compare the difficulty levels of different challenges. In general, if one enemy has twice as many health points as another, all other things being equal, it survives twice as long under assault, making it twice as hard to defeat.

RELATIVE DIFFICULTY AND POWER PROVIDED

You cannot determine how the player perceives the difficulty of a challenge through absolute difficulty alone. You must also take into account two more factors. The first is the amount of power that the game gives to the player to meet the challenge. *Power provided* measures, by means appropriate to the situation, the player's strength: the health and powers of his avatar, the size and makeup of his army, the performance characteristics of his racing car, or whatever factors apply. In the simple example described in the previous section, power provided would refer to the amount of damage the avatar can do when he hits the enemy and his resistance to damage: the number of health points that he has to lose before dying.

The *relative difficulty* is the difficulty of a challenge relative to the player's power to meet that challenge. For example, in a game like *World of Warcraft* (or any other RPG), a player playing a level 1 knight will find it much harder, in absolute terms, to defeat a large enemy than a small one. But a player playing a level 5 knight won't find it nearly so hard to defeat that same large enemy because the game provides a level 5 knight with so much more power than it provides a level 1 knight. The relative difficulty of defeating the enemy is governed by the power the player earns as her character levels up.

If the power the game provides to the player doesn't change throughout the game, then you may ignore this distinction between absolute and relative difficulty. But most games include an upgrade progression whereby the player gains power as the game progresses because the new powers keep the player interested in the game and give him the feeling of accomplishing more. As a result, when level designers build challenges into the game world, they must also take into account the power provided to the player to meet those challenges. The level designers have to know, for example, that by the time the player reaches the fourth level of the game, he will have earned three major weapon upgrades and a faster vehicle, so they set the difficulty of the fourth level's challenges relative to that level of power provided. To simplify managing the difficulty, many games don't allow the player to carry powers earned in one level over to the next one; instead, the level designers themselves set the amount of power provided separately for each level and take it into account accordingly as they devise challenges. In persistent worlds in which each individual player has his own amount of power provided, earned through his earlier play, the game must either warn players in advance against trying a mission that is too hard or flatly exclude them from such missions.

PERCEIVED DIFFICULTY AND IN-GAME EXPERIENCE

As they progress through a game, players learn to use the game's user interface more efficiently, and they learn at an intuitive level how the core mechanics of the game work. *In-game experience* at meeting any particular type of challenge may be measured by the amount of time the player has already spent meeting similar challenges within your game. (Remember that you cannot know how much previous experience the player has playing other games, which is why it's always good to offer her an optional tutorial.) The more in-game experience a player has, the easier she perceives a given type of challenge to be. Thus, when the level designers build a challenge into a level, they must take into account the amount of the player's in-game experience with the same type of challenge. If the player already has a lot of in-game experience with challenges of that type, the level designers should consider raising the challenge's absolute difficulty to compensate.

The *perceived difficulty* of a challenge—the difficulty that the player actually senses, and the type we are most concerned with—consists of the relative difficulty minus the player's experience at meeting such challenges. Remembering that relative difficulty is absolute difficulty minus power provided, we can put all these factors together into a single equation such that

perceived difficulty = absolute difficulty – (power provided + in-game experience)

Note that there are no units of measurement for these variables, so if you want to compute actual values for them, you will have to find a way to measure their quantities based on the challenges that you plan to include in your game. The equation serves more as a useful principle for you to understand than as a value you can really compute.

Creating a Difficulty Progression

In a balanced game, the perceived difficulty of challenges presented to the player either should not change or should rise, so the player feels that later challenges present greater difficulty than those at the beginning. (If a game becomes easier to play, players will definitely feel that the game is unbalanced.) To achieve this, you have to take into account the player's increasing in-game experience and build in appropriate increases in absolute difficulty. If you wish to, you can also build in increases in the power provided by the game. **Figure 15.3** shows this progression graphically. Notice the gap between the absolute and relative levels of difficulty. This gap represents power provided by the game to meet challenges, which widens steadily as the player gains power.

The gap between relative difficulty and perceived difficulty on the graph represents the player's increasing in-game experience as she plays. At the beginning of the game, the perceived difficulty exactly equals the relative difficulty because the player has no in-game experience at all. As time goes on, her perception changes as she gets more practice.

FIGURE 15.3
Absolute, relative, and perceived levels of difficulty

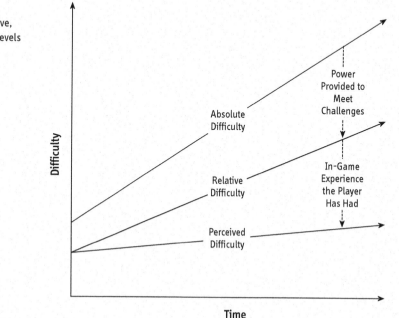

If the available power grows at exactly the same rate as the absolute difficulty goes up, the relative difficulty will be a flat line, as illustrated in **Figure 15.4**. In that case, a level 5 knight would find it exactly as hard to kill a level 5 troll in the middle of the game as a level 1 knight would find it to kill a level 1 troll at the beginning of the game. But relative difficulty should not be a flat line because when you factor in the player's increasing in-game experience, the perceived difficulty actually goes down—the game gets easier. Aim to increase the absolute difficulty of the challenges somewhat faster than you increase the available power to meet them. The gap between absolute and relative difficulty widens only slowly.

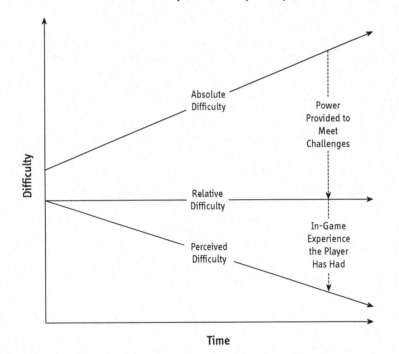

FIGURE 15.4
If relative difficulty is flat, perceived difficulty goes down as the player gains experience.

CHAPTER 15

WHEN PERCEIVED DIFFICULTY SHOULD NOT CHANGE

The perceived difficulty throughout the game should either remain flat or should rise. In most games, it rises. For some players, however, it should remain flat or rise only very slowly. Young children and infrequent gamers have a lower tolerance for frustration than more dedicated ones. Mobility-impaired players may not get as much benefit from increasing experience as fully able players in games with physical coordination challenges. If you are making a game specifically for these groups, try to keep the perceived difficulty level nearly flat throughout the course of the game. Don't trust your own instincts, however; as an expert player of your own game, it's hard for you to gauge how hard your game is. Watching members of your target audience play-test the game will help you to get this right.

NOTE In a game with more than five levels, the rate of difficulty should not increase as steeply as that shown in Figure 15.5. Also note that the figure doesn't illustrate the pacing within a level, only the general progress of the whole game.

Even if the perceived difficulty of a game rises only slowly, you do want the player to feel she attains bigger and bigger accomplishments as she goes. To achieve this, you must take into account all the factors pertaining to difficulty already discussed. Use the following guidelines:

▨ Increase the absolute difficulty of challenges over time.

▨ Increase the power available to the player to meet those challenges at a somewhat lower rate. (See the later section "Understanding Positive Feedback.")

▨ Be sure the player doesn't gain experience so fast that challenges start to feel as if they're getting easier rather than harder. Space challenges so that their relative difficulty increases slightly faster than the in-game experience increases.

▨ Play-test your game to look for any dramatic spikes or dips in the perceived difficulty of its challenges so you can iron them out. A sharp, unanticipated rise in the game's difficulty will discourage many players and may prevent them from finishing the game even if the difficulty quickly falls again.

▨ Start each game level at a perceived difficulty somewhat lower than that at which the preceding level ended, and increase the difficulty during the course of each level as well. Normally you achieve this by raising the absolute difficulty of each challenge the player faces throughout the level, and then you start the next level with easier challenges. Each game level should also take a little longer to play through and have a slightly steeper rate of difficulty growth than the one before. A graph explains this process best; **Figure 15.5** illustrates a game with only five levels. This sawtooth shape creates good pacing over the course of the game. Chapter 16, "General Principles of Level Design," discusses pacing at greater length.

FIGURE 15.5
A sawtooth difficulty progression across multiple game levels

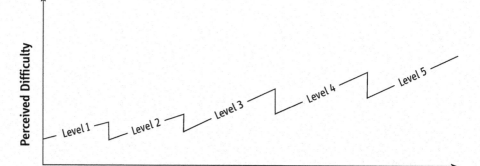

> ### DESIGN RULE Don't Jump Difficulty from Level to Level
>
> Do *not* introduce sudden difficulty jumps between the end of one level and the beginning of the next. There is a good chance the player ended his prior play session after completing the previous level and has not played it for some time, so he might have lost some of the benefit of his experience.

Establishing Difficulty Modes

In creating a single-player game, you should allow the player to choose how difficult she wants her experience to be, typically with three options labeled easy, normal, and hard, or something similar. When players make this choice, they're playing in a *difficulty mode,* such as easy mode or normal mode. (Don't confuse these with gameplay modes.)

Multiplayer games don't always offer different difficulty modes because in many multiplayer games, the player's skill determines how hard it is for others to beat him or for him to beat them. But in multiplayer games in which the environment itself sets challenges for the players, such as a road race, the players may want to choose the difficulty of the environment's challenges—to select easy, normal, or hard courses to race on, for example.

When you create a game that offers the player a choice of multiple difficulty modes, in effect you promise that the perceived difficulty of the game will never go above a certain point throughout a game level.

How you adjust the difficulty of challenges for different modes depends on the challenges and on the genre of your game. In action and action-adventure games, for example, designers normally give the enemies more health, allow them to do more damage, and make them more numerous. Designers also sometimes adjust the AI of enemies and artificial opponents, making them smarter or more aware of threats. Chapter 13 discusses how to adjust the absolute difficulty of different kinds of challenges.

NOTE Multiplayer games that are meant to be played by people of significantly varying skill, such as children and adults, sometimes allow each player to choose a difficulty level for themselves—a form of handicapping for the better players.

WHY OFFER DIFFICULTY MODES?

When you offer multiple difficulty modes, you allow the player to set the difficulty of the game to account for the two factors you cannot know or control: the player's previous experience with similar types of games and the player's native talent. Although nobody buys a game specifically because it offers multiple difficulty modes, a great many people *don't* buy games that they think might be too hard for them to play. Including multiple difficulty modes increases the market for your game by making it accessible to a broader range of players. In addition, difficulty modes give the player better value for his money at comparatively little development cost for you. Once players complete the game in an easy mode, they might enjoy playing it again in a harder mode. If it has only one mode, they're less likely to enjoy playing through it a second time.

Not all genres are suited to difficulty modes, and some designers feel that they are an outdated way to handle the variation in the players' native talent and previous experience. An alternative is to use techniques of dynamic difficulty adjustment (DDA), also sometimes called *adaptive difficulty*. (DDA appears in a later sidebar.) Although it might be desirable to use DDA only in an ideal world, in practice, not all teams have the resources to build and tune a DDA system. Furthermore, players like having difficulty modes and are used to them—which is a good reason to offer them.

DESIGN RULE Easy Mode Means *Easy!*

Some games, usually those built by game developers who are also hardcore gamers, offer the player an easy mode that isn't really easy at all. If you're going to call it "Easy Mode," it really should be easy for even an inexperienced player. Players choose Easy Mode for a reason; if they want a more challenging experience, they can choose a harder mode. Don't assume that you know what "easy" is. Try out your game on some inexperienced players and see how they react, then tune your Easy Mode for them.

In some cases, you may not be able to adjust the difficulty level of a challenge at all. With something like a static obstacle, such as a cliff the avatar must climb, the challenge is built into the shape of the cliff, and adjusting its difficulty would mean redesigning the landscape on the fly. Instead, give the player an alternative route that avoids the cliff climb in the easiest mode, but lock off or give a bonus for avoiding the easy route in the harder modes.

DYNAMIC DIFFICULTY ADJUSTMENT (DDA)

Over the years, game designers have made a number of efforts to create games that detect the player's level of skill and adapt themselves to change the player's experience accordingly. Several approaches have been tried:

- The first-person shooter game *Max Payne* automatically adjusts the strength of enemies and the amount of aiming assistance provided to the player based on her performance. The changes work to keep the player's experience at an appropriate level of difficulty, but they are invisible to the user.

- *Half-Life 2* checks the state of the avatar's health and ammunition when he breaks open a crate in the game world and adjusts the contents of the crate accordingly. If he is healthy and well supplied, he might find little or nothing, but if he is short of one of these resources, he might find medical kits or spare ammunition.

- The racing game *Burnout 2: Point of Impact* automatically changes the performance of computer-controlled drivers to keep them near the player's car regardless of how well or poorly she does, a technique called rubber banding. No matter what the skill level of the player, this approach ensures a close race. Unfortunately this system is easily exploitable and discourages improvement, since players are not rewarded for their increasing skill.

- *Crash Bandicoot,* an action game, offers the player extra shields against attack if he fails to get through a certain section too many times in a row. Players find this mechanism rather obvious. Furthermore, rather than being a global system like *Max Payne*'s, it had to be implemented separately for each region of the game where it offered extra shields.

- *Madden NFL 09* gave the player a series of explicit tests in its "Virtual Training Center," then adjusted the difficulty of the gameplay in the real game based on her performance in the tests.

- *God of War,* another action game, detects when the player is dying frequently and offers him the chance to play again in a lower difficulty mode. In this case, the game doesn't adapt its difficulty; it simply offers the player the chance to choose an easier mode. Some players complain that they find this patronizing; presumably others find it a relief.

DDA systems such as those used in *Max Payne* and *Burnout 2* are the subject of considerable debate within the game industry and among dedicated players. Some designers believe that no automated system can accurately predict how hard a player *wants* her experience to be, so they should not even be tried. In fact, as with everything else in game development, there are tradeoffs. Good DDA systems are time-consuming to build and tune, but they can significantly enhance the player's experience if done well. They are increasingly popular in mass-market games, in which the skill levels of the players can vary considerably and the players are less likely to be offended by discovering that a DDA system is in use.

continues on next page

DYNAMIC DIFFICULTY ADJUSTMENT (DDA) *continued*

You should not try to implement a DDA system in a beginner-level project. Learn to build and tune games in the conventional way first. However, if you are a more advanced designer or you have been assigned the task of developing one, read on.

Any DDA system requires two mechanics: a performance-evaluation system to measure how well the player is doing, and an adjustment mechanism to change the difficulty of the challenges he faces. How you do this will naturally depend a great deal on the kinds of challenges you're offering.

- Don't use DDA as a substitute for ordinary difficulty modes that the player can set. Players like to have the freedom to limit the maximum difficulty level of the game.

- Make it optional, a feature the player can accept or reject. DDA systems are often used in conjunction with player-settable difficulty modes.

- Use it to make the game harder but not easier. It is generally simpler to make a game more difficult than to make it easier. To make a game easier under computer control, the software has to determine the reason for the player's failure, which isn't always clear or measurable. Making a game harder doesn't depend as heavily on the computer's understanding of the reasons for the player's success.

- Never take something away from the player arbitrarily, especially something that he feels he's earned. It's OK to give the enemies more weapons; it's not OK to take away weapons from the player.

- Keep it subtle—this is the most important advice of all. The best DDA systems are the ones the players never even notice. *Max Payne* is a good example; *God of War* is a bad one.

As long as your adaptive-difficulty system remains an optional means of making the game extra challenging for the dedicated player, it will be less prone to the problems observed with such systems because the player cannot manipulate it to her advantage, and she can switch it off if it becomes a problem.

DDA is an advanced design topic, and there isn't room to cover all its nuances here. You can read more about the subject in the *Gamasutra* article "Difficulty Modes and Dynamic Difficulty Adjustment" (Adams, 2008).

Understanding Positive Feedback

Positive feedback occurs when a player's achievement causes changes to the state of
the game that make a subsequent achievement easier, which in turn makes further
achievements easier still, and so on. The term does not refer to the effect of increasing experience, but to a phenomenon of the core mechanics that occurs even if the
player's performance does not improve with experience. The core mechanics often
reward achievements with assets that the player can convert into power to make
further achievements easier. **Figure 15.6** shows a feedback relationship diagram.

NOTE This section
uses the word
achievement to refer
to an accomplishment
or feat, such as over-
coming a challenge.
It's not talking about
the symbolic rewards
some video games
give that are called
achievements.

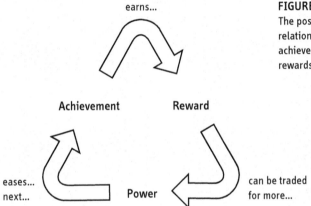

FIGURE 15.6
The positive feedback
relationship among
achievements,
rewards, and power

Monopoly, as usual, provides a classic example. When a player achieves a monopoly
by buying a group of related properties, the player may charge higher rents to any
opponent who lands on these properties—the owner's reward for the achievement.
The player may then use the money to purchase more property and collect more
monopolies, thus producing a better chance of earning still more money.

Some games feature an even closer relationship between achievement and power in
which the player's reward for achievement *is* power. The reward doesn't come in an
intermediate form, such as money, that must be converted into power by buying a
weapon or a spell. Whichever side loses a piece in a game of chess then plays with a
depleted force, so the player who takes the piece obtains more power relative to his
opponent. In PvP games such as chess, achieving the lead often confers some
advantage upon the leader that makes it easy for him to stay in the lead and difficult for the others to overtake him.

Not all games include positive feedback. If overcoming challenges does not produce
a reward that the player can use to help her overcome further challenges, no feedback cycle exists. In a javelin competition, a good throw of the javelin does not
produce additional power that influences subsequent throws.

Benefits of Positive Feedback

Positive feedback can benefit your game in two ways:

- **Positive feedback discourages stalemate.** A well-balanced PvP game should result in a stalemate only rarely, and PvE games should never end in stalemate. Positive feedback tends to bring games to an end because a player who takes a decided lead becomes unstoppable.

- **Positive feedback rewards success and provides that reward in a useful form rather than a cosmetic form, such as a higher score.** Even though the perceived difficulty of challenges may increase, thus requiring the player to work harder nearer the end of the game, she still feels rewarded by a sense of power and growth when she becomes able to do things she could not do at the beginning of the game. Because avatar growth is one of the key goals in RPGs, the positive feedback cycle serves as the central design feature of the internal economy of computer RPGs.

Controlling Positive Feedback

Although positive feedback generally benefits by helping bring a game to an appropriately timed end, especially in PvP games that involve direct conflict between the players, you must not allow positive feedback to operate so quickly that the game ends too soon or a player who falls behind never has any chance to catch up. Part of balancing your game will consist of adjusting your positive feedback cycle to prevent these problems.

Here are seven different ways of controlling the rate of positive feedback:

- **Don't provide too much power as a reward for success.** In chess, taking one of the opponent's pieces gives the player an added measure of power. In shogi (Japanese chess), the player can then add that piece to his own side, acquiring even more power. Introducing the piece directly would give the player too great an advantage; instead, it comes in as a weaker piece, which somewhat reduces the size of the reward. Similarly, in many war games, such as *Warcraft,* a player can destroy enemy factories, but he cannot capture them and use them to produce weapons for his own side. If he could do that, he would become unstoppable too quickly. (In real wars, armies often destroy their own production facilities and material to prevent them from falling into enemy hands for precisely this reason.)

- **Artificially limit the player's power.** Professional football in America used to have a positive feedback loop in which teams that performed well earned more money, enabling them to hire better players and therefore do better still. To break this loop, the National Football League implemented a salary cap, a rule that limits how much each team may spend on player salaries. This prevents rich teams from persistently outbidding poor teams for the best players. Teams can still earn big rewards, but they can't spend them on power. Shooter games that limit the number of guns a player can deploy at one time also restrict the player's power.

■ **Associate costs as well as benefits with player achievements.** Accomplishing something in a game should earn rewards, but it can also include a downside. You may do this explicitly or allow it to happen automatically as a function of the gameplay. In *Dungeon Keeper,* the player can convert enemy creatures to fight for her own side, but once she does so, she has to provide food, money, and living space for them—explicit costs associated with adding them to her army. A classic example from warfare is that the more territory you control, the longer a defensive perimeter you must maintain. Another is that the deeper you move into enemy territory, the longer your supply lines become.

■ **Raise the absolute difficulty level of challenges as the player proceeds.** This approach applies primarily to PvE games such as RPGs. As the player gains experience points and treasure through successful combat, he obtains more and more power through positive feedback. To continue to offer him meaningful challenges, increase the strength and numbers of the enemy. Defeating stronger enemies yields larger rewards, so the cycle continues. Near the end of the game, he fights enemies hundreds of times more difficult to beat—in absolute terms—than those that he fought at the beginning, and this gives him a great sense of accomplishment. But because you have matched the absolute difficulty of the challenges to the power you provide, the perceived difficulty remains under control.

■ **Allow collusion against the leader.** In games with three or more players, you can write the rules in such a way that the other players can collaborate against the player in the lead. The collaborating forces may be sufficient to overcome the effects of positive feedback when the power of a single player might not be. *Diplomacy* encourages collusion—forming alliances is the main point of the game.

■ **Define victory in terms unrelated to the feedback cycle.** If you define the victory condition of your game explicitly in terms of player rewards, power, or success at achievements that make up parts of the positive feedback cycle, then positive feedback will hasten victory. But you can also define victory in other terms. Taking a piece in chess confers an advantage to whichever player took it, but the victory condition in chess requires the player to checkmate her opponent's king, not to take the most pieces. Although a player may achieve the victory condition more easily with more pieces, it can also be useful to sacrifice a piece for strategic reasons.

■ **Use the effects of chance to reduce the size of the player's rewards.** RPGs do this to some degree by randomly varying the amount of loot that enemies yield to the player when they are defeated. By occasionally giving players a lower reward for their achievements, you slow down positive feedback.

Positive Feedback in Action

The set of graphs in **Figure 15.7** illustrates the effects of positive feedback, or its absence, in a variety of circumstances. Each graph shows the state of a hypothetical game between two players, A and B, over time. When the curve passes above the center line and into A's area, A leads; when it goes below the center, B leads. When the curve reaches the dotted line on one side or the other, the game ends and the player indicated wins.

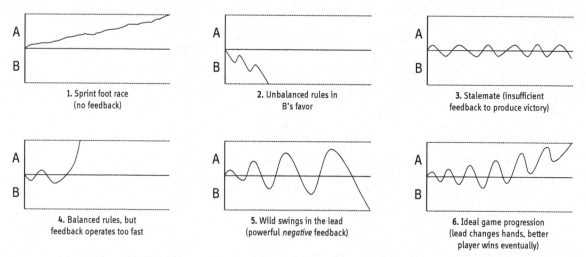

1. Sprint foot race
   (no feedback)

2. Unbalanced rules in
   B's favor

3. Stalemate (insufficient
   feedback to produce victory)

4. Balanced rules, but
   feedback operates too fast

5. Wild swings in the lead
   (powerful *negative* feedback)

6. Ideal game progression
   (lead changes hands, better
   player wins eventually)

FIGURE 15.7 Graphs showing the effects of different adjustments to positive feedback

Consider the following observations about these graphs:

▨ Graph 1 represents a game, such as a sprint foot race, in which no feedback loop exists to augment player power. A, the faster runner, wins.

▨ Graph 2's game lasts only a short time. B takes the lead and wins almost immediately. A's few efforts to catch up allow A to gain ground temporarily but ultimately fail. This graph describes an unfair game, badly balanced in favor of B.

▨ Graph 3 depicts a stalemate, with neither side ever getting far enough ahead for positive feedback to take hold and lead to victory. The game probably involves little positive feedback (or possibly none) and closely matched competitors.

▨ Graph 4 shows a game with fairly balanced rules but one in which positive feedback operates too quickly. B goes ahead, then A, then B again, and then A goes ahead just enough for a dramatic positive feedback cycle to make A unstoppable.

■ Graph 5 indicates a game with a feedback cycle that makes being in the lead a profound disadvantage, the effect of powerful negative feedback. A and B gain substantial leads and then alternately fall substantially behind so that the graph shows wild swings. *Mario Kart* and other multiplayer local games not intended to be taken too seriously sometimes use this mechanism.

■ Graph 6 shows an ideal game progression: The lead changes hands and both players have a good chance of winning the game for a while, but eventually A's superior play places her in a leading position that she never yields. The action of positive feedback ensures that B, the less-skilled player, cannot catch up, although B has a pretty good chance for about two-thirds of the game and perhaps could have won if A's attention had wavered; that is, the outcome wasn't a foregone conclusion.

Other Balance Considerations

This section addresses two undesirable qualities of unbalanced games, stagnation and triviality, that you should seek to avoid.

Avoiding Stagnation

Stagnation occurs in a PvE game when the game leaves the player in a position in which he simply does not know what to do next; he believes that he is stuck. (Don't confuse this with a stalemate, a situation in which the players definitely *cannot* go on no matter what.) Stagnation tends to be a result of a design that doesn't give the player enough information to proceed. First-person shooters that require a player to run all over the place trying to find the hidden switch that opens the level exit, *after* having killed all his opponents, stagnate. Once the player kills all the opponents, the level exit should be obvious.

Stagnation seldom occurs in PvP games because such games almost always put the competitors in direct conflict with one another and provide them with means to act against each other's forces. Stagnation occasionally happens when one player's forces are so reduced that there is little she can do. But because she usually loses the game soon afterward, this doesn't represent a serious stagnation problem. The most common complaint about stagnation in PvP games occurs in scenarios where the victory condition requires a player to destroy all enemy units, and one last enemy unit (often not even a combat unit) remains hidden in an obscure location. You can avoid this by setting a different victory condition, such as to destroy the enemy's headquarters instead of all her units.

Stagnation can be difficult to avoid in a sprawling action-adventure with so many different combinations and configurations that you can't reliably anticipate what the player may or may not try. However, you can still give the players information as they progress:

▤ Tackle stagnation passively by hiding in plain sight clues about how to proceed.

▤ Tackle stagnation actively by having the game detect when the player wanders around aimlessly; make the game provide a few gentle nudges to guide him in the right direction.

Never let the player feel bewildered. If he has to resort to outside assistance in order to proceed—whether by cheating, reading a strategy guide, or looking up the answers on the web—your game contains a design flaw.

Avoiding Trivialities

Players don't want to be bogged down in meaningless minutiae when they can be directing the big decisions. Forcing the player to decide where to store the gold when she must try to build an army and plan a campaign strategy merely distracts her with uninteresting details. It moves the player out of the flow state and into boredom. Likewise, any gameplay decision that has no real effect on the game world, or any decision that requires the player to pick from a slate of options that includes only one reasonable option, is trivial. Let the computer handle it. (This doesn't apply to non-gameplay decisions, such as self-expressive acts—choosing a team color may not affect the gameplay, but the player should still be allowed to do it.)

Sid Meier's Alpha Centauri handles this magnificently. In this game, the player can choose to handle every decision from overall control of the planet all the way down to production and direction of individual units, or he can let a computer-controlled manager control his bases and units. This accommodates players who want to micromanage every aspect of the game as well as those interested only in grand strategy. This is a superior design because it gives the player a choice. Other games force the player to do all the micromanagement, whether he wants to or not.

Trivial interactions or activities can add to the player's enjoyment when you use them well and not too often. Consider a cops and robbers game. The player's avatar, a police officer, patrols the city as usual, on the lookout for crime, when she spots a group of suspicious-looking characters on the corner. She stops the car, and the occupants immediately get out of the car, run down an alleyway, and vanish; the player won't meet these particular characters again, and they do not form part of the game's story. These characters provide local color rather than part of the gameplay. If you don't lead the player *too* far down the wrong path, you can use such trivial interaction to give the impression that there is more to the city than meets the eye.

Design to Make Tuning Easy

In the later stages of game development, you will spend a great deal of time tweaking and tuning your game to improve its balance and remove any dominant strategies or difficulty spikes that may have crept in. Here you'll find a few suggestions to make this process easier.

Chapter 14 explains that you should seek to generalize when you can, to create a set of mechanics that apply to a wide variety of entities rather than creating separate mechanics for each entity. So, for example, in any game that involves combat, try to create one set of mechanics that governs combat between units regardless of what types of units the combat involves. Not only does this simplify the programming—the developers can concentrate on implementing the core mechanics and then adding entities on top of those core rules, rather than coding each entity separately—it also simplifies tuning the design.

If each entity has its own mechanics, the mechanics for each entity must be tuned separately, which could potentially cause balance problems. If you use generalized mechanics as described in "Look for Patterns, Then Generalize" in Chapter 14, then once you get them into balance in general, any tweaking you need to do should not throw off the balance in unpredictable ways.

This book is not about programming or development techniques, but one trick is so useful that it's worth including here: Separate the code from the data. This lets designers tweak the game by trying different values for attributes without changing the code. Toward the end of the development cycle, you will spend a lot of time play-testing your game and refining its balance by changing the values of entities' attributes. You can store these data in a database—or even just a plain ASCII file—during development, moving them into a proprietary format for the final release.

Tweaking doesn't mean changing parameters randomly; that's a good way to waste time. The following suggestions should help you fine-tune your game efficiently:

- **Modify only one parameter at a time.** Adjust one parameter, then check the results, then adjust another parameter, and so on. This may seem tedious but it's very important. If you change more than one parameter at a time, you will have no idea which change you made produced the results that you got. A publisher will cancel a game if the developer can't get it tuned properly, and sometimes the problem is poor procedure.

- **When modifying parameters, make big adjustments, not small ones.** Brian Reynolds of Big Huge Games suggests beginning by doubling or halving the value of a parameter and checking the effect. Small adjustments may produce such subtle changes that you can't detect them. Make a large change, then iteratively reduce and test, moving toward the ideal value. Changing by a large factor makes it easier to zero in on your optimum setting.

TIP Always keep data that the core mechanics will use in a file that it reads when it starts up, or keep it accessible in real-time from a hidden designer's interface in the game. Never hard-code data into the program. This way you can change a detail and retest without having to recompile the program.

CHAPTER 15

▣ **Keep records.** Good testers keep close track of what they do so they don't end up wasting effort by trying the same thing twice. As a result, they can see the effects of the changes they've made and learn from experience.

▣ **Be sure your programmers use pseudo-random numbers.** As Chapter 14 explained, pseudo-random numbers let you control the effects of chance and hold the mechanics steady while you change parameters and test the result.

Summary

You have learned how to design games that are fair, avoiding dominant strategies and using chance in such a way that your game rewards skillful play. You have also seen how to manage difficulty so that the player's abilities match his challenges and keep him in the *flow* state of peak enjoyment. You now understand the role that positive feedback plays in games and how best to use it and control it. All these factors play a role in balancing a game, and if you keep them in mind, you should be able to adjust the core mechanics of your game to produce a challenging yet enjoyable experience for your player.

Design Practice EXERCISES

1. Devise a type of challenge that involves direct player control over one or more units *other* than conflict or racing challenges. Your type of challenge should involve units trying to accomplish some familiar task from the real world. (Your instructor may assign you a challenge type instead.) For your challenge, create three types of units in a transitive relationship with one another so that the attributes of the units determine that type A is better at the task than type B, and type B is better than type C. Document the challenge, the unit types, and the attributes that govern their suitability for the task. Then propose a shadow cost that balances the transitive relationship in a way that seems credible in the context of the challenge (such as the fuel-tank-size example in the racing game).

2. Design a game in which robots construct simple buildings consisting of floors, walls, and roofs, and assume that the foundations are already laid. (Don't worry about challenges or the victory condition for this exercise.) The construction tasks required include fetching different kinds of raw materials from stockpiles, transporting them to the building site, positioning them, and fastening them to the building. Decide for yourself what the raw materials will be; there must be at least four types. Devise names, attributes, and appropriate functions for at least six different kinds of robots that work together to perform these tasks; you may divide the robots' responsibilities any way you like, but do it in such a way that if any one type of robot is unavailable, the building cannot be completed. Include at least four attributes per type of robot. Document everything that you have created, and explain

how you have differentiated the robots orthogonally (which attributes each type possesses uniquely) as well as what features and abilities they all have in common.

Extra credit: Now adjust the robots' functions in such a way that some of their abilities overlap and if any one type of robot becomes unavailable, the others will still be able to complete the building, but no single robot can do it all.

3. Choose three different types of challenges from Chapter 13 and describe five versions of each type at different levels of absolute difficulty: very easy, easy, moderate, hard, and very hard (fifteen in all). Explain how each type of challenge differs for each level of absolute difficulty and give examples.

4. Modify the rules of checkers (draughts) to make the game asymmetric. Play-test the result with a friend to see if the game is still fair. Write a short paper explaining your changes, including types and numbers of units, types of moves allowed, and changes to the victory conditions for one or both sides.

5. *Monopoly* contains one game-balance weakness: The point at which one player becomes invincible due to the action of positive feedback is typically about an hour before the last player goes bankrupt and the game actually ends. Write a short paper proposing changes to the rules that would speed up the action of positive feedback in the later stages of the game without giving the first player who gets into the lead too much of an advantage in the early stages. Your proposed change must be fair: You cannot flatly offer the player in the lead a special advantage. While applying to all players, your rule change should be of the greatest benefit to the player with the largest amount of money. Explain how your proposal would work. (Hint: Your change may require a means of detecting that the game is in its later stages in order to come into effect then or to have its greatest impact then. Think about what is different between the early and later stages of the game and how a rule change might take advantage of that difference.)

Design Practice QUESTIONS

1. Is your game a PvP game or a PvE game?

2. Are the relationships among the player's options in the game largely transitive, intransitive, or a mixture of both?

3. If the relationships are transitive, how will you balance them so that each choice remains viable? Do you employ direct costs, shadow costs, or both? What will these costs be? How, if at all, will the player learn what they are? Or will the transitive options simply be upgrades from one another with no need to be balanced?

4. If your game includes intransitive relationships, what will you do to make them more interesting for the player and not too obvious?

5. Do you plan to give the player a choice of units to control or control over a variety of units? If so, how will you differentiate them? Will each unit have a unique role to play, with qualities it shares with no other, or will the qualities of some units overlap?

6. Does the game contain any elements that the player might perceive to be unfair?

7. If yours is a PvP game, are the capabilities of the forces symmetric or asymmetric? If they are asymmetric, in what ways do they differ and how will they be balanced? By adjusting costs? By changing rules or probabilities to compensate?

8. Do the game's challenges increase steadily in difficulty, or are there peaks and troughs, or spikes, in the difficulty level? If so, where are they?

9. How do you plan to change the absolute difficulty of your challenges? Do you plan to increase the power you provide to the player to meet the game's challenges? Will the player's perception of the game's difficulty go up with time or will it remain relatively flat?

10. What mechanisms, if any, will there be for changing the game's difficulty level? Hints? Shortcuts? A difficulty setting? How will the difficulty setting change the nature of the challenges offered? Will it make the enemies tougher or weaker, smarter or more stupid? Will it add or remove challenges entirely?

11. Does the game include positive feedback? If so, how will you control it to avoid runaway victory for the first player who gets ahead? A time delay? Negative feedback? A random factor?

12. How will the player know what to do next? What features does the game include to prevent the player feeling as if he is stuck?

13. To what degree is the player required to micromanage the game? Is the player obliged to look after small details? Are mechanisms available for the player to delegate some of these responsibilities to an automated process? If so, can the player be confident the automated process will make intelligent choices?

CHAPTER 16

General Principles of Level Design

If you have ever found yourself admiring the environment of a game or enjoying the way the game's challenges keep you guessing, you are appreciating the work of that game's level designer. The *level designer* creates not only the space in which the game takes place—its furnishings and backgrounds—but also the player's moment-by-moment experience of the game and much of its emotional context. Successful level designers draw on fundamental design principles that apply to any kind of game, such as ensuring the player always knows his short-term goals and the consequences of risks, as well as design principles specific to the type of game being designed. Level designers work closely with the game designer to make sure layouts are appropriate for the storyline and to achieve the atmosphere and pacing required to keep players engaged in the game world. Level design will not be a quick and easy process if you do it right. This chapter will identify 11 steps that the level designer takes, from initial handoff to user testing. The final section details problems to avoid in the level design process, including the key directive to never lose sight of your audience.

What Is Level Design?

Chapter 2, "Designing and Developing Games," described *level design* as the process of constructing the experience that will be offered directly to the player using components provided by the game designer. Note that the terms *game designer* and *level designer* are not interchangeable but refer to separate roles that, on larger development teams, are almost always played by different members of the team. On small or independent teams, however, the same person may do both. In the rest of this book, the word *you* means *the reader as game designer*, but in this chapter only, *you* indicates *the reader as level designer*.

Level designers create the following essential parts of the player's experience:

▪ **The space in which the game takes place.** If the game includes a simulated space, as most do, then level design includes creating that space using a 2D or 3D modeling tool. Although game designers determine what *kinds* of things will be in the game world, level designers determine precisely *what features* will be in each level of the game world and where these features will be. Level designers take the game designer's general plans for levels and make them specific and concrete.

- **The initial conditions of the level,** including the state of various changeable features (Is the drawbridge initially up or down?), the number of enemy characters the player faces, the amounts of any resources that the player controls at the beginning of the level, and the location of resources that may be found in the landscape. These examples were taken from an action-adventure; in a different genre the initial conditions will be different naturally.

- **The set of challenges the player will face within the level.** Many games offer challenges in a linear sequence; if they do, level designers determine what that sequence will be, construct a suitable space, and place the challenges within it. In other games, the challenges may be approached in a number of different possible sequences or in any order at all; see the sections "Layouts" and "Progression and Pacing," later in this chapter, for further discussion.

- **The termination conditions of the level,** ordinarily characterized in terms of victory and/or loss. In many games, levels can only be won but not lost, and in a few, such as the default mode in *SimCity,* levels can only be lost and never won.

- **The interplay between the gameplay and the game's story, if any.** The writer of the story must work closely with the level designer to interweave gameplay and narrative events.

- **The aesthetics and mood of the level.** Whereas the game designer and art director specify the overall tone of a level and artists create the specific models and textures, level designers take the general specifications and decide how to implement those plans. If the plan says, "Level 13 will be a scary haunted house," the level designers decide what kind of a house and *how* to make it feel scary and haunted.

Normally level designers construct all these parts using tools created specifically for the purpose. Some games, including *Little Big Planet* and *Half-Life 2,* actually ship their level design tools along with the game, so players can expand and customize the game world; if you own one of these games, you can practice level design by using those tools.

Level design could easily be the subject of an entire book. However, this chapter concentrates on introducing the general principles and the process of level design.

Key Design Principles

Two types of design principles will help you design a level: *universal level design principles* aimed at designing levels in any kind of game, and *genre-specific level design principles,* which focus on design issues specific to the different genres. This section addresses each of these in turn.

Universal Level Design Principles

Barbarossa: The [Pirate's] Code is more what you'd call "guidelines" than actual rules.

—PIRATES OF THE CARIBBEAN: THE CURSE OF THE BLACK PEARL

For some time, level designers have tried to define a set of principles to guide the level design process so that new games will avoid the errors of older ones. Considerable debate surrounds this issue, because not everyone agrees on which, if any, principle is truly universal. Examining the important principles constitutes a valuable exercise in any case, so we present a brief list here. Some principles apply as much to game design generally as they do specifically to level design, but because the level designer constructs the play environment and sets the challenges, she will be the one who puts these principles into practice.

- **Make the early levels of a game tutorial levels.** The entire section "Tutorial Levels," later in this chapter, is devoted to this extremely important topic.

- **Vary the pacing of the level.** This is also critically important. The later section "Progression and Pacing" addresses this.

- **When the player surmounts a challenge that consumes his resources, provide more resources.** This may seem obvious, but you might be surprised at how many games fail to do it. This, too, is addressed in "Progression and Pacing."

- **Avoid conceptual non sequiturs.** Unless your level is either intentionally surreal or meant to be funny, you shouldn't build elements that make no sense, such as rooms accessible only via ventilation shafts. Even more important, don't put dangers or rewards in places in which no sane person could possibly expect to find them. See the section "Avoid Conceptual Non Sequiturs," later in the chapter.

- **Clearly inform the player of her short-term goals.** At any given time, the player is working to achieve a whole hierarchy of challenges, from the overall victory condition of the game down to the problem occupying her attention (How do I get across this chasm?) at the immediate moment. (Chapter 13, "Gameplay," discusses the hierarchy of challenges at greater length.) While you do not always have to tell the player exactly what she needs to do to win (she may have to discover the long-term goal through exploration or observation), you should never leave her wondering what to do next; the current or next short-term goal should be obvious.

- **Be clear about risks, rewards, and the consequences of decisions.** When facing a challenge, the player should always have some idea of the benefits of success and the price of failure or, if the player has to make a decision, the likely consequences associated with his options. Old video games used to implement a *learn by dying* approach, which gave players no way to know what elements of the game world were dangerous and what weren't, so the avatars died repeatedly as the players learned. Industry professionals now consider this extremely bad design practice. Although the player should not necessarily know every detail of what consequences his decisions will produce, he should be able to make a reasonable guess based on the context in which you present the decision. If you give him a doorknob, it should open the door. It may *also* release a giant killer robo-camel into the room, but it should open the door first.

▨ **Reward the player for skill, imagination, intelligence, and dedication.** These four qualities distinguish a good player, and good players deserve to be rewarded. You may create rewards in many forms: powerups and other resources, shortcuts through the level, secret levels, mini-games, cut-scenes and other narrative material, or simple praise. Players like to be told when they've done a good job.

▨ **Reward in a large way, punish in a small way,** or to use an old adage, you catch more flies with honey than vinegar. The hope of success motivates players more than the fear of failure does. If a game repeatedly smacks them down hard, players will become discouraged and abandon the game with a feeling that they're being abused. Don't forget that the *duty to empathize* is one of the obligations of player-centric game design: Your primary objective is to give players an enjoyable experience. Build more rewards than punishments into your level.

▨ **The foreground takes precedence over the background.** Design the visual appearance of your level so that the player's attention is naturally drawn to her immediate surroundings. Don't make the background so complex that it distracts the player. Spend more of your machine's limited resources (polygons, memory, CPU time) on foreground objects than on background ones.

NOTE It is particularly challenging to the level designers to balance the difficulty of games intended for players of all ages.

▨ **The purpose of an artificial opponent is to put up a good fight and then lose.** Design your level so that the player will get better and better at overcoming the challenges until he succeeds at all of them. In a multiplayer competitive game, the skill and luck of the players decide who wins; but in a single-player game, you always want the player to win eventually, and it's up to you to make sure that happens. An unbeatable level is a badly designed level.

▨ **Implement multiple difficulty settings if possible.** Make your game accessible to a wider audience by allowing players to switch the difficulty of your game to easy, normal, or hard settings. In games with an internal economy, you should be able to tweak the numbers to adjust the difficulty to accommodate the player's preference; Chapter 15, "Game Balancing," addresses this in more detail.

THE 400 PROJECT

In 2001, veteran game designers Hal Barwood and Noah Falstein began assembling a list of design rules for video games, hoping eventually to compile a list of as many as 400 of them. So far, Barwood and Falstein's *400 Project* has gathered more than 100 rules from fellow designers; these represent the combined wisdom of many people. Rather than outright commandments, these are tools to guide your own creative work, as a ruler guides a pencil. Some of the rules conflict with others, and it will be up to you to decide when one rule is more important than another. You should download the rules and take them to heart as you design your game and the levels within it. You can find *The 400 Project* at www.finitearts.com/400P/400project.htm.

Genre-Specific Level Design Principles

Some principles of level design apply only to games within specific genres. Since there isn't room to present a comprehensive list of principles specific to each genre, this section offers *one* highly important genre-specific principle for each genre mentioned in Chapter 3, "The Major Genres." For more details on each genre, see the relevant e-book for that genre.

SHOOTER GAMES

Reward precision and timing. Shooter games vary enormously, from frenetic 2D button-mashers to slow-moving stealth games in which the player hardly ever fires at all. The one thing that they have in common is the player's need to hit what she is aiming at, which may be a moving target that shoots back. A player who shoots precisely should do better than one who misses a lot. In a stealth game, correctly anticipating the correct moment in a guard's patrol routine to sneak from one point of cover to another is a timing challenge. These skills are at the heart of the game and the game should reward performing them well.

ACTION AND ARCADE GAMES

Vary the pace. Action games (and especially the fast-and-furious arcade variety) put more stress on the player than any other genre does, so the universal principle of "vary the pace" applies more strongly to action games than to other genres; that is why it is the most important genre-specific principle as well. Players must be able to rest, both physically and mentally, between bouts of high-speed action.

STRATEGY GAMES

Reward planning. Strategic thinking means planning—anticipating an opponent's moves and preparing a defense, as well as planning attacks and considering an opponent's possible defensive moves. Design levels that reward planning. Give players defensible locations to build in and advantageous positions to attack from, but let the players discover these places for themselves.

ROLE-PLAYING GAMES

Offer opportunities for character growth and player self-expression. Character growth is a major player goal in any role-playing game (RPG); some players consider it even more important than victory. Every level should provide opportunities to achieve character growth by whatever means the game rewards—combat, puzzle solving, trade, and so on. RPGs also entertain by allowing players to express themselves; that is, to role-play. Every level should include opportunities for the player to make decisions that reflect the player's persona in the game.

SPORTS GAMES

Verisimilitude is vital. While not ordinarily broken into levels in the usual sense, sports games consist of individual matches played in different stadiums or courses with different teams or athletes, so you can think of each match played as a level. Level designers design the stadiums and sometimes the teams and athletes. More than in any other genre, players of sports games value a close relationship between the video game and the real world. The simulation of match play must be completely convincing; try to model each team and each stadium as closely as possible to the real thing—which includes not only appearances but the athletes' performance characteristics and the teams' coaching strategies.

VEHICLE SIMULATIONS

Reward skillful maneuvering. All vehicle simulations offer steering a vehicle as the primary player activity, and steering well, often in adverse circumstances, as the primary challenge. Construct levels that test the player's skill at maneuvering his vehicle and reward him for his prowess. Other challenges, such as shooting or exploring, should be secondary.

CONSTRUCTION AND SIMULATION GAMES

Offer an interesting variety of initial conditions and goals. Most construction and simulation games start the player with an empty space and let her build whatever she likes within the constraints of the game's internal economy. In such games, you won't need to do much level design. However, such a game can also offer the player an existing or partial construction and let her continue working from there, often with a goal to achieve within a certain time limit. These are normally called *scenarios* rather than *levels*, the difference being that a scenario, unlike a level, consists of a self-contained situation unrelated to any of the other scenarios. Typically the game allows players to try the scenarios in any order, and the gameplay (though not the goal) tends to be identical in each. Because you cannot alter the gameplay, scenario design becomes a matter of offering an interesting variety of initial conditions and goals. *SimCity 3000 Unlimited* comes with 13 scenarios, from reuniting East and West Berlin to preparing for a World Cup soccer match in Seoul.

ADVENTURE GAMES

Construct challenges that harmonize with their locations and the story. Adventure games offer much of their entertainment through exploration and puzzle solving. Designers set different chapters of an adventure game in different locations or landscapes to add novelty and interest to the experience. (A chapter is the adventure game equivalent of a level.) Create challenges that harmonize with the current level and with the current events in the story. In a room full of machinery, the challenges should involve machines; on a farm, the challenges should involve crops or farm animals. This principle applies to some extent to any game, but because story is so important in adventure games, the principle is especially important for that genre.

PUZZLE GAMES

Give the player clues about the correct solution state and his progress toward it. A puzzle in which the player has no idea what he is trying to achieve can be solved only by brute force trial-and-error, and that's no fun. A jigsaw puzzle's solution state is the picture on the front of the box, for example. If the object is to find a hidden solution state (as in the game hangman), then the player should get some kind of clues about whether or not he's getting close. You can give hints in a variety of ways depending the nature of the puzzle—by offering a hint if the player is taking a long time, or by letting him buy hints with points of some kind. The game *Guess the Food* gives hint points for each correct answer, and players can spend the points for hints if they get stuck.

Layouts

For games that involve travel, especially avatar-based games, the layout of the space significantly affects the player's perception of the experience. Over the years, a few common patterns have emerged, which this section introduces in simplified form. You should not hesitate to create any layout that your game needs.

NOTE This section addresses the layout of the space within a level that an avatar passes through. Don't confuse it with the sequence of levels themselves. Most games use a strictly linear sequence of levels.

Open Layouts

In an open layout, the player benefits from almost entirely unconstrained movement. An open layout corresponds to the outdoors, with an avatar in principle free to wander in any direction at any time. Even levels with open layouts, though, may include a few small regions that cannot be entered without difficulty or can be entered by only a single path (such as passing through a door into a building). War games make extensive use of open layouts, the *Battlefield* series being a particularly successful example. RPGs offer open layouts while the player goes adventuring outdoors, but typically they switch to network or combination layouts (described later) when the party goes indoors or underground.

Linear Layouts

A linear layout requires the player to experience the game's spaces in a fixed sequence with no side corridors or branches. It does not mean that the spaces are actually arranged in a line (see **Figure 16.1**). A player following a linear path can move only to the next area or to the previous area, and does not have to make any decisions about where to go next. A game in which all levels use linear layouts is often said to be *on rails* because, like a train on a track, the traveler goes wherever the predefined route takes her. Ordinarily, the player has no reason to go backward in a linear layout unless she forgot to pick up something that she needs. Linear layouts often require players to pass through one-way doors that actually prevent them from going back, so long as they have collected everything they need to go on. Be sure you don't lock a player out of a region that contains an item essential to her later progress—an elementary level design error.

Linear layouts naturally work well with linear stories; if your game features such a story, you might consider such a layout. See Chapter 11, "Storytelling," for more on linear stories.

FIGURE 16.1
A level with a linear layout

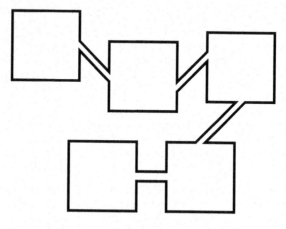

Traditional for side-scrolling action games and rail-shooters, the linear layout is otherwise uncommon nowadays. Today's designers of these kinds of games tend to favor the parallel layout.

FIGURE 16.2
A parallel layout

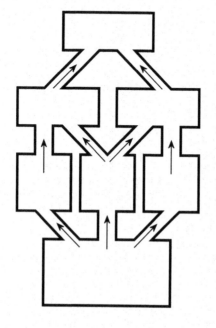

Parallel Layouts

A parallel layout—a modern variant of the linear layout—resembles a railroad switchyard with lots of parallel tracks and the means for the player to switch from one track to another at intervals. The player passes through the level from one end to another but may take a variety of paths to get there. See **Figure 16.2** for a much-simplified illustration.

Even though the parallel layout does not require players to pass through every available path, most players search them all anyway if the game lets them do so. One path may offer a greater risk and therefore a greater reward, while another path may give the player greater insights into the storyline. You can easily construct a parallel layout to reflect a foldback story structure. (See Chapter 11 for a discussion of story structures.)

You can also use parallel paths to provide shortcuts that let a player bypass particularly difficult challenges that lie on the more obvious path. If you do so, you may want to hide the entrance to the shortcut so only a dedicated explorer will find it. When you create a hidden entrance, you must provide some clue, however subtle, that it is there. Otherwise, finding it becomes a trial-and-error challenge, a sign of bad design. The original *Wolfenstein 3D* contained hidden rooms accessible only through wall panels that looked exactly like the rest of the wall, which forced players to check every single wall panel in the entire level to see which might conceal a hidden room.

Ring Layouts

In a ring layout, the path returns to its starting point, although you may include shortcuts that cut off a portion of the journey (see **Figure 16.3**). Designers mainly use ring layouts for racing games, in which players pass through the same space a number of times, facing challenges from the environment and each other along the way. Shortcuts require less time but should be proportionately more difficult than the regular route; balancing this will be a big part of the level designer's job.

Rings do not necessarily look like circles. Oval tracks or twisting road-racing tracks qualify as rings.

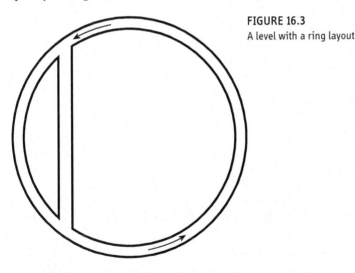

FIGURE 16.3
A level with a ring layout

Network Layouts

Spaces in a network layout connect to other spaces in a variety of ways. **Figure 16.4** shows a simple example. A large network poses a considerable exploration challenge; just learning the way around made up a significant part of the gameplay in old text adventure games. Modern graphical games that implement three-dimensional spaces usually present architecturally appropriate and logical networks (going downstairs from the ground floor of a building leads to the basement, for instance) but still offer plenty of opportunities to create enjoyable exploration challenges. See the section "Exploration Challenges" in Chapter 13 for further discussion.

A network layout gives the player considerable freedom about what path to take, so you will find it difficult to tell a story that requires a particular sequence of events in a network layout. This doesn't mean that you can't tell stories, only that your stories have to tolerate the player experiencing events in any sequence. To enforce *some* sequence, use a combination layout, described in the later section "Combinations of Layouts."

FIGURE 16.4
A simple network layout

In a network with a small number of major spaces, every space may be connected to every other space for maximum freedom of movement. This arrangement poses little exploration challenge to the player but makes an ideal fighting ground for deathmatch contests in games such as *Quake* because there are no choke points. Enemies may enter and exit in several directions, which prevents a player from guarding one particular location indefinitely.

Hub-and-Spoke Layouts

In the hub-and-spoke layout, the player begins in a central hub that ordinarily doesn't present significant challenges or dangers. As such, it serves as a place of comfort or safety, a base to which to return. To explore the rest of the world, the player follows a linear path out from the hub and then returns back to the hub on the same path (see **Figure 16.5**). The return journey should be quick—because the player covers old ground during the return—or should offer new opportunities for gameplay and new rewards as the player comes back. Normally you would also put a major challenge and a major reward at the outer end of the spoke.

This layout gives the player some choice about where he goes, which many players appreciate. For one thing, it allows them to abandon a level that they are finding difficult and try another one instead. You need not offer the player access to all the spokes at the beginning of the level, however; to make sure that the player doesn't try the harder challenges too soon, you can lock off some areas until the player tries the easier challenges available in other spokes. Note that if you unlock the spokes only one at a time, you effectively change the hub-and-spoke layout into a linear layout.

The *Spyro the Dragon* games use a hub-and-spoke plan. The games include several hubs, called *homeworlds,* each of which is the center of its level. Various spokes lead off from the hubs to areas with different themes.

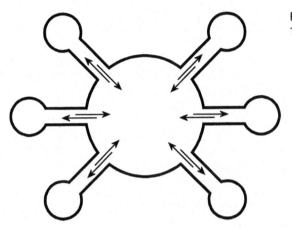

FIGURE 16.5
The hub-and-spoke layout

Combinations of Layouts

Many layouts combine aspects of each type of layout, providing, for instance, networked spaces to accomplish tasks within a larger linear framework. The layout in **Figure 16.6** corresponds to the story structure of many large RPGs, which tend to offer one major story arc and a large number of subplots or quests. Adventure games quite often use a combination structure too, letting players do considerable exploration in one area before moving on to another. A good many games also offer completely optional material in an otherwise linear design that the player can play through if she wants to—these are usually called *bonus levels.*

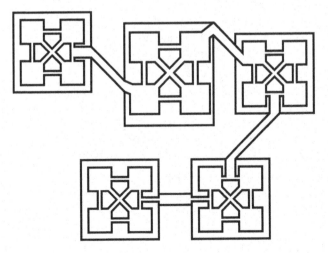

FIGURE 16.6
A combined linear and networked layout

Expanding on the Principles of Level Design

This section looks at a few particularly important issues in the list of universal design principles: atmosphere, pacing, and tutorial levels.

Atmosphere

The art director and lead game designer decide on the overall look of a game, the artists build the models, and the audio engineers create the sound effects. But it's up to the level designer to assemble all this material into a specific level in such a way that it's aesthetically coherent and creates the appropriate mood. A level designer does what in movies would be four or five jobs (set designer, lighting designer, special effects designer, Foley editor, and even cinematographer), because a level designer must look at the game world the way the player sees it—through the lens of the game's virtual camera.

As you work to establish the atmosphere of your game, you will use all the following tools:

■ **Lighting.** The placement and orientation of the lights in a level can create a sunny day, a moonlit night, or a dark alley. Soft morning light filtering in through a window creates a sense of warmth and well-being, whereas the odd glowing colored lights of a machine room evoke a sense of danger. The yellow of a sodium vapor street lamp or the harsh fluorescent lights of an office and any other lighting you choose must work with other aesthetic choices you make to set the mood of a level. What you choose *not* to light is just as important as what you choose *to* light.

■ **Color palette.** Just as the color palette of the avatar's clothes reflects her character, the color palette of the level reflects its mood. The color palette of the level will emerge from a combination of the original colors of the objects you place in it (created by the artists under neutral lighting conditions) plus the lighting that you add. Notice how television commercials use color to telegraph an emotion, calm you down, get you excited, or keep you interested in watching. Do some research on color and you will find many ways to create an effect in your level or elicit a particular response from the player.

■ **Weather and atmospheric effects.** Fog, rain, snow, and wind all create distinct impressions. So many games take place in indoor spaces that we sometimes forget the importance of weather to our moods. Dark, tumbling skies presage a storm and make us instinctively react with "Find shelter!," even in a video game. Fog creates mystery, while strong winds suggest instability and disturbances to come.

■ **Special visual effects.** When weapons recoil or screeching tires create smoke, when magic spells produce colored sparks or blood splashes across a wall, you're seeing visual effects. You can startle players, discomfit them, amuse them, or reward them, all with visual effects.

▧ **Music.** You won't write the music unless you're also a musician, but you may well choose the music of your level in conjunction with your game's audio director. The rhythm of the music helps to set the pace, and its timbre and key help to set the mood. Generally, but not always, music remains consistent throughout the level, part of its overall tone.

▧ **Ambient audio.** Like music, ambient audio contributes to the overall mood of a level. Notice how golf games use the sounds of birds singing and crickets chirping to suggest the peaceful outdoor tranquility of a golf course. The ambient audio can also vary with place and time, which tells the player something about where he is and helps him orient himself. Great steam engines churning create a feeling of power and danger; owls hooting and foxes crying tell us it's nighttime; the hubbub of talk and regular cries of vendors put us in a market square.

▧ **Special audio effects.** Audio effects naturally do for the ears what visual effects do for the eyes, and in some respects, they provide even more important information. From inside a car, you can't see the tires losing their grip on the road, but the squealing sound tells you you're on the edge of danger—you're pushing the vehicle to its limits.

Progression and Pacing

A large video game—one designed to be played for more than a single play session (though that might range from five minutes to an hour, say)—is almost always divided into a number of levels. If you want the player to experience those levels in a sequence, they should exhibit *progression* of some kind: changes from level to level that represent growth in some form, or narrative advancement, or both.

The *pacing* of a level refers to the frequency at which the player encounters individual challenges. A fast pace creates *stress,* offering challenges at a rapid rate while giving the player no opportunity to relax. (Chapter 13 defines stress and discusses the relationship between *stress* and *difficulty.*) A slow pace offers challenges at a slow rate and permits the player to take her time about addressing them.

This section of the chapter discusses both progression and pacing, and how to design them properly.

DESIGNING THE PROGRESSION

Games obviously need to change from level to level, but *how* should they change? Designer Mike Lopez has written a useful article on the subject in his "Gameplay Design Fundamentals" column for the *Gamasutra* webzine (Lopez, 2006). He identifies five game features that should exhibit progression throughout the game; these serve us as a starting point:

▧ **Mechanics.** Lopez uses this term to refer both to the core mechanics of the game and the actions available to the player. This book organizes these concepts differently, so we'll look at core mechanics here and actions later. Generally speaking, the core mechanics should become richer as the game goes along. In the early levels, especially the tutorial levels, the internal economy of the game should be easy for the player to learn. Later, the mechanics can become more intricate, as in games like the *Civilization* series. Many games also exhibit economic growth throughout the game, so the player is dealing with larger and larger quantities of resources—money, hit points, horsepower, or whatever the game deems to be of value.

▪ **Experience duration.** Except for the occasional atypical level (see the later section "Make Atypical Levels Optional"), it should take more and more time to play through each subsequent level. This rule is not absolute, but generally speaking, levels later in the game should be longer than those earlier in the game.

▪ **Ancillary rewards and environmental progression.** *Ancillary rewards* are unrelated to the gameplay: cut-scenes, trophies, unlockable content, and so on. (When the player gets to the end of *Silent Hill 3,* she earns the right to dress Heather, the avatar character, in new clothes and play the game again wearing them. This has no effect on the gameplay.) By *environmental progression* Lopez means enjoyable changes in the landscape of the game world, which makes sense when the game involves travel. Both of these provide novelty, one of the ways that video games entertain.

▪ **Practical gameplay rewards.** These are rewards that directly influence the player's future gameplay: new vehicles in driving games; new gear or skills in role-playing games; new moves or characters in fighting games; new technology in strategy games; and so on.

▪ **Difficulty.** Generally speaking, the perceived difficulty of the game should go up. It should go up quickly in games aimed at experienced players, and more slowly in casual games and those aimed at children. A few games such as *Bejeweled* have a flat difficulty curve because their challenges are based primarily on luck. Chapter 15 dealt with this issue extensively.

In addition to Lopez's list of features, you may wish to consider a few more:

▪ **Actions available to the player.** Lopez lumped these together with mechanics, but they aren't quite the same. A game can possess core mechanics that don't change much from level to level, yet still offer players new moves or other activities to perform as the game goes along. This is particularly noticeable in platform games. It's always a good idea to introduce new actions through a series of tutorial levels so that players can become skilled with one before learning the next one.

▪ **Story progression.** As your player progresses through the game, he should also progress through the story, if it has one. Exactly how this happens depends on a number of design decisions you must make: whether the plot is linear or not, and what mechanism causes the plot to advance. Chapter 11 addresses these details.

▪ **Character growth.** Video game characters often become more powerful through practical gameplay rewards, and sometimes they become more visually interesting through ancillary rewards such as new clothing. But you can also make them grow in a literary sense: become more mature, well-rounded people. A character who doesn't grow, especially over the course of several games, eventually begins to seem like a cartoon character with no emotional depth.

It will be easiest to implement these features if you organize your game into a number of discrete levels, each of which contains its own environment, starting conditions, victory condition, and so on. However, levels are naturally rather artificial. If you want to offer a strongly storylike experience, you may prefer to avoid having breaks between one level and the next, and try to create an entirely seamless experience. *Half-Life* is a famous example.

DESIGNING THE PACING

The pace you choose for your level will depend to a considerable extent on the genre of the game you're creating; players expect a faster- or slower-paced game depending upon the genre. The fastest-paced games of all, the old 2D side-scrolling or top-scrolling shooters, required players to move the joystick and bang the fire button continuously just to survive. Multiplayer deathmatch shooters such as *Quake* and its kin represent the modern equivalent. (Stealth games such as the *Rainbow Six* series, which involve careful planning, often move at a slow pace except for a brief wild flurry when the enemy comes into view.) Adventure games use the slowest pace because much of the activity consists of interactive dialogue (generally a story action rather than an action the player takes to surmount a challenge), exploration without much effort, and puzzle solving in which the players can take as long as they like. Play a variety of games and study their pacing. The companion e-book, *Fundamentals of Action and Arcade Game Design,* discusses pacing extensively because it is so important in that genre.

CLASSIC ARCADE PACING

In arcade games, especially old ones such as *Space Invaders*, the pace at which the player faces challenges becomes faster and faster as each level progresses. If the player succeeds in beating the level—destroying all the invading aliens—she gets a few seconds of rest before the next level begins. The next level offers identical challenges, but it starts at a faster pace than the previous level started and ends at a faster pace than the previous level ended. The pace of *Space Invaders* increases both within each level and from level to level until it overwhelms the player and she loses the game. She cannot win; she can only hope to get a high score.

This classic arcade pacing explains how arcade games used to make their money. This scenario is now considered a bit old-fashioned and inappropriate for console and PC games because they don't need to make the player lose to force her to put more money in the machine. However, with the continuing popularity of retro gaming, classic arcade pacing remains common in simple web-based games such as *Collapse!*

VARY THE PACING

As a general principle, the pacing of a level in any game, especially a game with physical challenges, should alternate between fast and slow periods, just as the tempo of movements in a symphony or the levels of excitement in an action movie vary. Players need moments to rest, both physically and mentally, and on the whole, the faster the pace of the level, the more important rest becomes. A particularly stressful challenge should be followed by a brief period with no challenges at all and then by easier challenges that gradually ramp up to more stressful ones again. This also gives the player a chance to savor the pleasant emotions that accompany success.

Varying the pace not only gives the player a rest from physical challenges, but it also produces a more balanced game. If overcoming a challenge requires spending a resource (ammunition or health or the like), then the more the player spends on a given challenge, the weaker and more vulnerable he is afterward. In his weakened state, he should not face another demanding challenge immediately. You should also make fresh supplies available to him immediately after he surmounts a challenge that costs him a lot of resources, as Chapter 15 explained. In shooter games, these traditionally take the form of boxes of ammunition and medical kits for restoring health, stored in an area immediately beyond a large group of enemies. In RPGs, enemies drop valuable resources when killed, thus helping to replenish the player's supply.

PACING IN *THE LORD OF THE RINGS*

For a wonderful example of varied pacing from literature, read *The Lord of the Rings*. Almost every major adventure or threat the Fellowship experiences in the first two volumes is followed by a period of rest and refreshment to heal wounds and, in particular, to replenish food supplies. The hobbits flee the Black Riders and take refuge with Farmer Maggot. They are caught in the Old Forest and rescued by Tom Bombadil. After the attack at Weathertop, they find shelter in Rivendell. After losing Gandalf in the Mines of Moria, they find succor in Lórien, and so on. This change of pace not only creates emotional variety for the reader, allowing her to enjoy the beauty and warmth of the heroes' places of shelter after the terrors of their journey, but it also makes the story more credible. No one can carry six months' worth of food on his back, so the supplies had to come from somewhere.

The Da Vinci Code, notwithstanding its financial success, is less credible in this regard. Involved in almost nonstop action from start to finish, the heroes never seem to need any sleep.

You can vary the pacing in a variety of ways: by creating an area free of challenges in which the player can simply explore; by creating an area that contains only low-stress challenges; or by making the player's avatar temporarily invulnerable or particularly strong as a reward for successfully overcoming a demanding challenge. You can also deliver a bit of the story through narrative: Watching a cut-scene, for example, gives the player a moment to relax.

You will find it easiest to vary the pacing in games that involve avatar travel through a linear space, because you can control the sequence in which the player confronts challenges. Games that give the player freedom to explore at will give you less control. In genres that use multipresent interaction models rather than avatar- or party-based ones, you may have little control at all. For example, in a real-time strategy game, the pacing depends to a large degree on the player's own style of play. Those who attack aggressively experience a faster pace than those who slowly build up huge armies before attacking.

OVERALL PACING

Although the pacing of a level should vary from time to time (depending on the genre), the overall pacing of the level should either remain steady or become more rapid as the player nears the end. A longstanding tradition in action games, and many other genres as well, calls for the inclusion of a *boss* to defeat at the end of the level: a particularly difficult challenge. Victory, and the end of the level, reward the player for defeating the boss, and this sometimes includes a cache of resources or treasure as well. Bosses, although something of a cliché, fit neatly into games with a Hero's Journey story structure. *Fundamentals of Action and Arcade Game Design* discusses bosses in greater detail.

TIP If your game is complex enough to need a manual, be sure to make the manual available for download from a website or page dedicated to the game. Players lose manuals.

Levels should not, in general, get easier and easier as they go along. If the player does well, *positive feedback* may come into play to make the game easier, and you will need to design the level, or the core mechanics, to reduce that effect. Chapter 15 discusses positive feedback at length, including various means of limiting it.

Tutorial Levels

Years ago, video games shipped with large manuals that explained how to play the games. Nowadays, however, all games should be designed so that the player can start playing immediately. A few complex games still use manuals, mostly in electronic form, but for detailed reference information rather than for instructions. Players still like to have manuals, but as many games are distributed in electronic form, you should make the manual available within the game so the player doesn't have to leave it to open the manual in another application.

Instead of instructions, games offer *tutorial levels*—early levels that teach the player how to play. Every commercial game except the simplest ones should include one or more tutorial levels. Although tutorial levels require more time and effort to build

TIP   If you discover that players are often uncertain about how to play, establish a Frequently Asked Questions (FAQ) web page for your game. Ideally, however, you will design the game so well that there won't be any frequently asked questions!

than a manual does to write, tutorial levels have a tremendous advantage: They let the player learn in a hands-on fashion. Players learn physical activities, such as how the control devices function in the game, far more quickly if they can try the actions for themselves.

Tutorial levels may be explicit or implicit. Explicit tutorial levels are separate from the main sequence of levels in the game and should be optional. For example, some sports games include a training camp feature that serves as a tutorial level, letting players learn the skills they need without actually playing a match. Experienced players can skip this part and go straight into regular play. Implicit tutorial levels are the first few levels of the game, carefully crafted so the player learns as he plays.

A tutorial level is not simply an easy level or a short level. A tutorial level should be a carefully crafted experience that explains the game's user interface (UI), key challenges, and actions to the player. Use voiceover narration, text superimposed on the screen, or a special mentor character to explain things. However, the player must be able to turn these features off or skip through them rapidly if he doesn't need them. Experienced players find it very frustrating to be forced to go through tutorial content that they already know.

As you design one or more tutorial levels for your game, consider these key principles:

- Introduce the game's features in an orderly sequence, starting with the most general and most often used features and proceeding to the more specialized and rarely used ones. Your tutorial should introduce each individual action that the game permits, but it need not discuss combinations of actions and what effects they may have. The players can work that out for themselves.

- Don't make all the game's features available at once. It will only confuse the player if she happens to select, by accident, a maneuver that you haven't introduced yet, which produces an effect on the screen that the player doesn't understand. Disable features until the tutorial introduces them.

- If the interface is complex, as interfaces tend to be in many war games and construction and management simulations, introduce the information over two or three tutorial levels.

- Highlight UI elements that appear on the screen with an arrow or a colored glow whenever your explanatory text or helpful guide character refers to them. Don't just say where these items appear on the screen and make the player look for them.

- Let the player go back and try things again as often as he wants, without any penalty for failure. All the costs of making a mistake that you might put into the ordinary game world should be switched off in the tutorial levels.

The Level Design Process

Now that you have learned the general *principles* of level design, let's turn to the *process*. Level design takes place during the elaboration stage of game design and, like the overall game design, is an iterative process. At points during the procedure, the level designers should show the work-in-progress to other members of the team for analysis and commentary. Early input from artists, programmers, and other designers prevents you from wasting time on overly complex levels, asking for features the programmers cannot implement, or making demands for artwork that the artists don't have time to meet.

At the 2004 Computer Game Technology Conference in Toronto, Canada, level designers Rick Knowles and Joseph Ganetakos of Pseudo Interactive presented an excellent lecture simply entitled "Level Design" (Knowles and Ganetakos, 2004). They described the 11-stage process by which their company builds levels, which is summarized here. The following sections assume that the development teams consist of game designers, artists, programmers, and sound designers, as well as you: the level designer.

Throughout the discussion of this process, you will notice a strong emphasis on the relationship between the level designer and the art team, and less emphasis on the relationship between the level designer and the audio or programming teams. The reason for this is that level designers build prototype artwork that the art team then uses as a blueprint from which to build final artwork that will actually go into the game. This requires that the level designers hand off their prototype to the art team and receive the final artwork back from the art team at particular stages in the process. The relationship with the programmers and the audio team is less sharply defined. Level designers request special features from these groups, and the project manager determines when and how that work gets done, but generally it doesn't involve handing off material *to* the audio or programming teams and receiving material back from them in the same way. Your relationship with the programmers and audio people is just as important as your relationship with the artists, but your interactions with them may be less formally scheduled.

A NOTE ON DUTIES AND TERMINOLOGY

The nature of a level designer's job varies considerably depending on both the genre of the game and the technology that implements it. A few years ago, level designers were not expected to possess either art or programming skills. As the size and complexity of games has increased, so has the size and complexity of the level designer's job. In modern 3D games, level designers often use 3D modeling tools to construct temporary—and sometimes even final—artwork to go into a game. (The term *model* refers to a three-dimensional geometric structure that depicts a single thing, such as a human, vehicle, tree, or the underlying landscape of a level.) Also, games now often include *scripting engines* that allow level designers to write small programs, or *scripts*, that control some aspects of the behavior of the level during play. Scripting engines normally implement scripting languages less powerful than the programming language used by the programmers, but the scripting language will be sufficient for defining the behavior of automated traps, doors, and other special events that may occur in the level. There isn't room in this book to teach you the skills you need to use such tools, but you can find many resources for learning to use them on the Internet and at colleges and universities.

For simplicity's sake, this section assumes that you are creating levels for a game that uses a 3D graphics engine to display a 3D game world. If you are making a 2D game, where it refers to models, think in terms of their 2D equivalents: *sprites* (2D art and animation) for movable objects and the *background* (a 2D painting, often made up of interchangeable rectangular tiles) for the landscape.

Design to Level Design Handoff

In the first stage, the game designers will tell you in a general way what they want for the level: its setting, mood, key gameplay activities, and events. You should then generate a list of features you want to appear in the level:

- Events that can be triggered by player action
- Props (objects that will be present in the level)
- Non-player characters (NPCs)

At this point you also create a rough overview map of the level, showing how the landscape varies and what props and NPCs will be in which areas. See **Figure 16.7** for an example from an unproduced driving game by Pseudo Interactive, set on islands inhabited by dinosaurs.

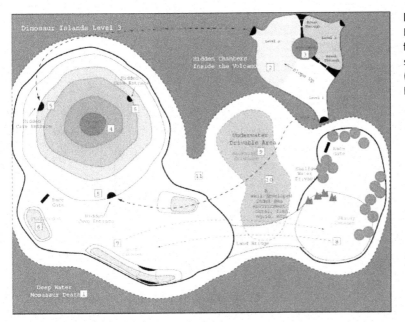

FIGURE 16.7
Rough level sketch for a driving game showing key features (Image courtesy Pseudo Interactive)

Planning Phase

Armed with the list and sketch created in the first stage, you now start to plan the level in detail. Use pencil and paper to work out the sequence of events, both what you expect the player(s) to do and how the game will respond. Begin to document your decisions in the following key areas: gameplay, art, performance, and code requirements.

GAMEPLAY

As you plan the gameplay for your level, you will need to consider all the following issues:

■ **Layout** (discussed extensively in the "Layouts" section earlier). Where can the player-controlled characters (avatar, party, or units) go and where can they not go? What creates these boundaries (physical obstacles or lethal dangers, for example)? What paths can they use to get there? Many parts of your level may be cosmetic: The player can see them but cannot reach them.

▓ **Areas devoted to major challenges or hazards.** Which areas carry strategic importance? Which will offer the biggest challenges? If the game involves combat, where would you like it to occur?

▓ **Pacing.** How will the intensity of action vary throughout the level? Where will the key events and the rest periods occur?

▓ **Termination conditions.** How does the player win or lose the level?

▓ **Resource placements.** Are deposits of weapons, health points, powerups, or any other resources hidden in the environment? Where? What resources, and how much?

▓ **Player start and end points.** Do the player-controlled characters begin the level at one or more specific locations? Where? Do the characters end at one or more locations? Where?

▓ **NPC positions and spawn points.** If NPCs—whether enemies, friends, or neutrals—appear in the level, where are they initially positioned? Can they suddenly appear in the level at a specific location or *spawn point* during play? Where?

▓ **Elevations.** How much vertical movement does the level permit and how does that affect play? Higher elevations naturally allow the player to see farther in first- and third-person perspectives; will this cause problems or constitute a positive feature of your level?

▓ **Secret areas**. Do you plan to incorporate hidden areas or secret shortcuts? Where will they be, and what clues will be available to suggest they might be present?

▓ **Special event issues.** What special events, unique to this level, can occur? Where will they occur? What will set them off? How do the special events reflect the setting and tone of the level?

▓ **Landmarks.** How does the player find her way around? How can she tell where she is? Establishing major landmarks will help her out.

▓ **Destruction.** Can any part of the level be destroyed or its landscape radically altered? Where does this happen and what causes it? How does it affect the gameplay? Does it have the potential to introduce anomalies, such as enemies who wander off the edge of the world and never return?

▓ **Storytelling.** How does the sequence of events the player experiences integrate with the game's story? Which events are dramatically meaningful and which are not? Where and when do you want cut-scenes or other narrative events to occur?

▓ **Save points and checkpoints.** Does the level include save points or checkpoints? Where? In games in which the player fails frequently and has to reload, positioning the save points is a critically important part of balancing the game.

ART

In the art-planning phase, you determine the *scope* of your level and how much artwork it will need. Scope refers to the magnitude and complexity of the level, both in terms of the number of objects and characters that it contains and the special events that it includes. You can make a serious error by choosing too large a scope, because if you overload your art staff, you may never get the level finished at all. See "Design Rule Get the Scope Right!," near the end of this chapter.

You already have your sketch and a general idea of what the environment will be like, whether on the sea floor, in outer space, or inside an anthill. First decide on the scale of the level: How big will this level be in the game world's units of measure? This will help you determine just how many other features the level needs. In almost every genre, if you've balanced the challenges correctly, the size of the level is directly proportional to the length of time that it takes the player to play through that level, so the scale you choose will, in a rough way, determine how much gameplay you can offer.

Next, start thinking about the kinds of objects that should be present in the level. Do research at the library or on the Internet for visual reference material to give you inspiration. Count the number of unique types of props that the level will require and plan in a general way where to put them. Certain generic items such as streetlights (or the infamous crates in first-person shooters) can simply be duplicated, but natural objects such as trees and boulders should come in several types, and the art team will need to know this. Try to avoid including too many identical objects in a level; it destroys realism (although you may be forced to go this route by the limitations of your target machine).

Either you or the art director will need to create a list of textures that the level will probably need. In an office, you may need tiles for the floor coverings, wood or metal for the desks, fabric for the chairs, and so on. Some offices may be streamlined, with severe geometric shapes, whereas others may be ornate, featuring a Louis XIV desk and antique chairs.

Work with the art team to decide on the visual appearance of any special effects that the artists will have to implement. It may take a while for the artists to come up with the visuals for a never-before-seen eruption of semisentient magma at zero gravity, so you need to plan ahead.

NOTE To save memory space in the machine and art development time, many games use a library of props that is available across all levels and try to keep the number of unique props in each level to a minimum. This creates a certain sameness to each level of the game, however. Provide as much visual diversity as you can afford.

CHAPTER 16

PERFORMANCE

Normally you think of performance as the programmers' problem, but it's up to the level designer not to build a world that bogs down the machine. You will need to sit down with the programmers and set some boundaries. How complex can the geometry be? How far into the distance will the graphics engine be able to render objects? How many autonomously moving units or creatures can the game support at one time? Know your machine's limitations as you plan your level.

CODE

Finally, as part of the planning process, identify specific requests that you intend to make of the programmers for features unique to this level. These may take the form of special events (sometimes called *gags*) that require coding, unique NPCs who appear only in this level but need their own behavior model and artificial intelligence, or special development tools you may require to build and test the level effectively. The more of these special coding problems you identify during planning and can discuss with the programmers in advance, the more likely that implementation will go smoothly.

Working through these steps results in an initial plan for the level. Don't expect the numbers and details in this plan to match exactly what you end up with in the finished level, but working out in advance as much as you can will ensure a smoother design process. Charging in without a plan and making it up as you go along creates more problems in the long run.

Prototyping

In this stage, you will build a prototype of the level. Much of this work will consist of using a 3D modeling tool to construct temporary models of the landscape and objects that can appear within it. The models you create will not end up in the game but will serve as blueprints from which the art team will create the final artwork.

The prototyping phase requires that at least part of the game engine be running so that you can load the model into it and test it. Your prototype should include such features as

■ The basic geometry (physical shape) of the game world created in a 3D modeling tool. If it's a 2D world, the prototype should show the layout of the 2D landscape.

■ Temporary textures to place on the geometry to give it a surface. Eventually these will be replaced by final textures created by the artists.

■ Temporary models of props (trees, furniture, buildings, and so on) and NPCs that will appear in the level so that you can put them where they belong in the landscape.

■ Paths planned for AI-driven NPCs—where they travel within the level.

■ A lighting design for the level, at least in general terms.

■ The locations of trigger points for key events. Placing these triggers and documenting what sets them off is referred to as *rigging*.

In some cases, you may be able to use final audio effects in your prototype; that is, the sound effects that will actually end up in the game. If those are not available from the audio team yet, use temporary sound effects and note that they will need to be replaced later.

Level Review

At this point, you have a working prototype of the level; if the programmers have the game engine running, you should be able to play your level in a rudimentary way. Hold a *level review,* inviting members of the design, art, programming, audio, and testing teams to get their feedback. Each should examine and play-test your prototype for potential problems that may come up in his own field when he is working on the real thing. The issues that the level review should address include these:

▨ **Scale.** Is the level the right size? Will it take too much or too little time to play through?

▨ **Pacing.** Does the flow of events feel right?

▨ **Difficulty.** Is the level easier or harder than you originally meant it to be? (This can be tricky to judge in a prototype, but the earlier you start looking at the question, the more time you have to tune it.)

▨ **Fun.** Is the level enjoyable overall? Does it have dull spots? In some genres such as puzzle games, it's normal to simply throw out levels that aren't fun enough. In games in which each level is part of a larger story, you have to fix them.

▨ **Placement of objects and triggers.** Are things where they need to be to make the level play smoothly and produce the experience you want?

▨ **Performance issues.** Is the level too complicated for the machine's processor to handle? The programmers should be able to flag any potential problems.

▨ **Other code issues.** Does the level call for software that represents a problem for the programmers? For example, a unique NPC that appears only in this level still needs its own AI; will this be an issue?

▨ **Aesthetics.** Is the level attractive and enjoyable to inhabit? Because the prototype uses temporary geometry and textures, a certain amount of imagination will be called for here.

Level Refinement and Lock-Down

After the level review, take the feedback you've received and refine the prototype, correcting any problems and implementing any new decisions made in the course of the review. This can require any amount of work, from tuning a few numbers to scrapping the entire design and starting over from scratch. When you think you've got it right, hold another review and make another refinement pass. Continue this process until everyone agrees (or the person in charge agrees) that the level is ready to go into full production.

At this point, lock the level design. Once a level is designated as *locked,* no additions or changes may be made except if grave problems are discovered. This corresponds to the lock-down that occurs in overall game design at the end of the concept stage. If you don't treat the level as locked, you could go on tuning and tweaking it forever, stretching out the development time and running up the budget.

Level Design to Art Handoff

With the level locked, it's time to hand off your prototype and all your design work to the artists who will use it as a blueprint to build the geometry, animations, and textures that will end up in the real game. If they don't know about your design from the level reviews already, you should sit down with the artists and give them a thorough briefing not only on how everything looks in the level, but where everything should be and how everything works. From this information, the art director will create a task list to construct all the content the level requires: models, textures, animations, special visual effects, and so on.

If your prototype has been relying on placeholder audio, at this point you will also need to provide details to the audio team about what the level will need in the way of final audio. Notify the programmers about any special code that is required for the level at this point so they can have it ready for the content integration stage. (*Content* refers to the non-software part of the game: artwork, audio, movies, and text.)

First Art and Rigging Pass

The project now enters the first art and rigging pass, during which the art team builds the real artwork and rigging. You may be working on other levels at the same time, but you should also stay in close touch with the art team—undoubtedly they will have questions. It may also be your responsibility to incorporate the content they create into the software to make sure that it all works.

Art to Level Design Handoff and Review

When the art team finishes the final artwork, the artists hand all their work back to you, and you should conduct another review. This will highlight any problems or errors with the artwork that need correcting.

Content Integration

At this point, you will assemble all the assets into the completed (but not yet tested) level—artwork, new code required by the level, audio, and any remaining tweaks to the lighting. You'll also adjust any remaining issues with the rigging, by repositioning characters, effects, and triggers as necessary.

Bug Fixing

Test the level at this point, looking for bugs in the code and mistakes in the content. This will be another iterative process, working back and forth between the art, audio, and code teams and yourself. After finishing your own testing, you hand off the level to the quality assurance (QA) department for formal testing.

User Testing and Tuning

In the last stage, you will need a test plan for the level and you will begin formal testing, known as *alpha testing*. At a large company, a QA department will create this plan; at a small one or on a student project, you will need to do this yourself. Ordinarily, this formal testing will be more thorough and strict than the testing you've already done; it will also find things that you missed because of your overfamiliarity with the material. During alpha testing you should also invite members of your target audience to play the game in your office while you watch to see if they are having problems with its usability or difficulty. When the level has been thoroughly tested, you may make it available for *beta testing* (testing by members of the general public outside your offices).

Pitfalls of Level Design

This chapter ends with a discussion of some important mistakes to avoid—classic errors of level design that, unfortunately, some designers continue to make.

Scope Carefully

The single most common error made by inexperienced level designers is to try to build something too big. (They almost never try to build something too small.) Everyone would love to make an epic such as a *Final Fantasy* game, but such games require huge production teams, giant budgets, and multiyear development cycles. And even among experienced professionals, epic projects often run late and go over budget.

You must design within the resources of your team, your budget, and the time you have available. Remember, scope refers not only to the size and complexity of the landscape but to the number of props, NPCs, and special events in the level. In order not to undertake an unrealistically large level, you must make lists of these things during the planning stage before you actually start constructing the prototype. The process of making these lists may surprise you by showing you just how much work goes into making even a relatively small level.

Before you choose a scope for your level, determine how much time and staff you have available, taking into account any vacations and holidays that may be coming up. Then assume that half of your team will be out sick for a week at some point during the development process—it's entirely possible. *Now* think again about the scope. How many models does your team think they can build in a day? How quickly can you detect an error, correct it, and test it again? Choose a level size that you and your team can manage. If you make a level too small, it's not easy to enlarge it, but at least you won't have the art team killing themselves to create all the content. If you make a level too big and find that there isn't time to complete everything, you'll have to either deliver a sparse, unfinished level or scramble to cut things out, which will almost certainly harm your level's balance and pacing.

> ## DESIGN RULE Get the Scope Right!
>
> Game projects fail for many reasons, but among the most common—especially among student projects—is overambition. It's critically important that you are sure your team can actually build the game you want to make; if they can't, you will end up making nothing.

Avoid Conceptual Non Sequiturs

At the beginning of the first level of *James Bond: Tomorrow Never Dies*, the player, in the persona of James Bond, sneaks into an enemy military outpost armed only with a pistol and faces numerous Russian guards; how many, he doesn't know. If he blows up some of the oil drums scattered somewhat randomly outside the outpost, he will find medical kits hidden inside, which he can use later to restore his health when wounded.

Hiding medical kits inside oil drums belongs to a class of design errors, usually made at the level design stage, called *conceptual non sequiturs*—game features that make no sense. No sane person would think of looking in an oil drum for a hidden medical kit. Furthermore, any thinking player would reason that if she's trying to sneak into an enemy military installation armed only with a pistol, causing a loud explosion right outside is not a good idea; several dozen people will come running to see what made the noise. She would further assume that any medical kit that *was* inside an oil drum when it blew up wouldn't be good for much afterward. Consequently, a reasonable player wouldn't blow up the oil drum and wouldn't get the benefit of the medical kit. In other words, the game punishes players for using their brains. It's simply poor design.

James Bond: Tomorrow Never Dies made the mistake of copying a 20-year-old cartoon-game mechanic—resources hidden in odd places—into a realistic game. A realistic game assumes that players can count on certain similarities between the real world and the game world (oil drums store oil, not medical kits; explosions destroy things rather than reveal things). No flight simulator bothers to explain gravity, for the same reason. The player of a realistic game expects the assumptions he makes in the real world to be valid in the game world. By violating these expectations with a conceptual non sequitur, *James Bond: Tomorrow Never Dies* became considerably harder for all but an experienced gamer who already knew the conventions of cartoon-style video games.

In short, avoid conceptual non sequiturs in realistic games. They discourage new players and make your game unnecessarily hard without making it more fun. Remember the principle that level designers should reward players for using their intelligence, not punish them for it.

Make Atypical Levels Optional

Level designers naturally like to vary the content of their levels, and it is good design practice to make creative use of the game's features or to set your levels in different environments to provide the novelty that players like.

Still, you should *not* create wildly atypical levels and force the player to play them to get through the game. Sometimes level designers create a level filled with only one kind of challenge—an action game level consisting of nothing but platform jumps, say, with no enemies to fight or treasure to find. Others like to take away some of the actions that a player uses routinely on other levels and force her to make do with a limited subset of actions for the duration. Some have created levels that borrow from a different genre entirely: a real-time strategy game level in which both sides control exactly one unit, thus turning the level into a strange sort of action game.

There are two reasons not to make these kinds of levels obligatory. First, it breaks the player's suspension of disbelief to be suddenly confronted with a situation that would never occur according to the rules of the game world as the player has already learned them. Second, it may actually make the game unwinnable for some players. If you create a level filled with only one kind of challenge, then a player who happens to be terrible at that kind of challenge—but who reasonably expected to make it through the game by being good at other kinds of challenges—might not be able to finish the game at all, stymied by one atypical level. And there may be many players who don't find that challenge as exciting as you do, who will find an entire level of it boring.

You shouldn't avoid making atypical levels at all; they can be a lot of fun. But make them optional—hidden levels the player can unlock through excellent play or side missions for extra points.

Don't Show the Player Everything at Once

As they say in theater, "Always leave them wanting more." This advice applies to the overall progression of the game, so both game designers and level designers need to be aware of it. If your players have faced every challenge, seen every environment, and used every action that you have to offer—all in a single level—then the rest of the game will be old hat for them. You have nothing further to offer but variations on a set of play mechanics and game worlds that they already know everything about. Let your game grow from level to level. Introduce new features gradually. Just as it all starts to seem a bit familiar, bring in a twist: a new vehicle, a new action, a new location, a new enemy, or a sharp change in the plot of the story.

Never Lose Sight of Your Audience

Level design, more than any other part of the game design and development process, brings with it the risk of building a game that your audience won't enjoy. *You* assemble all the components that the others provide, and when the player starts up the game, she finds herself in *your* environment. The game designers may decide on the types of challenges the game contains, but you decide when the player will face them, in what sequence, and in what combinations. Consequently, you, more than anyone else on the team, must apply the player-centric approach to every design decision you make. Go inside the mind of your player and try to imagine what it will be like to see it all for the first time.

Always remember that you are not the player. Your own personal circumstances have *nothing to do with the game*. You may be a 22-year-old male, but your player may well be a 10-year-old girl or a 50-year-old man. Understand the game's target audience and what that audience wants from the game; then make sure you give it to them—at all times!

TWINKIE DENIAL CONDITIONS

Since 1997, I have written a regular column called "The Designer's Notebook" for the *Gamasutra* developers' webzine. In the course of writing the column I have amassed a collection of design errors—mistakes to avoid—which I document in an annual column titled "Bad Game Designer, No Twinkie!" Many of these errors were suggested by other game designers or by angry gamers. The errors have come to be known as "Twinkie Denial Conditions." (A Twinkie is a snack cake often sold in vending machines; game developers frequently resort to vending machines for sustenance when they are working so late that all the pizza-delivery places are closed.) Some of the errors listed in this chapter are Twinkie Denial Conditions, but there are many more. You can find a complete list of Twinkie Denial Conditions with links to the articles in which they appeared at www.designersnotebook.com/Design_Resources/No_Twinkie_Database.

Summary

In this chapter, you explored level design, a key stage in the development of any video game. The level designer is responsible for actually presenting the game experience to the player by designing elements such as the space in which the game takes place, deciding what challenges a player will face at each level of the game, creating the atmosphere of the game world, and planning the pacing of events for each level. Level design is governed by universal principles as well as principles specific to the game's genre. In a strategy game, for example, the level design should reward planning; in a vehicle simulation, the level designer creates levels that test a player's skill at maneuvering her vehicle. An important aspect of level design is the actual layout of the level. Different stories require different layouts, but every layout should be designed to enhance the playing experience.

The level design process requires interaction among the game's design team, including artists, programmers, and the audio team. Attention to detail and a methodical approach to the steps of level design can help to prevent the kinds of level design pitfalls that will make your game infamous rather than famous.

Design Practice EXERCISES

1. Pick one of the layouts described in the chapter and, using pencil and paper, create a sketch of a level layout for a hypothetical first-person shooter. (Your instructor will tell you the required number of rooms or locations.) Mark in the layout all the necessary objects for your level. Mark the starting positions of all the enemies and where the trigger will be or what action will trigger them. If you include such things as traps or doors, mark where they are and what triggers change their state. Mark where supplies such as medical kits and ammunition will be placed. Be sure to consider the path your player will take, remembering that open spaces are good for outdoor exploration and that parallel, linear, network, or combination layouts are good for indoor spaces. Now make one list that contains all the different kinds of objects that you think you will need and another list of all of your textures. (Do not forget floors, walls, furniture, decorations, weapons, and resources such as ammunition and medical kits.)

2. Choose a game genre that involves avatar travel through the game world and create the background details (not the layout or placement of objects) of a typical level in that genre. In four or five pages, describe what your level looks like and what kinds of things happen in your level. Keep character backgrounds and back story, if there is one, to minimal details. Instead, focus on the atmosphere, the look and the sounds, the actions the player will take, the events the player will experience, and the motivation(s) that keep the player engaged. Be sure to document what features will set the mood and pace.

3. In two or three pages, explain a tutorial level of an existing game that you have played. How does the player learn the character's moves and capabilities? Remember universal principles and keeping the player interested enough to actually want to play the game. Do the player's skills build on each other, or are they all separate actions? Does the player get to customize his avatar, and if so, how? What, if anything, did the game leave for the player to discover on his own?

4. Choose two levels from two different games, one that has a great level design and one that is, in your opinion, lacking. Take two or three pages for each level and describe the design features that made the level great and the design pitfalls that detracted from the gameplay or undermined the story of the other level.

5. Go to www.finitearts.com/400P/400project.htm. Read up on Hal Barwood and Noah Falstein's *400 Project,* the concept of design rules, and the reasons why they are worth breaking or keeping. Choose four or five of the design principles/rules listed and write a page each on why you think they should be used or broken. Can you come up with any design rules that are not listed? If so, explain why you feel they should be considered for the *400 Project.*

Design Practice QUESTIONS

1. Where is it? What is the time and place?

2. What are the initial conditions of the level? What resources does the player start with? Are there additional resources in the landscape, and if so, which ones, how much, and where?

3. What is the layout of the level? What freedom of movement does the player have within it? In what sequence will she experience challenges, and to what extent can she change that sequence?

4. How will you keep the player informed of his short-term goals? How does he know what to do next?

5. What challenges will the player face there? What actions can she take?

6. What rewards and punishments are built into the level? How does the player win or lose the level?

7. How do you plan to control and vary the pacing?

8. What events in the level contribute to the story, if any? What narrative events might happen within the level?

9. What is the mood of the level? What is its aesthetic style? What will contribute to the player's experience of these things? Consider music, art, architecture, landscape, weather, ambient sounds and sound effects, and lighting.

CHAPTER 17

Design Issues
for Online Gaming

Online gaming has grown from a tiny fraction of the interactive entertainment business into a major market in its own right. In this chapter, you'll learn about some of the features and design challenges that set online gaming apart from the more traditional single-player or multiplayer local games. Online gaming is a technology rather than a genre, a mechanism for connecting players together rather than a particular pattern of gameplay. Therefore, this chapter addresses some of the design considerations peculiar to online games no matter what genre those games belong to. It's a huge topic, however, and there is room in this book only for the highlights.

Don't confuse online gaming, as this book uses the term, with online gambling or online casino gaming. Online gambling is a different industry, and is not covered here.

The second half of the chapter is devoted to online games that are *persistent worlds*, also known as massively multiplayer online games (MMOGs). Raph Koster, who was lead designer of both *Ultima Online* and *Star Wars Galaxies,* and Tess Snider, once a senior game systems programmer at Trion Worlds, Inc., provided a great deal of assistance with this material.

What Are Online Games?

This chapter uses the term *online games* to refer to multiplayer distributed games in which the players' machines are connected by a network. (This is as opposed to multiplayer local games in which all the players play on one machine and look at the same screen.) It doesn't include games that are distributed over the Internet but have no multiplayer gameplay, such as *Bejeweled*. It does include games played over a local area network (LAN), however; these also qualify as online games.

Advantages of Online Games

Some features of online games offer advantages to us as game developers, and some offer advantages to players, attracting people who might not otherwise play computer games.

Player Socializing

NOTE For further discussion of this topic, please read the excellent and insightful *Community Building on the Web: Secret Strategies for Successful Online Communities* by Amy Jo Kim (Kim, 2000).

Online games offer opportunities for social interaction. The social aspect enhances the players' enjoyment of the experience. Women represent a much greater proportion of the online game market than they do the single-player game market, in part because of the social aspect of these games.

The best-known systems that enable social interaction are typing text (*chatting*) and voice communication, although there are several others. When enough people get broadband access, online games could include video as well. A time might come when we see players dressing appropriately for their roles in the game so that they'll look cool on camera.

As the creator of such an online game, you're more than just a game designer; you must also be a social architect. This is actually your toughest challenge, far more difficult than designing the core mechanics of a single-player game. An online game is a petri dish for growing social situations, and it's nearly impossible to predict in advance what will happen there.

Human Intelligence Instead of Artificial Intelligence

In single-player games, the player competes against the computer, so the computer has to have enough artificial intelligence (AI) to be a good opponent; building the AI for a complex game presents a huge programming task and one that is difficult to get right. But if the players compete against each other, as they do in most online games, you don't usually need as much AI. The players provide all the intelligence required in many situations.

You can use AI in an online game if you want to: You might include non-player characters (NPCs) who need to behave intelligently, or you might design a game in which all the players play cooperatively against artificial opponents. Several popular games have limited NPCs but have some large opponents that the online players must work together to combat. *Guild Wars,* for example, encourages this type of play. The AI-controlled enemies are challenging to beat with a team of online friends and impossible for an individual. But many online games rely on their players to provide most of the intelligence in the game, and this can make the game easier to develop in that respect. A real-time strategy game, for example, still needs AI for its individual units when played online, but players supply the strategic and tactical thinking.

Online Gameplay Versus Local Multiplayer Gameplay

Multiplayer gameplay, whether online or local, offers great flexibility to the game designer, allowing purely competitive (everyone for himself), purely cooperative (us against the machine), or team-based (us versus them) play. In online play, a network links the players, who occupy (generally, but not necessarily) separate locations.

For most of their history, local play has been the standard mode of interaction for multiplayer console games: Each player holds a controller, and all players look at the TV. This has changed now that consoles routinely have network capability. Local play remains popular for certain genres, such as sports and music games, but most multiplayer play is now online.

PROBLEMS WITH LOCAL PLAY

Local play as just described presents the game designer with serious difficulties. For one thing, because all the players share the same TV, unless there are additional screens on the controllers, any user interface elements displayed must be duplicated for each player, taking up valuable screen space. If the game maintains a separate point of view for each player, you must subdivide the screen into little windows. Each player will find it harder to see a small individual window than the full screen image, and activity in the other players' windows will distract him.

More important, however, because local play uses a single display device, you have no way to hide information. Each player can see everything the others do. This works well for fighting games, but not as well for any game in which players might want to keep their activities secret—war games, for instance.

Finally, local play necessarily imposes limits on the number of people who can participate at one time. Consoles seldom support more than four players; PCs support even fewer. Even if you could add players indefinitely, the screen would become crowded with characters and other data, and the machine itself would bog down as the computing tasks grew.

BENEFITS OF NETWORKED PLAY

Online gaming solves all these problems. Each player uses her own screen, and the entire display supports only her gaming experience. The game can present her with her own unique perspective, including exactly as much information as the designer wants her to have and no more. And online games can support large numbers of people (although games requiring a central server may find the server capacity limiting); it's not uncommon for some games to support tens or hundreds of thousands of players online at a time. With an online game, players can always find other people to play with at any hour of the day or night.

NOTE Nintendo has made unusual advances in local multiplayer play that few other console designers have followed. The Wii U GamePad, which is the input device for the Wii U, includes a screen that allows the designer to display secret information only to the player who should see it. In a previous generation, the GameCube allowed players to plug in a Game Boy Advance and use it as a controller. Using the wireless connectivity of mobile phones, the Nintendo DS series also allows multiplayer local play in which each player has his own screen.

Disadvantages of Online Games

Playing games over a network, especially the Internet, presents the designer with certain challenges as well. This section discusses some of these technical issues, as well as the ongoing responsibilities of providing new content and customer service. You should also be aware that strangers playing your game anonymously over a network can cause social friction that can range from minor misbehavior to serious criminal offenses. This particular issue is addressed in a separate section, "Social Problems," later in the chapter.

Technical Issues

Although this is a book about game design rather than programming, you need to be aware of certain technical issues for online games that local games don't have to address. This section doesn't go into them in great detail, but aims to make you familiar with these technical considerations. If you design an online game, you will need to discuss them with your programming team.

COMMUNICATION MODELS

Your programming team will need to choose a communication model from the two currently in use in networked gaming. In the first, *client/server,* each player runs a program, called the *client,* on his computer, that communicates with a central program, the *server,* on a computer owned by a company providing the game service. In the client/server model, the server runs the game engine, sending packets of information to the various clients, and the clients merely present that information to the players.

The other model, *peer-to-peer,* involves direct communication between the players' computers. Implementation of peer-to-peer (sometimes abbreviated P2P) communication is quite straightforward for two-player games but becomes more complicated as more players are involved. The players' systems must decide which machine to designate as the *host*—that is, which will control the game while the others become *guests.* If the host logs out of the network, one of the guests' computers must take over and become the new host—preferably automatically and without anyone's noticing (this is known as *automated host migration,* a feature already supplied by Microsoft's DirectPlay facilities). Some companies also operate *matchmaking* services in which the company's server functions only to allow players to find one another and connect together in peer-to-peer networks. All of this is programming work that offline games don't have to bother with.

LATENCY

The Internet is designed for redundancy rather than speed, so it doesn't make any guarantees about how long a given packet of data will take to get from one point to another. This phenomenon is called *latency.* In many games, a faster connection translates into a gaming advantage, making players with high-speed connections more likely to win the game. You can design around this by making your game turn-based or trying to match up opponents on the basis of their connection speeds. At the moment, there is no one satisfactory answer.

DROPPED AND GARBLED PACKETS

What happens to your game if it doesn't get some of the information it needs because of a glitch in the network? Your system will require a mechanism for detecting a missing packet, or one containing bad data and requesting that the packet be resent from the server or host. Packets can also arrive out of order, which can cause confusion if your client receives information that a race car is about to cross the finish line, but the next packet indicates that the car is 100 yards back on the track instead. Every packet must have a unique serial number, in sequence, so that you can tell if one is missing or if packets are arriving in the wrong order. Fortunately, middleware companies are starting to offer software packages to help manage this problem.

It's Harder to Suspend Disbelief

For some players, gaming is a form of escapism that takes them away to a magical place, and they want it to stay magical while they're there. To them, it's particularly important that nothing occur in the game to break their suspension of disbelief, but in online games there will always be players who won't stay in character or who will talk about real-world issues and events while they're in the game. Unless there's a strong (and enforced) ethos of in-character role-playing, people who play in an online game have to accept that their imaginary world includes a lot of entirely real people.

The persistent world *World of Warcraft* offers players multiple versions of its game world with different versions imposing different rules on the player. In some versions, in-character role-playing is expected—although there is no real mechanism to enforce it.

The Need to Produce Content

When you're building a single-player game to be sold in retail stores, your job generally finishes when the gold master disc goes off to manufacturing. The players buy the game and you can go off to work on another project.

Online games don't work this way; they earn money either through advertising revenue, micropayments, or subscriptions. To keep people interested, you have to change things, and that means producing new content on an ongoing basis. This is expensive for the service provider and ties up skilled development staff. The problem is most obvious with persistent worlds, but even simple games need to be kept fresh. *FarmVille*, a popular browser game available via the Facebook social networking website, does not use 3D graphical environments, but the developers regularly add new gear for players to buy and things for them to do. Chapter 6, "Making Money from Your Game," discusses this issue further.

Customer Service

All game companies require customer service staff to help players with problems, but online games need far, far more of them. With offline games, players mostly need help with technical difficulties; for gameplay problems, they can buy strategy guides or find hints on the Internet. But in a live, online environment, players expect to get help immediately, and they demand help for a much larger range of issues than they do in offline games. Players expect customer service people not only to solve technical problems but also to explain the user interface, answer questions about game content, and enforce justice by investigating and punishing misbehavior by other players. Games for children must monitor chat interactions. With thousands of players logged on at any one time, providing these services can become very expensive.

Design Issues

The earliest online games, and many today as well, require the players to be logged on simultaneously. This is called *synchronous* gaming. It doesn't necessarily require that all the players are acting simultaneously; synchronous games can be either real-time or turn-based, but the players' actions are in some sense dependent on each other. This section addresses some design issues peculiar to synchronous online games: the problems presented by players arriving or disappearing during play, the pros and cons of real-time versus turn-based play. This section ends with a brief discussion of asynchronous games.

Arriving Players

Players can log on wanting to play your game at any time, and the game must be capable of dealing with them intelligently. In most noncomputer games, all the players must be present at the beginning of the match or it won't be fair. In *Monopoly*, for example, anyone who entered the game late would be at a significant disadvantage—the others would have already grabbed the best properties, and the game's built-in inflation would swiftly bankrupt newcomers.

The usual solution for this problem is to start new matches at frequent intervals and to have a waiting area, or *lobby*, where the players can hang around while they wait for a new match to begin. In a game that can be played with any number of players, such as bingo, you can simply start a new match, say, every three minutes, and whoever is waiting may play. In games requiring a fixed number of players, such as bridge, you will need to establish a matchmaking service that allows them to form groups and to wait (more or less patiently) for enough players to join a particular group; the game begins as soon as the required number of players arrives. The number of players needed for a game should be small, however, to minimize waiting times. Any game that requires more than about eight players risks alienating players who do not want to wait.

In some games, players can join almost immediately without any disadvantage—poker, for instance. Each hand takes little time, and new players can join at the end of the current hand. Tournament play, of course, has a definite start, and players cannot join after the game begins. For games of indefinite duration, such as persistent worlds, you can't do anything about the fact that some players possess advantages other players don't. The players who began the earliest and who devote the most time to play will always have an advantage (unless you allow players to purchase prebuilt characters for real money on eBay, but that just shifts the advantage from players who have the most time to players who have the most money). You can, however, prevent those advantages from spoiling the game for other players:

▪ **Get rid of the victory condition.** Without winners and losers, an online entertainment ceases to be a game per se and becomes a different kind of amusement. The player focuses on her own achievements rather than on defeating all the other players. In this case, the old cliché becomes apt: It's not whether you win or lose, but how you play the game. Persistent worlds, which are addressed later in the chapter, work on that basis.

▪ **Discourage competition between experienced players and newcomers.** You can measure the progress of your players and see to it that only those who are fairly matched come into direct conflict. Tournament chess uses a ranking system to do just that. A highly ranked player who beats a newcomer gets little or no reward for it. *Mafia Wars* permits only players with similar levels of experience to fight each other.

▪ **Be sure that direct competition is consensual.** If experienced players do get the chance to compete directly with newcomers, you should give the newcomers the option to refuse to play. No one should be forced to take part in an unfair competition. *World of Warcraft*, for example, offers some servers where players may fight each other (player-versus-player or PvP play) and some where they may not. The players may choose which kind of server to enter.

Disappearing Players

Just as players can appear at any time, they can log off at any time, or lose their connection to the game for technical reasons. If possible, your game should deal with this neatly and with minimal disruption to other players. In many games, such as racing games, players compete against one another in a free-for-all. If one player disappears, it doesn't make that much difference—his car vanishes from the track, and that's all. In effect, the player forfeits the race and the others continue. On the other hand, if the game requires players to work in teams, the disappearance of one player could put his team at a serious disadvantage. In games that require a fixed number of participants, your only options are to give the person a chance to reconnect, assuming the disappearance was a mistake, to include an AI element that can take over for the missing player, or to shut down the game.

Tournaments require special consideration. If players compete to get the best win-loss ratio, one might deliberately choose to log out rather than lose the game—which can deny the other person victory. Should the vanishing player be forced to forfeit? What if the disconnection was an accident, caused by a bad line? Unfortunately, there's no sure way to tell if it was.

You may find that one of the following suggestions solves the problem of vanishing players for your game:

▪ **The vanishing player forfeits the game.** This solution may unfairly penalize players who are disconnected by accident. It's a good solution only if the network connections are extremely reliable, such as a local area network. If the players run the risk of being disconnected accidentally and you are offering something valuable to the winner (such as a cash prize in a tournament), then you should not require vanishing players to forfeit the game. Online gambling games do not require the player to forfeit; they implement mechanisms for allowing a player to restart a game in the event of a disconnection.

▪ **Institute a penalty for disconnections that is less severe than forfeiture.** If a player disconnects in the middle of combat during an *EverQuest* session, the avatar remains in the game for a minute, taking additional damage. Unfortunately, the avatar doesn't fight very well by itself. On the MSN network, players who get disconnected once have 10 minutes to reconnect and resume the game; if they fail to do so, they forfeit or, in some games, an artificial player managed by the server takes over for them. If they get disconnected twice, they forfeit automatically. In many games, the game tries to reconnect to the player for a limited amount of time. In a turn-based game, such as poker, this has a minimal impact on the other players who have to wait for their turn anyway. Ultimately, the player is assumed to be away from his computer, and play continues without him until he reconnects.

▪ **Award victory to whomever is ahead in the game at the time of the disconnection.** This solution seems fair but means that the moment someone goes ahead, she can disconnect to deny her opponent a chance to catch up. Again, you should consider this only in circumstances in which it is difficult or impossible to disconnect intentionally.

▪ **Record it as a tie.** While this solution might motivate a losing player to disconnect intentionally, it still makes a fairly neutral solution.

▪ **Record it as a "disconnected game."** You then have to decide exactly what this means in the context of a tournament. If other players can view the records, they can tell when someone racks up a suspiciously high number of disconnections and avoid playing with that person. Or the server can determine that a player is being disconnected too often and prevent her from playing for a period of time.

▪ **Abandon the game entirely.** This is the fairest solution in the case of accidental disconnections, but it is unfair to whomever is leading if the player who is behind pulls the plug.

■ **Use referees.** The World Cyber Games, a large gaming tournament, keeps a log file during play, and in the event of disconnection, a referee can examine the file to adjudicate victory. If the players agree, they can also restart the match. This requires a human referee to be available, however, which adds to the operating costs.

There's no one right answer to this problem; it depends too much on the nature of the individual game. It's up to you as the designer to think about the problem and try to decide what's fair.

Real-Time Versus Turn-Based Games

Many online games take place in real time with each player acting simultaneously or at least independently of one another. This offers players maximum freedom; they always have something to do and can order their activities any way they like. It's also more immersive than turn-based gaming. Waiting your turn while other players act harms suspension of disbelief. Unfortunately, real-time gaming tends to make a strategy game into an action game. Whichever player moves his pieces fastest has the advantage. In games such as *Command & Conquer,* victory becomes a matter of establishing an efficient weapons-production system as quickly as possible.

Turn-based games remain popular in simpler online or mobile games. For this to work smoothly, you must include certain features:

■ **Limit the number of players in one game.** Four or five is a good maximum. With more than this, players will have to wait too long between turns and will grow impatient.

■ **Set a time limit on the length of a player's turn.** A slow player or one who has left to answer the phone mustn't be allowed to hold up the game. Both the player whose turn it is *and* all the other players should be able to see a countdown timer. Naturally, the length of time will vary depending on the sort of game; for a card game such as hearts, 10 seconds should be plenty.

■ **Determine a reasonable default action if the player runs out of time.** In games in which it's possible to pass, the best default might simply be to pass without acting, but in a game such as checkers, in which a move is required, the game will have to choose a move. It doesn't have to be a very smart move, however. It's up to the player to supply the intelligence; if she doesn't, it's her own fault.

■ **Let players do other things while waiting for their turn.** They should definitely be allowed to chat with one another, study the battlefield, organize their units, or do anything else that doesn't actually influence the gameplay.

A few games, such as *Age of Wonders II* or *Civilization IV,* allow all the players to take their turns simultaneously—that is, they each choose their next move at the same time, without knowing what the others are doing. Once they have all chosen (or a timer runs out), the turn ends, and the computer processes and displays the results of all the moves.

Note that some turn-based games permit very long turns in which players make only one move every 24 hours or exchange their moves by e-mail. *Draw Something* lets players take as long as they want between turns, but a single player can play with many other people at once, so even if one takes a long time responding, another may do so quickly, keeping the game moving. This can also allow novices to compete against more advanced players, because they're not under time pressure. Such games are becoming more common, especially in the mobile space.

Collusion

Collusion is a form of cheating in which players who are supposed to be opponents work together in violation of the rules. The rules of *Monopoly* explicitly prohibit collusion. The fact that the players are all in the same room, and usually have social obligations to one another, tends to enforce that rule. Unfortunately, you can't count on those factors in an online game. Some players will join an online multiplayer game with a deliberate, even avowed, intent to cheat. Because they're playing with strangers, they have no social relationship at stake, and because they're physically miles apart, no one can see them do it.

EXAMPLES OF COLLUSION

Computer games seldom have written rules because the designers assume that the game will enforce the rules automatically: The players simply can't make illegal moves, in most cases. However, software can't detect certain kinds of collusion between players.

Consider an online multiple-choice trivia game with three possible answers for each question. Each player receives the same question from the server and has a fixed length of time in which to enter an answer. When a player enters his answer, he immediately learns whether he was right or wrong. Correct answers earn points, and the player with the largest number of points at the end of the game wins.

Four players can easily collude at this game to guarantee that one of them will win. They all play on different machines in the same physical location—an Internet café, for instance. When a question appears, three of the players each immediately enter a different response—A, B, or C—and the fourth one waits. When the software informs one of these three players that she is correct, she immediately calls out her letter, and the fourth player enters it before the time runs out. This way the fourth player always enters the correct answer. Even with fewer than four players colluding this way, they can greatly increase the odds of winning.

You can easily defeat this form of collusion: You simply don't reveal the correct answer until the time for entering answers runs out. Players who enter an answer early simply have to wait to find out whether they answered correctly. But other forms of collusion can be more insidious. Online poker, for example, can involve players sharing information about their cards via instant messaging or some form of physical communication. There is no way for the system to account for external means of communication. If you offer a prize for the player who wins the greatest number of chess games in a certain length of time, for example, two players can collude to play each other, with one always trying to lose to the other as quickly as possible.

DESIGNING TO REDUCE COLLUSION

The designer of an online game must try to anticipate collusion as much as possible. Unfortunately, experience shows this to be extremely difficult. There are no limits on players' ingenuity or the lengths to which some will go. Even if your game doesn't offer a chat feature, players can play from two machines in the same room, call each other on mobile phones, or use any online chat facility to collude.

You can't prevent players from colluding, but you can design the game to minimize the effects of cheating. You should consider in what ways the following types of collusion might affect your game:

▪ **Sharing secret knowledge.** Does the player ever have secret knowledge that she can share to someone else's benefit? In the trivia game described previously, some players receive the correct answer before the time runs out. Withholding this information prevents collusion.

▪ **Passing cards (or anything else) under the table.** Does the game include mechanisms to transfer assets from one player to another? Is there any way to abuse these mechanisms?

▪ **Taking a dive.** What are the consequences if one player plays to lose deliberately? If you allow gambling on matches (even if only with play money or points), you should look out for this.

If you're designing a game in which the competition mode is supposed to be every player for herself, try imagining what would happen if you made it a team game in which you encouraged players to collaborate. If it's already a team game, try to imagine what would happen if one player on the team spied for the other team.

Asynchronous Games

By far the most significant change in online gaming has been the explosive growth of asynchronous games, especially casual games played on social media networks, such as Facebook. In an asynchronous game, the players' actions are not synchronized—they need not be logged on at the same time, nor do they ever have to wait for another player's turn (although they may choose to do so, or find it useful to coordinate their actions with another player).

Persistent worlds are largely asynchronous except when players choose to log in at the same time to go on a joint quest. However, they're different enough from other kinds of online games that they are discussed in a separate section, later in this chapter.

Many asynchronous games played on social networks provide in-game rewards to players for inviting friends to join. Games like *FarmVille* are primarily single-player games, because each player works toward his own goal at his own rate. However, they can advance faster and more successfully if they cooperate with each other by sharing virtual goods. This competition mode is seldom found in other kinds of games and might best be called *single-player cooperative*.

Asynchronous games mostly avoid the multiplayer competitive mode so that players don't have to wait for each other, except in the limited case of comparing high scores. Instead they tend to use single-player cooperative, multiplayer cooperative, or team-based modes. In the case of cooperative and team-based modes, each player's contribution to the overall goal has to be fairly independent of the others' contributions because of the asynchronous nature of the play. This works better for very large teams that don't rely too much on any one player's activities.

Asynchronous games avoid the problems of arriving and departing players because the nature of the play simply doesn't require that players be logged on at a specific time. Collusion is also less of a problem because these games are generally cooperative, so working together is encouraged rather than prohibited.

Technical Security

People feel a strong impulse to test the limits of computer software—to see what it will do with nonsensical inputs (such as firing upon their own troops in a war game). Similarly, players often think of ways to do things that the designers never intended or expected. Sometimes these unanticipated maneuvers, such as using the rocket launcher to propel the player upward in *Quake,* even become standard tactics.

Making unexpected but legal moves is not cheating; you can argue that designers should anticipate these tactics or that testers should discover them. But other forms of cheating, such as hacking the game's software or data files, are clearly unfair. In a single-player game, it doesn't really matter, but cheating in multiplayer games presents a more serious problem. People who wouldn't dream of cheating their close friends in person—say, playing poker around the living room table—happily cheat strangers when protected by the distance and anonymity that an online game offers.

Players have a moral right to expect a fair game when they're playing against other people, and they have a legal right to a fair game as well if they're playing for prizes of monetary value. Although all game software comes with a disclaimer that the publisher sells the software as is and without any warranty, the moment you start to give out prizes that are actually worth something, you must be very careful to ensure that your game is fair if you don't want to end up in court.

The legitimate players aren't the enemy, of course—the handful of cheaters are. We lock our doors at night not to protect ourselves from the honest majority of the population but to protect ourselves from the dishonest minority. You will have to design your game with the same consideration in mind.

Use a Secure Telecommunications Protocol

It takes an extremely dedicated hacker to tamper with the data stream between the client software and the server, but it takes only one. If the stakes are high enough, someone will decide the reward is worth the time spent. To foil hackers, your software must use a secure telecommunications protocol. Designing such a thing is a programming problem and is beyond the scope of this book, but if you're designing an online game, you should be sure that the telecommunications protocol you use provides the following features:

▦   First, all data should be encrypted to prevent users from understanding it outright. Each packet of data should be sent with suitable error-checking and error-correcting facilities, which will enable the software to detect whether the data has lost integrity in transmission. Even though Internet communications are far more reliable than the old modem-based systems were, it's always a good idea to verify that the arriving data is correct.

▦   Second, you might want to consider a *heartbeat* mechanism. In this system, your client software sends a short packet to your server at regular intervals, even when the client doesn't need to transmit data, simply to tell the server that the client is still present. This enables you to detect disconnections. If the nature of the game allows the client to remain silent indefinitely, the server doesn't know if the client has disconnected or if the player is just thinking.

▦   Each packet should include a unique serial number, to indicate the correct order of packets and to prevent spurious packets from being inserted by unauthorized means.

Don't Store Sensitive Data on the Player's Computer

Typically a game contains two kinds of data about a player. Your game needs to keep settings or preferences about the way the player appears and likes to play, as well as information that's actually relevant to the game state: the player's position, score, possessions, and so on. In *Monopoly,* for instance, the player's playing piece (hat, shoe, car, and so on) belongs in the former category; it doesn't matter to the state of the game which token the player uses. However, the player's properties, cash, and position on the board belong in the latter category; changes to those attributes affect the player's status in the game.

NOTE Mobile phone games tend to store sensitive data on the player's phone, contrary to this advice. For the moment, not many players know how to hack their phones to find and modify the data. That situation won't last forever, though, and it's still a risky practice.

This second kind of information shouldn't be stored on the player's own computer. Even with encryption techniques, you have to assume that someone will tamper with any data kept on the player's machine to give that player an unfair advantage. If your game truly generates too much sensitive data about each character to store it all on the server, at least store a checksum over the data when the player logs out so that when she logs back in again, you can check her data and determine whether it has been improperly modified in the meantime.

Don't Send the Player Data He Isn't Supposed to Have

A common characteristic of real-time strategy games is the *fog of war,* in which unexplored areas of the map appear dark and the player cannot detect movements of the enemy unless a friendly unit nearby can plausibly see them. Single-player games store all this information in the player's computer; it's just not visible to the player. Online games should not send any such hidden information to the player. If the player hacks the game to lift the fog of war, he can see unexplored areas and watch the movements of enemy units, giving him a significant advantage over his opponents.

Don't Let the Client Perform Sensitive Operations

In designing a client/server game, you must always strike a balance between the amount of processing that the server does and the amount that the client does. It saves CPU time on the server for you to offload as much of the processing work onto the client as you can, but it isn't always safe. Suppose, for example, that you're designing a simple role-playing game (RPG) in which the player occasionally encounters monsters and must fight them. It reduces the load on the server if the server sends the client some information about the current monster and lets the fight take place entirely on the player's computer. After the fight, the client sends a message back to the server reporting whether the player won, lost, or ran away, but this presents a danger: If the player hacks the client, she can program it to report that she wins every fight. In fact, the server, not the client, should perform the computations for the fight and determine whether the player won or lost.

Persistent Worlds

A good many online games are not really games at all by the definition you learned in Chapter 1, "Games and Video Games." Persistent worlds such as *World of Warcraft, Club Penguin,* and *EVE Online* constitute permanent environments in which players can play, retaining the state of their avatar from one session to another. Persistent worlds present a number of special problems and design requirements, which this section discusses at a general level. For a more in-depth discussion, read *Designing Virtual Worlds* by Richard Bartle (Bartle, 2003), and *Developing Online Games: An Insider's Guide* by Jessica Mulligan and Bridgette Patrovsky (Mulligan and Patrovsky, 2003).

Persistent worlds significantly predate today's popular graphical MMOGs. Since 1978, a small but dedicated community of developers has been building, playing, and studying text-based persistent worlds called *MUDs* (*multiuser dungeons* or *domains,* depending on whom you talk to) that could be played by groups of people over the Internet. In these worlds, in which players interact by typing commands, a rich culture of online role-playing evolved.

This book won't go into MUD design in any detail here; there is no commercial market for MUDs, and you can already find a vast amount of literature about the subject on the Internet. Many of the design problems of today's MMOGs, particularly those relating to social interactions among players, were solved—or at least studied—long ago in the MUD community.

How Persistent Worlds Differ from Ordinary Games

Part of the appeal of computer games is the environment in which the player finds herself: a fantasy world where magic really works or behind enemy lines in World War II. Another part is the role the gamer will play in the game: detective or pilot or knight-errant. Yet another is the gameplay itself, the nature of the challenges the player faces and the actions she may take to overcome them. And, of course, there is the goal of the game, its victory condition: to halt the enemy invasion or find the magic ring. The victory is usually the conclusion of a story that the player experiences and contributes to.

Persistent worlds offer some of these things but not all of them, and there are significant differences between the kinds of experiences that persistent worlds offer and those that conventional games offer.

STORY

Because persistent worlds have so many players, and because they are intended to continue indefinitely, the traditional narrative arc of a single-player game doesn't apply. Persistent worlds may offer storylike quests, but they always return to the world eventually; you can't have a once-and-for-all ending in the sense that a story does.

The setting of a persistent world consists of the environment itself and the overall conditions of life there. It can be a dangerous place or a safe one, a rich place or a poor one, a place of tyranny or a place of democracy. You can challenge players to respond to problems in the world as it is or to problems that you introduce, whether slowly or suddenly.

The goal is a quest or errand that the player undertakes as an individual or with others. Goals can be small-scale (eliminate the pack of wild dogs that has been marauding through the sheep flocks) or large-scale (everyone in the town gets together to rebuild the defenses in anticipation of an invasion). Most persistent worlds offer large numbers of quests from which players may choose.

NOTE Persistent worlds used to be commonly called massively multiplayer online role-playing games (MMORPGs), because the earliest ones belonged to the role-playing genre. More recently the industry has begun to call them massively multiplayer online games (MMOGs) instead, to reflect their growing diversity.

NOTE The MMOG *A Tale in the Desert* is unusual in that its world regularly comes to an end and starts again fresh in a new edition, called a Telling. Although the game persists for months at a time, it does not persist indefinitely.

As a designer, you probably want players to feel as if they are the first ones ever to undertake a particular quest, or to explore an area of the game world. Ordinary computer games allow you to evoke that feeling, because the game world is created fresh when the player starts up the game program. In a persistent world, on the other hand, only those who logged in on its first day of operation are the first to experience a quest or explore a new area. Furthermore, those who went before will always tell those who arrive later what to expect. In short, it's impossible to keep anything secret about a persistent world. As soon as a few players know it, they'll tell the other players.

Chapter 11, "Storytelling," introduced the *emergent narrative:* stories that emerge from the core mechanics of a game. In a persistent world, stories emerge not so much from the core mechanics as from interactions among the players. The best emergent stories (those that make the player feel as if he's participating in a story created by a great writer) occur in purely role-playing environments with almost no gamelike elements. In effect, the story experience in a persistent world comes about when the players are excellent role-players: good at acting and improvisational theater. As a designer, you cannot force good stories to emerge; it depends too much on the imagination and talent of the participants.

THE PLAYER'S ROLE

In a single-player, plot-driven game, the player's role is defined by the actions she is allowed to take and is constrained by the requirements of the story. In a persistent world, the player doesn't follow a single story line, so she may, in theory, choose from a larger variety of things to do and has more opportunities to define her own role. The early persistent worlds offered only a limited number of roles, but modern ones are increasingly rich and varied.

As the designer, you must supply an assortment of possible roles the player may take on and make those roles meaningful in your world. You should also give the player the freedom to change her role (though not always easily or immediately) as she sees fit. Because the world continues indefinitely without coming to a narrative conclusion, you can't expect the player to want to play the same way forever. Just as people change careers and hobbies over time, players need to be able to change roles.

GAMEPLAY

Finally, there's the question of the gameplay. Without a victory condition, you can't simply offer the player a predefined sequence of challenges and achievements as his ultimate objective. In the familiar persistent worlds designed like RPGs, the player's objective is to advance his character. He (usually) accomplishes this by fighting AI-controlled opponents, such as monsters, although he could also attain many other things as well: wealth, political power, fame (or notoriety), and so on.

TIP If your game offers too few things to do, it will fail. Your game design must be expansive. Even the coolest game mechanic becomes tiresome after a time. You have to supply alternative ways of playing or alternative ways of experiencing the world. Otherwise, the players will go to another world where they can have new experiences. You will need to release additions to the game or, better yet, completely different subgames embedded in the actual game.

In a single-player game, the player tries to read the designer's mind to some extent, to figure out what you want him to do, and then he does it. His play is often reactive, a response to challenges thrown at him. In a persistent world, the player decides for himself what he wants to do. He seeks out challenges if he feels like it, but he can spend all his time socializing if he prefers. His gameplay—and, indeed, the entire nature of the experience—is *expressive* and active rather than reactive. This quality of persistent-world play has profound effects on the design of such worlds, as you will see later in this section.

WHERE DOES *SECOND LIFE* FIT IN?

Second Life is a widely publicized online environment that allows users (known in the environment as *residents*) to build landscapes and a nearly unlimited variety of artifacts, including avatars and buildings, and sell them to one another. They may also interact with each other in a wide variety of ways. Users access the virtual world through a client, just as players of MMOGs do. However, unlike MMOGs, *Second Life* does not offer quests to achieve, combat or other types of challenges, a system for leveling characters up, or any of the other gameplay features typical of persistent worlds. It is simply an environment, and what happens in it is entirely up to the users. They can build their own games within the game world if they want to, but the system does not include many tools for implementing and enforcing the rules. All land in the game consists of islands in the sea that are owned by the residents (except for a few islands used for training new arrivals). Users must purchase an island in the sea from the operators, Linden Lab, if they want to construct their own environment. A built-in scripting language allows objects in the game to perform behaviors when a resident interacts with them.

Residents in *Second Life* may instantaneously teleport or fly their avatars to any location in the world that is not private (most are open). Residents use the virtual world for social interaction, personal expression, education, evangelism, and as a means of offering virtual goods and services for sale. A number of corporations and a small number of countries have opened "offices" in *Second Life* as a means of informing people about themselves.

Because every object and even the landscape in *Second Life* may be modified or deleted at any time, the user's client software must continually download the graphics for the virtual world. This is not true of most MMOGs, where the landscape is largely static and cannot be modified by the players. The constant data transmission required by *Second Life* creates a time lag in displaying the graphics that would be unacceptable in most MMOGs. *Second Life* is not intended for real-time play the way *World of Warcraft* is.

For the moment, *Second Life* is unique, or nearly so. It costs nothing to use, although residents must purchase Linden dollars (the in-game currency) with real money if they want to purchase in-world artifacts, and there is a price for some premium services. But it is not an MMOG.

The Four Types of Players

In 1997, MUD developer Richard Bartle wrote a seminal article called "Hearts, Clubs, Diamonds, Spades: Players Who Suit MUDs" for the first issue of the *Journal of Virtual Environments* (Bartle, 1997). He proposed that MUD players fall into four categories depending on whether they enjoy *acting on* (manipulating, exploiting, or controlling) or *interacting with* (learning about and communicating with) either the world or the other players (see **Figure 17.1**). Those who enjoy acting on other players he dubbed Killers, or clubs; those who enjoy interacting with other players he called Socializers, or hearts. Those who enjoy acting on the world he described as Achievers, or diamonds; those who enjoy interacting with the world he referred to as Explorers, or spades.

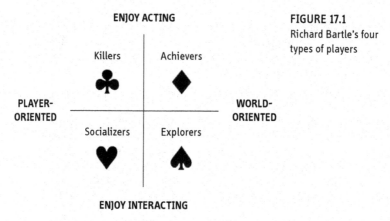

ENJOY ACTING

Killers   Achievers

PLAYER-   WORLD-
ORIENTED   ORIENTED

Socializers   Explorers

ENJOY INTERACTING

FIGURE 17.1
Richard Bartle's four types of players

Bartle went on to claim that a healthy MUD community required a certain proportion of each of these types of players and that adjusting the game design to attract or discourage any given type of player would tend to influence the numbers of others as well. In effect, a persistent world is a sort of ecology in which the players' styles of play influence the balance of the population. Bartle drew his data from personal observation rather than rigorous statistical analysis, so his conclusions can certainly be questioned. Nevertheless, his grouping of player types proved to be useful not only in the design of MUDs, but in graphical persistent worlds as well.

Creating an Avatar

Playing in persistent worlds is more than merely a form of gameplay; it's also a form of expression. The first thing a player does when she joins a persistent world is to create an avatar, or character who represents her in the game, one of the most expressive things she can do. Chapter 9, "Creative and Expressive Play," discusses avatar creation at greater length.

If you're making an online RPG that includes traditional avatar attributes such as speed, strength, and so on, consult the companion e-book *Fundamentals of Role-Playing Game Design* for more information.

Players like to maintain a profile listing some of their intangible attributes in order to identify and describe their avatars to other players. Profiles can include such things as

■ **Unique name or handle.** Unless your game allows totally anonymous play, people will need some way of identifying their avatars by name. That way, a player's name can appear in documents, on leader boards, in chat rooms and bulletin boards, and so on.

■ **Physical appearance.** People clearly need to be able to tell one character from another on the screen. The physical appearance of avatars should be as customizable as you can afford to make it. Even if appearance does not affect gameplay, players identify with and respond to physical appearances.

■ **History or experience.** Players like to record their characters' achievements for others to see. Records can include experience levels, quests undertaken, kills in battle, or any other accomplishments the player might be proud of. You'll have to decide whether some players will want to keep some of these things private and, if so, whether they should be allowed to.

■ **Reputation.** The system computes and stores the reputation as a number or symbol based on the player's play or on complaints or praise received about the player. (The eBay auction website includes a simple reputation system.) Some games use the reputation mechanism as a way of automatically tagging players who frequently take advantage of others. The reputation attribute warns other players, "This person is dangerous" or "This person is trustworthy." Beware, however: An automated system is subject to abuse through collusion if you don't place limits on it. If you offer a player the opportunity to repair a bad reputation through some apparently virtuous action such as donating money to another character, he can simply donate money repeatedly to a friend, who promptly donates it all back to him.

■ **Player autobiography.** It's fun for a player to make up a history for his character, a background that introduces that character to others in the world. It's another form of self-expression. However, if children play in your world, you will need to have a real person approve autobiographies for suitability.

You might or might not want to include important gameplay attributes in the player's profile; it depends on how making such information public affects the gameplay. Does allowing a player to hide attributes from the world constitute a legitimate part of gameplay or an unfair advantage? (Consider *Monopoly*, which does not allow players to hide their property cards under the table but allows everyone to see what all players own.)

SPORE: A MASSIVELY SINGLE-PLAYER ONLINE GAME

Spore broke new ground in a number of ways, and one was its use of the Internet. *Spore* is not a multiplayer online game in the usual sense. It does not maintain a single, central game world and players cannot interact with one another directly. However, when a player creates a creature or a building in the later levels of *Spore*, the game uploads the player's creation to a database stored on a server maintained by Electronic Arts, the publisher. These data are available to all other players, which means that one player's creature may appear in another player's world. This makes the player's experience of the game extremely rich, as creations from thousands of players may turn up in his game world. However, there is still no direct interaction with other players. A player can download a copy of another player's creature from the server (in fact, this happens automatically), but he cannot intentionally influence another player's experience. Will Wright, the designer, jokingly called *Spore* a massively single-player online game.

World Models

If you plan to offer more than just a chat room, you must give players something to do. The types of things that you give them to do and the rewards they earn for doing those things constitute the *world model*. Raph Koster identified five classic world models, although you can undoubtedly devise more. Yours may include elements from more than one of Koster's original five, listed here:

▨ **Scavenger model.** Players collect things and return them to places of safety. The game is primarily a large treasure hunt, and players don't risk losing anything they've collected.

▨ **Social model.** The world exists primarily to provide an expressive space. The fun comes from role-playing in character; most goals represent social achievement (political power, adulation, notoriety, and so on). Players use their characters' attributes as a basis for role-playing rather than computer-managed combat.

▨ *Dungeons & Dragons* **model.** In games based on this, the best-known model, the player is primarily in conflict with the environment, fighting NPCs for advancement and doing some scavenging along the way. Such games rely heavily on the functional attributes of the avatar for gameplay and include feedback mechanisms: Defeating enemies advances the character, which requires the game to offer tougher enemies next time. Such worlds tend to include quests as a form of narrative and a way of offering challenges to the players.

▨ **Player-versus-Player (PvP) model.** In this sort of world, players advance by defeating one another at contests, often characterized as combat. Players advance through a combination of their natural skill and rewards from winning battles. For this to work successfully, they need to be reasonably evenly matched; you can't have the old-timers beating up the newcomers all the time. *EVE Online* is perhaps the most cutthroat of the successful PvP games, with little in the rules to prevent players from abusing newcomers, although there are regions in which they will be safe as long as they stay within them.

▧ **Builder model.** This somewhat rare sort of world enables players to construct things and actually modify the world in which they play. *Minecraft* is the standout example at the moment, but there aren't that many like it. The builder model is a highly expressive form of entertainment. People get kudos not for their fighting skills, but for their aesthetic and architectural ones, both intangible qualities.

Avatar Death

In any persistent world that includes combat, you must decide whether it's possible for the player's avatar to die and what will happen if it does. As in other games, avatar death must be accompanied by a disincentive of some kind or combat will not be a meaningful part of gameplay. The trick is to find a disincentive that is proportional to the likelihood of the avatar's death. It is a question of balance: If the avatar can easily be killed through no fault of the player (such as through ignorance or bad luck), then the cost of dying—the disincentive—should be low, but if the player really has to be stupid to get her avatar killed, the cost should be high.

Some examples of penalties follow.

PERMANENT DEATH

In the most extreme case, the avatar dies and cannot be resurrected. The player loses all property that he owns (in which case you must decide what happens to that property) and must start over from scratch with a new avatar. This makes sense in games of short duration, but seldom in persistent worlds. Players in persistent worlds put too much time and effort into building up their avatars for you to ask them to start over.

RESURRECTION WITH TEMPORARILY REDUCED ATTRIBUTES

Designers commonly penalize the player for letting her avatar die by bringing the avatar back to life with reduced functional attributes—with less strength or perhaps less effective skills for a limited amount of time. In effect, you give the player a bit of a setback in her quest to grow a powerful avatar. Players find this irritating, so fear of incurring such a setback discourages risky play, but the penalty makes a certain amount of sense. If a gang of club-wielding trolls beats the avatar to death, the avatar ought to feel pretty lousy for a while when she comes back to life! In raids, healer characters can usually revive a dead avatar immediately by spending some of their own healing power. This makes the quest easier to achieve while still retaining a balancing factor; healers can't do this indefinitely.

NOTE In recent years a number of persistent worlds have lowered or even eliminated their penalties for avatar death, perhaps in an effort to recruit players who want a less difficult challenge. In some cases the avatar is simply displaced to another location and has to run back to where she came from, which is only a minor nuisance. Others that have free-to-play business models have taken a different approach: The player can pay to instantly revive her avatar without penalty.

RESURRECTION WITH SOME PROPERTY MISSING

Another classic disincentive for dying involves loss of money, gear, clothes, and other items in the avatar's inventory at the time. How much of his property he loses and what becomes of it can vary considerably from game to game. You can also allow players to have a vault in the game in which they can keep items that they're not carrying with them, and these items can remain safely in the vault for use by their resurrected avatar. You might as well include this feature because, if you don't, the players will create a second character that they never play with, known in MMOG parlance as a *mule*, to hold their primary avatar's things for them.

The Nature of Time

In a single-player computer game, you maintain a great deal of control over the relationship between game time and real time. Most games run at many times the speed of real time, and a player often experiences a simulated day in a game world in an hour or less of real time. You can also hand over control of the speed of time to the player when you want to; it's not uncommon for players in combat flight simulators to speed up time when flying to and from the combat zones and then slow down to real time again when they get there. Finally, you can skip time entirely—useful during periods when the player's avatar sleeps. You can blank the screen for a moment and then put up a text message that says, "8 hours later..." and continue with the game.

But you can't use any of these options in multiplayer games. Obviously you can't allow some players to move through time at different speeds than others, and you can't skip time unless you force all players to skip that time together. Although game time might be faster than real time, game time must proceed at the same fixed pace for everyone.

As a result, you must be careful about designing time-consuming activities. *EverQuest,* for example, employs a mechanism called *meditation,* in which players simply have to wait around for a while to restore their magic powers. There's no way to speed up this process—it literally does involve waiting. Nor can they log out of the game while meditating and log back in again later when the meditation process finishes. Players can't even switch to a different process on their computers. Verant Interactive, the developers of *EverQuest,* eventually built in a mini-game for players to play while waiting—a patch but not a real solution. If your game contains features so boring that you have to distract the players, you need to rethink the features.

Single-player games can be stopped and restarted at the player's discretion—a key consideration for designers of such games. If the player can save the game, he can essentially reverse time by going back to a previous point in the game and replaying the game from that point. This robs single-player games of some of the emotional impact of events because anything that happens, good or bad, can be reversed by reloading a saved version of the game. You can design the game to include some inevitable events, but of course, the more of these you include, the less interactive the game is.

In an online game, time is irreversible. Even if you had a convenient way to reverse time, you can't reasonably ask all your players to agree to reverse time to an earlier point (although the managers of some persistent worlds have had to roll back to a saved state when the game got into problems). In the ordinary course of events, when an event occurs in an online game, it's done and can't be undone.

Persistent World Economies

If the players in a persistent world can collect and trade things of value, then the world includes an economy. Economies are *much* easier to design and tune in a single-player game than they are in a persistent world. You can control the actions of a single person fairly strictly; in a persistent world, thousands of people interact within your game in ways that you might not have anticipated.

The original *Ultima Online* had a completely self-contained, closed economy with a fixed number of resources flowing around and around. You could mine iron ore, smelt it into iron, and forge the iron into weapons. Using the weapons would cause them to deteriorate, and when worn, they would return to the pool of raw iron ore available for mining. This last step wasn't strictly realistic, but it did close the loop.

The designers, however, didn't anticipate that players would hoard objects without using them. Because unused objects didn't go back into the pool, the iron ore quickly ran out, and as resources dwindled, inflation ran rampant. The players with hoards of iron had cornered the market and could charge extortionate fees for iron objects. Eventually, *Ultima Online's* proprietor could do nothing but adopt an open economy in which servers add new resources at intervals. One of *Ultima Online's* designers, Zack Simpson, discussed this at the 2000 Game Developers' Conference in a very informative lecture called "The In-Game Economics of *Ultima Online*" (Simpson, 2000).

It's essential in any economy that players not find a way to create something for nothing; that is, they shouldn't be able to return a resource to the system for more than they paid for it in the first place. Otherwise, they'll find a way to automate this process and generate an unlimited stream of that resource.

SECRETS TO SUCCESSFUL PERSISTENT WORLDS

Here are the secrets to a really long-lived, goal-oriented, persistent world of wide appeal:

- Have multiple paths of advancement (individual features are nice, but setting them up as growth paths is better).

- Make it easy to switch between paths of advancement (ideally, without having to start over).

- Make sure the milestones in the path of advancement are clear, visible, and significant (having 600 meaningless milestones doesn't help).

- Don't let your game feel like it is running out of significant milestones (try to make your ladder not feel finite).

Ownership is key: You have to give players a sense of ownership in the game. This is what will make them stay—it is a "barrier to departure." Social bonds are *not* enough because good social bonds extend outside the game. Instead, the ownership is in the context. If they can build their own buildings, build a character, own possessions, hold down a job, and feel a sense of responsibility for something that *cannot* be removed from the game—then they have ownership.

Social Problems

NOTE Raph Koster said, only partly joking, that the sole social rule in *Star Wars Galaxies* is, "Any behavior that hurts business is bad behavior."

Unfortunately, playing with strangers—particularly anonymous strangers—creates opportunities for a variety of types of misbehavior that can ruin the game for others. These range from simple rudeness to harassment, stalking, bullying, cheating in various forms, and outright fraud. Rudeness might not sound very serious, but it drives away other customers. (Persistently harassing other players online is called *griefing.*) Furthermore, if you want children to play your game, it is particularly important to make sure you offer a safe environment—you may even have a legal obligation to make sure adults don't use your game environment to abuse children—and that means hiring customer service people to monitor the players. Self-contained networks such as Nintendo's have some tools at their disposal to manage these problems, but on open networks such as the Internet, it's much harder.

Managing Chat

Every multiplayer game for machines that use keyboards should include a chat feature—a mechanism that enables players to send messages to one another. Voice chat, implemented with microphones, is now a common feature of online console games and many PC games as well. Depending on the nature of the game, players should be able to send private messages to one other individual, messages only to members of their own team (if any), or general broadcast messages to all other players who might reasonably be interested. In a game played by thousands of players, any one player should be able to broadcast messages only to those in her vicinity or on her team, whatever that might mean in the context of the game—the players at her table, the players in the same room of a dungeon, and so on.

Unfortunately, chat brings a new set of problems: the potential for rude, abusive, or harassing behavior. People who pay to play your game expect that others will meet certain minimum standards of civility. This is particularly important for games that will be played by children; parents rightfully want to protect their kids from abusive or offensive behavior. In a sporting event, the referee enforces rules that maintain these standards, or if there is no referee, then the collective authority of the other players must suffice. Online, it's much more difficult to police players' behavior.

LIMITED CONTENT

The surest solution is to restrict what players may say to each other. *Mario Kart* for the Nintendo Wii offers no voice chat and allows players only to choose remarks from a fixed list of phrases. Environments explicitly meant for children, such as *Webkinz*, also use this approach. This guarantees that they can't say anything offensive, but for adults, this limited list doesn't really meet the social need that chat supplies.

PROFANITY FILTERS

Designers have tried profanity filters, but they aren't fully reliable, and they sometimes produce laughable results. Words such as *damn* and *hell* are perfectly legitimate when talking about religion, even if they're considered swearing in another context—and don't think that people won't talk about religion when they're in your dungeon; they'll talk about everything under the sun. In any case, people can easily get around such filters by misspelling the words (and of course, profanity filters don't solve the problem for voice chat). A profanity filter should always be backed up by other means, such as online customer service representatives to whom players can report bad behavior.

COMPLAINT AND WARNING SYSTEMS

Some chat systems include complaint mechanisms designed to discourage online rudeness. Some online games give players a Report button they can click whenever they receive an offensive message. The offending message is, if it consists of text, automatically forwarded to someone in authority (usually online customer service staff), who can then investigate and take appropriate action: Warn the offender to mend his ways, kick him offline, or even ban his account.

The America Online Instant Messenger includes a fully automated system that allows users to warn each other, either anonymously or openly, when one participant behaves badly. A user can be warned once per message that she sends; the more warnings she receives, the less frequently the system permits her to send messages.

If she receives enough complaints, she may be unable to send any further messages for several hours. The record of the complaints is deleted over time, so a user's bad behavior is not held against her permanently. If she has behaved herself for a while, she can resume sending messages.

BLOCKING OTHER PLAYERS

Some chat mechanisms allow a player to hide messages from other individuals whose behavior they find offensive, a practice called "blocking" or "muting." The player simply selects the name of a person he wants to ignore, and he no longer receives chat messages from that person, no matter what the person writes. You can permit this to take place silently (the other player doesn't know she's being ignored) or automatically send a message telling her that she has been ignored—the online equivalent of deliberately turning your back on someone. This mechanism is both effective—the users have full control over whom they hear from and whom they don't—and inexpensive because it doesn't require staff intervention. You should also include the ability to turn off chat entirely if players simply don't want to hear from anyone else.

MODERATED CHAT SPACES

The most effective, but also the most expensive, way of keeping order in a chat space is to give one person authority to discipline the others at all times. Internet Relay Chat uses this method; the creator of a chat room exercises the authority to kick people out. If the enforcer also participates in the game, this method is subject to abuse. When people set up their own online matches among their friends, you can let them police themselves; but when they are paying someone to arrange the game for them (as in a matchmaking service or persistent world), the moderator must be an impartial representative of the game's provider—a customer service agent, in effect, whether paid or unpaid.

The Player-Killer (PK) Problem

No aspect of the design of persistent worlds has been debated more than this one simple question: Should players' avatars be allowed to kill one another? The next few sections summarize some of the issues so that you can make an informed decision for your own game.

Most designers offer persistent worlds resembling RPGs in that players advance in skill and power through combat. It's generally more interesting if this combat occurs against another player rather than against an NPC for several reasons. First, another player's avatar is more likely to be carrying interesting and valuable objects worth looting (if the game permits looting) than a randomly generated NPC; unlike an NPC, another player will have kept only valuable items and gotten rid of anything not worth keeping. Second, fighting another player is a social experience, which an

NPC cannot offer. Finally, a player can use his human intelligence to put up a better fight; an NPC has to use AI, which is seldom as sophisticated.

THE *ULTIMA ONLINE* EXPERIENCE

Initially the designers of *Ultima Online* permitted players to kill one another without restraint (except in towns), hoping that players would establish their own justice mechanisms within the game. Unfortunately, the world quickly began to resemble present-day Somalia: unremitting random violence, feuds, continual victimization of the weak by the strong, and petty warlords or gangs of bandits controlling areas of turf. Players engaging in this behavior became known as *player-killers,* or PK players. No satisfactory solution arose from the players, partly because the software did not offer any genuinely painful punishment mechanisms for them to use against offenders. (In real life, we either lock murderers away for a very long time or kill them permanently, neither of which any for-pay persistent world can afford to do.) Designers then tried a variety of automated mechanisms for encouraging justice, but players found ways of exploiting most such mechanisms. In the end, the developers threw up their hands and divided the world into *shards* (separate, independent versions of the world) with different rules for each. Some allowed PvP combat, and others did not. Approximately 80 percent of the players chose to play in non-PvP shards.

JUSTICE MECHANISMS

Koster offers the following summary of approaches to regulating PvP combat, whether fatal or not:

⬛ **No automated regulation.** Anyone can attack anyone, and administrators or social mechanisms (vigilante justice) deal with rogue players. Koster estimates that as much as 40 percent of the potential audience will avoid this type of game because they don't like PvP.

⬛ **Flagging of criminals.** Player killing is considered a criminal act within the game's rules: not prevented by the system, but wrong. The server automatically detects criminal behavior and flags the criminals, who become fair game for others to attack. The system can also reduce the attributes of criminals, in effect penalizing them for their behavior. This can be used for thievery and other crimes as well as murder, matching the reduction to the severity of the crime. Single-player RPGs use a version of this system too: Players may behave in good or bad ways, but those who behave badly frequently suffer penalties—NPCs will not talk to them or trade with them, for example.

⬛ **Reputation systems.** This is similar to flagging, except that players decide when to report someone for criminal behavior and can choose not to do so. In practice, they almost always do, however.

▪ **PvP switch.** Players indicate their willingness to fight other players by setting a switch (a binary attribute) in their profile, becoming either a PvP player, who can attack and be attacked, or a non-PvP player, who cannot attack or be attacked. You can use this switch to give temporary consent for duels and arena-based combat. Unfortunately, this mechanism creates suspension-of-disbelief problems when players use area-effect weapons such as a magic fireball spell: Three PvP players get roasted by a fireball that leaves a non-PvP player in the same vicinity untouched because he cannot be attacked.

▪ **Safe games; no PvP allowed.** This is the least troublesome solution, but even this approach has its hazards. Players will still find ways of abusing one another—for example, by luring an unsuspecting newcomer into an area where he will be attacked by a monster. Koster estimates that this approach will cost you up to 20 percent of your potential audience, that 20 percent being those players who like PvP.

You can also divide the world into safe and dangerous geographic zones, but in practice people tend to either stay in the safe zones or play near the edges, hoping to lure a potential victim over the line without her realizing it.

FACTION-BASED PVP

A number of persistent worlds allow players to belong to factions. These can be as small as gangs or as large as entire nations at war. The rules enable players to attack members of enemy factions but not members of their own faction—in effect, it's team play. Different factions control different regions, so players can generally tell safe areas from unsafe areas. For the most part, this arrangement solves the random violence problem that initially plagued *Ultima Online*.

THE BOTTOM LINE ON PLAYER KILLING

You cannot please everybody, so you will benefit from deciding *whom* you want to please and tailoring your environment to them. In a game that allows player killing, a certain number of players will inevitably abuse the system, exploiting their superior strength to victimize weaker players without ever putting themselves at risk. You can't please them without also providing them with victims who *won't* be pleased, so it's not worth trying. Ultimately, you need to bear two things in mind:

▪ **It's a fantasy world.** That means it's supposed to be enjoyable, escapist entertainment. People don't fantasize about being harassed, bullied, or abused. A fair contest among consenting players is one thing; perpetual harassment or an ambush by a gang is quite another. In fact, the law is finally beginning to catch up with game systems, and cyber-bullying is being recognized as a form of real-world harassment, even if it takes place in a fantasy world.

■ **People pay to play.** This makes your world distinctly different from the real world. The real world doesn't owe us anything; we survive as best we can. But as a game provider, you've taken the players' money, so you have obligations to them. Just exactly what those obligations are is open to debate, of course, but if players don't feel that you are meeting your obligations, they will leave.

PLAYER EXPECTATIONS

Players have higher expectations of the virtual world than of the real world. For example, players expect all labor to result in profit; they expect life to be fair; they expect to be protected from aggression before the fact, not just have to seek redress after the fact; they expect problems to be resolved quickly; and they expect that their integrity will be assumed to be beyond reproach. In other words, they expect too much, and you will not be able to supply it all. The trick is to manage their expectations.

Summary

Multiplayer games are harder to design than single-player ones, online games are harder still, and persistent worlds are the hardest of all. It's a bit like the difference between cooking for yourself and planning a dinner party. When you're cooking for yourself, you decide what you want, make it, and eat it. When you're planning a dinner party, you have to take into account more variables: who likes what food, who gets along with whom, and what entertainment should you offer in addition to the food. A dinner party requires more work ahead of time—but it's a lot more fun than eating by yourself, too. The flexibility and power of online gaming enables you to create entertainment experiences that you simply can't produce in other forms.

Design Practice QUESTIONS

1. How do you plan to deal with the issue of new players arriving in the middle of a long game? Get rid of the victory condition, or find a way to make sure that players are matched with those of similar ability?

2. What will happen to the gameplay when a player suddenly goes offline? How will it affect the other players' experience of the game (what they see and hear)? Does it disrupt the balance of the game? Will it make the challenges easier or harder? Is the game even meaningful anymore?

3. What happens to the game's score when a player vanishes? Is the game still fair?

4. Does your game offer a player an advantage of some kind for intentionally disconnecting himself (whether by preventing him from losing or by sealing his own victory)? Is there any way to minimize this without penalizing players who are disconnected accidentally?

5. In a turn-based game, what mechanism will you use to prevent a player from stalling play for the other players? Set a time limit? Allow simultaneous turns? Implement a reasonable default if the player does nothing?

6. If you offer a chat mechanism, what features will you implement to keep it civil? Filters? A complaint system? An ignore system? Or will your game require moderated chat spaces?

7. Is your game designed to prevent (or alleviate) collusion? Because you can't prevent players from talking to each other on the phone as they play, how will you address this? Or can you design your game in such a way that collusion is part of the gameplay, as in *Diplomacy?*

GLOSSARY

A

absolute difficulty The difficulty of a challenge, taking into account both the *intrinsic skill required* and the *stress* on the player, as compared to the trivial case of a similar challenge. See also *relative difficulty* and *perceived difficulty*.

abstract (adjective) A quality of a game that indicates it bears little relationship to the real world and the player may not rely on his understanding of the real world in playing the game; its rules are arbitrary. Abstract is one end of the *realism* scale; the other end is *representational*.

abstract (verb) To remove a complex mechanism from a simulation (often a mechanism intended to simulate a real-world phenomenon) and replace it with a simpler mechanism or none at all.

accelerometer A device that measures acceleration. Placed inside a game controller, it can detect when the player moves the controller. An accelerometer is at the heart of the Nintendo Wii controller and within smart phones.

action game A game whose gameplay consists primarily of physical coordination challenges.

action-adventure A hybrid genre of *action game* and *adventure game*. The action-adventure is now more popular than either of its two constituents.

actions Player behaviors permitted by the *rules*. Many game actions are intended to overcome *challenges*, but others serve to add to the player's enjoyment in other ways.

active challenge A challenge to the player that requires special mechanics to implement and determine whether the player has overcome it. Puzzles or enemies are active challenges. Contrast with *passive challenge*.

adaptive music A technique of modifying or even generating music in real time to react to events in a game.

adventure game An interactive story in which the player takes the role of the protagonist. Puzzle-solving and conceptual reasoning challenges form the majority of the gameplay; physical coordination challenges are few or nonexistent.

agency The player's ability to affect future events in a story, possibly including the ending, by taking *dramatic actions*. Also sometimes called *dramatic freedom*.

AI See *artificial intelligence*.

analog device A user input device that can transmit a range of numeric values to indicate its current state or the amount that it has changed from its previous state. A slider, commonly used to implement a throttle in flight simulators, is an analog device.

art-driven game A game whose design is driven primarily by visual aesthetics.

artificial intelligence (AI) A suite of programming techniques that allow a computer to mimic human behavior in certain domains. Video games use AI to provide artificial opponents for players to play against, among other functions.

asymmetric game A game in which the players do not start with identical conditions, do not play by the same rules, or do not seek to achieve the same victory condition.

asynchronous play Play (usually in an online game) in which players' activities are not synchronized. The players need not be logged on to the network at the same time but may join and leave the game at any point without interfering with the progress of the game.

atomic challenge A challenge that the player faces immediately during play. One of the lowest-level challenges in the *hierarchy of challenges*. A challenge that is not composed of other subchallenges.

attract loop A continuously cycling noninteractive demonstration on an arcade game designed to attract the attention of passersby.

attributes Data values that describe one or more qualities of a character or unit. These may be symbolic, numeric, or collections of data. For descriptions of the different kinds of attributes, see *characterization attributes, status attributes, functional attributes,* and *cosmetic attributes.*

augmented reality A form of computerized interaction in which computer-presented data and input mechanisms are combined with real-world events. The game is said to augment the player's experience of the real world (and, for that matter, the real world augments the player's experience of the game).

automated storytelling See *emergent storytelling.*

automation Generally speaking, having a computer do something that a human would otherwise do. In game design, including a game feature that simplifies the complexity of playing the game by having the computer handle certain activities for the player, especially if they are particularly difficult, or repetitive, or uninteresting. Auto-targeting in shooter games is an example of automation.

avatar A fictional character in a game with whom the player identifies as the personification of herself within the game world. The character need not be human; it may even be a vehicle.

avatar-based interaction model An *interaction model* in which the player is represented by a single character, vehicle, or other entity in the game world. The key point of this relationship is that the player may influence the game world only through the avatar actions and, therefore, only those regions of the game world where the avatar is present.

B

backgrounder A document that describes the personality, attitudes, and other characteristics of a game character.

back story The imaginary history that precedes the game-world time when the game takes place; sometimes also the imaginary background of a non-player character or avatar.

balance In a player-versus-player game, the design task of making the game fair to all players. In a player-versus-environment game, the design task of managing the difficulty level of the game.

binary device A user input device that transmits only two states, turned on and turned off. Contrast with *analog device.*

boss A large and particularly difficult challenge that must be overcome, typically the last one required to complete a *level* of a game.

bot An artificially intelligent opponent, usually in a first-person shooter, that players may implement as a modification to the game.

branch point A point in the overall plot of an interactive story at which the player's path through the plot may go in different directions. At a branch point, some factor (most frequently a player action) selects a direction that the path will take. Also called a *node.*

branching story An interactive story whose plot is preplanned by the designer but may take alternative paths as a result of actions the player takes.

broad interface A user interface that offers many options to the player at once, making them quick to use at the cost of being time-consuming to learn and daunting to new players. Compare with *deep interface.*

C

camera model The point of view ordinarily adopted by the game's *virtual camera* when displaying the *game world,* along with instructions about how the camera should behave during play. The camera model is one component of a *gameplay mode.* Some camera models include artificial intelligence that attempt to make the camera move automatically to show the scene from a particularly desirable viewpoint. Non-intelligent camera models that keep the camera relatively fixed are sometimes called *perspectives,* for example, the top-down perspective.

cartoon physics An implementation of physical laws that differ from Newtonian physics in such a way that the game looks and behaves like an animated cartoon.

challenge A nontrivial task the player seeks to perform to move toward the game's goals.

character level A numeric *status attribute* that roughly describes a character's power to perform certain activities. In role-playing games, characters rise from level to level with experience.

characterization attributes Attributes that describe something fundamental about a character or unit and change only slowly by small amounts or not at all. Maximum speed might be a characterization attribute for a vehicle. See *attributes.*

cheat (noun) An action, usually obscure and undocumented, that adjusts the game's internal economy to assist the player. If the player can type a sequence of keystrokes that makes her avatar permanently invincible, she has enabled a cheat. Many cheats are undocumented shortcuts designed to assist the testing process.

cheat (verb) (1) To violate the rules of a game to one's own advantage as a player. (2) To draw a game world object in such a way that its appearance conflicts with its supposed perspective. Most usually used to draw buildings at a slight angle in the top-down perspective to enable the viewer to see their side as well as their roofs.

checkpoints Locations in a game level at which the game may be saved (or is automatically saved) or at which the avatar will be reincarnated if he dies.

collectible A game world object that is in the player's interest to find and collect.

combinatorial explosion An undesirable property of branching stories in which the number of plot lines grows to unmanageable numbers as each line offers more and more branch points.

combo move A rapid sequence of joystick movements and button presses that must be performed perfectly to produce an avatar action. Usually found in fighting games.

competition A form of play in which players are trying to achieve mutually exclusive goals.

competition mode One of a variety of different forms of competitive or cooperative play, such as team play or multiplayer cooperative play. Many video games allow players to choose a competition mode.

compound entity An entity made up of more than one datum. An entity describing the wind that included both speed and direction would be a compound entity consisting of two *attributes,* one for wind speed and one for direction.

computer role-playing game (CRPG) Term used to distinguish computerized role-playing games from noncomputerized tabletop role-playing games.

concept See *game concept.*

concept art Sketches drawn during the early stages of game design to give developers and publishers an idea of how game world features and characters may look in the game. Concept art is not incorporated into the final product.

concept stage The first major stage of game design in which the designer works to turn an idea for a game into a *game concept.*

conflict challenge A challenge requiring the direct opposition of forces under the player's control. Not to be confused with *conflict of interest.*

conflict of interest The defining quality of a game in formal *game theory:* a situation in which the players seek mutually incompatible outcomes.

constrained creative play Creative play artificially constrained by rules. The rules may impose physical, aesthetic, or economic limitations on what the player may create. Contrast with *freeform creative play.*

contestant-based interaction model An *interaction model* in which the player acts like a contestant in a TV game show. Interactions consist of answering questions, choosing correct answers, and making simple strategic decisions.

context-sensitive camera model A *camera model* in which the camera moves in response to the events and circumstances of the game rather than being fixed with respect to the game world or the avatar.

continuous scrolling A characteristic of scrolling 2D *camera models* where the landscape scrolls continuously in one direction; the player has limited, if any, control over the avatar and is focused on whatever appears. Also called *forced scrolling.*

converter A mechanic, sometimes automated, that converts one or more resources into one or more other resources.

cooperation A form of play in which the players act together to achieve the same goals.

core mechanics A symbolic and mathematical model of the game's rules that can be implemented algorithmically; specifically, those rules that operate throughout the whole game. Mechanics that are created specifically for use in particular levels, or that control the behavior of individual non-player characters that are not always present, are not considered core mechanics.

cosmetic attributes Attributes of a character, vehicle, or other object that affect only its appearance, not its interaction with the core mechanics of the game. The paint color of a car is a cosmetic attribute. Contrast with *functional attributes*.

crane To move the game's virtual camera up or down in space.

crippleware Software distributed under the *freemium* model whose free version lacks so much functionality that it is not worth having.

crowdfunding A technique for raising money to undertake a project by asking large numbers of potential buyers to contribute small amounts of money to its development in advance.

CRPG See *computer role-playing game*.

cut-scenes Short, noninteractive visual sequences that momentarily interrupt play.

D

deadlock A condition of the game's *internal economy* in which either (a) a production mechanism cannot begin to operate because it requires a *resource* that is not available and no way exists to produce the needed resource, or (b) a production mechanism ceases to operate because it has run out of some needed input resource and no way exists to produce the needed resource. Deadlocks are caused by the presence of a *feedback loop* or a *mutual dependency* in the flow of resources.

deathmatch A multiplayer competitive competition mode.

deep interface A user interface that presents options in a hierarchy or sequence of menus, making them relatively easy to find at the cost of being slow to use for experienced players. Compare with *broad interface*.

degree of freedom The number of possible dimensions that an input device can move through.

designer-driven game A game whose designer retains all creative control. Such games usually reflect the designer's own personal desires rather than a wish to entertain others.

desktop model An *interaction model* that mimics a computer or a real desktop.

dev kit or **development kit** A specialized hardware device and accompanying software that make it possible to build a game for a proprietary home console machine. Normally available only to developers who have a license from the console manufacturer.

dialogue tree A structure documenting player dialogue choices and non-player character responses to those choices in a *scripted conversation* that can be drawn on paper in a diagram that looks rather like a tree. Each player option produces a new branch in the tree.

difficulty One of several measures that determine how hard a game is to play. See *absolute difficulty, relative difficulty,* and *perceived difficulty.*

dimensions Collections of related properties that define how the player experiences the *game world,* for example, the physical dimension, emotional dimension, ethical dimension, and so on.

dolly To move the game's virtual camera forward or backward along a line in the same direction that it is facing.

dominant strategy A *strategy* so effective that the player has no reason to use any other. A game containing a dominant strategy is said to be poorly *balanced.*

downloadable content Extra content that the player can download to enhance or extend a game.

drain A mechanic that permanently removes *resources* from the game world without introducing anything in exchange.

dramatic action An action the player takes that changes the direction of the plot line and, thus, future events in the story as the player will experience it. Many player actions contribute to a story but are not dramatic actions; they do not change the future.

dramatic compression A quality of a story such that repetitive or irrelevant events are left out of the telling.

dramatic freedom See *agency.*

dramatic tension An audience's sense that an important problem or situation in a story is not yet resolved, leaving them wondering how it will come out. Do not confuse with *gameplay tension.* Usually called "conflict" by screenwriters.

dungeon exit See *level exit.*

E

Easter egg An undocumented feature or detail in a game left for the player to find.

elaboration stage The second and longest stage of game design, during which the designers elaborate on the game concept they built during the *concept stage*.

embedded narrative Narrative material that is written by the designer and built into the game software (embedded) during development. See *narrative* and *narrative events*, and contrast with *emergent narrative*.

emergence A quality of a game that arises from the operation of its mechanics rather than preplanned events established by the designer. Contrast with *progression*.

emergent storytelling or **emergent narrative** A system of interactive storytelling in which the story's events are produced by the core mechanics, rather than being written by the designer in advance.

emotes Animations of an avatar that the player can trigger voluntarily to show emotion, usually to other players in a multiplayer game.

emotional resonance A quality of a game such that it evokes in the player the emotional responses that the designer intends for it to.

entity A datum or collection of data that describes some object, character, quantity, or state of affairs in the game. See *simple entity* and *compound entity*.

exchange A pair of lines of dialogue in a *dialogue tree* consisting of a player's line and a non-player character's response to that line.

exclusionary material Content or features, such as racial or sexual content, that tend to drive players away from a game they might otherwise like.

experience points (XP) A resource earned by the player through combat and other activities in a *role-playing game*.

explicit challenge A challenge the player is explicitly told about by the game. Typically the explicit challenges are the *victory condition* and the *atomic challenges*.

F

factories Entities, usually characterized as buildings, under player control that convert or produce resources of use to the player.

fair (1) In a player-versus-player game, a perception on the part of the players that the rules do not create advantages for one player over another other than by the operation of chance. (2) In a player-versus-environment game, player expectations that the game will be winnable using ordinary skill and common sense.

feature lock The point during game development beyond which no new features may be introduced into the game. After feature lock the game may be tested and tuned, but new features may not be added.

feedback (1) Information provided to the player to let him know the effects of his actions upon the game world and other data he may need to evaluate his status and plan future actions. Used in the context of user interfaces. See *feedback element.* (2) A phenomenon occurring in automated internal economies; see *feedback loop* for further information. (3) A common phenomenon occurring in the *balance* of a game so that the player's successful efforts make the game easier or harder. See *positive feedback* and *negative feedback.*

feedback element An audible or visible part of the user interface that informs the player about the effects of his actions upon the game world and other data he may need to evaluate his status and plan future actions. Sound effects and visible *indicators* are feedback elements.

feedback loop In an *internal economy,* a situation in which some of the resources produced by a production mechanism must either (a) be used to initiate the production mechanism in the first place or (b) be fed back into the production mechanism to keep it operating. Feedback loops run the risk of creating a *deadlock.*

fighting games A subgenre of action game in which the gameplay consists primarily of hand-to-hand combat.

first playable level The first level created by the level design team that actually includes representative gameplay, as opposed to being a prototype or mockup. It should be a typical example of a level, not the first level that the player will play.

first-person perspective A *camera model* always used with *avatar-based interaction models* in which the *virtual camera* displays the *game world* from the point of view of the avatar's own eyes.

first-person shooter (FPS) A *shooter* game in which the game world is displayed from the *first-person perspective.* Also sometimes called a POV (point of view) shooter and, in Europe, an egoshooter.

five factor model A psychological model of human personality traits centered around given domains: openness to new experiences, conscientiousness, extraversion, agreeableness, and neuroticism. The designer, Jason VandenBerghe, has mapped these traits to a variety of player motivations.

flowboard A document that describes a game's *structure*—the relationships between its various *gameplay modes* and when the game transitions from one mode to another. Also sometimes called a "wireframe," although this term is ambiguous, because it also refers to a 3D model's raw polygon data.

fog of war (1) The technique of hiding unexplored regions of a terrain from the player using an aerial perspective by showing them as featureless, usually black or clouds. (2) The technique of hiding regions or some aspects of terrain, even if previously explored, from a player using an aerial perspective, if the player has no *units* in the region to see what is going on there. Typically used in war games to prevent the player from observing enemy troop movements unless she has units nearby to see them.

foldback story A variant of a *branching story* in which the branching plot lines eventually return to an inevitable event that the player will experience regardless of his choices before branching out again.

forced scrolling See *continuous scrolling.*

FPS See *first-person shooter.*

freeform creative play Creative play constrained only by the options that the game offers and the technological limitations of the machine but not by rules. Contrast with *constrained creative play.*

freemium A business model for earning money from a product by giving away the product for free, but charging customers for premium features.

free-roaming camera A *camera model* used in 3D *game worlds,* normally with *multi-present interaction models,* in which the *virtual camera* may move anywhere around the world, often under player control.

functional attributes Attributes of an avatar or other character that influence gameplay through their effect on the core mechanics. Contrast with *cosmetic attributes.*

G

game A type of *play* activity conducted in the context of a *pretended* reality in which the participant(s) try to achieve at least one arbitrary, nontrivial *goal* by acting in accordance with *rules.*

game concept A statement of a group of design choices sufficient to convey, among other things, what a game will be like to play, for what audience it is intended, and on what machine it will run.

game engine That part of the game's software that implements the *core mechanics.*

game theory A branch of mathematics aimed at discovering optimal solutions in situations where the parties to the situation have a *conflict of interest.*

game treatment A document that presents the game in a broad outline to someone who's already interested in it and wants to hear more about it.

game tree A hypothetical specification of all possible future events in a game, which can be drawn on paper in a diagram that looks like a tree, as future choices branch out. Normally used only for two-player, turn-based games.

game world An imaginary universe in which the events of the game take place. Most computer game worlds are simulated two- and three-dimensional spaces containing characters and objects.

gameplay The challenges presented to a player and the actions the player is permitted to take, both to overcome those challenges and to perform other enjoyable activities in the game world.

gameplay mode A collection of features of a game that strongly influence the player's experience of the game at any given time. The features that make up a gameplay mode are: a) the subset of the game's *gameplay* that the core mechanics offer at any particular time; b) the *camera model* with which the user interface displays the *game world;* and c) the *interaction model* offered by the user interface, by which the player acts upon the world. Whenever any of these features changes significantly, the game has entered a new gameplay mode.

gameplay tension The player's uncertainty about whether she will overcome the challenges she faces and, in a player-versus-player game, what her opponent will do next. Do not confuse with *dramatic tension.*

gamer dedication A scale that measures the extent to which gamers are dedicated to playing video games and learning about the game industry, using a variety of metrics.

genre A category of games characterized by particular kinds of challenges, regardless of setting or game-world content. Games that include challenges from several different genres are called *hybrids.*

global mechanic A mechanic that operates throughout the game regardless of which gameplay mode the game may be in.

goals Desired results or conditions that the player seeks to achieve. The goals of a game need not be achievable, so long as players can work toward them. Games usually have many goals, defined by the *hierarchy of challenges.* The *victory condition,* if the game has one, is always one of these goals.

granularity The frequency with which the game presents *narrative* elements to the player.

griefing Intentional harassment of another player, or an entire group of players, outside the social norms of an online game. Griefing can vary from being a mild annoyance to a serious real-world crime if it takes the form of personal threats or sexual harassment of children.

group play A form of social play in which members of a group take turns at playing a single-player game while the others watch. Also called hotseat play.

H

handicap An adjustment to the rules of the game (often of the *victory condition*) intended to balance differential skill among the players and give the less skilled a better chance of winning against superior players.

harmony An aesthetic quality of a game such that it feels as if all its elements—visual, auditory, gameplay, and others—belong together and complement each other.

head-up display (HUD) The technique of displaying *indicators* superimposed on the *main view* in a user interface rather than in a separate window of their own. Previous editions of this book called these superimposed indicators *overlays*.

heartbeat A technical mechanism for determining whether or not a player on a network is still connected to a server (or to another player). The player's client software sends a short data packet to the server at regular intervals to indicate that the player is connected.

hierarchy of challenges A theoretical hierarchy of goals the player tries to achieve at any given moment, consisting (from the top down) of completing the entire game, winning the current level, completing a sub-mission within the level, if any, and so on down to the challenge immediately facing her at the moment, an *atomic challenge*.

high concept A very short description, no more than two or three sentences long, that conveys the most important aspects of an idea for a game.

HUD Short for *head-up display.*

hypersexualized Quality of a character whose sexual attributes have been exaggerated to an extreme extent.

I

immersion The feeling of being submerged in a form of entertainment and unaware that you are experiencing an artificial world. Players become immersed in several ways: tactically, strategically, and narratively.

immutable rules Rules that cannot change during play.

implicit challenge A challenge the player is not told about directly but must infer from the rules, observation of the game, trial and error, or by knowing what the *explicit challenges* are.

in-app purchases (IAPs) Purchases that a player makes with real money within a game to buy new features of a game, to speed up the game, or to prolong gameplay.

indicator Any visual user interface element that shows the status of some important value in the game and changes continually as the value changes. Digits, power bars, lights, gauges, *small multiples*, and many other design elements are used as indicators.

influence map A map maintained internally by the game software that records how a building in the game world landscape influences the area around it. Used to simplify logistics by having units in the neighborhood of the building receive support automatically.

in-game events Events performed by the core mechanics of a game as part of an *interactive story.*

in-game experience Experience the player has gained from confronting a particular type of challenge during the course of a game. A factor in computing the *perceived difficulty* of a challenge at a given point in the game.

intangible resource A resource that does not occupy space in the game world or has to be managed as a physical object. Happiness could be an intangible resource. Compare with *tangible resource.*

interaction model The means by which the player projects his will into the game world, which is facilitated by the user interface. The interaction model is one component of a *gameplay mode*. Common interaction models include *avatar-based, party-based, multipresent, contestant-based,* and *desktop.*

interactive fiction Text-only adventure games played by typing on a keyboard.

interactive story A story that a player interacts with by contributing *player events* and possibly by changing its plot through *dramatic actions.*

internal economy The subset of the *core mechanics* that deals with the numeric relationships among entities in the game and the way those relationships change over time and in response to events in the game.

intrinsic skill required The amount of skill a player must have to meet a challenge independently of time pressure, as compared to the trivial case of the same challenge. One component of *absolute difficulty.*

L

lag A delay between a player giving a command and an online game responding to it. See *latency.*

LAN parties Multiplayer networked play in which all the players are in the same room or building but each has her own machine networked to the others over a local-area network (LAN).

latency A measure of the length of time required for data to be transmitted from a sender to a receiver over a network, often caused by overcrowding on the network. When a player plays a game over a network with high latency, he experiences delays in the apparent responsiveness of the game, a phenomenon called *lag*.

level Ordinarily refers to a portion of a video game, usually with its own victory condition, that the player must complete before moving on to the next portion. Levels are often, but not always, completed in a prescribed sequence. In storytelling terms, levels may be thought of as chapters; in war games, they are missions; in fighting games, they are individual bouts; in simulations, they are scenarios. Used with a qualifier, however, the word may take on a different meaning. See *character level.*

level exit In a game that involves exploration, the standard transition point from the current *level* to the next.

level warp In a game that involves exploration, a transition point other than the standard level exit that enables the player to jump to the next level (or even several levels ahead) without completing the current level.

leveling up or **leveling** In a game that implements *character levels,* the attainment of some accomplishment (usually arriving at a threshold number of *experience points*) that causes the character to gain a level and with it an increase in *characterization attributes.*

license A contract between the owner of an intellectual property such as a character, movie, book, or sports league, and a game developer or publisher to acquire the rights to use that property in games. The term *license* is often used to refer to the property itself, as in "Electronic Arts has the *Harry Potter* license." The term also refers to purchasing the rights to use other intellectual property, such as fonts, images, middleware, and proprietary platforms.

limited series A series of episodes in a long-running, but ultimately limited, story. Plot lines may carry over from one episode to another, and there will be one major plot thread across the entire series as well.

linear stories Stories in which the player's actions do not change her experience of the plot.

localization The process of modifying game content to make the game suitable for sale in a country other than the one for which it was originally developed.

loss condition An unambiguous true-or-false condition that determines when a player has lost a game. Not all games have a loss condition. Many games cannot be lost; they simply remain unfinished.

M

Machinations A graphical diagramming language and simulation tool devised by Joris Dormans to enable easy display and rapid prototyping of *internal economies.*

magic circle Term coined originally by Johan Huizinga to refer to physical locations in which special social rules of behavior apply. Subsequently adopted by the game industry and other fictional media as follows: The magic circle is a theoretical concept related to the act of *pretending* that occurs when we choose to play a game. When we begin to *play* and agree to abide by the *rules,* we enter the magic circle. Within the magic circle, actions that would be meaningless in the real world take on meaning in the context of the game.

main view The portion of the screen that displays the player's primary view of the game world.

mana An expendable resource of magical power consumed by casting magic spells. The word is of Polynesian origin, although in that context its meaning is considerably more complex.

manager game A sports game in which the player may exercise the functions of a team's manager but may not play matches.

market-driven game A game whose features are included simply because they are known to appeal to a given market, whether or not those features are consistent with the game's real premise.

microgames Games that last only a few seconds. Players must be able to grasp the *rules* instantly upon being presented with the game.

mini-map A small, dynamically updated map of a *game world,* usually displayed in the corner of the screen in the *primary gameplay mode,* for quick reference. A mini-map that is centered on the avatar and whose orientation changes to reflect the direction the avatar is facing is usually called a *radar screen.*

mixed reality See *augmented reality.*

model sheet A sheet of paper containing a large number of drawings or renderings of a single character showing a number of different poses and facial expressions.

mods Player-created modifications to a game that provide new content and sometimes new ways to play the game.

monster generator A device visible in the environment that serves as a *source* for enemies entering the game world. A monster generator may be destroyed or otherwise prevented from introducing enemies; contrast with *spawn point.*

Monte Carlo simulation A way of evaluating the performance of a system by running the system hundreds or thousands of times with random inputs, and analyzing the results statistically to see if they are within acceptable bounds.

moveset A list of animations that shows how a character can move, both voluntarily and involuntarily.

multiplayer distributed gaming Playing games among multiple players at distributed locations (such as over a network), which enables each to have her own video screen and individual view of the game world. Contrast with *multiplayer local gaming.*

multiplayer local gaming Playing games in the same room with other people, all looking at the same video screen. This approach makes it impossible to provide individual players with secret information.

multipresent interaction model An *interaction model* in which the player may influence many areas of the game world at one time.

mutable rules Rules that can be changed during a game according to other rules that define how the changes may take place.

mutual dependency A condition of an *internal economy* in which two processes each require the output of the other as an input in order to function. If one of the input supplies is diverted elsewhere and no more becomes available, a *deadlock* will occur.

N

narrative Noninteractive story material that is presented by the game to the player, consisting of *narrative events*. It differs from *in-game events* in that narrative is written as part of the design process rather than being produced by the core mechanics.

narrative events Events that are shown to the player through narration rather than through the action of the player or the core mechanics. Equivalent to *embedded narrative.*

native talent The inherent ability that a player brings to a game.

natural language Ordinary language as spoken or written by human beings.

negative feedback A phenomenon of the game's *balance* such that successful player actions make subsequent challenges more difficult and unsuccessful actions make them easier. Negative feedback has the property of keeping the game's difficulty constant.

networked play Play among characters on computers connected together by a network. See *multiplayer distributed gaming.*

node See *branch point.*

nonlinear stories Stories whose plot line can change in response to *dramatic actions* on the part of the player.

non-player character (NPC) A simulated character in a video game who is not an avatar for a player. The behavior of an NPC is normally governed by *artificial intelligence*.

NPC See *non-player character*.

O

object (of a game) See *goals*.

one-way door Any mechanism in a game that prevents a player from returning to a space or experiencing a part of a story's plot that he has already experienced before. It need not be an actual door.

overlay See *head-up display*.

P

pace The rate at which the player is obliged to interact with the game; the speed at which the game presents challenges.

pan To turn the game's virtual camera about its vertical axis.

parallax scrolling A display technique in which a layer of background objects in 2D environments scroll by more slowly than a layer of foreground objects, creating the impression that they are farther away. Normally used in the *side-scrolling perspective* to create an illusion of depth.

party A group of characters, normally under the control of one or more players, who act cooperatively in a game, most commonly a role-playing game.

party-based interaction model An *interaction model* in which the player influences the *game world* through a *party* of characters who generally stay together in one area but may sometimes separate briefly. The player controls most or all the members of the party.

passive challenge A challenge presented to the player by a static obstacle, that does not require extra mechanics to implement. A maze is a passive challenge. Contrast with *active challenge*.

pathfinding An artificial intelligence technique for finding a route from one point in a landscape to another while avoiding obstacles along the way.

pay-to-win A business model for earning money from games such that players who spend more money have a competitive advantage against players who spend less money.

perceived difficulty The player's actual perception of how hard a challenge is to overcome. It takes into account four factors: *intrinsic skill required, stress, power provided* by the game, and the player's *in-game experience* at surmounting similar challenges.

perfect information A quality of a game such that each player has full knowledge of her own status and the other players' status including all previous actions taken; no information is hidden, and there is no element of chance.

permanent upgrade An upgrade to the capabilities of the player's avatar or units that lasts for the remainder of the game.

persistent world A large online game with no definite beginning or ending that allows players to join, play, and depart at any time. Most frequently implemented as a server-based computer role-playing game played over the Internet.

perspective One of several *camera models* in which the game's *virtual camera* remains largely fixed with respect either to an avatar or a game world. For example, the camera in a *first-person perspective* always remains fixed relative to the avatar. The previous edition of this book referred to all camera models as perspectives.

phablet A mobile smartphone large enough to be used as a small tablet computer.

plan-and-build A construction play mechanic in which the player plans a new object at a location in the environment and the resources necessary to construct it are consumed over time as the object is built. Contrast with *purchase-and-place*.

platformers Action or action-adventure games in which a common avatar action involves jumping on and off platforms in the game world.

play Nonessential human activities that are usually, but not always, recreational as well. One of the four key elements of a game.

player events Actions performed by the player as part of an interactive story.

player-centric An approach to game design that requires the designer to empathize with the player and concentrate on entertaining that player.

player-killing Nonconsensual combat among players in an online game, usually between unfairly matched players, whereby the more powerful attacks the weaker to take his possessions (if the game allows it), or simply to annoy or bully him.

positional audio The technique of adjusting the volume and apparent position of a source of sound in the game world in real time to reflect the avatar's physical relationship to the source.

positive feedback A phenomenon of the game's *balance* such that successful player action makes subsequent challenges easier.

power provided The resources, actions, capabilities, and other game features under the player's control that enable her to meet challenges.

powerup An object in the game world that, when found by a character (usually the avatar), gives that character added powers.

presentation layer Another term for the *user interface.*

pretending The mental ability to establish a notional reality that the pretender knows is different from the real world. One of the four key elements of a game.

previous experience The amount of time the player has spent playing games similar to the one under development. This factor influences the *perceived difficulty* of the game but lies outside the designer's knowledge or control.

primary gameplay mode The *gameplay mode* in which the player spends the largest part of her time in the game. In a few games, the player divides her time equally between two or more gameplay modes, but these are rare.

procedural rhetoric Using a game's mechanics to convey a message to a player, so that he will come to understand it through the act of playing rather than being told explicitly.

production mechanism A mechanic that either is a source of a resource or converts an unusable resource (such as buried gold) into a usable one.

progression A game feature in which the player is presented with a predesigned sequence of challenges (or possible variety of sequences), ordered by the designer. Contrast with *emergence.*

pseudo-random numbers Numbers generated by an algorithm in the computer that reproduces the same sequence of numbers each time it is used, if given the same initial seed value.

purchase-and-place A construction play mechanic in which the player purchases a new object by expending some resource and immediately places it in the game world. Contrast with *plan-and-build.*

puzzle A mental challenge with at least one correct solution state that the player must find.

PvE Short for player-versus-environment. A type of game in which the player seeks to overcome challenges provided by the game's environment but does not compete with or oppose other players directly. Most single-player non-networked games are PvE games.

PvP Short for player-versus-player. A type of game in which multiple players compete to see who will be the winner or, in a *persistent world,* who will prevail in a particular conflict between players. In a single-player PvP game, the sole human player plays against an artificial opponent simulated by the computer.

Q

quick-save A game feature that allows the player to save the game state instantly with a single button-press, without interrupting play.

quick start mode A game setting that allows the player to enter gameplay quickly with a standard or randomized set of reasonable defaults so as to avoid having to design and customize an avatar or make other decisions before starting to play.

R

radar screen See *mini-map*.

realism A continuous scale upon which the game's relationship to the real world is measured. One end of the scale is *abstract* (little or no relationship); the other end is *representational* (very close relationship). Different aspects of the game may have their own levels of realism (such as the graphics and the physics), which combine to form the game's overall level of realism.

relative difficulty A measure of the difficulty of a challenge relative to the *power provided* by the game to meet the challenge. Relative difficulty is computed from the *absolute difficulty* of the challenge and the power provided.

representational A quality of a game such that the game represents ideas and relationships familiar from the real world, such as gravity, money, death, parenthood, or fear, and presents its game world in a photorealistic way. Representational games expect players to apply some of their understanding of the real world to the game world. The opposite end of the *realism* scale from *abstract*.

representative player A hypothetical player of the game being designed who represents a typical example of someone in the game's target audience. In *player-centric* game design, the designer must keep the representative player in mind at all times.

requirements specification A document stating what features and performance characteristics a proposed product must have.

resources Entities in the game world that may be created, destroyed, gained, lost, transferred from place to place or from player to player, or converted into other entities. Resources must be measured in numeric quantities. If an entity in a game never changes and cannot be traded, such as a hill in a war game, then the entity is not a resource.

rigging The process part of level design that involves deciding where key events will take place in that level and what will trigger their occurrence. Also used for the process of preparing a 3D model to be animated.

role-playing game (RPG) A game in which the player controls one or more characters, typically designed by the player, and guides them through a series of adventures or quests. Character growth in power and abilities is usually, but not necessarily, a key feature of the genre.

roll To rotate the game's virtual camera about a line through the lens, so that the horizon is no longer level. Also called *tilt*.

royalty A percentage of a product's profits that is paid to its creator by its publisher. If a developer is entitled to a 10 percent royalty and his publisher earns a net profit from his game of $20, the developer gets $2.

RPG See *role-playing game.*

rules Instructions that dictate to the player how to play. Rules normally include lists of required, permitted, and prohibited actions; the sequence of play; the challenges and actions that make up the gameplay; the goals of the game; the termination conditions of the game; definitions of the meanings of symbols in the game (its semiotics); and any metarules if some of the rules are changeable. In noncomputerized games, the players must also implement any bookkeeping operations (such as the function of the bank in *Monopoly*), and these operations are also governed by rules. Such rules for bookkeeping operations also exist in video games, but the players are not aware of them because the software implements them.

S

sandbox mode A *gameplay mode* in which the player is not presented with a *victory condition*. This mode has few restrictions on what he may do and offers no guidance on what he should do.

save slot A numbered, or sometimes named, feature of a game that allows the game to be saved in progress and resumed later. Games that use save slots typically offer only a fixed number of slots.

scalar variable A variable quantity consisting of exactly one value, such as the amount of money in a bank account. The value changes, but there's only one value at any given time. Contrast with *vector variable.*

scope A term referring in a general way to the total amount of work required to build and test an entire game or one level of a game. This includes building and integrating all the assets and all the code and testing the result.

scripted conversation A technique that allows a player to have a conversation with a non-player character (NPC) in a game by selecting a line of dialogue from a menu of options. Her avatar says the line, the NPC responds, and the player receives a new menu of lines to choose from. Scripted conversations may be documented with a *dialogue tree.*

scrum A project management process that includes the process of creating and testing features of new software in short iterations.

self-defining play Game activities that allow the player to choose, customize, or construct an avatar, thus defining the player's imaginary self in the game.

serial A series of episodes in an indefinitely long story with a consistent world, in which plot lines continue from one episode to the next. This is the classic soap opera format.

serious game Game that is designed to solve a real-world problem through play.

shadow costs Secondary or hidden costs that lie behind the apparent costs of goods or services.

shell menu A menu of options implemented by game software outside the game world. Chiefly used for loading and saving games and customizing the user interface.

shooter A subgenre of action games whose primary challenge is shooting.

side quest A quest or mission, usually found in a role-playing game, that the player is free to accept or reject without his decision affecting the progress of the main storyline.

side-scrolling perspective A *camera model* normally used with *avatar-based interaction models* in which the game's *virtual camera* follows the *avatar* through a 2D *game world* presented in a side view.

sightseeing Play whose purpose is simply to allow the player to admire the scenery in a game, without any associated challenge. Exploration that is not difficult.

simple entity An entity containing a single datum, such as a number or a symbolic value. The number of points a player has scored is a simple entity.

simulation A mathematic or symbolic model of a real-world situation.

single-player cooperative A competition mode in which multiple players work toward their own individual goals in separate games, but may communicate and give assistance to each other within the game.

skill tree A diagram showing the sequence by which a player may add new skills to her avatar or the characters in her party in a role-playing game.

small multiple A visual *indicator* used to show an amount by displaying multiple copies of a small image on the screen. The number of lives remaining in an action game is often shown as a small multiple of pictures of the avatar; as the player gains or loses lives, pictures are added or removed.

source A mechanic that introduces resources into the game world without requiring anything in exchange.

spawn point A location in the game world where enemies appear (which means it is also a *source*). Sometimes also used to refer to locations where the avatar reappears after dying, typically in multiplayer first-person shooter games. Normally the player cannot interfere with the operation of a spawn point, and often the spawn point is visually indistinguishable from the rest of the environment.

status attributes Attributes that describe the current state of a character or unit and may change frequently. Current speed and current health are examples. See *attributes*.

stealth learning Learning that occurs without the player being aware of it.

story A credible and coherent account of dramatically meaningful events, whether true or fictitious.

storytelling engine A part of the game's software that is responsible for presenting noninteractive narrative content (such as video or scrolling text) when called upon to do so.

strategy A plan or approach for playing and winning a game.

stress The time pressure placed on a player while he tries to complete a challenge. Stress is one element of the challenge's *absolute difficulty*.

structure of a game The relationships among a game's *gameplay modes,* including a specification of the circumstances in which the game switches from one mode to another.

survival horror A subgenre of action or action-adventure games that uses some of the qualities of horror movies: lone protagonists, disturbing images, and startling attacks.

suspension of disbelief Term originally coined by Samuel Taylor Coleridge to refer to a reader's willing choice to believe in the fantasies of romantic poetry despite their incredibility. Subsequently adopted by the game industry and other fictional media and significantly redefined. See *immersion*, which is now used synonymously, for the game industry's definition.

symmetric game A game in which all the players begin with the same initial conditions (resources, starting positions, and so on), are trying to achieve the same goals, and play by the same rules. Such a game is usually considered to be *fair* and is generally easier to *balance* than an *asymmetric game*.

synchronous play Play (usually of an online game) in which the players must be participating in the game at the same time, although they may be taking turns. Contrast with *asynchronous play*.

T

tangible resource A resource that represents physical objects that exist in the game world, usually take up space, and can be stored or transported there. Cows can be tangible resources. Compare with *intangible resource.*

tech tree Short for *technology tree.*

technology tree A diagram that represents the available sequences in which a player may upgrade her *units* in a strategy game by means of research. The diagram is tree-shaped because at intervals it branches, allowing the player to choose one particular sequence or another.

technology-driven game A game designed to show off a particular technological achievement or feature.

teleporter A mechanic, often implemented in the game world as a visible object, that transports a character instantaneously from one place in the world to another.

temporary upgrade An upgrade in the capabilities of a player's avatar or units that lasts for less time than the remainder of the game—either until the end of the current level, until a fixed number of real-time seconds has elapsed, or until some resource has been consumed.

termination condition An unambiguous true-or-false condition that determines when a game has ended. Not always identical to a victory or loss condition; a race ends not after one runner wins but after the final runner crosses the finish line.

third-person perspective A *camera model* intended for use with *avatar-based interaction models* in which the *virtual camera* follows the *avatar* as he moves around the *game world.*

tilt To cause the game's virtual camera to look up or down.

tooltip A small floating text box that appears when a mouse cursor hovers over an icon to explain what the icon stands for and disappears when the cursor moves away.

top-down perspective A *camera model* in which the *virtual camera* displays the 2D *game world* from directly overhead. Its 3D equivalent is the *free-roaming* camera model.

top-scrolling perspective A *camera model* in which the *virtual camera* displays the 2D *game world* from directly overhead and the world scrolls by from the top to the bottom of the screen at a constant rate; most often used in *avatar-based gameplay modes* involving vehicles.

toy A physical object that a person can play with, typically in an unstructured fashion and without any formal rules (though the player may invent rules of his own if he wishes).

trader An on-demand mechanic, often implemented as a non-player character, that exchanges resources with the players and NPCs for other resources. A trader does not create or destroy resources but changes their ownership.

treatment A document, typically about 20 pages long, intended to describe a game in enough detail to allow a funding agency to decide whether or not to fund a developer to build a prototype of the game.

truck To move the game's virtual camera laterally, perpendicular to the direction that it is facing.

tuning stage The final stage of game design in which designers refine the core mechanics and other aspects of the design without adding any new features.

tutorial level A *level* whose purpose is to teach the player about the *user interface* and the game's *atomic challenges* and its actions.

twitch game A game whose primary challenges are physical, concentrating chiefly on reaction-time tests. A subgenre of *action games*.

U

unique entity An entity describing an object, character, or datum of which there is only one example in the game world.

unique selling points Unique characteristics of a game that will make it stand out in the marketplace.

unit In a strategy game, a combatant or support entity (such as a transport vehicle) under the control of one of the players or an artificial opponent.

unlimited series A series of story episodes set in a consistent world, each of which is self-contained so that the series may go on indefinitely and the episodes may be viewed or read in any order.

upgrade A change to gameplay that gives the player an advantage or capability she did not formerly possess. It usually occurs in one of two forms: as an improvement in the performance of her avatar or units or as a new action that was not previously available. The term is commonly used in role-playing games and strategy games; in action games, usually it refers to improvements that the player can purchase some-how. Improvements that are provided by the gameplay in action games are more commonly called *powerups*. See *permanent upgrade* and *temporary upgrade*.

user interface The collection of presentation elements and control elements that mediate between the player in the real world and the game world. User interfaces translate player actions performed on the machine's input devices into game-world actions, and they translate game-world events and other data into images and sounds produced by the machine's output devices.

V

variable scrolling A characteristic of 2D scrolling camera models in which the landscape scrolls under, or behind, the avatar in response to his movements. Contrast with *continuous scrolling*.

vector variable A set of related numbers that collectively describe something. In physics, a vector normally describes how to get from one point in space to another (on a 2D plane this requires two numbers, an angle and a distance). In games, any collection of related data can be considered a vector. Data describing the amount of water available at each point on a map would be considered a vector.

victory condition An unambiguous true-or-false condition that determines when a player has won the game or the current *level*. The highest challenge in the *hierarchy of challenges*. Not all games have a victory condition. Many construction and management simulations can be lost (by running out of resources) but not won.

video game A game mediated by a computer.

virtual camera A hypothetical camera that displays the *game world* in the main view. Some 3D engines simulate a virtual camera almost as if it were a real camera, including such optical features as lens focal length, depth of field, and lens flare. Design decisions about how the virtual camera behaves set the *camera model* of the current *gameplay mode*.

W

walkthrough mode A mode of play that allows the player to walk through an environment that he has constructed to see what it looks like from the inside; this mode is used mostly by construction and management simulations to allow the player to examine his own work. Not the same as *sightseeing*.

wildcard enemy In an action game, an enemy that attacks the player at unpredictable times, outside the ordinary waves of enemies.

REFERENCES

INTRODUCTION

Poole, Steven. 2004. *Trigger Happy: Videogames and the Entertainment Revolution.* Reprint edition. New York: Arcade Publishing.

CHAPTER 1

Bateman, Chris. 2008. "Top Ten Videogame Emotions." Weblog post at *Only a Game,* available at onlyagame.typepad.com/only_a_game/2008/04/top-ten-videoga.html (referenced 3 August 2013).

Consalvo, Mia. 2009. "There Is No Magic Circle." *Games and Culture* 4(4) 408–417.

Dini, Dino. 2004. "Gameplay Cinderella." *Develop* 41 (July, 2004) p. 31.

Gee, James Paul. 2004. *What Video Games Have to Teach Us About Learning and Literacy.* New York: Palgrave Macmillan.

Gee, James Paul. 2005. *Why Video Games Are Good for Your Soul.* Altona, Victoria, Australia: Common Ground.

Huizinga, Johan. 1971. *Homo Ludens: A Study of the Play Element in Culture.* Boston: Beacon Press.

Juul, Jesper. 2002. "The Open and the Closed: Games of Emergence and Games of Progression." In F. Mäyrä (Ed.) *Proceedings of Computer Games and Digital Cultures Conference,* Tampere, Finland, June 2002, pp. 323–329.

Koster, Raph. 2004. *A Theory of Fun for Game Design.* Scottsdale, AZ: Paraglyph Press.

Moriarty, Brian. 1997. "Listen: The Potential of Shared Hallucinations." Lecture delivered at the Game Developers' Conference, Santa Clara, CA, 1997. At http://ludix.com/moriarty/listen.html (referenced October 26, 2013).

Rollings, Andrew, and Dave Morris. 2003. *Game Architecture and Design: A New Edition.* Indianapolis: New Riders Games.

Salen, Katie, and Eric Zimmerman. 2003. *Rules of Play: Game Design Fundamentals.* Cambridge, MA: MIT Press.

Samuels, Arthur. 1959. "Some Studies in Machine Learning Using the Game of Checkers." *IBM Journal of Research and Development* 3:211–229.

CHAPTER 2

Adams, Ernest, and Joris Dormans. 2012. *Game Mechanics: Advanced Game Design*. San Francisco: Peachpit Press.

Bateman, Chris, and Richard Boon. 2006. *21st Century Game Design*. Hingham, MA: Charles River Media.

Elling, Kaye. 2006. "Inclusive Games Design." Lecture delivered at the Animex International Festival of Animation and Computer Games, University of Teesside, Middlesbrough, UK, February 2006. Slides available in PowerPoint format at www.designersnotebook.com/Media/Inclusive_Games_Design.ppt (referenced October 26, 2013).

Ray, Sheri Graner. 2003. *Gender Inclusive Game Design: Expanding the Market*. Hingham, MA: Charles River Media.

Rollings, Andrew, and Dave Morris. 2003. *Game Architecture and Design: A New Edition*. Indianapolis: New Riders Games.

Schwaber, Ken. 2004. *Agile Project Management with Scrum*. Redmond, WA: Microsoft Press.

CHAPTER 4

Devor, Holly. 1989. *Gender Blending*. Bloomington, IN: Indiana University Press.

Durchin, Jesyca. 2000. "Developing Software for Girls." Lecture delivered at the Game Developers Conference, San Jose, CA, March 2000.

Elling, Kaye. 2006. "Inclusive Games Design." Lecture delivered at the Animex International Festival of Animation and Computer Games, University of Teesside, Middlesbrough, UK, February 2006. Slides available in PowerPoint format at www.designersnotebook.com/Media/Inclusive_Games_Design.ppt (referenced September 30, 2013).

Entertainment Software Association. 2013. "2013 Essential Facts about the Computer and Video Game Industry." Report available online at www.theesa.com/facts/pdfs/ESA_EF_2013.pdf (referenced September 30, 2013).

Ip, Barry, and Ernest Adams. 2002. "From Casual to Core: A Statistical Mechanism for Studying Gamer Dedication." Article in the *Gamasutra* webzine, June 6, 2002. Available at www.gamasutra.com/view/feature/2988/from_casual_to_core_a_statistical_.php (referenced October 5, 2013).

Jones, Gerard. 2002. *Killing Monsters: Why Children Need Fantasy, Super Heroes, and Make-Believe Violence*. New York: Basic Books.

Kim, Scott. "Designing Web Games That Make Business Sense." Lecture delivered at the 2001 Game Developers' Conference. Available at www.scottkim.com/thinkinggames/GDC01/webgamesbusinesssense.html (referenced October 5, 2013).

Matthews, G., Deary, I. J., & Whiteman, M. C. 2009. *Personality Traits*. Cambridge: Cambridge University Press.

Miller, Carolyn Handler. 2008. *Digital Storytelling, Second Edition: A Creator's Guide to Interactive Entertainment*. Burlington, MA: Focal Press.

Ray, Sheri Graner. 2003. *Gender Inclusive Game Design: Expanding the Market*. Hingham, MA: Charles River Media.

Saint-Exupéry, Antoine de. 1968. *The Little Prince*. Translated by Katherine Woods. New York: Harcourt.

VandenBerghe, Jason. 2012. "The 5 Domains of Play: Applying Psychology's Big 5 Motivation Domains to Games." Lecture delivered at the 2012 Game Developers' Conference, San Francisco, CA, March 2012. Slides available at www.darklorde.com/2012/03/the-5-domains-of-play-slides (referenced October 1, 2013).

CHAPTER 7

Alexander, Christopher et al. 1977. *A Pattern Language*. Oxford, UK: Oxford University Press.

CHAPTER 8

Jones, Gerard. 2002. *Killing Monsters: Why Children Need Fantasy, Super Heroes, and Make-Believe Violence*. New York: Basic Books.

CHAPTER 9

Rouse, Richard. 2000. "Designing Design Tools." Article in the *Gamasutra* webzine, March 23, 2000, at www.gamasutra.com/view/feature/3443/designing_design_tools.php (referenced October 26, 2013).

CHAPTER 10

Campbell, Joseph. 1972. *The Hero with a Thousand Faces*. Bollingen reprint edition. Princeton, NJ: Princeton University Press.

Collins, Karen. 2008. *Game Sound: An Introduction to the History, Theory, and Practice of Video Game Music and Sound Design*. Cambridge, MA: MIT Press.

Maestri, George. 2006. *Digital Character Animation 3*. Berkeley, CA: New Riders.

Meretzky, Steve. 2001. "Building Character: An Analysis of Character Creation." Article in the *Gamasutra* webzine, November 20, 2001, at www.gamasutra.com/resource_guide/20011119/meretzky_01.htm (referenced October 26, 2013).

Poole, Steven. 2001. "Lara's Story." *The Guardian.* June 15, 2001.

Vaughn, William. 2012. *Digital Modeling.* Berkeley, CA: New Riders.

Vogler, Christopher. 1998. *The Writer's Journey: Mythic Structure for Writers.* Second edition. Studio City, CA: Michael Wiese Productions.

CHAPTER 11

Adams, Ernest. 2004. "How Many Endings Does a Game Need?" Designer's Notebook column in the *Gamasutra* webzine, December 22, 2004, at www.gamasutra.com/features/20041222/adams_01.shtml (referenced October 26, 2013).

Bateman, Chris, ed. 2006. *Game Writing: Narrative Skills for Videogames.* Hingham, MA: Charles River Media.

Campbell, Joseph. 1972. *The Hero with a Thousand Faces.* Bollingen reprint edition. Princeton, NJ: Princeton University Press.

LeBlanc, Marc. 2000. "Formal Design Tools: Emergent Complexity, Emergent Narrative." Lecture delivered at the Game Developers' Conference, San Jose, CA, March 2000. Slides available in PowerPoint format at http://algorithmancy.8kindsoffun.com/gdc2000.ppt (referenced October 26, 2013).

Vogler, Christopher. 1998. *The Writer's Journey: Mythic Structure for Writers.* Second edition. Studio City, CA: Michael Wiese Productions.

CHAPTER 12

Bateman, Chris, ed. 2006. *Game Writing: Narrative Skills for Videogames.* Hingham, MA: Charles River Media.

Brandon, Alexander. 2004. *Audio for Games: Planning, Process, and Production.* Indianapolis: New Riders Games.

Garrett, Jesse James. 2010. *The Elements of User Experience: User-Centered Design for the Web and Beyond, Second Edition.* Indianapolis: New Riders Publishing.

Sanger, George. 2003. *The Fat Man on Game Audio: Tasty Morsels of Sonic Goodness.* Indianapolis: New Riders Games.

Tufte, Edward. 2001. *The Visual Display of Quantitative Information.* Second edition. Cheshire, CT: Graphics Press.

CHAPTER 13

Cousins, Ben. 2004. "Elementary Game Design." *Develop* 44 (October, 2004) p. 51.

CHAPTER 14

Adams, Ernest, and Joris Dormans. 2012. *Game Mechanics: Advanced Game Design*. San Francisco: Peachpit Press.

Crawford, Chris. 1986. *Balance of Power: International Politics as the Ultimate Global Game*. Redmond, WA: Microsoft Press. Now available in HTML format at www.erasmatazz.com/library/my-books/balance-of-power.html (referenced September 28, 2013).

Juul, Jesper. 2002. "The Open and the Closed: Games of Emergence and Games of Progression." In F. Mäyrä (Ed.) *Proceedings of Computer Games and Digital Cultures Conference*, Tampere, Finland, June 2002, pp. 323–329.

Koster, Raph. 2011. "Social Mechanics for Social Games." Lecture delivered at the Game Developers' Conference, San Francisco, CA, February 2011. Slides available in PDF format at www.raphkoster.com/wp-content/uploads/2011/02/Koster_Social_Social-mechanics_GDC2011.pdf (referenced September 26, 2013).

CHAPTER 15

Adams, Ernest. 2008. "Difficulty Modes and Dynamic Difficulty Adjustment." Designer's Notebook column in the *Gamasutra* webzine, May 14, 2008, at www.gamasutra.com/view/feature/3660/the_designers_notebook_.php (referenced October 26, 2013).

Csikszentmihalyi, Mihalyi. 1991. *Flow: The Psychology of Optimal Experience*. Reprint edition. New York: Harper Perennial.

Sirlin, David. 2000. "Rock, Paper, Scissors in Strategy Games." At www.sirlin.net/articles/rock-paper-scissors-in-strategy-games.html (referenced October 26, 2013).

Smith, Harvey. 2003. "Orthogonal Unit Differentiation." Lecture delivered at the Game Developers' Conference, San Francisco, CA, March 2003. Slides available in PowerPoint format at www.planetdeusex.com/witchboy/gdc03_OUD.ppt (referenced October 26, 2013).

CHAPTER 16

Barwood, Hal, and Noah Falstein. "The 400 Project." At www.finitearts.com/400P/400project.htm (referenced October 26, 2013).

Knowles, Rick, and Joseph Ganetakos. 2004. "Level Design." Lecture delivered at the Computer Game Technology Conference, Toronto, Ontario, April 2004. Slides available at www.designersnotebook.com/public/ld_overview.zip (referenced October 26, 2013).

Lopez, Mike. 2006. "Gameplay Design Fundamentals: Gameplay Progression." Article in the *Gamasutra* developers' webzine, November 28, 2006, at www.gamasutra.com/features/20061128/lopez_01.shtml (referenced May 25, 2009).

CHAPTER 17

Bartle, Richard. 1997. "Hearts, Clubs, Diamonds, Spades: Players Who Suit MUDs." *Journal of Virtual Environments* (formerly the *Journal of MUD Research*) 1.

Bartle, Richard. 2003. *Designing Virtual Worlds.* Indianapolis: New Riders Games.

Kim, Amy Jo. 2000. *Community Building on the Web: Secret Strategies for Successful Online Communities.* Berkeley, CA: Peachpit Press.

Mulligan, Jessica, and Bridgette Petrovsky. 2003. *Online Games: An Insider's Guide.* Indianapolis: New Riders Games.

Simpson, Zack Booth. 2000. "The In-Game Economics of *Ultima Online.*" Lecture delivered at the Game Developers' Conference, San Jose, CA, March 2000. Available online at www.mine-control.com/zack/uoecon/uoecon.html (referenced October 26, 2013).

INDEX

INDEX

INDEX

INDEX

Fundamentals
of Game Design

You understand the basic concepts of game design: gameplay, user interfaces, core mechanics, character design, and storytelling. Now you want to know how to apply them to individual game genres. These focused guides give you exactly what you need. They walk you through the process of designing for game genres and show you how to use the right techniques to create fun and challenging experiences for your players.

Fundamentals of Music, Dance, and Exercise Game Design
Fundamentals of Role-Playing Game Design
Fundamentals of Vehicle Simulation Design
Fundamentals of Adventure Game Design
Fundamentals of Action and Arcade Game Design

For a complete listing visit **peachpit.com/ernestadams**